Rick Steves'

FRANCE
BELGIUM &
THE NETHERLANDS
2002

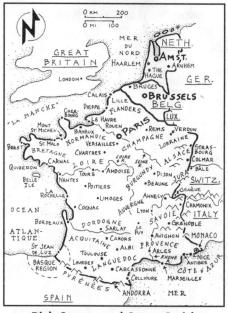

Rick Steves and Steve Smith

AVALON
TRAVEL

Other ATP travel guidebooks by Rick Steves
Rick Steves' Best of Europe
Rick Steves' Europe Through the Back Door
Rick Steves' Europe 101: History and Art for the Traveler (with Gene Openshaw)
Rick Steves' Mona Winks: Self-Guided Tours of Europe's Top Museums
    (with Gene Openshaw)
Rick Steves' Postcards from Europe
Rick Steves' Germany, Austria & Switzerland
Rick Steves' Great Britain
Rick Steves' Ireland (with Pat O'Connor)
Rick Steves' Italy
Rick Steves' Scandinavia
Rick Steves' Spain & Portugal
Rick Steves' Florence (with Gene Openshaw)
Rick Steves' London (with Gene Openshaw)
Rick Steves' Paris (with Steve Smith and Gene Openshaw)
Rick Steves' Rome (with Gene Openshaw)
Rick Steves' Venice (with Gene Openshaw)
Rick Steves' Phrase Books: German, French, Italian, Spanish/Portuguese,
    and French/Italian/German

Thanks to Steve's wife, Karen Lewis Smith, for her help on covering French
cuisine and children's activities.

Avalon Travel Publishing, 5855 Beaudry Street, Emeryville, CA 94608

First printing January 2002.
Printed in the United States of America by R. R. Donnelley.

For the latest on Rick's lectures, guidebooks, tours, and public television series,
contact Europe Through the Back Door, Box 2009, Edmonds, WA 98020,
tel. 425/771-8303, fax 425/771-0833, www.ricksteves.com, or e-mail:
rick@ricksteves.com.

ISSN 1084-4406
ISBN 1-56691-355-1

Europe Through the Back Door Editors: Risa Laib, Jacquie Maupin,
    Lauren Mills
Avalon Travel Publishing Editor: Kate Willis
Research Assistance: Cameron Hewitt, Tom Clark, Colleen Cox
Copy Editor: Donna Leverenz
Production & Typesetting: Kathleen Sparkes, White Hart Design
Design: Linda Braun
Cover Design: Janine Lehmann
Maps: David C. Hoerlein
Cover Photo: Arc de Triomphe, Paris, France; © Jeff Greenberg/
    Unicorn Stock Photos

Distributed to the book trade by Publishers Group West, Berkeley, California

CONTENTS

Top Destinations in France, Belgium, and the Netherlands

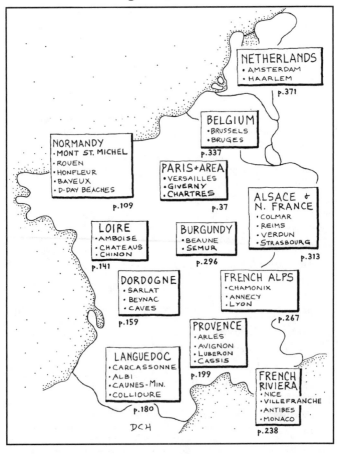

NETHERLANDS
- AMSTERDAM
- HAARLEM

p.371

BELGIUM
- BRUSSELS
- BRUGES

p.337

NORMANDY
- MONT ST. MICHEL
- ROUEN
- HONFLEUR
- BAYEUX
- D-DAY BEACHES

p.109

PARIS & AREA
- VERSAILLES
- GIVERNY
- CHARTRES

p.37

ALSACE & N. FRANCE
- COLMAR
- REIMS
- VERDUN
- STRASBOURG

p.313

LOIRE
- AMBOISE
- CHATEAUS
- CHINON

p.141

BURGUNDY
- BEAUNE
- SEMUR

p.296

DORDOGNE
- SARLAT
- BEYNAC
- CAVES

p.159

FRENCH ALPS
- CHAMONIX
- ANNECY
- LYON

p.267

PROVENCE
- ARLES
- AVIGNON
- LUBERON
- CASSIS

p.199

LANGUEDOC
- CARCASSONNE
- ALBI
- CAUNES-Min.
- COLLIOURE

p.180

FRENCH RIVIERA
- NICE
- VILLEFRANCHE
- ANTIBES
- MONACO

p.238

DCH

INTRODUCTION

You've made a great choice. France is Europe's most diverse, tasty, and, in many ways, exciting country to explore. And for extra travel thrills, this book takes you north through the best of Belgium and the Netherlands.

France is nearly as big as Texas, with 58 million people and 460 different cheeses. *Diversité* is a French forte. This country features three distinct mountain ranges (the Alps, the Pyrenees, and the Central), the different-as-night-and-day Atlantic and Mediterranean coastlines, cosmopolitan cities (such as Paris, Lyon, and Nice, all featured in this book), and sleepy villages. From its Swisslike Alps to its *molto* Italian Riviera and from the Spanish Pyrenees to *das* German Alsace, you can stay in France, feel like you've sampled much of Europe, and never be more than a short stroll from a good *vin rouge*.

Belgium and the Netherlands, called the Low Countries because nearly half their land is below sea level, are easy to overlook, surrounded by mega-Europe. We've spliced these into our France guide so that your memories can include some Bruges lace, Belgian waffles, a dike hike, and a few Dutch masters. If ever an area was a travel cliché come true, it's the Low Countries.

After years of researching and tour guiding together, Rick Steves and Francophile Steve Smith have teamed up to write this book. For 14 years we have worked hard to discover and describe France's most interesting destinations, and give you tips on how to use your time and money most efficiently. France, Belgium, and the Netherlands are a many-faceted cultural fondue. Each of our recommended destinations is a dripping forkful (complete with instructions on how to enjoy the full flavor without burning your tongue).

This book covers the predictable biggies and mixes in a healthy dose of "Back Door" intimacy. Along with the Eiffel Tower, Mont St. Michel, and the French Riviera, you'll take a bike tour of the Loire, marvel at 15,000-year-old cave paintings, and take a canoe ride down the lazy Dordogne River. You'll find a *magnifique* hill town perch to catch a Provençal sunset, ride Europe's highest mountain lift, and touch the quiet Romanesque soul of village Burgundy. Just as important, you'll meet the intriguing people who run your hotel or bed-and-breakfast.

Rick Steves' France, Belgium & the Netherlands is a tour guide in your pocket—actually, two tour guides in your pocket. Places covered are balanced to include the most famous cities and intimate villages, from jet-setting beach resorts to the traditional heartland. We've been selective, including only the most exciting sights and romantic villages. For example, there are *beaucoup de* beautiful châteaux in the Loire region. We recommend just the best. And while there are dozens of Loire towns to base in, we recommend the top two.

The best is, of course, only our opinion. But after more than 25 busy years of travel writing, lecturing, tour guiding, and Francophilia between us, we've developed a sixth sense for what tickles the traveler's fancy.

This Information Is Accurate and Up-to-Date

This book is completely updated every year. Most publishers of guidebooks that cover a region from top to bottom can afford an update only every two or three years (and even then it's often by letter). Since this book is selective, covering only the places we think make the top month of sightseeing, we can update it each summer. Of course, even with an annual update, things change. But, if you're traveling with the current edition of this book, we guarantee you're using the most up-to-date information available (for the latest, see www.ricksteves.com/update). This book will help you have an inexpensive, hassle-free trip. Use this year's edition. Saving a few bucks by traveling on old information is not smart. If you're packing an old book, you'll learn the seriousness of your mistake...in Europe. Your trip costs at least $10 per waking hour. Your time is valuable. This guidebook saves lots of time.

Planning Your Trip

This book is organized by destinations. Each of these destinations is a mini-vacation on its own, filled with exciting sights and homey, affordable places to stay. For each chapter, you'll find the following:

Planning Your Time, a suggested schedule with thoughts on how to best use your limited time.

Orientation material, including tourist information, city transportation, and an easy-to-read map designed to make the text clear and your arrival smooth.

Sights with ratings: ▲▲▲—Don't miss; ▲▲—Try hard to see; ▲—Worthwhile if you can make it; No rating—Worth knowing about.

Sleeping and **Eating**, with addresses, phone and fax numbers, and, when available, e-mail addresses of our favorite hotels and restaurants, from budget bargains to worthwhile splurges.

Transportation Connections to nearby destinations by train and route tips for drivers.

The handy **appendix** includes telephone tips, a festival calendar, a climate chart, and French survival phrases.

Browse through this book, choose your favorite destinations, and link them up. You'll travel like a temporary local, getting the absolute most out of every mile, minute, and dollar. You won't waste time on mediocre sights because, unlike other guidebooks, we cover only the best. Since your major financial pitfall is lousy, expensive hotels, we've worked hard to assemble the best accommodation values for each stop. As you travel the route we know and love, we're happy you'll be meeting some of our favorite Europeans.

Trip Costs

Five components make up your total trip cost: airfare, surface transportation, room and board, sightseeing/entertainment, and shopping/miscellany.

Airfare: Don't try to sort through the mess. Find and use a good travel agent. A basic round-trip United States-to-Paris flight costs $700 to $1,100 (even cheaper in winter), depending on where you fly from and when. Always consider saving time and money in Europe by flying "open jaw" (into one city and out of another). Flying into Nice or Amsterdam and out of Paris costs roughly the same as flying round-trip to Paris. You can get cheaper round-trip flights to London or Amsterdam, but the cost of train tickets (to get you back to London or Amsterdam for your flight home) will eliminate most of your savings. Many find relaxed, Mediterranean Nice infinitely easier than Paris as a starting point for their trips.

Surface Transportation: For a three-week whirlwind trip of our recommended destinations in France, allow $500 per person for public transportation (trains and key buses), or $600 per person (based on 2 people sharing) for a three-week car rental, tolls, gas, and insurance. Car rental is cheapest if arranged from the United States. Train passes are normally available only outside of Europe. You may save money by simply buying tickets as you go (see "Transportation," below).

Room and Board: You can thrive in France and the Low Countries on $70 a day per person for room and board (allow $80 a day for Paris). A $70-a-day budget allows $10 for lunch, $15 for dinner, and $45 for lodging (based on 2 people splitting the cost of a $90 double room that includes breakfast). That's doable. Students and tightwads do it on $40 a day ($20 per bed, $20 for meals and snacks). But budget sleeping and eating requires the skills and information covered later in this chapter (and in much greater depth in my book *Rick Steves' Europe Through the Back Door*).

Sightseeing and Entertainment: In big cities, figure $5 to $8 per major sight (Louvre-$6.50, Anne Frank House-$7), $2 for minor ones (climbing church towers), $10 for guided walks, and $25 for bus tours and splurge experiences (concerts in Paris' Sainte-Chapelle or a ride on the Chamonix gondola). An overall average of $15 a day works for most. Don't skimp here. After all, this category directly powers most of the experiences all the other expenses are designed to make possible.

Shopping and Miscellany: Figure $2 per ice-cream cone, coffee, or soft drink. Shopping can vary in cost from nearly nothing to a small fortune. Good budget travelers find that this category has little to do with assembling a trip full of lifelong and wonderful memories.

Prices, Times, and Discounts

The prices in this book, as well as the hours and telephone numbers, are accurate as of mid-2001. Europe is always changing, and we know you'll understand that this, like any other guidebook, starts to yellow even before it's printed. With the materialization of the euro currency in 2002, exchange rates and prices will likely fluctuate.

In Europe you'll be using the 24-hour clock. After 12:00 noon, keep going—13:00, 14:00, and so on. For anything over 12, subtract 12 and add p.m. (for example, 14:00 is 2 p.m.).

While discounts for sights and transportation generally are not listed in this book, seniors (60 and over), students (with International Student Identification Cards), and youths (under 18) can get big discounts—but only by asking. Teachers are also given discounts or free admission to many sights in France (identification required, Council Travel issues an International Teacher ID Card, call U.S. tel. 800/2-COUNCIL, www.counciltravel.com).

Exchange Rates

We've priced things throughout this book in local currencies. France, Belgium, and the Netherlands have adopted the euro currency.

> 1 euro (€) = about $0.90, and €1.10 = about $1.

To convert prices in euros into dollars, take 10 percent off the price in euros: €10 = about $9, and €25 = about $22. For information on the euro, see the European Central Bank's Web site: www.euro.ecb.int.

When to Go

Late spring and fall are best. Wildflowers proliferate in May and June, while September brings the grape harvest and drier weather. In the latter half of October, France glistens with fall colors and no crowds. Europeans vacation in July and August, jamming the Riviera, Provence, Dordogne, and the Alps (July 15–Aug 20 is the worst), leaving the rest of the country reasonably tranquil. And, while many French businesses close in August, the traveler hardly notices. Winter travel is OK—you'll find gray, generally mild weather in the south (unless the wind is blowing), cold weather in the north, and rain everywhere. October, November, and December are generally drier and warmer months than January, February, and March, particularly in southern France. While Holland is a festival of flowers in the spring, the Low Countries have considerably shorter summers and drearier winters than southern France. Sights and tourist information offices keep shorter hours, and some tourist activities (like English-language castle tours) vanish altogether.

Sightseeing Priorities
Depending on the length of your trip, here are our recommended priorities. The material in this book could keep
you wonderfully entertained for at least a month in France,
Belgium, and the Netherlands.

France:

3 days:	Paris and maybe Versailles
5 days, add:	Normandy
7 days, add:	The Loire
10 days, add:	Dordogne, Carcassonne
14 days, add:	Provence, the Riviera
18 days, add:	Burgundy, Chamonix
21 days, add:	Alsace, Champagne

For a day-by-day itinerary for this three-week trip, geared for drivers
and train travelers, see "Whirlwind Three-Week Tour" below.

Belgium and the Netherlands:
With cheap flights from the United States, minimal culture shock,
almost no language barrier, and a well-organized tourist trade,
the Low Countries are a good place to start a European trip.

2 days:	Amsterdam, Haarlem
3–4 days, add:	Bruges
5–6 days, add:	Brussels
7 days, add:	Side trips from Amsterdam (e.g., Enkhuisen, The Hague)

Red Tape, Business Hours, and Holidays
You need a passport but no visa or shots to travel in France,
Belgium, and the Netherlands.

You'll find much of rural France closed weekdays from noon
to 14:00 (lunch is sacred). On Sunday and during the numerous
holidays (see below), most French businesses are closed (family
is sacred), though small markets such as *boulangeries* (bakeries) are
open until noon, and museums are open all day. On Monday many
businesses are closed until 14:00 and often all day. Smaller towns are
often quiet and downright boring on Sundays and Mondays. Saturdays are like weekdays. Note that on any day, sights stop admitting
people 30 to 60 minutes before they close.

Be wary of holiday weekends, which make many places busier
than summer with crowded trains, roadways, and hotels. The French
are experts at the four-day getaway, and you're no match when
it comes to driving and hotel-finding during these peak periods.

Whirlwind (Kamikaze) Three-Week Tour of France by Car or Train

Day   By Car

1   Fly into Paris, pick up car, visit Giverny and/or Rouen, overnight in Honfleur (save Paris sightseeing for end of trip).

2   09:00–Depart Honfleur, 10:00–Caen World War II Museum, 12:00–Drive to Arromanches for lunch and museum, 15:00–American cemetery, 16:00–Point du Hoc, 17:00–German cemetery, dinner and overnight in Bayeux.

3   09:00–Bayeux tapestry and church, 13:30–Mont St. Michel, 16:00–Drive to Dinan, 17:00–Arrive in Dinan for one Brittany stop, sleep in Dinan.

4   10:00–Depart Dinan and drive to Loire, 14:00–Tour Chambord, 17:00–Arrive in Amboise, sleep in Amboise.

5   08:45–Depart Amboise, 09:00–Chenonceaux, 11:30–Cheverny château and lunch, 14:00–Possible stop in Chaumont, back in Amboise for Leonardo's house and free time in town, sleep in Amboise.

6   08:30–Depart Amboise, morning stop in Chauvigny, lunch at Mortemart, 13:30–Oradour-sur-Glane, 14:30–Drive to Beynac, 17:30–Wander Beynac or tour its castle, dinner and overnight in Beynac.

7   09:00–Browse the town and market of Sarlat, 12:00–Font de Gaume tour, 14:00–More caves, castles, or canoe extravaganza, dinner and sleep in Beynac.

8   09:00–Depart Beynac, 10:00–Short stop at Cahors bridge, 12:30–Arrive in Albi, couscous lunch, 14:00–Tour church and Toulouse-Lautrec Museum, 16:00–Depart for Carcassonne, 18:00–Explore, have dinner, and sleep in Carcassonne.

9   10:30–Depart Carcassonne, 11:00–Lastours castles or Minerve, 15:30–Pont du Gard, 16:30–Drive to Arles, 17:30–Set up for evening in Arles.

10   All day for Arles and Avignon, evening back in Arles.

11   08:30–Depart Arles, 09:00–Les Baux, 11:00–Depart Les Baux, 12:00–Lunch and wander in Isle sur la Sorgue, 14:00–Luberon hill-town drive, 16:00–Depart for the Riviera, 19:00–Arrive in Nice or Antibes.

12   Sightsee in Nice and Monaco, then sleep in Nice or Antibes.

13   Morning free, 12:00–Drive north, sleep at Clelles (urbanites sleep in Lyon).

14 Morning drive north, long stop in Annecy, in afternoon
        arrive in Chamonix. With clear weather do Aiguille
        du Midi.

15 All day for the Alps.

16 09:00–Depart Chamonix, 12:00–Lunch in Brancion,
        14:00–Depart, 15:00–Arrive in Beaune for Hôtel Dieu
        and wine tasting, sleep in Beaune.

17 09:00–Depart for Burgundy village treats or get to Alsace
        early. Arrive in Colmar after 3.5-hour drive.

18 09:00–Unterlinden Museum, 10:00–Free in town,
        14:00–Wine Road villages, evening back in Colmar.

19 08:00–Depart Colmar, 12:00–Lunch, tour Verdun battle-
        field, 15:00–Depart, 16:00–Arrive Reims, church and
        champagne, 18:00–Turn in car at Reims, picnic-dinner
        celebration on train, 21:00–Collapse in Paris hotel.

20 Sightsee Paris, tour over.

continued on next page

Whirlwind Tour (continued)
Day By Train and Bus
All times are approximate. Fewer buses and trains run on Sunday.

1   Fly into Paris, find your hotel, go for an afternoon walk.
2   All day to sightsee in Paris.
3   Head to Giverny in morning (about 08:00, depart Paris by train to Vernon, check bags at station, then bus or taxi to Giverny), early afternoon train to Rouen (check bags at station), sightsee there, then head to Honfleur (from Rouen, take late afternoon train to Le Havre—about 16:15—then catch bus to Honfleur—about 17:30), sleep in Honfleur.
4   Morning in Honfleur, midday bus to Caen, then train to Bayeux, see tapestries in the afternoon. Sleep in Bayeux.
5   All day for D-Day beaches by minivan excursion or one-day car rental, late afternoon train (about 17:00) to Pontorson, taxi to Mont St. Michel, sleep on Mont St. Michel, tour abbey at night (sound-and-light show).
6   Early morning walk around the island, 09:00–Bus to Pontorson, 10:00–Train to Caen, transfer to Tours, transfer to Amboise, sleep in Amboise.
7   All day to tour the Loire, sleep in Amboise.
8   Early-morning train to Sarlat (with transfers at Tours and Bordeaux St. Jean), afternoon in Sarlat, sleep in Sarlat or Beynac (note: it's possible to visit Oradour-sur-Glane on this day; see Amboise and Sarlat "Transportation Connections," on pages 151 and 166).
9   All day in the Dordogne, morning train to Les Eyzies (Grotte de Font de de Gaume), taxi back, afternoon canoe trip, sleep in Sarlat or Beynac.

In 2002 these times can be busy anywhere in France: Easter week (March 29–April 6), Labor Day weekend (May 1–5), VE Day and Ascension weekend (May 8–12), Pentecost weekend (May 17–20, religious holiday on May 19), Bastille Day (July 14), Assumption (Aug 15), All Saints' Day weekend (Oct 30–Nov 1, religious holiday on Nov 1), Armistice Day (Nov 11), and the winter holidays (late Dec–early Jan). Many sights close on the actual holiday (check with the local TI).

Banking
Bring your ATM, credit or debit card, and some traveler's checks in dollars. Listed hotels rarely accept American Express.
   The best and easiest way to get cash in euros is to use the

10 Morning train to Carcassonne (transfer in Souillac or Bordeaux and in Toulouse), afternoon wall walk, sleep in Carcassonne.

11 Morning train to Arles, sleep in Arles.

12 Morning train to Nîmes, late-morning bus to Pont du Gard (about 11:00), early-afternoon bus from Pont du Gard to Avignon (about 13:30), afternoon in Avignon, evening train back to Arles, sleep in Arles.

13 Morning bus to Les Baux (about 08:30), midday return to Arles, afternoon train to Nice, stroll the promenade, sleep on the Riviera.

14 Morning in Nice's old city, bus to Monaco, see changing of the guard and casino, return to Nice for beach time or Chagall museum, sleep in Nice.

15 Take a vacation from your vacation and spend a day on the beach. Spend part of the day in Antibes or take the bus to St. Paul-de-Vence.

16 Choose between urban or rural: Morning train to Lyon, visit Lyon, sleep there. Or take the scenic train to Digne/Grenoble and sleep in a remote mountain village en route (see "Transportation Connections—Nice").

17 Morning in Lyon, midday train to Annecy, visit Annecy, late-afternoon train to Chamonix, sleep in Chamonix. Or train from your remote village to Grenoble and Annecy (visit if time allows), then train to Chamonix.

18 All day to hike in the Alps, sleep in Chamonix.

19 Train to Colmar, sleep in Colmar.

20 All day in Alsace, sleep in Colmar (or evening train to Paris if you must leave the next day).

21 Train to Paris.

omnipresent French bank machines (always open, lower fees, quick processing; you'll need a four-digit PIN—numbers only, no letters—with your Visa or MasterCard). Before you go, verify with your bank that your card will work. Bring two cards in case one gets damaged. "Cash machine" in French is *distributeur automatique des billets*, or *D.A.B.* (day-ah-bay).

Regular banks usually have the best rates for cashing traveler's checks. For a large exchange it pays to compare rates and fees. Exchange rates and transaction fees can vary wildly. The Bank of France (Banque de France) offers the best rates but has branches only in larger cities. French banking hours vary, though most are open Monday through Friday from 09:00 to 16:30. Some branches open Saturday morning, and many are closed on Monday. Post offices, train stations, and tourist offices usually change money if you can't get to a bank. Post offices (which take cash or American Express traveler's checks) give a good rate, have longer hours, and charge no fee. Don't be petty about changing traveler's checks. The greatest avoidable money-changing expense is having to waste time every few days returning to a bank. Change 10 days' or two weeks' worth of money, get big bills, stuff them in your money belt, and travel!

Just like at home, credit (or debit) cards work easily at hotels, restaurants, and shops, but small businesses (like bed-and-breakfasts) accept payment only in local currency. Smart travelers function with hard local cash.

The Language Barrier and That French Attitude

You've no doubt heard that the French are "mean and cold and refuse to speak English." This is an out-of-date preconception left over from the de Gaulle days. The French are as friendly as any other people. Parisians are no more disagreeable than New Yorkers. And, without any doubt, the French speak more English than Americans speak French. Be reasonable in your expectations: Waiters are paid to be efficient, not chatty. And small-town French postal clerks are every bit as speedy, cheery, and multi-lingual as ours are back home.

The biggest mistake most Americans make when traveling in France is trying to do too much with limited time. Hurried, impatient travelers who miss the subtle pleasures of people-watching from a sun-dappled café and taking walks in the country-side often misinterpret French attitudes. By slowing your pace and making an effort to understand French culture, you're much more likely to have a richer experience. The French take great pride in their culture, clinging to their belief in cultural superiority despite the fact that they're no longer a world superpower. Let's face it—it's tough to keep on smiling when you've been crushed by a Big Mac, Mickey-Moused by Disney, and drowned in instant cof-fee. Your hosts are cold only if you decide to see them that way. Polite and formal, they respect the fine points of culture and tradition. In France, strolling down the street with a big grin on your face (and saying hello to people you don't know) is a sign of senility, not friendliness (seriously). The French think that Americans, while friendly, are hesitant to pursue more serious friendships. Recognize sincerity and look for kindness. Give the French the benefit of the doubt.

Communication difficulties in France are exaggerated. To hurdle the language barrier, bring a small English/French dictio-nary, a phrase book (look for ours), a menu reader, and a good supply of patience. If you learn only five phrases, learn and use these: *bonjour* (good day), *pardon* (pardon me), *s'il vous plaît* (please), *merci* (thank you), and *au revoir* (good-bye). The French place great importance on politeness. Begin every encounter with "*Bonjour madame/monsieur*" and end every encounter with "*Au revoir madame/monsieur.*"

The French are language perfectionists—they take their language (and other languages) seriously. Often they speak more English than they let on. This isn't a tourist-baiting tactic but is timidity on their part to speak another language less than fluently. Start any conversation with "*Bonjour, madame/monsieur. Parlez-vous anglais?*" and hope they speak more English than you speak French. In transactions, a small notepad and pen minimize misunderstandings about prices. Have vendors write the price down.

In Belgium and the Netherlands, forget the language barrier. Except in smaller, nontouristy towns, most young or well-educated people speak English (along with other languages). In southern Belgium, French is foremost; in northern Belgium and the Netherlands, it's Dutch, but English is a close second.

Travel Smart

Upon arrival in a new town, lay the groundwork for a smooth departure. Reread this book as you travel and visit local tourist information offices. Slow down and appreciate the friendliness of the local people. Ask questions. Most locals are eager to tell you about their town's history and point you in their idea of the right direction. Buy a phone card and use it for reservations and confirmations. Wear your money belt. Those who expect to travel smart, do.

Train travelers: Look for the tips on trains and buses later in this chapter. Drivers: Read our driving tips and study the examples of road signs in this chapter.

Maximize rootedness by minimizing one-night stands. Mix intense and relaxed periods. Every trip (and every traveler) needs at least a few slack days. Pace yourself. Assume you will return.

As you read through this book, note special days (holidays, festivals, market days, and days when sights are closed). Plan ahead for banking, laundry, post office chores, picnics, and Sundays (particularly if traveling by train). Sundays have pros and cons, as they do for travelers in the United States (special events and weekly markets, limited hours, shops and banks closed, limited public transportation, no rush hours). Saturdays are virtually weekdays. Popular places are even more popular on weekends and inundated on three-day weekends (most common in May).

Tourist Information

Except in Paris, the tourist information office is your best first stop in any new city. If you're arriving in town after the office closes, try calling ahead or picking up a map in a neighboring town. In this book we refer to tourist offices as TIs (for Tourist Information). Throughout France and the Low Countries, you'll find TIs are usually well-organized and have English-speaking staffs. Most will help you find a room by calling hotels (for a small fee) or giving you a complete listing of available bed-and-breakfasts. Towns with a lot of tourism generally have English-speaking guides available for private hire (about $100 for a 2-hour guided town walk).

The French call their TIs by different names. *Office de Tourisme* and *Bureau de Tourisme* are used in cities, while *Syndicat d'Initiative* or *Information Touristique* are used in small towns. Look also for *Accueil* signs in airports and at popular sights in France. These are info booths staffed with seasonal helpers who provide tourists with limited, though generally sufficient, information. French TIs are often closed from noon to 14:00.

Tourist Offices, U.S. Addresses

Each country's national tourist office in the United States is a wealth of information. Before your trip, request any specific information you may want (such as city maps and schedules of upcoming festivals).

French Government Tourist Office: For questions and brochures (on regions, barging, the wine country, and so on), call 410/286-8310. Ask for the Discovery Guide. Materials delivered in four to six weeks are free; there's a $4 shipping fee for information delivered in 5 to 10 days.

Their Web site is www.franceguide.com and their offices are ...

In **New York:** 444 Madison Ave., 16th floor, New York, NY 10022, fax 212/838-7855, e-mail: info@francetourism.com.

In **Illinois:** 676 N. Michigan Ave. #3360, Chicago, IL 60611-2819, fax 312/337-6339, e-mail: fgto@mcs.net.

In **California:** 9454 Wilshire Blvd. #715, Beverly Hills, CA 90212, fax 310/276-2835, e-mail: fgto@gte.net.

Belgian National Tourist Office: 780 3rd Ave. #1501, New York, NY 10017, tel. 212/758-8130, fax 212/355-7675, www.visitbelgium.com, e-mail: info@visitbelgium.com. Hotel and city guides, list of Jewish sites, brochures for ABC lovers—antiques, beer, and chocolates. Ask for a Brussels map.

Netherlands Board of Tourism: 355 Lexington Ave., 19th floor, New York, NY 10017, tel. 888/GO-HOLLAND, fax 212/370-9507, www.goholland.com, e-mail: info@goholland.com. Great country map, events calendar, seasonal brochures, $3 donation requested for mailing.

Recommended Guidebooks

Consider some supplemental travel information, especially if you're traveling beyond our recommended destinations.

Considering the improvements they'll make in your $3,000 vacation, $25 or $35 for extra maps and books is money well spent. One simple budget tip can easily save the price of an extra guidebook.

France: Lonely Planet's *France* is well-researched, with good maps and hotel recommendations for low- to moderate-budget travelers (but it's not updated annually). The highly opinionated, annually updated *Let's Go: France* (St. Martin's Press) is ideal for students and vagabonds. The popular skinny green Michelin guides are dry but informative, especially if you're driving. They're known for their city and sightseeing maps and for their concise and helpful information on all major sights. English editions, covering most of the regions you'll want to visit, are sold in France for about $12 (or $20 in the U.S.). Consider *Rick Steves' Paris* (see below). Of the multitude of other guidebooks on France and Paris, many are high on facts and low on opinion, guts, or personality. To better understand the French, read *French or Foe* (by Polly Platt) and *Fragile Glory* (by Richard Bernstein). *The Course of French History* (by Pierre Goubert) provides a reasonably succinct and readable summary of French history.

Belgium and the Netherlands: For the same reason that this region only appears as an add-on to our France book, the Low Countries seem to fall through the cracks in most travel publishers' catalogs. You'll find skimpy chapters in the big all-Europe books or too much information in the various city or country guidebooks covering the region.

Rick Steves' Books and Videos

Rick Steves' Europe Through the Back Door 2002 gives you budget travel tips on minimizing jet lag, packing light, planning your itinerary, traveling by car or train, finding budget beds without reservations, changing money, avoiding rip-offs, outsmarting thieves, hurdling the language barrier, staying healthy, taking great photographs, using your bidet, and lots more. The book also includes chapters on 35 of my favorite "Back Doors," three of which are in France and Belgium.

Rick Steves' Country Guides are a series of eight guidebooks—including this book—covering the Best of Europe, Great Britain, Ireland, Germany/Austria/Switzerland, Italy, Spain/Portugal, and Scandinavia. All are updated annually and come out in December and January.

My **City Guides** cover Paris, London, and Rome (available in January), and—new for 2002—Venice and Florence (available in March). These practical guides offer in-depth coverage of the sights, hotels, restaurants, and nightlife in these grand cities, along with illustrated tours of their great museums.

Rick Steves' Europe 101: History and Art for the Traveler (with Gene Openshaw, 2000) gives you the story of Europe's people, history, and art. Written for smart people who were sleeping in their history and art classes before they knew they were going to Europe, *101* really helps Europe's sights come alive.

Rick Steves' Mona Winks (with Gene Openshaw, 2001) gives you fun, easy-to-follow, self-guided tours of Europe's top 25 museums and cultural sites, including Amsterdam's Rijks-museum and Van Gogh Museum and Paris' Louvre, Orsay, Rodin Museum, Palace of Versailles, and a walk through historic Paris.

My *Rick Steves' French Phrase Book* (1999) is a fun, practical tool for independent budget travelers. This handy book has every-thing you'll need while traveling in France and much of Belgium, including a menu decoder, conversational starters for connecting with locals, and an easy-to-follow telephone template for making hotel reservations.

My latest television series, *Rick Steves' Europe*, features a new show on Paris. Of a combined total of 68 episodes (from my new series and the original series, *Travels in Europe with Rick Steves*), I have 12 half-hour shows on France, Belgium, and the Netherlands. These air on public television throughout the United States. They are also available as information-packed home videos, along with my 90-minute slide-show lecture on France, Belgium, and the Netherlands (call us at 425/771-8303 for our free newsletter/catalog).

Rick Steves' Postcards from Europe, my autobiographical book, packs 25 years of travel anecdotes and insights into the ultimate 3,000-mile European adventure. Through my guidebooks, I share my favorite European discoveries with you. *Postcards* (set partly in France and the Netherlands) introduces you to my favorite European friends.

All of my books are published by Avalon Travel Publishing (www.travelmatters.com).

Maps

The maps in this book, drawn by Dave Hoerlein, are concise and simple. Dave, who is well-traveled in France and the Low Countries, has designed the maps to help you locate recom-mended places and get to the TIs, where you'll find more in-depth maps (often free) of the cities or regions. For an overall map of Europe, consider my Rick Steves' Europe Planning Map—geared to travelers' needs—with sightseeing destinations listed prominently (for our free newsletter/ catalog, contact us at 425/771-8303 or www.ricksteves.com).

Don't skimp on maps. Michelin maps are available throughout

France at bookstores, newsstands, and gas stations (for €5.50, half the U.S. price). Train travelers can do fine with Michelin's #989 France map (1:1,000,000). For better detail, pick up the yellow 1:200,000-scale maps as you travel. Drivers should consider the soft-cover Michelin France atlas (the entire country at 1:200,000, well-organized in a $20 book with an index and maps of major cities). Learn the Michelin key to get the most sightseeing value out of their maps.

Tours of France by Rick Steves and Steve Smith

Travel agents can tell you about all the normal tours, but they won't tell you about ours. At Europe Through the Back Door, we organize and lead tours covering the highlights of this book. Choose from "Paris and the Heart of France" (14 days), "Provence and the South of France" (15 days), and the "Best of Village France" (18 days). These depart each year from April through October, are limited to 24 people per group, and have two guides and big, roomy buses. We also offer one-week off-season getaways to Paris (20 people maximum). For details, call us at 425/771-8303 or check www.ricksteves.com.

Transportation

By Car or Train?

Cars are best for three or more traveling together (especially families with small kids), those packing heavy, and those scouring the countryside. Trains and buses are best for solo travelers, blitz tourists, and city-to-city travelers. Because so many of your destinations are likely to be small places like Honfleur, Mont St. Michel, D-Day beaches, Loire châteaux, Dordogne caves, and villages in Provence and Burgundy, trains and buses require great patience, planning, and more time. Seriously evaluate the value of a train or bus detour and focus on fewer key destinations.

Trains

Train stations are usually centrally located in cities, making hotel hunting and sightseeing easier. Schedules change by season, weekday, and weekend. Verify train schedules shown in this book (to study ahead on the Web, check www.reiseauskunft.bahn.de /bin/query.exe/en). Bigger stations have helpful information agents (often in red vests) roaming the station and *Accueil* offices or booths capable of answering rail questions more quickly than the information or ticket windows.

For France, the nationwide information line for train schedules and reservations is 08 36 35 35 35 (the message prompts you to push "9" for a sales agent—ask for an English-speaking agent

The French Rail System

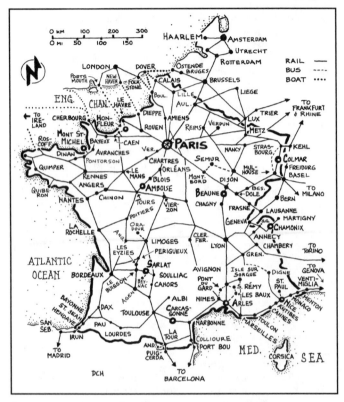

and hope for the best). This incredibly helpful, timesaving service costs €0.35 per minute from anywhere in France (call to confirm schedules and make TGV reservations, allow 5 min per call). The time and energy you save easily justifies the telephone torture, particularly when making seat reservations (phoned reservations must be picked up at least 30 min prior to departure).

France's rail system (SNCF) sets the pace in Europe. Its super TGV system has inspired bullet trains throughout the world. The TGV runs at 170 to 220 mph. Its rails are fused into one long, continuous track for a faster and smoother ride. The TGV has changed commuting patterns in much of France and put most of the country within daytrip distance of Paris. The Eurostar English Channel tunnel train to Britain and the Thalys bullet train to Brussels are two more links in the grand

Cost of Public Transportation

Prices listed are for 2001. My free *Rick Steves' Guide to European Railpasses* has the latest on 2002 prices. To get the railpass guide, call us at 425/771-8303 or visit www.ricksteves.com/rail (you can order most passes online). France-only passes are not valid on Thalys or Paris-Berlin night train.

FRANCE FLEXIPASS

	Adult 1st class	Adult 2nd class	Senior 1st class	Youth 1st class	Youth 2nd class
Any 3 days in 1 month	$210	$180	$199	$150	$130
Extra rail days (max 6)	34	30	30	24	20

Seniors 60+, Youth under 26. Kids 4–11 half adult fare.

FRANCE FLEXI SAVERPASS

	Adult 1st cl.	Adult 2nd cl.	Senior 1st cl.
Any 3 days in 1 month	$171	$146	$159
Extra rail days (max 6)	30	30	27

Prices are per person for two or more traveling together. OK to mix kids and adults (kids 4–11 half adult fare) but senior rates (age 60+) cannot be mixed with adults or kids on the same pass.

FRANCE RAIL & DRIVE PASS

France: The map shows approximate point-to-point one-way 2nd class rail fares in $US. Add up fares for your itinerary to see whether a railpass will save you money.

Any 3 days of rail and 2 days of Avis rental car in 1 month.

Car category	1st cl	2nd cl	Extra car day
Economy	$199	$175	$49
Compact	209	185	55
Intermediate	220	199	70
Small automatic	229	205	79

Rail and Drive prices are approximate per person, two traveling together. Solo travelers pay about $100 extra, third and fourth members of a group need only buy the equivalent flexi railpass. Extra rail days (7 max) cost $29 per day for first or second class. You can add up to 6 extra car days. To order a France Rail & Drive pass, call your travel agent or Rail Europe at 800/438-7245.

EURAIL SELECTPASSES

This pass covers travel in three adjacent countries (for instance: France–Benelux–Germany). For details, visit www.ricksteves.com/rail or see *Rick Steves' Guide to European Railpasses.*

	1st cl Selectpass	1st cl Saverpass	2nd cl Youthpass
5 days in 2 months	$328	$280	$230
6 days in 2 months	360	306	252
8 days in 2 months	420	358	294
10 days in 2 months	476	406	334

Saverpass: price is per person for 2 or more adults traveling together at all times.
Youthpasses: Under age 26 only. Kids 4-11 pay half adult fare; under 4: free.

Train Tips

- Arrive at the station with plenty of time before your departure to find the right platform, confirm connections, and so on. In small towns, your train may depart before the station opens; go directly to the tracks and find the overhead sign that confirms your train stops at that track.
- Check schedules in advance. Upon arrival at a station, find out your departure possibilities. Large stations have a separate information window or office; at small stations, the regular ticket office gives information.
- Write the date on your "flexi" pass each day you travel.
- Validate tickets (not passes) and reservations in orange machines before boarding. If you're traveling with a pass and have a reservation for a particular trip (e.g., TGV), you must validate the reservation.
- Before getting on a train, confirm that it's going where you think it is. For example, ask the conductor or any local passenger on the platform, "*Ah Bayeux?*" (To Bayeux?).
- Some trains split cars en route. Make sure your train car is continuing to your destination by asking, "Set vwa-ture vah ah Bayeux?" ("This car goes to Bayeux?").
- If a seat is reserved, it will be labeled *réservé*, with the cities to and from which it is reserved.
- Verify with the conductor all transfers you must make ("Correspondance ah?" means "Transfer where?").
- To guard against theft, keep your bags right overhead; don't store them on the racks at the end of the car.
- Note your arrival time so you'll be ready to get off.
- Use the trains' free WCs before you get off (a bird in the hand).

Bus Tips

- Read the train tips above and use those that apply.
- TIs often have regional bus schedules and can help plan your trip.
- Service is sparse on Sunday. Wednesday bus schedules are often different during the school year.
- Be at stops at least five minutes early.
- On schedules, *en semaine* means Monday through Saturday.

Key Phrases

- *Bonjour, monsieur/madame, parlez vous anglais?* Phonetics: bohn-zhoor, muhs-yur/mah-dahm, par-lay-voo ahn-glay? Meaning: Hello, sir/madame, do you speak English?
- *Je voudrais un depart pour ___* (destination), *pour le ___* (date), *vers ___* (general time of day), *la plus direct possible.* Phonetics: zhuh voo-dray day-par poor ___ (destination), poor luh ___ (date), vayr ___ (time), lah ploo dee-rek poh-see-bluh. Meaning/Example: I would like a departure for Amboise, on 23 May, about 09:00, the most direct way possible.

European train system of the 21st century. The fastest TGV Mediterranean line opened in 2001, with trains screaming from Paris' city center and Charles de Gaulle airport to Avignon in 2.5 hours and to Nice in 5.5 hours.

The most economical railpass for a focused tour of France, Belgium, and the Netherlands is the Eurail Selectpass for $476 (2001 price), which gives you 10 travel days (within a 2-month period) in three adjacent countries. Other railpass possibilities include a five-country Europass (with BeNeLux added) or a pricey 17-country Eurailpass (best for a whirlwind trip of Europe). All of these passes give a 15 percent discount to two or more companions traveling together.

Those traveling solely in France will save money with a France Railpass (available only outside France, through travel agents, or Europe Through the Back Door; call us at 425/771-8303 for our free railpass guide or find it at www.ricksteves.com). For roughly the cost of a Paris-Avignon-Paris ticket, the France Railpass offers three days of travel (within a month) anywhere in France. You can add up to six additional days for the cost of a two-hour ride each. (The Flexi Saver gives two traveling together a 20 percent discount.) Each day of use allows you to take as many trips as you want in a 24-hour period (you could go from Paris to Chartres, see the cathedral, then continue to Avignon, stay a few hours, and end in Nice—though I don't recommend it). Buy second-class tickets in France for shorter trips and spend your valuable railpass days wisely.

If traveling *sans* railpass, inquire about the many point-to-point discount fares possible (for youths, those over 60, married couples, families, travel during off-peak hours, and more). While Eurailers (over 26) automatically travel first class, those buying individual tickets should remember that second-class tickets, available to people of any age, provide the same transportation for 33 percent less. Adults (but not seniors) also have a choice of first or second class with the France Railpass.

Reservations, while generally unnecessary for non-TGV trains, are advisable during busy times (e.g., Fri and Sun afternoons and particularly holiday weekends, see above under "Red Tape, Business Hours, and Holidays"), and are required for any TGV train (€1.50–9) and for *couchettes* (berths, €15) on night trains. Even railpass holders need reservations for the TGV trains. To avoid the more expensive reservation fees, avoid traveling at peak times; ask at the station. Validate (*composter*) all train tickets and reservations in the orange machines located before the platforms. (Watch others and imitate.)

For mixing train and bike travel, ask at stations for information booklets: *Train + Velo* (France) and *Treins en Fiets* (the Netherlands).

Cars, Rail 'n' Drive Passes, and Buses

Car rental is cheapest if arranged in advance through your home-town travel agent. The best rates are weekly with unlimited mileage or leasing (see below). You can pick up and drop off just about anywhere, anytime. Big companies have offices in most cities. Small rental companies can be cheaper but aren't as flexible.

When you drive a rental car, you are liable for its replacement value. CDW (Collision-Damage Waiver) insurance gives you the peace of mind that comes with zero- or low-deductible coverage for about $15 a day. A few "gold" credit cards provide this coverage for free if you use their card for the rental; quiz your credit-card company on the worst-case scenario. Or consider the $6-a-day policy offered by Travel Guard (U.S. tel. 800/826-1300, www.travelguard.com).

For a trip of three weeks or more, leasing is a bargain. By technically buying and then selling back the car, you save lots of money on tax and insurance (CDW is included). Leasing, which you should arrange from the United States, usually requires a 22-day minimum contract, but Europe by Car leases cars in France for as few as 17 days for $500 (U.S. tel. 800/223-1516, www.europebycar.com). Belgium and the Netherlands are also particularly good for leasing.

You can rent a car on the spot just about anywhere. In many cases this is a worthwhile splurge. All you need is your American driver's license and money (about €60/day, with 100 kilometers included). Campanje, a Dutch company, specializes in used VW campers fully loaded for camping through Europe. Rates run about $500 per week for a four-person camper van (minimum 4 weeks), including tax and insurance. Ask about discounts for early booking and off-season and long-term rental (For a brochure, write to P.O. Box 9332, 3506 GH Utrecht, Netherlands, tel. 31/30-244-7070, fax 31/30-242-0981, www.xs4all.nl/~campanje).

Rail 'n' drive passes allow you to economically mix car and train travel (available only outside of France, from your travel agent). Generally, big-city connections are best done by train, and rural regions are best done by car. With a rail 'n' drive pass you get an economic "flexi" railpass with "flexi" car days. This allows you to combine rail and drive into one pass—you can take advantage of the high speed and comfort of the TGV trains for longer trips, and rent a car for as little as one day at a time for those regions that are difficult to get around in without one (like the Loire, the Dordogne, and Provence), all for a very reasonable package price. Within the same country, you can pick up a car in one city and drop it off in another city with no problem. While you're only required to reserve the first car day, it's safer to reserve all days, as cars are not always available on short notice.

Regional buses take over where the trains stop. You can get almost anywhere by rail and bus if you're well-organized, patient,

Standard European Road Signs

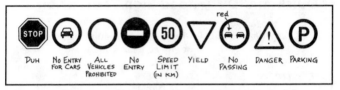

and have enough time. Review our bus schedule information and always verify times at the local tourist office or bus station, calling ahead when possible. A few bus lines are run by SNCF (France's rail system) and are included with your railpass, but most bus lines are independent of the rail system and are not covered by railpasses. Train stations often have bus information where train-to-bus connections are important—and vice versa for bus companies. On Sunday, regional bus service virtually disappears.

Regional minivan excursions offer organized day tours of regions where bus and train service is useless. For the D-Day beaches, châteaux of the Loire Valley, the *Route du Vin* in the Alsace, and wine-tasting in Burgundy, we list companies providing this helpful service at reasonable rates. Some of these minivan excursions offer just transportation between the sights; others add a running commentary and regional history.

Driving

An international driver's license is not necessary for France, Belgium, and the Netherlands. Seat belts are mandatory, and children under age 10 must be in the back seat. Gas (*essence*) is expensive—about $4.50 per gallon. Diesel (*gazole*) is less—about $3.50 per gallon. It's worth renting a diesel car if you can. Gas is most expensive on autoroutes and cheapest at big supermarkets (closed at nights and Sundays). Many gas stations close on Sunday.

Go metric. A liter is about a quart, four to a gallon. A kilometer is six-tenths of a mile. I figure kilometers to miles by cutting them in half and adding back 10 percent of the original (120 km: 60 + 12 = 72 miles, 300 km: 150 + 30 = 180 miles).

Four hours of autoroute tolls cost about $20, but the alternative to these super "feeways" is often being marooned in rural traffic. Autoroutes usually save enough time, gas, and nausea to justify the splurge. Mix high-speed "autorouting" with scenic country-road rambling (be careful of sluggish tractors on country roads). You'll usually take a ticket when entering an autoroute and pay when you leave, though shorter sections have periodic unmanned toll booths, which you can pay by dropping coins into a basket (change given), or by inserting a credit card (keep a good supply of coins in your ashtray).

Quick-and-Dirty Road Sign Translation

Céder le Passage:	Yield
Centre Commercial:	Grouping of large, suburban stores (not city center)
Centre-Ville:	City center
Doublage Interdit:	No passing
Feu:	Traffic signal
Horadateur:	Remote parking meter, usually at the end of the block
Parc de Stationnement:	Parking lot
Parking/	
Stationnement Interdit:	No parking
Priorité à Droite:	Right of way
Rue Pietonne:	Pedestrian-only street
Sauf Riverains:	Local access only

Signs Unique to Autoroutes:

Bouchon:	Traffic jam ahead
Fluide:	No slowing ahead, fluid conditions
Peage:	Toll
Telepeage:	Toll booths—for locals with automatic toll payment only
Toutes/	
Autres Directions:	All/other directions (leaving city)

Roads in France are classified into departmental (D), national (N), and autoroutes (A). D routes (usually yellow lines on maps) are slow and often the most scenic. N routes (usually red lines) are the fastest after autoroutes (orange lines). Green road signs are for national routes; blue are for autoroutes. There are plenty of good facilities, gas stations, and rest stops along most French roads.

Here are a few French road tips: In city centers, traffic merging from the right normally has the right of way (*priorité à droite*), though cars entering France's many suburban roundabouts must yield. When navigating through cities, approach intersections cautiously, stow the map, and follow the signs to *centre-ville* (downtown) and from there to the tourist information office (*Office de Tourisme*). When leaving (or just passing through), follow the signs for *Toutes Directions* or *Autres Directions* (meaning anywhere else) until you see a sign for your specific destination. While the French are eating (12:00–14:00), many sights (and gas stations) are closed, so you can make great time driving. The French drive fast and live to tailgate.

Parking is a headache in the larger cities, and theft is a problem throughout France. Ask your hotelier for ideas, and pay to park at well-patrolled lots (blue "P" signs direct you to parking lots in French cities). Most parking structures require that you take a ticket and prepay at a machine just before leaving. Or use the curbside metered parking (usually free 12:30–14:00, 19:00–09:00, and in August). Look for a small machine selling time (called *horadateur*, usually 1 per block), plug in a few coins (about €0.75 gets an hour), push the green button, and get a receipt showing the amount of time you have, then display it inside your windshield. Keep a pile of coins in your ashtray for parking meters, public rest rooms, Laundromats, and short stints on autoroutes.

Biking

Throughout France and the Low Countries, you'll find areas where public transportation is limited and where bicycle touring is a good idea for some. For many, biking is a romantic notion that is less so after the first hill—seriously evaluate your physical condition and understand the limitations bikes present. We've listed bike-rental shops where appropriate. The TI will always have addresses. For a good touring bike, allow about $10 for a half day and $16 for a full day. Pay more for better equipment; generally the best is available through bike shops, not at TIs or train stations. If you haven't been on a bike in a while, start with an easy ride.

Telephones, Mail, and E-mail

An efficient card-operated system has virtually replaced coin-operated public phones throughout Europe. Each country offers phone cards good for use only in telephones within its borders (though you can use them for international calls). Insert the card in the phone and dial away.

France: Buy a **phone card** (*une télécarte*) from any post office or train station or from most newsstands and tobacco shops (*tabac*). Pick up a *télécarte* at the beginning of your trip and use it for hotel reservations, calling TIs, and phoning home. France has two denominations of phone cards: *une petite* costs about €7; *une grande* about €15. When you use the *télécarte* (simply take the phone off the hook, insert the card, and wait for a dial tone), the price of the call (local or international) is automatically deducted.

France's latest phone card (Kertel, pron: care-tel) is not inserted into the phone, but allows you to dial from the comfort of your hotel (or anywhere) and charge the call to the card for lower rates than with a *télécarte* (€8 and €15 cards available). It's simple to use, instructions are provided in English, and the card is sold wherever *télécartes* are sold. And while per-minute rates are cheaper with Kertel than a *télécarte*, it's slower to use (more numbers to dial), so local calls are quicker with a *télécarte* from a phone booth.

USA Direct Services: Despite the expense, some travelers prefer to use American calling cards (AT&T, MCI, and Sprint numbers listed in appendix). Calling-card calls were a fine deal until direct-dial rates were cut in half. Now it's cheaper to make your international calls using a European phone card (whether French or Kertel, Belgian, or Dutch). Definitely avoid using your American calling card for calls between European countries; it's far cheaper to call direct.

Dialing Direct: France has a dial-direct, 10-digit telephone system. There are no area codes. To call to or from anywhere in France, including Paris, you dial the 10 numbers directly.

To call France from another country, start with the international access code of the country you're calling from (00 for European countries and 011 from the United States and Canada), dial France's country code (33), and then drop the initial zero of the 10-digit local number and dial the remaining nine digits. For example, the phone number of one of our favorite hotels in Paris is 01 47 05 49 15. To call it from home, dial 011-33-1 47 05 49 15.

To dial out of France, start your call with its international code (00), then dial the country code of the country you're calling. To call our office in the United States, dial 00 (France's international access code), 1 (U.S. country code), then 425/771-8303 (our area code plus local number).

For a list of **international access codes and country codes**, see the appendix. European time is six/nine hours ahead of the east/west coast of the United States.

Belgium and the Netherlands: Belgium uses a direct-dial system like France (no area codes). To call anywhere within Belgium, you dial the same nine-digit number. To make an international call to Belgium, dial the international access code (011 for U.S./Canada, 00 for Europe), Belgium's country code (32), then the local number without its initial zero.

The **Netherlands**' phone system uses area codes. To make a call within a city, you dial the local number without the area code. To make a long distance call within the country, include the code. To call internationally, dial the international access code (011 for U.S./Canada, 00 for Europe), the Netherlands' country code (31), the area code without its initial zero, and the local number. Example: The number of a recommended hotel in Haarlem is 023/532-4530. To call it within Haarlem, dial 532-4530. To call it from Amsterdam, dial 023/532-4530. To call it from the United States, dial 011 (U.S. international access code), 31 (Netherlands country code), 23 (Haarlem's area code without the initial zero), and 532-4530.

Cell Phones: Affluent travelers like to buy cell phones (about $60 on up) in Europe to use for making local and international calls. The cheaper phones generally work only if you're making calls from the country where you purchased it (e.g., a phone bought in France won't work in Belgium). Pricier phones allow you to call from any country, but it'll cost you about $40 per country to outfit the phone with the necessary chip and pre-paid phone time. If you're interested, stop by any European shop that sells cell phones (you'll see an array of phones prominently displayed in the store window). Depending on your trip and budget, ask for a phone that works only in that country or one that can be used throughout Europe. And, if you're really on a budget, skip cell phones and use European phone cards instead.

Mail: The hours of French post offices (called PTT for Postal, Telegraph, and Telephone) vary, though most are open weekdays from 08:00 to 19:00 and Saturday morning from 08:00 to 12:00. Small-town PTTs open at 09:00 and close for lunch from 12:00 to 14:00. Stamps and phone cards are also sold at *tabac* (tobacco) shops. It costs about €0.70 to mail a postcard to the United States.

To arrange for mail delivery, reserve a few hotels along your route in advance and give their addresses to friends. Or you can use American Express Company's mail services (available to anyone who has at least one American Express traveler's check). Allow 10 days for a letter to arrive. Phoning is so easy that we've dispensed with mail stops altogether.

E-mail: E-mail use among European hoteliers is increasing. Cybercafés are popular in most cities, giving you reasonably inexpensive and easy Internet access. Ask for the nearest cyber-café at the TI or at your hotel (some have Internet stations in their lobbies).

Sleeping

In France and the Low Countries, accommodations are a good value and easy to find. Choose from one- to three-star hotels (two stars is our mainstay), bed-and-breakfasts, hostels, and camp-grounds. We like places that are clean, small, central, traditional, inexpensive, friendly, and not listed in other guidebooks. Most places we list have at least five of these seven virtues.

Hotels

In this book the price for a double room will normally range from $30 (very simple, toilet and shower down the hall) to $140 (maximum plumbing and more), with most clustering around $60. Rates are higher in Paris and other popular cities. A triple and a double are often the same room, with a small double bed and a sliver single, so a third person sleeps very cheaply. Most hotels have a few singles, triples, and quads. While groups sleep cheap, traveling alone can be expensive—a single room usually costs about the same as a double.

Sleep Code

To give maximum information in a minimum of space, we use these codes to describe accommodations listed in this book. Prices listed are per room, not per person.

S = Single room (or price for one person in a double).

D = Double or Twin. French double beds can be very small.

T = Triple (generally a double bed with a single).

Q = Quad (usually two double beds).

b = Private bathroom with toilet and shower or tub.

s = Private shower or tub only. (The toilet is down the hall.)

CC = Accepts credit cards (Visa and MasterCard, rarely American Express).

no CC = Does not accept credit cards; pay in local cash.

SE = Speaks English. This code is used only when it seems predictable that you'll encounter English-speaking staff.

NSE = Does not speak English. Used only when it's unlikely you'll encounter English-speaking staff.

* = French hotel rating system, ranging from zero to four stars.

According to this code, a couple staying at a "Db-€70, CC, SE" hotel would pay a total of 70 euros (or about $63) for a double room with a private bathroom. The hotel accepts credit cards or cash in payment, and the staff speaks English.

French receptionists often don't mention the cheaper rooms. Study the room price list posted at the desk. Understand it. You'll save an average of $15 if you get a room with a shower "down the hall" rather than in your room; ask for a room without a shower (*sans douche*) rather than with a shower (*avec douche*). A room with a bathtub (*salle de bain*) costs $5 to $10 more than a room with a shower (*douche*) and is generally larger. A double bed (*grand lit*) is $5 to $10 cheaper than twins (*deux petits lits*), though rooms with twin beds tend to be larger and French double beds are generally smaller than American double beds. Queen-size beds are rare. Hotels often have more rooms with tubs than showers and are inclined to give you a room with a tub (which the French prefer). If you prefer a double bed and a shower, you need to ask for it—and you'll save up to $20. If you'll take twins or a double, ask for a *chambre pour deux* (room for two) to avoid being needlessly turned away.

The French have a simple hotel rating system (0–4 stars) that depends on the amenities offered. One- and two-star hotels are the best budget values, though some three-star hotels (and even a few 4-star hotels) justify the extra cost. More than two stars generally buys unnecessary amenities (mini-bars, 24-hour receptionist, etc.). Unclassified hotels (no stars) can be bargains or depressing dumps. Look before you leap, and lay before you pay (upon departure). Hotels in France must charge a daily tax (*tax du séjour*) that is normally added to the bill. It varies from €0.50 to €1 per person per day depending on the number of stars the hotel has. While some hotels include it in the price list, most add it to your bill.

You'll have the option of breakfast at your hotel, which is pleasant and convenient, but paying €5.50 for coffee, croissant, and bread is not a great value. Some hotels offer a buffet breakfast (about €8), adding cereals, fruit, cheese, and yogurt alongside the bread and croissants. While it's pricey, we usually spring for it. Hotels rarely require you to have breakfast, though some include it in the price (they are noted in this book). Many travelers enjoy coffee and a croissant for less at the corner café.

Some hotels strongly encourage their peak-season guests to take half-pension; that is, breakfast and either lunch or dinner. By law, they can't require you to take half-pension unless you are staying three or more nights, but, in effect, many do during summer. While the food is usually good, it limits your ability to shop around. We've indicated where we think *demi-pension* is a good value.

France is littered with sterile, ultramodern hotels, usually located on cheap land just outside of town, providing drivers with low-stress accommodations. The antiseptically clean and cheap Formule 1 and ETAP chains (€24–40/room for up to 3 people), the more hotelesque Ibis hotels (€50–70 for a double), and the cushier Mercure and Novotels hotels (€70–107 for a double) are all run by the same company, Accor. While far from quaint, these can be a good value; check their Web site at www.accorhotels .com. A smaller, up-and-coming chain, Kyriad, has its act together, offering good prices and quality (reservations tel. 01 64 62 48 41 or toll free 08 25 00 30 03). For a long listing of various hotels throughout France, see www.france.com.

Rooms are safe. Still, keep cameras and money out of sight. Towels aren't routinely replaced every day; drip-dry and conserve. If that French Lincoln-log pillow isn't your idea of comfort, American-style pillows (and extra blankets) are usually in the closet or available on request. For a pillow, ask for *un oreiller, s'il vous plaît* (un oar-ray-yay, see-voo-play). Many hotels will ask you to sign their *Livre d'Or* (a book for client comments). They take this seriously and enjoy reading your remarks.

Making Reservations

It's possible to travel at any time of year without reservations, but given the high stakes, erratic accommodations values, and the quality of the gems we've found for this book, we'd highly recommend calling ahead for rooms several days in advance. Reserve farther ahead for the busiest times: summer (June–Aug) and holiday weekends throughout the year (May is loaded; see "Red Tape, Business Hours, and Holidays," above).

If you know exactly which dates you need and really want a particular place, reserve before you leave home. This is especially important for Paris, which can be tight anytime (May, June, Sept, and Oct are worst).

If you prefer to book rooms as you go, make a habit of calling between 10:00 and 11:00 on the day you plan to arrive, when the hotelier knows who'll be checking out and just which rooms will be available.

Don't be afraid to call. We've taken great pains to list telephone numbers with long-distance instructions (see "Telephones, Mail, and E-mail," above, and the appendix). Most hotels listed are accustomed to English-only speakers. A hotel receptionist will trust you and hold a room until 16:00 without a deposit, though some will ask for a credit-card number. Please honor (or cancel by phone) your reservations. *If you must cancel, give at least two days' notice.* These family-run businesses lose money if they turn away customers while holding a room for someone who doesn't show up. Long distance is cheap and easy from public phone booths. Don't let these people down—we promised you'd call and cancel if for some reason you won't show up. Don't needlessly confirm rooms through the tourist office; they'll take a commission.

When reserving from home, phone and fax costs are reasonable, e-mail is a steal, and simple English works. To fax, use the form in the appendix (online at www.ricksteves.com/reservation). If you're writing a letter, add the zip code and confirm the need and method for a deposit. A two-night stay in August would be "2 nights, 16/8/02 to 18/8/02"—Europeans write the date as day/month/year, and European hotel jargon uses your day of departure.

If you send a reservation request and receive a response with rates stating that rooms are available, this is not a confirmation. You must confirm that the rates are fine and that indeed you want the room. One night's deposit is generally required. A credit card will usually be accepted as a deposit, though you may need to send a signed traveler's check or a bank draft in the local currency. If you give your credit-card number for the deposit, the hotel may bill one night's stay to your card (most let you know this in advance). Don't give your credit-card number as a deposit unless you're absolutely sure you want to stay there on the dates you requested and are clear that they have a room available. If you don't show up, you'll be billed for one night, and if you cancel in advance, you may not receive your entire deposit back. Reconfirm your reservations a few days in advance for safety.

Bed-and-Breakfasts

B&Bs offer double the cultural intimacy for a good deal less than most hotel rooms. This book and local tourist offices list B&Bs.

France: *Chambres d'hôte* (CH) are found mainly in the smaller towns and the countryside. They are listed by the owner's family name. While some post small *Chambres* or *Chambres d'hôte* signs in their front windows, many are found only through the local tourist office. We list reliable CHs that offer a good value and/or unique experience (such as CHs in renovated mills, châteaux, and wine *domaines*). Doubles with breakfast generally cost between €30 and €45 (breakfast may or may not be included—ask). While your hosts will rarely speak English, they will almost always be enthusiastic and delightful.

Belgium and the Netherlands: B&Bs in the Low Countries are common in well-touristed areas. Hosts usually speak English and are interesting conversationalists. Local TIs can book you into a B&B much cheaper than a hotel (though it's even cheaper to use our B&B listings and book direct). B&Bs are more important for budget travelers here than in France.

Hostels

Hostels charge about $14 per bed. Get a hostel card before you go (contact Hostelling International, tel. 202/783-6161, www.hiayh .org). Travelers of any age are welcome if they don't mind dorm-style accommodations or meeting other travelers. Travelers without a hostel card can generally spend the night for a small extra "one-night membership" fee. Cheap meals are sometimes available, and kitchen facilities are usually provided for do-it-yourselfers. Expect youth groups in spring, crowds in the summer, snoring, and incredible variability in quality from one hostel to the next. Family rooms are sometimes available on request, but it's basically boys' dorms and girls' dorms. You usually can't check in before 17:00 and must be out by 10:00. There is often a 23:00 curfew. Official hostels are marked with a triangular sign that shows a house and a tree. In France, ask for an *auberge de jeunesse*.

Camping

In Europe, camping is more of a social than an environmental experience. It's a great way for American travelers to make European friends. Camping costs about $12 per campsite per night, and almost every destination recommended in this book has a campground within a reasonable walk or bus ride from the town center and train station. A tent and sleeping bag are all you need. Many campgrounds have small grocery stores and washing machines, and some even come with discos and miniature golf. Hot showers are better at campgrounds than at many hotels. Local TIs have camping information. You'll find more detailed information in the *Michelin Camping Guide* (available at most French bookstores) or the thorough *Guide Officiel Camping/Caravaning (Fédération Française de Camping et de Caravaning)*.

Eating in France

The French eat long and well. Relaxed lunches, three-hour dinners, and endless hours sitting in outdoor cafés are the norm. They have a legislated 35-hour workweek and a self-imposed 36-hour eat-week. Local cafés, cuisine, and wines become a high-light of any French adventure—sightseeing for your palate. Even if the rest of you is sleeping in cheap hotels, let your taste buds travel first class in France. (They can go coach in England.) You can eat well without going broke—but choose carefully: You're just as likely to blow a small fortune on a mediocre meal as you are to dine wonderfully for $15.

Breakfast

Petit déjeuner (puh-tee day-zhu-nay) is typically *café au lait*, hot choc-olate, or tea; a roll with butter and marmalade; and a croissant. We carry fruit and a package of *Vache Qui Rit* (Laughing Cow) cheese to supplement the morning marmalade. While breakfasts are available at your hotel (about €5.50), they're cheaper at corner cafés (no cof-fee refills). It's fine to buy a croissant or roll at a bakery and eat it with your cup of coffee at a café. If your hotel offers a buffet break-fast (usually cereal, yogurt, cheese, fruit, and bread), spring for it. If the morning egg urge gets the best of you, drop into a café and order *une omelette* or *oeufs sur le plat* (fried eggs). You could also buy or bring plastic bowls and spoons from home, buy a box of French cereal and a small box of milk, and eat in your room before heading out for coffee.

Picnics

For most lunches—*déjeuner* (day-zhuh-nay)—we picnic or munch a take-away sandwich from a *boulangerie* (bakery), or a crepe from a *crêperie*.

  French picnics can be first-class affairs and adventures in high cuisine. Be daring. Try the smelly cheeses, ugly pâtés, sissy quiches, and minuscule yogurts. Local shopkeepers are accus-tomed to selling small quantities of produce. Try the tasty salads to go and ask for a plastic fork (*une fourchette en plastique;* oon foor-shet en plah-steek).

  Gather supplies early; you'll want to visit several small stores

to assemble a complete meal, and many close at noon. Look for
a *boulangerie*, a *crémerie* (cheeses), a *charcuterie* (deli items, meats,
and pâtés), an *épicerie* or *alimentation* (small grocery with veggies,
drinks, and so on), and a *pâtisserie* (delicious pastries). Open-air
markets (*marchés*) are fun and photogenic and close about noon
(local TIs have details). Local *supermarchés* offer less color and
cost, more efficiency, and adequate quality. Department stores
often have supermarkets in the basement. On the outskirts of
cities, you'll find the monster *hypermarchés*. Drop in for a glimpse
of hyper-France in action.

Café Culture
French cafés (or brasseries) provide light meals and a refuge from
museum and church overload. They are carefully positioned spots
from which to watch the river of local life flow by. It's easier to
sit and feel comfortable in a café when you know the system.

Check the price list first. Prices, which must be posted prominently, vary wildly between cafés (main-square cafés are more
expensive than those on small alleys). Cafés charge different prices
for the same drink depending upon where you want to be seated.
Prices are posted: *comptoir* (counter/bar) and the more expensive
salle (seated). Don't pay for your drink at the bar if you want to
sit at a table (as you might do at home).

Your waiter won't overwhelm you with friendliness. Notice
how hard they work. They almost never stop. Cozying up to clients
(French or foreign) is probably the last thing on their minds.

The standard menu items are the *croque monsieur* (grilled ham
and cheese sandwich) and *croque madame* (*monsieur* with a fried egg
on top). The *salade composée* (sah-lahd com-po-zay) is a hearty chef's
salad. To get salad dressing on the side, order *la sauce a côté* (lah soce
ah co-tay). Sandwiches are least expensive but plain unless you buy
them at the *boulangerie* (bakery). To get more than a piece of ham
(*jambon*) on a baguette, order a sandwich *jambon-crudité* (crew-dee-
tay), which means garnished with lettuce, tomatoes, cucumbers, and
so on. Omelets come lonely on a plate with a basket of bread. The
plat du jour (daily special) is your fast, hearty €8 to €11 hot plate.
Regardless of what you order, bread is free; to get more, just hold
up your bread basket and ask, *"Encore, s'il vous plaît."* While prices
include service, tip, and tax, it's polite to round up for a drink or
meal well-served (e.g., if your bill is €19, leave €20); this bonus tip
generally isn't more than 5 percent of the bill.

If you order coffee, here's the lingo:
- *un express* (uh nex-press) = shot of espresso
- *une noisette* (oon nwah-zette) = espresso with a shot of milk
- *café au lait* = coffee with lots of milk. Also called *un grand
  crème* (uh grahn krem; big) or *un petit crème* (uh puh-tee
  krem; average)

- *un café allongé* (uh kah-fay ah-low-zhay) = cup of coffee, closest to American style
- *un décaffiné* (uh day-kah-fee-nay) = decaf; can modify any of the above drinks

By law the waiter must give you a glass of tap water with your coffee if you request it; ask for *Un verre d'eau, s'il vous plaît* (uh vayr dough, see-voo-play). For more café drink suggestions, see "Drinks," below.

Restaurants

Choose restaurants filled with locals, not places with big neon signs boasting, "We Speak English." Consider our suggestions and your hotelier's opinion, but trust your instinct. If the menu (*la carte*) isn't posted outside, move along. Refer to our restaurant recommendations to get a sense of what a reasonable meal should cost.

La carte is the menu; if you ask for *le menu*, you'll get a fixed-price meal. This fixed-price *menu* gives you a choice of soup, appetizer, or salad (*entrée*); a choice of three or four main courses (*plat principal*) with vegetables; plus a cheese course and/or a choice of desserts. (The same *menu* can cost €6 more at dinner.) Most restaurants offer a reasonable *menu-enfant* (kids' menu). Service is included, but wine or drinks are generally extra. Wines are often listed in a separate *carte des vins*; ask for *un vin ordinaire* (van or-din-air) if all you want is table wine. Tipping (*pourboire*) is unnecessary as service is always included, though if you enjoyed the service, it's polite to leave a few euros (€1–2 per person if you *really* appreciated the service, none if you didn't).

If you'd prefer ordering *à la carte*, ask the waiter for help in deciphering *la carte*. Go with the waiter's recommendations and anything *de la maison* (of the house), unless it's organ meat (*tripes, rognons, andouillette*). Galloping gourmets should bring a menu translator (the *Marling Menu Master* is excellent).

Remember, the *entrée* is the first course and *le plat principal* is the main course. *Le plat du jour* (plate of the day) is usually a one-course (main) daily special served with vegetables (usually €8–11), served all day at bistros and cafés but only at lunch (when available) at restaurants. Soft drinks and beer cost €1.50 to €3 (about $1.20–2.40), and a bottle or carafe of house wine—which is invariably good enough for Rick, if not always Steve—costs €5.50 to €11 ($4.40–8.80). To get a waiter's attention, simply say, "*S'il vous plaît.*"

Restaurants tend to be better value in the countryside than in Paris. If you're driving, look for red-and-blue *Relais Routier* decals, indicating that the place is recommended by the truckers' union.

Drinks

In stores, unrefrigerated soft drinks and beer are one-third the price of cold drinks. Milk and boxed fruit juice are the cheapest drinks. Avoid buying drinks to go at streetside stands; you'll find them far cheaper in a shop. Try to keep a water bottle with you. Water quenches your thirst better and cheaper than anything you'll find in a store or café. We drink tap water throughout France and the Low Countries.

The French often order bottled water with their meal (*eau minérale*; oh mee-nay-rahl). If you'd rather get a free pitcher of tap water, ask for *une carafe d'eau* (oon kah-rahf doh). Otherwise, you may unwittingly buy bottled water.

To save money when ordering a beer at a café or restaurant, ask for a beer on tap (*une pression*; oon pres-yon) or a draft beer (*un demi*; uh duh-mee); either is less expensive than a bottled beer. House wine is cheaper by the "pitcher" (*pichet*; pee-shay) than a bottle (*bouteille*; boo-teh-ee). If all you want is a glass of wine (about €1–3), ask for *un verre de vin* (uh vehr duh van).

You could drink away your children's inheritance if you're not careful. The most famous wines are the most expensive, while lesser-known taste-alikes remain a bargain (see our regional suggestions in each chapter). If you like brandy, try a *marc* (regional brandy, e.g., *marc de Bourgogne*) or an Armagnac, cognac's cheaper twin brother. *Pastis*, the standard aperitif, is a sweet anise or licorice drink that comes on the rocks with a glass of water. Cut it to taste with lots of water. France's best beer is Alsatian; also try Krônenburg or the heavier Pelfort. *Une panaché* (pan-a-shay) is a very refreshing French shandy (lemonade and beer). For a fun, bright, nonalcoholic drink, order *un diabolo menthe* (7-Up with mint syrup). The ice cubes melted after the last Yankee tour group left.

Traveling with Kids

France is kid-friendly, partly because so much of it is rural. It's easy to find restaurants with kids' menus. (We travel with a plastic container of peanut butter brought from home and smuggle small jars of jam from breakfast for food emergencies.) Choose hotels with pools (many listed in this book, most in the south) and attached restaurants so the kids can go back to the room and play while you finish a pleasant dinner. Minimize hotel changes by planning three-day stops.

To make your trip fun for everyone in the family, mix heavy-duty sights with kids' activities (playing miniature golf, renting bikes, and riding the little tourist trains popular in many French towns). Swap baby-sitting duties with your partner if one of you wants to take in an extra sight. Our kids' favorite places were Mont St. Michel, the Alps, Loire châteaux, Carcassonne, and Paris (especially the Eiffel Tower and Seine River boat ride). For memories that will last long after the trip, keep a family journal. Pack a small diary and a glue stick. While relaxing at a café over a *citron pressé* (lemonade), take turns writing the days' events and include mementos such as ticket stubs from museums, post-cards, or a stalk of lavender.

Stranger in a Strange Land

We travel all the way to Europe to enjoy differences—to become temporary locals. You'll experience frustrations. Certain truths that we find "God-given" or "self-evident," such as cold beer, ice in drinks, bottomless cups of coffee, hot showers, body odor smelling bad, and bigger being better, are suddenly not so true. One of the benefits of travel is the eye-opening realization that there are logical, civil, and even better alternatives. The fact that Americans treat time as a commodity can lead to frustrations when dealing with other cultures. For instance, while an American "spends" or "wastes" time, a French person merely "passes" it. You will find no cup holders in French cars—drinks are to be enjoyed slowly, with friends. A will-ingness to go local (and at a local tempo) ensures that you'll enjoy a full dose of European hospitality.

If there is a negative aspect to the European image of Ameri-cans, it's that we can appear big, loud, aggressive, impolite, rich, and a bit naive. While Europeans look bemusedly at some of our Yankee excesses—and worriedly at others—they nearly always afford us individual travelers all the warmth we deserve.

Back Door Manners

While updating this book, we heard over and over again that our readers are considerate and fun to have as guests. Thank you for traveling as temporary locals who are sensitive to the culture. It's fun to follow you in our travels.

Send Us a Postcard, Drop Us a Line

If you enjoy a successful trip with the help of this book and would like to share your discoveries, please fill out and send the survey at the end of this book to us at Europe Through the Back Door, Box 2009, Edmonds, WA 98020. We personally read and value all feedback. Thanks in advance—it helps a lot.

For our latest travel information, tap into our Web site: www.ricksteves.com. For any updates to this book, check www.ricksteves.com/update. Rick's e-mail address is rick@ricksteves.com. Anyone is welcome to request a free issue of our *Back Door* quarterly newsletter.

Judging from all the positive feedback and happy postcards we receive from travelers who have used this book, it's safe to assume you'll enjoy a great, affordable vacation—with the finesse of an independent, experienced traveler.

From this point, "we" (your coauthors) will shed our respective egos and become "I."

Thanks, and *bon voyage*!

BACK DOOR TRAVEL PHILOSOPHY
As Taught in *Rick Steves' Europe Through the Back Door*

Travel is intensified living—maximum thrills per minute and one of the last great sources of legal adventure. Travel is freedom. It's recess, and we need it.

Experiencing the real Europe requires catching it by surprise, going casual... "Through the Back Door."

Affording travel is a matter of priorities. (Make do with the old car.) You can travel—simply, safely, and comfortably—anywhere in Europe for $80 a day plus transportation costs. In many ways, spending more money only builds a thicker wall between you and what you came to see. Europe is a cultural carnival; time after time you'll find that its best acts are free, and the best seats are the cheap ones.

A tight budget forces you to travel close to the ground, meeting and communicating with the people, not relying on service with a purchased smile. Never sacrifice sleep, nutrition, safety, or cleanliness in the name of budget. Simply enjoy the local-style alternatives to expensive hotels and restaurants.

Extroverts have more fun. If your trip is low on magic moments, kick yourself and make things happen. If you don't enjoy a place, maybe you don't know enough about it. Seek the truth. Recognize tourist traps. Give a culture the benefit of your open mind. See things as different but not better or worse. Any culture has much to share.

Of course, travel, like the world, is a series of hills and valleys. Be fanatically positive and militantly optimistic. If something's not to your liking, change your liking. Travel is addictive. It can make you a happier American as well as a citizen of the world. Our Earth is home to six billion equally important people. It's humbling to travel and find that people don't envy Americans. They like us but, with all due respect, they wouldn't trade passports.

Globe-trotting destroys ethnocentricity. It helps you understand and appreciate different cultures. Travel changes people. It broadens perspectives and teaches new ways to measure quality of life. Many travelers toss aside their hometown blinders. Their prized souvenirs are the strands of different cultures they decide to knit into their own character. The world is a cultural yarn shop. And Back Door Travelers are weaving the ultimate tapestry. Come on, join in!

PARIS

Paris offers sweeping boulevards, sleepy parks, world-class art galleries, chatty crêpe stands, Napoleon's body, sleek shopping malls, the Eiffel Tower, and people watching from outdoor cafés. Climb the Notre-Dame and the Eiffel Tower, cruise the Seine and the Champs-Elysées, and master the Louvre and Orsay Museums. Save some after-dark energy for one of the world's most romantic cities. Many people fall in love with Paris. Some see the essentials and flee, overwhelmed by the huge city. With the proper approach and a good orientation, you'll fall head over heels for Europe's capital city.

Planning Your Time
Paris in One, Two, or Three Days

Day 1
Morning: Follow "Historic Core of Paris" Walk (see "Sights," below), featuring Ile de la Cité, Notre-Dame, Latin Quarter, and Sainte-Chapelle (consider lunch at nearby Samaritaine view café).
Afternoon: Visit the Pompidou Center (at least from the outside), then walk to the Marais neighborhood: visit the place des Vosges and consider touring the Carnavalet Museum or the Jewish Art and History Museum nearby.
Evening: Cruise Seine River or take Paris by Night bus tour.

Day 2
Morning: Follow Champs-Elysées Walk from Arc de Triomphe down the grand Champs-Elysées boulevard to Tuileries Gardens.
Afternoon: Complete your walk through the Tuileries (several lunch cafés in the park), then tour the Louvre.
Evening: Enjoy Trocadero scene and twilight ride up Eiffel Tower.

Daily Reminder

Monday: The catacombs and these museums are closed today—Orsay, Rodin, Marmottan, Montmartre, Carnavalet, and Versailles; the Louvre is especially crowded, but the Richelieu wing stays open until 21:45. Some small stores don't open until 14:00. The rue Cler market is dead. Some restaurants and banks are closed. It's discount night at most cinemas.

Tuesday: Many museums are closed today, including the Louvre, Picasso, Cluny, and Pompidou Center. The Eiffel Tower, Orsay, and Versailles are particularly busy today.

Wednesday: All sights are open, the Louvre until 21:45. The weekly *Pariscope* magazine comes out today. School is out, so many child-related sights are open (and busy). Some cinemas offer discounts.

Thursday: All sights are open (except the Sewer Tour). The Orsay is open until 21:45. Department stores are open late.

Friday: All sights are open (except the Sewer Tour). Afternoon trains and roads leaving Paris are crowded; TGV reservation fees are higher.

Saturday: All sights are open (except the Jewish Art and History Museum). The fountains run at Versailles (July–Sept). Department stores are busy. The Jewish Quarter is quiet.

Sunday: Some museums are two-thirds price all day and/ or free the first Sunday of the month, thus more crowded (e.g., Louvre, Orsay, Rodin, Cluny, Pompidou, and Picasso). The fountains run at Versailles (early April–early Oct). Most of Paris' stores are closed on Sunday, but shoppers will find relief in the lively Marais neighborhood—the Jewish Quarter—and in Bercy Village where many stores are open. Look for organ concerts at St. Sulpice and possibly other churches. The American Church usually offers a free evening concert at 18:00 (Sept–May). Most recommended restaurants in the rue Cler neighborhood are closed for dinner.

Day 3
Morning: Tour the Orsay Museum.
Afternoon: Either tour the Rodin Museum and Napoleon's Tomb or visit Versailles (take RER direct from Orsay).
Evening: Take Montmartre Walk, featuring Sacré-Coeur.

Orientation

Paris is split in half by the Seine River, divided into 20 *arrondissements* (proud and independent governmental jurisdictions), and circled by a ring-road freeway (the *périphérique*). You'll find Paris easier to navigate if you know which side of the river you're on, which *arrondissement* you're in, and which subway (Métro) stop you're closest to. If you're north of the river (the top half of any city map), you're on the Right Bank (*rive droite*). If you're south of it, you're on the Left Bank (*rive gauche*). Most of your sightseeing will take place within five blocks of the river.

Arrondissements are numbered, starting at Notre-Dame (ground zero) and moving in a clockwise spiral out to the ring road. The last two digits in a Parisian zip code are the *arrondissement* number. The notation for the Métro stop is "Mo." In Parisian jargon, Napoleon's tomb is on *la rive gauche* (the Left Bank) in the 7*ème* (7th *arrondissement*), zip code 75007, Mo: Invalides. Paris Métro stops are used as a standard aid in giving directions, even for those not using the Métro. As you're tracking down addresses, these definitions will help: *place* (square), *rue* (road), and *pont* (bridge).

Tourist Information

Avoid the Paris tourist offices—long lines, short information, and a €0.75 charge for maps. This book, the *Pariscope* magazine (described below), and one of the freebie maps available at any hotel are all you need. The main TI is at 127 avenue des **Champs-Elysées** (daily 09:00–20:00, tel. 08 36 68 31 12—phone tree, or 01 49 52 53 10), but the other TIs are less crowded: at **Gare de Lyon** (daily 08:00–20:00, tel. 01 43 43 33 24, answered by live English-speaker), at the **Eiffel Tower** (May–Sept daily 11:00–18:42, yes, 18:42, closed off-season, tel. 01 45 51 22 15), and at the **Louvre** (Wed–Mon 10:00–19:00, closed Tue). Both **airports** have handy TIs (called ADP) with long hours and short lines (see "Transportation Connections," below). For a complete list of museum hours and scheduled English-language museum tours, pick up the free *Musées, Monuments Historiques, et Expositions* booklet from any museum.

Pariscope: The *Pariscope* weekly magazine (or one of its clones, €0.50 at any newsstand) lists museum hours, art exhibits, concerts, music festivals, plays, movies, and nightclubs. Smart tour guides and sightseers rely on this for all the latest (www.pariscope.fr in French).

Web Sites: This short list is entertaining and at times useful: www.bonjourparis.com (a newsy site that claims to offer a virtual trip to Paris with interactive French lessons, tips on wine and food, and news on the latest Parisian trends), www.paris-touristoffice.com (the official site for Paris' TIs, offering practical information on hotels, special events, museums, children's activities, fashion, nightlife, and more), and www.paris-anglo.com (similar to bonjourparis .com with informative stories on visiting Paris, plus a directory of over 2,500 English-friendly businesses).

Maps: While Paris is littered with free maps, they don't

Paris Overview

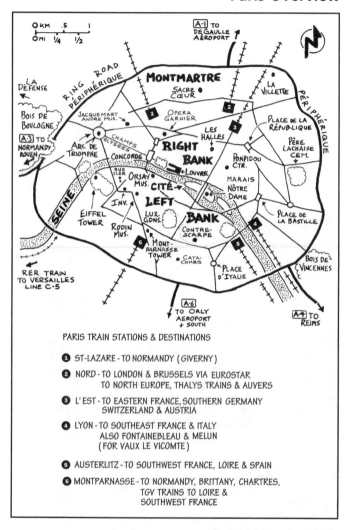

O KM   .5   1
O MI 1/4 1/2

LA DÉFENSE

RING ROAD PÉRIPHÉRIQUE

A-1 TO DE GAULLE AÉROPORT

MONTMARTRE

SACRÉ CŒUR

LA VILLETTE

PÉRIPHÉRIQUE

BOIS DE BOULOGNE

JACQUEMART ANDRE MUS.

OPÉRA GARNIER

① ②

PLACE DE LA RÉPUBLIQUE

A-3 TO NORMANDY ROUEN

CHAMPS ELYSÉES

ARC DE TRIOMPHE

CONCORDE

LES HALLES

RIGHT BANK

③

PÈRE LACHAISE CEM.

RUE CLER

ORSAY MUS.

CITÉ

Louvre

POMPIDOU CTR.

MARAIS

SEINE

INV.

LEFT BANK

NÔTRE DAME

EIFFEL TOWER

RODIN MUS.

LUX. GDNS.

CONTRE-SCARPE

PLACE DE LA BASTILLE

④

⑥ MONT-PARNASSE TOWER

CATA-COMBS

⑤

BOIS DE VINCENNES

RER TRAIN TO VERSAILLES LINE C-5

PLACE D'ITALIE

A-6 TO ORLY AÉROPORT + SOUTH

A-4 TO REIMS

PARIS TRAIN STATIONS & DESTINATIONS

❶ ST-LAZARE - TO NORMANDY (GIVERNY)

❷ NORD - TO LONDON & BRUSSELS VIA EUROSTAR
   TO NORTH EUROPE, THALYS TRAINS & AUVERS

❸ L'EST - TO EASTERN FRANCE, SOUTHERN GERMANY
   SWITZERLAND & AUSTRIA

❹ LYON - TO SOUTHEAST FRANCE & ITALY
   ALSO FONTAINEBLEAU & MELUN
   (FOR VAUX LE VICOMTE)

❺ AUSTERLITZ - TO SOUTHWEST FRANCE, LOIRE & SPAIN

❻ MONTPARNASSE - TO NORMANDY, BRITTANY, CHARTRES,
   TGV TRAINS TO LOIRE &
   SOUTHWEST FRANCE

show all the streets. You may want the huge Michelin #10 map of Paris. For an extended stay, I prefer the pocket-size, street-indexed *Paris Pratique* (€6) with an easy-to-use Métro map.

Bookstores: There are many English-language bookstores in Paris where you can pick up guidebooks (for nearly double their American price), including: Shakespeare & Company (daily

12:00–24:00, some used travel books, 37 rue de la Boucherie, across river from Notre-Dame, tel. 01 43 26 96 50), W. H. Smith (248 rue de Rivoli, Mo: Concorde, tel. 01 44 77 88 99), and Brentanos (37 avenue de L'Opéra, Mo: Opéra, tel. 01 42 61 52 50).

American Church: The American Church is a nerve center for the American émigré community. It distributes a free, handy, and insightful monthly English-language newspaper called the *Paris Voice* (with useful reviews of concerts, plays, and current events; available at about 200 locations in Paris, www.parisvoice.com) and an advertisement paper called *France—U.S.A. Contacts* (full of useful information for those seeking work or long-term housing). The church faces the river between the Eiffel Tower and Orsay Museum (reception open Mon–Sat 09:30–22:30, Sun 09:00–19:30, 65 quai d'Orsay, Mo: Invalides, tel. 01 40 62 05 00).

Arrival in Paris

By Train: Paris has six train stations, all connected by Métro, bus, and taxi. All have ATMs, banks or change offices, information desks, telephones, cafés, lockers (*consigne automatique*), newsstands, and clever pickpockets. Hop the Métro to your hotel (see "Getting around Paris," below).

By Plane: For detailed information on getting from Paris' airports to downtown Paris (and vice versa), see "Transportation Connections" at the end of this chapter.

Helpful Hints

Theft Alert: Use your money belt and never carry a wallet in your back pocket or a purse over your shoulder. Thieves thrive in tourist areas and the Métro (at stations and in subway cars).

Museums: Most museums offer reduced prices on Sunday. Many sights stop admitting people 30 to 60 minutes before they close, and many begin closing rooms 45 minutes before the actual closing time. For the fewest crowds, visit very early, at lunch, or very late. Most museums have slightly shorter hours October through March. French holidays can really mess up your sightseeing plans (Jan 1, May 1, May 8, July 14, Nov 1, Nov 11, and Dec 25). See "Daily Reminder" in this chapter for other "closed" days. The best Impressionist art museums are the Orsay, Orangerie, and Marmottan.

Paris Museum Pass: In Paris there are two classes of sightseers: those with a museum pass and those who stand in line. Serious sightseers save time and money by getting this pass. Sold at museums, main Métro stations (including Ecole Militaire and Bastille stations), and TIs, it pays for itself in two admissions and gets you into most sights with no lining up (€13/1 day, €26/3 consecutive days, €39/5 consecutive days; no youth discounts). You can buy one on any day at any sight where it's valid (though supply can be limited at big sights like the Louvre, best to buy elsewhere). The pass is not activated until the first time you use it (you enter the date on the pass).

Included sights (and entry fee without the pass) you're likely to visit: Louvre (€7), Orsay (€7), Sainte-Chapelle (€5.50), Arc de Triomphe (€6), Orangerie (€6), Napoleon's Tomb (€6), Carnavalet Museum (€5.50), Conciergerie (€5.50), Sewer Tour (€4), Cluny Museum (€6), Pompidou Center (€5), Notre-Dame towers (€5.50) and crypt (€3), Picasso Museum (€5), and Rodin Museum (€4). Outside Paris, the pass covers Versailles (€7) and its Trianons (€5), Château de Fontainebleau (€5.50), and Château Chantilly (€6). Notable sights not covered: Eiffel Tower, Montparnasse Tower, Marmottan Museum, Garnier Opéra, Jacquemart-André Museum, Jewish Art and History Museum, Grande Arche at La Défense, Jeu de Paume Exhibition Hall, Catacombs, new Paris story film, and the ladies of Pigalle.

Tally it up—but remember, an advantage of the pass is that you skip to the front of virtually all lines, saving hours of waiting, especially in summer (though everyone must pass through the slow-moving metal-detector lines, and some places can't accommodate a bypass lane, such as Notre-Dame's tower). With the pass, you'll pop painlessly into sights that you're walking by (even for a few minutes) that might otherwise not be worth the expense (e.g., Paris crypt, Conciergerie, Victor Hugo's House, Panthéon). Try to avoid buying your museum pass at a major museum, where supply can be spotty and lines long—remember they are sold at TIs, including those at the airports, and at key Métro stations. The free museum and monuments directory that comes with your pass lists the latest hours, phone numbers, and specifics on what kids pay. The cutoff age for free entry varies from 5 to 18. Most major art museums let young people under 18 in for free.

Telephone Cards: Pick up the essential France *télécarte* at any *tabac* (tobacco shop), post office, newsstand, or TI (*une petite télécarte* is about €7; *une grande* is about €15). Smart travelers check things by telephone. Most public phones use *télécartes*. France's latest phone card, Kertel (pron: care-tel), allows you to dial from any phone, even from your hotel room (sold wherever *télécartes* are sold).

Useful Telephone Numbers: American Hospital—01 46 41 25 25, English-speaking pharmacy—01 45 62 02 41 (24 hrs, Mo: Georges V), Police—17, U.S. Embassy—01 43 12 22 22, Paris and France directory assistance—12, AT&T operator—0800 99 00 11, MCI—0800 99 00 19, Sprint—0800 99 00 87. (See appendix for additional numbers.)

Toilets: Carry small change for pay toilets, or walk into any sidewalk café like you own the place and find the toilet in the back. The toilets in museums are free and generally the best you'll find, and, if you have a museum pass, you can drop into almost any

museum for the clean toilets. Modern, supersanitary, street-booth
toilets provide both relief and a memory (coins required, don't
leave small children inside unattended). Keep some toilet paper
or tissues with you as some toilets are poorly supplied.

Getting around Paris

By Métro: Europe's best subway is divided into two systems—
the Métro (for puddle-jumping everywhere in Paris) and the RER
(which connects suburban destinations with a few stops in central
Paris). You'll be using the Métro for almost all your trips (runs
daily from 05:30–00:30). Occasionally you'll find the RER more
convenient as it makes fewer stops (like an express bus).

In Paris you're never more than a 10-minute walk from a Métro
station. One ticket takes you anywhere in the system with unlimited
transfers. Save 40 percent by buying a *carnet* (car-nay) of 10 tickets
for €9 at any Métro station (a single ticket is €1.30, kids 4–10 pay
€4.75 for a *carnet*). Métro tickets work on city buses, though one
ticket cannot be used as a transfer between subway and bus.

The new, overpriced, single or multiday *Paris Visite* Métro pass
gives you free run of all Métro, RER, and bus routes in central Paris
(and discounts at minor sights). You're better off buying *carnets* of
10 tickets (see above) and getting three days' use out of one *carnet*
(most travelers use 3–4 tickets/day). The *Paris Visite* pass covers
three progressively larger zones (zones 1–3, 1–5, and 1–8; sold at
any Métro station, no photo required). Zones 1 through 3 include
central Paris and virtually all tourist needs (1 day-€8.50 for adults/
€4.50 for kids under 12; 2 days-€13.75/€7; 3 days-€18.30/€9;
and 5 days-€27/€13.75; no 4-day option). Zones 4 through 8 add
suburban destinations, such as Versailles, Disneyland Paris, and the
airports, for which you're better off buying individual tickets. The
pass begins when you validate it (on bus or at Métro turnstile)
and lasts for the consecutive number of days purchased. Note that
tourists can no longer can buy the cheaper *Carte Orange* week- or
month-long passes; these are now available only for French residents.

To get to your destination, determine the closest "Mo" stop
and which line or lines will get you there. The lines have numbers,
but they're best known by their direction or end-of-the-line stop.
(For example, the La Défense/Château de Vincennes line runs
between La Défense in the west and Vincennes in the east.)

Once in the Métro station, you'll see blue-and-white signs
directing you to the train going in your direction (e.g., "direction:
La Défense"). Insert your ticket in the automatic turnstile, pass
through, and reclaim and keep your ticket until you exit the system. Fare inspectors regularly check for cheaters and accept
absolutely no excuses from anyone. I repeat, keep that ticket
until you leave the Métro system.

Transfers are free and can be made wherever lines cross.

Paris

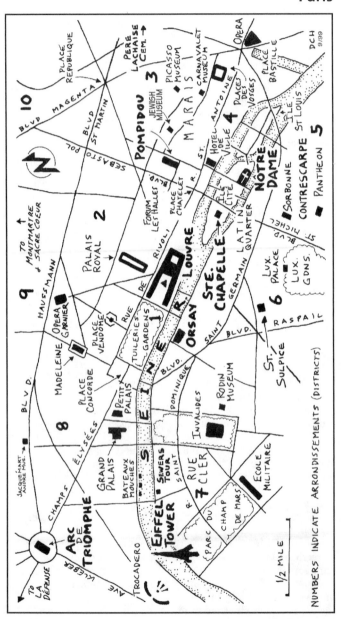

Key Words for the Métro and RER

- *direction* (dee-rek-see-ohn): direction
- *ligne* (leen-yuh): line
- *correspondance* (kor-res-pohn-dahns): transfer
- *sortie* (sor-tee): exit
- *carnet* (kar-nay): cheap set of 10 tickets
- *Pardon, madame/monsieur* (par-dohn, mah-dahm/mes-yur): Excuse me, lady/bud.
- *Je descend* (juh day-sahn): I'm getting off.
- *Donnez-moi mon porte-monnaie!*: Give me back my wallet!

Etiquette

- When waiting at the platform, get out of the way of those exiting their train. Board only once everyone is off.
- Avoid using the hinged seats when the car is jammed; they take up valuable standing space.
- In a crowded train, try not to block the exit. If you're blocking the door when the train stops, step out of the car and to the side, let others off, then get back on.
- Talk softly in the cars. Listen to how quietly Parisians can communicate and follow their lead.
- When leaving or entering a station, hold the door open for the person behind you.
- On escalators, stand on the right, pass on the left.

When you transfer, look for the orange *correspondance* (connections) signs when you exit your first train, then follow the proper direction sign.

Before you *sortie* (exit), check the helpful *plan du quartier* (map of the neighborhood) to get your bearings, locate your destination, and decide which *sortie* you want. At stops with several *sorties*, you can save lots of walking by choosing the best exit.

Thieves spend their days in the Métro. Be on guard. For example, if your pocket is picked as you pass through a turnstile, you end up stuck on the wrong side while the thief strolls away. Any jostle or commotion (especially when boarding or leaving trains) is likely the sign of a thief or team of thieves in action.

Paris has a huge homeless population and over 11 percent unemployment; expect a warm Métro welcome from panhandlers, musicians, and those selling magazines produced by the homeless community.

By RER: The RER (*Réseau Express Régionale*, pron. air-ay-air) is the suburban train system serving destinations such as Versailles, Disneyland Paris, and the airports. These routes are indicated by thick lines on your subway map and identified by letters A, B, C, and so on. The RER works like the Métro but can be speedier (if it serves your destination directly) because it makes only a few stops within the city. One Métro ticket is all you need for RER rides within central Paris. You can transfer between the Métro and RER systems with the same ticket. Unlike the Métro, you need to insert your ticket in a turnstile to exit the RER system, and, also unlike in the Métro, signage can vary between RER stations, meaning you have to pay attention and verify that you're heading the right direction (RER lines often split at the end of the line, leading to different signed *Destinations*—study your map and you'll do fine). To travel outside the city (to Versailles or the airport, for example), you'll need to buy a separate, more expensive ticket at the station window before boarding; make sure your stop is served by checking the signs over the train platform (not all trains serve all stops).

By City Bus: The trickier bus system is worth figuring out. Métro tickets are good on both bus and Métro, though you can't use the same ticket to transfer between the two systems. One ticket gets you anywhere in central Paris, but, if you leave the city center (shown as zone 1 on the diagram on board the bus), you must validate a second ticket. While the Métro shuts down about 00:30, some buses continue much later. Schedules are posted at bus stops. Handy bus-system maps (*plan des autobus*) are available in any Métro station and are provided in your *Paris Pratique* map book if you invest (€6).

Big system maps, posted at each bus and Métro stop, display the routes. Individual route diagrams show the exact routes of the lines serving that stop. Major stops are painted on the side of each bus. Enter through the front doors. Punch your Métro ticket in the machine behind the driver, or pay the higher cash fare. Get off the bus using the rear door. Even if you're not certain you've figured it out, do some joyriding (outside of rush hour). Lines #24, #63, and #69 are Paris' most scenic routes and make a great introduction to the city. Bus #69 is particularly handy, running between the Eiffel Tower, rue Cler (recommended hotels), Orsay, Louvre, Marais (recommended hotels), and Père Lachaise Cemetery. The handiest bus routes are listed for each hotel area recommended (see "Sleeping," below).

By Taxi: Parisian taxis are almost reasonable. A 10-minute ride costs about €8 *sans baggage* (versus €1 to get anywhere in town on the Métro). You can try waving one down (a glowing white light on the roof means it's free), but it's easier to ask your hotel to call for you or ask for the nearest taxi stand (*Où est une station de taxi?*; oo ay oon stah-see-ohn duh taxi). Taxi stands are indicated by a circled *T* on many city maps, including Michelin's #10 Paris. A typical taxi takes up to three people (maybe 4 if you're polite and pay €2 extra);

groups can use a *grand taxi*, which must be booked in advance (ask your hotel to call). If a taxi is summoned by phone, the meter starts as soon as the call is received. Higher rates are charged at night from 19:00 to 7:00, all day Sunday, and to either airport. There's a €1 charge for each piece of baggage. For a tip, round up to the nearest euro (minimum €0.50. Taxis are tough to find on Friday and Saturday nights, especially after the Métro closes (around 00:30). If you need to catch a train or flight early in the morning, consider booking a taxi the night before.

By Foot: Be careful! Parisian drivers are notorious for ignoring pedestrians. Never assume you have the right-of-way, even in a crosswalk. When crossing a street, keep your pace constant and don't stop suddenly. By law, drivers must miss pedestrians by one meter/three feet (1.5 meters/5 feet in the countryside). Drivers carefully calculate your speed and won't hit you, provided you don't alter your route or pace. Watch out for a lesser hazard: *merde*. Parisian dogs decorate the city's sidewalks with 16 tons of droppings a day. People get injured by slipping in it.

Organized Tours of Paris

Bus Tours: Paris Vision offers handy bus tours of Paris, day and night (advertised in hotel lobbies); its "Illuminated Paris" tour is much more interesting (see "Nightlife in Paris," below). Far better daytime bus tours are the hop-on hop-off double-decker bus services connecting Paris' main sights while providing running commentary (ideal in good weather when you can sit on top; see also Bâteau-Bus under "Boat Tours," below).

Two companies provide this service: **L'Open Tours** and **Les Cars Rouges** (pick up their brochures showing routes and stops from any TI or on their buses). The yellow buses of L'Open Tours provide more extensive coverage, with three different routes rolling by most of the important sights in Paris (the Paris Grand Tour offers the best introduction). Tickets are good for any route. Buy your tickets from the driver (€23/1-day ticket, €25/2-day ticket, kids 4–11 pay €11.50 for 1 or 2 days). Two or three buses depart hourly from about 10:00 to 18:00; expect to wait 10 to 20 minutes at each stop. You can hop off at any stop, then catch a later bus following the same circuit. You'll see these bright yellow, topless double-decker buses all over town—pick one up at the first important sight you visit, or start your tour at the Eiffel Tower stop (the first street on nonriver side of the tower, tel. 01 42 66 56 56). **Les Cars Rouges'** bright red buses offer largely the same service with fewer stops on a single, Grand Tour Route for less money (2-day tickets, €21-adult, €10-kids 4–12, tel. 01 53 95 39 53).

Boat Tours: Several companies offer one-hour boat cruises on the Seine (by far, best at night). The huge, mass-production **Bâteaux-Mouches** boats depart every 20 to 30 minutes from pont de l'Alma's right bank, the centrally located pont Neuf, and right in front of the Eiffel Tower, and are convenient to rue Cler hotels (€7, €4 for ages 4–12 and over 65, daily 10:00–22:30, useless taped explanations in 6 languages and tour groups by the dozens, tel. 01 42 25 96 10). The smaller and more intimate **Vedettes de pont Neuf** depart only once an hour from the center of the pont Neuf (twice an hour after dark), but they come with a live guide giving explanations in French and English and are convenient to Marais and Contrescarpe hotels (€8.50, €4 for ages 4–12 and over 65, tel. 01 46 33 98 38). From early April to early November, **Bâteau-Bus** operates boats on the Seine, connecting seven key stops about every 25 minutes: Eiffel Tower, Champs-Elysées, Orsay/place de la Concorde, Louvre, Notre-Dame, Hôtel de Ville, and St. Germain-des-Près. Pick up a schedule at any stop (or TI) and use the boats as a scenic alternative to the Métro. Tickets are available for one day (€10, €5.50 under 12) and two days (€12, €6 under 12). Boats run from 10:00 to 19:00, and until 21:00 June through September. **Paris Canal** departs twice daily for three-hour, one-way cruises between the Orsay and Parc de la Vilette. You'll cruise up the Seine, then along a quiet canal through nontouristy Paris, accompanied by English explanations (€15, €8.50 for kids 4–11, €11.50 for ages 12–25). One-way trips depart from near the Orsay at 9:30 from quai Anatole France, and from Parc de la Vilette (at Folie des Visites du Parc) at 14:30 (tel. 01 42 40 96 97).

Walking Tours: Paris Walking Tours offers a variety of excellent two-hour walks nearly daily for €10 (tel. 01 48 09 21 40 for recorded schedule in English, fax 01 42 43 75 51, www .pariswalkingtours.com). They focus on the Marais, Luxembourg Gardens, Garnier Opéra, Montmartre, and Hemingway's Paris. Ask about their family-friendly tours. Call ahead a day or two to learn their schedule and starting point. No reservations are required. These are thoughtfully prepared, humorous, and relaxing walking tours led by British or American guides. Don't hesitate to stand close to the guide to hear. For Lost Generation fans, **Paris Literary Promenades** takes you through areas once popular with literary giants, from Joyce to Beckett to Hemingway (€9, late May–mid-Oct, daily except Wed at 14:30 and 19:00, 2 hrs, tours depart from place de l'Odeon, tel. 01 48 07 80 72 or cellular 06 03 27 73 52). You can also hire a Parisian as your personal guide. Arnaud Servignat (tel. 06 72 77 94 50, e-mail: arnotour @noos.fr) and Marianne Siegler (tel. 01 42 52 32 51) are licensed local guides who freelance for individuals and families ($150/ 4 hrs, $250/day).

Bike Tours: Mike's Bullfrog Bike Tours—like a frat party on wheels—attracts a college crowd for its boisterous three- to four-hour rolls through Paris (€20, May–Nov daily at 11:00, also at 15:30 June–July, no CC, in English, no bikes or reservations

needed, meet at south pillar of Eiffel Tower, cellular 06 09 98 08
60, www.mikesbiketours.com).
   Excursion Tours: Many companies offer minivan and
big-bus tours to regional sights (including all daytrips described
below). **Paris Walking Tours** are the best, with informative and
fun afternoon visits to the Impressionist artist retreats of Giverny
and Auvers-sur-Oise (€47–56, includes admissions, see "Walking
Tours," above). **Paris Vision** offers mass-produced, full-size bus
and minivan tours to several popular regional destinations, including the Loire Valley, Champagne region, D-Day beaches, and
Mont St. Michel. Their minivan tours are more expensive but
more personal, in English, and offer pickup at your hotel (€130–
200/person). Their full-size bus tours are multilingual and cost
about half the price of a minivan tour—worth it for some simply
for the ease of transportation to the sights (full-size buses depart
from 214 rue de Rivoli, Mo: Tuileries, tel. 01 42 60 30 01, fax
01 42 86 95 36, www.parisvision.com).

Sights—The "Historic Core of Paris" Walk
(This information is distilled from the Historic Paris Walk chapter
in *Rick Steves' Mona Winks*, by Gene Openshaw and Rick Steves.)
   Allow four hours for this self-guided tour, including sightseeing. Start where the city did—on the Ile de la Cité. Face Notre-
Dame and follow the dotted line on the "Core of Paris" map (within
this chapter). To get to Notre-Dame, ride the Métro to Cité, Hôtel
de Ville, or St. Michel and walk to the big square facing the...
   ▲▲**Notre-Dame Cathedral**—This 700-year-old cathedral is
packed with history and tourists. Study its sculpture and windows,
take in a Mass, eavesdrop on guides, and walk all around the
outside (free, daily 08:00–18:45, €2.50 for treasury open daily
09:30–17:30—not covered by museum pass, free English tours
normally Wed and Thu at 12:00 and Sat at 14:30, Sun Masses at
08:00, 08:45, 10:00, 11:30, 12:30, and 18:30, Mo: Cité, Hôtel de
Ville, or St. Michel). Climb to the top for a great view of the city;
you get 400 steps for only €5.50 (entrance outside, daily April–
Sept 09:00–18:00, Oct–March 10:00–17:30). There are clean
€0.50 toilets in front of the church near Charlemagne's statue.
   The **cathedral facade** is worth a close look. The church is
dedicated to "Our Lady" (Notre-Dame). Mary is center stage—
cradling Jesus, surrounded by the halo of the rose window. Adam
is on the left and Eve is on the right.
   Below Mary and above the arches is a row of 28 statues
known as the Kings of Judah. During the French Revolution,
these Biblical kings were mistaken for the hated French kings.
The citizens stormed the church, crying, "Off with their heads!"
All were decapitated but have since been recapitated.
   Speaking of decapitation, look at the carving above the

Core of Paris

doorway on the left. The man with his head in his hands is
St. Denis. Back when there was a Roman temple on this spot,
Christianity began making converts. The fourth-century bishop
of Roman Paris, Denis, was beheaded. But these early Christians
were hard to keep down. The man who would become St. Denis
got up, tucked his head under his arm, and headed north until
he found just the right place to meet his maker: Montmartre.
(Athough the name "Montmartre" comes from the Roman
"Mount of Mars," later generations—thinking of their beheaded
patron St. Denis—preferred a less pagan version, "Mount of
Martyrs.") The Parisians were convinced of this miracle, Christianity gained ground, and a church soon replaced the pagan temple.

Medieval art was OK if it embellished the house of God and
told Bible stories. For a fine example, move to the base of the
central column (at the foot of Mary, about where the head of

St. Denis could spit if he was real good). Working around from the left, find God telling a barely created Eve, "Have fun but no apples." Next, the sexiest serpent I've ever seen makes apples à la mode. Finally, Adam and Eve, now ashamed of their naked-ness, are expelled by an angel. This is a tiny example in a church covered with meaning.

Now move to the right and study the carving above the **central portal**. It's the end of the world, and Christ sits on the throne of Judgment (just under the arches, holding his hands up). Below him an angel and a demon weigh souls in the balance. The "good" stand to the left, looking up to heaven. The "bad" ones to the right are chained up and led off to...Versailles on a Tuesday. The "ugly" ones must be the crazy sculpted demons to the right, at the base of the arch.

Wander through the interior. You'll be routed around the ambulatory, much as medieval pilgrims would have been. Don't miss the rose windows filling each of the transepts. Back outside, walk around the church through the park on the riverside for a close look at the flying buttresses.

The neo-Gothic 90-meter (300-foot) **spire** is a product of the 1860 reconstruction. Around its base are apostles and evange-lists (the green men) as well as Viollet-le-Duc, the architect in charge of the work. Notice how the apostles look outward, bless-ing the city, while the architect (at top, seen from behind the church) looks up, admiring his spire.

The archaeological **crypt** is a worthwhile 15-minute stop with your museum pass (€3, Tue–Sun 10:00–17:30, closed Mon, enter 100 meters/325 feet in front of church). You'll see Roman ruins, trace the street plan of the medieval village, and see dia-grams of how the earliest Paris grew and grew, all thoughtfully explained in English.

If you're hungry near Notre-Dame, the nearby Ile St. Louis has inexpensive *crêperies* and grocery stores open daily on its main drag. Plan a picnic for the quiet bench-filled park immediately behind the church (public WC).

Behind Notre-Dame, squeeze through the tourist buses, cross the street, and enter the iron gate into the park at the tip of the island. Look for the stairs and head down to reach...

▲▲**Deportation Memorial (Mémorial de la Déportation)**— This memorial to the 200,000 French victims of the Nazi concen-tration camps draws you into their experience. As you descend the steps, the city around you disappears. Surrounded by walls, you have become a prisoner. Your only freedom is your view of the sky and the tantalizing glimpse of the river below.

Enter the single-file chamber ahead. Inside, the circular plaque in the floor reads, "They descended into the mouth of the earth and they did not return." A hallway stretches in front of you, lined with 200,000 lighted crystals, one for each French citizen that died. Flickering at the far end is the eternal flame of hope. The tomb of the unknown deportee lies at your feet. Above, the inscription reads, "Dedicated to the living memory of the 200,000 French deportees sleeping in the night and the fog, exterminated in the Nazi concentration camps."

Above the exit as you leave is the message you'll find at all Nazi sights: "Forgive but never forget." (Free, April–Sept daily 10:00–12:00, 14:00–19:00, Oct–March daily 10:00–12:00, 14:00–17:00, east tip of island near Ile St. Louis, behind Notre-Dame, Mo: Cité.)

Ile St. Louis—Look across the river to the Ile St. Louis. If the Ile de la Cité is a tug laden with the history of Paris, it's towing this classy little residential dinghy laden only with boutiques, famous sorbet shops, and restaurants (see "Eating in Paris," below). This island wasn't developed until much later (18th century). What was a swampy mess is now harmonious Parisian architecture. The pedestrian bridge, pont Saint Louis, connects the two islands, leading right to rue Saint Louis en l'Ile. This spine of the island is lined with interesting shops. A short stroll takes you to the famous Bertillon ice-cream parlor (#31). Loop back to the pedestrian bridge along the parklike quays (walk north to the river and turn left). This walk is about as peaceful and romantic as Paris gets.

Before walking to the opposite end of the Ile de la Cité, loop through the Latin Quarter (as indicated on the map). From the Deportation Memorial, cross the bridge onto the Left Bank and enjoy the riverside view of the Notre-Dame and window shop among the green book stalls, browsing through used books, vintage posters, and souvenirs. At the little park and church (over the bridge from the front of Notre-Dame), venture inland a few blocks, basically arcing through the Latin Quarter and returning to the island two bridges down at place St. Michel.

▲**Latin Quarter**—This area, which gets its name from the language used here when it was an exclusive medieval university district, lies between Luxembourg Gardens and the Seine, centering around the Sorbonne University and boulevards St. Germain and St. Michel. This is the core of the Left Bank—it's crowded with international eateries, far-out bookshops, street singers, and jazz clubs. For colorful wandering and café sitting, afternoons and evenings are best (Mo: St. Michel).

Along rue Saint-Severin, you can still see the shadow of the medieval sewer system (the street slopes into a central channel of bricks). In the days before plumbing and toilets, when people still went to the river or neighborhood wells for their water, "flushing" meant throwing it out the window. Certain times of day were flushing times. Maids on the fourth floor would holler "*Garde de l'eau!"* ("Look out for the water!") and heave it into the streets, where it would eventually be washed down into the Seine.

Consider a visit to the Cluny Museum for its medieval art and unicorn tapestries (listed under "Sights—Southeast Paris," below).

Place St. Michel (facing the St. Michel bridge) is the traditional core of the Left Bank's artsy, liberal, hippie, Bohemian district of poets, philosophers, winos, and tourists. In less-commercial times, place St. Michel was a gathering point for the city's malcontents and misfits. Here, in 1871, the citizens took the streets from the government troops, set up barricades *Les Mis*–style, and established the Paris Commune. In World War II, the locals rose up against their Nazi oppressors (read the plaques by St. Michel fountain). And in the spring of 1968, a time of social upheaval all over the world, young students—battling riot batons and tear gas—took over the square and demanded change.

From place St. Michel, look across the river and find the spire of Sainte-Chapelle church and its weathervane angel (below). Cross the river on pont St. Michel and continue along boulevard du Palais. On your left you'll see the high-security doorway to Sainte-Chapelle. But first, carry on another 30 meters (100 feet) and turn right at a wide pedestrian street, the rue de Lutece.

Cité "Métropolitain" Stop—Of the 141 original turn-of-the-19th-century subway entrances, this is one of 17 survivors now preserved as a national art treasure. The curvy, plantlike ironwork is a textbook example of Art Nouveau, the style that rebelled against the erector-set squareness of the Industrial Age (e.g., Mr. Eiffel's tower).

The flower market right here on place Louis Lepine is a pleasant detour. On Sundays this square chirps with a busy bird market. And across the way is the Prefecture de Police, where Inspector Clouseau of *Pink Panther* fame used to work and where the local resistance fighters took the first building from the Nazis in August 1944, leading to the Allied liberation of Paris a week later.

Pause here to admire the view. Sainte-Chapelle is a pearl in an ugly architectural oyster, part of a complex of buildings that includes the Palace of Justice (to the right of Sainte-Chapelle, behind the fancy gates). Return to the entrance of Sainte-Chapelle. Everyone needs to pass through a metal detector to get in. Free toilets are ahead on the left. The line into the church may be long. (Museum-card holders can go directly in; pick up the excellent English info sheet.) Enter the humble ground floor of...

▲▲▲**Sainte-Chapelle**—This triumph of Gothic church architecture is a cathedral of glass like no other. It was speedily built from 1242 to 1248 for St. Louis IX (France's only canonized king) to house the supposed Crown of Thorns. Its architectural harmony is due to the fact that it was completed under the direction of one architect in only six years—unheard of in Gothic times. (Notre-Dame took more than 200 years to build.)

The design clearly shows an Old Regime approach to worship. The basement was for staff and other common folk. Royal Christians worshiped upstairs. The ground-floor paint job, a 19th-century restoration, is a reasonably accurate copy of the original.

Climb the spiral staircase to the **Chapelle Haute**. Fill the place with choral music, crank up the sunshine, face the top of the altar, and really believe that the Crown of Thorns was there, and this becomes one awesome space.

"Let there be light." In the Bible, it's clear: Light is divine. Light shining through stained glass was a symbol of God's grace shining down to earth. Gothic architects used their new technology to turn dark stone buildings into lanterns of light. The glory of Gothic shines brighter here than in any other church.

There are 15 separate panels of stained glass (6,500 square feet—two-thirds of it 13th-century original), with more than 1,100 different scenes, mostly from the Bible. In medieval times, scenes like these helped teach Bible stories to the illiterate.

The altar was raised up high to better display the relic—the Crown of Thorns—around which this chapel was built. The supposed crown cost King Louis three times as much as this church. Today it is kept in the Notre-Dame Treasury and shown only on Good Friday.

Louis' little private viewing window is in the wall to the right of the altar. Louis, both saintly and shy, liked to go to church without dealing with the rigors of public royal life. Here he could worship still dressed in his jammies.

Lay your camera on the ground and shoot the ceiling. Those ribs growing out of the slender columns are the essence of Gothic.

Books in the gift shop explain the stained glass in English. There are concerts (€15–23) almost every summer evening. (€5.50 entry, €8 combo-ticket with Conciergerie, daily April–Sept 09:30–18:30, Oct–March 10:00–17:00, Mo: Cité, tel. 01 48 01 91 35 for concert information.)

Palais du Justice—Back outside, as you walk around the church exterior, look down and notice how much Paris has risen in the 800 years since Sainte-Chapelle was built. You're in a huge complex of buildings that has housed the local government since ancient Roman times. It was the site of the original Gothic palace of the early kings of France. The only surviving medieval parts are the Sainte-Chapelle church and the Conciergerie prison.

Most of the site is now covered by the giant Palais de Justice, home of France's supreme court (built in 1776). "*Liberté, Egalité, Fraternité*" over the doors is a reminder that this was also the headquarters of the revolutionary government.

Now pass through the big iron gate to the noisy boulevard

du Palais and turn left (toward the Right Bank). On the corner is the site of the oldest public clock (built in 1334) in the city. While the present clock is said to be Baroque, it somehow still manages to keep accurate time.

Turn left onto quai de l'Horologe and walk along the river. The round medieval tower just ahead marks the entrance to the Conciergerie. Pop in to visit the courtyard and lobby (free). Step past the serious-looking guard into the courtyard.

Conciergerie—This former prison is a gloomy place. Kings used it to torture and execute failed assassins. The leaders of the Revolution put it to similar good use. The tower next to the entrance, called "the babbler," was named for the painful sounds that leaked from it.

Look at the stark lettering above the doorways. This was a no-nonsense revolutionary time. Everything, even lettering, was subjected to the test of reason. No frills or we chop 'em off.

Step inside; the lobby, with an English-language history display, is free. Marie Antoinette was imprisoned here. During a busy eight-month period in the Revolution, she was one of 2,600 prisoners kept here on the way to the guillotine. The interior, with its huge vaulted and pillared rooms, echoes with history but is pretty barren (€5.50, €8 with Sainte-Chapelle, daily April–Sept 09:30–18:30, Oct–March 10:00–17:00, good English descriptions, Mo: Cité). You can see Marie Antoinette's cell, housing a collection of her mementos. In another room, a list of those made "a foot shorter at the top" by the "national razor" includes ex-King Louis XVI, Charlotte Corday (who murdered Marat in his bathtub), and the chief revolutionary who got a taste of his own medicine, Maximilien Robespierre.

Back outside, wink at the flak-proof vested guard and turn left. Listen for babbles and continue your walk along the river. Across the river you can see the rooftop observatory—flags flapping—of the Samaritaine department store, where this walk will end. At the first corner, veer left past France's supreme-court building and into a sleepy triangular square called place Dauphine. Marvel at how such quaintness could be lodged in the midst of such greatness as you walk through the park to the end of the island. At the equestrian statue of Henry IV, turn right onto the bridge and take refuge in one of the nooks on the Eiffel Tower side.

Pont Neuf—This "new bridge" is now Paris' oldest. Built during Henry IV's reign (around 1600), its 12 arches span the widest part of the river. The fine view includes the park on the tip of the island (note Seine tour boats), the Orsay Museum, and the Louvre. These turrets were originally for vendors and street entertainers. In the days of Henry IV, who originated the promise of "a chicken in every pot," this would have been a lively scene.

Directly over the river, the first building you'll hit on the Right Bank is the venerable old department store, Samaritaine.

▲**Samaritaine Department Store Viewpoint**—Enter the store
and go to the rooftop. Ride the glass elevator from near the pont
Neuf entrance to the ninth floor (you'll be greeted by a WC—
check out the sink). Pass the 10th-floor *terrasse* for the 11th-floor
panorama (tight spiral staircase; watch your head). Quiz yourself.
Working counterclockwise, find the Eiffel Tower, Invalides/
Napoleon's Tomb, Montparnasse Tower, Henry IV statue on
the tip of the island, Sorbonne University, the dome of the
Panthéon, Sainte-Chapelle, Notre-Dame, Hôtel de Ville (city
hall), Pompidou Center, Sacré-Coeur, Opéra, and Louvre. The
Champs-Elysées leads to the Arc de Triomphe. Shadowing that—
even bigger, while two times as distant—is the Grande Arche de
la Défense. You'll find light, reasonably priced, and incredibly
scenic meals on the breezy terrace, and a supermarket in the
basement. (Rooftop view is free, daily 09:30–19:00, Mo: Pont
Neuf, tel. 01 40 41 20 20.)

Sights—Paris' Museums near the Tuileries Gardens

The newly renovated Tuileries Gardens was once private property of kings and queens. Paris' grandest public park links
these museums.

▲▲▲**Louvre**—This is Europe's oldest, biggest, greatest, and maybe
most-crowded museum. There is no grander entry than through
the pyramid, but metal detectors create a long line at times. To
avoid the line, you have two choices: Museum-pass holders can use
the group entrance in the pedestrian passageway between the pyramid and rue de Rivoli (facing the pyramid with your back to the
Tuileries Gardens, go to your left, which is north; under the arches
you'll find the entrance and escalator down). Or anyone can get
into the Louvre from the slick underground Carrousel shopping
mall that connects with the museum; enter the mall either at
99 rue de Rivoli at the door with the red awning or get off the
Métro at the "Palais Royal/Musée du Louvre" stop and follow
signs to "Musée du Louvre" (don't get off at the "Louvre Rivoli"
Métro stop, which is farther away).

Pick up the free *Louvre Handbook* in English at the information
desk under the pyramid as you enter. Don't try to cover the entire
museum. The 90-minute English-language tours, which leave six
times daily except Sunday, boil this overwhelming museum down
to size (€5.50, tour tel. 01 40 20 52 09). Clever €5 digital audioguides (after ticket booths, at top of stairs) give you a receiver and
a directory of about 130 masterpieces, allowing you to dial a (rather
dull) commentary on included works as you stumble upon them.
Rick Steves' and Gene Openshaw's museum guidebook, *Rick
Steves' Mona Winks* (buy in United States), includes a self-guided
tour of the Louvre.

Paris' Museums near the Tuileries Gardens

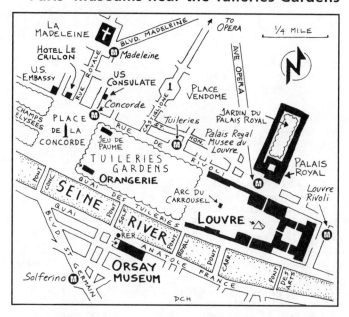

If you can't get a guide, start in the Denon wing and visit the **highlights**, in this order: Michelangelo's *Slaves*; Ancient Greek and Roman works (Parthenon frieze, *Venus de Milo*, Pompeii mosaics, Etruscan sarcophagi, Roman portrait busts, *Nike of Samothrace*); Apollo Gallery (jewels); French and Italian paintings in the Grande Galerie (a 400-meter hike and worth it); the *Mona Lisa* and her Italian Renaissance roommates; the nearby neoclassical collection (*Coronation of Napoléon*); and the Romantic collection, with works by Delacroix (*Liberty at the Barricades*) and Géricault (*Raft of the Medusa*).

Cost: €7, €5 after 15:00 and on Sunday, free on first Sunday of month and for those under 18, covered by museum pass. Tickets good all day. Reentry allowed.

Hours: Wednesday through Monday 09:00 to 18:00, closed Tuesday, all wings open Wednesday until 21:45, Richelieu Wing (only) open until 21:45 on Monday. Galleries start closing 30 minutes early. Closed January 1, Easter, May 1, November 1, and Christmas Day. Crowds are worst on Sunday, Monday, Wednesday, and mornings. Save money by visiting after 15:00. (You can enter the pyramid for free until 21:30. Go in at night and see it glow.) Tel. 01 40 20 51 51, recorded info tel. 01 40 20 53 17 (www.louvre.fr).

The newly renovated Richelieu wing and the underground shopping-mall extension add the finishing touches to Le Grand Louvre Project (which started in 1989 with the pyramid entrance). To explore this most recent extension of the Louvre, enter through the pyramid, walk toward the inverted pyramid, and uncover a post office, a handy TI and SNCF office, glittering boutiques and a dizzying assortment of good-value eateries (up the escalator), and the Palais-Royal Métro entrance. Stairs at the far end take you right into the Tuileries Gardens, a perfect antidote to the stuffy, crowded rooms of the Louvre.

Jeu de Paume—This one-time home to the Impressionist art collection (which is now located in the Orsay) hosts rotating exhibits of top contemporary artists (€6, not covered by museum pass, Tue 12:00–21:30, Wed–Fri 12:00–19:00, Sat–Sun 10:00–19:00, closed Mon, on place de la Concorde, just inside Tuileries Garden on rue de Rivoli side, Mo: Concorde).

L'Orangerie—After a two-year renovation, this museum of Impressionist art is due to reopen sometime in 2002. For specifics, ask at a TI or another museum (i.e., Louvre, Orsay). This small, quiet, and often-overlooked museum houses Monet's water lilies, many famous Renoirs, and a scattering of other great Impressionist works. The breezy round rooms of water lilies are two of the most enjoyable rooms in Paris (price and hours not set, located in Tuileries Garden near place de la Concorde, Mo: Concorde).

▲▲▲**Orsay Museum**—Paris' 19th-century art museum (actually, art from 1848–1914) includes Europe's greatest collection of Impressionist works. The museum is housed in a former train station (Gare d'Orsay) across the river and a lovely 15-minute walk downstream from the Louvre through the Tuileries Gardens. (The RER-C train line zips you right to "Musée d'Orsay"; the Métro stop Solferino is 3 blocks south of the Orsay.)

Until the summer of 2002, the main entry to the Orsay will be closed for renovation, and you will enter at a temporary entry facing the river.

Start on the ground floor. The "pretty" conservative-establishment art is in the south side. Then cross into the brutally truthful and, at that time, very shocking art of the realist rebels and Manet (north side of ground floor). Then ride the escalators at the far end (detouring at the top for a grand museum view) to the series of Impressionist rooms (Monet, Renoir, Dégas, et al).

Don't miss the Grand Ballroom (room 52, Arts et Decors de la IIIème République) and Art Nouveau on the mezzanine level. The restaurant Le Salon de Thé du Musée, near the ballroom, is worth a peek or even a lunch stop (affordable salad bar).

Cost and Hours: €7; €5 after 16:15, on Sunday, and for ages 18 to 25; free for youth under 18 and for anyone on the first Sunday of the month (June 20–Sept 20 Tue–Sun 09:00–18:00, Sept 21–June 19 Tue–Sat 10:00–18:00, Sun 09:00–18:00, Thu until 21:45 all year, closed Mon, last entrance 45 min before closing, galleries start closing 30 min early). Tickets are valid all day. The Orsay is covered by the museum pass. Pass holders can enter to the left of the main entrance (during the renovation, they can walk to the front of the line and show their passes). Ask for a free floor plan in English. English-language tours usually run daily except Sunday at 11:30, cost €5.50, take 90 minutes, and are also available on audioguide (€5). The Orsay is very crowded on Tuesday, when the Louvre is closed. Tel. 01 40 49 48 48.

Sights—Southwest Paris: The Eiffel Tower Neighborhood

▲▲▲**Eiffel Tower**—It's crowded and expensive but worth the trouble. Go early (by 08:45) or late in the day (after 20:00 in summer, otherwise 18:00) to avoid most crowds; weekends are worst. Pilier Nord (the north pillar) has the biggest elevator and, therefore, the fastest-moving line. It takes two elevators to get to the top (transfer at level 2), which means two lines and very long waits if you don't go early or late. A TI/ticket booth is between the Pilier Nord and Est (east pillar). The stairs (yes, you can walk up partway) are next to the Jules Verne restaurant entry. A sign in the jammed elevator tells you to beware of pickpockets.

The tower is 300 meters tall (1,000 feet), 15 centimeters (6 inches) taller in hot weather, covers 2.5 acres, and requires 50 tons of paint. Its 7,000 tons of metal are spread out so well at the base that it's no heavier per square inch than a linebacker on tiptoes. Visitors to Paris may find *Mona Lisa* to be less than expected, but the Eiffel Tower rarely disappoints, even in an era of skyscrapers.

Built a hundred years after the French Revolution (and in the midst of an Industrial one), the tower served no function but to impress. Bridge-builder Gustave Eiffel won the contest for the 1889 Centennial World's Fair by beating out such rival proposals as a giant guillotine. To a generation hooked on technology, the tower was the marvel of the age, a symbol of progress and of man's ingenuity. To others, it was a cloned-sheep monstrosity. The writer Maupassant routinely ate lunch in the tower just so he wouldn't have to look at it.

Delicate and graceful when seen from afar, it's massive—even a bit scary—from close up. You don't appreciate the size until you walk toward it; like a mountain, it seems so close but takes forever to reach. There are three observation platforms, at 60, 120, and 270 meters (200, 400, and 900 feet); the higher you go, the more you pay. Each requires a separate elevator (and a line), so plan on at least 90 minutes if you want to go to the top and back. The

Eiffel Tower to Invalides

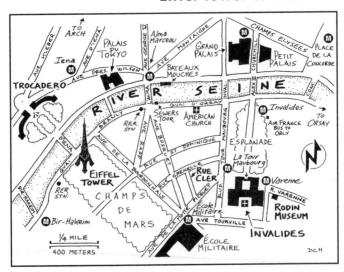

view from the 120-meter high (400 feet) second level is plenty.
As you ascend through the metal beams, imagine being a worker,
perched high above nothing, riveting this giant erector set
together. On top, all of Paris lies before you, with a panorama
guide. On a good day you can see for 65 kilometers (40 miles).

The first level has exhibits, a post office (daily 10:00–19:00,
cancellation stamp will read Eiffel Tower), snack bar, WCs, and
souvenirs. Read the informative signs (in English) describing the
major monuments, see the entertaining free movie on the history
of the tower, and don't miss a century of fireworks, including the
entire millennium blast, on video. Then consider a drink or a
sandwich overlooking all of Paris at the snack café (outdoor tables
in summer) or at the city's best view bar/restaurant, **Altitude 95**
(€15 lunches, €34–46 dinners, dinner seatings at 19:00 and 21:00,
reserve well ahead for a view table; before you ascend to dine,
drop by the booth between the north-*nord* and east-*est* pillars to
pick up a pass that enables you to skip the line; tel. 01 45 55 20 04,
fax 01 47 05 94 40).

The second level has the best views (walk up the stairway
to get above the netting), a small cafeteria, WCs, and an Internet gimmick to have your photo at the Eiffel Tower sent into
cyberspace (*La Gallerie des Visiteurs*).

It costs €4 to go to the first level, €7 to the second, and €10
to go all the way for the 270-meter view (900 feet, not covered
by museum pass). On a budget? You can climb the stairs to the

second level for only €3 (March–Sept daily 09:00–24:00, Oct–Feb 09:30–23:00, shorter lines at night, Mo: Trocadero, RER: Champ de Mars, tel. 01 44 11 23 23).

The best place to view the tower is from Trocadero Square to the north (a 10-min walk across the river, and a happening scene at night). Consider arriving at the Trocadero Métro stop, then walking toward the tower. Another great viewpoint is the long, grassy field, le Champ de Mars, to the south (after about 20:00 the *gendarmes* look the other way as Parisians stretch out or picnic on the grass). However impressive it may be by day, it's an awesome thing to see at twilight, when the tower becomes engorged with light and virile Paris lies back and lets night be on top.

▲**Paris Sewer Tour (Egouts)**—This quick and easy visit takes you along a few hundred meters of underground water tunnel lined with interesting displays, well-described in English, explaining the evolution of the world's longest sewer system. (If you lined up Paris' sewers, they would reach beyond Istanbul.) Don't miss the slide show, the fine WCs just beyond the gift shop, and the occasional tours in English (€4, covered by museum pass, Sat–Wed 11:00–17:00, closed Thu–Fri, where pont de l'Alma greets the Left Bank, Mo: Alma Marceau, RER Pont de l'Alma, tel. 01 47 05 10 29).

▲▲**Napoleon's Tomb and Army Museum (Les Invalides)**— The emperor lies majestically dead inside several coffins under a grand dome—a goose-bumping pilgrimage for historians. Napoleon is surrounded by the tombs of other French war heroes and a fine military museum in Hôtel des Invalides. Check out the interesting World War II wing. Follow signs to the "crypt" to find Roman Empire–style reliefs listing the accomplishments of Napoleon's administration. The restored dome glitters with 26 pounds of gold (€6, students and kids 12–17-€5, under 12 free, daily April–Sept 09:00–17:45, Oct–March 10:00–16:45, Napoleon's Tomb open June 15–Sept 15 until 18:45, Mo: La Tour Maubourg or Varennes, tel. 01 44 42 37 72).

▲▲**Rodin Museum**—This user-friendly museum is filled with passionate works by the greatest sculptor since Michelangelo. See *The Kiss*, *The Thinker*, *The Gates of Hell*, and many more. Don't miss the room full of work by Rodin's student and mistress, Camille Claudel (€4, €2.75 on Sun and for students, free for youth under 18 and for anyone first Sun of month; €0.75 for gardens only, which may be Paris' best deal as many works are well-displayed in the beautiful gardens; Tue–Sun 09:30–17:45, closed Mon and at 17:00 off-season; near Napoléon's Tomb, 77 rue de Varennes, Mo: Varennes, tel. 01 44 18 61 10). There's a good self-serve cafeteria as well as idyllic picnic spots in the family-friendly back garden.

▲▲**Marmottan**—In this private, intimate, less-visited museum, you'll find more than 100 paintings by Claude Monet (thanks to his son Michel), including the *Impressions of a Sunrise* painting that gave the movement its start—and name (€6, not covered by museum pass, Tue–Sun 10:00–17:30, closed Mon, 2 rue Louis Boilly, Mo: La Muette, follow museum signs 6 blocks through a delightful kid-filled park to museum, tel. 01 44 96 50 33). Combine this fine museum with a stroll down one of Paris' most pleasant shopping streets, the rue de Passy (from La Muette Métro stop).

Sights—Southeast Paris: The Latin Quarter

▲**Latin Quarter**—This Left Bank neighborhood, just opposite the Notre-Dame, is the Latin Quarter. (For more information and a walking tour, see "Historic Core of Paris" Walk, above.) This was the center of Roman Paris. But its touristic fame relates to the Latin Quarter's intriguing artsy, bohemian character. This was perhaps Europe's leading university district in the Middle Ages—home, since the 13th century, to the prestigious Sorbonne University. Back then, Latin was the language of higher education. And, since students here came from all over Europe, Latin served as their linguistic common denominator. Locals referred to the quarter by its language: Latin. In modern times this became the center of Paris' café culture. The neighborhood's main boulevards (St. Michel and St. Germain) are lined with cafés—once the haunts of great poets and philosophers, but now the hangouts of tired tourists. While still youthful and artsy, the area has become a tourist ghetto filled with cheap North African eateries.

▲▲**Cluny Museum (Musée National du Moyen Age)**—This treasure trove of medieval art fills the old Roman baths, offering close-up looks at stained glass, Notre-Dame carvings, fine gold-smithing and jewelry, and rooms of tapestries—the best of which is the exquisite *Lady with the Unicorn*. In five panels, a delicate-as-medieval-can-be noble lady introduces a delighted unicorn to the senses of taste, hearing, sight, smell, and touch (€6, €4 on Sun; Wed–Mon 09:15–17:45, closed Tue, near the corner of boulevards St. Michel and St. Germain, Mo: Cluny, tel. 01 53 73 78 00).

St. Germain des Prés—A church was first built on this site in A.D. 452. The church you see today was constructed in 1163. The area around the church hops at night with fire-eaters, mimes, and scads of artists (Mo: St. Germain-des-Prés).

▲**St. Sulpice Organ Concert**—For pipe-organ enthusiasts, this is a delight. The Grand-Orgue at St. Sulpice has a rich history, with a line of 12 world-class organists (including Widor and Dupre) going back 300 years. Widor started the tradition of opening the loft to visitors after the 10:30 service on Sundays. Daniel Roth continues to welcome guests in three languages while playing five keyboards at once. The 10:30 Sunday Mass is followed by a high-powered 25-minute recital at 11:40. Then, just after noon, the small, unmarked door is opened (left of entry as you face the rear). Visitors scamper like 16th notes up spiral stairs, past the

Latin Quarter

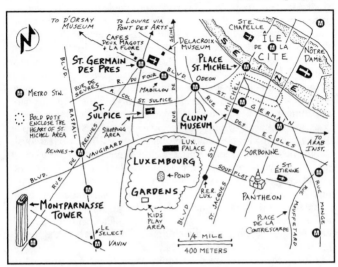

18th-century Stairmasters that were used to fill the billows, into a world of 7,000 pipes, where they can watch the master performing the next Mass. You'll generally have 30 minutes to kill (there's a plush lounge) before the organ plays; visitors can leave at any time. If late or rushed, show up around 12:30 and wait at the little door. As someone leaves you can slip in (Mo: St. Sulpice or Mabillon). The nearby St. Germain market is open Sundays and worth a stop.

▲▲**Luxembourg Gardens**—Paris' most beautiful, interesting, and enjoyable garden/park/recreational area is a great place to watch Parisians at rest and play. The brilliant flower plantings are completely changed three times a year, and the boxed trees are brought out of the *orangerie* in May. Challenge the card and chess players to a game (near the tennis courts), or find a free chair near the main pond and take a breather. Notice any pigeons? A poor Ernest Hemingway used to hand hunt (read: strangle) them here. Paris Walking Tours offers a good tour of the park (see "Organized Tours," above). The grand neoclassical domed Panthéon, now a mausoleum housing the tombs of several great Frenchmen, is a block away and is only worth entering if you have a museum pass. The park is open until dusk (Mo: Odéon, RER: Luxembourg). If you enjoy the Luxembourg Gardens and want to see more, visit the elegant Parc Monceau (Mo: Monceau) and the colorful Jardin des Plantes (Mo: Jussieu or Gare d'Austerlitz, RER: Luxembourg).

Montparnasse Tower—This 59-floor superscraper—it's cheaper and easier to get to the top than to that of the Eiffel Tower—

offers one of Paris' best views, since the Eiffel Tower is in it and
Montparnasse Tower isn't. Buy the photo guide to the city, then
go to the rooftop and orient yourself (€8, not covered by museum
pass, daily in summer 09:30–23:30, off-season 10:00–22:00, disappointing after dark, entrance on rue l'Arrivé, Mo: Montparnasse).
This is efficient when combined with a daytrip to Chartres, because
trains to Chartres depart from the Montparnasse train station.

▲**Catacombs**—These underground tunnels contain the anonymous
bones of six million permanent Parisians. In 1785 the Revolutionary
government of Paris decided to make its congested city more spacious and sanitary by emptying the city cemeteries (which traditionally surrounded churches) into an official ossuary. The perfect locale
was the many kilometers of underground tunnels from limestone
quarries, which were, at that time, just outside the city. For decades,
priests led ceremonial processions of black-veiled, bone-laden carts
into the quarries where they were stacked into piles 1.5 meters high
(5 feet) and as much as 24 meters deep (80 feet) behind neat walls
of skull-studded tibia. Each transfer was completed with the placement of a plaque indicating the church and district where that pile
of bones originated and the date they arrived.

From the entry of the Catacombs, a spiral staircase leads
18 meters down (60 feet). Then you begin a 1.5-kilometer-long
(1 mile) subterranean walk. After several blocks of empty passageways, you ignore a sign announcing: "Halt, this is the empire of
the dead." Along the way, plaques encourage visitors to reflect upon
their destiny: "Happy is he who is forever faced with the hour of his
death and prepares himself for the end every day." You emerge far
from where you entered, with white limestone-covered toes, telling
anyone in the know you've been underground gawking at bones.
Note to wannabe Hamlets: An attendant checks your bag at the
exit for stolen souvenirs (€5, not covered by museum pass, 1 place
Denfert-Rochereau, Mo: Denfert-Rochereau, Tue–Fri 14:00–16:00,
Sat–Sun 9:00–11:00, 14:00–16:00, closed Mon, tel. 01 43 22 47 63).

Sights—Northwest Paris
▲▲**Place de la Concorde and the Champs-Elysées**—This
famous boulevard is Paris' backbone and greatest concentration
of traffic. All of France seems to converge on the place de la
Concorde, the city's largest square. It was here that the guillotine
took the lives of thousands—including King Louis XVI and Marie
Antoinette. Back then it was called the place de la Revolution.

Catherine de Médici wanted a place to drive her carriage, so
she started draining the swamp that would become the Champs-
Elysées. Napoléon put on the final touches, and it's been the place
to be seen ever since. The Tour de France bicycle race ends here,
as do all parades (French or foe) of any significance. While the
boulevard has become a bit hamburgerized, a walk here is a must.

Take the Métro to the Arc de Triomphe (Mo: Etoile) and saunter down the Champs-Elysées (Métro stops every few blocks: FDR, George V, and Etoile).

▲▲▲**Arc de Triomphe**—Napoléon had the magnificent Arc de Triomphe commissioned to commemorate his victory at the Battle of Austerlitz. There's no triumphal arch bigger (50 meters/ 164 feet high, 40 meters/130 feet wide). And, with 12 converging boulevards, there's no traffic circle more thrilling to experience— either behind the wheel or on foot (take the underpass). An elevator or a spiral staircase leads to a cute museum about the arch and a grand view from the top, even after dark (€6, June–Sept daily 09:30–23:00, Oct–May daily 9:30–22:00, Mo: Etoile, use underpass to reach arch, tel. 01 43 80 31 31).

▲**Le Palais Garnier (a.k.a. "The Old Opera")**—This grand palace of the belle époque (late 19th century) was built for Napoleon III and finished in 1875. (After completing this project, Opéra architect Garnier went south to design the casino in Monte Carlo.) From the grand Avenue de l'Opéra—once lined with Paris' most fashionable haunts—the newly restored facade seems to say "all power to the wealthy." While huge, the actual theater seats only 2,000. The real show was before and after, when the elite of Paris— out to see and be seen—strutted their elegant stuff in the extravagant lobbies. Think of the grand marble stairway as a theater itself. As you wander the halls and gawk at the decor, imagine the place filled with the beautiful people of the day. The massive foundations straddle an underground lake (creating the mysterious world of the Phantom of the Opera). Tourists can peek from two boxes into the actual red velvet theater to see Marc Chagall's colorful ceiling (1964) playfully dancing around the eight-ton chandelier. Note the box seats next to the stage—the most expensive in the house with an obstructed view of the stage, but just right if you're there only to be seen. The elitism of this place prompted Mitterand to have a people's opera house built in the 1980s (symbolically on place de la Bastille, where the French Revolution began). This left the Garnier Opéra home only to a ballet and occasional concerts. While the library-museum is of interest to opera buffs, anyone will enjoy the second-floor grand foyer and Salon du Glacier, iced with decor typical of 1900 (€5, daily 10:00–17:00 except when in use for performance, English tours summers only, normally at 14:00, call to confirm; enter through the front off place de l'Opéra, Mo: Opéra, tel. 01 40 01 22 53). American Express and the *Paris Story* film are on the left side of the Opéra, and the venerable Galeries Lafayette department store is just behind.

Paris Story **Film**—This entertaining film gives a good and painless overview of Paris' turbulent, brilliant past, covering 2,000 years in 45 fast-moving minutes. Its cushy chairs make an ideal break from bad weather and sore feet and make it fun with kids (€8, kids 6–18-€5, families with 2 kids and 2 parents-€21, not covered by the museum pass, shows are on the hour daily 09:00–18:00, next to Opéra at 11 rue Scribe, Mo: Opéra, tel. 01 42 66 62 06).

▲▲**Musée Jacquemart-André**—This thoroughly enjoyable museum showcases the lavish home of a wealthy, art-loving, 19th-century Parisian couple. After wandering the grand boulevards, you now get inside for an intimate look at the lifestyles of the Parisian rich and fabulous. Edouard André and his wife Nélie Jacquemart—who had no children—spent their lives and fortunes designing, building, and then decorating a sumptuous mansion. What makes this visit so rewarding is the fine audioguide tour (in English, free with admission). And to make it even more memorable, the place is strewn with paintings by Rembrandt, Botticelli, Uccello, Mantegna, Bellini, Boucher, Fragonard—enough to make a painting gallery famous. Plan on spending an hour with the audioguide (€8, not covered by museum pass, daily 10:00–18:00, elegant café, 158 boulevard Haussmann, Mo: Miromesnil, tel. 01 42 89 04 91).

▲**Grande Arche de La Défense**—The centerpiece of Paris' ambitious skyscraper complex (La Défense) is the Grande Arche. Built to celebrate the 200th anniversary of the 1789 French Revolution, the place is big—38 floors on more than 200 acres. It holds offices for 30,000 people. Notre-Dame Cathedral could fit under its arch. The La Défense complex is an interesting study in 1960s land-use planning. More than 100,000 workers commute here daily, directing lots of business and development away from downtown and allowing central Paris to retain its more elegant feel. This aspect makes sense to most Parisians, regardless of whatever else they feel about the controversial complex. You'll enjoy city views from the Arche elevator (€7, under €2.75–5, not covered by museum pass, daily 10:00–19:00, includes a film on its construction and art exhibits, RER or Mo: La Défense, follow signs to Grande Arche or get off 1 stop earlier at Esplanade de la Défense and walk through the interesting business complex, tel. 01 49 07 27 57).

Sights—North Paris: Montmartre
▲**Sacré-Coeur and Montmartre**—This Byzantine-looking church, while only 130 years old, is impressive. It was built as a "praise the Lord anyway" gesture after the French were humiliated by the Germans in a brief war in 1871. The church is open daily until 23:00. One block from the church, the place du Tertre was the haunt of Toulouse-Lautrec and the original Bohemians. Today it's mobbed by tourists and unoriginal bohemians but still fun (go early in the morning to beat the crowds). Wander down rue Lepic to the two remaining windmills (once there were 30). Rue des Saules leads to Paris' only vineyard. Métro: Anvers (an extra Métro ticket buys your way up the funicular and avoids the stairs) or the closer but less scenic Abbesses. A taxi to the top of the hill saves time and sweat.

Pigalle—Paris' red-light district, the infamous "Pig Alley," is at the foot of Butte Montmartre. *Ooh la la*. More shocking than dangerous. Walk from place Pigalle to place Blanche, teasing desperate barkers and fast-talking temptresses. In bars, a €150 bottle of cheap champagne comes with a friend. Stick to the bigger streets, hang on to your wallet, and exercise good judgment. Cancan can cost a fortune, as can con artists in topless bars. After dark, tour buses line the streets. Tour guides make big bucks by bringing their groups to touristic nightclubs like the Moulin Rouge (Mo: Pigalle and Abbesses).

Sights—Northeast Paris: Marais Neighborhood and More

The Marais neighborhood extends along the right bank of the Seine from the Pompidou Center to the Bastille. It contains more pre-Revolutionary lanes and buildings than anywhere else in town and is more atmospheric than touristy. It's medieval Paris. This is how much of the city looked until, in the mid-1800s, Napoleon III had Baron Haussmann blast out the narrow streets to construct broad boulevards (wide enough for the guns and ranks of the army, too wide for revolutionary barricades), creating modern Paris. Originally a swamp (*marais*) during the reign of Henry IV, this area became the hometown of the French aristocracy. In the 17th century, big shots built their private mansions (*hôtels*) close to Henry's place des Vosges. When strolling the Marais, stick to the west-east axis formed by rue Ste. Croix de la Bretonniere, rue des Rosiers (heart of Paris' Jewish community), and rue St. Antoine. On Sunday afternoons, this trendy area pulses with shoppers and café crowds.

▲**Place des Vosges**—Study the architecture in this grand square: nine pavilions per side. Some of the brickwork is real, some is fake. Walk to the center, where Louis XIII sits on a horse surrounded by locals enjoying their community park. Children frolic in the sandbox, lovers warm benches, and pigeons guard their fountains while trees shade this retreat from the glare of the big city. Henry IV built this centerpiece of the Marais in 1605. As hoped, this turned the Marais into Paris' most exclusive neighborhood. As the nobility flocked to Versailles in a later age, this, too, was a magnet for the rich and powerful of France. With the Revolution, the aristocratic elegance of this quarter became working-class, filled with gritty shops, artisans, immigrants, and Jews. **Victor Hugo** lived at #6, and you can visit his house (€3, Tue–Sun 10:00–17:40, closed Mon, 6 place des Vosges, tel. 01 42 72 10 16). Leave the place des Vosges through the doorway at southwest corner of the square (near the 3-star Michelin restaurant, l'Ambrosie) and pass through the elegant **Hotel de Sully** (great example of a Marais mansion) to rue St. Antoine.

▲▲**Pompidou Center**—Europe's greatest collection of far-out

Marais Neighborhood Walk

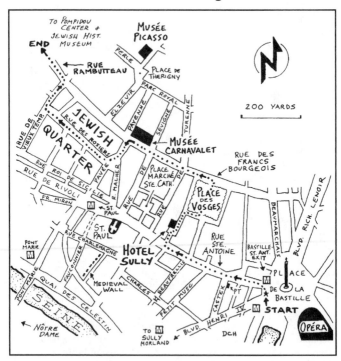

modern art, the Musée National d'Art Moderne, is housed on the top floor of this newly renovated and colorful exoskeletal building. Once ahead of its time, this 20th-century art (remember that century?) has been waiting for the world to catch up with it. After so many Madonnas and Children, a piano smashed to bits and glued to the wall is refreshing (€5, audioguide-€4, Wed–Mon 11:00–21:00, closed Tue, to use escalator you need a ticket for the museum or a museum pass, good mezzanine-level café is cheaper than cafés outside, Mo: Rambuteau, tel. 01 44 78 12 33).

The Pompidou Center and its square are lively, with lots of people, street theater, and activity inside and out—a perpetual street fair. Kids of any age enjoy the fun, colorful fountain (called *Homage to Stravinsky*) on the square.

▲▲**Museum of Art and History of Judaism (Hôtel d'Aignan)**— This remarkable museum, located in a beautifully restored Marais mansion, tells the story of Judaism throughout Europe, from the Roman destruction of Jerusalem to the theft of famous artwork during World War II. Helpful audioguides and many English explanations make this an enjoyable history lesson. Move along at your own speed. The emphasis of the museum is to illustrate the cultural unity maintained by this continually dispersed population. You'll learn about the history of Jewish traditions, from bar mitzvahs to menorahs, and see exquisite traditional costumes and objects around which daily life revolved. Don't miss the explanation of the Dreyfus affair, a major event in early-1900 French politics. You'll also see photographs of and paintings by famous Jewish artists, including Chagall, Modigliani, and Soutine. The small section devoted to the deportation of Jews from Paris is very moving (€6, ages 18–25-€4, under 18 free, not covered by museum pass, Mon–Fri 11:00–18:00, Sun 10:00–18:00, closed Sat, 71 rue du Temple, Mo. Rambuteau or Hôtel de Ville, tel. 01 53 01 86 53).

▲**Picasso Museum (Hôtel Salé)**—This is the world's largest collection of Pablo Picasso's paintings, sculpture, sketches, and ceramics and includes his personal collection of Impressionist art. It's well-explained in English and worth ▲▲▲ if you're a fan (€5, Wed–Mon 09:30–18:00, closed Tue, 5 rue Thorigny, Mo: St. Paul or Chemin Vert, tel. 01 42 71 25 21).

▲▲**Carnavalet Museum**—The tumultuous history of Paris is well-displayed in this converted Marais mansion. Unfortunately, explanations are in French only, but many displays are fairly self-explanatory. You'll see paintings of Parisian scenes, French Revolution paraphernalia, old Parisian store signs, a small guillotine, a model of 16th-century Ile de la Cité (notice the bridge houses), and rooms full of 15th-century Parisian furniture (€5.50, Tue–Sun 10:00–17:40, closed Mon, 23 rue de Sévigné, Mo: St Paul, tel. 01 42 72 21 13).

Promenade Plantée Park—This three-kilometer (2-mile) narrow garden walk, once a train track and now a joy, runs from place de la Bastille (Mo: Bastille) along avenue Daumesnil to Saint-Mandé (Mo: Michel Bizot). Part of the park is elevated. At times you'll walk along the street until you pick up the next segment. From place de la Bastille, take avenue Daumesnil (past Opéra building) to the intersection with avenue Ledru Rollin. Walk up the stairs and through the gate (free, opens Mon–Fri at 08:00, Sat–Sun at 09:00, closes at sunset).

▲**Père Lachaise Cemetery**—Littered with the tombstones of many of the city's most illustrious dead, this is your best one-stop look at the fascinating, romantic world of permanent Parisians. The place is confusing, but maps will direct you to the graves of Chopin, Molière, Edith Piaf, Oscar Wilde, Gertrude Stein, Héloïse, and Abelard. In section 92, a series of statues memorializing the war makes the French war experience a bit more real (open until dusk, helpful €1.50 maps at flower store near entry, across street from Métro stop, Mo: Père Lachaise or bus #69).

Disappointments de Paris

Here are a few negatives to help you manage your limited time:

La Madeleine is a big, stark, neoclassical church with a postcard facade and a postbox interior. The famous aristocratic deli behind the church, Fauchon, is elegant, but so are many others handier to your hotel.

Paris' **Panthéon** (nothing like Rome's) is another stark neo-classical edifice, filled with mortal remains of great Frenchmen who mean little to the average American tourist.

The **Bastille** is Paris' most famous nonsight. The square is there, but confused tourists look everywhere and can't find the famous prison of Revolution fame. The building's gone and the square is good only as a jumping-off point for Promenade Plantée Park (see "Sights—Northeast Paris," above).

Finally, the **Latin Quarter** is a frail shadow of its characteristic self. It's more Tunisian, Greek, and Woolworth's than old-time Paris. The café life that turned on Hemingway and endeared boul' Miche and boulevard St. Germain to so many poets is also trampled by modern commercialism.

Best Shopping

Forum des Halles is a huge subterranean shopping center. It's fun, mod, and colorful but lacks a soul (Mo: Les Halles). The **Galeries Lafayette** behind the old Opéra Garnier is your best elegant, Old World, one-stop Parisian department store/shopping center (Mo: Opéra). Also visit the adjacent **Printemps** store and the historic (as well as handy) **Samaritaine** department store in several buildings near pont Neuf (Mo: Pont Neuf). Ritzy shops surround the Ritz Hotel at place Vendôme (Mo: Tuileries).

Palace of Versailles

Every king's dream, Versailles was the residence of the French king and the cultural heartbeat of Europe for about 100 years—until the Revolution of 1789 ended the notion that God deputized some people to rule for Him on earth. Louis XIV spent half a year's income of Europe's richest country turning his dad's hunting lodge into a palace fit for a divine monarch. Louis XV and Louis XVI spent much of the 18th century gilding Louis XIV's lily. In 1837, about 50 years after the royal family was evicted, King Louis Philippe opened the palace as a museum. Europe's next-best palaces are Versailles wanna-bes.

Information: A helpful TI is just past Sofitel Hôtel on your walk from the station to the palace (May–Sept daily 09:00–19:00, Oct–April daily 09:00–18:00, tel. 01 39 24 88 88, can order Versailles tickets online but they're easy to buy on-site, www.chateauversailles.fr). You'll also find information booths inside

Versailles

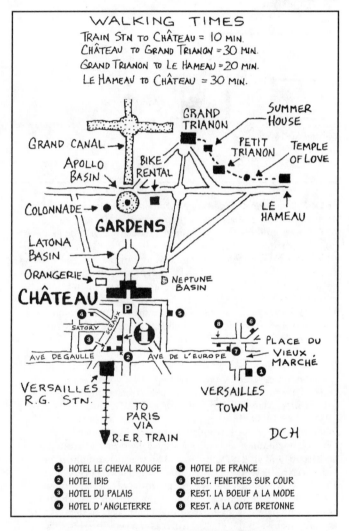

WALKING TIMES
TRAIN STN TO CHÂTEAU = 10 MIN.
CHÂTEAU TO GRAND TRIANON = 30 MIN.
GRAND TRIANON TO LE HAMEAU = 20 MIN.
LE HAMEAU TO CHÂTEAU = 30 MIN.

❶ HOTEL LE CHEVAL ROUGE ❺ HOTEL DE FRANCE
❷ HOTEL IBIS ❻ REST. FENETRES SUR COUR
❸ HOTEL DU PALAIS ❼ REST. LA BOEUF A LA MODE
❹ HOTEL D'ANGLETERRE ❽ REST. A LA COTE BRETONNE

the château (doors A, B-2, and C). The useful brochure, *Versailles Orientation Guide*, explains your sightseeing options.

Ticket Options: The self-guided, one-way romp through the State Apartments, including the Hall of Mirrors, costs €7 (covered by museum pass; €5.50 after 15:30, on Sun, or for ages 18–25; under 18 free). The entry fee is payable at doors A, C,

Entrances to Versailles

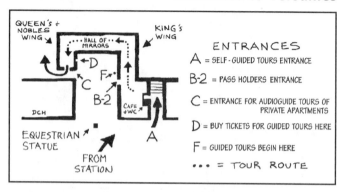

or D. If you want a guided tour through the other sections, you need to pay the €7 base price, then pay extra for the tour.

Tours: Add €4 for a 60-minute guided tour of lesser-known nobles' apartments (like those of the well-coiffed Madame Pompadour) or €6 for a 90-minute guided tour of the King's Private Apartments (Louis XV, Louis XVI, and Marie Antoinette), the chapel, and Opera House. Pay and get your tour appointment at entrance D. Tour times are normally all allotted for the day by 13:00. Tours leave from door F (across the courtyard from door D). Two informative but dry audioguide tours are available. Choose between €4 for Louis XIV's Private Apartments at door C, or €3.50 for the State Apartments and Hall of Mirrors at doors A or B-2. Both audioguide tours are sold until one hour before closing. Tours aren't covered by the museum pass. If you have extra time before your tour, wander through the State Apartments or gardens.

Hours: May through September Tuesday through Sunday 09:00 to 18:30, October through April Tuesday through Sunday 09:00 to 17:30, closed Monday, last entry 30 minutes before closing. In summer, Versailles is especially crowded around 10:00 and 13:00, and all day Tuesday and Sunday. To minimize crowds, either arrive by 09:00 or after 15:30 (admission is cheaper after 15:30, but you'll miss the last guided tours of the day, which generally depart around 15:00); tour the gardens after the palace closes. The palace is great late. On my last visit, at 18:00, I was the only tourist in the Hall of Mirrors...even on a Tuesday.

Time to Allow: Six hours round-trip from Paris (1 hour each way in transit, 2 hours for palace, 2 for gardens).

Self-Guided Tour: For the basic self-guided tour, join the line at entrance A if you need to pay admission. Those with a museum pass are allowed in through entrance B-2 without a wait. Enter the palace and take a one-way walk through the

State Apartments from the "King's Wing," through the magnificent Hall of Mirrors, and out via the "Queen's Wing."

The Hall of Mirrors was the ultimate hall of the day—75 meters long (250 feet), with 17 arched mirrors matching 17 windows with royal garden views, 24 gilded candelabra, eight busts of Roman emperors, and eight classical-style statues (7 are ancient originals). The ceiling is decorated with stories of Louis' triumphs. Imagine this place filled with silk gowns and powdered wigs, lit by thousands of candles. The mirrors—a luxurious rarity at the time—were a reflection of a time when aristocrats felt good about their looks and their fortunes. In another age altogether, this was the room in which the Treaty of Versailles was signed, ending World War I.

Before going downstairs at the end, take a stroll clockwise around the long room filled with the great battles of France murals. If you don't have *Rick Steves' Paris* or *Rick Steves' Mona Winks*, the guidebook called *The Châteaux, The Gardens, and Trianon* gives a room-by-room rundown.

Palace Gardens: The gardens offer a world of royal amusements. Outside the palace is L'Orangerie. Louis, the only one who could grow oranges in Paris, had an orange grove on wheels that could be wheeled in and out of his greenhouses according to the weather. A promenade leads from the palace to the Grand Canal, an artificial lake that, in Louis' day, was a mini-sea with nine ships, including a 32-cannon warship. France's royalty used to float up and down the canal in Venetian gondolas.

While Louis cleverly used palace life at Versailles to "domesticate" his nobility, turning otherwise meddlesome nobles into groveling socialites, all this pomp and ceremony hampered the royal family as well. For an escape from the public life at Versailles, they built more intimate palaces as retreats in their garden. Before the Revolution, there was plenty of space to retreat—the grounds were enclosed by a 40-kilometer-long fence.

The beautifully restored **Grand Trianon Palace** is as sumptuous as the main palace but much smaller. With its pastel-pink colonnade and more human scale, this is a place you'd like to call home. The nearby **Petit Trianon**, which has a fine neoclassical exterior with a skippable interior, was Marie Antoinette's favorite residence (€5 for both, €3 after 15:30, covered by museum pass, April–Oct Tue–Sun 12:00–18:00, closed Mon, Nov–March 12:00–17:00).

You can almost see princesses bobbing gaily in the branches as you walk through the enchanting forest, past the white marble temple of love (1778) to the queen's fake-peasant **Hamlet** (*Hameau*; interior not tourable). Palace life really got to Marie Antoinette. Sort of a back-to-basics queen, she retreated farther and farther from her blue-blooded reality. Her happiest days were at the hamlet, under a bonnet, tending her perfumed sheep and her manicured gardens in a thatch-happy wonderland.

Getting around the Gardens: It's a 30-minute hike from the palace, down the canal, past the two mini-palaces to the hamlet. You can rent bikes (€6/hr). The pokey tourist train runs between the canal and château (€5, 5/hr, 4 stops, you can hop on and off as you like, nearly worthless commentary).

Garden Hours: Except for fountain-filled weekends (see below), the gardens are free and open from 7:00 to sunset (as late as 21:30). There's a sandwich kiosk and a decent restaurant at the canal.

Fountain Spectacles: Classical music fills the king's backyard and the garden's fountains are in full squirt on Saturdays from July through September and on Sundays from early April through early October (schedule for both days: 11:00–12:00, 15:30–17:00, and 17:20–17:30). On these "spray days," the gardens cost €5 (ages 18–25-€3.50, free if under 18, not covered by museum pass, ask for map). Louis had his engineers literally reroute a river to fuel these fountains. Even by today's standards, they are impressive. For more information, pick up the map of the fountain show (*Les Grandes Eaux Musicales*) at any information booth. Also ask about the impressive *Les Fêtes de Nuit* nighttime spectacle (on some Sat, July–mid-Sept).

Getting There: Take the RER-C train (€5 round-trip, 30 min one-way) to Versailles R.G. or "Rive Gauche" (not Versailles C.H., which is farther from the palace). Trains named "Vick" leave about five times an hour for the palace from these RER stops: Invalides, Champ de Mars, Musée d'Orsay, St. Michel, Pont de l'Alma, and Gare d'Austerlitz. Any train named Vick goes to Versailles; don't board other trains. Get off at Versailles Rive Gauche (the end of the line), turn right out of the station, then left at the first boulevard. It's a 10-minute walk to the palace.

Your Eurailpass covers this inexpensive trip, but it uses up a valuable "flexi" day. Instead of using your pass, consider seeing Versailles on your way in or out of Paris. To get free passage, show your railpass at an SCNF ticket window (for example, at the Les Invalides or Musée d'Orsay RER stops) and get a *contremarque de passage*; keep this ticket to exit the system.

When returning from Versailles, look through the windows past the turnstiles for the departure board. Any train leaving Versailles goes as far as downtown Paris (they're marked "all stations until d'Austerlitz"). If you're uncertain, confirm with a local by asking, "*À Paris?*" ("To Paris?").

Allow €35 (each way) for a taxi from Paris to Versailles. To cut your park walking by 50 percent, consider having the taxi drop you at the Hamlet (*Hameau*).

Town of Versailles (zip code: 78000): After the palace closes and the tourists go, the prosperous, wholesome town of Versailles

Chartres

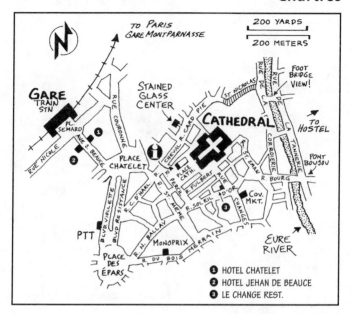

To Paris Gare Montparnasse

200 YARDS
200 METERS

FOOT BRIDGE VIEW!

GARE TRAIN STN

STAINED GLASS CENTER

CATHEDRAL

TO HOSTEL

PL. SEMARD

① ②

RUE COURONNE

AVE J. BEAUCE

RUE NICOLE

PLACE CHATELET

CHEVAL R. CARD. PIE

ST. NICHOLAS

CORROIERIE

TANNERIE

PONT BOUJOU

R. PERCHE

R. ST. MEME

R. C. D'HART.

BLVD VIOLETTE

BLVD RESISTANCE

R. N. BALLAY

MONOPRIX

R. DU BOIS

MERRAIN

PTT

PLACE DES ÉPARS

B. FULBERT

R. SOLEIL

ST. EMAN

R. BOURG

COV. MKT.

③

R. D'OR

CHANGES

EURE RIVER

① HOTEL CHATELET
② HOTEL JEHAN DE BEAUCE
③ LE CHANGE REST.

feels a long way from Paris. The central market thrives on place du Marché on Sunday, Tuesday, and Friday until 13:00 (leaving the RER station, turn right and walk 10 min). Consider the wisdom of picking up or dropping your rental car in Versailles rather than in Paris. In Versailles, the Hertz and Avis offices are at Gare des Chantiers (Versailles C.H., served by Paris' Montparnasse station). Versailles makes a fine home base; see Versailles accommodations (and recommended restaurants) under "Sleeping," below.

More Day Trips from Paris

▲▲▲Chartres—In 1194, a terrible fire destroyed the church at Chartres that housed the much-venerated veil of Mary. With almost unbelievably good fortune, the monks found the veil miraculously preserved in the ashes. Money poured in for the building of a bigger and better cathedral—decorated with 2,000 carved figures and some of France's best stained glass. The cathedral feels too large for the city because it was designed to accommodate huge crowds of pilgrims. One of those pilgrims, an impressed Napoleon, declared after a visit in 1811: "Chartres is no place for an atheist." Rodin called it "the Acropolis of France." British Francophile Malcolm Miller or his assistant give great "Appreciation of Gothic" tours Monday through Saturday, usually at noon

Paris Day Trips

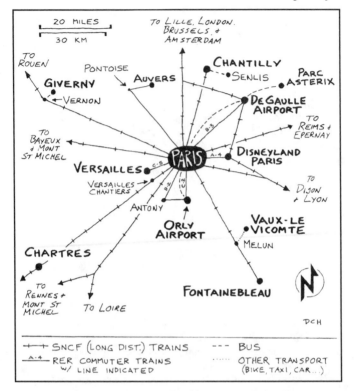

and 14:45 (verify times in advance, no tours off-season, call TI at 02 37 18 26 26). Each €6 tour is different; many people stay for both tours. Just show up at the church (daily 7:00–19:00).

Explore Chartres' pleasant city center and discover the picnic-friendly park behind the cathedral. The helpful **TI**, next to the cathedral, has a map with a self-guided tour of Chartres (Mon–Sat 09:00–19:00, Sun 09:00–17:30, tel. 02 37 18 26 26). Chartres is a one-hour train trip from the Gare Montparnasse (about €11 one-way, 10/day). To stay overnight, try the comfy **Hôtel Chatelet***** (Sb-€56–72, Db-€66, extra person-€9, streetside rooms cheaper, CC, 6 avenue Jehan de Beauce, tel. 02 37 21 78 00, fax 02 37 36 23 01, e-mail: hchatel@club-internet.fr) or the basic **Hôtel Jehan de Beauce**** (S-€24, D-€27, Ds-€31, Db-€37–47, Tb-€38, CC, 19 avenue Jehan de Beauce, tel. 02 37 21 01 41, fax 02 37 21 59 10).

▲**Giverny**—Monet spent 43 of his most creative years here (1883–1926). Monet's gardens and home are unfortunately split by a busy road and very popular with tourists. Buy your ticket, walk through the gardens, and take the underpass into the artist's famous lily-pad land. The path leads you over the Japanese Bridge, under weeping willows, and past countless scenes that leave artists aching for an easel. Back on the other side, stroll through his more robust, structured garden and his mildly interesting home. The jammed gift shop at the exit is Monet's actual skylit studio.

While lines may be long and tour groups may trample the flowers, true fans still find magic in those lily pads. Minimize crowds by arriving before 10:00 (get in line) or after 16:00 (€5.50, €4 for gardens only, April–Oct Tue–Sun 10:00–18:00, closed Mon and Nov–March, tel. 02 32 51 94 65).

Take the Rouen-bound train from Paris' Gare St. Lazare station to Vernon (about €21 round-trip, long gaps in service, know schedule before you go). From the Vernon train station to Monet's garden (4 kilometers/2.5 miles away), take the Vernon-Giverny bus (4/day, scheduled to meet most trains), hitch, taxi (€11 for up to 3, €12 for 4, tel. 07 76 08 50 78), or rent a bike at the bar opposite the station (€12, tel. 02 32 21 16 01, crummy ride on a busy road). Get return bus times from the ticket office in Giverny (note that driver sometimes skips last pickup), or ask them to call a taxi if you don't see one waiting at the bus stop (tel. 02 32 51 70 17 or 06 07 34 36 68). Bus stops are in the parking lot across from the entry to Monet's home and just beyond the American Impressionist Art Museum. Big tour companies do a Giverny day trip from Paris for around $60.

The **American Impressionist Art Museum** (turn left when leaving Monet's place and walk 90 meters/300 feet) is devoted to American artists who followed Claude to Giverny. This bright, modern gallery has a good little Mary Cassatt section and gives us a rare chance to see French people appreciating our artists (same price and hours as Monet's home).

To sleep two blocks from Monet's home, try the adorable **Hôtel La Musardiere**** (Db-€46–69, Tb-€63–73, CC, 132 rue Claude Monet, 27620 Giverny, tel. 02 32 21 03 18, fax 02 32 21 60 00).

▲▲**Disneyland Paris**—Europe's Disneyland is basically a modern remake of California's, with most of the same rides and smiles. The main difference is that Mickey Mouse speaks French (and you can buy wine with your lunch). My kids went ducky. Locals love it. It's worth a day if Paris is handier than Florida or California. Crowds are a problem (tel. 01 64 74 30 00 for the latest). If possible, avoid Saturday, Sunday, Wednesday, school holidays, and July and August. After dinner, crowds are gone, and you'll walk right onto rides that had a 45-minute wait three hours earlier. To avoid lines at the five most popular rides, get a free FASTPASS at the entry (punch in machines at rides to reserve a ride). You'll also save time by buying your tickets ahead (at airport TIs, over 100 Métro stations, or along the Champs-Elysées at the TI, Disney Store, or Virgin Megastore). Food is fun but expensive. Smuggle in a picnic (€37, kids 3–11-€29, €18 for all ages from 17:00–23:00 in summer, kids under 3 always free, about 25 percent cheaper off-season, daily April–June 09:00–20:00; July–Aug 09:00–23:00; Sept–March Mon–Fri 10:00–20:00, Sat–Sun 09:00–20:00, tel. 01 60 30 60 30, fax 01 60 30 60 65, www.disneylandparis.com).

Disney brochures are in every Paris hotel. The RER (about €7 each way, direct from downtown Paris to Marne-la-Vallee in 30 min) drops you right into the park. The last train back to Paris leaves shortly after midnight.

To sleep reasonably at the huge Disney complex, try **Hôtel Sante Fe**** with shuttle service to the park every 12 minutes (Db-€214 includes breakfast and 2-day park pass, CC, tel. 01 60 30 60 30, fax 01 60 30 60 65).

Nightlife in Paris

Paris is brilliant after dark. Save energy from your day's sightseeing and get out at night. Whether it's a concert at Sainte-Chapelle, an elevator up the Arc de Triomphe, or a late-night café, experience the city of light lit. If a **Seine River cruise** appeals, see "Organized Tours of Paris," page 47.

The *Pariscope* magazine, in French, offers a complete weekly listing of music, cinema, theater, opera, and other special events (€0.50 at any newsstand, www.pariscope.fr). The *Paris Voice* newspaper, in English, has a monthly review of Paris entertainment (available at any English-language bookstore, French-American establishments, or the American Church, www.parisvoice.com).

Music
Jazz Clubs

With a lively mix of American, French, and international musicians, Paris has been an internationally acclaimed jazz capital since World War II. You'll pay from €6 to €24 to enter a jazz club (1 drink may be included; if not, expect to pay €5–9 per drink; beer is cheapest). See *Pariscope* magazine under "Musique" for listings, or, better, the American Church's *Paris Voice* paper for a good monthly review, or drop by the clubs to check out their calendars posted on the front door. Music starts after 22:00 in most clubs. Some offer dinner concerts from about 20:30 on. Here are a few good bets:

Caveau de la Huchette, a characteristic old jazz club for visitors, fills an ancient Latin Quarter cellar with live jazz and frenzied dancing every night (€9 weekday, €12 weekend admission, €5 drinks, Tue–Sun 21:30–02:30 or later, closed Mon, 5 rue de la Huchette, Mo: St. Michel, recorded info tel. 01 43 26 65 05).

For a hotbed of late-night activity and jazz, go to the two-block-long rue des Lombards, at boulevard Sebastopol, midway between the river and Pompidou Center (Mo: Chatelet). **Au Duc des Lombards**, right at the corner, is one of the most popular and respected jazz clubs in Paris, with concerts generally at 21:00 (42 rue des Lombards, tel. 01 42 33 22 88). **Le Sunset** and **le Sunside** sit side by side a block west, offering more traditional jazz— Dixieland, big band—and fewer crowds, with concerts generally at 21:00 (60 rue des Lombards, Sunset tel. 01 40 26 46 60, Sunside tel. 01 40 26 21 25).

At the more down-to-earth and mellow **Le Cave du Franc Pinot**, you can enjoy a glass of chardonnay at the main-floor wine bar, then drop downstairs for a cool jazz scene (good dinner-and-jazz values as well, located on Ile St. Louis where Pont Marie meets the island, 1 quai de Bourbon, Mo: Pont Marie, tel. 01 46 33 60 64).

Classical Concerts

For classical music on any night, consult *Pariscope* magazine; the "Musique" section under "Concerts Classiques" lists concerts (free and fee). Look for posters at the churches. Churches that regularly host concerts include St. Sulpice, St. Germain-des-Près, Basilique de Madeleine, St. Eustache, St. Julien-le-Pauvre, and Sainte-Chapelle. It's worth the €15 to €23 entry for the pleasure of hearing Mozart surrounded by the stained glass of the tiny Sainte-Chapelle. Look also for daytime concerts in parks like the Luxembourg Gardens. Even the Galeries Lafayette department store offers concerts. Many are free (*entrée libre*), such as the Sunday atelier concert sponsored by the American Church (18:00, not every week, Sept–May, 65 quai d'Orsay, Mo: Invalides, RER: Pont de l'Alma, tel. 01 40 62 05 00).

Opera

Paris is home to two well-respected operas. The Opéra Garnier, Paris' first opera house, hosts opera and ballet performances. Come here for less expensive tickets and grand belle époque decor (Mo: Opéra, tel. 01 44 73 13 99). The Opéra de la Bastille is the massive modern opera house that dominates place de la Bastille. Come here for state-of-the-art special effects and modern interpretations of classic ballets and operas (Mo: Bastille, tel. 01 43 43 96 96). For tickets, call 01 44 73 13 00, go to the opera ticket offices (open 11:00–18:00), or, best, reserve on the Web at www.ticketavenue .com (for both operas).

Bus Tours

Paris Illumination Tours, run by Paris Vision, connect all the great illuminated sights of Paris with a 100-minute bus tour in 12 languages. Double-decker buses have huge windows, but customers continuing to the overrated Moulin Rouge get the most desirable front seats. You'll stampede on with a United Nations of tourists, get an audioguide, and listen to a tape-recorded spiel (interesting but occasionally hard to hear). Uninspired as it is, this provides an entertaining first-night overview of the city at its floodlit and scenic best (bring your city map to stay oriented as you go). Left-side seats are marginally better. Visibility is fine in the rain. You're entirely on the bus except for one five-minute cigarette break at the Eiffel Tower viewpoint (adult-€23, kids under 11 ride free, departures at 20:30 nightly all year, also 21:30 April–Oct only, departs from Paris Vision office at 214 rue de Rivoli, across the street from Mo: Tuileries). These trips are sold through your hotel (brochures in lobby) or direct at the address listed above. Look also for the same tour by minivan—pickup is at your hotel, the driver is a qualified guide, and there's a maximum of seven clients (€46/ person, kids ages 4–11-€23, tel. for bus and minivans 01 42 60 30 01, fax 01 42 86 95 36, www.parisvision.com).

Sleeping in Paris
(€1.10 = about $1, country code: 33)

Sleep Code: **S** = Single, **D** = Double/Twin, **T** = Triple, **Q** = Quad, **b** = bathroom, **s** = shower only, **CC** = Credit Cards accepted, **no CC** = Credit Cards not accepted, * = French hotel rating system (0–4 stars).

I've focused on three safe, handy, and colorful neighborhoods: rue Cler, Marais, and Contrescarpe. For each, I list good hotels, helpful hints, and restaurants (see "Eating," below). Before reserving, read the descriptions of the three neighborhoods closely. Each offers different pros and cons, and your neighborhood is as important as your hotel for the success of your trip.

Reserve ahead for Paris, the sooner the better. Conventions clog Paris in September (worst), October, May, and June (very tough). In August, when Paris is quiet, some hotels offer lower rates to fill their rooms (if you're planning to visit Paris in the summer, the extra expense of an air-conditioned room can be money well spent). Most hotels accept telephone reservations, require prepayment with a credit-card number, and prefer a faxed follow-up to be sure everything is in order. For more information, see "Making Reservations" in this book's Introduction.

French hotels are rated by stars (indicated in this book by an *). One star is simple, two has most of the comforts, and three is generally a two-star with a mini-bar and fancier lobby (though I've tried to find three-star hotels that merit the expense; four stars offer more luxury than you have time to appreciate).

Old, characteristic, budget Parisian hotels have always been cramped. Retrofitted with elevators, toilets, and private showers (as most are today), they are even more cramped. Even three-star hotel rooms are small and often not worth the extra expense in

Paris. Some hotels include the hotel tax (*taxe du séjour*, about €0.60–0.90 per person per day), though most will add this to your bill. Two- and three-star hotels are required to have an English-speaking staff. Nearly all hotels listed will have someone who speaks English.

Recommended hotels have an elevator unless otherwise noted. Quad rooms usually have two double beds. Because rooms with double beds and showers are cheaper than rooms with twin beds and baths, room prices vary within each hotel.

You can save as much as €15 by finding the increasingly rare room without a private shower, though some hotels charge for down-the-hall showers. Singles (except for the rare closet-type rooms that fit only 1 twin bed) are simply doubles used by one person. They rent for only a little less than a double. Continental breakfasts average €6, buffet breakfasts (baked goods, cereal, yogurt, and fruit) cost €7.75 to €9.25. Café or picnic breakfasts are cheaper, but hotels usually give unlimited coffee.

Get advice from your hotel for safe parking (consider long-term parking at Orly Airport and taxi in). Meters are free in August. Garages are plentiful (€14–23/day, with special rates through some hotels). Self-serve Laundromats are common; ask your hotelier for the nearest one (*Où est un laverie automatique?*; ooh ay uh lah-vay-ree auto-mah-teek).

If you have any trouble finding a room using our listings, try one of these helpful Web sites: www.parishotel.com and www.hotelboulevard.com. You can select from various neighborhood areas (e.g., Eiffel Tower area), give the dates of your visit and preferred price range, and presto—they'll list options with rates. You'll find the hotels listed in this book to be better located and objectively reviewed, though as a last resort these services are handy.

Rue Cler Orientation

Rue Cler, a villagelike pedestrian street, is safe, tidy, and makes me feel like I must have been a poodle in a previous life. How such coziness lodged itself between the high-powered government district and the wealthy Eiffel Tower and Invalides areas, I'll never know. This is a neighborhood of wide, tree-lined boulevards, stately apartment buildings, and lots of Americans. The American Church, American library, American University, and many of my readers call this area home.

Become a local at a rue Cler café for breakfast or join the afternoon crowd for *une bière pression* (a draft beer). On rue Cler, you can eat and browse your way through a street full of tart shops, delis, cheeseries, and colorful outdoor produce stalls. For an after-dinner cruise on the Seine, it's just a short walk to the river and the Bâteaux-Mouches (see "Organized Tours of Paris," above).

Your neighborhood **TI** is at the Eiffel Tower (May–Sept

daily 11:00–18:42, no kidding, tel. 01 45 51 22 15). The Métro
station (Ecole Militaire) and a **post office** are at the end of
rue Cler on avenue de la Motte Piquet, and there's a handy
SNCF office at 78 rue St. Dominique (Mon–Fri 09:00–19:00, Sat
10:00–12:20, 14:00–18:00). The Banque Populaire (across from
Hôtel Leveque) changes money. Rue St. Dominique is the area's
boutique-browsing street. The Epicerie de la Tour **grocery** is
open until midnight (197 rue de Grenelle).

The **American Church and College** is the community center
for Americans living in Paris and should be one of your first stops
if you're planning to stay a while (reception open Mon–Sat 09:00–
22:30, Sun 09:00–19:30, 65 quai d'Orsay, tel. 01 40 62 05 00). Pick
up copies of the *Paris Voice* for a monthly review of Paris entertainment, and *France-U.S.A. Contacts* for information on housing and
employment through the community of 30,000 Americans living
in Paris. The interdenominational service at 11:00 on Sunday, the
coffee hour after church, and the free Sunday concerts (18:00, not
every week, Sept–May only) are a great way to make some friends
and get a taste of émigré life in Paris.

Afternoon *boules* (lawn bowling) on the esplanade des
Invalides is a relaxing spectator sport. Look for the dirt area to
the upper right as you face the Invalides.

You should try at least one of these helpful **bus routes:**
Line #69 runs along rue St. Dominique and serves Les Invalides,
Orsay, Louvre, Marais, and Père-Lachaise cemetery. Line #92
runs along avenue Bosquet and serves the Arc de Triomphe and
Champs-Elysées in one direction and the Montparnasse Tower in
the other. Line #87 runs on avenue de la Bourdonnais and serves
St. Sulpice, Luxembourg Gardens, and the Sevres-Babylone shopping area. Line #28 runs on boulevard La Tour Maubourg and
serves the St. Lazare station.

Sleeping in the Rue Cler Neighborhood
(7th arrondissement, Mo: Ecole Militaire, zip code: 75007)
Rue Cler is the glue that holds this pleasant neighborhood
together. From here you can walk to the Eiffel Tower, Napoleon's
Tomb, the Seine, and the Orsay and Rodin Museums.

Many of my readers stay in this neighborhood. If you want to
disappear into Paris, you'll do it better at the hotels away from the
rue Cler or in the other neighborhoods I list. And if nightlife matters, sleep elsewhere. The first seven hotels listed below are within
Camembert-smelling distance of rue Cler; the others are within a
5- to 10-minute stroll. Warning: The first two hotels are popular
with my readers.

Hôtel Leveque** is ideally located, with a helpful staff
and a singing maid. It's a big place with well-designed rooms
that have all the comforts (S-€53, Db-€84–91, Tb-€114,

breakfast-€7, first breakfast free for readers of this book, CC,
air-con planned for 2002, 29 rue Cler, tel. 01 47 05 49 15,
fax 01 45 50 49 36, www.hotel-leveque.com, e-mail: info
@hotelleveque.com).

Hôtel du Champ de Mars**, with charming, pastel rooms
and helpful English-speaking owners Françoise and Stephane
and right-hand man Slim, is a cozier rue Cler option. The hotel
has a Provence-style, small-town feel from top to bottom. Rooms
are small but comfortable and a very good value. Single rooms
can work as tiny doubles (Sb-€66, Db-€72–76, Tb-€92, CC, 30
meters off rue Cler at 7 rue de Champ de Mars, tel. 01 45 51 52
30, fax 01 45 51 64 36, www.hotel-du-champ-de-mars.com,
e-mail: stg@club-internet.fr).

Hôtel Cadran*** charges too much for its fine location
and cozy lobby. Rooms are tight and narrow but air-conditioned
(Sb-€148, Db-€165, CC, 10 rue de Champs de Mars, tel. 01 40
62 67 00, fax 01 40 62 67 13, www.cadran.com).

Hôtel Relais Bosquet*** is modern, spacious, and a bit
upscale, with snazzy, air-conditioned rooms and big beds (Sb-
€123–148, standard Db-€140, spacious Db-€163, extra bed-€31,
parking-€14, CC, 19 rue de Champ de Mars, tel. 01 47 05 25 45,
fax 01 45 55 08 24, www.relaisbosquet.com).

Hôtel Beaugency***, on a quieter street just off rue Cler,
has small but comfortable rooms, a lobby you can stretch out in,
and friendly Nadine in charge (Sb-€104, Db-€111, Tb-€127,
buffet breakfast, CC, 21 rue Duvivier, tel. 01 47 05 01 63, fax 01
45 51 04 96, www.hotel-beaugency.com).

Hôtel la Motte Piquet**, at the end of rue Cler, is reasonable, spotless, and cozy (Ss-€54, Sb-€60–69, Db-€69–79, CC,
most rooms face a busy street, 30 avenue de la Motte Piquet,
tel. 01 47 05 09 57, fax 01 47 05 74 36).

Sleeping near rue Cler: The following listings are a 5- to 10-
minute walk west of rue Cler and are listed in order of proximity.

Hôtel Prince**, just across avenue Bosquet from the Ecole
Militaire Métro stop, has fair-value rooms, many overlooking a
busy street (Db-€74–97, CC, 66 avenue Bosquet, tel. 01 47 05 40
90, fax 01 47 53 06 62).

Hôtel le Tourville**** is the most classy and expensive of
my Paris listings. This four-star gem is surprisingly intimate and
friendly, from its welcoming lobby to its air-conditioned, pastel
rooms and vaulted breakfast area (small standard Db-€138, superior Db-€170, Db with private terrace-€215, extra bed-€15.50,
CC, 16 avenue de Tourville, Mo: Ecole Militaire, tel. 01 47 05 62
62, fax 01 47 05 43 90, e-mail: hotel@tourville.com).

Hôtel de Turenne**, with comfortable, air-conditioned
rooms, is a great value when it's hot, and it has five truly single
rooms (Sb-€61, Db-€71–81, Tb-€96, extra bed-€9.50, CC,

Rue Cler Hotels

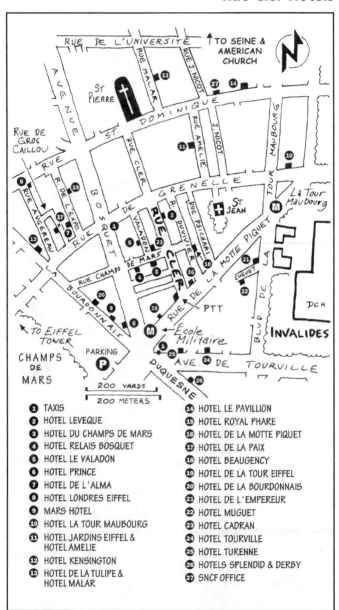

1. TAXIS
2. HOTEL LEVEQUE
3. HOTEL DU CHAMPS DE MARS
4. HOTEL RELAIS BOSQUET
5. HOTEL LE VALADON
6. HOTEL PRINCE
7. HOTEL DE L'ALMA
8. HOTEL LONDRES EIFFEL
9. MARS HOTEL
10. HOTEL LA TOUR MAUBOURG
11. HOTEL JARDINS EIFFEL & HOTEL AMELIE
12. HOTEL KENSINGTON
13. HOTEL DE LA TULIPE & HOTEL MALAR
14. HOTEL LE PAVILLION
15. HOTEL ROYAL PHARE
16. HOTEL DE LA MOTTE PIQUET
17. HOTEL DE LA PAIX
18. HOTEL BEAUGENCY
19. HOTEL DE LA TOUR EIFFEL
20. HOTEL DE LA BOURDONNAIS
21. HOTEL DE L'EMPEREUR
22. HOTEL MUGUET
23. HOTEL CADRAN
24. HOTEL TOURVILLE
25. HOTEL TURENNE
26. HOTELS SPLENDID & DERBY
27. SNCF OFFICE

20 avenue de Tourville, tel. 01 47 05 99 92, fax 01 45 56 06 04, e-mail: hotel.turenne.paris7@wanadoo.fr).

Hôtel Londres Eiffel*** is my closest listing to the Eiffel Tower and Champs de Mars park. It offers small but thought-fully appointed rooms, cozy public spaces, and an Internet station. Helpful Esther and Cedric take good care of their guests (Sb-€90–102, Db-€103–112, Tb-€135, CC, use handy bus #69 or the RER Alma stop, 1 rue Augerau, tel. 01 45 51 63 02, fax 01 47 05 28 96, www.Londres-Eiffel.com).

Mars Hôtel**, with an ambitious, engaging new owner, is a solid midrange value with mostly spacious rooms and a beam-me-up-Jacques, coffin-sized elevator. The front rooms are noisier but have a view of the Eiffel Tower (€70, large Db-€85, extra bed-€18.50, CC, 117 avenue de la Bourdonnais, tel. 01 47 05 42 30, fax 01 47 05 45 91).

Hôtel de la Bourdonnais***, best known for its renowned restaurant, is a perfectly Parisian place. It mixes Old World elegance with professional service, generally spacious rooms, and pleasant public spaces (Sb-€110, Db-€130, Tb-€140, Qb-€150, Qb suite-€200, CC, 111 avenue de la Bourdonnais, tel. 01 47 05 45 42, fax 01 45 55 75 54, www.hotellabourdonnais.fr).

Hôtel Kensington** feels less personal but is a good value with warmly decorated rooms (Sb-€53, Db-€67–82, CC, 79 avenue de la Bourdonnais, tel. 01 47 05 74 00, fax 01 47 05 25 81, www.hotel-kensington.com).

Hôtel de la Paix is bare-bones basic and cheap (S-€29, Ds-€51, Db-€54, Tb-€74, no CC, no elevator, no frills, 19 rue du Gros-Caillou, tel. 01 45 51 86 17, fax 01 45 55 93 28).

Hôtel de la Tulipe** is a unique place two blocks from rue Cler toward the river, with artistically decorated rooms (each one different) above a wood-beamed lounge and a peaceful, leafy courtyard (Db-€105–110, Tb-€140, CC, no elevator, cable TV, 33 rue Malar, tel. 01 45 51 67 21, fax 01 47 53 96 37, www.hoteldelatulipe.com).

Sleeping near Métro stop La Tour Maubourg: The next four listings are within two blocks of the intersection of avenue de la Motte Piquet and Les Invalides.

Hôtel le Pavillon** is a quiet place with unrealized potential, set back from the street. A small courtyard greets clients, its pastel rooms are adequate, but bathrooms need work (Sb-€72, Db-80€, CC, family suites-€105, 54 rue St. Dominique, tel. 01 45 51 42 87, fax 01 45 51 32 79, e-mail: patrickpavillon@aol.com).

Hôtel Les Jardins Eiffel*** is a bit pricey but merits its three stars with professional service, a spacious lobby, outdoor patio, and comfortable, air-conditioned rooms—some with private balconies. Ask for a room *avec petit balcon* (Sb-€92–128, Db-

€100–152, extra bed-€21, parking-€17/day, CC, 8 rue Amelie, tel. 01 47 05 46 21, fax 01 45 55 28 08, e-mail: eiffel@unimedia.fr).

What the roomy **Hôtel de l'Empereur**** lacks in personality, it makes up for in value. Its pleasant rooms offer all the comforts except air-conditioning. Streetside rooms have views but some noise; fifth-floor rooms have small balconies and better views (Sb-€68–72, Db-€73–82, Tb-€103, Qb-€118, CC, 2 rue Chevert, tel. 01 45 55 88 02, fax 01 45 51 88 54, www.hotelempereur.com).

Reserve early for the **Hôtel Muguet****, a peaceful and clean hotel where you get three-star comfort for the price of two. The hotel offers sharp, air-conditioned rooms, a small garden court-yard, and several good family rooms (Sb-€85, Db-€94–102, Tb-€130, CC, 11 rue Chevert, tel. 01 47 05 05 93, fax 01 45 50 25 37, www.hotelmuguet.com).

Lesser values: Given this fine area, these are acceptable last choices. **Hôtel Malar*** (Db-€78–86, CC, 29 rue Malar, tel. 01 45 51 38 46, fax 01 45 55 20 19, www.hotelmalar.com); **Hôtel de la Tour Eiffel**** (Sb-€61, Db-€76, Tb-€79, CC, 17 rue de l'Exposition, tel. 01 47 05 14 75, fax 01 47 53 99 46, Muriel speaks English); **Hôtel Royal Phare**** (Db-€61–74, CC, facing Ecole Militaire Métro stop, 40 avenue de la Motte Piquet, tel. 01 47 05 57 30, fax 01 45 51 64 41); **Hôtel Amelie**** (Db-€87, CC, 5 rue Amelie, tel. 01 45 51 74 75, fax 01 45 56 93 55); **Hôtel de l'Alma***** (Db-€114, CC, 32 rue de l'Exposition, tel. 01 47 05 45 70, fax 01 45 51 84 47, e-mail: almahotel @minitel.net); **Derby Eiffel Hôtel***** (Db-€116–139, CC, air-con, 5 avenue Duquesne, tel. 01 47 05 12 05, fax 01 47 05 43 43, e-mail: info@derbyeiffelhotel.com); **Hôtel Splendid***** (Db-€122–145, CC, most rooms have Eiffel Tower views, 29 avenue Tourville, tel. 01 45 51 24 77, fax 01 44 18 94 60, e-mail: splendid@club-internet.fr); and the basic, overpriced **Hôtel La Serre*** (Db-€84, CC, has good location on rue Cler but generates readers' complaints for its rude staff and bizarre hotel practices—you can't see room in advance or get a refund, 24 rue Cler, across from Hôtel Leveque, Mo: Ecole Militaire, tel. 01 47 05 52 33, fax 01 40 62 95 66).

These are last resorts. The following two hotels are decent and well-located, but are poorly and erratically run by the same rude owner. **Hôtel La Tour Maubourg*****, with spacious Old World rooms, overlooks a lawn within sight of Napoleon's tomb (Sb-€107, Db-€122–137, CC, includes breakfast, immediately at La Tour Maubourg Métro stop, 150 rue de Grenelle, tel. 01 47 05 16 16, fax 01 47 05 16 14). **Hôtel Valadon****, one block west of rue Cler, is small, quiet, and sleekly furnished. Avoid the musty, windowless basement room (Sb-€61, Db-€78–86, CC, 16 rue Valadon, tel. 01 47 53 89 85, fax 01 44 18 90 56).

Hôtel Valadon**, one block west of rue Cler, is small, quiet, and has generously sized rooms with sleek furnishings. Avoid the musty, windowless basement room (Sb-€61, Db-€78–86, CC, unpredictable owners, 16 rue Valadon, tel. 01 47 53 89 85, fax 01 44 18 90 56, www.hotelvaladon.com).

Hôtel La Tour Maubourg*** feels like a slightly faded, elegant manor house with spaciously comfortable Old World rooms and a rigid owner. It overlooks a cheery green lawn within sight of Napoleon's tomb (Sb-€107, Db-€122–137, suites for up to 4 people-€168–274, CC, includes breakfast, immediately at La Tour Maubourg Métro stop, 150 rue de Grenelle, tel. 01 47 05 16 16, fax 01 47 05 16 14, www.latour-maubourg.fr).

Marais Orientation

Those interested in a more Soho–Greenwich Village locale should make the Marais their Parisian home. The Marais is a more happening area than rue Cler, with great access to many museums: Picasso, Carnavalet, Jewish History, and Pompidou Center. It's narrow, medieval Paris at its finest, where elegant stone mansions sit side by side with trendy bars, antique shops, and slick boutiques. Only 15 years ago it was a forgotten Parisian backwater, but now the Marais is one of Paris' most popular residential, tourist, and shopping areas.

The nearest **TIs** are in the Louvre (Wed–Mon 10:00–19:00, closed Tue) and Gare de Lyon (daily 08:00–20:00, tel. 01 43 43 33 24, answered by live English speaker). The **Banque de France** changes money, with good rates and long lines (Mon–Fri 09:00–11:45, 13:30–15:30, closed Sat–Sun, at corner of rue St. Antoine and place de la Bastille). Most banks and other services are on the main drag, rue de Rivoli/St. Antoine. You'll find one **taxi stand** on the north side of rue St. Antoine, where it meets rue Castex, and another on the south side of St. Antoine, in front of the St. Paul church.

The new Bastille opera house, Promenade Plantée Park, place des Vosges (Paris' oldest square), the Jewish Quarter (rue des Rosiers), and nightlife-happening rue de Lappe are all nearby. Be sure to stroll into place des Vosges after dark. The massive budget **department store** is BHV, next to Hôtel de Ville. Marais **post offices** are on rue Castex and on the corner of rues Pavée and Francs Bourgeois.

Helpful **bus routes:** Line #69 on rue St. Antoine takes you to the Louvre, Orsay, Rodin, and Napoleon's Tomb and ends at the Eiffel Tower. Line #86 runs down boulevard Henri IV, crossing Ile St. Louis and serving the Latin Quarter along boulevard St. Germain. Line #96 runs on rues Turenne and Francois Miron and serves the Louvre and boulevard St. Germain (near Luxembourg Gardens). Line #65 serves the train stations Austerlitz, Est, and Nord from place de la Bastille.

Sleeping in the Marais Neighborhood
(4th arrondissement, Mo: St. Paul or Bastille, zip code: 75004)

The Marais runs from the Pompidou Center to the Bastille (a 15-min walk), with most hotels located a few blocks north of the main east-west drag, rue de Rivoli/St. Antoine. It's about 15 minutes on foot from any hotel in this area to Notre-Dame, Ile St. Louis, and the Latin Quarter. Strolling home (day or night) from Notre-Dame along the Ile St. Louis is marvelous.

The St. Paul Métro stop puts you right in the heart of the Marais, while the Hôtel de Ville stop serves its western end, and the Bastille stop serves its eastern limit.

Hôtel Castex** is a clean, well-run, and cheery place—a great value with comfortable rooms, many stairs, and a good location on a relatively quiet street. Reserve by phone and leave your credit-card number (Sb-€47, Db-€55–58, Tb-€74, CC, no elevator, just off place de la Bastille and rue St. Antoine, 5 rue Castex, Mo: Bastille, tel. 01 42 72 31 52, fax 01 42 72 57 91, e-mail: info@castexhotel.com). The owners have another decent-value hotel two Métro stops away in a less-appealing location that often has rooms when others don't: **Hôtel de la République**** (Sb-€53, Db-€61, CC, cable TV, 31 rue Albert Thomas, 75010 Paris, Mo: République, tel. 01 42 39 19 03, fax 01 42 39 22 66, www.republiquehotel.com).

Grand Hôtel Jeanne d'Arc**, a warm, welcoming place with thoughtfully appointed rooms, is ideally located for connoisseurs of the Marais. Rooms on the street can be noisy until the bars close. Sixth-floor rooms have a view, and corner rooms are wonderfully bright in the City of Lights. Reserve this place way ahead (small Db-€70, standard Db-€94, Tb-€109, good Qb-€125, CC, 3 rue Jarente, Mo: St. Paul, tel. 01 48 87 62 11, fax 01 48 87 37 31).

Hôtel Bastille Speria***, a short block off the Bastille, feels family-run while offering business-type service. The 45 plain but cheery rooms have air-conditioning and thin walls. It's English-language friendly, from the *Herald Tribune*s in the lobby to the history of the Bastille posted in the elevator (Sb-€90–98, Db-€100–125, Tb-€143, CC, 1 rue de la Bastille, Mo: Bastille, tel. 01 42 72 04 01, fax 01 42 72 56 38, e-mail: speria@micronet.fr).

Hôtel Lyon-Mulhouse**, with half of its rooms on a busy street just off place de la Bastille, is a good value. Rooms are large and pleasant (Sb-€55–75, Db-€65–85, Tb-€75–95, Qb-€102, CC, 8 boulevard Beaumarchais, tel. 01 47 00 91 50, fax 01 47 00 06 31, e-mail: hotelyonmulhouse@wanadoo.fr).

Hôtel de la Place des Vosges** is well-located on a quiet street just off place des Vosges. The owners plan to renovate all rooms in 2002 (Sb-€84–99, Db-€107–122, prices are estimates, CC, elevator starts one floor up, 12 rue de Biraque, Mo: St. Paul,

Marais Hotels

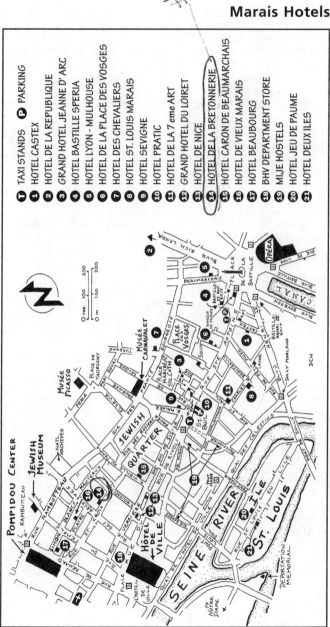

- **T** TAXI STANDS **P** PARKING
- **1** HOTEL CASTEX
- **2** HOTEL DE LA REPUBLIQUE
- **3** GRAND HOTEL JEANNE D'ARC
- **4** HOTEL BASTILLE SPERIA
- **5** HOTEL LYON - MULHOUSE
- **6** HOTEL DE LA PLACE DES VOSGES
- **7** HOTEL DES CHEVALIERS
- **8** HOTEL ST. LOUIS MARAIS
- **9** HOTEL SEVIGNE
- **10** HOTEL PRATIC
- **11** HOTEL DE LA 7 eme ART
- **12** GRAND HOTEL DU LOIRET
- **13** HOTEL DE NICE
- **14** HOTEL DE LA BRETONNERIE
- **15** HOTEL CARON DE BEAUMARCHAIS
- **16** HOTEL DE VIEUX MARAIS
- **17** HOTEL BEAUBOURG
- **18** BHV DEPARTMENT STORE
- **19** MIJE HOSTELS
- **20** HOTEL JEU DE PAUME
- **21** HOTEL DEUX ILES

tel. 01 42 72 60 46, fax 01 42 72 02 64, e-mail: hotel.place.des
.vosges@gofornet.com).

Hôtel des Chevaliers***, a little boutique hotel one block
northwest of place des Vosges, offers small, pleasant rooms with
modern comforts. Rooms off the street are quiet (Db-€114–130,
CC, skip overpriced breakfast, 30 rue de Turenne, Mo: St. Paul,
tel. 01 42 72 73 47, fax 01 42 72 54 10).

Hôtel Sévigné** is less personal but central, offering sufficient
rooms at fair prices with the cheapest breakfast in Paris—€3.50
(Sb-€56, Db-€60–63, Tb-€69, CC, 2 rue Malher, Mo: St. Paul,
tel. 01 42 72 76 17, fax 01 42 78 68 26, www.le-sevigne.com).

Hôtel Pratic* has a terrific location on a fun, people-friendly
square and charges accordingly. Its stairs are many and its overpriced rooms are modern, but nothing special (Db-€90, CC, no
elevator, 9 rue d'Ormesson, Mo: St. Paul, tel. 01 48 87 80 47,
fax 01 48 87 40 04, e-mail: practic.hotel@wanadoo.fr).

Hôtel St. Louis Marais**, well-situated between the
river and rue St. Antoine, has a fine lobby and cozy if pricey
rooms (small Db-€108, standard Db-€125, CC, no elevator,
1 rue Charles V, tel. 01 48 87 87 04, fax 01 48 87 33 26, www
.saintlouismarais.com).

Hôtel de 7ème Art**, two blocks south of rue St. Antoine,
is a relaxed, Hollywood-nostalgia place, run by young, friendly,
hip Marais types, with a full-service café/bar and Charlie Chaplin
murals. Most rooms are adequate, but the few large double rooms
at €107 are plenty nice (Sb or Db-€82–93, large Db-€107–125,
extra bed-€21, CC, 20 rue St. Paul, Mo: St. Paul, tel. 01 44 54
85 00, fax 01 42 77 69 10, e-mail: hotel7art@wanadoo.fr).

MIJE Youth Hostels: The Maison Internationale de la
Jeunesse des Etudiants (MIJE) runs three classy old residences
clustered a few blocks south of rue St. Antoine. Each offers simple,
clean, single-sex, one- to four-bed rooms for families and travelers
under the age of 30 (exceptions are made for families). Prices
are per person; you can pay more to have your own room or be
roomed with as many as three others (Sb-€37, Db-€27, Tb-€24,
Qb-€22, no CC, includes breakfast but not towels, which you
can get from a machine; required membership card-€2.50
extra/person; rooms locked 12:00–15:00 and at 01:00). **MIJE
Fourcy** (cheap dinners, 6 rue de Fourcy, just south of rue Rivoli),
MIJE Fauconnier (11 rue Fauconnier), and the best, **MIJE
Maubisson** (12 rue des Barres), share the same contact information (tel. 01 42 74 23 45, fax 01 40 27 81 64, www.mije.com)
and Métro stop (St. Paul). Reservations are accepted.

Sleeping near the Pompidou Center: The remaining hotels
are farther west and closer to the Pompidou Center than to
place Bastille.

Hôtel de Nice**, on the Marais' busy main drag, is a cozy

Charming Double 122

"Marie Antoinette does tie-dye" place. Its narrow halls are littered with paintings, and rooms are filled with lots of thoughtful touches. Twin rooms, which cost the same as doubles, are larger but on the street side—with effective double-paned windows (23 rooms, Sb-€58, Db-€92, Tb-€110, CC, 42 bis rue de Rivoli, Mo: Hôtel de Ville, tel. 01 42 78 55 29, fax 01 42 78 36 07).

Hôtel de la Bretonnerie***, three blocks north and east of Hôtel de Ville, is a fine Marais splurge. It has elegant decor and tastefully decorated rooms with an antique, open-beam warmth (standard Db-€105, Db with character-€136, the standard Db has enough character for me, family-friendly suites-€175, CC, closed Aug, between rue du Vielle du Temple and rue des Archives at 22 rue Sainte Croix de la Bretonnerie, Mo: Hôtel de Ville, tel. 01 48 87 77 63, fax 01 42 77 26 78, www.bretonnerie.com).

At the inexpensive, laid-back **Grand Hôtel du Loiret****, you get what you pay for (S-€37, Sb-€47–60, D-€42, Db-€56–73, Tb-€70–82, CC, just north of rue de Rivoli, 8 rue des Garçons Mauvais, Mo: Hôtel de Ville, tel. 01 48 87 77 00, fax 01 48 04 96 56, e-mail: hoteloiret@aol.com).

Hôtel Caron de Beaumarchais***, its lobby cluttered with bits from an elegant 18th-century Marais house, rents rooms that antique collectors would appreciate (Db-€135–150, CC, air-con, 12 rue Vielle du Temple, Mo: Hôtel de Ville, tel. 01 42 72 34 12, fax 01 42 72 34 63, www.carondebeaumarchais.com).

Hôtel de Vieux Marais**, tucked away on a quiet street two blocks east of the Pompidou Center, offers bright and fairly spacious rooms with air-conditioning, simple decor, and we-try-harder owners. Say hello to Leeloo, the hotel hound (Sb-€95–105, Db-€105–120, extra bed-€23, CC, just off rue des Archives at 8 rue du Platre, Mo: Rambuteau/Hôtel de Ville, tel. 01 42 78 47 22, fax 01 42 78 34 32).

Hôtel Beaubourg*** is a good three-star value within spitting distance of the Pompidou Center. The rooms are wood-beam comfy, and public spaces are warm and pleasant (Db-€104–113, some with balconies-€122, includes breakfast, CC, 11 rue Simon Lefranc, Mo: Rambuteau, tel. 01 42 74 34 24, fax 01 42 78 68 11, e-mail: htlbeaubourg@hotellerie.net).

Sleeping near the Marais on Ile St. Louis: The peaceful, residential character of this island and its central location have drawn Americans for decades, allowing hotels to charge top euro for their generally standard though comfortable rooms. There are no budget values here, but the island's coziness and proximity to the Marais, Notre-Dame, and the Latin Quarter compensate for high room rates. These hotels are on the island's main drag, the rue St. Louis en l'Ile, where I list several restaurants (see "Eating," below).

Hôtel Jeu de Paume**** is the most expensive hotel I list in Paris. When you enter its magnificent lobby—with high ceilings and half-timbered walls—you'll understand why. It has fine public spaces and charming rooms, most of which face a central garden (Db-€210–255, Db-suite-€415–445, CC, 54 rue St. Louis en l'Ile, tel. 01 43 26 14 18, fax 01 40 46 02 76, www.JeudePaumehotel.com).

Hôtel Des Deux Iles*** is the best value on the island, with an appealing lobby and well-appointed rooms. The owners charge a small-room price for some larger rooms—ask (Sb-€122, Db-€140, CC, air-con, must cancel 1 week in advance or pay fees, 59 rue St. Louis en l'Ile, tel. 01 43 26 13 35, fax 01 43 29 60 25, www.hotel-ile-saintlouis.com). Its sister hotel, **Hôtel de Lutece*****, is next door (#65) with the same rates but smaller rooms (CC, tel. 01 43 26 13 35, fax 01 43 29 60 25).

Contrescarpe Orientation

This lively, colorful neighborhood is like Montmartre with fewer tourists. It's just south of the Latin Quarter, encompassing the area between Luxembourg Gardens and rue Monge.

The nearest **TI** is at the Louvre Museum. The **post office** (PTT) is between rue Mouffetard and rue Monge at 10 rue de l'Epée du Bois. Place Monge hosts a colorful **outdoor market** on Wednesday, Friday, and Sunday until 13:00. The **street market** at the bottom of rue Mouffetard bustles daily except Monday (Tue–Sat 08:00–12:00, 15:30–19:00, Sun 08:00–12:00, 5 blocks south of place Contrescarpe). Lively cafés at place Contrescarpe hop with action from the afternoon into the wee hours. **Bus #47** runs along rue Monge north to Notre-Dame, the Pompidou Center, and Gare du Nord.

The flowery Jardin des Plantes park is just east, and the sublime Luxembourg Gardens are just west. Both are ideal for afternoon walks, picnics, naps, and kids. The doorway at 49 rue Monge leads to a hidden **Roman arena** (Arènes de Lutèce). Today, *boules* players occupy the stage while couples cuddle on the seats. Admire the Panthéon from the outside (it's not worth paying to enter), and peek inside the exquisitely beautiful St. Etienne-du-Mont church.

Sleeping in the Contrescarpe Neighborhood
(5th arrondissement, Mo: place Monge, zip code: 75005)

Hotels here are a 20-minute walk from Notre-Dame, Ile de la Cité, and Ile St. Louis, and a 5- to 10-minute walk to the Luxembourg Gardens and the grand boulevards St. Germain and St. Michel. Fewer tourists sleep in Contrescarpe, and I find the hotel values generally better than in most other neighborhoods. Most hotels listed are on or very near rue Mouffetard, the spine of this area, running from the perfectly Parisian place Contrescarpe south to rue Bazelles. Two thousand years ago, rue Mouffetard was the principal Roman road south to Italy. Today, this small,

Contrescarpe Hotels and Restaurants

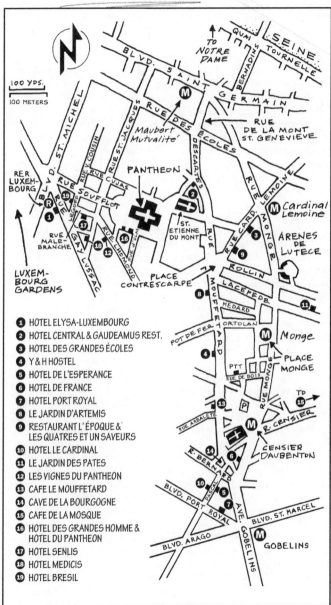

- **1** HOTEL ELYSA-LUXEMBOURG
- **2** HOTEL CENTRAL & GAUDEAMUS REST.
- **3** HOTEL DES GRANDES ÉCOLES
- **4** Y & H HOSTEL
- **5** HOTEL DE L'ESPERANCE
- **6** HOTEL DE FRANCE
- **7** HOTEL PORT ROYAL
- **8** LE JARDIN D'ARTEMIS
- **9** RESTAURANT L'ÉPOQUE & LES QUATRES ET UN SAVEURS
- **10** HOTEL LE CARDINAL
- **11** LE JARDIN DES PATES
- **12** LES VIGNES DU PANTHEON
- **13** CAFE LE MOUFFETARD
- **14** CAVE DE LA BOURGOGNE
- **15** CAFE DE LA MOSQUE
- **16** HOTEL DES GRANDES HOMME & HOTEL DU PANTHEON
- **17** HOTEL SENLIS
- **18** HOTEL MEDICIS
- **19** HOTEL BRESIL

...andering street has a split personality. The lower part thrives in the daytime as a pedestrian market street. The upper part sleeps during the day but comes alive after dark, teeming with bars, restaurants, and nightlife. These hotels are listed in order of proximity to the Seine and Notre-Dame.

Hôtel Central* defines unpretentiousness, with a charming location; a steep, slippery, castlelike stairway; so-so beds; and simple rooms (all with showers, though toilets are down the hall). It's a fine budget value (Ss-€27–29, Ds-€37–41, no CC, no elevator, 6 rue Descartes, Mo: Cardinal Lemoine, tel. 01 46 33 57 93).

Hôtel des Grandes Ecoles*** is simply idyllic. A short alley leads to three buildings that protect a flowering garden courtyard, preserving a sense of tranquility that is rare in a city this size. Rooms are spacious and comfortable with large beds. This romantic place is deservedly popular, so call well in advance (Db-€90–114, extra bed-€15, parking-€20, CC, 75 rue de Cardinal Lemoine, Mo: Cardinal Lemoine, tel. 01 43 26 79 23, fax 01 43 25 28 15, www .hotel-grandes-ecoles.com, mellow Marie speaks some English).

Sleeping between the Panthéon and Luxembourg Gardens: The following five hotels are a five-minute walk from place Contrescarpe. For these listings, the RER stop Luxembourg (with direct connections to the airports) is closer than the nearest Métro stop, Maubert Mutualité. The first two face the Panthéon's right transept.

Hôtel du Panthéon*** offers a seductively comfy lobby and rooms decorated in "country French." Rooms are well-designed, with air-conditioning and every comfort. Fifth-floor rooms have balconies, but sixth-floor rooms have the best views (Db-€190–220, CC, tel. 01 43 54 32 95, fax 01 43 26 64 65, www.hoteldupantheon.com).

Hôtel des Grandes Hommes*** has spacious, wood-beamed rooms, which are scheduled for renovation in 2002 (Db-€190–230, prices are estimates, CC, 17 place du Panthéon, tel. 01 46 34 19 60, fax 01 43 26 67 32, e-mail: reservation @hoteldesgrandeshommes.com).

Hôtel Senlis** hides quietly two blocks from Luxembourg Gardens with modest rooms, all with beamed ceilings and TVs (Sb-€65, Db-€70–85, Tb-€95, Qb-€107, CC, 7 rue Malebranche, tel. 01 43 29 93 10, fax 01 43 29 00 24, e-mail: hoteldesenlis@wanadoo.fr).

Hôtel Brésil** lies one block from Luxembourg Gardens and offers less character, and some smoky rooms, at reasonable rates (Sb-€62, Db-€62–85, CC, 10 rue le Goff, tel. 01 43 54 76 11, fax 01 46 33 45 78, e-mail: hoteldubresil@wanadoo.fr).

Hôtel Medicis is as cheap, stripped-down, and basic as it gets with a soiled linoleum charm, a helpful owner, and a great location (S-€15, D-€30, 214 rue St. Jacques, tel. 01 43 54 14 66, Denis SE).

Hôtel Elysa-Luxembourg*** sits on a busy street at Luxembourg Gardens and charges top euro for its plush, air-conditioned
rooms (Sb-€107, Db-€134, CC, 6 rue Gay Lussac, tel. 01 43 25
31 74, fax 01 46 34 56 27, www.elysa_luxembourg.fr).

Sleeping at the bottom of rue Mouffetard: Of my recommended accommodations in the Contrescarpe neighborhood, these
are farthest from the Seine and other tourists and lie in an appealing
work-a-day area. They may have rooms when others don't.

Y&H Hostel offers a great location; easygoing, English-
speaking management; Internet access; kitchen facilities; and basic
but acceptable hostel conditions (beds in 4-bed rooms-€18, beds
in double rooms-€21, sheets-€2.50, no CC, rooms closed
11:00–16:00 but reception stays open, 02:00 curfew, reservations
require deposit, 80 rue Mouffetard, Mo: Cardinal Lemoine, tel. 01
47 07 47 07, fax 01 47 07 22 24, e-mail: smile@youngandhappy.fr).

Hôtel de l'Esperance** gives you nearly three stars for
the price of two. It's quiet, pink, fluffy, and comfortable, with
thoughtfully appointed rooms complete with canopy beds, hair
dryers, and a flamboyant owner (Sb-€70, Db-€72–86, small
Tb-€101, CC, 15 rue Pascal, Mo: Censier-Daubenton, tel.
01 47 07 10 99, fax 01 43 37 56 19).

Hôtel le Cardinal*** is a new, well-designed hotel with pleasing decor, air-conditioning, and modern comforts (Sb-€93, standard
Db-€115, large Db-€185, Tb-€205, CC, 20 rue Pascal, tel. 01 47
07 41 92, fax 01 47 07 43 80, e-mail: hotelcardinal@aol.com).

Hôtel de France**, set on a busy street, has fine, modern
rooms and hardworking, helpful owners (Jean and Christine).
The best and quietest rooms are *sur le cour* (on the courtyard),
though streetside rooms are fine (Sb-€62, Db-€74–78, CC,
requires 1 night nonrefundable deposit, 108 rue Monge, Mo:
Censier-Daubenton, tel. 01 47 07 19 04, fax 01 43 36 62 34,
e-mail: hotel.de.fce@wanadoo.fr).

Don't let **Hôtel Port Royal***'s lone star fool you—this place is
polished bottom to top and has been well-run by the same family for
66 years. Its clean and comfy rooms come at fair prices. Ask for a
room off the street (S-€35–46, Db-€63–73, no CC, climb stairs
from rue Pascal to busy boulevard de Port Royal, 8 boulevard de
Port Royal, Mo: Gobelins, tel. 01 43 31 70 06, fax 01 43 31 33 67).

Sleeping and Eating near Paris, in Versailles

For a laid-back alternative to Paris within easy reach of the big
city by RER train (5/hr, 30 min), Versailles, with easy, safe parking
and reasonably priced hotels, can be a good overnight stop (see
map on page 71). Park in the château's main lot while looking for
a hotel or leave your car there overnight (free from 19:30–08:00).
Get a map of Versailles at your hotel or at the TI. Be sure to explore
the pleasant town center around place du Marché Notre-Dame

(15-min walk, veer left out of the château), where you'll find a variety of reasonable restaurants, cafés, and a few cobbled lanes (market days Sun, Tue, and Fri until 13:00). Rue Satory is another pedestrian-friendly street with restaurants (near recommended Hôtel d'Angleterre, 10-min walk, go right out of the château).

Hôtel Le Cheval Rouge**, built in 1676 as Louis XIV's stables, now houses tourists. It's a block behind place du Marché in a quaint corner of town on a large, quiet courtyard with free, safe parking and sufficiently comfortable rooms (Ds-€49, Db-€58–72, Tb-€86, Qb-€90, CC, 18 rue Andre Chenier, tel. 01 39 50 03 03, fax 01 39 50 61 27).

Ibis Versailles** offers fair value, modern comfort, but no air-conditioning (Db-€71, cheaper weekend rates can't be reserved ahead, CC, across from RER station, 4 avenue du General de Gaulle, tel. 01 39 53 03 30, fax 01 39 50 06 31).

Hôtel du Palais, facing the RER station, has clean, sharp rooms, and the cheapest I list in this area. Ask for a quiet room off the street (Ds-€43, Db-€49, extra person-€11, CC, miles of stairs, 6 place Lyautey, tel. 01 39 50 39 29, fax 01 39 50 80 41).

Hôtel d'Angleterre**, away from the frenzy, is a tranquil old place with comfortable and spacious rooms. Park nearby in the palace lot (Db-€56–72, extra bed-€15, CC, just below palace to the right as you exit, 2 rue de Fontenay, tel. 01 39 51 43 50, fax 01 39 51 45 63).

Hôtel de France***, in an 18th-century townhouse, offers four-star value, with air-conditioned, appropriately royal rooms, a pleasant courtyard, comfy public spaces, a bar, and a restaurant (Db-€125–130, Tb-€168, CC, just off parking lot across from château, 5 rue Colbert, tel. 01 30 83 92 23, fax 01 30 83 92 24, www.hotelfrance-versailles.com).

Eating: You'll find nothing but food establishments lining the old market square (place du Marché). These places are on or near the square and all are good for lunch or dinner. **La Boeuf à la Mode** offers fine, traditional cuisine right on the square (€23 *menu*, 4 rue au Pain, tel. 01 39 50 31 99). **Fenêtres sur Cour** is the romantic's choice; it feels like you're dining in an Impressionist painting (closed Mon all year and Tue–Wed eves in summer, just below market square in antique village, on place de la Geole, tel. 01 39 51 97 77). **A la Cote Bretonne** is the place to go for crêpes in a cozy setting (a few steps off the square on the traffic-free rue des Deux Ponts, #12).

EATING IN PARIS

Paris is France's wine and cuisine melting pot. While it lacks a style of its own (only French onion soup is truly Parisian), it draws from the best of France. Paris could hold a gourmet's Olympics and import nothing.

Picnic or go to bakeries for quick take-out lunches. Many Parisian department stores have huge supermarkets hiding in the basement, and top-floor cafeterias offering affordable, low-risk, low-stress, what-you-see-is-what-you-get meals.

Stop at a café for a lunch salad or *plat du jour*, but linger longer over dinner. You can eat well, restaurant style, for €15 to €23. Your hotel can usually recommend nearby restaurants in the €15 range. Remember, cafés are happy to serve a *plat du jour* (garnished plate of the day, about €11) or a cheflike salad (about €9) day or night, while restaurants expect you to enjoy a full dinner.

To save piles of euros, review the budget eating tips in this book's introduction and consider dinner picnics (great take-out dishes available at *charcuteries*).

Romantic Picnic Spots: My favorite dinner-picnic places are the pedestrian bridge (pont des Arts) across from the Louvre, with unmatched views and plentiful benches; the Champ de Mars park under the Eiffel Tower; and the western tip of Ile St. Louis, overlooking Ile de la Cité. Bring your own dinner feast and watch the riverboats or the Eiffel Tower light up the city for you.

Restaurants

Restaurants open for dinner around 19:00, and small local favorites get crowded after 21:00. Most of the restaurants listed below accept credit cards.

My recommendations are centered around the same three great neighborhoods I list accommodations for (above); you can come home exhausted after a busy day of sightseeing and have a good selection of restaurants right around the corner. And evening is a fine time to explore any of these delightful neighborhoods, even if you're sleeping elsewhere.

Most restaurants we've listed in these areas have set priced *menus* between €15 and €30. In most cases, the few extra euros you pay for not choosing the least expensive option is money well-spent, as it opens up a variety of better choices. You decide.

If you are traveling outside of Paris, save your splurges for the countryside, where you'll enjoy regional cooking for less money.

Eating in the Rue Cler Neighborhood

The rue Cler neighborhood isn't famous for its restaurants. That's why I enjoy eating here. Several small, family-run places serve great dinner *menus* for €15 and *plats du jour* for €9 to €12. My first two recommendations are easygoing cafés, ideal if what you want is a light dinner (good dinner salads) or more substantial but simple meals.

Café du Marché, with the best seats, coffee, and prices on rue Cler, serves hearty salads and good €9 *plats du jour* for lunch

Rue Cler Restaurants

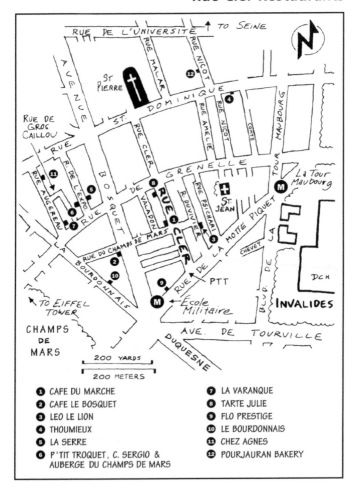

● CAFE DU MARCHE
● CAFE LE BOSQUET
● LEO LE LION
● THOUMIEUX
● LA SERRE
● P'TIT TROQUET, C. SERGIO &
   AUBERGE DU CHAMPS DE MARS

● LA VARANQUE
● TARTE JULIE
● FLO PRESTIGE
● LE BOURDONNAIS
● CHEZ AGNES
● POURJAURAN BAKERY

or dinner to a trendy, smoky, mainly French crowd. Arrive before 19:30 or wait at the bar. A chalkboard listing the plates of the day—each a meal—will momentarily be hung in front of you (at the corner of rue Cler and rue Champ de Mars).

Café le Bosquet is a vintage Parisian brasserie. Come here for a bowl of French onion soup, a salad, or a three-course set *menu* (€16 *menu*, many choices, closed Sun, 46 avenue Bosquet, tel. 01 45 51 38 13).

Leo le Lion, a warm, charming souvenir of old Paris, is

popular with locals. Expect to spend €23 per person for fine *à la carte* choices (closed Sun, 23 rue Duvivier, tel. 01 45 51 41 77).

Thoumieux, the neighborhood's classy, traditional Parisian brasserie, is deservedly popular. It's big and dressy with formal but good-natured waiters. Skip the *menu* and order *à la carte* (allow €30/person with wine, 79 rue St. Dominique, tel. 01 47 05 49 75).

I like browsing the handful of fine places that line rue de l'Exposition, one block west of avenue Bosquet between rue St. Dominique and rue de Grenelle. Each of these places is a hard-working, mom-and-pop organization with plenty of charm and a distinct ambience. Eat early with tourists or late with locals. **Restaurant La Serre**, at #29, has fun atmosphere but an unpredictable staff (*plats* €8–11, daily from 19:00, often a wait after 21:00, good onion soup and duck specialties, tel. 01 45 55 20 96, Marie-Alice and Philippe speak English). **Le P'tit Troquet**, across the street at #28, is delightfully Parisian, popular with locals, and gracefully run by Dominique—allow €24 per person for dinner (closed Sun–Mon, tel. 01 47 05 80 39). **La Casa di Sergio**, at #20, is where I go in Paris for gourmet Italian cuisine served family style by Sicilian Sergio. Sergio says he's waited his entire life to open a restaurant like this. While not cheap, the food is remarkable. Sit down and let Sergio do the rest (€26–34 *menus*, closed Wed, tel. 01 45 51 37 71). The softly lit tables and red velvet chairs of **Auberge du Champ de Mars**, at #18, draw a romantic crowd (€15 *menu*, expensive wines, closed Sun).

These three places are closer to the Champs de Mars park. Just off rue de Grenelle, the friendly and unpretentious **La Varanque** is a good budget bet, with €9 *plats* and a €12 *menu* (27 rue Augereau, tel. 01 47 05 51 22). **Chez Agnes** is tiny, a good value, and run by engaging Agnes (closed Mon, next to recommended Hôtel Londres Eiffel at 1 rue Augereau, tel. 01 45 51 06 04). For a truly special occasion, the **Le Bourdonnais** has one Michelin star and a warm, intimate feel. Micheline Croat, your hostess, will take good care of you (€64 *menu*, 113 avenue de la Bourdonnais, tel. 01 47 05 47 96).

Picnicking: The rue Cler is a moveable feast that gives "fast food" a good name. The entire street is clogged with connoisseurs of good eating. Only the health-food store goes unnoticed. A festival of food, the street is lined with people whose lives seem to be devoted to their specialty: polished produce, rotisserie chicken, crêpes, or cheese squares.

For a magical picnic dinner at the Eiffel Tower, assemble it in no fewer than five shops on rue Cler and lounge on the best grass in Paris (the police don't mind after dusk), with the dogs, Frisbees, a floodlit tower, and a cool breeze in the Parc du Champ de Mars.

The **crêpe stand** next to Café du Marché does a wonderful top-end dinner crêpe for €4. Asian delis (generically called *Traiteur Asie*) provide tasty low-stress, low-price, take-out treats (2 with tables on rue Cler—1 across from Hôtel Leveque, the other near rue du Champs de Mars). For a variety of savory quiches or a tasty pear-and-chocolate tart, try **Tarte Julie's** (take-out or stools, 28 rue Cler). The elegant **Flo Prestige** *charcuterie* is open until 23:00 and offers mouthwatering meals to go (at the École Militaire Métro stop).

Eating in the Marais Neighborhood

The sidewalks of the Marais are filled with locals and tourists in search of a good meal from, unfortunately, an abundance of average eateries. I've worked hard to find the best in this area where too often you must choose between the quality of the atmosphere or the cuisine. The Ile St. Louis is a short walk away (see below) and offers those staying in the Marais a pleasant alternative for restaurants.

For starters, stroll rue Vieille du Temple (near rue des Rosiers), home to several lively cafés providing traditional fare (some even serve Sunday brunch) and a handful of good restaurants worth the detour. **Au Petit Fer à Cheval,** named for its horseshoe-shaped bar, is an authentic gem with mirrored walls and tiled floors. To avoid crowds, come for lunch, an early dinner, or a nightcap. The restaurant in back serves daily specials to diners seated on old wooden Métro seats (daily until 24:00, 30 rue Vieille du Temple, tel. 01 42 72 47 47,). **Le Colimacon**, at #44, is a romantic little place offering two-course (€14) or three-course (€20) *menus* of traditional cuisine including *magret de canard aux fruits de saison* (duck breast with a sauce of seasonal fruit, closed Tue eves, reservations required, tel. 01 48 87 12 01).

Vegetarians will appreciate the excellent cuisine at popular **Picolo Teatro** (closed Mon, near rue des Rosiers, 6 rue des Ecouffes, tel. 01 42 72 17 79) or **L'As du Falafel**, which serves the best falafels on rue des Rosiers at #34.

You'll find several places that rely more on the quality of their charming location than their cuisine at the tiny square, place du Marché Ste. Catherine. For reliably good cuisine with a Basque emphasis, find **L'Auberge de Jarente** (€18 *menu*, closed Sun–Mon, just off the square at 7 rue Jarente, tel. 01 42 77 49 35).

Dinners under the candlelit arches of place des Vosges are *très* romantic. The mod and pastel **Nectarine** at #16 is a teahouse serving good salads, quiches, and reasonable *plats du jour* both day and night (tel. 01 42 77 23 78). **Ma Bourgogne** is bigger, darker, and more traditional (allow €38/person with wine, open daily, dinner reservations smart, no CC, at northwest corner, tel. 01 42 78 44 64). Just off place des Vosges, **L'Impasse** (or **Chez Robert**) is a cozy neighborhood bistro located on a quiet alley

Marais Restaurants

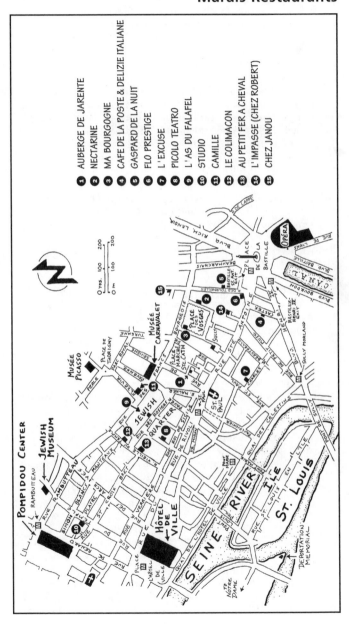

1 AUBERGE DE JARENTE
2 NECTARINE
3 MA BOURGOGNE
4 CAFE DE LA POSTE & DELIZIE ITALIANE
5 GASPARD DE LA NUIT
6 FLO PRESTIGE
7 L'EXCUSE
8 PICOLO TEATRO
9 L'AS DU FALAFEL
10 STUDIO
11 CAMILLE
12 LE COLIMAÇON
13 AU PETIT FER A CHEVAL
14 L'IMPASSE (CHEZ ROBERT)
15 CHEZ JANOU

next to a Laundromat. Clean your clothes while you dine from a classic bourgeois *menu* with a variety of €6 first courses, €13.50 second courses, and €6 desserts (closed Sun, 4 impasse Guemenee, tel. 01 42 72 08 45). A few blocks west you'll find **Camille,** a traditional corner brasserie with white-aproned waiters serving €9 salads and very French *plats du jour* for €15 (daily, 24 rue des Francs-Bourgeois at corner of rue Elzevir, tel. 01 42 72 29 50).

The next places sit near the intersection of rues Castex and St. Antoine. For a break from French cooking, find a table at the tiny and *très* tasty **Trattoria Delizie Italiane** (closed Sun–Mon, 6 rue Castex, tel. 01 44 54 00 33). On the other side of rue St. Antoine, **Gaspard de la Nuit** is cozy and a worthwhile step up with a good €24 *menu* (a block off rue St. Antoine at 6 rue des Tournelles, tel. 01 42 77 90 53). If the weather's nice, grab a table on the terrace at **Chez Janou,** a Provençal bistro, then make your selection from a tempting *à la carte* menu (CC, at corner of rue des Tournelles and rue Roger-Verlomme, 2 rue Roger-Verlomme, tel. 01 42 72 28 41).

Near Hôtel du 7ème Art, splurge at the romantic and dressy **L'Excuse** (€30 *menu,* closed Sun, reserve ahead, 14 rue Charles V, tel. 01 42 77 98 97).

Closer to the Pompidou Center, the **Studio** is wonderfully located on a 17th-century courtyard below a dance school. The tasty salads, €12 *plats du jour,* and Tex-Mex food are good day or night (41 rue de Temple, tel. 01 42 74 10 38).

Picnicking: Picnic at the peaceful place des Vosges (park closes at dusk). Hobos stretch their euros at the supermarket in the basement of the **Monoprix** department store (near place des Vosges on rue St. Antoine), and connoisseurs prefer the gourmet take-out places all along rue St. Antoine, such as **Flo Prestige** (open until 23:00, on the tiny square where rue Tournelle and rue St. Antoine meet). A few small grocery shops are open until 23:00 on rue St. Antoine (near intersection with rue Castex). An **open-air market,** held Sunday morning, is just off place de la Bastille on boulevard Richard Lenoir.

For a cheap breakfast, try the tiny *boulangerie/pâtisserie* where the hotels buy their croissants (coffee machine-€0.50, baby quiches-€1.50, *pain au chocolat*-€0.75, 1 block off place de la Bastille, at corner of rue St. Antoine and rue de Lesdiguieres).

Eating in the Contrescarpe Neighborhood

There are a few diamonds in this otherwise rough area for fine dining. Most come here for the lively and cheap eateries that line rues Mouffetard and du Pot-de-Fer. Study the many *menus,* compare crowds, then dive in and have fun (see map on page 93).

Le Jardin d'Artemis is one of the better values on rue Mouffe-tard at #34 (€13.50 and €21 *menus*), though **Restaurant l'Epoque**

is the best place I found for fine cuisine at moderate prices (basic
€13.50 *menu*, €19 *menu* is worth the extra euros, a block off place
Contrescarpe at 81 rue Cardinal Lemoine, tel. 01 46 34 15 84).
Across the street, **Les Quatres et Une Saveurs** is a hard-core,
gourmet vegetarian place and worth a detour (closed Mon, 72 rue
Cardinal Lemoine, tel. 01 43 26 88 80). **Le Jardin des Pates** is popular with less strict vegetarians, serving pastas and salads at fair prices
(near Jardins des Plantes, 4 rue Lacepede, tel. 01 43 31 50 71).
    The next two places are near the Panthéon. **Gaudeamus**,
with a low-profile café on one side and a cozy bistro on the other,
has friendly owners and cheap *menus* (daily, just below the Panthéon, 47 rue Montagne Ste. Genevieve, tel. 01 40 46 93 40).
Les Vignes du Panthéon has Old World appeal and is popular
with locals (allow €23 for *à la carte*, closed Sat–Sun, 4 rue des
Fossés, tel. 01 43 54 80 81).

Eating on Ile St. Louis

The Ile St. Louis is popular with Americans for good reason: It's
a romantic and peaceful place to window shop for plenty of prom-
ising dinner possibilities. Cruise the island's main street for a
variety of good options, from cozy *crêperies* to romantic restaurants.
After dinner, sample Paris' best sorbet and ice cream at any place
advertising "les glaces Berthillon" (the original Berthillon shop is
at 31 rue St. Louis en l'Ile). Then stroll across to the Ile de la
Cité to see an illuminated Notre Dame.
    All listings below line the rue St. Louis en l'Ile and begin
at the end of the island closest Notre Dame. **Café Med**, at #77,
serves inexpensive salads, crêpes, and lighter *menus* in a cheery
setting (open daily). Nearby at #72, **Coin Sud** offers much of the
same with warmer ambience. **La Castafiore**, at #51-53, serves fine
Italian in a black-and-white-tile atmosphere (€28 *menu*). Farther
down, **Au Gourmet de l'Isle**, is a fun, good bet with a €25 *menu*
(closed Mon–Tue). Almost next door, **l'Auberge de la Reine
Blanche** is worth a visit for its consistently good cuisine and
pleasant owners (open daily).
    For a crazy, touristy, cellar atmosphere and hearty, fun
food, feast at **La Taverne du Sergeant Recruiter**. The "Sergeant Recruiter" used to get young Parisians drunk and stuffed
here, then sign them into the army. It's all-you-can-eat, including wine and service, for €31 (daily from 19:00, #41, tel. 01 43
54 75 42). There's a near-food-fight clone next door at **Nos
Ancêtres Les Gaulois** ("Our Ancestors the Gauls," daily from
19:00, tel. 01 46 33 66 07).

Transportation Connections—Paris

Paris is Europe's rail hub, with six major train stations, each
serving different regions: Gare de l'Est (east-bound trains),

Gare du Nord (northern France and Europe), Gare St. Lazare (northwestern France), Gare d'Austerlitz (southwest France and Europe), Gare de Lyon (southeastern France and Italy), and Gare Montparnasse (northwestern France and TGV service to France's southwest). Any train station can give you schedule information, make reservations, and sell tickets for any destination. Buying tickets is handier from an SNCF neighborhood office (e.g., Louvre, Invalides, Orsay, Versailles, airports) or at your neighborhood travel agency—worth their small fee (SNCF signs in their window indicate they sell train tickets). For schedule information, call 08 36 35 35 35 (€0.50/min, English sometimes available).

Gare du Nord: Serves northern France and several international destinations. To **Brussels** (21/day, 1.5 hrs, cheaper by bus, see "Buses," below), **Bruges** (18/day, 2 hrs, change in Brussels, 1 direct), **Amsterdam** (10/day, 4 hrs; cheaper by bus, see "Buses," below), **Copenhagen** (1/day, 16 hrs, 2 night trains), **Koblenz** (6/day, 5 hrs, change in Köln), **London** via Eurostar Chunnel (17/day, 3 hrs, tel. 08 36 35 35 39, www.raileurope.com, www .eurostar.co.uk; for details, see below). **By Banlieue/RER lines to**: **Chantilly-Gouvieux** (hrly, fewer on weekends, 35 min), **Charles de Gaulle airport** (2/hr, 30 min, runs 05:30–23:00, track 4).

Gare de l'Est: Serves eastern France and points east. To **Colmar** (12/day, 5.5 hrs, change in Strasbourg, Dijon, or Mulhouse), **Strasbourg** (14/day, 4.5 hrs, many require changes), **Reims** (12/day, 1.5 hrs), **Verdun** (5/day, 3 hrs, change in Metz or Chalon), **Munich** (5/day, 9 hrs, some require changes, night train), **Vienna** (7/day, 13–18 hrs, most require changes, night train), **Zurich** (10/day, 7 hrs, most require changes, night train), **Prague** (2/day, 14 hrs, night train).

Gare Montparnasse: Serves Lower Normandy and Brittany and offers TGV service to Loire Valley and southwestern France. To **Chartres** (20/day, 1 hr, Banlieue lines), **Pontorson-Mont St. Michel** (5/day, 4.5 hrs, via Rennes, then take bus; or take train to Pontorson via Caen, then bus from Pontorson), **Dinan** (7/day, 4 hrs, change in Rennes and Dol), **Bordeaux** (14/day, 3.5 hrs), **Sarlat** (5/day, 6 hrs, change in Bordeaux, Libourne, or Souillac), **Toulouse** (11/day, 5 hrs, most require change, usually in Bordeaux), **Albi** (7/day, 6–7.5 hrs, change in Toulouse, also night train), **Carcassonne** (8/day, 6.5 hrs, most require changes in Toulouse and Bordeaux, direct trains take 10 hrs), **Tours** (14/day, 1 hr).

Gare du Lyon: Offers TGV and regular service to southeastern France, Italy, and other international destinations. To **Melun** (hrly, 30 min), **Fontainebleau** (nearly hrly, 45 min), **Beaune** (12/day, 2.5 hrs, most require change in Dijon), **Dijon** (15/day, 1.5 hrs), **Chamonix** (9/day, 9 hrs, change in Lyon and St. Gervais, direct night train), **Annecy** (8/day, 4–7 hrs), **Lyon**

(16/day, 2.5 hrs), **Avignon** (9/day in 2.5 hrs, 6/day in 4 hrs with change), **Arles** (14/day, 5 hrs, most with change in Marseille, Avignon, or Nîmes), **Nice** (14/day, 5.5–7 hrs, many with change in Marseille), **Venice** (3/day, 3/night, 11–15 hrs, many require changes), **Rome** (2/day, 5/night, 15–18 hrs, many require changes), **Bern** (9/day, 5–11 hrs, most require changes, night train).

Gare St. Lazare: Serves Upper Normandy. To **Giverny** (train to Vernon, 5/day, 45 min; then bus or taxi 10 min to Giverny), **Rouen** (15/day, 75 min), **Honfleur** (6/day, 3 hrs, via Lisieux, then bus), **Bayeux** (9/day, 2.5 hrs, some with change in Caen), **Caen** (12/day, 2 hrs).

Gare d'Austerlitz: Provides non-TGV service to the Loire Valley, southwestern France, and Iberia. To **Amboise** (8/day in 2 hrs, 12/day in 1.5 hrs with change in St. Pierre des Corps), **Cahors** (7/day, 5–7 hrs, most with changes), **Barcelona** (1/day, 9 hrs, change in Montpellier, night trains), **Madrid** (2 night trains only, 13–16 hrs), **Lisbon** (1/day, 24 hrs).

Buses: The main bus station is Gare Routière du Paris-Gallieni (28 avenue du General de Gaulle, in suburb of Bagnolet, Mo: Gallieni, tel. 01 49 72 51 51). Buses provide cheaper, if less comfortable, transportation to major European cities; you'll pay about $24 to get from Paris to Brussels (compared to $80 second-class by train) and $33 from Paris to Amsterdam compared to $100 second-class by train (Eurolines tel. 08 36 69 52 52, www.eurolines.com).

The Eurostar Train to London

The fastest and most convenient way to London is by rail. Eurostar is the speedy passenger train that zips you from downtown Paris to London (17/day, 3 hrs) faster and easier than flying. The train goes 190 mph in France but a doddering 80 mph in England. (When the English segment gets up to speed the journey time will shrink to 2 hours.) The actual tunnel crossing is a 20-minute, black, silent, 100-mile-per-hour nonevent. Your ears won't even pop. Eurostar trains also run direct to London from Charles de Gaulle Airport or even Disneyland Paris.

Channel fares are reasonable but complicated. For the latest, call 800/EUROSTAR in the United States. These are prices from 2001: The "Leisure Ticket" is affordable ($219 first class, $139 second class, 50 percent refundable up to 3 days before departure). "Full Fare" first class costs $279 and includes a meal (a dinner departure nets you more grub than breakfast); "full fare" second class costs $199 (fully refundable even after departure date). Discounts are available to railpass holders ($155/first class, $75/second class, railpass must include France or Britain), seniors over 60 ($189/first class only), youths under 26 ($79/second class), and children under 12 (about half the fare of your ticket).

Cheaper seats can sell out. Book from home if you're ready to commit to a date and time. Compare fares sold by U.S. rail agents (www.raileurope.com) and French agents (www.eurostarplanet.com, French only). If you're ready to commit to a date, time, and U.S. prices, you can book by calling 800/EUROSTAR, visiting www .raileurope.com, or by having your travel agent do it all for you (prices do not include FedEx ticket delivery).

Buy your Eurostar ticket in Paris at any train station, neighborhood SNCF office, most travel agencies, or by phone (tel. 08 36 35 35 39). Those with a railpass pay about €85 (second class) one-way, any day. Without a railpass, a same-day round-trip on a Saturday or Sunday costs €154. Various deals are available. For instance, if you stay over on a Saturday night, you'll pay €115 for a second-class round-trip (7-day advance purchase necessary). Round-trip tickets over a Saturday are often cheaper than the basic one-way fare...you know the trick. Note that first-class and business-class fares are substantially higher.

Charles de Gaulle Airport

Paris' primary airport has three main terminals: T-1, T-2, and T-9. Air France uses T-2; charters dominate T-9, and U.S. carriers use T-1. Terminals are connected every few minutes by a free *navette* (bus), and the RER (Paris subway) stops at T-1 and T-2 terminals. The TGV train station is at T-2. There is no bag storage at the airport.

Those flying to or from the United States will probably use T-1, and the information that follows is for that terminal. The "Meeting Point" is ground zero for tourist information, with free maps, museum passes, and brochures (daily 07:00–22:00). A Relay store sells Kertel phone cards. A bank (with lousy rates) is near gate 16. An American Express cash machine and an ATM are near gate 32. Car-rental offices are on the arrival level from gates 10 to 22; the SNCF (train) office is at gate 22. For flight information, call 01 48 62 22 80.

Those departing from this terminal will find restaurants, a PTT (post office), a pharmacy, boutiques, and a handy grocery store one floor below the ticketing desks at level 2.

Transportation between Charles de Gaulle Airport and Paris: Three efficient public-transportation routes, taxis, and airport shuttle vans link the airport's T-1 and T-2 terminals with central Paris. At T-1 (where most land), **RER trains** run every 15 minutes to central Paris. From gate 36, take the elevator down to level (*niveau*) 2, walk outside, cross the street, and catch the green bus to *Roissypole*. Transfer to RER trains there (€8, stops at Gare du Nord, Chatelet, St. Michel, and Luxembourg Gardens). When coming to the airport from Paris, T-1 is the first RER stop at Charles de Gaulle, T-2 is the second stop. The **Roissy Bus** runs every 15 minutes between gate 30 and Paris' Opéra Garnier (€8, 40 min, buy ticket inside terminal at gate 30; the Opéra stop is on rue Scribe at the American Express office). The **Air France Bus** leaves every 15 minutes from gate 34 and serves the Arc de Triomphe and Porte Maillot in about 40 minutes for €10, and the Montparnasse Tower in 60 minutes for €11 (from any of these stops you can reach your hotel by taxi). The RER Roissy Rail, Roissy Bus, and Air France bus described above serve the T-2 terminal as efficiently and economically as T-1. For most people, the RER Roissy Rail works best. A **taxi** ride with luggage costs about €38; a taxi stand is at gate 20. The **Disneyland Express bus** departs from gate 32. The **TGV station** is at T-2 (from gate 36, take elevator down to *niveau* 2, walk outside, cross the street, and catch the red bus to T-2).

For a stress-free trip between either of Paris' airports and downtown, consider an **airport shuttle minivan**, ideal for single travelers or families of four or more. Reserve from home, and they'll meet you at the airport (€23 for 1 person, €27 for 2, €41 for 3, €55 for 4, plan on a 30-min wait if you ask them to pick you up at the airport). Choose between **Airport Connection** (tel. 01 44 18 36 02, fax 01 45 55 85 19, www.airport-connection.com) or **Paris Airport Services** (tel. 01 49 62 78 78, fax 01 49 62 78 79, www.magic.fr/pas, e-mail: pas@magic.fr).

Sleeping at or near Charles de Gaulle Airport: Hôtel Ibis**, outside the RER Roissy Rail station for T-1 (the first RER stop coming from Paris), offers standard and predictable accommodations (Db-€85, CC, near *navette* bus stop, free shuttle bus to either terminal takes 2 min, tel. 01 49 19 19 19, fax 01 49 19 19 21, e-mail: h1404@accor-hotels.com), as does **Novotel***** (Db-€133–145, CC, tel. 01 49 19 27 27, fax 01 49 19 27 99). A 15-minute drive from the airport is another Ibis hotel in the village of Roissy with shuttle service.

Drivers wanting to avoid rush-hour traffic may consider sleeping north of Paris in the medieval town of Senlis (15 min north of airport) at **Hostellerie de la Porte Bellon** (Db-€65, CC, in center at 51 rue Bellon, near rue de la République, tel. 03 44 53 03 05, fax 03 44 53 29 94).

Orly Airport

This airport feels small. Orly has two terminals: Sud and Ouest. International flights arrive at Sud, as I assume you will. After exiting Terminal Sud's baggage claim (near gate H), you'll be greeted by signs directing you to city transportation, car rental, and so on. Turn left to enter the main terminal area, and you'll find exchange offices with bad rates, an ATM machine, the ADP (a quasi–tourist office that offers free city maps and basic sightseeing information, open until 23:00), and an SNCF French rail desk (closes at 18:00, sells train tickets and even Eurailpasses, next to the ADP). Downstairs is a sandwich bar, WCs, a bank (same bad rates), a newsstand (buy *télécarte* phone card), and a post office (great rates for cash or American Express traveler's checks). Car-rental offices are located in the parking lot in front of the terminal. For flight info on any airline serving Orly, call 01 49 75 15 15.

Transportation between Paris and Orly Airport: There are three efficient public-transportation routes, taxis, and a couple of airport shuttle services linking Orly Sud and central Paris. The gate locations listed below apply to Orly Sud, but the same transportation services are available from both terminals. The **Air France bus** (outside gate G) runs to Paris' Invalides Métro stop (€8, 4/hr, 30 min) and is best for those staying in or near the rue Cler neighborhood (from Invalides terminal, take the Métro 2 stops to Ecole Militaire to reach recommended hotels). The **Jetbus #285** (outside gate F, €5, 4/hr) is the quickest way to the Paris subway and the best way to the recommended hotels in the Marais and Contrescarpe neighborhoods (take Jetbus to Villejuif Métro stop, buy a *carnet* of 10 Métro tickets, then take the Métro to the Sully Morland stop for the Marais area, or the Censier-Daubenton or place Monge stops for the Contrescarpe area). If coming to the airport, make sure your train serves Villejuif, as the route splits at the end of the line.

The **Orlybus** (outside gate H, €5.50, 4/hr) takes you to the Denfert-Rochereau RER-B line and the Métro, offering subway access to central Paris. The **Orlyval trains** are overpriced (€9) and require a transfer at the Antony stop to reach RER line B (serving Luxembourg, Chatelet, St. Michel, and Gare du Nord stations in central Paris). **Taxis** are to the far right as you leave the terminal, at gate M. Allow €26 for a taxi into central Paris.

Airport shuttle minivans are ideal for single travelers or families of four or more (see "Charles de Gaulle Airport," above, for the companies to contact; from Orly, figure about €18 for 1 person, €12/person for 2, less for larger groups and kids).

Sleeping near Orly Airport: The only reasonable airport hotel is **Hôtel Ibis**** (Db-€61, CC, tel. 01 56 70 50 60, fax 01 56 70 50 70). The **Hôtel Mercure***** provides more comfort for a price (Db-€114, tel. 01 46 87 23 37, fax 01 46 87 71 92). Both have free shuttles to the terminal.

NORMANDY

Apple orchards, dramatic coastlines, half-timbered towns, and thatched roofs accent the green, rolling hills of Normandy. Parisians call Normandy "the 21st *arrondissement*." It's their escape—the nearest beach. The British call this area close enough for a weekend away.

Viking Norsemen settled here in the ninth century, giving Normandy its name. William the Conqueror invaded England from Normandy in the 11th century. To see his victory commemorated in a remarkable tapestry, weave Bayeux into your trip. In Rouen, France's greatest cheerleader, Jeanne d'Arc (Joan of Arc), was convicted of heresy and burned at the stake by the English, against whom she had rallied France during the Hundred Years' War.

The rugged, rainy coast of Normandy harbors tiny fishing villages such as little Honfleur, which today harvests more charm than fish. The cliffhanger coast, two hours south of Honfleur, was the scene of a WWII battle that changed the course of history. South of the D-Day beaches, on the border of Brittany, is the almost surreal island abbey of Mont St. Michel, rising serene and majestic, oblivious to its tides of tourists.

Planning Your Time

Honfleur, the D-Day beaches, and Mont St. Michel each merit an overnight visit. If you're driving between Paris and Honfleur, Giverny (see Paris chapter) or Rouen (sights closed Tue) are easy stops; by train they're best as daytrips from Paris. The WWII museum in Caen works well as a stop between Honfleur and Bayeux (and the D-Day beaches), and it's wise not to arrive before 17:00 at Mont St. Michel. Dinan, only 40 minutes from Mont St. Michel

Normandy

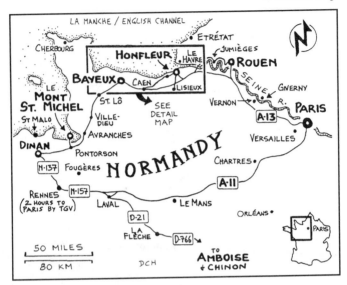

(1 hr by train), offers an enchanting introduction to Brittany. Some enjoy Mont St. Michel as a daytrip from Dinan.

Getting around Normandy

Trains serve Rouen, Caen, Bayeux, Mont St. Michel (via Pontorson), and Dinan, with reasonable service from Paris but marginal service between these sights. Plan ahead and you'll manage. Buses make Giverny, Honfleur, Arromanches, and Mont St. Michel accessible to train stations in nearby towns, though Sundays have little if any bus service. Mont St. Michel is a headache by train except from Paris.

Cuisine Scene—Normandy

Known as the land of the four Cs (Calvados, Camembert, cider, and *crème*), Normandy specializes in cream sauces, organ meats (sweetbreads, tripe, and kidneys—"the gizzard salads" are great), and seafood (*fruits de mer*). Dairy products are big here. Local cheeses are Camembert (mild to very strong), Brillat-Savarin (buttery), Livarot (spicy and pungent), Pavé d'Auge (spicy and tangy), and Pont l'Evéque (earthy flavor). Normandy is famous for its powerful Calvados apple brandy, Benedictine brandy (made by local monks), and three kinds of alcoholic apple ciders (*cidre* can be *doux*—sweet, *brut*—dry, or *bouche*—sparkling and the strongest). Look also for Poiret, a tasty pear cider.

ROUEN

This 2,000-year-old city of 100,000 people mixes dazzling Gothic
architecture, soaring half-timbered houses, and contemporary
bustle like no other in France. Medieval Rouen (pron. ru-ohn)
was France's second largest city, with 40,000 residents (only Paris
had more), and walked a political tightrope between England and
France for centuries. It was an English base during the Hundred
Years' War. William the Conqueror made Rouen his home 900
years ago; 300 years later, Joan of Arc was burned here.

Orientation: Rouen's sights, hotels, and train station are within a 15-minute walk of the river on its right (northern) bank (*rive
droite*). The streets Jeanne d'Arc, des Carmes, and de la République
each cross the river and slice through the heart of Rouen.

Tourist Information: The TI faces the cathedral. Pick up
their map highlighting a walking tour (in French only), information
on Rouen's museums, and a brochure on the Route of the Ancient
Abbeys—described below (May–Sept Mon–Sat 09:00–19:00, Sun
09:30–12:30, 14:00–18:00; Oct–April Mon–Sat 09:00–18:00, Sun
10:00–13:00, tel. 02 32 08 32 40, www.mairie-rouen.fr).

Arrival in Rouen

By Train: Rue Jeanne d'Arc cuts down from Rouen's station (24-hr
lockers available) through the town center to the Seine River. Walk
from the station down rue Jeanne d'Arc to rue du Gros Horloge.
This pedestrian mall in the medieval center connects the open-air
market and Jeanne d'Arc church (to your right) with the cathedral
and TI (to your left). To go to the start of the Rouen walking tour
(described below), turn right on rue du Gros Horloge (you'll see the
sweeping roof of the modern Eglise Jeanne d' Arc). Rouen's new
subway whisks you from the train station to the Palais de la Justice
in one stop (€1.25), one block above rue du Gros Horloge.

By Car: Follow signs to *centre-ville* (city center) and *rive droite*
(right bank) and park along the river (metered until 19:00) or in
one of many underground lots (near cathedral is best, about €5.50
overnight). If you get turned around (and you probably will in this
city of narrow one-way streets), aim for the cathedral spires.

Walking Tour of Rouen

For a quick dose of Rouen's Gothic and half-timbered wonders,
begin at the Jeanne d'Arc church and follow the route described
below (most sights on this route close 12:00–14:00). The ruins
of the old St. Sauveur church near the entry to the Jeanne d'Arc
church make a good seat and starting point. Sit here.

▲**Eglise Jeanne d'Arc**—This modern church is a tribute to
Jeanne d'Arc. Nineteen-year-old Jeanne was burned at the
stake on this square in 1431.

The church, completed in 1979, feels Scandinavian inside and

Rouen

1 HOTEL CATHEDRALE
2 HOTEL CARDINAL
& BRASSERIE SAINT PAUL
3 Hotel NOTRE DAME
4 LA MIRABELLE & PARIS
MARAICHERS RESTAURANTS
5 AUBERGE SAINT MACLOU

out—reminding us again of Normandy's Nordic roots. Pick up an English pamphlet describing the church (closed 12:30–14:00, public WC 30 meters from church doors). The colorful outdoor market behind the church closes for the day at 12:30.

Now turn around. With the town's lacy Gothic skyline and half-timbered buildings solidly on vertical hold, it's hard to imagine the town devastated by WWII bombs. Its restoration attests to the French commitment to their people-friendly city centers (rather than to suburban sprawl).

The striking **half-timbered houses** (14th–19th centuries) that line Rouen's streets remind us that there's more oak than stone in this region. Cantilevered floors were standard until about 1520. These top-heavy designs made sense because city land was limited, property taxes were based on ground-floor square footage, and the cantilevering minimized unsupported spans on upper floors. Rouen's historic wealth was due largely to its location as the last bridge across the Seine before the Atlantic and its inland river port.

Rue du Gros Horloge—This has been Rouen's main pedestrian and shopping street since Roman times. It links the Eglise Jeanne d'Arc and the Cathédrale Notre Dame and shows off the impressive Renaissance (1528) public clock, le Gros Horloge. Admire the clock and sculpture in the arch from below.

Take the first left after the old clock and in a block you'll see the...

Palace of Justice—This impressive Flamboyant Gothic palace was largely restored after WWII bombing, though the western facade remains littered with pockmarks from German guns. Returning to rue du Gros Horloge, turn left and continue to rue du Bec, where a plaque up on your left commemorates the assassination in Texas of the explorer (and native Rouen son), Cavelier de la Salle, who gave Louisiana to France. Continue to...

▲▲Cathédrale Notre Dame—Grab a seat on the shady benches on the right in the square. This is the church Monet painted at various times of day from an apartment he rented solely for this purpose opposite the cathedral (one of the paintings is in Rouen's Musée des Beaux Arts, four others are at Musée d'Orsay in Paris). This soaring exterior is considered one of France's most beautiful, a fine example of the last overripe stage of Gothic architecture called Flamboyant—flamelike. Notice how many statues are missing from niches in the facade. The ugly concrete buildings across from the cathedral are a fine example of function over form. Enter the cathedral and make a marvel-at-the-Gothic circuit inside, stopping halfway down the nave on the right to see photos showing the severe WWII bomb damage. You'll find helpful English explanations in small plaques near the side chapels. This cathedral is far brighter than it should be; only a few original stained-glass windows—behind the altar—survived the bombing.

Leave the cathedral via the left (northern) transept. Enjoy the Gothic facade behind you as you exit and then turn right to rue St. Romain. This fine old medieval lane leads a few blocks to St. Maclou Church. A plaque on your right (under the ruined Gothic arch) identifies the site of an old chapel, where Joan of Arc was sentenced to death—and where she was proclaimed innocent 25 years later. Take a look down rue des Chanoines (next left) for a half-timbered fantasy. Rue St. Romain leads to the...

St. Maclou Church—Study the unique bowed facade. Inside, walk to the end of the choir and look back at the stained glass framed by the suspended crucifix.

Leaving the church, turn right and right (giving the boys on the corner a wide berth) and wander past a fine wall of half-timbered buildings fronting rue Martainville. Within a block, a passageway on the left leads to...

Aître St. Maclou—Find the well in the center of this half-timbered courtyard. Notice the ghoulish carvings around you. This cemetery for 14th-century plague victims is now an art school. Peek in on the young artists. Examples of their art are in the new exhibition rooms near the entrance. A black cat watches you leave the courtyard.

Return right onto rue Martainville and stroll toward the leaning towers. Take a right on rue Damiette, passing half-timbered antique shops that lead to Rouen's third fine Gothic church, St. Ouen. A thousand-year-old Danish rune stone stands by the church door, reminding locals of their Nordic heritage. The park behind this church is perfect for a picnic. In front of St. Ouen, rue Hôpital takes you back to rue Jeanne d'Arc and the station or your car.

Sights—Rouen

(Sights are closed Tuesdays.)

▲**Musée des Beaux Arts**—This crowd-free, well-organized museum beautifully displays paintings from all periods, including works by Caravaggio, Rubens, Veronese, Steen, Géricault, Ingres, Delacroix, and the Impressionists. Don't miss Monet's painting of Rouen's cathedral and the room dedicated to Gericault. Pick up the museum plan at the ticket desk. Key rooms have excellent English descriptions on small, portable boards and even have clever foldaway stools (€3.25 Wed–Mon 10:00–18:00, some rooms close 12:30–13:30, closed Tue, 26 bis rue Jean Lecanuet, 3 blocks below station).

Museum of Ironworks (Musée le Seq des Tournelles)—This surprisingly interesting museum in a defunct Gothic church contains nothing but iron objects, many over 1,500 years old. Locks, keys, tools, even coffee grinders—virtually anything made out of iron is on display (€2.30, Wed–Mon 10:00–13:00, 14:00–18:00, closed Tue, no English explanations, behind Musée des Beaux Arts, 2 rue Jacques Villon).

La Tour de Jeanne d'Arc—Originally eight towers such as this formed the medieval fortifications of Rouen. Joan was kept here before burning at the stake on place du Vieux Marche—where the Jeanne d'Arc church now stands. This tower is only worth seeing from the outside (note the moat). Only the second floor has English explanations, and there's no view from the top (€1.50, rue du Donjon, between Musée des Beaux Arts and train station).

Sights—Near Rouen

The Route of Ancient Abbeys (La Route des Anciennes Abbayes)—The route is punctuated with abbeys, apples, Seine

River views, and pastoral scenery. Drivers follow the D-982 west of Rouen. By bus, take #30, which follows the route of ancient abbeys (4/day, none Sun, 50 min one-way to Jumièges, depart from Rouen's bus station at 25 rue des Charrettes, tel. 02 35 52 92 00, see map).

Stop to admire the Romanesque church at the **Abbey of St. Georges de Boscherville**, but skip the €3.80 abbey grounds. The romantically ruined abbey at **Jumièges** is worth the entry fee (follow the river on D-65 from Duclair for a more scenic approach). Founded in 654, it was destroyed by Vikings, only to be rebuilt by William the Conqueror (€3.20, daily mid-April–mid-Sept 09:30–19:00, mid-Sept–mid-April 09:30–13:00, 14:30–17:30, helpful English handout). The Auberges des Ruines across the street makes a good lunch stop. Cross the Seine between Jumièges and Honfleur on the €1.50 car ferry at Duclair, or on one of three suspension bridges. The €5.50 it costs to cross the Pont de Normandie (bridge between Rouen and Honfleur) isn't worth it.

Sleeping and Eating in Rouen
(€1.20 = about $1, country code: 33, zip code: 75000)
Sleep Code: **S** = Single, **D** = Double/Twin, **T** = Triple, **Q** = Quad, **b** = bathroom, **s** = shower only, **CC** = Credit Cards accepted, **no CC** = Credit Cards not accepted, **SE** = Speaks English, **NSE** = No English, * = French hotel rating system (0–4 stars).

All of these hotels are within two blocks of the cathedral; directions are given from the cathedral. The first two hotels are equally good.

The central, welcoming **Hôtel Cardinal**** is a great value. All of its spotless and comfortable rooms look right onto the cathedral; some have private balconies and a few are ideal for families. It's to the right of the cathedral as you face it (Sb-€41–56, Db-€48–65, Tb-€75, Qb-€81, extra bed-€9, good breakfast buffet-€6.25, CC, elevator, cable TV, 1 place de la Cathédrale, tel. 02 35 70 24 42, fax 02 35 89 75 14).

The central **Hôtel de la Cathédrale**** welcomes you with a flowery, umbrella-filled courtyard; a cozy, wood-beamed breakfast room; and decent rooms (Sb-€45–53, Db-€53–61, no CC, elevator, 12 rue St. Romain, outside left transept of the cathedral, tel. 02 35 71 57 95, fax 02 35 70 15 54, www.hotel-de-la-cathedrale.fr, e-mail: contact@hotel-de-la-cathedrale.fr, friendly Nathalie SE).

Hôtel Notre Dame** is also welcoming, with spacious, comfortable rooms—some with cathedral views (Db-€41-55, Tb-€56, CC, Internet access, cable TV, hair dryers, 4 rue de Savonnerie, 2 blocks from river below cathedral, tel. 02 35 71 87 73, fax 02 35 89 31 52).

Eating: Two of Rouen's best moderately priced seafood restaurants are both on place du Vieux Marché across from the

church of Joan of Arc: **La Mirabelle** (tel. 02 35 71 58 21) and
Paris Maraichers (tel. 02 35 71 57 73). Many inexpensive alterna-
tives are between the St. Maclou and St. Ouen churches, such as
Auberge St. Maclou just to the left of St. Maclou church (closed
Sun–Mon, 222 rue St. Martainville, tel. 02 35 71 06 67). **Brasserie
St. Paul**, next to the recommended Hôtel Cardinal, is also good.

Transportation Connections—Rouen

Rouen is well served by trains from Paris, through Amiens to
other points north, and through Caen to other destinations
west and south.

By train to: Paris' Gare St. Lazare (15/day, 75 min),
Bayeux (3/day, 3 hrs, change in Caen), **Pontorson-Mont St.
Michel** (3/day, 4 hrs, change in Caen and Pontorson, then bus
to Mont St. Michel or taxi, see "Transportation Connections—
Mont St. Michel," below).

By train and bus to Honfleur (5/day, 1.5 hrs, train to
Le Havre then bus over Pont de Normandie to Honfleur—Le
Havre's bus station is 1 block from train station, turn left out
of station and cross big boulevard; or in 2 hrs via Lisieux—train
from Rouen to Lisieux then bus to Honfleur).

HONFLEUR

Honfleur (ohn-flur), which escaped the bombs of World War II,
actually feels as picturesque as it looks. Gazing at its cozy harbor,
lined with skinny, soaring houses, it's easy to overlook the historic
importance of this port. For over a thousand years, sailors have
enjoyed Honfleur's ideal location, where the Seine meets the
English Channel. William the Conqueror received supplies
shipped from Honfleur, and Samuel de Champlain sailed from
here in 1608, discovering the St. Lawrence Waterway and
Quebec City. Honfleur was also a favorite of 19th-century
Impressionists: Monet, Dufy, and Boudin all painted here.

Today's Honfleur, long eclipsed by the gargantuan port of
Le Havre just across the Seine, happily uses its past as a bar
stool and sits on it.

Orientation: All of Honfleur's interesting streets and activities are a short walk from the old port (Vieux Bassin). Honfleur
is low on sights but high on ambience and art galleries. Snoop
around the streets behind place Berthelot and Eglise Ste. Catherine for some of Normandy's oldest half-timbered homes.

Tourist Information: The TI is in the left end of the flashy
glass public library (*Mediathéque*) on quai Lepaulmier, two blocks
from the Vieux Bassin toward Le Havre. Pick up the handy town
map and information on Normandy. The TI sells a handy **museum
pass** (€7.75, valid for the rest of the year), a good deal only if you
plan to visit at least three sights that charge admission (Easter–Oct

Mon–Sat 09:30–12:30, 14:00–18:30, no midday closing in summer, Sun 10:00–17:00; Nov–Easter Mon–Sat 9:00–12:00, 14:00–18:00, closed Sun, tel. 02 31 89 23 30, www.ville-honfleur.fr).

Arrival in Honfleur

By Bus: If you're arriving from Lisieux or Deauville, the first bus stop in Honfleur (Albert Sorel) is closer to most hotels (walk down rue de la République to the harbor). The other stop is south of the port at the bus station (*gare routière*), has a useful information counter (see "Transportation Connections," below), and is closer to Hôtels Absinthe, Cascades, and de la Tour. Walk up rue des Fosses with Hôtel Moderne on your left to reach the center.

By Car: Follow *centre-ville* signs and park as close to the old port (Vieux Bassin) as possible. Parking is tight in Honfleur. The pricey *parking du Bassin* is across from the TI (€1.50/1 hr, €7.75/day), the cheaper *parking priviligié* is just beyond, down the quai de la Tour and across the small bridge (€1.50/3 hrs, €3/day). Inquire at your hotel where you can park for free.

Sights—Honfleur

▲▲**Eglise Ste. Catherine**—As I stepped inside this church, my first thought was, "If you could turn it over it would float." This unusual church was built in the 15th century by naval architects— logical in this shipbuilding town. It replaced a ruined stone church. Rough-hewn wood beams give it a feel-good warmth you don't find in stone churches. In the last months of World War II, a bomb fell through the roof but didn't explode. The exterior is a wonderful conglomeration of wood-shingle, brick, and half-timbered construction.

The church's bell tower was built across the square to lighten the load on the roof of the wooden church and to minimize fire hazards. (Tower and church open 09:00–18:30 in summer, otherwise 09:00–12:00, 14:00–18:00.) The church is free. In the tower, the room that has a few church artifacts is not worth the €1.50.

▲**Eugène Boudin Museum**—This pleasant, airy museum houses a variety of early Impressionist paintings by artists you may not recognize. Look for scenes of Honfleur and nearby Deauville. Norman costumes are on the second floor (€4, mid-March–Sept Wed–Mon 10:00–12:00, 14:00–18:00, Oct–mid-March 10:00–12:00, 14:30–17:00, closed Tue year-round, elevator, no photos, rue de l'Homme de Bois, tel. 02 31 89 54 00).

Maisons Satie Museum—Located in composer Erik Satie's birth home and interesting only for his fans, this museum has rooms with modern-art interpretations of his compositions (€4.60, daily 10:30–18:00, until 19:00 in summer, free English audioguide, 67 boulevard Charles V).

Museums of Old Honfleur—Two museums combine to paint

Honfleur

❶ HOTEL DAUPHIN	❽ TO BAR DE LA SALLE DES FETES ROOMS
❷ HOTEL DES LOGES	❾ TO MADAME BELLEGARDE ROOMS
❸ HOTEL DES CASCADES	❿ LA TORTUE RESTAURANT
❹ HOTEL LE CHEVAL BLANC	⓫ AU PETIT MAREYEUR RESTAURANT
❺ HOTEL LE CHAT	⓬ AUBERGE DU VIEUX CLOCHER
❻ HOTEL ABSINTHE	⓭ LA CIDRERIE BAR
❼ HOTEL DE LA TOUR	⓮ PERROQUET VERT & L'ALBATROSS BARS

a picture of daily life in Honfleur since the Middle Ages. The **Musée de la Marine**, located in an old church right on Vieux Bassin, offers an interesting collection of ship models and marine paraphernalia. The **Musée d'Ethnographie et d'Art Populaire**, located in the old prison (which you'll pass through) behind Musée de la Marine, re-creates typical rooms, cramming them with objects of daily life from various eras (€3 for both or €2.30 each, Tue–Sun 10:00–12:00, 14:00–18:00, closed Mon, ask for English explanation).

Boat Excursions—Boats to Pont de Normandie (see below) depart from in front of Hôtel Cheval Blanc (€6-adult, €4.60-child, Easter–Nov, 50 min, tel. 02 31 89 41 80). The 30-minute excursions on Honfleur's harbor on the *Calypso* are less interesting (€3.80).

Côte de Grace Walk—For good exercise and a bird's-eye view over Honfleur and Pont de Normandie, take the short, steep walk up to the Côte de Grace viewpoint (from Eglise Ste. Catherine, walk past Hôtel Dauphin and up rue Brûlée, turn right on rue Eugene Boudin, then turn left at the top and climb la Rampe de Mont Joli; best early in the morning or at sunset).

Saturday Morning Farmers' Market—The area around Eglise Ste. Catherine is transformed into a colorful market each Saturday morning from 09:00 to 12:30.

▲**Normandie Bridge**—The 2.1-kilometer-long (1.3-mile-long) Pont de Normandie is the longest cable-stayed bridge in the western world. This is a key piece of a super-freeway that links the Atlantic ports from Belgium to Spain (€5.50 to take car across). View the bridge from Honfleur (better from an excursion boat or above the town on the Côte de Grace; best when floodlit) or visit the free Exhibition Hall (under tollbooth on Le Havre side, daily 08:00–19:00). The Seine finishes its winding 500-mile journey here. From its source, it drops only 450 meters (1,500 feet). It flows so slowly that in certain places a stiff breeze can send it flowing upstream.

Sleeping in Honfleur
(€1.10 = $1, country code: 33, zip code: 14600)
Honfleur is busy on weekends and holidays and in the summer. English is widely spoken. Off-season rates plunge; the lower room rates listed below are for off-season (generally Oct–May).

A modern **launderette** (Lavomatique) is a block to the right and behind the TI (daily 07:00–20:00, 4 rue Notre Dame).

Hôtel Dauphin** is a solid and central midrange bet, with a family feel, a homey lounge/breakfast room, many stairs, and an Escher-esque floor plan. The rooms are quite comfortable, some with open-beam ceilings and all with new beds and some street noise (Db-€46–61, Tb-€70–104, pay-as-you-go breakfast upgrades include cereal-€0.75, yogurt-€0.75, fruit-€0.75, and freshly squeezed juice-€1.85, CC, all rooms theoretically smoke-free, a stone's throw from church at 10 place Berthelot, tel. 02 31 89 15 53, fax 02 31 89 92 06, www.hotel-du-dauphin.com, friendly Valerie SE).

Hôtel des Loges**, next to the Dauphin, is tranquil and very sharp, with many tastefully renovated rooms and pleasant common areas (Db-€52–63, Tb-€54, CC, 18 rue Brûlée, tel. 02 31 89 38 26).

Hôtel Le Chat*** offers wood beams and mostly large,

quasi-classy rooms in a historic, ivy-covered stone building across from the Ste. Catherine church (Db-€63–84, CC, restaurant, place Ste. Catherine, tel. 02 31 14 49 49, fax 02 31 89 28 61, e-mail: hotel.lechat@honfleur.com).

Hôtel Le Cheval Blanc*** is a good three-star splurge right on the water, with port views from every tastefully decorated room, new beds, and a rare (in this town) elevator. It's a big, half-timbered place with no restaurant (Sb-€67–78, Db-€70–198, most Db-€81–136, includes good buffet breakfast, CC, cancel with less than a week's notice and lose €38—otherwise deposit returned at year's end, 2 quai de Passagers, tel. 02 31 81 65 00, fax 02 31 89 52 80, www.hotel-honfleur.com).

Hôtel des Cascades*, tired but adequate, is well-located a block north of the harbor (Db-€31–46, third person-€8 more, dinner required on summer weekends, CC, facing rue Montpensier at 17 place Thiers, tel. 02 31 89 05 83, fax 02 31 89 32 13, Melanie SE).

Hôtel Absinthe*** is a small, tastefully restored hotel with seven very comfortable rooms behind the restaurant le Bistro du Port. Jacuzzi tubs, wood-beamed decor, and a cozy lounge with fireplace make this a good splurge (Db-€84–114, Db suite-€206, extra bed-€23, CC, 1 rue de la Ville; if no receptionist, keys available in restaurant Absinthe across the alley, tel. 02 31 89 23 23, fax 02 31 89 53 60, www.absinthe.fr).

Hôtel de la Tour*** is a modern, no-brainer hotel with easy, free parking and spacious, cookie-cutter rooms (Sb-€44–64, Db-€53–73, loft family rooms-€76–107, CC, mini-bars, elevator, 3 quai de la Tour, near bus terminal and TI, tel. 02 31 89 21 22, fax 02 31 89 53 51, www.hoteldelatourhonfleur.com).

Chambres d'hôte offer a good option here (the TI has a long list), though most are at least 1.5 kilometers from the center of Honfleur. The following two are a short walk from the center.

Bargain rooms are tucked above the *très* local **Bar de la Salle des Fêtes**, where French is spoken with a shy smile by Monsieur and Madame Leguyon (D-€28, nifty studio with kitchenette-€31–40, place Albert Sorel, at bus stop Albert Sorel, 300 meters from harbor out rue de la République, tel. 02 31 89 19 69 or 06 13 31 22 03).

Gentle **Madame Bellegarde** offers comfortable rooms in her pleasant home (Db-€29, a family-friendly Tb with kitchenette and great bathroom view-€47, 54 rue St. Leonard, 10-min uphill walk from TI, 3 blocks up from St. Leonard church in nontouristy part of Honfleur, look for sign in window, tel. 02 31 89 06 52).

Eating in Honfleur

Eat seafood here. It's a tough choice between the hard-to-resist waterfront tables of the many look-alike places lining Vieux

Bassin (a walk along the port is mandatory after dark) and those with more solid reputations on small side streets.

Several good restaurants line rue de l'Homme de Bois, such as the unpretentious **La Tortue** (€15 and €21 *menus*, closed Tue off-season, 36 rue de l'Homme de Bois, tel. 02 31 89 04 93). Better still, enjoy Honfleur's best affordable seafood in the *charmant* **Au Petit Mareyeur** (€19 *menu*, closed Mon–Tue, reservations necessary, 4 place Hamelin, tel. 02 31 98 84 23). The classy and intimate **Auberge du Vieux Clocher** will tempt any romantic (€19 and €26 *menus*, closed Sun and Wed except in summer, reserve ahead, 9 rue de l'Homme de Bois, tel. 02 31 89 12 06). Near the bottom of the street, **La Cidrerie** is a cozy cider bar with fresh crêpes, Calvados, and ambience (closed Tue–Wed, set back on cathedral side of place Hamelin at #26).

Nightlife in Honfleur centers on the old port. Two bar/cafés sit 50 meters apart on the tall-skinny-building side of the port and divide Honfleur's after-hours clientele by age: the **Perroquet Vert** is 40-something, while **l'Albatross** is clearly Generation X.

Transportation Connections—Honfleur

Buses connect Honfleur with Le Havre, Caen, Deauville, and Lisieux, where you'll catch a train to other points. While train and bus service are usually coordinated, ask at Honfleur's helpful bus station for the best connection for your trip (Mon–Fri 09:00–12:15, 14:30–17:30, Sat 09:15–12:15, closed Sun, tel. 02 31 89 28 41). Railpass holders will save money by connecting though the nearest city, as bus fares increase with distance.

By bus and train to: Bayeux (5/day, 2.5 hrs, bus to Lisieux or quicker via Caen, then train to Bayeux), **Rouen** (5/day, 90 min, bus over Pont de Normandie to Le Havre, train to Rouen, or in 2 hrs via Lisieux), **Paris'** Gare St. Lazare (5/day, 3 hrs; 1 hr bus to Lisieux or Deauville, then 2 hr train to Paris; buses from Honfleur meet most Paris trains).

BAYEUX

Only 10 kilometers (6 miles) from the D-Day beaches, Bayeux was the first city liberated after the landing, and it makes a great home base for visiting the area's sights. Even without its famous tapestry and proximity to the D-Day beaches, Bayeux would be worth a visit for its pleasant *centre-ville* and awe-inspiring cathedral.

Orientation: Navigating Bayeux is a breeze on foot or by car. Look for the cathedral spires and follow the signs to *centre-ville* or *tapisserie* to reach the city center (from the train station it's a 15- to 20-min walk or a €5 taxi to any of the recommended hotels). Market days are Wednesday (on pedestrian rue St. Jean) and Saturday (bigger, on place St. Patrice). Both end at noon.

Tourist Information: The TI is on the bridge (Pont St.

Jean). Pick up a town map, the excellent *D-Day Landings and the Battle of Normandy* brochure, bus schedules, and regional information (June–mid-Sept Mon–Sat 09:00–19:00, Sun 09:30–12:00, 14:30–18:00; mid-Sept–May daily 09:00–12:00, 14:00–18:00, Internet access, on Pont St. Jean leading to pedestrian street rue St. Jean, tel. 02 31 51 28 28, www.bayeux-tourisme.com).

Bike Rental: Try Monsieur Roue (€14/day, boulevard W. Churchill, tel. 02 31 92 27 75).

Bayeux History—The Battle of Hastings
The most memorable date of the Middle Ages is probably 1066 because of this pivotal battle. England's King Edward was about to die without an heir, and the question was who would succeed him: Harold, an English noble, or William, the Duke of Normandy? Harold was captured during a battle in Normandy. To gain his freedom, he promised William that, when the ailing King Edward died, he would allow William to ascend the throne. Shortly after that oath was taken, Harold was back in England, Edward died, and Harold grabbed the throne. William, known as William the Bastard, invaded England to claim the throne he reasoned was rightfully his. Harold met him in southern England at the town of Hastings, where their forces fought a fierce 14-hour battle. Harold was killed and his Saxon forces were routed. William—now "the Conqueror"—marched on London to claim his throne, becoming King of England as well as Duke of Normandy. The advent of a Norman king of England muddied the political waters, setting in motion 400 years of conflict between England and France not to be resolved until the end of the Hundred Years' War in 1453.

The Norman Conquest of England brought England into the European mainstream. The Normans established a strong central English government. They brought with them the Romanesque style of architecture (e.g., the Tower of London and Durham Cathedral) that the English call "Norman." Historians speculate that had William not succeeded, England would have remained on the fringe of Europe (like Scandinavia), and French culture (and language) would have prevailed in the New World.

Sights—Bayeux
Note that the €6.25 ticket for the Bayeux Tapestry gets you into the Baron Gerard Museum and Hôtel du Doyon (both listed below) but not the WWII museum.

▲▲▲**Bayeux Tapestry**—Actually woolen embroidery on linen cloth, this document—precious to historians—is a 70-meter (230-foot) cartoon telling the story of William the Conqueror's rise from Duke of Normandy to King of England and his victory over Harold at the Battle of Hastings. Long and skinny, it was designed to hang from the nave of Bayeux's cathedral.

Your visit has three parts (explaining the basic story of the battle three times—which was about right for me): First, you'll walk through a "mood-setting images on sails" room into a room with a replica of the tapestry with extensive explanations. You'll then continue to a room designed to set the cultural scene for the battle. Next, a 15-minute AV show in the cinema up one flight gives a relaxing dramatization of the event. Finally, you'll get to the real McCoy. It's worth the €0.75 (have exact change) and the wait for the headphones, which give a top-notch, fast-moving, 20-minute scene-by-scene narration complete with period music. If you lose your place, you'll find subtitles in Latin. Remember, this is a piece of Norman propaganda—the English (the bad guys, referred to as *les goddamns*, after a phrase the French kept hearing them say) are shown with mustaches and long hair; the French (*les* good guys) are clean-cut and clean shaven (€6.25, mid-March–mid-Oct daily 09:00–18:30, until 19:00 May–August, mid-Oct–mid-March daily 09:30–12:30, 14:00–18:00, tel. 02 31 92 05 48). Arrive by 09:00 or late in the day to avoid crowds. When buying your ticket, get the English film times. If you're rushed and the cinema schedule doesn't match yours, skip the film. If possible, see the 14-minute film first, exit the way you entered, and backtrack to see the replica before the original tapestry (because cinema-goers pile into the original tapestry room after each film).

▲▲**Bayeux Cathedral**—This massive building towers over Bayeux. Walk inside. The view of the nave from the top of the steps is as good as Gothic gets. Historians believe the tapestry originally hung here. Imagine it proudly circling the congregation, draped around the nave from the mini-arches just below the big and bright upper windows of the clerestory. The nave's huge, round lower arches are Romanesque (11th century) and decorated with the same zigzag pattern that characterizes this "Norman" art in England. But this nave is much brighter because of the later Gothic windows of the top half of the nave. The finest example of 13th-century "Norman" Gothic is in the choir (the fancy area behind the central altar). For maximum 1066 atmosphere, step into the crypt (below central altar). Study the frescoed angels and the ornately carved 11th-century capitals decorated with Roman-style acanthus leaves and gray meanies (free, daily 09:00–18:00, until 19:00 July–Aug). The cathedral is beautifully illuminated after dark.

Baron Gerard Museum—This museum, located outside the cathedral's left transept, houses a collection of porcelain and lace and a modest painting gallery (free with ticket to tapestry, daily 10:00–12:30, 14:00–18:00, in summer until 19:00 with no midday closing).

Hôtel du Doyen—Watch lace workers design and make intricate lace as they did in the 1600s and see examples of their finest works

Bayeux

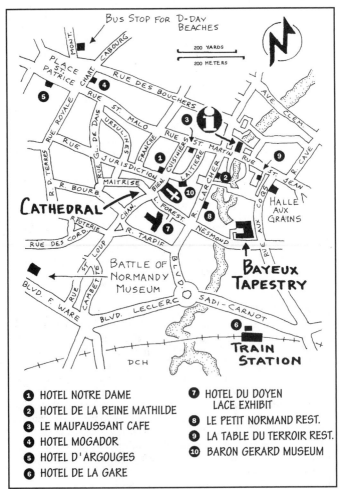

BUS STOP FOR D-DAY BEACHES

200 YARDS
200 METERS

PLACE ST. PATRICE

RUE DES BOUCHERS

CATHEDRAL

BATTLE OF NORMANDY MUSEUM

BAYEUX TAPESTRY

HALLE AUX GRAINS

BLVD. LECLERC

SADI-CARNOT

BLVD. F. WARE

TRAIN STATION

DCH

1 HOTEL NOTRE DAME
2 HOTEL DE LA REINE MATHILDE
3 LE MAUPAUSSANT CAFE
4 HOTEL MOGADOR
5 HOTEL D'ARGOUGES
6 HOTEL DE LA GARE

7 HOTEL DU DOYEN LACE EXHIBIT
8 LE PETIT NORMAND REST.
9 LA TABLE DU TERROIR REST.
10 BARON GERARD MUSEUM

over the years (free with ticket to tapestry, located outside cathedral's right transept, same hours as Baron Gerard Museum).

▲**Bayeux Memorial Museum/Battle of Normandy**—This museum, providing a good overview of the Battle of Normandy, features tanks, jeeps, uniforms, and countless informative displays, plus a good 30-minute film (€5.20, May–mid-Sept daily 09:30–18:30, mid-Sept–April closes 12:30–14:00, on Bayeux's ring road, 20 min on foot from center, tel. 02 31 51 46 90).

Sleeping in Bayeux
(€1.10 = $1, country code: 33, zip code: 14400)

Hotels are a good value here. Also see "Sleeping in and near Arromanches," below.

Hôtel Notre Dame*, right across from the cathedral, needs attention but has spacious, frumpy-dumpy rooms with peely wall-to-ceiling carpeting (ask for a room with a view of the cathedral). Hustling Annick, who takes care of your every need, assumes you'll dine in the hotel's reasonable restaurant; you'll probably be quoted prices including dinner (D-€31, Db-€43, Tb-€55, Qb-€71, CC, 44 rue des Cuisiniers, tel. 02 31 92 87 24, fax 02 31 92 67 11, e-mail: hotel-notre-dame@welcome.to).

Hôtel de Reine Mathilde**, one block from the cathedral on the street just below it, has modern and comfortable rooms (Db-€45, Tb-€57–66, CC, 23 rue Larcher, tel. 02 31 92 08 13, fax 02 31 92 09 93).

Le Maupassant Café is dead center and offers 10 immaculate and modern rooms over a café at bargain rates (S-€24–26, D/Db-€31–34, Tb-€46, Qb-€55–61, 19 rue St. Martin, tel. 02 31 92 28 53, fax 02 31 02 35 40).

The next two hotels are a 15-minute walk from the TI up rue St. Martin.

Hôtel Mogador** is a solid two-star bet with friendly Monsieur Mencaroni at the helm. Choose between cozy wood-beamed rooms on the busy square or immaculate, comfortable rooms off the street (Sb-€35, Db-€40–44, Tb-€52, CC, easy parking, good breakfast, 20 rue Alain Chartier/place St. Patrice, tel. 02 31 92 24 58, fax 02 31 92 24 85, SE).

For three-plus-star comfort at two-star prices, stay at the impeccable **Hôtel d'Argouges****. Every room is warmly decorated and meticulously cared for by the owners, M. and Mme. Ropartz. Named for its builder, Lord d'Argouges, this tranquil retreat has a châteaulike feel and a lovely private garden. Just off the huge place St. Patrice, look for an archway with a brown sign (Sb-€47, Db-€63–73, several fantastic family suites-€85–113, extra bed-€14, the garden annex has fine doubles from €47–63, private parking, CC, 21 rue St. Patrice, tel. 02 31 92 88 86, fax 02 31 92 69 16, e-mail: dargouges@aol.com).

Desperate train travelers can bed down in the basic, unwelcoming **Hôtel de la Gare**'s* simple rooms (S-€15, D-€16, Db-€33, T-€22, Tb-€47, 26 place de la Gare, tel. 02 31 92 10 70).

Eating in Bayeux

Bayeux's old city centers around the pedestrian rue St. Jean, which is lined with *crêperies*, cafés, and the best *charcuterie* in town (salads and quiches to go, across from Hôtel Churchill). **La Table du Terroir** is run by a butcher, so meat is the game in this fun,

traditional place where clients share monastic plank-tables
(€9 lunch *menu*-no choice, dinner *menus* from €15, 42 rue St.
Jean, tel. 02 31 92 05 53). The **Brasserie Guillaume** at Hôtel
Reine Mathilde offers a good selection of salads and inexpensive
lunch options. The restaurants at **Hôtel Notre Dame** (€15
menu, see "Sleeping," above) and **Le Petit Normand** (*menus*
start at €13, 35 rue Larcher) each merit their fine reputations.

Transportation Connections—Bayeux

By train to: Paris' St. Lazare (9/day, 2.5 hrs, 3 require change in
Caen), **Amboise** (7/day, 5–6 hrs, change in Caen and Tours, or
Paris Montparnasse and Tours-St. Pierre des Corps), **Rouen** (3/day,
3 hrs, change in Caen), **Honfleur** (5/day, 2.5 hrs; train to Lisieux or
Caen, then bus to Honfleur; trip is quicker via Caen), **Pontorson-
Mont St. Michel** (2/day, 2 hrs to Pontorson, with a convenient
late-afternoon departure; from Pontorson bus to Mont St. Michel,
see "Transportation Connections—Mont St. Michel," below).

   By bus to the D-Day beaches: Bus Vert serves the area
(about €2.30 one-way to the beaches). Line #74 leaves Bayeux
(St. Patrice stop) about 12:00 for Arromanches and returns 90
minutes later. Line #70 has a 12:00 trip that serves the American
cemetery and returns 75 minutes later (confirm schedule, particularly for Wed; catch the bus at Bayeux train station or place St.
Patrice—a 15-min walk up rue St. Martin from the center, veer
right through the square to bus shelters).

D-DAY BEACHES

Along the 120 kilometers (75 miles) of Atlantic coast north of
Bayeux, stretching from Sainte Marie du Mont to Ouistreham,
you'll find WWII museums, monuments, cemeteries, and battle
remains left in tribute to the courage of the British, Canadian,
and American armies who successfully carried out the largest
military operation in history. It was on these beautiful beaches,
at the crack of dawn, June 6, 1944, that the Allies finally gained a
foothold in France and Nazi Europe began to crumble.

> *"The first twenty-four hours of the invasion will be
> decisive . . . the fate of Germany depends on the outcome . . .
> for the Allies, as well as Germany, it will be the longest day."*
>   —Field Marshall Erwin Rommel to his aide,
>   April 22, 1944. From *The Longest Day*.

Getting around the D-Day Beaches

On Your Own: A car is ideal, particularly for three or more
people (the Bayeux TI lists rental agencies), though biking can
work for some (rent a bike in Bayeux at M. Roue's shop for
€14/day, boulevard W. Churchill, tel. 02 31 92 27 75). Buses

connect Bayeux and Arromanches (see "Transportation Connections—Bayeux," above) to allow you to see the most impressive D-Day (*Jour J* in French) sights.

By Taxi: Figure €16 one-way from Bayeux to Arromanches and €26 from Bayeux to the American cemetery (up to 6 persons). Ask about "waiting rates" and rates for combining several stops (tel. 02 31 92 92 40).

By Tour: Several companies offer good half- and full-day excursions to the D-Day beaches from Bayeux. These are not guided tours; you get an English-speaking driver and transportation between key sights (for fully guided tours of the beaches, see Caen's Battle of Normandy Museum, below). **Bus Fly Excursions** offers well-prepared four-hour tours (€32, cash only, includes Pointe du Hoc, American cemetery, Longues-sur-Mer, and Arromanches); they also offer daytrips to Mont St. Michel for about €53 (tel. 02 31 22 00 08 or 02 33 39 23 52, fax 02 31 92 35 10, www.busfly.com). **Victory Tours** offers similar tours for less (half day-€28, full day-€53, tel. 02 31 51 98 14, www.lignerolles.homestead.com). Book these tours in advance.

Sights—D-Day Beaches

Most museums will slightly reduce your entry fee if you have a full-price ticket from another museum.

▲▲▲**Caen's Battle of Normandy Museum (le Memorial)**—Caen (pron. cah), the modern capital of lower Normandy, has the best World War II museum in France. Officially named the Memorial for Peace (*le Memorial*), its intent is to put the Battle of Normandy in a broader context. Your visit has four parts: the lead-up to World War II, the actual Battle of Normandy, the video presentations, and the ongoing fight for peace.

The museum is brilliant. Begin with a downward spiral stroll, tracing (almost psychoanalyzing) the path of Europe from World War I to the rise of fascism to World War II.

The lower level gives a thorough look at how World War II was fought—from General de Gaulle's London radio broadcasts to Hitler's early missiles to wartime fashion.

You then see a series of three powerful movies (20 min each, for all languages, the cycle starts every 20 min—a clock at the end of the lower-level exhibits lets you plan your time). Ninety percent of the incredible D-Day footage is real, with a bit taken from the movie *The Longest Day*.

The memorial then takes you beyond World War II to the Gallery of Nobel Prizes. This is a celebration of the courageous work of people such as Andrei Sakharov, Elie Wiesel, and Desmond Tutu, who understand that peace is more than an absence of war.

The finale is a walk through the U.S. Armed Forces Memorial Garden. I was a bit bothered by the mindless laughing of

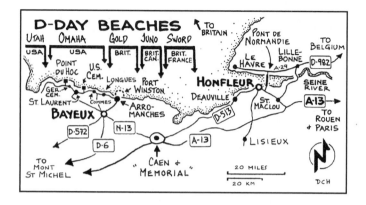

lighthearted children unable to appreciate their blessings. Then I read on the pavement, "From the heart of our land flows the blood of our youth, given to you in the name of freedom." And their laughter made me happy.

Cost and Hours: €11.75 (free for WWII veterans, €10 for other veterans, free admission and nursery for kids under 10). The museum is open daily usually from 09:00 to 19:00 (until 20:00 mid-July–Aug, closes at 18:00 Nov–Feb, ticket office closes 75 min before museum). Allow a minimum of 2.5 hours for your visit, including an hour for the videos; no guided tours (tel. 02 31 06 06 44—as in June 6, 1944, fax 02 31 06 01 66, www.memorial-caen.fr).

Tours: The museum runs seven-person minivan guided tours of the D-Day beaches. Tours include entry to Caen's Battle of Normandy Museum and four-hour tours of the D-Day beaches, including Longues-sur-Mer, Arromanches, Omaha Beach, American Cemetery, and Pointe du Hoc (€45 for morning departure, €60 for afternoon departure, daily departures April–Sept at 09:00 and 14:00, Oct–March at 13:00 only, contact Caen Museum for details and to reserve and pay in advance, CC).

Getting to Museum: It's on the ring-road freeway (*périphérique nord*) in Caen (sortie #7, look for signs to *le Memorial*). By train, it's two hours from Paris (14/day) or 15 minutes from Bayeux (10/day); take bus #17-Memorial from Caen's train station (exit right out of station, second shelter, buses every 15 min, or taxi-€9 one-way).

The City of Caen: WWII bombs may have lain waste to 75 percent of the buildings, but today's Caen (population 115,000) bristles with confidence, students, and a well-restored old city. Train travelers may find Caen more convenient than Bayeux for touring the region's sights. The **TI** is on place St. Pierre, 10 blocks across the canal from the station (walk up Avenue du

6 Juin, tel. 02 31 27 14 14). The looming château and pedestrian streets are within a few blocks of the TI. **Hôtel de France****, a three-minute walk from the station, has plain but sleepable rooms (Db–€42–48, CC, 10 rue de la Gare, turn right out of station, right on first main street, and you'll see signs, tel. 02 31 52 16 99, fax 02 31 83 23 16).

▲▲▲**Arromanches (Musée du Débarquement)**—The first-ever prefab harbor was created by the British in this town. As it was Churchill's brainchild, it was named Port Winston. Walk along the seafront promenade and imagine 18 old ships and 115 football field–size cement blocks (called Mulberries) being towed across the English Channel and sunk right here to create an 11-kilometer-long (7-mile-long) breakwater and harbor for landing 54,000 vehicles and 500,000 troops in six days. You can still see remains of the temporary harbor and visit the beachfront museum, where this incredible undertaking is recreated with models, maps, mementos, and two short audiovisual shows—ask for English (€5.50, May–Aug daily 09:00–19:00, April and Sept 09:00–18:00, Oct–Dec and Feb–March 09:00–12:30, 13:30–17:00, closed Jan, tel. 02 31 22 34 31).

Walk to the top of the bluff behind the museum for the view (€1.50 to park if you came by car) and ponder how, from this makeshift harbor, the liberation of Europe commenced. Skip the 360-degree screen showing *The Price of Freedom* (too loud, no coherent story, €3.75, 2 showings/hr, last at 18:40).

The Town of Arromanches: This small town, ground zero for the D-Day invasion, is mesmerizing if you can ignore the trinket shops. Get up on those cliffs and walk the beach. The **TI** is across the parking lot from the museum on rue Colonel Rene Michel (daily 10:00–12:00, 14:00–18:00, no midday closing in summer, tel. 02 31 21 47 56, www.arromanches.com). The population of tiny Arromanches just reached 500 persons (about the same as on June 6, 1944). There's a supermarket (above the town by the parking lot), a post office, and an ATM near the museum. To summon the town's only taxi, dial 06 07 83 44 48. For accommodations, see "Sleeping," below.

Longues Sur Mer—Several German bunkers, guns intact, are left guarding against seaborne attacks on the city of Arromanches (the €4.60 booklet is helpful, skip the €4 tour). Walk to the observation post for a great view over the channel (located between Arromanches and Port en Bessin; turn right at signal in Longues sur Mer). You can drive right down to the water by continuing down the small road past the parking lot.

▲▲▲**American Cemetery at St. Laurent**—On a bluff just above Omaha Beach, the 9,400 brilliant white-marble crosses and Stars of David glow in memory of Americans who gave their lives to free Europe on the beaches below, where fighting was particularly intense. Notice the names and home states inscribed on the crosses. Behind the monument, surrounded by roses, are the names of 1,557 missing or unidentified soldiers. France has given the United States free permanent use of this 172-acre site. It is immaculately maintained by the American Battle Monuments Commission. Pick up the handout in the small office as you enter. The trail to the beach below is open from 09:00 to 18:00, off-season until 17:00 unless wild boars (*sangliers*) are prowling about.

German Military Cemetery—To ponder German losses, drop by this somber, thought-provoking resting place of 21,000 German soldiers. While the American cemetery is the focus of American visitors, visitors here speak in hushed German. The site is glum, with two graves per simple marker and dark crosses that huddle together in groups of five. It's just south of Point du Hoc (right off N-13 in village of La Cambe, 22 km west of Bayeux; follow signs to *Cimetiére Allemand*).

▲▲**Pointe du Hoc**—During the D-Day invasion, 225 U.S. rangers attempted a castle-style assault of the German-occupied cliffs by using grappling hooks and ladders borrowed from London fire departments. Only 90 survived. German bunkers and bomb craters remain as they were found (20 min by car west of American Cemetery in St. Laurent, just past Vierville-sur-Mer). A museum dedicated to the rangers is in nearby Grandcamp-Maisy.

Sleeping in Arromanches and near the D-Day Beaches
(€1.10 = about $1, country code: 33)

To feel the pulse of World War II, sleep near the beach. Light-hearted **Pappagall Hôtel d'Arromanches**** is a good value, with smartly appointed rooms, a fun bar, and cheery restaurant (Db in summer-€63, otherwise Db-€41–50, includes breakfast, skip half-pension, 2 rue Colonel Rene Michel, 14117 Arromanches, tel. 02 31 22 36 26, fax 02 31 22 23 29). **Hôtel de la Marine**** is less welcoming but offers beach views from most of its comfy rooms (some squishy beds) and from its elegant restaurant (Db-€48–63, Tb-€61–73, family rooms-€85–116, CC, restaurant *menus* from €15, quai du Canada, tel. 02 31 22 34 19, fax 02 31 22 98 80, e-mail: mcverdier@caramail.com). For evening fun, try the bar at **Pappagall Hôtel d'Arromanches** or **Pub Marie Celeste**, right around the corner on rue de la Poste.

Sleeping near Arromanches
(€1.10 = $1, country code: 33)

Chambres d'hôte litter the coast (the TIs in Bayeux and Arromanches have long lists). It's worth the effort to track down **Andre and Madeleine Sebires'** working farmhouse with four

homey and cheap rooms and a pleasant garden. It's in tiny Ryes
(between Bayeux and Arromanches) at the Ferme du Clos Neuf—
and tough to find. Try these directions from Arromanches: Take
D-87, enter Ryes and pass the church on the left; then, at first
junction, turn right onto rue de la Forge (look for the faded *chambres* signs) and continue until you cross a tiny bridge. Turn right
just after the bridge onto rue de la Triangle and follow small sign
on right to Le Clos Neuf. If the Sebires prove too elusive, call
from Ryes, and they'll come get you (Sb-€26, Db-€31, Tb-€38,
includes breakfast, zip code: 14400, tel. 02 31 22 32 34, NSE).

Or consider the almost mystical **Château du Bosq** in Commes.
Seven kilometers (4 miles) from Bayeux, this *très* rustic, 700-year-
old château comes with turrets, a water-filled moat, a peaceful
restaurant, and minimally decorated rooms (though serious renovations are planned for 2002 and prices will increase). It's quiet:
no TV, no phones, no noise, no kidding (D-€29, Db-€46–69,
Tb-€69, extra bed-€11, between Arromanches and American
Cemetery, 14520 Commes, tel. 02 31 92 52 77, fax 02 31 92 26 71).

MONT ST. MICHEL
The distant silhouette of this Gothic island-abbey sends the tired
sightseer's spirits soaring. Mont St. Michel, which through the ages
has been among the top four pilgrimage sites in Christendom, floats
like a mirage on the horizon, though it does show up on film.

The causeway, built in 1878, stopped the water from flowing
around the island, which in turn contributed to the filling in of the
bay around Mont St. Michel—so it's no longer an island. A new
bridge is planned (construction to begin in 2002) that will allow the
water to circulate and turn Mont St. Michel into an island again.

Orientation
Mont St. Michel is connected by a three-kilometer causeway to the
mainland and surrounded by a sandy mud flat. Your visit features a
one-street village that winds up to the fortified abbey. Between
10:00 and 16:00, tourists trample the dreamscape (try to remember
that this street was just as jammed with earnest pilgrims 800 years
ago). A ramble on the ramparts offers mud-flat views and an escape
from the tourist zone. The only worthwhile entry is the abbey itself,
at the summit of the island.

Daytime Mont St. Michel is a touristy gauntlet—worth a stop,
but a short one will do. The tourist tide recedes late each afternoon.
On nights from autumn through spring, the island is abbey-quiet,
the illumination, beautiful. Poets prefer evenings here.

Arrive late and depart early if you can. The abbey interior
(which isn't an essential visit anyway) should be open until midnight from May through September (off-season until 22:00).
Consider bringing a dinner picnic (see "Eating," below); there

Mont St. Michel Area

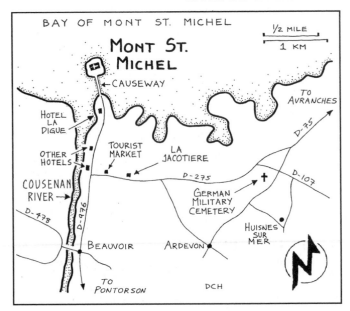

are no grocery shops on the island, but there's a handy tourist *super-marché* at the mainland end of the causeway (daily 08:30–20:00).

Tourist Information: The overwhelmed TI (and WC) is to your left as you enter Mont St. Michel's gates. They have *chambres d'hôte* listings, English tour times for the abbey, bus schedules, and the tide table, *Horaires des Marées*, which is essential if you explore outside Mont St. Michel (daily 09:00–19:00 in summer, off-season 09:00–12:30, 14:00–18:00, tel. 02 33 60 14 30, www .manchetourisme.com). A post office (PTT) and ATM are 50 meters beyond the TI.

Tides: The tides here (which rise 17 m/56 ft) are the largest and most dangerous in Europe. During a flood tide, the ocean rushes in at 20 kilometers (12.5 miles) per hour. In medieval times, the tides clocked in "at the speed of a galloping horse." Even today, the undertow can sweep a slow horse (or tourist) away. High tides (*grandes marées*) lap against the tourist-office door (where you'll find tide hours posted).

Parking: Very high tides rise to the edge of the causeway—leaving the causeway open but any cars parked below it under water. Safe parking is available at the foot of Mont St. Michel (€2.30); you will be instructed where to park under high-tide conditions. There's plenty of parking, provided you arrive off-season or early or late in high season. Make a note of your parking sector and plan on a 15-minute walk to the island from your car.

Sights—Mont St. Michel

The Village below the Abbey—Mont St. Michel's main street of shops and hotels leads to the abbey. With only 30 full-time residents, the village lives solely for tourists. After the TI, check the tide warnings posted on the wall and admire the huge doors you're walking through. Before the drawbridge, on your left, peek through the door of Restaurant Le Mère Poulard. Watch the colorful action as a traditional omelet is whipped up by this virtual theater-kitchen. Don't spend €23 for this edible tourist trap but enjoy the show as old-time-costumed cooks beat omelets, daddy, eight to the bar.

As you pass through the old drawbridge, Mont St. Michel greets you with the most touristy street this side of Tijuana (remember those pilgrims). You can trudge through the crowds uphill past several gimmicky museums to the abbey (all island hotel receptions are located on this street). Or better, if the abbey's your goal, climb the first steps on your right after the drawbridge and then turn right or left at the top; the ramparts lead all the way up and up to the abbey in either direction (quieter if you turn right). Public WCs are next to the TI, halfway up, and at the abbey entrance. You can attend Mass at the tiny St. Pierre church (Thu and Sun at 11:00, opposite Hôtel la Vielle Auberge).

▲▲**Abbey of Mont St. Michel**—Mont St. Michel has been an important pilgrimage center since A.D. 708, when the Archangel Michael told the bishop of Avranches to "build here and build high." With uncanny foresight, he reassured the bishop, "If you build it…they will come." Today's abbey is built on the remains of a Romanesque church, which was built on the remains of a Carolingian church. Saint Michael, whose gilded statue decorates the top of the spire, was the patron saint of many French kings, making this a favored sight for French royalty through the ages. As you enter, imagine the headaches and hassles the monks ran into while building it. They had to ferry the granite from across the bay (then deeper and without the causeway) and make the same hike you just did—with more luggage.

The visit is a one-way route through interesting—but barren—Gothic rooms. The situation of this abbey is its most impressive feature. You'll explore the church, delicate cloisters, and refectory (where the monks ate in austere silence) and then climb down into the dark, damp Romanesque foundations. A highlight is the giant tread wheel, which six workers would power hamster-style to haul two-ton loads of stones and supplies from the landing below. This was used right up until the 19th century.

You won't find any English explanations posted in the abbey,

Mont St. Michel

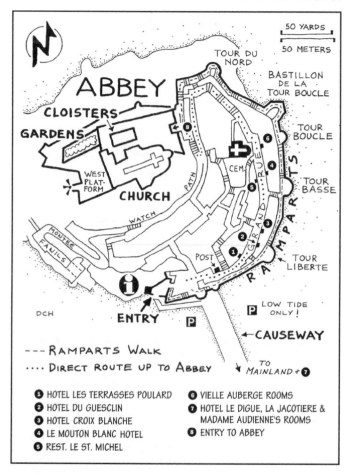

50 YARDS

50 METERS

TOUR DU NORD

BASTILLON DE LA TOUR BOUCLE

ABBEY

CLOISTERS

GARDENS

TOUR BOUCLE

WEST PLAT-FORM

CEM.

RUE

CHURCH

TOUR BASSE

PATH

WATCH

GRANDE

RAMPARTS

MONTEE FANILS

POST

TOUR LIBERTE

DCH

ENTRY

P

P   LOW TIDE ONLY!

← CAUSEWAY

--- RAMPARTS WALK

.... DIRECT ROUTE UP TO ABBEY

↓ TO MAINLAND & ❼

❶ HOTEL LES TERRASSES POULARD
❷ HOTEL DU GUESCLIN
❸ HOTEL CROIX BLANCHE
❹ LE MOUTON BLANC HOTEL
❺ REST. LE ST. MICHEL

❻ VIELLE AUBERGE ROOMS
❼ HOTEL LE DIGUE, LA JACOTIERE & MADAME AUDIENNE'S ROOMS
❽ ENTRY TO ABBEY

but then, there's not a lot to explain. Still, you'll better appreciate the site by renting an **audioguide** (€3.80, €5.35 for 2) or taking a 75-minute English-language **tour** (free, tip requested, 4–6 tours/day, first tour usually at 10:00, last at 17:00, confirm tour times at TI, meet at top terrace in front of church, groups can be large). For some, the tours make a short story long.

Admission and hours: €6.25 entry (mid-May–mid-Sept daily 09:00–18:30, spring and fall 09:30–17:00, closes at 16:00 in winter, ticket office closes 60 min earlier, abbey also open summer eves—see "Evening on Mont St. Michel," below, tel. 02 33 89 80 00.)

Buy your ticket to the abbey and keep climbing. Allow 20 minutes to climb at a steady pace from the TI. When you leave the abbey, make a hard right at the bottom of the steps (just past the WCs) to see more of the village and avoid crowds.

Evening Visits: On summer evenings, the gardens are open 19:00 to 21:00, and the abbey interior is open from 21:00 to 24:00. With laser lights, mood music, and videos, it's like a self-guided sound-and-light show. The €8 entry includes the garden and abbey; arrive about 20:30 and do both (nightly July–Aug, weekends only in Sept).

▲▲**Stroll around Mont St. Michel**—To resurrect that Mont St. Michel dreamscape and evade all those tacky tourist stalls, walk out on the mudflats around the island. At low tide it's reasonably dry and a great memory. This can be extremely dangerous, so be sure to double-check the tides. Remember the scene from the Bayeux tapestry where Harold rescues Normans from the quicksand? It happened somewhere in this bay. You may notice groups hiking in from the muddy horizon. Attempting this without a local guide is reckless.

▲▲▲**Evening Views on Mont St. Michel**—After dark, the island is magically floodlit. Views from the ramparts are sublime. You must exit the island and walk out on the causeway a few hundred meters to best appreciate this magical place.

German Military Cemetery (Cimetière Militaire Allemand)— Located five kilometers from Mont St. Michel near tiny Huisnes-sur-Mer, this somber but thoughtfully presented cemetery/ mortuary houses the remains of 12,000 German soldiers and offers insight into their lives with letters they sent home (English translations). From the lookout, there are sensational views over Mont St. Michel.

Sleeping on or near Mont St. Michel
(€1.10 = $1, country code: 33, zip code: 50116)
Sleeping on the island, inside the walls, is the best way to experience Mont St. Michel, though drivers should consider the *chambres d'hôtes* listed below. On the island, most hotels are tired and impersonal, and some pad their profits by requiring guests to buy dinner from their restaurant. Several are closed from November until Easter. Because most visitors only daytrip here, you should be able to find a room at almost any time of the year. Still, reserve ahead if possible.

On Mont St. Michel: These hotels are listed in order of altitude (the first are lowest on the island and closest to parking).

Hôtel les Terrasses Poulard***, 50 meters after the TI, has the most polished and priciest rooms on the island (Db-€76– 145, CC, tel. 02 33 60 14 09, fax 02 33 60 37 31). The impersonal **Hôtel du Guesclin**** offers good clean rooms at competitive rates (Db-€43–72, Tb-€84, no CC, tel. 02 33 60 14 10, fax 02 33 60 45 81). **Hôtel Croix Blanche***** needs a face-lift but has a few loft triples and some good-view doubles (Sb-€72, Db-€80–87, Tb/Qb-€110–136, extra bed-€16, CC, tel. 02 33 60 14 04, fax 02 33 48 59 82, e-mail: hotel.croix-blanche@gofornet.com). **Le Mouton Blanc** has decent, generally cozier rooms (Db-€61, Tb/Qb-€72–92, CC, tel. 02 33 60 14 08, fax 02 33 60 05 62). The comfortable rooms offered at **Restaurant le St. Michel,** across from Le Mouton Blanc, are the best value on the island (Db-€38–53, no CC, no dinner requirements but a good restaurant, tel. & fax 02 33 60 14 37, Patricia, Philippe, and Freddo SE). The rooms at **Vielle Auberge**, owned by a moody woman, are among the next best for the price, but don't let her talk you into more room than you need (Db-€55, Db with view-€64, Db with view and terrace-€102, extra bed-€16, CC, tel. 02 33 60 14 34, fax 02 33 70 87 04).

On the Mainland: Modern hotels gather at the mainland end of the causeway, offering soulless but cheaper rooms with easy parking and a cheesy Coney Island feel. The friendly **Hôtel de la Digue***** is the best and most convenient. Most rooms are spacious and cushy (ask for a room with private terrace on the riverside: *chambre avec petit balcon sur la Couesnon*). You can dine with a partial view of Mont St. Michel at their well-respected restaurant (small Db-€54, spacious Db-€72, Tb-€78, Qb-€79–88, CC, tel. 02 33 60 14 02, fax 02 33 60 37 59, www.ladigue.fr).

Chambres d'Hôte

Simply great values, these places are in the village of Ardevon, a few minutes' drive from the island toward Avranches. Charming Madame Brault's stone farmhouse, **La Jacotière**, is closest (walkable to the causeway), with six immaculate, modern rooms and great views of Mont St. Michel from her picnic-perfect garden (Db-€35, studio with view-€40, extra bed-€9, no CC, tel. 02 33 60 22 94, fax 02 33 60 20 48, SE). About 1.5 kilometers down the road you'll find the equally charming **Madame Audienne**'s rustic stone farmhouse with five simple rooms (5 more are underway), four of which have views of Mont St. Michel (Sb-€23, Db-€34, Tb-€41, includes breakfast, no CC, relaxing garden, tel. 02 33 60 23 56, daughter Estelle speaks a little English).

Train travelers may prefer sleeping in dismal Pontorson, a 15-minute drive from Mont St. Michel (zip code, 51170). **Hôtel Vauban****, across from the train station, is quiet and comfortable (D-€31, Db-€38–49, Tb-€52, 2 boulevard Clemenceau, tel. 02 33 60 03 84, fax 02 33 60 35 48).

Eating on Mont St. Michel

Puffy omelets (*omelette Montoise*) are the island's specialty. Also look for mussels and seafood platters, locally raised lamb (fed on the saltwater grass), and Muscadet wine (dry, cheap, and white). I let Patricia and Phillipe cook for me at the light-hearted and reasonable **Le St. Michel** (good omelets and mussels, tel. 02 33 60 14 37), across from Hôtel le Mouton Blanc. **Hôtel de la Digue** offers more refined cuisine on the mainland at the foot of the causeway (expensive wine list, see "Sleeping," above). The tourist *supermarché*, near Hôtel de la Digue, has what you need for a romantic picnic (daily 08:30–20:00), though you can buy sandwiches and drinks to go on the island. Picnic in the small park below the abbey (to the left as you look up at the abbey).

Transportation Connections—
Mont St. Michel

The nearest train station is in Pontorson (called *Pontorson-Mont St. Michel*), 15 minutes from Mont St. Michel by bus (4/day Mon–Fri, 2/day Sun, evening trains have no bus connection). Taxis from Pontorson to Mont St. Michel (or vice versa) cost about €13, €17 after 19:00 and on weekends/holidays; look for others to share a cab (tel. 02 33 60 26 89). Three daily buses also run directly from Mont St. Michel to Rennes (1.75 hrs) with connections to many destinations.

By bus and train to: **Paris** (6/day, 4 hrs, via 1.75-hr bus to Rennes then train to Paris Montparnasse, or via 15-min bus to Pontorson then train to Paris with change in Rennes or Caen), **Bayeux** (2/day, 2.5 hrs, bus to Pontorson, then direct train), **Dinan** (3/day, 2 hrs, bus to Pontorson, then train with change in Dol, or in 4 hrs via bus to Rennes then train with change in Dol), **St. Malo** (3/day, 1.5 hrs, bus to Pontorson, then train with change in Dol), **Amboise** (4/day, 7 hrs, bus to Pontorson then train with changes in Caen and Tours' main station; or 8 hrs via bus to Rennes then train with changes at Paris Montparnasse and St. Pierre des Corps).

By bus from Mont St. Michel to: **St. Malo** (2/day, 75 min direct), **Rennes** (2/day, morning and evening, 70 min, Couriers Bretons bus, tel. 02 99 19 70 70).

BRITTANY

The Couesnon River marks the border between Normandy and Brittany. It hits the sea just west of Mont St. Michel, leaving the island barely in Normandy. The peninsula of Brittany is rugged, with an isolated interior, a well-discovered coast, strong Celtic ties, and a passion for crepes (which they call *galettes*). This region of independent-minded locals is linguistically and culturally quite different from Normandy and, for that matter, the rest of France. The coastal route from Mont St. Michel through the oyster-famous town of Cancale (good lunch stop), Pointe du Grouin (good hiking), and on to the historic walled city of St. Malo gives a good introduction to this province.

DINAN

If you have time for only one stop in Brittany, do Dinan. This perfectly preserved ancient city is conveniently located and offers Brittany's best medieval center (1 hour from Mont St. Michel). Dinan feels real.

Orientation

Dinan's old city is contained within its medieval ramparts, climbing steeply uphill east to west from the river Rance to huge place du Guesclin. Place des Merciers is ground zero for most activities in Dinan.

Tourist Information: Pick up a map at the TI and ask about boat trips on the Rance river (June–Sept 09:00–19:00, Oct–May 09:00–12:00, 14:00–18:00, skip overpriced tourist magazine, near Château de Dinan on 9 rue du Château, tel. 02 96 87 69 76).

Arrival in Dinan: To get to the center from the train station (no lockers), either take a minibus (2/hr) or a 30-minute walk (left out of station up rue Deroyer, right on rue Thiers, then cross huge place Duclos-Pinot and walk up rue Marchix). Dinan is confusing for drivers; follow *centre-ville* signs to the station. From there, take the streets (listed above as the walking route arrival by train) to reach the massive place du Guesclin (free parking except July–Sept).

Markets: Thursday is market day until 12:30 on place du Guesclin. Wednesday is flea-market day on place St. Saveur.

Sights—Dinan

Quick Self-Guided Walking Tour—Start at the TI. Walk down rue de l'Horloge to the lookout tower, Tour de l'Horloge (€2.50, 160 steps, fantastic views, April–Sept 10:00–18:00, Oct–March 14:00–18:00), then continue down rue de l'Horloge and turn left into Dinan's historic commercial center, the place des Merciers. The half-timbered, arcaded buildings are Dinan's oldest. They date from the time when property taxes were based on the square footage of your ground floor. To provide shelter from both the taxes and the rain, owners built out their first floors. Turn right where the square ends and then rappel partway down rue Jerzual (for *crêperies*, boutiques, and stiff knees). Crossing under the medieval gate (Porte Jerzual), turn right and climb to the only accessible section of the ramparts. Enjoy the view and then double back down the ramparts. From here, you have two choices, depending on your stamina:

If you're feeling fit, continue down to the old port (where the town was founded). Then, for a breath of Brittany, cross the old bridge, turn right, and follow the river trail 30 minutes to the pristine little village of Lehon, where you'll find a café/*crêperie*.

If your legs disagree, skip the old port. Jog right after exiting the gate of the ramparts above the Porte Jerzual and take the first left uphill to the Jardins Anglais (English Gardens). Survey Dinan's port and the Rance valley. Then peek inside the very Breton Basilique St. Sauveur (bordering the park, English handout inside).

Château de Dinan—The donjon (keep) and nearby walls are all that's left of Dinan's once massive castle. Skip it; there are no English explanations and the view from the top is not worth the climb.

River Boat Trips—Consider a scenic river cruise to St. Malo. Boats depart from Dinan's port at the bottom of rue Jerzual (€16 one-way, €21 round-trip, schedules depend on tides, get details at TI).

Sleeping and Eating in Dinan
(€1.10 = $1, country code: 33, zip code: 22100)

Hôtel de l'Arvor** is a good, central, midrange value with modern rooms wrapped in an old stone facade (standard Db-€45, larger Db-€60, CC, 5 rue Pavie, tel. 02 96 39 21 22, fax 02 96 39 83 09).

Hôtel les Grandes Tours offers small but sharp rooms and private parking (S/D-€31, Sb/Db-€44–47, Tb/Qb-€68, parking-€4.60, CC, 6 rue du Château, tel. 02 96 85 16 20, fax 02 96 85 16 04, e-mail: carregi@wanadoo.fr).

Hôtel La Tour de l'Horloge** is an 18th-century manor house located dead center with adequate rooms (skip the "outside" rooms on the alley, Db-€41–53, Tb-€64, Qb-€77, no CC, 5 rue de la Chaux, tel. 02 96 39 96 92, fax 02 96 85 06 99, e-mail: hiliotel@wanadoo.fr, SE).

At **Hôtel de la Duchesse Anne***, friendly Giles offers reasonable comfort, a small bar, and an unpretentious restaurant on the huge place du Guesclin (Db-€43–46, Tb-€56, Qb-€70, includes breakfast, no CC, 10 place du Guesclin, tel. 02 96 39 09 43, fax 02 96 87 57 26).

Hôtel Du Théâtre is Dinan's bargain, with no stars but clean and cheery rooms over a small café opposite the TI (S-€15.50, D-€20, Db-€27–32, no CC, 2 rue Ste. Claire, tel. 02 96 39 06 91, NSE).

Hôtel de France**, facing the train station, provides good rooms at fair rates over a pleasant café (Sb-€39, Db-€44, Tb-€56, Qb-€61, no CC, 7 place du Novembre 11, tel. 02 96 39 22 56, fax 02 96 39 08 96).

Eating: Try any of the cozy *crêperies* in the old city. If you're not in the mood for crêpes, try my favorite restaurant, **Le St. Louis**, just around the corner from Hôtel les Grandes Tours. Flames from the fireplace flicker on wood beams and white tablecloths (€15 *menu*, great salad bar and desserts, closed Wed except in summer, 9 rue de Lehon, tel. 02 96 39 89 50). If you need more dining elegance, **La Fleur de Sel** has it (*menus* from €19, just off place du Guesclin at 7 rue Ste. Claire, tel. 02 96 85 15 14). You'll find several cozy restaurants in the old port (steep walk down rue Jerzual); **Les Terrasses** sits right on the river and has a good €15 *menu* (also good just for a drink on its huge terrace, tel. 02 96 39 09 60).

Transportation Connections—Dinan
By train to: Paris (7/day, 3.5 hrs, change in Dol and Rennes), **Pontorson-Mont St. Michel** (3/day, 2 hrs, change in Dol, then bus or taxi from Pontorson), **St. Malo** (7/day, 1 hr, change in Dol), **Amboise** (4/day, 5–6 hrs, probable changes in Dol, Rennes, Le Mans, and Tours' St. Pierre des Corps).

ST. MALO AND FOUGÈRES
▲**St. Malo**—Come here to experience *the* Breton beach resort. Stroll high up on the impressive ramparts that circle the entire old city, eat seafood, walk as far out on the beaches as the tides allow, then return to Dinan for the night. An easy day trip, St. Malo is a 45-minute drive or a one-hour bus or train ride from Mont St. Michel or Dinan. The excellent **TI** is at Esplanade St. Vincent (tel. 02 99 56 64 48).
▲**Fougères**—This very Breton city is a delightful stop for drivers traveling between the Loire châteaux and Mont St. Michel. Fougères has one of Europe's largest medieval castles, a fine city center, and a panoramic park viewpoint (from St. Leonard church in the Jardin Public). Try one of the café/ *crêperies* near the castle, such as the tempting Crêperie des Remparts, one block uphill from the castle. Pick up a city map and castle description in English at the castle entrance. The interior is grass and walls.

THE LOIRE

The Loire River, which glides east to west across France and separates north from south, gave its name to this popular tourist region. The Loire Valley is carpeted with fertile fields, crisscrossed by rivers and streams, and studded with hundreds of castles and palaces in all shapes and sizes. The medieval castles explain the area's strategic value during the Hundred Years' War. Renaissance palaces replaced medieval castles when a "valley address" became a must among the hunt-crazy rich and royalty. Today, the Loire Valley has a split personality: It's one of France's most important agricultural regions, and a burgeoning bedroom community of Paris, thanks to the TGV bullet trains that link this pastoral area with Paris in under an hour.

Many travelers find the Loire a good first or last stop on their French odyssey (5 TGV trains/day connect Paris' Charles de Gaulle Airport in 1 hour with the city of Tours, which has car rental agencies at the station).

Planning Your Time

Use Amboise (good for Eurailers or drivers) or Chenonceaux (good for drivers) as a home base for touring the famous châteaux northeast of Tours: Chenonceau, Blois, Chambord, Chaumont-sur-Loire, and Cheverny. Use Chinon or Azay le Rideau as your home base to visit the châteaux west of Tours: Chinon, Azay le Rideau, Langeais, and Villandry. If you're renting a car, pickup at Tours' suburban St. Pierre station is a snap (1 hour by train from Paris).

A day and a half is sufficient to sample the best châteaux. (Many find the Loire manageable as a daytrip from Paris; see "By Minibus Tours," below.) Consider this plan: Visit Chenonceau (in town of Chenonceaux) early when crowds are smaller, spend midday at Chambord, and enjoy Cheverny late (the hunting dogs are fed at 17:00). Extend your day by attending a sound-and-light show offered at many châteaux (usually June–Sept). Lights, sound effects, and, occasionally, actors help recreate the château's history. Some are interesting, some are dull; all start late. Get details at the specific château or local TI and read my reviews.

If arriving by car, try to see one château on your way in (e.g., Chambord if arriving from the north, Langeais from the west, or Azay le Rideau from the south). If arriving by train from Paris, consider a stop in Blois and the bus excursion to Chambord and Cheverny (see "Getting around the Loire Valley," below, or go directly to Amboise and try to visit Le Clos Lucé that afternoon).

Don't go overboard on château-hopping. Two châteaux, possibly three (if you're a big person), make up the recommended daily dosage. Famous châteaux are least crowded early, at lunchtime, and late. Most open around 09:00 and close between 18:00 and 19:00. During the off-season, many close from 12:00 to 14:00 and at 17:00.

A good one-day plan for those with no car and no money for a minivan tour is to catch the once-per-day Amboise-Chenonceaux bus (see "Getting around the Loire Valley," below) and spend the afternoon enjoying Amboise, its château, and Leonardo's place, Le Clos Lucé.

If you're driving to the Dordogne from the Loire, the A-20 autoroute via Limoges (and Oradour-sur-Glane) is fastest, and, at least for now, free.

Getting around the Loire Valley

By Train: With easy access from Amboise, Tours is the transport hub for hard-core train travelers. The châteaux of Chenonceau, Langeais, Chinon, and Azay le Rideau have some train and/or bus service from Tours' main station (although Chenonceaux is better by bus or bike from Amboise). In Tours, there are two important train stations and a bus station with service to several châteaux: The main train station is called "Tours SNCF," and the smaller TGV station is "St. Pierre des Corps." Check the schedules carefully, as service is sparse on some lines.

By Bus: There's one bus per day from Amboise to Chenonceaux, (departs Amboise at 10:54, returns from Chenonceaux at 12:40, allowing you about 90 min at the château). From mid-May until early September, there's also a handy excursion bus from the Blois train station (20 min by train from Amboise) that serves Chambord and Cheverny, giving you 90 minutes at each château (€10 includes bus fare and discounts on château entries; departs Blois station at 9:10, returns at 13:10; or departs Blois at 13:20, returns at 18:00). For details, call the Blois TI at 02 54 90 41 41.

By Minibus Tour: Pascal Accolay runs **Acco-Dispo**, a small, personal minibus company with good all-day château tours from Amboise and Tours. Costs vary with the itinerary; figure €21 to

The Loire Valley

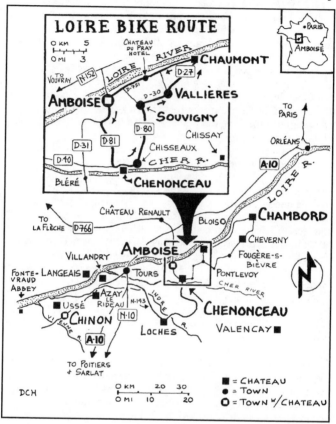

€28 for a half-day and €37 to €43 for an all-day tour. English is the primary language. While you'll get a fun and enthusiastic running commentary on the road, covering each château's background as well as the region's contemporary scene, you're on your own at each château (and you pay the admission fee). All-day tours depart about 08:30, afternoon tours depart about 12:50. Both return to Amboise around 18:30. Several itinerary options are available; most include Chenonceau. Reserve two to three days ahead if possible; groups are small, ranging from two to eight château-hoppers. (Daytrippers from Paris find this service convenient; after a one-hour ride on the TGV to Tours, they're met near the central station and delivered there at the end of the day.) Ask about Acco-Dispo's multiday tours of the Loire and Brittany (daily, free hotel pickups, 18 rue des Vallées in Amboise, tel. 06 82 00 64 51, fax 02 47 23 15 73, www.accodispo-tours.com). **Excursions SNCF** also provides daily minibus and big bus tours from Tour's SNCF station to a variety of châteaux (€15–25, half-day departures at 09:00 and 13:15 from bus platform 6, tel. 02 47 05 46 09, fax 02 47 58 71 73, e-mail: info@ligeris.com).

By Taxi: A taxi from Amboise to Chenonceaux costs about €16. Your hotel can call one for you. The meter doesn't start until you do.

By Rental Car: Cars are best rented at either of Tours' train stations; they are also available in Amboise (see "Amboise—Helpful Hints," below).

By Bike: Cycling options are endless in this region where the elevation gain is generally manageable (still, many find even the shortest rides exhausting and too time-consuming). Amboise, Blois, and Chinon make the best bike bases. From Amboise, allow an hour to Chenonceaux (warning: the first 3 km are uphill). Only the most fit and serious bikers can ride to Chaumont in 90 minutes and connect Amboise, Chenonceaux, and Chaumont with an all-day 60-kilometer pedal (see Loire Valley map in this chapter for details). From Blois by bike to Chambord is a manageable 75-minute, one-way ride, but adding Cheverny makes a grueling, full-day, 50-kilometer round-trip. Most can do the pleasant bike ride from Chinon to Ussé (big hill when leaving Chinon), and some will find the energy to continue to Langeais. Only those in top shape will enjoy continuing on to Villandry (see "Chinon," below). Call the Blois TI for bike-rental information (tel. 02 54 90 41 41).

Cuisine Scene—Loire Valley

Here in "the garden of France," anything from the earth is bound to be good. Loire Valley rivers produce fresh trout (*truite*), salmon (*saumon*), and smelt (*éperlau*), which are often served fried (*friture*). *Rillettes*, a stringy pile of cooked then whipped pork, makes for a cheap, mouthwatering sandwich spread (use lots of mustard and add a baby pickle, called a *cornichon*). The area's fine goat cheeses include Crottin de Chavignol (*crottin* means horse dung, which is what this cheese, when aged, resembles), Saint-Maure Fermier (soft and creamy), and Selles-sur-Cher (mild). For dessert, try a delicious *tarte Tatin* (upside-down caramel-apple tart). The best and most expensive white wines are the Sancerres and Pouilly-Fumés. Less expensive but still tasty are Tourraine Sauvignons and the sweeter Vouvrays. The better reds come from Chinon and Bourgeuil.

AMBOISE

Straddling the widest part of the Loire, Amboise slumbers in the shadow of its hilltop château. A castle has overlooked the Loire from Amboise since Roman times. Leonardo da Vinci retired

here... just one more fine idea. The town is busily preparing
for the 550th anniversary in 2002 of da Vinci's birth in 1452;
ask about special events at the TI (or, to plan ahead, check
www.amboise-valloire.com).

As the royal residence of François I, Amboise wielded far
more importance than you'd imagine from a lazy walk down
the pleasant pedestrian-only commercial zone at the base of the
palace. With or without a car, Amboise is an ideal small-town
home base for exploring the best of château country.

Orientation: Amboise (pop. 11,000) covers both sides of
the Loire and an island in the middle. The station is on the north
side of the river, but everything else is on the south (château) side,
including the TI.

Tourist Information: The information-packed TI is in
the round building on the riverbank at quai du Général de Gaulle
(Mon–Sat 09:00–19:00, Sun 10:00–12:00, 15:00–18:00, tel. 02 47
57 09 28, www.amboise-valloire.com). Their city map shows
restaurants, hotels, and château information, including the time
and place of English-language sound-and-light shows. They
can reserve a room for you in a hotel or *chambre d'hote*, but first
peruse the photo album of regional *chambres d'hôte*. Ask about
city walking tours in English.

Arrival in Amboise

By Train: Amboise's train station, with a post office and taxi stand,
is birds-chirping peaceful (tel. 02 47 23 18 23). Turn left out of the
station, make a quick right, and walk down rue de Nazelles five
minutes to the bridge that leads you over the Loire and into town.
Within three blocks of the station, you'll find a recommended hotel,
B&B, and bike-rental shop.

By Car: Drivers set their sights on the flag-festooned
château capping the hill. Most recommended accommodations
and restaurants cluster just downriver of the château. Park on
the street near your hotel or near the TI.

Helpful Hints

Information: The Michelin Green Guide to the Loire provides a
good historical and architectural background on the region and
each château. English versions are sold for about €11 (40 percent
off the U.S. price) at most tourist shops.

Bike Rental: Rent a bike for about €11 per half day and
€14 per full day (leave your passport or a photocopy of it). Two
reliable places are **Locacycle** (daily 09:00–19:00, near TI at 2 rue
Jean-Jacques Rousseau, tel. 02 47 57 00 28, English spoken) and
Cycles Richard, (Mon–Sat, closed 12:00–14:00, located on train-
station side of river, just past bridge at 2 rue de Nazelles, tel. 02
47 57 01 79, NSE).

Amboise

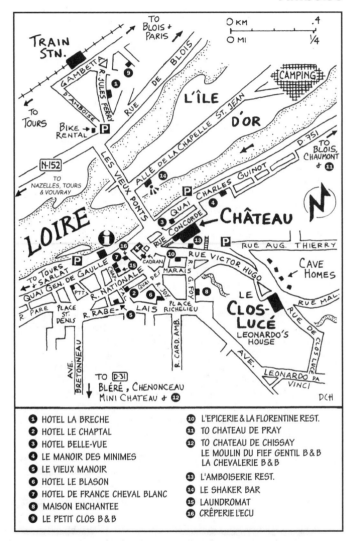

- ❶ HOTEL LA BRECHE
- ❷ HOTEL LE CHAPTAL
- ❸ HOTEL BELLE-VUE
- ❹ LE MANOIR DES MINIMES
- ❺ LE VIEUX MANOIR
- ❻ HOTEL LE BLASON
- ❼ HOTEL DE FRANCE CHEVAL BLANC
- ❽ MAISON ENCHANTEE
- ❾ LE PETIT CLOS B&B
- ❿ L'EPICERIE & LA FLORENTINE REST.
- ⓫ TO CHATEAU DE PRAY
- ⓬ TO CHATEAU DE CHISSAY
     LE MOULIN DU FIEF GENTIL B&B
     LA CHEVALERIE B&B
- ⓭ L'AMBOISERIE REST.
- ⓮ LE SHAKER BAR
- ⓯ LAUNDROMAT
- ⓰ CRÊPERIE L'ECU

Car Rental: Avis is expensive (across from Amboise TI, tel. 02 47 57 01 54, fax 02 47 23 22 47); **Garage Jourdain** is less (downriver from TI at 105 route de Tours, tel. 02 47 57 17 92, fax 02 47 57 77 50). Both close Monday through Friday from 12:00 to 14:00 and at 18:00 weekdays, 17:00 on Saturdays, and all day Sunday.

Laundromat: The handy coin-op Lav'centre is a block from rue Chaptal toward the château on 9 allée du Sergent Turpin (daily 07:00–21:00, Oct–May until 20:00). The door locks at closing time; leave beforehand or you'll trigger the alarm system.

Chocolate Fantasy: An essential and historic stop for chocoholics is **Bigot Patisserie & Chocolatier.** Ask about tours of their shop (near the château, on place Michel Debré).

Sights—Amboise

▲▲**Le Clos Lucé**—In 1516, Leonardo da Vinci packed his bags (and several of his favorite paintings, including the *Mona Lisa*) and left an imploding Rome for better working conditions in the Loire Valley. This "House of Light" is the plush palace where he spent his last three years. France's Renaissance king François I set Leonardo up here just so he could enjoy his intellectual company. There's a touching sketch in Leonardo's bedroom of François comforting his genius pal on his deathbed. The house thoughtfully recreates (with adequate English information) the everyday atmosphere Leonardo enjoyed as he pursued his passions to the very end. Of all the palaces I've seen on the Loire, this is the one where I'd live. The ground floor is filled with sketches recording the storm patterns of Leonardo's brain and models of his remarkable inventions (built by IBM, according to his notes). It's hard to imagine that this Roman candle of creativity died nearly 500 years ago. The garden café is reasonable and appropriately meditative; above it is a French-only video about Leonardo (€6 entry, Sept–June daily 10:00–19:00, July–Aug 09:00–20:00, get the English handout). It's a 15-minute walk from the TI, up past troglodyte homes (unsafe parking lot at Le Clos Lucé).

▲**Château d'Amboise**—The royal residence of Francois I, this was used in the Middle Ages to greet royal pilgrims en route from Paris to Spain's Santiago de Compostela. Leonardo da Vinci is said to have designed the château's vaulted spiral staircases. Pick up the fine, free English tour flier as you enter. The lacy, petite chapel (first stop) is Flamboyant Gothic, with two fireplaces "to comfort the king" and a plaque "evoking the final resting place" of Leonardo. Where he's actually buried, no one seems to know. Continue into and through the well-furnished château—which, though much larger in the 15th century, still feels plenty big. Your last stop is the horsemen's tower, a brick ramp—climbing 40 meters (131 feet) in five spirals—designed to accommodate a mounted soldier in a hurry (€6.25, March–Oct daily 09:00–18:00, until 19:30 in summer, off-season closes 12:00–14:00 and at 17:00, tel. 02 47 57 00 98).

Caveau des Vignerons—This small cave offers free tastings of regional wines, cheeses, and foie gras (April–Sept 10:00–19:00, under Amboise's château across from recommended l'Epicerie restaurant).

La Maison Enchantée—Push the buttons and watch dolls dance in 25 different settings (adult-€5.30, child-€3.80, April–Oct Tue–Sun 10:00–12:00, 14:00–18:00, summers 10:00–19:00, Nov–March Tue–Sun 14:00–17:00, walk down rue de la Tour from château to 7 rue du General Foy, tel. 02 47 23 24 50).

Mini-Château—This five-acre park on the edge of Amboise (on the route to Chenonceaux) shows all the Loire châteaux in 1:25-scale models, forested with 600 bonsai trees and laced together by a model TGV train. It's a fun introduction to the real châteaux you'll be visiting. The English brochure is essential (adult-€10, kids ages 4–16-€7, April–Sept daily 10:00–18:00, 9:00–19:00 in summer, off-season closes at 17:00, tel. 02 47 23 44 44). You'll find other kid-oriented attractions at Mini-Château; skip the donkey show but consider playing a round of mini-golf and feeding the fish in the moat (a great way to get rid of that old baguette).

▲**Château d'Amboise Sound-and-Light Show**—This is one of the region's best shows. While it's entirely in French, you can buy the English translation for €4.60. Volunteer locals from toddlers to pensioners recreate the life of François I with costumes, jugglers, impressive light displays, and fireworks (adults-€15.50, kids ages 6–14-€5.50, June–Aug Wed and Sat 22:30–24:00, dress warmly, details at TI).

Sleeping in Amboise
(€1.10 = about $1, country code: 33, zip code: 37400)
Sleep Code: **S** = Single, **D** = Double/Twin, **T** = Triple, **Q** = Quad, **b** = bathroom, **s** = shower only, **CC** = Credit Cards accepted, **no CC** = Credit Cards not accepted, **SE** = Speaks English, **NSE** = No English, * = French hotel rating system (0–4 stars).

Amboise is busy in the summer, but there are lots of hotels and *chambres d'hôte* (CH) in and around the city; the TI can help with reservations. Except for the first hotel and the first CH, all listings are in the old town center.

Hotels
Hôtel La Brèche** is a refuge run by a "we try harder" family and has spotless, comfortable rooms and a peaceful garden with Ping-Pong and a few ducks. It's 10 minutes from the city center and 100 meters from the train station. Many rooms overlook the garden; those on the street are generally larger and the room off the garden is family perfect. Half-pension is required in the summer, and it gets you a prize-winning dinner for an extra €12.20 per person—I spring €3 more for the *menu du terror*. Box lunches are also available for €8.40 (S/D-€26, Sb/Db-€50, Tb-€49–55, Qb-€56–60, a few good family rooms-€64–69, CC, 26 rue Jules Ferry, tel. 02 47 57 00 79, fax 02 47 57 65 49, www.labreche-amboise.com, Pierre and mother Annick SE).

Hôtel Belle-Vue*** overlooks the river where the bridge hits the town. This hotel has spacious public rooms and effective double-paned windows. Half of its comfortable rooms overlook the château; four come with huge, shared terraces (Db-€56–62, Tb-€68–76, Qb-€80–90, CC, elevator, 12 quai Charles-Guinot, tel. 02 47 57 02 26, fax 02 47 30 51 23).

Hôtel Le Blason**, with friendly staff and a good restaurant, is a half-timbered, old building on a square five blocks from the river, with small, bright, and modern rooms on a noisy street (Sb-€44, Db-€49, Tb-€54, CC, quieter rooms in back and on top floor, easy parking, 11 place Richelieu, tel. 02 47 23 22 41, fax 02 47 57 56 18, e-mail: leblason@wanadoo.fr, Agnes SE).

Hôtel Le Chaptal** is basic, cheap, central and *très* frumpy, with birds in the lobby and decent rooms—quieter off the street—but marginal beds (Db-€32–35, Tb-€40, Qb-€46, CC, 13 rue de Chaptal, tel. 02 47 57 14 46, fax 02 47 57 67 83, NSE). In summer they request that you dine in their cheery, inexpensive dining room.

Le Manoir des Minimes****, a renovated 17th-century mansion, feels a bit overdone with precious furniture but works for those seeking luxury in Amboise. Rooms are modern and large (Db-€100–115, deluxe Db-€130–150, 3–4 person suites-€190–225, extra bed-€20, CC, 34 quai Charles Guinot, 3 blocks upriver from bridge, tel. 02 47 30 40 40, fax 02 47 30 40 77, e-mail: manoir-les-minimes@wanadoo.fr).

Le Vieux Manoir is a better high-end splurge. American ex-pat Gloria Bellnap (a wealth of information) has completely restored this secluded but central manor home with an attention to detail that Martha Stewart would appreciate. The lovely breakfast room opens to immaculate gardens, the public spaces are American-cozy, and the six bedrooms would make an antique collector drool (rooms $110–150, includes hearty breakfast, easy parking, no CC, pay in euros or U.S. dollars, personal check or cash, 13 rue Rabelais, tel. & fax 02 47 30 41 27, www.le-vieux-manoir.com).

Hôtel de France Cheval Blanc* rents simple, spotless, and comfortable rooms above a café across from the TI at fair rates (D-€24, Db-€30–401, T-€31, Tb-€41–58, CC, no elevator, 6 quai du General de Gaulle, tel. 02 47 57 02 44, fax 02 47 57 69 54). *Rue* (street) rooms have double-paned windows but some traffic noise seeps in. *Cour* (courtyard) rooms are quieter.

Le Petit Clos *chambre d'hote* has three cheery, cottage-type ground-floor rooms on a quiet, picnic-perfect private garden. Charming Madame Roullet speaks a leetle English (Db-€54, family room for up to 5 people-€107, no CC, includes big, farm-fresh breakfast with homemade everything, easy parking, 3 blocks from station, turn left out of station and follow tracks to 7 rue Balzac, tel. 02 47 57 43 52).

Sleeping near Amboise

Also see "Sleeping in Chenonceaux," below.

You'll feel a hint of the original medieval fortified castle behind the Renaissance elegance of the 750-year-old **Château de Pray******. The dining room is splendid and the chef is talented (€39–48 *menus*, reservations required). The pool is below the château (Db-€93–168, Tb-€107–198, Qb-€130–230, CC, 5-min drive upriver from Amboise, toward Chaumont on the D-751, tel. 02 47 57 23 67, fax 02 47 57 32 50, e-mail: chateau.depray@wanadoo.fr).

Château de Chissay****, a five-minute drive east of Chenonceaux, offers a noble experience. Perched above a valley in a private park, this storybook 15th-century château was home to two French kings. Now it's home to a large swimming pool, regal rooms, professional service, and is a royal value if you land a standard room (Sb-€70, standard but beautiful Db-€77–90, spacious Db-€140, suites-€185–245, rooms with valley views are more costly but worth it, optional dinner from €32, CC, no elevator, 41400 Chissay, tel. 02 54 32 32 01, fax 02 54 32 43 80, e-mail: chateau-chissay@wanadoo.fr).

Château de Nazelles *chambre d'hote* is for those wanting a château hotel experience *sans* the pretension. Young, charming, and English-speaking Monsieur and Madame Fructus have tastefully restored this historic 16th-century hillside castle, which was once home to the original builder of Chenonceau. Trails lead into the forest above, a pool is sculpted under the cliffs, and lush gardens with views over Amboise greet guests (Db-€85–90, includes breakfast, CC, tel. & fax 02 47 30 53 79, www.chateau -nazelles.com). From Amboise, take the N-152 toward Tours, turn right on the D-5, then left in Nazelles-Negron on the D-1 and quickly veer right above the post office (PTT) to 16 rue Tue la Soif; look for small *Gîtes* sign.

For a "Peter Mayle does the Loire" experience 15 minutes from Amboise and Chenonceaux, sleep at Roger and Ann's beautifully renovated 16th-century mill house, **Le Moulin du Fief Gentil**, where you get four acres and a backyard pond (fishing possible), smartly decorated rooms, and a splendid common living room. If Ann is cooking, splurge for dinner (Db-€70–90, dinner-€27/person, no CC, 37150 Bléré, tel. 02 47 30 32 51, fax 02 47 30 22 38, www.fiefgentil.fr.fm, e-mail: fiefgentil @wanadoo.fr). It's located on the edge of Bléré (from Bléré, follow signs toward Luzille).

Closer to Amboise, the bargain *chambres* at **La Chevalerie** are family-friendly in every way—total seclusion in a farm setting, a swingset, a tiny fishing pond, common kitchens, and connecting rooms wrapped in a warm reception (Db-€37, Tb-€49, Qb-€61, no CC, 37150 La Croix en Touraine, from Amboise take D-31 toward Bléré and look for the sign on your left after about 4 km, tel. 02 47 57 83 64).

Le Fleuray is a positively charming small hotel and is popular with other guidebooks (Db-€74–90, CC, 10 min up river from Amboise in Cangey, tel. 02 47 56 09 25, fax 02 47 56 93 97, www.lefleurayhotel.com).

Eating in Amboise
Reasonable local eateries abound in Amboise. I like dining near the château on or near place Michel Debré: L'Amboiserie is a good value with a large selection and a pleasant upstairs terrace (7 rue Victor Hugo, tel. 02 47 39 50 40). L'Epicerie is the romantic's choice at 46 place Michel Debré (excellent €17.50 *menu*, tel. 02 47 57 08 94). Next door at #50, La Florentine is kid-friendly, with good pizza and pasta (tel. 02 47 57 49 49).

Near the pedestrian street rue Nationale, Crêperie L'Ecu is good and quiet (closed Mon, indoor/outdoor seating, 7 rue Corneille) and Le Cadran offers low-cost, low-stress pizza and grilled foods (under the arch at 14 rue Nationale, tel. 02 47 30 53 60). In any weather, La Brèche's cozy restaurant with outdoor terrace is a good value (see "Hotels," above); the walk home includes a floodlit château. On the island, across from the château, the bar Le Shaker offers scenic cocktails and outdoor tables with late-night château views. Or consider making the short drive to Chenonceaux for dinner with Laurent and Sophie at Hôtel La Roseraie (see "Sleeping and Eating in Chenonceaux," below).

Transportation Connections—Amboise
Twelve 15-minute trains per day link Amboise to the regional train hub of St. Pierre des Corps (suburban Tours). From there you'll find reasonable connections to distant points (including the TGV to Paris Montparnasse). Transferring in Paris can be the fastest way to reach many destinations, even in the south.

By train to: Paris (20/day, 1.5 hrs, 8/day direct to Paris Austerlitz and 12/day to Paris Montparnasse with change at St. Pierre de Corps), Sarlat (4/day, 6 hrs, change at St. Pierre des Corps then TGV to Libourne or Bordeaux St. Jean, then train through Bordeaux vineyards to Sarlat), Limoges (near Oradour-sur-Glane, 9/day, 4 hrs, change at St. Pierre des Corps and Vierzon or at Les Aubrais-Orleans and Vierzon, then tricky bus connection from Limoges to Oradour-sur-Glane), Pontorson-Mont St. Michel (4/day, 7 hrs, changes at Tours main station, Caen, then bus from Pontorson; or 8 hrs with changes at St. Pierre des Corps, Paris Montparnasse, then bus from Rennes), Bayeux (9/day, 5–6 hrs, changes in Caen and Tours, or at Paris Montparnasse and St. Pierre des Corps).

Châteaux Northeast of Tours

Either Amboise (above) or Chenonceaux (below) make a good home base for exploring these châteaus.

▲▲▲**Chenonceau** (shuh-non-so)—The toast of the Loire, this 15th-century Renaissance palace arches gracefully over the Cher River. One look and you know it was designed by women: The original builder's wife designed the part of the château that parallels the river; Diane de Poitiers, mistress of Henry II, added an arched bridge across the river. She enjoyed her lovely retreat until Henry died (pierced in a jousting tournament on rue St. Antoine in Paris' Marais district) and his vengeful wife, Catherine de Médici, unceremoniously kicked her out (and into the château of Chaumont). Catherine added the three-story structure on Diane's bridge. She died before completing her vision of a matching château on the far side of the river, but not before turning Chenonceau into the local aristocracy's place to see and be seen. This castle marked the border between free and Nazi France in World War II. Dramatic prisoner swaps took place here. Chenonceau is self-tourable (pick up the English translation), with piped-in classical music, glorious gardens, and uninspired summertime sound-and-light shows (château entry-€7.75, skip the €1.50 Musée de Cires—wax museum, sound-and-light show-€7.75, mid-March–mid-Sept daily 09:00–19:00, early closing off-season, tel. 02 47 23 90 07). Just to confuse proofreaders, Chenonceau is the name of the château, Chenonceaux the name of the town (pronounced the same).

There are three trains per day from Tours and one bus per day from Amboise (departs Amboise at 10:54, departs Chenonceaux at 12:40, allowing 90-min visit of château). To beat the crowds, arrive at 08:45 or after 17:30 and plan on a 15-minute walk from the parking lot to the château. The **TI** is on the main road from Amboise as you enter the village (tel. 02 47 23 94 45). You can taste the wine from Chenonceaux's vineyards for €1.50; look for signs in the parking lot.

Sleeping and Eating in Chenonceaux: If you prefer a quiet village and have a car, set up in sleepy little Chenonceaux (zip code: 37150). **Hostel du Roy**** is a bargain, with simple, comfortable rooms, a quiet garden courtyard, and a basic restaurant (Db-€35–40, Tb/Qb-€40–49, CC, 9 rue Dr. Bretonneau, 5-min walk to château, tel. 02 47 23 90 17, fax 02 47 23 89 81, www.hostelduroy.com, Nathalie SE). **Hôtel La Roseraie***** is a wonderful place. While English-speaking Laurent and Sophie spoil you, their delightfully decorated, country-classy rooms will enchant you (Db-€44–84, a few grand family rooms-€73–114, CC, free parking, heated pool, rental bikes, and a wood-beamed dining room where I dress up and splurge for a great dinner—€16/€21/€29 *menus*, located dead center on main drag at 7 rue Dr. Bretonneau, hard-to-read sign, tel. 02 47 23 90 09, fax 02 47 23 91 59, www.charminghotel.com).

Relais Chenonceaux***, across from Hôtel La Roseraie, pales in comparison but has modern, wood-finished rooms and a flowery patio (Db-€46–64, Tb-€63–72, Qb-€76, CC, tel. 02 47 23 98 11, fax 02 47 23 84 07, www.chenonceaux.com). **Au Gateau de Breton** is a friendly, reasonable, and good restaurant for lunch or dinner (closed Tue–Wed, 16 rue Dr. Bretonneau, tel. 02 47 23 90 14).

▲▲**Blois** (pron. blah)—With quick access to Chambord (bus or car, see "Getting around the Loire Valley," above), a fresh coat of paint, dolled-up pedestrian areas, and a dynamite château, Blois is a good urban stop in this mostly rural region. The **Château Royal** is in the city center, with no nearby forest, river, or lake. It's an easy walk from the train station, near ample underground parking, and just above the TI. Pick up an English brochure and read the English room display signs at this well-orchestrated castle. This château was home to Louis XII and François I, and is where Catherine de Médici spent her last night. Begin in the courtyard where four different wings, ranging from Gothic to classical, surround you and underscore the importance of this château over many centuries. Your visit to the château's interior begins in the dazzling Hall of the Estates General and continues to a great display of gargoyles, models, and other odds and ends in a small lapidary museum, up through several gorgeously tiled and decorated royal rooms, and ends in a fine arts museum with a 16th-century who's who portrait gallery and interesting ironworks room (château entry-€6, combo-ticket with sound-and-light show-€11, April–Sept daily 09:00–18:00, until 19:00 July–Aug, Oct–March 09:00–12:30, 14:00–17:30, occasional tours in English, sound-and-light show many evenings April–Sept).

The **TI** is just below the château (April–Sept daily 09:00–19:00, Oct–March Mon–Sat 09:00–12:30, 14:00–18:00, Sun 09:30–12:30, 3 avenue Jean Laigret, tel. 02 54 90 41 41). Save time to explore the city center using the TI's handy walking-tour brochure; the brown and purple routes are best.

▲▲▲**Chambord** (sham-bor)—With 440 rooms and 365 fireplaces, this place is big. Surrounded by Europe's largest enclosed forest park, teeming with wild deer and boar, it began as a simple hunting lodge for bored Blois counts. François I, using 1,800 workmen over 15 years, made a few modest additions and created this "weekend retreat" (you'll find his signature salamander everywhere). Highlights are the huge double-spiral staircase designed by Leonardo da Vinci, second-floor vaulted ceilings, enormous towers on all corners, a pincushion roof of spires and chimneys, and a 33-meter (107-foot) lantern supported by flying buttresses. To see what happens when you put 365 fireplaces in your house, wander through the forest of spires on the rooftop (fine views). Only 80 of its rooms are open to the public—and that's plenty. Focus on the well-furnished first floor (ground level and second floors have bare rooms featuring "the hunt"). This château requires good information to make it come alive. The brochure is useless. Better options are the free 30-minute tour (check times at entry, longer tours usually at 12:30—€3.80) or rent the €3.80 audioguide (second earphone-€1.50). Because most rooms are unfurnished, some travelers are content simply seeing this château from the outside (€6.40, April–Sept daily 09:30–18:15, until 19:15 in summer, off-season closes at 17:15, tel. 02 54 50 40 00). From April through September, many evening visits to the château (21:30–24:00) are accompanied by music and mood lighting (€12.50, or €14 for a day-and-night ticket). Also look for horse-riding demonstrations (€7, June–Sept daily, mid-morning, tel. 02 54 20 31 01, www.chambord-horse-show.fr).

Chambord's **TI**, next to the souvenir shops, has information on bike rentals and *chambres d'hôte* (tel. 02 54 20 34 86). One daily 40-minute bus connects Chambord with Blois' train station on weekdays, but the Blois excursion bus is better (€10, departs Blois at 09:10 and 13:20; for more info, see "Getting around the Loire Valley," above).

Sleeping in Chambord: To wake up with Chambord out your window, try **Hôtel du Grand St-Michel****. It comes with Old World hunting-lodge charm, an elegant dining room (*menus* for €16 and €21), and a chance to roam the château grounds after the peasants are run out (Db-€47, big Db with view of château-€70, worth the extra cost, extra person-€11.50, CC, 41250 Chambord, tel. 02 54 20 31 31, fax 02 54 20 36 40).

▲▲▲**Cheverny** (sheh-vayr-nee)—The most lavish furnishings of all the Loire châteaux decorate this stately hunting palace. Those who complain that the Loire châteaux have stark and barren interiors missed Cheverny. This château was built in 1634 and has been owned by the same family ever since. Family pride shows in its flawless preservation and intimate feel. The viscount's family still lives on the third floor—you'll see some family photos. Cheverny was spared by the French Revolution; the owners were popular then, as today, even among the village farmers. Barking dogs remind visitors that the viscount still loves to hunt. The kennel (200 meters in front of the château) is especially interesting at dinnertime when the 70 hounds are fed (April–Nov at 17:00, Dec–March at 15:00). The dogs—half English foxhound and half French bloodhound or *Poitevin*—are fed by trainers who know each dog by name (they all look the same to me). If a dog misbehaves, it gets an immediate cold bath. The trophy room next door bristles with 2,000 stag antlers (€5.50, pick up English self-guided tour brochure at château, not where you buy your ticket; June–mid-Sept daily 09:15–18:30, mid-Sept–May daily 09:30–12:00, 14:15–17:00, tel. 02 54 79 96 29).

Cheverny village has a small grocery and several cafés.

The town is easy to reach from Blois by excursion bus (see "Getting around the Loire Valley," above).

Fougères sur Bièvre (foo-zher soor bee-eh-vruh)—This feudal castle is worth a look even if you don't go inside. Located a few minutes from Cheverny on the way to Chenonceaux and Amboise, it's right in the village (constructed for defense, not hunting) and was built over the small river (unlimited water supply during sieges). It has been completely renovated, and, while there are no furnishings, you'll see models of castle-construction techniques. Contemplate the impressive roof structure, gaze through loop holes, stand over drop holes in the main tower (hot oil, anyone?), and ponder two medieval latrines demonstrating how little toilet technology has changed in 800 years. Posters throughout (French only) describe modern renovation techniques (€4, April–Sept daily 09:30–12:00, 14:00–18:00, Oct–March closes at 16:30, helpful English handout).

▲▲**Chaumont-sur-Loire** (show-mon-soor-lwahr) **and the Festival of Gardens**—Chaumont's first priority was defense; a castle has been here since the 900s (you'll appreciate its strategic location on the long climb up). Today's château offers an asymmetrical mix of Gothic and Renaissance architecture, well-furnished rooms, and good views. Built mostly in the 15th and 16th centuries, this place was force-swapped by Catherine de Médici for Diane de Poitier's Chenonceau; you'll see tidbits about both women inside. Louis XVI, Marie Antoinette, Voltaire, and Benjamin Franklin all spent time here. The chest in room 7 weighs over 1,000 pounds, and the floor tiles in room 9 are dazzling. Back outside, the fancy royal horse houses (*écuries*) are worthwhile for first timers. From mid-June to mid-October, the *Festival des Jardins*—Festival of Gardens—is a gardener's dream (you'll find it across the small footbridge). The superb displays vary each year according to theme (€5 château only, €7 with stables, add €2.50 for Festival of Gardens, daily March–Sept 09:30–18:00, Oct–Feb 10:00–16:30, English handout available, tel. 02 54 51 26 26).

Loches and Valancay (lohsh, vah-lahn-say)—Overlooked Loches, located about 30 minutes south of Amboise, would be my choice for the best Loire home base, were it more central. This pretty town sits on the region's loveliest river, the Indre, and offers an appealing mix of medieval monuments, stroll-worthy streets, and fewer tourists. The castle dominates the skyline and is worth a short visit (good views, sound-and-light shows in summer). The Wednesday street market is small but lively. **Hôtel George Sand***** is right on the river with a well-respected restaurant, an idyllic terrace, and rustically comfortable rooms (Db-€47–70, a few large Db-€110, CC, no elevator, 300 meters south of TI at 39 rue Quintefol, tel. 02 47 59 39 74, fax 02 47 91 55 75).

The nearby Renaissance château of **Valancay** is a massive, lavishly furnished structure with echoes of Talleyrand (Napoleon's prime minister), lovely gardens, and many kid-friendly summer events such as fencing demonstrations (€6, March–Nov daily 09:30–18:00, until 19:30 in summer, closed Dec–Feb, audioguide available, tel. 02 54 00 10 66).

CHINON

This pleasing town straddles the Vienne River and hides its ancient cobbles under a historic castle. Chinon (shee-non) is best known today for its popular red wines (tasting opportunities abound), but for us it makes the best home base for seeing the sights west of Tours: Azay le Rideau, Villandry, Langeais, Ussè, and the Abbey of Fontevraud.

Everything of interest to travelers is between the château and the river. The **TI** has bike rentals, *chambres d'hôte* listings, wine-tasting details, and a handy English-language self-guided tour of the town (May–Sept daily 9:00–19:00, Oct–April Mon–Sat 10:00–12:00, 14:00–18:00, in village center on place Hofhein, tel. 02 47 93 17 85).

Bike Rental: Rent bikes at Agnes Sorel Hôtel (helpful owners suggest routes, 4 quai Pasteur, tel. 02 47 93 04 37).

Sights—Chinon

▲▲**Château de Chinon**—Don't underestimate this crumbled castle, especially if you're looking for a stark medieval comparison to châteaux of the lavish hunting-lodge variety. Henry II and Eleanor of Aquitaine loved this castle, and it was here that Joan of Arc first encouraged Charles VII to take the throne. It's a steep walk up from the town of Chinon, but the views are sensational. What remains of this 12th-century castle is well-presented in English by tour-on-your-own pamphlets or, better, on unusually good live tours (6/day in summer, 4/day in winter, free with ticket, call for hours). Start in the "exposition room" with a short, automated history of the château (every other show presented in English) and end at the impressive *donjon* (keep) housing a three-floor museum about Joan of Arc. For information broadcast on a loudspeaker in English, press the English button by the door at the exit of each room. Enjoy the stunning views from the top (€4.50, mid-March–Oct daily 09:00–19:00, Nov–mid-March 09:00–12:00, 14:00–17:30, tel. 02 47 93 13 45).

Sleeping and Eating in Chinon
(€1.10 = about $1, country code: 33, zip code: 37500)
Hotels are a good value in Chinon. If you sleep here, walk out to the river after dark for a floodlit view of the castle walls.

Hôtel Diderot**, an appealing 18th-century manor house on the eastern edge of town, offers comfortable rooms surrounding a peaceful courtyard. Ground-floor rooms on the courtyard are a bit dark but have private patios. There are a few good family rooms (Sb-€41–52, Db-€49–64, extra bed-€13, CC, 4 rue Buffon, tel. 02 47 93 18 87, fax 02 47 93 37 10, e-mail: hoteldiderot@wanadoo.fr, friendly Rachel and Laurent speak enough English).

Hôtel Agnes Sorel, a 10-minute walk west of the TI, is intimate and cozy with welcoming owners (Stephane and Catherine) and 10 traditionally furnished rooms, a few with river views and four rooms in an annex surrounding a flowery courtyard (Db-€43–69, Db suite-€92, T/Qb suite-€107, CC, rental bikes, 4 quai Pasteur, tel. 02 47 93 04 37, fax 02 47 93 06 37).

The central **Hôtel le Jeanne d'Arc**, with clean linoleum rooms above a café, is this town's budget value with no stars, no fluff, lots of stairs, and an owner with an attitude (Sb-€27, Db-€30–34, CC, 11 rue Voltaire, tel. 02 47 93 02 85, fax 02 47 98 43 72).

Eating: The **Crêperie du Grand Carroi** makes great crêpes at reasonable prices (closed Tue, just off pedestrian rue Voltaire at 30 rue du Grand Carroi). **Les Années 30** is my favorite restaurant in town (€21 *menus*, 78 rue Voltaire, tel. 02 47 93 37 18). For an incredible experience and a meal you won't soon forget, drive 15 minutes to Villandry and dine at the farmhouse **Etape Gourmande**. Have your hotel reserve for you (75–115F *menus*, daily 12:00–15:00, 19:30–21:30, closed mid-Nov–mid-March, Domaine de la Giraudiere, 1 km from château toward Druye, call to reserve, tel. 02 47 50 08 60).

Châteaux West of Tours
▲**Azay le Rideau** (ah-zay luh ree-doh)—Most famous for its romantic reflecting-pond setting, serene Azay le Rideau sits in a beautiful park with an interior that is far more interesting if you rent the €4.50 audioguide (€5.50 entry, April–Sept daily 09:00–18:00, until 19:00 in summer, imaginative €9.90 sound-and-light show May–late Sept, Nov–March 9:00–12:30, 14:00–17:30, tel. 02 47 45 42 04).

The delightful town center may convince you to set up here. If you do, **Hôtel Biencourt**** is ideal, near the château and a very good value with light, airy rooms in a restored convent (Ds-€34, Db-€43–52, extra bed-€8, CC, 7 rue de Balzac, 37190 Azay le Rideau, tel. 02 47 45 20 75, fax 02 47 45 91 73, friendly Isabelle SE). For dinner, **La Ridelloise** is small, modest, and a good value (*menus* from €12, 36 rue Nationale, tel. 02 47 45 63 53). Azay's **TI** is behind Hôtel Le Grand Monarque on place l'Europe (April–Oct daily 09:00–13:00, 14:00–18:00, Nov–March Tue–Sat 14:00–18:00, tel. 02 57 45 44 40).

▲▲**Langeais** (lahn-zhay)—This epitome of a medieval castle, complete with a moat, drawbridge, lavish defenses, and turrets, is elegantly furnished and has basic English descriptions in each room. Langeais, which provides a good feudal contrast to the other, more playful châteaux, is the area's fourth-most-interesting castle after Chenonceau, Chambord, and Cheverny (€6, April–Oct daily 09:00–18:30, until 21:00 in summer, Nov–March closes 12:00–14:00 and at 17:00, tel. 02 47 96 72 60, frequent train service from Tours).

▲**Villandry** (▲▲▲ for gardeners, vee-lahn-dree)—This otherwise mediocre castle has the region's best gardens, immaculately maintained and arranged in elaborate geometric patterns; the garden overlook behind the château is terrific. Skip the château interior but don't miss the fine *Four Seasons of Villandry* slide show (€7, €5.25 for gardens, Easter–Sept daily 09:00–19:00, Oct–Easter closes at 17:30, tel. 02 47 50 02 09).

Ussè (oos-seh)—This château, famous as the "*Sleeping Beauty* castle," is worth a quick photo stop for its fairy-tale turrets and gardens, but don't bother touring it. The best view, with reflections and a golden-slipper picnic spot, is from just across the bridge.

▲**Abbaye de Fontevraud** (fohn-tuh-vroh)—Located 15 minutes west of Chinon, this well-presented 12th-century abbey housed nuns and monks and was run by powerful women. The tombs of Henry II, Eleanor of Aquitaine, and Richard the Lionhearted are in the austerely beautiful church. Don't miss the one-of-a-kind medieval kitchen (€5.50, June–mid Sept daily 09:00–19:00, mid Sept–May 09:30–12:00, 14:00–18:00, 5 tours/day in English, or tour it alone using the informative handout, tel. 02 41 51 71 41).

DORDOGNE

The Dordogne River Valley is a dreamy blend of natural and man-made beauty. Walnut orchards, tobacco fields, dense forests, and canoes line the river while hundreds of stone fortresses stand guard on cliffs above, a testament to this region's importance in the Middle Ages. During the brutal Hundred Years' War, this lazy river separated Britain and France. Today's Dordogne carries more tourists than goods and struggles to manage its popularity with British and Dutch tourists.

The joys of the region include rock-sculpted villages, fertile farms surrounding I-could-retire-here cottages, film-gobbling vistas, relaxed canoe rides, and a local cuisine worth loosening your belt for. The Dordogne's most thrilling sights are its caves, decorated with prehistoric artwork. The cave of Font-de-Gaume has the greatest ancient cave paintings still open to the public (15,000 years old).

To explore this beautiful river valley, sleep in or near Beynac if you have a car and in Sarlat if you don't. If you're visiting in summer, consider splurging for a rare air-conditioned room.

Planning Your Time

You'll need a minimum of a day and a half to explore this magnificent region. Your sightseeing obligations are prehistoric cave art, the Dordogne River Valley, the town of Sarlat, and, if you have a bit more time, the Lot River Valley (best done when heading to or from the south). You'll want a full roll of film for the riverfront villages and medieval castles, and a waterproof camera for your canoe trip. Call well in advance to reserve a ticket to the cave art at Grotte de Font-de-Gaume or ask your hotel for help when you reserve your room (see below under

"Sights—Cro-Magnon Caves in the Dordogne Region").
This area is inundated with tourists in August.

For drivers: A good (but tiring) driving day might go something like this: Morning and lunch in Sarlat, 13:00-Cave tour, 15:00-Two-hour canoe trip, 17:30-Tour Beynac castle with river view, 19:00-Walk behind the castle to the goose farm, 20:30-Dine. This also works well with a cave tour as the first or last stop of the day. For part or most of a second day, explore the twisting alleys in Beynac and La Roque-Gageac, tour the castle at Castlenaud, or drive the lesser-traveled Vézère River connecting Les Eyzies, La Roque St. Christophe, and the Lascaux II cave at Montignac (canoes available on the Vézère). With a third day and a car, head upriver to explore Rocamadour, Gouffre de Padirac, and storybook villages such as Carennac and Loubressac.

As you drive in or out the day before or after (connecting the Dordogne with the Loire and Carcassonne), break the long drives with stops in Oradour-sur-Glane to the north (the A-20 autoroute from Soulliac is currently free and provides quick access to Oradour and the Loire Valley), and by all means cruise the Lot Valley on your way south (from Cahors to Cajarc).

For train travelers: A good day for train travelers based in Sarlat: Morning train to Les Eyzies, see Font-de-Gaume caves, train or taxi back to Sarlat and arrange an afternoon canoe trip (pickup possible in Sarlat) or hire a taxi for an all- or part-day excursion (see "Getting around the Dordogne," below). With good preparation, train travelers can fit in more stops (see "Transportation Connections—Sarlat," below).

Getting around the Dordogne

This region is a joy with a car but tough without. You could rent a car or a bike (in Sarlat or Les Eyzies), hire an all-day taxi service (see below), or get to Beynac and toss your itinerary into the Dordogne.

By Bike or Moped: Bikers find the Dordogne scenic but awfully hilly, with crowded roads. Consider a moped, if you dare. Rent bikes and mopeds in Sarlat at Peugeot Cycles (36 avenue Thiers, tel. 05 53 28 51 87, fax 05 53 28 50 08) or at Budget Car rental (listed below). A scenic Dordogne Valley loop ride is described in "Sights—Along the Dordogne River," below.

By Train: Train service is sparse. Trains run from Sarlat almost to the Font-de-Gaume caves in Les Eyzies (transfer in Le Buisson), but leave you in Les Eyzies for four hours (which is about right for visiting the museum and Font-de-Gaume caves, bike rental available in Les Eyzies). You'll probably find the caves in Cougnac more accessible (5-min taxi from Gourdon which is on the Brive-Toulouse line).

By Car: In Sarlat, you can rent a car at **Europcar** (le Pontet, place de la Lattre de Tassigny, tel. 05 53 30 30 40, fax 05 53 31 10 39) or **Budget** (Centre Commercial du Pontet, tel. 05 53 28 10 21, fax 05 53 28 10 92).

By Custom Taxi/Minivan Excursions: These taxi services offer customized tours (split the cost with up to 7 travelers, find partners at your hotel): Friendly Philippe, owner of **Allo-Taxi Philippe** likes Americans, speaks English, and has a new vehicle with leather interior and raised seats for better viewing. He will custom design your tour, help with cave reservations, and give running commentary on his region during your excursion. Many pickup locations are possible, including Bordeaux's airport and remote train stations (€25 per hour for up to 7, tel. 05 53 59 39 65, cellular 06 08 57 30 10, e-mail: allophilippetaxi@orange.fr). **Allo Sarlat Taxi** is another taxi service that does excursions (tel. 05 53 59 02 43, cellular 06 80 08 65 05). For taxi service from Sarlat to Beynac or La Roque-Gageac, allow €15 (€22 at night); from Sarlat to Les Eyzies allow €26 (€38 at night and on Sun).

Cuisine Scene—Dordogne River Valley

Gourmets flock to this area for its geese, ducks, and wild mushrooms. The geese produce (involuntarily) the region's famous *foie gras* (they're force-fed, denied exercise, and slaughtered for their livers). *Foie gras* tastes like butter and costs like gold. The duck specialty is *confit de canard* (duck meat preserved in its own fat—sounds terrible but tastes great). *Pommes Sarladaise* are mouthwatering, thinly sliced potatoes fried in duck fat and commonly served with *confit de canard*. Wild truffles are dirty black mushrooms that farmers traditionally locate with sniffing pigs and then charge a fortune for (€457 per kilo, $190 per pound). Native cheeses are Cabécou (a silver-dollar-sized, pungent, nutty-flavored goat cheese) and Echourgnac (made by local Trappist monks). You'll find walnuts (*noix*) in salads, cakes, and liqueurs. Wines to sample are Bergerac (red and white) and Cahors (a full-bodied red). The *vin de noix* (sweet walnut liqueur) is perfect before dinner.

Dordogne Market Days

Market day is a major event in this cuisine-rich area and should be high among your priorities. Try to visit at least one of these markets (they end at 12:00).

Sunday:	St. Cyprien (good market, 5 min west of Beynac)
Monday:	Les Eyzies (near Grotte de Font-de-Gaume)
Tuesday:	Cenac (canoe float begins here), Le Bugue (great market, 20 min west of Beynac)
Wednesday:	Sarlat (bustling market)
Thursday:	Domme
Friday:	Le Buisson (transfer point to Les Eyzies), Souillac (transfer point to Cahors, Carcassonne)
Saturday:	Sarlat, Cahors (both are worthwhile)

SARLAT

Sarlat (sar-lah) is a pedestrian-friendly banquet of a town, scenically set amid forested hills. There are no blockbuster sights here, just a seductive tangle of cobblestone alleys peppered with beautiful buildings and *foie gras* stores (geese hate Sarlat). The town is just the right size: Large enough to have a theater with four screens and small enough so that everything is an easy stroll from the town center. Sarlat has been a haven for writers and artists throughout the centuries and remains so today.

Orientation

Rue de la République slices like an arrow through the circular old town. Sarlat's smaller half has few shops and many quiet lanes; all of the action lies east of rue de République. Get lost.

Tourist Information: The cramped, English-speaking TI, in the center on place de la Liberté, has free maps of the city and region, *chambres d'hôte* listings, and the useful *Guide Pratique* booklet, which lists bus and train schedules as well as car, bike, and canoe rentals (April–Nov Mon–Sat 09:00–19:00, Sun and Dec–March daily 10:00–12:00, 14:00–18:00, tel. 05 53 31 45 45, www.sarlat-tourisme.com). Ask about occasional English walking tours (€3.80, 90 min, meet at the TI).

Arrival in Sarlat

By Car: Drivers will find this small town surprisingly busy, and parking can be a headache, particularly on market days. Try along avenue Gambetta in the north end of town or in one of the signed lots along the ring road. Be careful not to park on a market street on Tuesday or Friday nights.

By Train: Train travelers have a mostly downhill 20-minute walk to the center (consider a taxi, about €6). Turn left out of the station and follow avenue de la Gare as it curves downhill, then turn right on avenue Thiers to reach the center.

Helpful Hints

Laundry: One of the two launderettes (both daily 09:00–22:00) is across from the recommended Hôtel Couleverine (self-serve or leave and pick up); the other is at 74 avenue de Selves, near recommended Hôtel de Selves.

Bike Rental: see "Getting Around the Dordogne," above.

Sights—Sarlat

▲▲**Stroll through Sarlat**—The helpful three-panel *City of Sarlat* brochure (€4, on sale at many shops and the TI) gives an informative walking tour of the city. As you stroll the curving alleys and diagonal streets and appreciate its many historic buildings, remember Sarlat is a medieval town at its

base. Merchants renovated their homes in the style that was
fashionable at the time, which in Sarlat's case was often Renaissance. For evidence of Renaissance renovations, look for
rectangular windows and grand stairways in courtyards. People
unable to afford home renovations kept their Gothic gables
and spiral stairways.

Start by exploring the musty **cathedral** that began as an
abbey and today shows an eclectic mix of styles from the 1200s
to the 1700s. Exit from the right transept. Snoop through a few
quiet courtyards and then turn left, making your way toward the
rear of the cathedral. Climb up the steps to that medieval space
capsule, the **Lantern of the Dead** (*Lanterne des Morts*). Big shots
were buried here in the Middle Ages. Exit right (with your back
to the lantern). Turn right and climb to the top of this lane for a
good look back over Sarlat. Meander back down to place de la
Liberté, ground zero for market days, and find the small square
with the bronze geese (once a bustling goose market). Remember
to save time to prowl the quiet side of town (the other side of rue
de la République).

▲**Open-Air Markets**—Outdoor markets thrive on Wednesday
morning and all day Saturday. Saturday's market is best in the
morning (produce and food vendors leave at noon) and seems
to swallow the entire town. The best market after Sarlat's is in
St. Cyprien on Sunday.

Sleeping in Sarlat
(€1.10 = about $1, country code: 33, zip code: 24200)
Sleep Code: **S** = Single, **D** = Double/Twin, **T** = Triple, **Q** = Quad,
b = bathroom, **s** = shower only, **CC** = Credit Cards accepted,
no CC = Credit Cards not accepted, **SE** = Speaks English, **NSE** =
No English, * = French hotel rating system (0–4 stars).

Even with summer crowds, Sarlat is the train traveler's best
home base. In July and August many hotels require half-pension.
The hotels below are listed in approximately the order you would
find them, starting at the upper, north end of the city on rue de
Selves. The first four hotels are in the town center.

Hôtel de la Madeleine*** is a grand place with elegant
lounges, hotelesque service, and cavernous, air-conditioned rooms
(Sb-€56–68, Db-€63–78, Tb-€88, Qb-€100, garage parking-
€5.50, CC, elevator, at north end of ring road at 1 place de la
Petite Rigaudie, tel. 05 53 59 10 41, fax 05 53 31 03 62, e-mail:
hotel.madeleine@wanadoo.fr, SE).

Hôtel des Recollets** is popular and offers modern comfort
under heavy stone arches, with smartly decorated rooms, big beds,
and a mellow courtyard on Sarlat's quiet side (Db-€50–60, Tb-
€56–66, Qb-€72–81, no restaurant, CC, 4 rue Jean-Jacques
Rousseau, 3 blocks down rue de la République from Hôtel de la

Sarlat

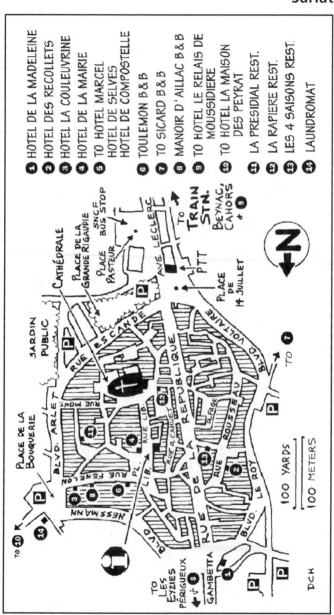

1. HOTEL DE LA MADELEINE
2. HOTEL DES RECOLLETS
3. HOTEL LA COULEUVRINE
4. HOTEL DE LA MAIRIE
5. TO HOTEL MARCEL
   HOTEL DE SELVES
   HOTEL DE COMPOSTELLE
6. TOULEMON B&B
7. TO SICARD B&B
8. MANOIR D' AILLAC B&B
9. TO HOTEL LE RELAIS DE MOUSSIDIERE
10. TO HOTEL LA MAISON DES PEYRAT
11. LA PRESIDIAL REST.
12. LA RAPIERE REST.
13. LES 4 SAISONS REST.
14. LAUNDROMAT

Madeleine, tel. 05 53 31 36 00, fax 05 53 30 32 62, www.hotel
-sarlat-recollets.com, Christophe SE).

Hôtel La Couleuvrine** has formal management but
plenty of medieval character in its somewhat faded but cozy
rooms. Families enjoy *les châmbres familles*, and a few rooms
have private terraces (Db-€42–52, Tb-€60, CC, elevator,
on ring road at 1 place de la Bouquerie, tel. 05 53 59 27 80, fax
05 53 31 26 83, www.hotels-restau-dordogne.org/couleuvrine).
Half-pension is encouraged at busy periods and in summer
(figure €67 per person for room, breakfast, and dinner, with
fine cuisine in an elegant restaurant).

Hôtel de la Mairie** plays second fiddle to its café. It's
young and basic, with big rooms right on the main square
(Ds-€34, Db-€40–45, Ts-€42–51, Qb-€65, CC, place de la
Liberté, check in at café, tel. & fax 05 53 59 05 71, SE).

The next three listings are a five-minute walk down avenue
Gambetta from Hôtel de la Madeleine.

Hôtel Marcel* is a simple souvenir of old Sarlat with a
dark, wood-beamed lobby and flowery wallpaper (Db-€38–51,
50 rue de Selves, no CC, tel. 05 53 59 21 98, fax 05 53 30 27 77).
Closer to the center, **Hôtel de Selves***** is sleek and modern,
with pastel decor surrounding a swimming pool and quiet garden
(Sb-€56–80, Db-€66–84, Db with balcony-€92, extra bed-€20,
garage-€6, CC, elevator, sauna, air-con, 93 avenue de Selves, tel.
05 53 31 50 00, fax 05 53 31 23 52, e-mail: hotel.sarlat@magic.fr).

Hôtel de Compostelle** is cheaper and less snazzy than
Hôtel de Selves but has modern rooms and a few good family
suites (Db-€52, Tb-66, Qb-€70–77, CC, elevator, 64 avenue
de Selves, tel. 05 53 59 08 53, fax 05 53 30 31 65).

Chambres d'Hôtes in Sarlat
These *chambres d'hôtes* are all great bargains, very central, and
compare well with the hotels listed.

Friendly English-speaking Pierre-Henri **Toulemon** has
three large, great-value rooms in a 17th-century home a few
blocks from the TI (Db-€35–43, €4.75 per extra person up to 5,
no CC, 4 rue Magnanat, look for big steps from northeast corner
of place de la Liberté, tel. 05 53 31 26 60, cellular 06 08 67 76
90, www.toulemon.com). The old-fashioned **Sicards** rent three
fine rooms in a newer home just off the ring road on the southeastern edge of the old town, a five-minute walk from the TI
(Sb-€27, Db-€29–32, Tb-€35, no CC, Le Pignol, rue Louis
Arlet, tel. 05 53 59 14 28, NSE). **Le Manoir d'Aillac** is friendly
and has three well-furnished rooms with a separate entry in
a very central historic building (open mid-May–mid-Sept,
Db-€40, Tb-€46, no CC, 13 rue Fenelon, tel. 05 53 59 02 63,
e-mail: josef.paulsen@wanadoo.fr, SE).

Sleeping near Sarlat

Many golden stone hotels surround Sarlat for those preferring to be close yet rural (with easy parking). **Hôtel le Relais de Moussidiere*****, five minutes below Sarlat off the road to Beynac, offers affordable luxury in a lovely setting, with a huge pool, private terraces, and an almost tropical feel (fine "standard" Db-€92–100, bigger Db-€122, CC, in Moussidiere Basse, just south of Sarlat on road to Bergerac, tel. 05 53 28 28 74, fax 05 53 28 25 11, www.chateauxhotels.com/moussidiere). **Hôtel La Maison des Peyrat**** is a cheaper, less polished refuge in a vine-strewn home with donkeys, quiet gardens, and a smashing pool, a five-minute drive above Sarlat (Db-€55–90, extra person-€15.50, optional dinner and breakfast-€21, CC, follow brown signs from eastern edge of Sarlat's ring road up through suburbs, Le Lac de la Plane, tel. 05 53 59 00 32, fax 05 53 28 56 56).

Eating in Sarlat

Sarlat is packed with good restaurants, most of which serve local specialties. For a truly fine experience in a historic building, dine inside or on the outdoor courtyard at **La Presidial** (*menu* from €17, closed Mon, rue Landry, tel. 05 53 28 92 47). **La Rapière**, opposite the cathedral, provides wood-beam coziness and fine regional cuisine (*menus* from €18, June–Sept daily, closed Sun off-season, place de la Cathedrale, tel. 05 53 59 03 13). The recommended **Hôtel La Couleuvrine** is a well-respected and elegant good bet (*menus* from €18). On the quieter side, just off rue de la République, **Les 4 Saisons** offers a good €18 *menu* (June–Sept daily, closed Wed off-season, 2 Côte de Toulouse, tel. 05 53 29 48 59). Drivers can go to Beynac or La Roque-Gageac for a beautiful setting and excellent value (see "Eating in and near Beynac," below).

Transportation Connections—Sarlat

Sarlat's TI has schedules. Soulliac and Perigueux are the train hubs for points within the greater region. For all destinations below, you can go west via the Libourne/Bordeaux line (transferring in either city depending on your connection), or east via SNCF bus to Souillac (covered by railpass). I've listed the fastest path in each case. Sarlat train info: tel. 05 53 59 00 21.

By train to: Paris (7/day, allow 6 hrs; 3/day with change in Libourne or Bordeaux St. Jean, then TGV; and 4/day via bus to Souillac then train with possible change in Brive-la-Gaillarde), **Amboise** (3/day, 5 hrs, via Libourne or Bordeaux St. Jean, then TGV to St. Pierre des Corps, then local train to Amboise), **Limoges/Oradour-sur-Glane** (difficult trip, 5/day, 3–4 hrs; 3/day via bus to Souillac and train to Limoges, then bus to Oradour; 2/day with change in Le Buisson and Perigueux), **Cahors** (5/day,

2–3 hrs, bus to Souillac, then train to Cahors), **Albi** and **Carcassonn**e (2/day in 4.5 hrs with changes in Le Buisson, Agen, and Toulouse; 3/day in 6–7 hrs via bus to Souillac then train with changes possible in Brive-la-Gaillarde and Toulouse).

To Beynac: Beynac is accessible only by taxi (€15) or bike (best rented in Sarlat).

BEYNAC

The feudal village of Beynac (bay-nak) tumbles down a steep hill from its massive castle to the river far below and sees fewer tourists than its big brother, Sarlat. You'll have the Dordogne River at your doorstep and a perfectly preserved medieval village winding like a sepia film set from the beach to the castle above. The floodlit village is always open for evening strollers. Some of the film *Chocolat* was filmed here, adding to its popularity with tourists (for another *Chocolat* setting, see also "Sights—Near Semur-en-Auxois" in Burgundy chapter).

Orientation

This vertical village climbs steeply uphill from the river to the château. Pay to park at lots on the river, way up at the castle (follow signs to Château de Beynac), or halfway between. A trail follows the river toward Castlenaud (begins across from Hôtel Bonnet), with great views back toward Beynac (ideal at night) and, for able route finders, a healthy hike to Castlenaud (1 hr).

Tourist Information: The helpful TI (Corinne SE) is at the village riverside parking lot (April–Sept daily 10:00–12:00, 14:00–18:00, closed Sun off-season, tel. & fax 05 53 29 43 08, www.perigord.tm.fr). Pick up the *Plan de Beynac* (in English) for a simple, self-guided walking tour. The post office (with ATM) is across the street.

Sights—Beynac

▲Château de Beynac—This brooding, cliff-clinging castle soars 150 meters (500 feet) above the Dordogne River. During the Hundred Years' War, the castle of Beynac housed the French, while the British set up their headquarters across the river at Castelnaud. From the condition of the castles, it looks like France won. The sparsely furnished castle is most interesting for the valley views. Tour it on your own from 12:15 to 13:45; otherwise you must go with a free French-speaking guide. Pick up the English translation (€6, mid-March–mid-Nov, tours 10:00– 18:00, July–Aug last tour begins at 18:00, tel. 05 53 29 50 40).

River Cruise Trips—Boats leave from Beynac's riverside parking lot and give a mildly interesting, relaxing 50-minute cruise of the Dordogne with English explanations (€6, about every 30 min from 10:00–18:00, Easter–Oct, tel. 05 53 28 51 15).

Heart of the Dordogne

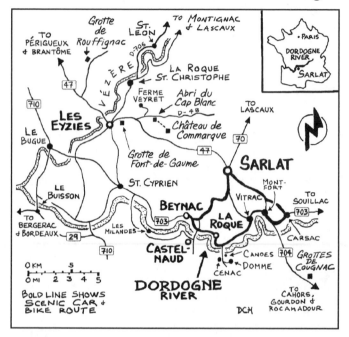

Foie Gras in the Making—You can witness (evenings only) the force-feeding of geese (*la gavage*) at many places. Look for *gavage* signs but beware: You are expected to buy and locals know that Americans are squeamish. Friendly Madame Gauthier's farm offers a peek at the *gavage* and is down the road behind Château de Beynac (park there or walk 10 min from château through parking lot and away from river—you'll see signs, demonstrations 18:00–19:30, tel. 05 53 29 51 45).

Sleeping in Beynac
(€1.10 = about $1, country code: 33, zip code: 24220)
Those with a car should sleep in or near Beynac. With hotel pickup services and taxis, even those without a car may find Beynac worth the trouble. The tiny Beynac TI posts a listing on its door of all accommodations with prices and current availability. You must pay to park in the riverfront lot between 10:00 and 19:00. Leave nothing in your car at night as theft is a problem.

Hôtel Bonnet**, on the eastern edge of town, offers reasonable comfort, river views from many of rooms (some noise, though windows are double paned), a peaceful backyard garden, and a well-respected restaurant that feels like a hunting lodge (Db-€47–56, Tb-€58, free parking or €3 in their garage, CC, tel. 05 53 29 50 01, fax 05 53 29 83 74, e-mail: hbonnet@free.fr).

Hôtel du Château** is dead center with many amenities, including a pool, bar, and terrace café, and has big plans to renovate its 18 run-down rooms (Db-€43, extra person-€9, CC, tel. 05 53 29 50 13, fax 05 53 28 53 05, www.hotel -restaurant-du-chateau.com).

The restaurant Hostellerie Malleville, next door to Hôtel du Chateau, offers 12 quiet, cozy rooms in an annex up the street at their **Hôtel Pontet**** (Db-€43, Tb-€53, Qb-€57, CC, includes use of pool at their other hotel in nearby Vézac, check in at Hostellerie Malleville, tel. 05 53 29 50 06, fax 05 53 28 28 52).

Le Café de la Rivière, just above Hostellerie Malleville, has two airy and pleasant rooms and even more pleasant owners, Hamish and Xinthe (British ex-pats). The rooms are next to a garden café and have river views and some road noise through the double-paned windows (Db-€46–53, no CC, tel. 05 53 28 35 49, e-mail: hamish.xinthe@wanadoo.fr).

Chambres Residence Versailles sits above, and does the name justice with immaculate rooms that Louis would have appreciated, laundry facilities, a quiet terrace and garden, and, best of all, the welcoming Fleurys (Db-€46, 3 rooms have fine views, includes English breakfast, no CC, Route du Château, tel. & fax 05 53 29 35 06, NSE). With the river on your right, take the small road—wedged between the hill and Hôtel Bonnet—800 meters up, turn right at the *atelier menuisier* (woodworkers' workshop), and continue 100 meters farther.

Sleeping near Beynac, in Vézac
For motellike comfort, drive two kilometers east from Beynac to Vézac and try either the more polished **Relais des 5 Châteaux**** (Db-€42–47, extra person-€12.50, CC, good restaurant, nice pool, tel. 05 53 30 30 72, fax 05 53 31 19 39, e-mail: 5chateaux @perigord.com), or the quieter and more basic **l'Oustal**, with a pool, Ping-Pong, and volleyball (Db-€47, Db-€52, Tb-€55–60, Qb-€64–69, higher-priced rooms face pool, families should ask for their loft rooms—*chambres mezzanine*, CC, 24220 Vézac, tel. 05 53 29 54 21, fax 05 53 28 28 52).

Eating in Beynac
You'll dine well in air-conditioned comfort at **Hôtel du Château** and better, for a bit more, under the wood beams of **Hôtel Bonnet** (see "Sleeping," above, for both). **Taverne des Remparts** is a good value high above the town; I can't imagine leaving Beynac without relaxing at their view-perfect café—best at night (closed Mon, CC, call to reserve, tel. 05 53 29 57 76, across from castle,

Jerome and Sophie SE). Above Hostellerie Malleville at **Le Café de la Rivière**, Hamish and Xinthe serve low-stress, less traditional food (even hamburgers) on a beautiful terrace with valley views (tel. 05 53 28 35 49). **La Petite Tonnelle** is intimate, welcoming, and reasonable (100 meters from river on road to castle, tel. 05 53 29 95 18). Beynac also offers a dreamy dinner-picnic site. Walk up the hill (easier said), pass the château, continue out of the village, and turn right at the cemetery and walk about 50 meters.

Sights—Along the Dordogne River

▲▲▲**Dordogne Valley Scenic Loop Ride or Drive**—The most scenic stretch of the Dordogne lies between Carsac and Beynac. From Sarlat, follow signs toward Cahors and Carsac, then veer right to Eglise de Carsac (visit this tiny Romanesque church if it's open). From Carsac, follow the river via Montfort, La Roque-Gageac, and Beynac. Bikers, note that the round-trip from Sarlat totals about 45 kilometers (28 miles). Less ambitious bikers will find the 30-kilometer (18-mile) loop ride from Sarlat to La Roque-Gageac to Beynac and back to Sarlat sufficient. This trip works just as well from Beynac.

▲▲**Castelnaud**—Château de Beynac's crumbling rival looks a little less mighty, but the inside packs a medieval punch. Several rooms display weaponry and artifacts from the Hundred Years' War. The courtyard comes with a 46-meter-deep well (drop a pebble) and an entertaining video showing catapults, which litter the grounds, in action. The rampart views are as unbeatable as the siege tools outside the walls are formidable. Borrow the English explanations from the ticket lady for the room-by-room story (€6, May–Sept daily 10:00–19:00, July–Aug 09:00–20:00, Oct–April 10:00–18:00, Dec–Feb closes for lunch and at 17:00, from the river it's a steep hike through a pleasant peasant village, the car park is closer, tel. 05 53 31 30 00). You can stop here halfway through your canoe trip or take a one-hour hike from Beynac along a difficult-to-follow riverside path (it hugs the river as it passes though campgrounds and farms).

▲**La Roque-Gageac**—A few minutes upriver from Beynac, La Roque (the rock), as the locals call this village, is impressively wedged between river and cliffs. This place can be busy, as road traffic and pedestrians are funneled to the riverfront road. Get off the road and find the back alleys, and for views, wander up the narrow tangle of lanes that seem to disappear into the cliffs. La Roque was once a thriving port, exporting Limousin oak to Bordeaux for wine barrels. Find the old ramp leading down to the river. Look for markers showing the water levels of three floods and ask someone about the occasional rock avalanches from above. The sky-high **Fort Troglodyte** is a good energy-burner but offers little more than views (€4, get English explanation, daily 10:00–19:00). The small **TI** is in a parking lot at the east end of town (Easter–Sept only, daily 10:00–12:00, 14:00–18:00, tel. 05 53 29 17 01).

Sleeping in La Roque: For a small splurge, enjoy a romantic dinner and, better yet, stay overnight at the reasonable **Hôtel Belle Etoile****. It has classic decor, a cozy bar, river views from most rooms (best rooms on main floor), and a great restaurant (closed Mon). The hotel is closed from October through March (Db-€47–76, no CC, no half-pension requirement, reserve private parking ahead, 24250 La Roque-Gageac, tel. 05 53 29 51 44, fax 05 53 29 45 63, e-mail: hotel.belle-etoile@wanadoo.fr, friendly Danielle SE). The modest **Hôtel Café Tabac** sits next door with five small, clean, and cheap rooms above a local bar (Ds-€30, no CC, 3 rooms have river views, tel. 05 53 29 51 63, NSE). At the eastern edge of the village, **Hôtel Gardette**** has well-kept rooms (5 with river views), good rates, a terrace café, and a new pool planned (Ds-€30, Db-€38–46, CC, at main parking lot, 24250 La Roque-Gageac, tel. 05 53 29 51 58, fax 05 53 28 38 73, e-mail: egardette@aol.com).

Domme—The reason to climb the hill to this over-boutiqued town is for the magnificent valley view. Turn your back on the trinkets and have a view drink, or, better, stay at the splendid **Hôtel l'Esplanade***** with the best view rooms in the Dordogne and an excellent, though pricey, restaurant (Db with view-€73, Db with view and balcony-€114, extra person-€12.50, CC, air-con, 24250 Domme, tel. 05 53 28 31 41, fax 05 53 28 49 92, e-mail: esplanade.domme@wanadoo.fr). Just below, in overlooked little Cénac, **Madame Barry's La Touille Chambres** is friendly, quite comfortable, and a great value (Db-€40, Tb-€52, no CC, 24250 Cénac St. Julien, just west of Renault Garage, tel. 05 53 28 35 25, cellular 06 08 60 91 58).

▲▲▲Dordogne Canoe Trips—For a refreshing break from the car or train, explore the riverside castles and villages of the Dordogne by canoe. Several outfits rent plastic two-person canoes (and 1-person kayaks) and will pick you up at an agreed-upon spot. If Beynac is your home base, make sure the outfit allows you to get out in Beynac. For €20, two can paddle the best two-hour stretch from Cénac to Beynac (includes shuttle, call ahead to arrange if you don't have a car, in summer the usual pickup time in Beynac is 09:00). In Cénac, look for **Dordogne Randonées** (coming from Sarlat or Beynac, take the first left after crossing the bridge to Cénac, tel. 05 53 28 22 01, e-mail: randodordogne @wanadoo.fr). In La Roque-Gageac, **Canoe-Dordogne** rents canoes for the pleasant two-hour float to Château Milandes (€20, tel. 05 53 29 58 50). While you need to be in decent shape for the longer trips, it's OK if you're a complete novice—the only white-water you'll encounter will be your partner frothing at the views.

You'll get a life vest and, for a few extra euros, a watertight bucket. Beach your boat wherever you want to take a break. The best two stops are the village of La Roque-Gageac and the castle at Castelnaud.

Cro-Magnon Caves in the Dordogne Region

There are four caves in this region with original cave paintings that tourists can still admire: the top-quality Grotte de Font-de-Gaume (tours in English offered only in summer); the immense Grotte de Rouffignac; the smaller yet interesting Grotte de Cougnac (some tours in English, fewer crowds); and the well-organized and impressive Grotte du Pech Merle (some English tours; listed under "Sights—Southeast of the Dordogne," below). Train travelers may find the Grottes de Cougnac most accessible (see below). Dress warmly for any cave visit, even if it's hot outside.

The first four cave sights—Grotte de Font-de-Gaume, Grotte de Rouffignac, Roque St. Cristophe, and Abri du Cap-Blanc—are within a 20-minute drive of Les Eyzies. The last two sights—Lascaux and Grotte de Cougnac—are a 30-minute drive from Sarlat (in opposite directions).

Les Eyzies-de-Tayac—This town is the overrun touristy hub of this cluster of historic caves, castles, and rivers and only merits a stop for its museum (see below). The **TI** rents bikes (July–Aug Mon–Sat 09:00–19:00, Sun 10:00–12:00, 14:00–18:00, otherwise Mon–Sat 09:00–12:00, 14:00–18:00, Sun 10:00–12:00, 14:00–17:00, tel. 05 53 06 97 05, fax 05 53 06 90 79). The train station is a level 500 meters from the center (turn right out of the station).

National Museum of Prehistory—This museum makes a good first stop in your prehistory lesson. Appropriately located on a cliff ledge (across from TI), it has four small rooms with good English explanations. Among its many prehistoric artifacts are everyday tools, impressively sculpted clay bison, and a variety of human and animal skeletons dating from 50,000 B.C. (€4.50, July–Aug daily 09:30–19:00, mid-March–June and Sept–mid-Nov Wed–Mon 09:30–12:00, 14:00–18:00, closes Tue except July–Aug and at 17:00 mid-Nov–mid-March).

Sleeping near Les Eyzies: Just 10 minutes by car from Les Eyzies, the remote hilltop farm at **Ferme Veyret** is as real as it gets. Mama greets you with a huge smile and nary a word of English, son cooks, and daughter does everything else. The rooms are comfortable, spotless, and furnished like grandma's with modern conveniences like hair dryers. You'll be expected to dine here, and you'd be a fool not to, as dinner includes everything from *apéritif* to *digestif*, with five courses in-between and wine throughout (Db-€41 per person, includes breakfast and dinner, big pool, cows, pigs, en route to Abri du Cap-Blanc, look for yellow signs, 24620 Les Eyzies de Tayac, tel. 05 53 29 68 44, fax 05 53 31 58 28).

The Dordogne Region

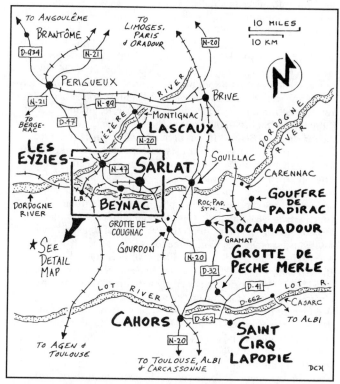

Caves near Les Eyzies-de-Tayac

▲▲▲**Grotte de Font-de-Gaume**—Even if you're not a connoisseur of Cro-Magnon art, you'll dig this cave. It's the last cave in Europe with prehistoric (polychrome) painting still open to the public, and its turnstile days are numbered. On a carefully guided and controlled 100-meter walk, you'll see about 20 red-and-black bison—often in elegant motion—painted with a moving sensitivity. Your guide—with a laser pointer and great reverence—will trace the faded outline of the bison and explain how 15,000 years ago, cave dwellers used local minerals and the rock's natural contour to give the paintings dimension. The paintings were discovered by the village schoolteacher in 1901. Tickets are now limited to 200 a day, since heavy-breathing tourist hordes damage the art by raising and lowering the temperature and humidity levels.

Visits are by appointment only. Reserve in advance by phone; your hotel can make the call. Summertime spots are booked a month in advance. Even off-season, it's smart to call ahead and get a time. Request an English tour (usually summers only) and arrive 30 minutes early or lose your spot. You'll find it interesting even in French, but ask for the English brochure and read through the books in the gift shop before you go (€5.50, Thu–Tue 09:00–12:00, 14:00–17:30, closed Wed and at 17:00 Nov–Feb, no photography or large bags, tel. 05 53 06 86 00, fax 05 53 35 26 18). Drivers who can't get a spot here (or who want to see completely different caves) should try the caves at Rouffignac (see below) or aim for the more remote Grotte du Pech Merle, an hour east of Cahors (see "Sights—Southeast of the Dordogne," below).

▲**Abri du Cap-Blanc**—In this prehistoric cave (just up the road from Font-de-Gaume), early artists used the rock's natural contours to add dimension to their sculpture. The small museum, with English explanations, will prepare you, and the useful English handout will guide you. Look for places where the artists smoothed or roughed the surfaces to add depth. In this single stone room, your French-speaking guide will spend 30 minutes explaining 14,000-year-old carvings. Impressive as these carvings are, their subtle majesty bypasses some. Free tours leave on the half hour (€4.75, July–Aug Wed–Mon 09:30–19:00, April–Oct Wed–Mon 10:00–12:00, 14:00–18:00, closed on Tue and Nov–March, tel. 05 53 29 21 74). The sight is well-signed, three kilometers after Grotte de Font-de-Gaume on the road to Sarlat.

▲▲**Grotte de Rouffignac**—This is the second-best cave in the area after Font-de-Gaume. Dress warmly; the visit lasts 70 minutes and extends one kilometer into the hillside. In this extensive cave, a French-speaking guide escorts you on a small train, stopping to point out engravings of mammoths (done with wood sticks—many of those vertical lines are prehistoric bear-claw scratches) and brilliant black paintings of rhinos, bison, horses, mammoths, and reindeer. The most interesting stop is at the end as you descend from the train into a vault of ceiling paintings (notice the original level of the floor through the end of this cave; the artists had to crawl to this place and draw while lying on their backs). The horse is amazing. The helpful guides make time to answer questions in English but lead the tour in French (€5.75, daily 10:00–11:30, 14:00–17:30, opens at 09:00 in summer July–Aug, closed Nov–March, no reservations, tours leave about every 30 min, best strategy is to arrive before opening time and take the first tour—afternoons are busier, and the summertime 14:00 lineup can be ugly, tel. 05 53 05 41 71). It's well-signed from the route between Les Eyzies and Perigueux; allow 20 minutes from Les Eyzies.

Roque St. Christophe—Like hanging gardens over the Vézère River, these extensive, cliff-hugging ledges and caves (no paintings) were inhabited from 50,000 years ago to the Middle Ages, and help paint a picture of life before written history. They'll pique your interest with their sheer size, multiple levels, and stunning setting. The €1.50 English handout is well-done and essential (€5.75, daily March–Oct 10:00–18:00, Nov–Feb 11:00–17:00, tel. 05 53 50 70 45, lots of steps, 8 km north of Les Eyzies, follow signs to Montignac, good café/snack bar). Adorable St. Leon, just north of Roque St. Christophe, makes a nice lunch or coffee stop.

▲▲**Lascaux**—The region's most famous cave paintings are at Lascaux, 22 kilometers north of Sarlat and Les Eyzies. In the interest of preservation, these caves are closed to tourists. But the adjacent Lascaux II copy caves are impressive in everything but authenticity. At Lascaux II, the reindeer, horses, and bulls of Lascaux I are painstakingly reproduced by top artists using the same dyes, tools, and techniques their predecessors did 15,000 years ago. Anyone into caveman art will appreciate the thoughtful explanations. It's worth working your schedule around English tour times (€7.75, July–Aug daily 09:30–19:00, Sept–June Tue– Sun 10:00–12:00, 14:00–17:30; call ahead for English tour times, 5 tours/day in July–Aug, on demand in off-season; from mid-April–mid Sept tickets are sold only at Montignac TI, caves 2.5 km south of Montignac, TI tel. 05 53 51 95 03). Pleasant Montignac is worth a wander.

Sleeping near Lascaux: The **Hôtel Château de Fleunie***** offers regal 15th-century château accommodations, a pool, and a restaurant (Db-€56–122, *menus* from €21, CC, 24570 Condat sur Vézère, tel. 05 53 51 32 74, fax 05 53 50 58 98, www.lafleunie.com).

▲**Grotte de Cougnac**—Located 30 kilometers south of Sarlat, this less-touristy cave is handy for drivers and accessible to train travelers. The cave offers impressive rock formations and a more intimate look at Cro-Magnon cave art. It's five kilometers north of Gourdon, just off the D-704, near the delightful town of Payrignac. Gourdon is a 15-minute train ride from Souillac (4/day) and a five-minute taxi ride from the cave (€5.25, July–Aug daily 09:00–18:00, otherwise 09:30–11:00, 14:00–17:00, English book available, 70-min tours, some in English, call ahead, tel. 05 65 41 47 54).

Sights—North of the Dordogne, near Limoges

▲▲▲**Oradour-sur-Glane**—Located two hours north of Sarlat and 25 kilometers west of Limoges, this is one of the most powerful sights in France. French schoolchildren know this town well. Most make a pilgrimage here. *La Ville Martyr*, as it is known, was machine-gunned and burned on June 10, 1944, by Nazi troops. The Nazis were either seeking revenge for the killing of one of their officers (by French resistance fighters in a neighboring village) or simply terrorizing the populace in preparation for the upcoming Allied invasion (this was 4 days after D-Day). With cool, German attention to detail, the Nazis methodically rounded up the entire population of 642 townspeople. The women and children were herded into the town church, where they were teargassed and machine-gunned. Plaques mark the place where the town's men were grouped and executed. The town was then set on fire, its victims left under a blanket of ashes. Today, the ghost town, left untouched for nearly 60 years, greets every pilgrim who enters with only one English word: Remember.

The new **underground museum** (*Centre de la Memoire*) provides a good social and political context for the event, including home videos of locals before the attack and disturbing footage of the actual event (€5.50, daily 09:00–19:00, closes at 18:00 Nov–April). Hushed visitors walk the length of Oradour's main street, past gutted, charred buildings in the shade of lush trees, to the underground memorial on the market square (rusted toys, broken crucifixes, town mementos under glass). Visit the cemetery where most lives ended on June 10, 1944, and finish at the church with its bullet-pocked altar (entry to Oradour village is free, same hours as the museum).

Public transport here is a challenge. Four daily buses connect Limoges with Oradour in 20 minutes (10-min walk from Limoges train station to bus stop on place Winston Churchill). Consider a taxi. Limoges is a stop on an alternative train route between Amboise and Sarlat.

Mortemart—With a car and extra time, visit this nontouristy village (15 min northwest of Oradour on D-675). You'll find a medieval market hall, a few cafés, and a sweet château (good picnic benches behind). **Hôtel Relais**** offers five rooms over a well-respected restaurant (Db-€46, Tb-€60, CC, *menus* from €15.50, 87330 Mortemart, tel. & fax 05 55 68 12 09).

Sights—Southeast of the Dordogne

Some find this remote, less-visited section of the Dordogne even more beautiful than the area around Sarlat. Follow the Dordogne upriver east from Souillac to explore the *charmant* villages of Martel, Carennac, Loubressac, Bretenoux, and the impressively situated château de Castelnau-Bretenoux. Just below are the Tom Sawyer–like Gouffre de Padirac and the cliff-hanging Rocamadour.

Rocamadour (▲▲ after dark)—Found one hour east of Sarlat, the dramatic rock-face setting and medieval charm of this historic pilgrimage town can be trampled by daily hordes of tourists. Those who arrive late and spend the night enjoy fewer crowds and a floodlit fantasy. Those who come only during the day might wonder why they did, as there's little to do here except to climb the steps as pilgrims did (and some still do) or cheat and take the elevator to a few churches and stare at the view. Rocamadour has three basic levels: the bottom-level pedestrian street with shops and restaurants, the chapel level 143 steps up (or €1 elevator, €2 round-trip) with a snazzy Museum of Sacred Art (€4.75, excellent English handout), and a private château at the very top (€2.50 elevator, €4 round-trip, skip the €2.30 château view). Eight hundred years ago there were even more tourists climbing these steps, as this was an important stop on the famous pilgrimage route to Santiago de Compostela in Spain. In 1244, these steps attracted a crusade-bound Saint Louis (he built Sainte-Chapelle in Paris). There are two **TIs:** the glassy TI that you come to first in l'Hospitalet (above Rocamadour) and down in La Cité Medievale on the level pedestrian street (July–Aug daily 10:00–20:00, otherwise 10:00–12:30, 14:00–18:00, tel. 05 65 33 22 00). Ask about occasional English tours of the chapels. Trains (transfer in Brive-la-Gaillarde) leave you five kilometers (3 miles) from the village (€8 taxi, tel. 05 65 33 63 10). Drivers can approach Rocamadour in two ways: They can park at the top (then walk down a series of switchbacks or take the elevator down—€4 round-trip, follow signs to *Parking Château)* or drive to the bottom (then walk or elevator up—€2 round-trip).

Sleeping in and near Rocamadour: Every hotel has a restaurant where they'd like you to dine. **Hôtel des Pelerins****, near the western end of the pedestrian street in La Cité Medievale, has immaculate, comfortable rooms; the best have balconies and face the valley (Db-€41, Db with view and balcony-€53, Tb-€56, CC, tel. 05 65 33 62 14, fax 05 65 33 72 10, www.terminus-des-pelerins.com). **Hôtel Sainte Marie**** has a privileged location 143 steps above the main pedestrian drag (take the elevator) and rumpled rooms, most with great views (D-€31, Db-€49, Tb-€53, Qb-€57, no CC, tel. 05 65 33 63 07, fax 05 65 33 69 08).

You can sleep peacefully eight kilometers (5 miles) from Rocamadour in the sublime *chambre d'hôte* **Moulin de Fresquet.** Gracious Gerard has restored an ancient mill complete with antique-furnished rooms, outdoor terraces, and a duck pond—with ducks for pets, not for dinner. If Gerard is cooking, eat here (Db-€51–67, dinner-€18, 46500 Gramat, tel. 05 65 38 70 60, cellular 06 08 85 09 21, fax 05 65 33 60 13, www.moulindefresquet.com, SE).

Idyllic little Carennac also makes a good home base for this area. Stay in the simple, friendly **Hôtel des Touristes*** (Db-€38, extra person-€7.75, no CC, tel. 05 65 10 94 31, fax 05 65 39 79 85) or the more cushy **Hôtel Fenelon**** (Db-€44–55, Tb-€56–64, CC, pool, tel. 05 65 10 96 46, fax 05 65 10 94 86).

▲▲**Gouffre de Padirac**—Twenty minutes from Rocamadour is a fascinating cave (lots of stalagmites but no cave art). Buy the cheapest English language booklet on the caves, read it while you wait in line, and you'll be well-briefed to follow the 70-minute French-language tour through this huge system of caverns. You'll ride elevators, hike along a buried stream, and even take a subterranean boat ride; dress warmly (€7.75, April–Oct daily 9:00–12:00, 14:00–18:00, long lines at 14:00; no lunch closing in July–Aug, closed Nov–March; daytrips organized from Rocamadour TI; tel. 05 65 33 64 56).

▲▲▲**Lot River Valley**—Ninety minutes south of the Dordogne, the overlooked Lot River meanders under stubborn cliffs, past idyllic villages, and through a stunningly beautiful valley. The fortified bridge at Cahors, prehistoric cave paintings at Grotte du Pech Merle, and breathtaking town of St. Cirq Lapopie are remarkable sights in this valley—each within a half hour of the others. These sights are worthwhile for drivers connecting the Dordogne with Albi or Carcassonne, or as a long daytrip from Sarlat. With extra time, spend a night in St. Cirq Lapopie (see below), and, with more time, continue upriver to Cajarc (those going to or coming from the south can scenically connect with Albi via Villefranche de Rouergue and Cordes-sur-Ciel).

Pont Valentré at Cahors—One of Europe's finest medieval monuments, this fortified bridge was built in 1308 to keep the English out of Cahors. It worked. Learn the story of the devil on the center tower. The steep trail on the noncity side leads to great views (keep climbing, avoid branch trails, be careful if trail is wet) and was once the route to Santiago de Compostela. Just past the city-side end of the bridge is Le Cèdre, a wine shop/café/souvenir stand with delightful owners; say *bonjour* to Marie-Danielle and Jean-Claude and ask to sample Cahors' black wine and *foie gras* (duck is cheaper than goose and just as tasty). They have reasonable salads and sandwiches and can ship wine to the United States. If you need an urban fix, stroll the pedestrian-friendly alleys between Cahor's cathedral and the river.

▲▲**Grotte du Pech Merle**—About 30 minutes east of Cahors, this cave with prehistoric paintings of mammoths, bison, and horses rivals the better-known ones at Grotte de Font-de-Gaume. The cave is filled with interesting stalactite and stalagmite formations. I liked the mud-preserved Cro-Magnon footprint. Call to reserve a time (English spoken). Start at the museum with a film subtitled in English, then descend to the caves. If you can't join an English tour, ask for the English translation booklet. In summer, arrive by 09:30 or call to reserve a spot (€6.75, €5.75 off-season, Easter–Oct daily 09:30–12:00, 13:30–17:00, closes earlier off-season, tel. 05 65 31 27 05, fax 05 65 31 20 47).

▲▲**St. Cirq Lapopie**—Beg, borrow, or steal a night in St. Cirq Lapopie (san sear lah-poh-pee). Clinging to a ledge 180 meters (600 feet) above the Lot River, this spectacularly situated village defies gravity. And while you need to be careful of summer crowds, St. Cirq has not yet been marred by boutiques and remains wonderfully tranquil after-hours. Wander the rambling footpaths and uneven lanes, find the best light for your memories, and appreciate where you are. You'll find ideal picnic perches, a few galleries, and several restaurants. The **TI** is located across from Auberge du Sombral (tel. 05 65 31 29 06). St. Cirq has 18 rooms, 10 of which are at the cozy, central **Auberge du Sombral****, run with style by Madame Haldeveled (Db-€53–72, excellent €17 *menu*, CC, tel. 05 65 31 26 08, fax 05 65 30 26 37, phone better than fax, closed mid-Nov–March). **Hôtel de la Pelissaria*****, at the lower end of the village, has eight carefully tended rooms cascading down the hill amid terraced gardens, offers postcard views up to the main village, and is . . . idyllic (Db-€63–114, CC, tiny pool, no restaurant, tel. 05 65 31 25 14, fax 05 65 30 25 52, e-mail: lapelissariahotel@minitel.net).

LANGUEDOC

From the 10th to the 13th centuries, this powerful and independent region ruled most of southern France between the Rhône River and the Pyrenees mountains. The brutal Albigensian (Cathar) Crusades began here in 1208 and ultimately led to Languedoc's demise and eventual incorporation into the state of France.

The name *languedoc* comes from the *langue* (language) its people spoke: *Langue d'oc* ("language of Oc," *Oc* for the way they said "yes") was the dialect of southern France; *langue d'oil* was the dialect of northern France (where *oil*, later to become *oui*, was the way of saying "yes"). As Languedoc's power faded, so did its language.

The Moors, Charlemagne, and the Spanish have all called this area home. You'll see, hear, and feel the strong Spanish influence. I'm lumping Albi in with the Languedoc region, though locals don't think of it as true Languedoc.

While sharing many of the same attributes as Provence (climate, wind, grapes, and sea), this sunny, intoxicating, south-westernmost region of France is allocated little time by most travelers. Today, Languedoc is largely overlooked and is most famous for its inexpensive yet tasty wines.

Planning Your Time

Key sights in Languedoc are Albi, Carcassonne, Minerve, the Cathar castle ruins, and Collioure. Albi makes a good day or overnight stop between the Dordogne region and Carcassonne. Plan your arrival at Carcassonne carefully: Arrive late in the afternoon, spend the night, and leave by noon the next day, and you'll miss the daytrippers. Collioure is your Mediterranean beach town vacation-from-your-vacation. To find the Cathar castle ruins and Minerve, you'll need wheels of your own and

Languedoc

a good map. If you're driving, the most exciting Cathar castles—
Peyrepertuse and Queribus—work well as stops between
Carcassonne and Collioure. No matter what transport you use,
Languedoc is a logical stop between the Dordogne and Provence
or on the way to Barcelona, which is just over the border.

Getting around Languedoc

Albi, Carcassonne, and Collioure are accessible by train (though
connections to Albi can be awkward), but a car is essential for
seeing the remote sights. Pick up your rental car in Albi, Carcassonne, or Collioure and buy the local Michelin map #83. Roads
can be pencil-thin, and traffic slow—lower your ambitions. East
of Montauban, the D-115 from Bruniquel (along the l'Averyon

River then south to Cordes) is dreamy, and the D-964 south of Bruniquel to Gaillac is a scenic route to Albi (see "Route of the Bastides," below). Drivers continuing north should consider the beautiful but slow drive through the Lot River Valley via Ville-franche de Rouergue and Cajarc (see "Sights—Southeast of the Dordogne," in the previous chapter).

Cuisine Scene—Languedoc

Hearty peasant cooking and full-bodied red wines are Langue-doc's tasty trademarks. Be adventurous. *Cassoulet*, an old Roman concoction of goose, duck, pork, mutton, sausage, and white beans, is the main-course specialty. You'll also see *cargolade*, a stew of snail, lamb, and sausage. Local cheeses are Roquefort and Pelardon (a nutty-tasting goat cheese). Corbières, Miner-vois, and Côtes du Roussillon are the area's good-value red wines. The locals distill a fine brandy, Armagnac, which tastes just like cognac and costs less.

The Cathars

The Cathars were a heretical group of Christians who grew in num-bers under a tolerant rule in Languedoc from the 11th through the 13th centuries. They saw life as a battle between good (the spiritual) and bad (the material) and considered material things evil and of the devil. While others called them "Cathars" (from the Greek word for "pure") or "Albigenses" (for their main city, Albi), they called them-selves simply "friends of God." Cathars focused on the teachings of St. John and recognized only baptism as a sacrament. Because they believed in reincarnation, they were vegetarians.

Travelers encounter the Cathars in their Languedoc sightsee-ing because of the Albigensian Crusades (1209–1240s). The king of France wanted to consolidate his grip on southern France. The pope needed to make a strong point that the only acceptable Chris-tianity was Roman style. Both found self-serving reasons to wage a genocidal war against these people—who never amounted to more than 10 percent of the local population and who coexisted happily with their non-Cathar neighbors. After a terrible generation of torture and mass burnings, the Cathars were wiped out. The last Cathar was burned in 1321.

Today, tourists find haunting castle ruins (once Cathar strongholds) high in the Pyrenees and eat hearty *salade Cathar*.

ALBI

Those coming to see the basilica and the Toulouse-Lautrec Museum will be pleasantly surprised by Albi's sienna-toned bricks and the half-timbered buildings that line the town's many traffic-free streets. Lost in the Dordogne-to-Carcassonne shuffle and overshadowed by its big brother Toulouse, unpretentious Albi awaits your visit with minimal tourist trappings. Train travelers with limited time may find the detour to Albi too time-consuming.

Orientation: Albi's sights, pedestrian streets, and hotels cluster within a 10-minute walk of the basilica. The **TI** is between the basilica and Toulouse-Lautrec Museum (July–Aug Mon–Sat 09:00–19:30, Sept–June Mon–Sat 09:00–12:30, 14:00–18:00, Sun all year 10:30–12:30, 14:00–17:30, tel. 05 63 49 48 80).

Arrival in Albi

By Train: There are two stations in Albi; you want *Albi-Ville*. From the station, take a left onto avenue Marechal Joffre, walking past the Hôtel Regina, and then another left on avenue General de Gaulle; cross place Laperouse, keeping left of the gardens, then follow the signs to *cathédrale* and to Albi's old city. Lockers are available at the station.

By Car: Follow signs to *centre-ville* and *cathédrale* and park in front of the basilica.

Sights—Albi

Pick up a map of the city center at the TI (get the purple *circuit poupre* walking tour in English) and follow its suggested walking tour, reading the English information posted at key points along the way. On this walk you'll see...

▲▲▲**Basilique Ste. Cécile**—This 13th-century fortress/basilica was the nail in the Albigensian coffin. Both the imposing exterior and the stunning interior of this cathedral drive home the message of the Catholic (read "universal") Church. The extravagant porch looks like the afterthought it was. The interior is an explosion of colors and geometric shapes framing a vivid *Last Judgment*. Even with the gaping hole that was cut from it to make room for a newer pipe organ, the *Last Judgment* makes its point in a way that would stick with any medieval worshiper (June–Sept 08:30–18:45, Oct–May closes 12:00–14:30 and at 18:30). The choir is worth the small admission, and the sound-and-light show—*Son et Lumière Spectacle*, offered in summer—is worth staying up for (€4.75, 22:00, ask at TI).

▲▲**Musée Toulouse-Lautrec**—The Palais de la Berbie (once the fortified home of the archbishop) has the world's best collection of Lautrec's paintings, posters, and sketches. The artist, crippled from youth and therefore on the fringe of society, had an affinity for people who didn't quite fit in. He painted the dregs of Parisian society because they were his world. His famous Parisian-nightlife posters are here. The top floor houses a skippable collection of contemporary art (€4, €3 audioguide, April–May daily 10:00–12:00, 14:00–18:00; July–Aug daily 09:00–18:00; Oct–March Wed–Mon 10:00–12:00, 14:00–17:00; tel. 05 63 49 48 70). The gardens below have fine views.

Albi

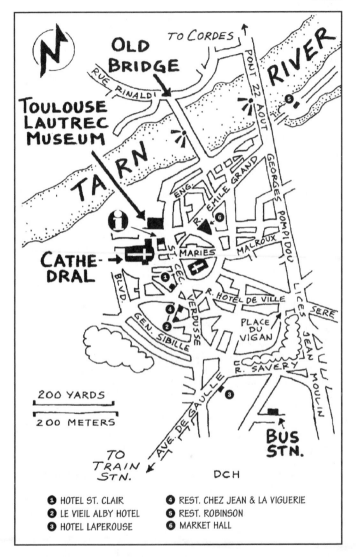

① HOTEL ST. CLAIR
② LE VIEIL ALBY HOTEL
③ HOTEL LAPEROUSE
④ REST. CHEZ JEAN & LA VIGUERIE
⑤ REST. ROBINSON
⑥ MARKET HALL

Eglise St. Salvy and Clôitre—This is an OK church with fine cloisters. Delicate arches surround an enclosed courtyard, providing a peaceful interlude from the shoppers that fill the pedestrian streets (open all day).

La Cave des Vignerons—This wine cave presents regional wines in an appealing setting (across from basilica, where rue des Fargues meets the square).

Market Hall—The quiet Art Nouveau market is good for picnic-gathering and people-watching (Tue–Sun until 13:00, closed Mon, 2 blocks from basilica).

City Views—For great views of Albi and the Tarn River, walk or drive past the basilica down to either the Pont-Vieux or the newer and higher Pont 22 Aout 1944.

Sights—Near Albi

▲**Route of the Bastides**—The hilly terrain north of Albi made hospitable ground for medieval villages to organize around for defensive purposes. Here, fortified villages (*bastides*) spill over hill-tops, above rivers, and between wheat fields and forests, creating a worthwhile detour for drivers. Connect these *bastides*: Castelnau de Montmiral (wonderful main square, 10 min from Albi), tiny Bruniquel, vertical Penne, too-popular Cordes-sur-Ciel, and, if you really want to get off the beaten path, the ridge-top village of Najac.

Cordes-sur-Ciel—Hill town–lovers can't resist this brilliantly situated, well-preserved, and crowded medieval marvel just 25 kilometers north of Albi. Cordes, once an important Cathar base, is now filled with boutiques and too many tourists on weekends and in the summer, but is quieter off-season. It's a long, steep walk up to the town from the lower parking lots (€2.30, first hour is free); take the €2 shuttle bus (4/hr, buy tickets at parking meter or from driver, departs from place Jeanne Ramel-Cals, next to TI). Trains get you as far as Cordes-Vindrac, where a taxi-bus will shuttle you five kilometers to Cordes (€4, tel. 05 63 56 14 80). Cordes has two **TI**s, one at the base of the hill town and another in the center (Sept–June 10:30–12:30, 14:00–18:00, July–Aug 10:00–19:00, tel. 05 63 56 00 52). The rustic **Hostellerie de Vieux Cordes***** at the top is the place to stay; some rooms have valley views (Db-€44–61, CC, 21 rue St. Michel, 81170 Cordes, tel. 05 63 53 79 20, fax 05 63 56 02 47, www.cordes@thuries.fr).

Najac—This is Cordes *sans* crowds and appropriate only for hill town nuts, as it requires a serious detour. This narrow *bastide* caps a high ridge and lies beneath a ruined castle. At the welcoming **Hôtel du Barry****, all rooms have great views and the restaurant justifies the detour (Db-€54–60, prices are per person and include breakfast and dinner, CC, free parking, 12270 Najac, tel. 05 65 29 74 32, fax 05 65 29 75 32, www.oustaldelbarry.com).

Gorges du Tarn—Adventure-lovers can canoe, hike, or drive the stunning Tarn River gorge by heading east from Albi to Millau, then following the gorge all the way to St. Enimie. Roads are slow but spectacular. The best base for canoeing is in tiny La Malene (40 km northeast of Millau). Stay in the simple but comfortable

Auberge de l'Emarcadere (Db-€38, Tb-€46, CC, tel. 04 66 48
51 03, fax 04 66 48 58 94), or in the country-luxurious **Manoir
de Montesquiou** (Db-€64–95, big Db-€125, extra bed-€15.25,
you'll be expected to dine at its great restaurant-€28, CC, tel. 04
66 48 51 12, fax 04 66 48 50 47, www.manoir-montesquiou.com).

Sleeping and Eating in Albi
(€1.10 = about $1, country code: 33, zip code: 81000)
Sleep Code: **S** = Single, **D** = Double/Twin, **T** = Triple, **Q** = Quad,
b = bathroom, **s** = shower only, **CC** = Credit Cards accepted,
no CC = Credit Cards not accepted, **SE** = Speaks English,
NSE = No English, * = French hotel rating system (0–4 stars).

   Hôtel St. Clair**, offering steep stairs, a small courtyard,
and fine rooms, is decorated with a loving touch (Db-€40–49,
Tb-€56–66, CC, 2 blocks from basilica in pedestrian zone on
rue St. Clair, tel. 05 63 54 25 66, fax 05 63 47 27 58, e-mail:
micheleandrieu@hotmail.com, Michele SE). **Le Vieil Alby
Hôtel****, located in the heart of Albi's pedestrian area, has good
rooms and a worthwhile restaurant (Sb-€40–50, Db-€41–55,
Tb-€58, garage-€7, CC, 25 rue Toulouse-Lautrec, tel. 05 63
54 14 69, fax 05 63 54 96 75). **Hôtel Laperouse****, run by
gentle M. Chartrou, is one block from the old city and a 10-
minute walk to the train station. It has easy parking, a quiet
garden, and a big pool, and is a good value—spring for a room
with balcony over the pool (Sb/Db-€34–56, CC, 21 place
Laperouse, tel. 05 63 54 69 22, fax 05 63 38 03 69).

   Eating: Albi is filled with inexpensive restaurants specializing in organ meats. Several good places line the rue Toulouse-
Lautrec (2 blocks from Hôtel St. Clair). **Chez Jean** (opposite
Hôtel St. Clair) is fun and simple. **La Viguerie** at #7 stands
above the rest in price, quality, and ambience (€21 *menu*, tel.
05 63 54 76 44). At #25, the recommended **Le Vieil Alby Hôtel**
restaurant is traditional and reliable (*menus* from €14.50). For
a fun experience, find **Le Robinson**, where Lices Georges
Pompidou meets the river. A path leads down to the river to
this vine-strewn paradise (reasonable *menus*, 142 rue Eurand
Branly, tel. 03 63 46 15 69). For more happening café action,
head to the grand place du Vigan.

Transportation Connections—Albi
You'll connect to just about any destination through Toulouse.
   By train to: Toulouse (11/day, 70 min), **Carcassonne**
(9/day, 2.5 hrs, change in Toulouse), **Sarlat** (2/day in 4.5 hrs
with changes in Toulouse, Agen, and Le Buisson; or 3/day in 6–7
hrs via Souillac with changes possible in Brive-la-Gaillarde and
Toulouse, then bus from Souillac), **Paris** (7/day, 6–7.5 hrs change
in Toulouse, then TGV, night train).

Carcassonne Overview

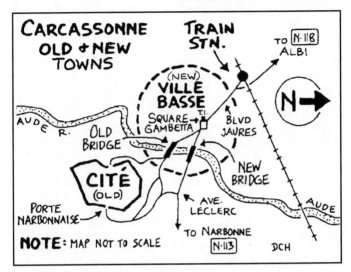

CARCASSONNE

Medieval Carcassonne is a 13th-century world of towers, turrets, and cobblestone alleys. It's a walled city and Camelot's castle rolled into one, frosted with too many tourists. At 10:00 the sales-people stand at the doors of their main-street shops, their gauntlet of tacky temptations poised and ready for their daily ration of customers. A quieter Carcassonne rattles in the early morning or evening breeze, so spend the night. If you're sensitive to crowds, consider sleeping in nearby Caunes-Minervois (see "Sleeping near Carcassonne," below), or rent a bike and cruise the Canal du Midi's level towpath (see "Sights—Carcassonne," below).

Locals like to believe that Carcassonne got its name this way: 1,200 years ago, Charlemagne and his troops besieged this fortress/town (then called La Cité) for several years. A cunning townsperson named Madame Carcas saved the town. Just as food was running out, she fed the last bits of grain to the last pig and tossed him over the wall. Splat. Charlemagne's bored and frustrated forces, amazed that the town still had enough food to throw fat party pigs over the wall, decided they would never succeed in starving the people out. They ended the siege and the city was saved. Madame Carcas *sonne*-d (sounded) the long-awaited victory bells, and La Cité had a new name: Carcas-sonne. Historians, however, suspect that Carcassonne is a Frenchified version of the town's original name (Carcas).

From Rick's journal on his first visit to Carcassonne:

"Before me lives Carcassonne, the perfect medieval city. Like
a fish that everyone thought was extinct, somehow Europe's
greatest Romanesque fortress city has survived the centuries.
I was supposed to be gone yesterday, but here I sit imprisoned
by choice—curled in a cranny on top of the wall. The wind blows
away the sounds of today, and my imagination 'medievals' me.
The moat is one foot over and 100 feet down. Small plants and
moss upholster my throne."

Orientation

Contemporary Carcassonne is neatly divided into two cities: The
magnificent La Cité (fortified city) and the lively *ville basse* (modern downtown). Two bridges connect the two parts, the busy Pont
Neuf and the pedestrian-only Vieux Pont, both with great views.

Tourist Information: Carcassonne has three TIs: one in the
train station, one in La Cité, and one in the *ville basse*. The handy
La Cité TI is just to your right as you enter the main gate called
Narbonnaise (daily 09:00–18:00, until 19:00 July–Aug). The TIs at
the train station and in the *ville basse* (on place Gambetta, near huge
French flags at 15 boulevard Camille Pelletan) share the same hours
(Mon–Sat 09:00–12:15, 14:00–18:30, closed Sun, tel. 04 68 10 24).
Pick up the map of La Cité with English explanations, get English
tour times for Château Comtal, and ask about festivals.

Arrival in Carcassonne

By Train: The train station is located in the *ville basse*, a 30-
minute walk from La Cité. Ask at the station TI about the free
navette (shuttle bus) signed "La Cité," or walk straight out of the
station and find buses #2 or #8 opposite the McDonald's (you
may have to transfer at place Gambetta, 2/hr, €0.75, pay driver).
Or you can continue on foot past McDonalds, up the pedestrian
street, to the heart of the *ville basse*. From there, a left on rue de
Verdun takes you to place Gambetta and across Pont Vieux to
La Cité. Figure €8 for a taxi from the train station to La Cité.
While there's no baggage check at the station, you can check
bags across the street at Hôtel Terminus (€2.30 per bag).

By Car: Following signs to La Cité, you'll come to a large
parking lot (€3) and a drawbridge (Porte Narbonnaise) at the
walled city's entrance. If staying inside the walls, show your
reservation (verbal assurances won't do) and park free in the
outside lot, then drive into the city after 18:00. Theft is common—
leave nothing in your car at night.

Sights—Carcassonne

▲▲▲**Medieval Wall Walk**—You'll enter La Cité via Porte Narbonnaise. This principal access was made crooked for defensive
purposes. To avoid claustrophobic crowds that jam the main street,

Carcassonne's La Cité

- ❶ HOTEL LE DONJON &
  JARDIN DE LA TOUR RESTAURANT
- ❷ HOTEL DES REMPARTS &
  RESTAURANT L'AUBERGE DU GRAND PUITS
- ❸ YOUTH HOSTEL
- ❹ HOTEL MONTMORENCY
- ❺ CELLIER DES VIGNERONS
- ❻ HOTEL ESPACE CITE
- ❼ CHAMBRE D'HOTE
- ❽ LA TABLE RONDE REST.
- ❾ LE SAINT JEAN RESTAURANT
- ❿ TO HOTEL GRAND TERMINUS
  & HOTEL BRISTOL
- ⓫ HOTEL TROIS COURONNES

turn left after entering Porte Narbonnaise and walk between the walls (*les lices*), entering La Cité from a back door farther down (several access points available). La Cité is a medieval fortress first constructed during the time of the Roman Empire. It was partially reconstructed in 1844 as part of a program to restore France's important monuments. Walk much of the outer wall (no charge; in town, follow signs to *lices*). The higher inner walls are mostly

`

inaccessible, except for those in Château Comtal. Savor every step and view.

▲**Carcassonne Terre d'Histoire**—A busy medieval fair fills up most of the first three weeks of August. Don't miss the jousting tournament (*spectacle équestre*), usually at 18:00.

▲▲▲**Walk to Pont Vieux**—For the best view back onto the floodlit city, hike down to the old bridge. As you exit the Narbonnaise Gate, go left on rue Nadaud to rue Gustave, then turn left onto rue Trivalle. Ask, "*Où est le Pont Vieux?*" (oo ay luh pohn vee-uh). Return via the back-door entry to La Cité near Basilique St. Nazaire.

Basilique St. Nazaire—Enter this church and slowly walk down the center. Notice the Romanesque arches supporting the aisle and the delicately vaulted Gothic arches over the altar. Enjoy the explosion of color of the 14th-century stained glass. This is one of the best examples of Gothic architecture in southern France.

Château Comtal—Carcassonne's third layer of defense was originally built in 1125 but was completely redesigned in later reconstructions. Peek into the inner courtyard, ask about the free English tours (generally 2–4/day May–Sept), and admire the towers (€5.50, daily June–Sept 09:00–19:00, Oct–May 09:30–12:30, 14:00–18:00).

Cellier des Vignerons—Duck into this snappy wine bar to sample from a vast selection of local wines and enjoy the peaceful outdoor terrace. You are expected to buy a bottle if you taste, but prices are reasonable (13 rue du Grand Puits).

Canal du Midi—Completed in 1681, this sleepy, 250-kilometer (155-mile) canal connects France's Mediterranean and Atlantic coasts. Before railways, Canal du Midi was jammed with commercial traffic. Today it's busy with pleasure craft. Look for the slow-moving hotel barges strewn with tanned and well-fed vacationers. The towpath that spans the length of the canal makes for ideal, level biking. The canal runs right in front of the train station in Carcassonne (bike rental behind station at **Location VTT**, 25 Ave des Corbières, tel. 04 68 24 03 03, reserve ahead if possible).

Sleeping in Carcassonne
(€1.10 = about $1, country code: 33, zip code: 11000)
Sleep Code: **S** = Single, **D** = Double/Twin, **T** = Triple, **Q** = Quad, **b** = bathroom, **s** = shower only, **CC** = Credit Cards accepted, **no CC** = Credit Cards not accepted, **SE** = Speaks English, **NSE** = No English, ***** = French hotel rating system (0–4 stars).

Sleeping in Carcassonne's La Cité
Sleep in or near the old walls. In the summer, when La Cité is jammed with tourists, consider sleeping in quieter Caunes-Minervois (see "Sleeping near Carcassonne," below). Several

places, including a hostel, offer rooms inside the walls. Except for the mid-July–mid-August peak, there are plenty of rooms.

Best Western's **Hôtel Le Donjon***** offers tight but well-appointed rooms, a mood-setting lobby, and a great location inside the walls (Db-€72–97, Tb-€72–113, parking-€5, CC, air-con, elevator, tel. 04 68 11 23 00, fax 04 68 25 06 60, e-mail: hotel .donjon.best.western@wanadoo.fr).

Hôtel des Remparts***, another Best Western hotel, is right by the castle. Its 12th-century staircase leads to modern rooms, some with views of the ramparts (same rates as Le Donjon, 5 place de Grand Puits; to book rooms at des Remparts, call or drop by Hôtel Le Donjon, above).

The *chambre d'hôte* across from Hôtel des Remparts (inquire in small boutique) rents one double room and two huge apartment-like rooms that could sleep five and have a kitchenette and private terrace (Db-€49, Tb-€53, Qb-€64, family deals, stocked fridge and self-serve breakfast included, no CC, tel. & fax 04 68 25 16 67).

The **Auberge de Jeunesse** (youth hostel) is clean and well-run, with an outdoor garden courtyard, self-service kitchen, TV room, bar, video games, and a welcoming ambience. If you ever wanted to bunk down in a hostel, do it here—all ages welcome. Only July is tight. Nonmembers pay €3 extra (dorm bed-€11.60, sheets-€2.60, 2 doubles, a few quads, otherwise 6 to a room, includes breakfast, no CC, open all day, rue de Vicomte Trencavel, tel. 04 68 25 23 16, fax 04 68 71 14 84, www.hostelbooking.com). They also offer their guests (not the public) reasonably priced minivan excursions to otherwise inaccessible sights.

Sleeping near La Cité

At **Hôtel Montmorency****, Cecile and Stephane are perfect hosts with fine rooms that are knocking at the door of La Cité's drawbridge and entry. Gaze at the walls from the cool of the pool or from terrace tables (Db-€46–69, Tb-€69, Qb-€84, breakfast-€6, CC, free parking, 2 rue Camille Saint-Saëns, tel. 04 68 11 96 70, fax 04 68 11 96 79, www.lemontmorency.com, e-mail: le.montmorency@wanadoo.fr).

Hôtel Espace Cité**, two blocks downhill from Hôtel Montmorency, is sterile and modern but handy for drivers (Db-€50, Tb-€58, Qb-€66, small rooms, CC, air-con, 132 rue Trivalle, tel. 04 68 25 24 24, fax 04 68 25 17 17, www.hotelespacecite.fr).

Hôtel Trois Couronnes*** offers the only view rooms of La Cité I could find, just across the Pont Vieux, if you can get by the awful exterior (Db with view-€107, CC, elevator, 2 rue des Couronnes, 15-min walk from train station, tel. 04 68 25 36 10, fax 04 68 25 92 92).

Near the train station: Grand Hôtel Terminus***, while a bit faded, is friendly, turn-of-the-century grand, and worth ducking into for its lobby alone. Just across from the station, the rooms are sufficiently comfortable with high ceilings (Db-€73, Tb-€90, no CC, elevator, 2 avenue Marechal Joffre, tel. 04 68 25 25 00, fax 04 68 72 53 09). **Hôtel Bristol****, on the canal facing the station, has adequate rooms at fair rates (Db-€38–52, Tb-€54, Qb-€58, CC, elevator, 7 avenue Foch, tel. 04 68 25 07 24, fax 04 68 25 71 89).

Sleeping near Carcassonne

To experience unspoiled, tranquil Languedoc, sleep surrounded by vineyards, a 15-minute drive from Carcassonne, in the unspoiled village of Caunes-Minervois (zip code: 11600). Comfortably nestled in the foothills of the Montaigne Noire, Caunes-Minervois offers an eighth-century abbey, two cafés, a good pizzeria, a few wineries, and very few tourists. My two hotel recommendations sit side by side in the heart of the village, with owners eager to help you explore their region. Delightful Americans Terry and Lois Link take good care of you at **L'Ancienne Boulangerie**, where rooms are designed with care, the beds are tops, and the breakfast terrace will slow your pulse (S-€25, Sb-€40, D-€35, Db-€60, a lofty family room-€15 per extra person, includes breakfast, no CC, tel. 04 68 78 01 32, e-mail: ancienneboulangerie@compuserve.com, www.caunes-minervois.com). **Hôtel d'Alibert****, a wonderfully Old World place with traditionally French rooms, is run by Frederic with relaxed panache (large Db-€46–61, extra person €15.50, no CC, tel. 04 68 78 00 54, e-mail: frederic.alibert@wanadoo.fr). Don't skip a meal in his terrific restaurant (closed Sun–Mon). Closer to Carcassonne, British Diana and Chris of **La Ferme de la Sauzette** warmly welcome travelers in their cottagelike farmhouse with five antiqued rooms and the possibility of a home-cooked dinner (Sb-€50, Db-€56–64, Tb-€76, dinner with wine-€23, no CC, take D-142 south from Carcassonne 5 km to Cazilhac, Sauzette is on the left, 3 km from Cazilhac town hall [*mairie*] along D56 in direction of Villefloure, 11570 Villefloure, tel. 04 68 79 81 32, fax 04 68 79 65 99, www.lasauzette.com).

Eating in La Cité

Skip the touristy joints lining the main drag. **Le Jardin de la Tour** is inviting and reliable (*menus* from €14, near Hôtel du Donjon, tel. 04 68 25 71 24). Dine peacefully with views of the inner château and good cuisine at **Le St. Jean** (*menus* from €14, behind Hôtel des Remparts), or dine cheaply with Jacques Brel at **L'Auberge du Grand Puits** (hearty *salade Cathar* and *cassoulet*, place des Grands Puits, tel. 04 68 71 27 88). **La Table Ronde** is also good (€12.20 *menu*, 30 rue du Plô, tel. 04 68 47 38 21).

Picnics can be gathered at the small *alimentation* (grocery) on the main drag (generally open until 20:00). For your beggar's banquet, picnic on the city walls. For fast, cheap, hot food, look for places on the main drag with quiche and pizza to go.

Transportation Connections—Carcassonne

By train to: Sarlat (2/day in 4.5 hrs with changes in Toulouse, Agen, and Le Buisson; or 3/day in 6–7 hrs via Souillac with changes possible in Brive-la-Gaillarde and Toulouse, then bus from Souillac), **Arles** (6/day, 3 hrs, 3 require changes in Narbonne and Nîmes or Avignon), **Nice** (6/day, 6–9 hrs, fastest via change in Marseille), **Paris**' Gare Montparnasse (8/day, a few direct in 10 hrs or in 6.5 hrs by TGV with changes in Toulouse and possibly Bordeaux), **Toulouse** (hrly, 1 hr), **Barcelona** (3/day, 5 hrs, change in Narbonne and Port Bou, the border town).

Sights—Languedoc

These sights are worth a visit only if you're driving. Peyrepertuse and Queribus make ideal stops between Carcassonne and Collioure (allow 2 hours from Carcassonne on narrow, winding roads).

▲▲▲**Châteaux of Hautes Corbières**—Two hours south of Carcassonne, in the scenic foothills of the Pyrenees, lies a series of surreal, mountain-capping castle ruins. The Maginot Line of the 13th century, these sky-high castles were strategically located between France and the Spanish kingdom of Roussillon. As you can see by flipping through the picture books in Carcassonne tourist shops, these castles' crumpled ruins are an impressive contrast to the restored walls of Carcassonne. Bring a good map (lots of tiny roads) and sturdy walking shoes—prepare for a climb and be wary of slick stones.

The most spectacular is the château of **Peyrepertuse**. The ruins seem to grow right out of a narrow splinter of cliff. The views are so sensational you feel you can reach out and touch Spain. Let your imagination soar, but watch your step as you try to reconstruct this eagle's nest (€3.80, May–Sept 09:00–sunset, Oct–April 10:00–sunset, tel. 04 68 45 40 55). Canyon-lovers will enjoy the detour to the nearby and narrow **Gorges de Galamus**, just north of St. Paul de Fenouillet. Closer to the D-117, **Queribus** towers above (steep hike) and is famous as the last Cathar castle to fall. It was left useless when the border between France and Spain was moved (in 1659) farther south into the high Pyrenees (€3.80, get the English pamphlet, April–Oct daily 09:00–sunset, Nov–March weekends only 10:00–sunset).

▲**Abbaye de Fontfroide**—Hidden in the Corbières mountains, this beautiful abbey is a worthwhile detour just 10 kilometers south of Narbonne (exit 38 from A-9 autoroute). Founded in 1093, this once-powerful Cistercian abbey worked the front lines against the spread of Catharism. The assassination of one of its monks unleashed the terrible Albigensian Crusades. Today's abbey is privately owned and well-restored, with 3,000 roses, sublime cloisters, a massive church, and a monk's dormitory amid total isolation. Call ahead for English tours or visit on a French-only tour with printed English explanations (€6, daily Sept–June 10:00–12:00, 14:00–17:00, July–Aug 09:30–18:30, hrly tours, tel. 04 68 45 18 31).

Châteaux of Lastours—Sixteen kilometers north of Carcassonne (forget public transportation), these four ruined castles cap a barren hilltop and offer drivers the most accessible look at the region's Cathar castles. From Carcassonne, follow signs to Mazamet, then Conques sur Orbiel, then Lastours. In Lastours you must park at the lot as you enter the village, then walk to the old factory (look for "accueil" signs) to the slick new ticket office (get the English information on the castles). It's a 20-minute uphill walk to the castles, and you can explore the remains of a few medieval homes at the end. These four castles were the inheritance of sons from a ruler who wanted to treat each fairly. Drive high to the *Belvedere* for a panorama overlooking the castles (€3 for access to the castles and *Belvedere* viewpoint daily April–Sept 10:00–18:00, Oct 10:00–17:00, closed Nov–March).

▲**Minerve**—A onetime Cathar hideout, spectacular Minerve is sculpted out of a deep canyon that provided a natural defense. Strong as it was, it didn't keep out the pope's army. The village was razed during the vicious Albigensian Crusades. The view from the small parking lot alone (€1.50) justifies the detour. Cross the bridge on foot, then wander into the village to its upper end and a ruined tower. A path leads down to the river from here (watch your step as you descend); you can reenter the village from the riverbed at its lower end.

Minerve has two pleasant cafés, one hotel, an intriguing museum of prehistory, a few wine shops—and not much more. Stay here and melt into southern France (literally, if it's summer); you won't regret it. Sleep and eat at the friendly and cozy **Relais Chantovent** (Sb-€36, Db-€37–47, Tb-€43, Qb-€50, ask for the new rooms, CC, Minerve 34210, tel. 04 68 91 14 18, fax 04 68 91 81 99). People travel great distances to dine at their moderately priced restaurant (closed Sun–Mon), so reserve early.

Minerve is between Carcassonne and Beziers, 15 kilometers northeast of Olonzac and 40 minutes by car from Carcassonne. It's an ideal stop between Provence and Carcassonne. In the mood for wine-tasting? The **Trois Blasons Cave des Vignerons** in Azillanet (just west of Minerve) has a fine selection of regional wines. For a more personal experience, say *bonjour* to my friends Monsieur and Madame Remaury, who offer a good selection and an exquisite setting from which to sample the local product (a leetle Engleesh spoken; coming from Minerve, it's just past Azillanet, look for signs to **Domaine de Pech d'Andre** on your left, tel. 04 68 91 22 66).

COLLIOURE

Collioure, while surrounded by less appealing resorts, is blessed
with an ideal climate (the temperature has not dropped below
55 degrees in 4 years) and a romantic setting. By Mediterranean
standards, this seaside village should be overrun—it has everything.
Like an ice-cream shop, Collioure offers 31 flavors of pastel houses
and six petite, scooped-out, and pebbled beaches sprinkled lightly
with beachgoers. This sweet scene, capped by a winking lighthouse,
sits under a once-mighty castle in the shade of the Pyrenees.

Come here to unwind and do nothing. Even with its crowds
of French vacationers in peak season (July and August are
jammed), Collioure is what many are looking for when heading
to the Riviera—a sunny, relaxing splash in the Mediterranean.

Orientation

Collioure's sights and hotels gather near Château Royal. Most
shopping, sights, and hotels are in the old town, across the drainage
channel from the château. There are good views to the old town
from across the bay near the recommended Hôtel Boramar.
Evenings are best in Collioure—as the sky darkens, yellow lamps
reflect warm pastels and deep blues.

Tourist Information: The TI is behind the main beachfront cafés at 5 place du 18 Juin (Sept and June Mon–Sat
09:00–12:00, 14:00–19:00, closed Sun and at 18:30 Oct–May,
July–Aug Mon–Sat 09:00–20:00, Sun 10:00–12:00, 15:00–18:00,
tel. 04 68 82 15 47, www.collioure.com).

Laundromat: Laverie 3L will do your laundry while you
do your relaxing (daily July–Aug 09:00–19:00, otherwise daily
09:00–12:00, 15:00–18:00, 1 block up from post office at 28 rue
de la République, tel. 04 68 98 04 17).

Car Rental: Consider Garage Renault, opposite the
Laundromat on rue de la République (tel. 04 68 82 08 34).

Taxi: Call 04 68 82 27 80 or 04 68 82 09 30.

Arrival in Collioure

By Train: Walk out of the station, turn right, and follow the
road downhill for about 10 minutes until you see Hôtel Fregate
(hotels are listed from this point).

By Car: Parking is tricky here, and downright difficult in
summer. Follow Collioure *centre-ville* signs. Look for a parking
spot on the street or, if you have no luck, follow Gare SNCF signs
(use pay lot at the train station until you find better). Ask your
hotel for parking suggestions and take everything out of the car.

Sights—Collioure

Check your ambition at the station. Enjoy a slow coffee, snuggle
into the pebble-sand beach, and lose yourself in the old city's

Collioure

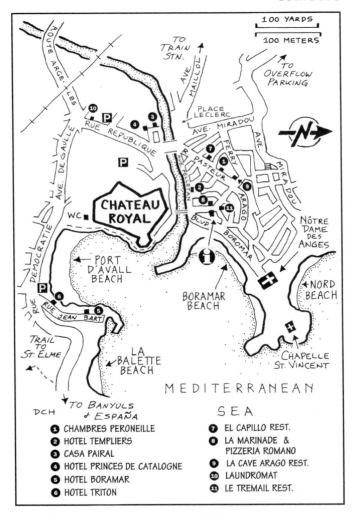

100 YARDS

100 METERS

ROUTE ARGELES

TO TRAIN STN.

AVE. MAILLOL

TO OVERFLOW PARKING

PLACE LECLERC

AVE. MIRADOU

AVE. DE GAULLE

RUE REPUBLIQUE

N

AVE. MIRADOU

FERRY

PASTEUR

ARAGO

CHATEAU ROYAL

WC.

AVE. DEMOCRATIE

BLVD. BORAMAR

NÔTRE DAME DES ANGES

PORT D'AVALL BEACH

RUE JEAN BART

BORAMAR BEACH

NORD BEACH

TRAIL TO ST. ELME

LA BALETTE BEACH

CHAPELLE ST. VINCENT

MEDITERRANEAN SEA

DCH

TO BANYULS & ESPAÑA

❶ CHAMBRES PERONEILLE
❷ HOTEL TEMPLIERS
❸ CASA PAIRAL
❹ HOTEL PRINCES DE CATALOGNE
❺ HOTEL BORAMAR
❻ HOTEL TRITON

❼ EL CAPILLO REST.
❽ LA MARINADE & PIZZERIA ROMANO
❾ LA CAVE ARAGO REST.
❿ LAUNDROMAT
⓫ LE TREMAIL REST.

narrow, hilly streets. The 800-year-old **Château Royal** (€3, daily June–Sep 10:00–17:15, Oct–March 09:00–16:15, great ramparts and views, mildly interesting exhibits on local history and contemporary art) and the waterfront **Notre Dame des Anges** church are worth exploring. On walls along the waterfront, the **Chemin de Fauvism** (Path of Fauvism) displays copies of Derain's and Matisse's works inspired by Collioure (TI has details).

Consider renting a paddleboat or taking a **Promenade sur Mer** motorboat excursion (€7 for a 60-min motorboat trip, departures hrly in summer, 5/day off-season, leaves from break-water near château, tel. 04 68 81 43 88). The TI has information on hikes into the hills (the ruined castle of St. Elme, 1.5 km in 1 hour straight up, offers the best views).

Collioure produces well-respected wines. Many wine shops offer relaxed tastings of the locally produced sweet Banyuls and Collioure reds and rosés. Try **Les Caves du Roussillon,** with a great selection and good prices (9 avenue General de Gaulle).

Sights—Near Collioure

Enchanting **Ceret** awaits 40 kilometers away with fountains and mountains at its front door and an excellent modern art museum with works by Picasso, Mirò, Chagall, and more (€6, daily 10:00–18:00). This makes a fine daytrip from Collioure (allow 50 min to Ceret by car, or train to nearby Perpignan and bus from there, get details at the TI). The 40-minute coastal drive via the Col de Banyuls into Spain is beautiful and well worth the countless curves, even if you don't venture past the border. Train travelers can make a daytrip to Spain, to either Barcelona (3.5 hrs one-way) or, closer, Figueres and its Salvador Dalí museum (get schedules at station).

Sleeping in Collioure

(€1.10 = about $1, country code: 33, zip code: 66190)
You have two good choices for hotel location: tucked behind the château in the old city (closer to train station) or in a quieter area across the bay, with views of the old city (10-min walk from château).

In the Old City: Directions to the following places are given from the big Hôtel Fregate, at the entrance to the old city. The cheapest rooms in the old city are the simple, clean, and comfortable rooms at Monsieur and Madame **Peroneille's Chambres,** on the pedestrian street two blocks past Hôtel Fregate (Ds-€39, Db-€42, Tb-€59, Qb-€67, no CC, rooms in main building are pricier but infinitely better than those in annex, ask to see rooftop terrace, 20 rue Pasteur, tel. 04 68 82 15 31, fax 04 68 82 35 94). The artsy and eternally hip **Hôtel Templiers**,** one block from Hôtel Fregate, has a complacent staff but rents delightfully decorated rooms, some with views (Db-€53–63, CC, 12 avenue l'Amiraute, tel. 04 68 98 31 10, fax 04 68 98 01 24, e-mail: info@hotel-templiers.com). Opposite Hôtel Fregate, Collioure's best splurge is the Mediterranean-elegant **Casa Pairal***,** with a cozy lounge and fine air-conditioned rooms around a garden courtyard and pool (small Db-€69–75, pleasant Db-€79–93, big Db-€88–123, Tb-€131–152, extra bed-€20, garage-€6, CC, impasse Palmiers, tel. 04 68 82 05 81, fax 04 68 82 52 10, www.roussillhotel.com, SE).

For American style and efficiency, try **Princes de Catalogne's***** spacious, comfortable, and air-conditioned rooms (Db-€56–69, Tb/Qb-€96–111, CC, next to Casa Pairal, rue des Palmiers, tel. 04 68 98 30 00, fax 04 68 98 30 31, www .hotelprincescatalogne.com).

Across the Bay: On the view side of the bay, your best bet is the **Hôtel Boramar****. Get a room with a terrace facing the sea or sleep elsewhere (Db without view-€43, Db with view-€52, Tb with view-€58, CC, rue Jean Bart, tel. 04 68 82 07 06). Next door, the neon-pink **Hôtel Triton**** is impersonal but has acceptable rooms at fair rates, many with fine views (Ds-€44, Db-€53, Tb-€60, CC, verify prices first, rue Jean Bart, tel. 04 68 98 39 39, fax 04 68 82 11 32).

Eating in Collioure

In the old city, **El Capillo** is a good value (2 rue Pasteur, tel. 04 68 82 48 23) and **La Marinade** is better for seafood (€18 *menu*, near TI at 14 place du 18 Juin, tel. 04 68 82 09 76). **Le Tremail** serves fine seafood and duck specialties to contented clients one block from the bay (16 bis rue de la Prud Homie, tel. 04 68 82 16 10). **Pizzeria Romana,** across from the TI, is cheap, fun, and quirky (6 place du 18 Juin). For a lively, local, and smoky *tapas*-bar experience, find **La Cave Arago** (18 rue Pasteur, open Thu–Sun, tourists tolerated). I love buying something to go (*à emporter*) and finding a romantic spot to eat along the water.

Transportation Connections—Collioure

By train to: Carcassonne (9/day, 2 hrs, 6 require change in Narbonne), **Paris** (5/day, 6.5 hrs with changes in Perpignan or Montpellier and Lyon then TGV to Gare Montparnasse, 1 direct train to Gare d'Austerlitz in 10 hrs), **Barcelona** (2/day, 3 hrs, change in Cerbère), **Avignon/Arles** (7/day, 3.5 hrs, many transfer points possible). The train station ticket office closes at 17:45 (tel. 04 68 82 05 89). Consider handy night trains to Paris, key Italy destinations, and Geneva.

PROVENCE

This magnificent region is shaped like a giant wedge of quiche. From its sunburnt crust fanning out along the Mediterranean coast from Nîmes to Nice, it stretches north along the Rhône Valley to Orange. The Romans were here in force and left many ruins—some of the best anywhere. Seven popes, great artists such as van Gogh, Cézanne, and Picasso, and author Peter Mayle all enjoyed their years in Provence. The region offers a splendid recipe of arid climate (except for occasional brutal winds known as the *mistral*), captivating cities, exciting hill towns, dramatic scenery, and oceans of vineyards.

Explore the ghost town that is ancient Les Baux and France's greatest Roman ruin, Pont du Gard. Spend your starry, starry nights where van Gogh did, in Arles. Uncover its Roman past, then find the linger-longer squares and café corners that inspired Vincent. Youthful but classy Avignon bustles in the shadow of its brooding pope's palace. It's a short hop from Arles or Avignon into the splendid scenery and villages of the Côtes du Rhône and Luberon regions that make Provence so popular today. And if you need a Provençal beach fix, consider Cassis, barely east of Marseille.

Planning Your Time
Make Arles or Avignon your sightseeing base (hotels are a far better value in Arles). Italophiles prefer smaller Arles, while poodles pick urban Avignon. To measure the pulse of Provence, spend at least one night in a smaller town. Vaison la Romaine is ideal for those heading to/from the north, and Isle sur la Sorgue is centrally located between Avignon, the wine route, and the Luberon (all described below). The small port town of Cassis is a worthwhile Mediterranean meander between Provence and

Provence

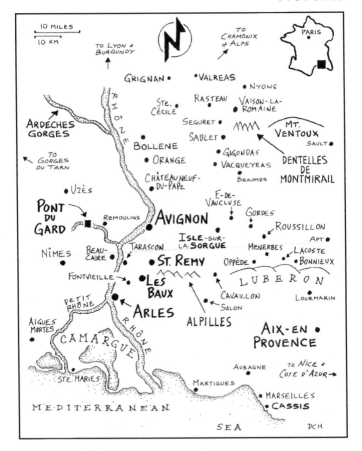

the Riviera. Everything is accessible by public transit. You'll want a full day for sightseeing in Arles (best on Wed or Sat, when the morning market rages), a half day for Avignon, and a day or two for the villages and sights in the countryside.

Getting around Provence

By Car: The yellow Michelin map of this region is essential for drivers. Avignon (population 100,000) is a headache for drivers; Arles (population 35,000) is easier, though it still requires urban driving skills. Park only in well-watched spaces and leave nothing in your car. For some of Provence's most scenic drives, follow my daytrip routes (see "Villages of the Côtes du Rhône: A Loop Trip for Wine and Village Lovers" and "Not Quite a Year in Provence: The Hill Towns of Luberon," below). If you're heading north from Provence, consider a three-hour detour through the spectacular Ardeches Gorges (see Côtes du Rhône loop trip, below).

By Bus or Train: Public transit is good between cities and marginal to small towns. Frequent trains link Avignon, Arles, and Nîmes (about 30 min between each), and buses connect smaller towns. Les Baux is accessible by bus from Arles. Pont du Gard, St. Rémy, Vaison la Romaine, and some Côtes du Rhône villages are all accessible by bus from Avignon. While a tour of the villages of Luberon is possible only by car or bus excursion from Avignon, nearby Isle sur la Sorgue is an easy hop by train from Avignon. The TIs in Arles and Avignon have information on bus excursions to regional sights that are hard to reach *sans* car (€18/half day, €30/full day). Cassis has train service via Marseille or Toulon.

Cuisine Scene—Provence

The almost extravagant use of garlic, olive oil, herbs, and tomatoes makes Provence's cuisine France's liveliest. To sample it, order anything *à la Provençale*. Among the area's spicy specialties are *ratatouille* (a thick mixture of vegetables in an herb-flavored tomato sauce), *brandade* (a salt cod, garlic, and cream mousse), *aioli* (a garlicky mayonnaise often served atop fresh vegetables), *tapenade* (a paste of puréed olives, capers, anchovies, herbs, and sometimes tuna), *soupe au pistou* (vegetable soup with basil, garlic, and cheese), and *soupe à l'ail* (garlic soup). Look also for *riz Camarguaise* (rice from the Camargue) and *taureau* (bull meat). Banon (wrapped in chestnut leaves) and Picodon (nutty taste) are the native cheeses. Provence also produces some of France's great wines at relatively reasonable prices. Look for Gigondas, Sablet, Côtes du Rhône, and Côte de Provence. If you like rosé, try the Tavel. This is the place to splurge for a bottle of Châteauneuf-du-Pape.

Provence Market Days

Provençal market days offer France's most colorful and tantalizing outdoor shopping. The best markets are Tuesday in Vaison la Romaine; Wednesday in St. Rémy; Thursday in Nyons; Saturday in Arles, Uzès, and Apt; and, best of all, Sunday in Isle sur la Sorgue. Crowds and parking problems abound at these popular events— arrive by 09:00, or, better, sleep in the town the night before.

Monday:	Cadenet (near Vaison la Romaine)
Tuesday:	Vaison la Romaine, Tarascon, and Gordes
Wednesday:	St. Rémy, Arles, and Violes (near Vaison la Romaine)
Thursday:	Nyons, Beaucaire, Vacqueyras, and Isle sur la Sorgue

Friday:	Remoulins (Pont du Gard), Bonnieux, Châteauneuf-du-Pape, and Lourmarin
Saturday:	Arles, Uzès, Valreas, and Apt (near Luberon hill towns)
Sunday:	Isle sur la Sorgue, Mausanne (near les Baux), Coustelet (local produce only), and Beaucaire

ARLES

By helping Julius Caesar defeat Marseille, Arles earned the imperial nod and was made an important port city. With the first bridge over the Rhône River, Arles was a key stop on the Roman road from Italy to Spain, the Via Domitia. After reigning as a political hotspot of the early Christian church (the seat of an archbishopric for centuries) and thriving as a trading city on and off until the 18th century, Arles all but disappeared from the map. Van Gogh settled here a hundred years ago but left only memories. American bombers destroyed much of Arles in World War II. Today, Arles thrives again with one of France's few communist mayors. This compact city is alive with great Roman ruins, an eclectic assortment of museums, made-for-ice-cream pedestrian zones, and squares that play hide-and-seek with visitors.

Orientation

Arles faces the Mediterranean and turns its back to Paris. Its spaghetti street plan disorients the first-time visitor. Landmarks hide in the medieval tangle of narrow, winding streets. Everything is deceptively close. While Arles sits on the Rhône, it completely ignores the river. The elevated riverside walk provides a direct route to the excellent Ancient History Museum, an easy return to the station, and fertile ground for poorly trained dogs. Hotels have free city maps, but Arles works best if you simply follow street-corner signs pointing you toward the sights and hotels of the town center. Racing cars enjoy Arles' medieval lanes, turning sidewalks into tightropes and pedestrians into leaping targets. The free "Starlette" minibus-shuttle circles the town's major sights every 20 minutes, but does not serve the Ancient History Museum, so it isn't very helpful (just wave at the driver and hop in; Mon–Sat 07:30–19:30, never on Sun). It does serve the train station, the only stop you pay for (€0.80).

Tourist Information: The main TI is on the ring road, esplanade Charles de Gaulle (April–Sept daily 09:00–18:45, Oct–March Mon–Sat 09:00–17:45, Sun 10:30–14:30, tel. 04 90 18 41 20). There's also a TI at the train station (April–Sept Mon–Sat 09:00–13:00, 14:00–18:00, closed Sun, Oct–March 09:00–13:00 only, closed Sun). Both TIs can reserve a hotel room (€0.75 fee). Pick up the good city map and information on the Camargue Wildlife area. Ask about bullfights and bus excursions to regional sights.

Arrival in Arles

By Train and Bus: Both stations are next to each other on the river and a 10-minute walk from the center. Lockers are not available. Pick up a city map at the train station TI and get the bus schedule to Les Baux at the bus station (tel. 04 90 49 38 01). To reach the old town, walk to the river and turn left.

By Car: Follow signs to *centre-ville*, then follow signs toward *gare SNCF* (train station). You'll come to a huge roundabout (place Lamartine) with a Monoprix department store to the right. Park along the city wall or in nearby lots (€1/hr, €2.60/4 hrs; pay attention to "no parking" signs on Wed and Sat until 13:00). Theft is a big problem. From place Lamartine, walk into the city through the two stumpy towers or take bus #1 (€0.80, 2/hr).

Helpful Hints

Supermarket: A big, handy Monoprix supermarket/department store is on place Lamartine (Mon–Sat 08:30–19:25, closed Sun).

Laundromats: One is at 12 rue Portagnel (daily 07:00–21:00). Another, nearby at 6 rue Cavalarie, near place Voltaire (daily 07:00–21:00, later once you're in), has a confusing central-command panel: €3 for wash (push machine number on top row), €1.50 for 25 minutes of dryer (push dryer number on third row 5 times slowly), €0.30 for flakes (button #11). Dine at the recommended L'Arlatan restaurant (across the street, see "Eating in Arles," below) while you clean.

Public Pools: There are two public pools in Arles (one indoor and one outdoor). Ask at the TI or your hotel.

Taxis: Arles' taxis charge a minimum €9 fee. Nothing in town is worth a taxi ride (figure €33–41 to Les Baux or St. Rémy, tel. 04 90 96 90 03).

Bike Rental: Try the Peugeot store (15 rue du Pont, tel. 04 90 96 03 77). While Vaison la Romaine and Isle sur la Sorgue make better biking bases (see below), rides to Les Baux (very steep climb) or into the Camargue work from Arles, providing you're in great shape (forget it in the wind).

Car Rental: Consider ADA (cheapest, 22 avenue Stalingrad, tel. 04 90 52 07 27), Avis (at train station, tel. 04 90 96 82 42), or Europcar (downtown at 2 bis avenue Victor Hugo, tel. 04 90 93 23 24).

Sights—Arles' Museums

The very handy monument pass (*le pass monuments*) covers Arles' many sights and is valid for one week (€10, €7.75 under 18, sold at each sight). Otherwise, it's €3 per sight and museum (€5.50 apiece for the Ancient History Museum and the Arlaten Folk Museum). While any sight is worth a few minutes, many aren't worth the individual admission. Many sights begin closing rooms 30 minutes early.

Arles

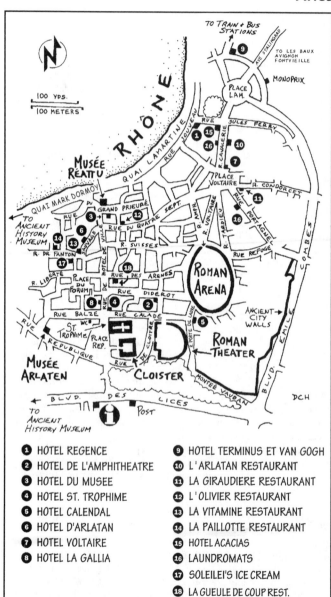

1 HOTEL REGENCE
2 HOTEL DE L'AMPHITHEATRE
3 HOTEL DU MUSEE
4 HOTEL ST. TROPHIME
5 HOTEL CALENDAL
6 HOTEL D'ARLATAN
7 HOTEL VOLTAIRE
8 HOTEL LA GALLIA

9 HOTEL TERMINUS ET VAN GOGH
10 L'ARLATAN RESTAURANT
11 LA GIRAUDIERE RESTAURANT
12 L'OLIVIER RESTAURANT
13 LA VITAMINE RESTAURANT
14 LA PAILLOTTE RESTAURANT
15 HOTEL ACACIAS
16 LAUNDROMATS
17 SOLEILEI'S ICE CREAM
18 LA GUEULE DE COUP REST.

▲▲▲**Ancient History Museum (Musée de L'Arles Antique)**—
Begin your visit of Arles in this superb, air-conditioned museum.
Models and original sculpture (with the help of the free English
handout) recreate the Roman city of Arles, making work-a-day
life and culture easier to imagine. Notice what a radical improve-
ment the Roman buildings were over the simple mud-brick homes
of the pre-Roman inhabitants. Models of Arles' arena even illustrate the moveable stadium cover, good for shade and rain. While
virtually nothing is left of Arles' chariot racecourse, the model
shows that it must have rivaled Rome's Circus Maximus. Jewelry,
fine metal and glass artifacts, and well-crafted mosaic floors make
it clear that Roman Arles was a city of art and culture. The finale
is an impressive row of pagan and early Christian sarcophagi
(2nd–5th centuries). In the early days of the Church, Jesus was
often portrayed beardless and as the good shepherd—with a lamb
over his shoulder.

Built at the site of the chariot racecourse, this museum is
a 20-minute walk from Arles along the river. Turn left at the
river and follow it to the big modern building just past the new
bridge—or take bus #1 (€0.80) from boulevard des Lices and the
TI (€5.50, March–Oct daily 09:00–19:00, Nov–Feb 10:00–18:00,
tel. 04 90 18 88 88).

▲▲▲**Roman Arena (Amphithéâtre)**—Nearly 2,000 years ago,
gladiators fought wild animals here to the delight of 20,000
screaming fans—cruel. Today matadors fight wild bulls to the
delight of local fans—still cruel. While the ancient third row of
arches is long gone, three towers survive from medieval times,
when the arena was used as a fortress. In the 1800s, it corralled
200 humble homes and functioned as a town within the town.
Climb the tower. Walk through the inner corridors of this 132-
by-105-meter oval and notice the similarity to modern-day stadium floor plans. And, if you don't mind the gore, a bullfight is
an exciting show (€3, May–Sept 09:00–18:30, Oct 09:00–17:30,
and Nov–April 10:00–16:30).

Classical Theater (Théâtre Antique)—Precious little survives
from this Roman theater, which served as a handy town quarry
throughout the Middle Ages. Two lonely Corinthian columns
look from the stage out over the audience. The 10,000 mostly
modern seats are still used for concerts and festivals. Take a stroll
backstage through broken bits of Rome; you can see much of the
theater by peeking through the fence (€3, May–Sept 09:00–11:30,
14:00–18:30, Oct and April 09:00–11:30, 14:00–17:30, Nov–March
10:00–11:30, 14:00–16:30).

Musée Réattu—Housed in a beautiful, 15th-century mansion,
highlights of this mildly interesting, mostly modern art collection
are 57 Picasso drawings (some two-sided and all done in a flurry of
creativity—I liked the bullfights best), a room of Henri Rousseau's

Camargue watercolors, and an unfinished painting by the neo-classical artist Réattu, none with English explanations (€3, plus €1.50 for special exhibits, April–Sept daily 09:00–12:00, 14:00–18:30, Oct and March until 17:00, Nov–Feb until 16:00, 10 rue de Grand Prieuré, tel. 04 90 96 37 68).

▲**Musée Arlaten**—This cluttered folklore museum, given to Arles by Nobel Prize winner Frederic Mistral (see "Place du Forum," below), overflows with interesting odds and ends of Provence life. It's like a failed 19th-century garage sale: shoes, hats, wigs, old photos, bread cupboards, and a model of a beetle-dragon monster, all crammed too close together to really appreciate. If you're fond of folklore, this museum is for you (€5.50, April–Sept daily 09:00–12:30, 14:00–18:00, Oct–March until 17:00, 29 rue de la République, tel.04 90 96 08 23).

▲▲**St. Trophime Cloisters and Church**—This church, named after a third-century bishop of Arles, sports the finest Romanesque west portal (main doorway) I've seen anywhere. But first enjoy place de la République. Sit on the steps opposite the church. The **Egyptian obelisk** used to be the centerpiece of Arles' Roman Circus. Watch the peasants—pilgrims, locals, and street musicians. There's nothing new about this scene. Like a Roman triumphal arch, the church trumpets the promise of Judgment Day. The tympanum (the semicircular area above the door) is filled with Christian symbolism. Christ sits in majesty, surrounded by symbols of the four evangelists (Matthew—the winged man, Mark—the winged lion, Luke—the ox, and John—the eagle). The twelve apostles are lined up below Jesus. Move closer. This is it. Some are saved and others aren't. Notice the condemned—a chain gang on the right bunny-hopping over the fires of hell. For them, the tune trumpeted by the three angels on the very top is not a happy one. Ride the exquisite detail back to a simpler age. In an illiterate medieval world, long before the vivid images of our Technicolor time, this message was a neon billboard over the town's square. A chart just inside the church (on the right) helps explain the carvings. On the right side of the nave, a fourth-century early-Christian sarcophagus is used as an altar.

The adjacent **cloisters** are the best in Provence (enter from square, 20 meters to right of church). Enjoy the sculpted capitals of the rounded Romanesque columns (12th century) and the pointed Gothic columns (14th century). The second floor offers only a view of the cloisters from above (same cost and hours as the Roman arena).

More Sights—Arles

▲▲**Place du Forum**—Named for the Roman Forum that stood here, this café-crammed square is always lively and best at night. Only two columns from a second-century temple survive. They are incorporated into the wall of Hôtel Nord Pinus. Van Gogh lounged under these same plane trees—his *Le Café de Nuit* was painted from this square. The bistros on the square, while no place for a fine dinner, put together a good salad, and when you sprinkle in the ambience, that's €8 well spent. The guy on the pedestal is Frederic Mistral; he received the Nobel Prize for literature in 1904. He used his prize money to preserve and display the folk identity of Provence—by founding the Arlaten Folk Museum—at a time when France was rapidly centralizing.

▲▲**Wednesday and Saturday Markets**—On these days until noon, Arles' ring road erupts into an outdoor market of fish, flowers, produce, and you-name-it (boulevard Emile Combes on Wed, boulevard Lices on Sat). Join in, buy flowers, try the olives, sample some wine, and swat a pickpocket. On the first Wednesday of the month, it's a grand flea market.

Fondation Van Gogh—A ▲▲ sight for his fans, this small gallery features works by several well-known contemporary artists who pay homage to Vincent through their thought-provoking interpretations of his art (€4.60, not covered by monument passes, April–mid Oct daily 10:00–19:00, mid-Oct–March Tue–Sun 10:00–12:30, 14:00–17:30, facing Roman arena at 24 bis Rond Point des Arènes).

▲▲**Bullfights (Courses Camarguaise)**—Occupy the same seats fans have used for nearly 2,000 years and take in one of Arles' most memorable experiences—a bullfight *à la Provençale* in an ancient arena. Three classes of bullfights take place here. The *course protection* is for aspiring matadors; it's a daring dodge-bull game of scraping hair off the angry bull's nose for prize money offered by local businesses (no blood). The *trophée de l'avenir* is the next class, with amateur matadors. The *trophée des as excellence* is the real thing à la Spain: outfits, swords, spikes, and the whole gory shebang (tickets €4.60–9.15; Easter–Oct Sat, Sun, and holidays; skip the "rodeo" spectacle, tel. 04 90 96 03 70 or ask at TI). There are nearby village bullfights in small wooden bullrings nearly every weekend (TI has schedule).

The Camargue—Knocking on Arles' doorstep, this is one of the few truly "wild" areas of France, where pink flamingos, wild bulls, and the famous white horses wander freely amid rice fields, lagoons, and mosquitoes. It's a ▲▲▲ sight for nature-lovers and boring for others. The D-37 that skirts the Etang de Vaccarès lagoon has some of the best views. The **Musée Camarguais** actually does a good job describing (in English) the natural features and traditions of the Camargue and has a 3.5-kilometer (2-mile) nature trail. It's 12 kilometers from Arles on the D-570 toward Ste. Marie de la Mer; at the *Mas du Pont de Rousty* farmhouse, look for signs (€4.60, May–Sept daily 09:15–17:45, Wed–Mon Oct–March 10:15–16:45, closed Tue off-season, tel. 04 90 97 10 82). Buses serve the Camargue (and the museum) from Arles' train station (tel. 04 90 96 36 25).

Sleeping in Arles
(€1.10 = about $1, country code: 33, zip code: 13200)
Sleep Code: **S** = Single, **D** = Double/Twin, **T** = Triple, **Q** = Quad,
b = bathroom, **s** = shower only, **CC** = Credit Cards accepted,
no CC = Credit Cards not accepted, **SE** = Speaks English,
NSE = No English, * = French hotel rating system (0–4 stars).

Hotels are a great value here; many are air-conditioned,
though few have elevators. All except the last are central. The
first three are closer to the train station.

Hôtel Régence** sits on the river with immaculate and
comfortable rooms, good beds, safe parking, and easy access to
the train station (Db-€30–46, Tb-€40–55, Qb-€56, choose
river-view or quiet, air-con courtyard rooms, CC, 5 rue Marius
Jouveau, from place Lamartine turn right immediately after passing through towers, tel. 04 90 96 39 85, fax 04 90 96 67 64,
www.hotel-regence.com, e-mail: contact@hotel-regence.com).

Hôtel Acacias**, just off place Lamartine and inside the
old city walls, is a modern new hotel owned by Hôtel Régence
(above). It's a pastel paradise, with rooms that are a smidge too
small but have all the comforts, including cable TV, hair dryers,
and air-conditioning (Db-€46–65, Tb-€69–74, Qb-€78, buffet
breakfast-€5.50, CC, elevator, 1 rue Marius Jouveau, tel. 04 90
96 37 88, fax 04 90 96 32 51, www.hotel-acacias.com, e-mail:
contact@hotel-acacias.com).

Hôtel Terminus et van Gogh* has bright, basic rooms in
van Gogh colors, facing a busy roundabout at the gate of the old
town, a long block from the train station. This building appears
in the painting of van Gogh's house; the artist's house was bombed
in World War II (Db-€30–37, CC, 5 place Lamartine, tel. &
fax 04 90 96 12 32).

Hôtel du Musée** is a quiet, delightful, manor-home hideaway with 20 comfortable air-conditioned rooms, a flowery two-
tiered courtyard, and a cool art-gallery lounge. The rooms in the
new section are worth the few extra euros and steps. The relaxed
Dubreuils speak some English (Sb-€37–46, Db-€46–61, Tb-
€60–64, Qb-€75, parking-€7, breakfast-€6, CC, no elevator,
11 rue du Grande Prieuré, follow signs to Musée Réattu, tel.
04 90 93 88 88, fax 04 90 49 98 15, www.hoteldumusee.com.fr,
e-mail: contact@hoteldumusee.com.fr).

Hôtel St. Trophime** is another fine old mansion converted
to a hotel with a grand entry, charming courtyard, broad halls,
large rooms, and (rare in Arles) an elevator, but no air-conditioning
(standard Db-€47, larger, off-street Db-€55, Tb-€63, huge Qb-
€70, CC, 16 rue de la Calade, near place de la République, tel.
04 90 96 88 38, fax 04 90 96 92 19).

Hôtel de l'Amphithéâtre**, a boutique hotel, is small,
friendly, and *très* cozy, with thoughtfully decorated rooms, a

pleasant atrium breakfast room, and air-conditioning. Ask about the new family rooms planned for 2002 (Db-€44–64, Tb-€84, CC, parking-€4, 5 rue Diderot, 1 block from arena, tel. 04 90 96 10 30, fax 04 90 93 98 69, www.hotelamphitheatre.fr, SE).

Hôtel Calendal**, located between the Roman arena and classical theater, should be three stars. It's Provençal chic with a large outdoor courtyard, smartly decorated rooms, Internet access, and seductive ambience (Db facing street-€40–55, Db facing garden-€60–65, Db with balcony-€75, Tb-€70, Qb-€80, breakfast-€6.50, CC, air-con, reserve ahead for parking-€10, 5 rue Porte de Laure, just above arena, tel. 04 90 96 11 89, fax 04 90 96 05 84, www.lecalendal.com, SE).

Hôtel d'Arlatan***, built over the site of a Roman basilica, is classy in every sense of the word. It has sumptuous public spaces, a tranquil terrace, designer pool, and antique-filled rooms, most with high wood-beamed ceilings and stone walls. In the lobby of this 15th-century building, a glass floor looks down into Roman ruins (Db-€84–137, Db/Qb suites-€152–229, great €10 buffet breakfast, parking-€11, CC, elevator, air-con, 26 rue du Sauvage, 1 block off place du Forum, tel. 04 90 93 56 66, fax 04 90 49 68 45, www.hotel-arlatan.fr, SE).

Starving artists can afford these two clean but spartan places: friendly **Hôtel Voltaire*** rents 12 small rooms with great balconies overlooking a caffeine-stained square a block below the arena (D-€24, Ds-€27, Db-€30, third or fourth person-€8 each, CC, 1 place Voltaire, tel. 04 90 96 49 18, fax 04 90 96 45 49). **Hôtel La Gallia**, with small but clean rooms, is a steal (Ds-€23, Db-€25, no CC, above lively café, 22 rue de l'Hôtel de Ville, tel. 04 90 96 00 63).

Sleeping near Arles, in Fontvieille
(See also "Sleeping in Les Baux," below.) Many drivers, particularly those with families, prefer staying in the peaceful countryside with good access to the area's sights. Just 10 minutes from Arles and Les Baux, and 20 minutes from Avignon, little Fontvieille slumbers in the shadows of its big-city cousins (though it has its share of restaurants and boutiques). **Le Peiriero***** is a tired mommy or daddy's dream come true with a vast grassy garden, massive pool, Ping-Pong table, badminton, and (believe it or not) three miniature golf holes. This complete retreat also comes with an appealing terrace café, good restaurant, and spacious loft family rooms, capable of sleeping up to five, with full bathrooms on both levels (the higher prices in each category are for rooms over the garden, Db-€69–81, Tb-€76–88, Tb loft-€104, add €7.75 per extra person, breakfast buffet-€7.35, CC, air-con, free parking, 34 avenue de Les Baux, just east of Fontvieille on road to Les Baux, tel. 04 90 54 76 10, fax 04 90 54 62 60, www.hotel-peiriero.com).

Le Domaine de la Forest is a restored farmhouse with modern apartments for five to six people (kitchen, 2 bedrooms, private terrace). Surrounded by vineyards and rice fields, this rural refuge offers a pool, swings, and a volleyball court. While most spend a full week, shorter stays are possible off-season (nightly-€92, weekly rental required in summer-€534, from Arles take D-17 toward Fontvieille and look for *Gîtes Ruraux* signs, route de L'Aqueduc Romain, just off D-82, 13990 Fontvieille, tel. 04 90 54 70 25, fax 04 90 54 60 50, www.domaine-laforest.com).

Eating in Arles

Great atmosphere and mediocre food at fair prices await on place du Forum; **L'Estaminet** probably does the best dinner. Elsewhere, near Hôtel Régence, **L'Arlatan** is friendly and unpretentious, serving a fine meal and great desserts (€16 *menu*, closed Wed, opposite Laundromat at 7 rue Cavalerie, tel. 04 90 96 24 85). Just up the street on place Voltaire, **La Giraudière** offers good regional cooking (€17.50 *menu*, closed Tue, tel. 04 90 93 27 52). Near Hôtel du Musée, **L'Olivier** is my Arles splurge, offering exquisite Provençale cuisine (€26 *menu*, 1 bis rue Réattu, reserve ahead, tel. 04 90 49 64 88). Locals reserve early for the few tables at **Gueule de Loup** (€23/€38 *menus*, 97 rue des Arenes, tel. 04 90 96 96 69). Vegetarians and carnivores appreciate **La Vitamine**'s good selection of salads and pastas, and the owners appreciate you— show this book and enjoy a free *kir* (closed Sun, just below place du Forum on 16 rue Dr. Fanton, tel. 04 90 93 77 36). Almost next door, **La Paillotte** specializes in traditional Provençale cuisine (€14.50 *menu*, 28 rue Dr. Fanton, tel. 04 90 33 15). For the best ice cream in Arles, find **Soleilei's**; all ingredients are natural, with unusual flavors such as *fadoli*, an olive oil ice cream (across from recommended La Vitamine restaurant at 9 rue Dr. Fanton).

Transportation Connections—Arles

By bus to: Les Baux (4/day, 30 min, none on Sun, less from Nov–March, ideal departure about 08:30 with a return from Les Baux about 11:20 or 12:40), **Camargue/Ste. Marie de la Mer** (8/day Mon–Sat, less on Sun, 1 hr). Buses depart from Arles bus station and from 16 boulevard Clemenceau downtown (tel. 04 90 49 38 01).

By train to: Paris (17/day, 2 direct TGVs in 4 hrs, 15 with change in Avignon in 5 hrs), **Avignon** (14/day, 20 min, check for afternoon gaps), **Carcassonne** (6/day, 3 hrs, 3 with change in Narbonne), **Beaune** (10/day, 4.5 hrs, 9 with change in Nîmes or Avignon and Lyon), **Nice** (11/day, 4 hrs, 10 with change in Marseille), **Barcelona** (2/day, 6 hrs, change in Montpellier), **Italy** (3/day, change in Marseille and Nice; from Arles it's 4.5 hrs to Ventimiglia on the border, 9.5 hrs to the Cinque Terre, 8 hrs to Milan, 11 hrs to Florence, or 13 hrs to Venice or Rome).

AVIGNON

Famous for its nursery rhyme, medieval bridge, and brooding Palace of the Popes, contemporary Avignon bustles and prospers behind its mighty walls. During the 68 years (1309–1377) that Avignon starred as the *Franco Vaticano*, it grew from a quiet village to the thriving city it remains. Today it combines a huge student population with a white-collar, sophisticated city feel. Street mimes play to international crowds enjoying Avignon's sprawling cafés and many boutiques. If you're here in July, be prepared for the rollicking theater festival and reserve your hotel months early. Clean, polished, and popular Avignon is more impressive for its outdoor ambience than its museums and monuments. See the pope's palace, then explore its thriving streets and beautiful vistas from the Parc de Rochers des Doms.

Orientation

The cours Jean Jaurés (which turns into rue de la République) leads from the train station to place de l'Horloge and the Palace of the Popes, splitting Avignon in two. The larger right (eastern) half is where the action is. Climb to the parc de Rochers des Doms for a fine view, enjoy the people scene on place de l'Horloge, meander the back streets (see "Sights—Walking Tour Of Avignon's Back Streets," below), and lose yourself in a quiet square. Avignon's shopping district fills the traffic-free streets where rue de la République meets place de l'Horloge (creamy gelato just off place de l'Horloge, where St. Agricol meets Joseph-Vernet). Walk or drive across Pont Daladier (bridge) for a great view of Avignon and the Rhône River.

Tourist Information: The main TI is between the train station and the old town at 41 cours Jean Juarés (April–Sept Mon–Sat 09:00–18:00, closed Sun; Oct–March Mon–Fri 09:00–18:00, Sat 09:00–13:00, 14:00–17:00, Sun 10:00–12:00, longer hours during July festival, tel. 04 32 74 32 74, www.avignon-tourisme.com). A branch TI is inside the city wall at the entrance to Pont St. Bénezet (April–Oct only, daily 9:00–19:00). Pick up the handy *Guide Pratique* (info on car and bike rental, hotels, and museums) as well as their Avignon discovery guide, which includes several good (but tricky to follow) walking tours. Ask about English walking tours of Avignon (€7.75, Tue and Thu at 10:00, depart from the main TI). They also have regional bus and train schedules to all destinations described in this chapter and information on bus excursions to popular regional sights (including the wine route, Luberon, and Camargue). Many of Avignon's sights are closed on Tuesdays.

Arrival in Avignon

By Train: TGV passengers need to take the free shuttle bus (*navette*, 4/hr, 15 min) from the space-age new TGV station to the main station in central Avignon (car rental is available at the TGV station; nothing within walking distance). All other trains serve the main station (baggage check available). From the main station, walk through the city walls onto the cours Jean Juarés (TI 3 blocks down at #41). The bus station (*gare routière*) and car rentals are 100 meters to the right of the train station, near the Ibis hotel.

By Car: Drivers enter Avignon following *centre-ville* signs. Park close to Pont St. Bénezet, either outside the wall or in the big structure just inside the walls and use that TI. Figure €1.50/hr and €8/day for pay lots. Hotels have advice for smart overnight parking. Leave nothing in your car.

Helpful Hints

Book Ahead for July: During the July festival, rooms are rare— reserve way early or stay in Arles or St. Rémy (see "Sleeping in Arles," above, or "Sleeping in St. Rémy" under "Sights near Les Baux," below).

Laundromat: Handy to most hotels is the Laundromat at 66 place St. Corps, where rue Agricol Perdiguier ends (daily 7:00–20:00).

English Bookstore: Try Shakespeare Bookshop (Tue–Sat 9:30–12:30, 14:00–18:30, closed Mon, 155 rue Carreterie, in Avignon's northeast corner, tel. 04 90 27 38 50).

Sights—Avignon

▲**Palace of the Popes (Palais des Papes)**—In 1309, a French pope was elected (Pope Clement V). At the urging of the French king, His Holiness decided he'd had enough of unholy Italy. So he loaded his carts and moved north to peaceful Avignon for a steady rule under a supportive king. The Catholic Church literally bought Avignon (then a two-bit town), and popes resided here until 1403. From 1378 on, there were twin popes, one in Rome and one in Avignon, causing a schism in the Catholic Church that wasn't fully resolved until 1417.

The pope's palace is two distinct buildings: one old and one older. Along with lots of big, barren rooms, you'll see frescoes, tapestries, and some beautiful floor tiles. The audioguide tour does a decent job of overcoming the lack of furnishings and gives a thorough history lesson while allowing you to tour this largely empty palace at your own pace. Enjoy the view and windswept café at the tower (€7, €8.50 during art exhibits, April–Oct daily 09:00–19:00, July–Aug until 20:00, Nov–March 09:00–17:45, ticket office closes 1 hr earlier, tours in English twice daily March–Oct, call 04 90 27 50 74 to confirm, at north end of town on place du Palais).

Musée du Petit Palais—This palace superbly displays medieval Italian painting and sculpture. Since the Catholic Church was

Avignon

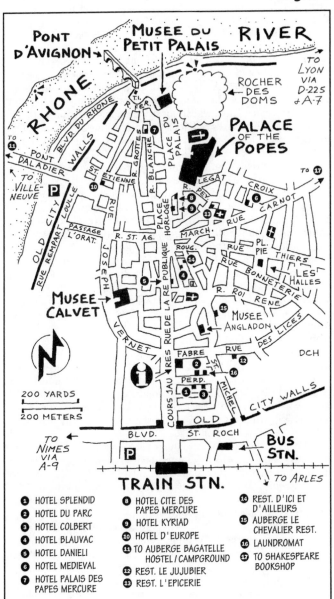

PONT D'AVIGNON

MUSEE DU PETIT PALAIS

RIVER

RHONE

TO LYON VIA D-225 & A-7

ROCHER DES DOMS

PALACE OF THE POPES

TO ⑪

PONT DALADIER

TO VILLE-NEUVE

BLVD. DU RHONE

WALLS

ST. ETIENNE

R. GROTES

R. FER.

R. BLANCHE

PLACE DU PALAIS

T.I.

⑦

R. LEGAT

R. PEY

CROIX

TO ⑰

CARNOT

⑥

⑧

⑨

⑬

OLD CITY

LOULLE

P

⑩

RUE

PASSAGE L'ORAT.

R. ST. AG.

JOSEPH

MARCH.

ROUG.

RUE

RUE

PIE

PL. PIE

THIERS

LES HALLES

RUE BONNETERIE

⑭

Rue Rempart

⑤

④

RES RUE DE LA RE PUBLIQUE

R. ROI RENE

MUSEE CALVET

VERNET

⑮

MUSEE ANGLADON

DES LICES

DCH

N

FABRE

RUE

⑫

200 YARDS

200 METERS

COURS JAU

ⓘ

②

ST

⑯

PERP.

①

③

MICHEL

CITY WALLS

OLD

TO NIMES VIA A-9

BLVD.

ST. ROCH

P

BUS STN.

TRAIN STN.

TO ARLES

① HOTEL SPLENDID
② HOTEL DU PARC
③ HOTEL COLBERT
④ HOTEL BLAUVAC
⑤ HOTEL DANIELI
⑥ HOTEL MEDIEVAL
⑦ HOTEL PALAIS DES PAPES MERCURE

⑧ HOTEL CITE DES PAPES MERCURE
⑨ HOTEL KYRIAD
⑩ HOTEL D'EUROPE
⑪ TO AUBERGE BAGATELLE HOSTEL / CAMPGROUND
⑫ REST. LE JUJUBIER
⑬ REST. L'EPICERIE

⑭ REST. D'ICI ET D'AILLEURS
⑮ AUBERGE LE CHEVALIER REST.
⑯ LAUNDROMAT
⑰ TO SHAKESPEARE BOOKSHOP

the patron of the arts, all 350 paintings deal with Christian themes. Visiting this museum before going to the Palace of the Popes gives you a sense of art and life during the Avignon papacy (€4.60, Wed–Mon 09:30–13:00, 14:00–17:30, closed Tue, at north end of place du Palais).

▲**Parc de Rochers des Doms and Pont St. Bénezet**—Hike above the Palace of the Popes for a panoramic view over Avignon and the Rhône valley. At the far end, drop down a few steps for a good view of pont St. Bénezet. This is the "Sur le pont d'Avignon" of nursery-rhyme fame, whose construction and location were inspired by a shepherd's religious vision. Imagine a 22-arch, 1,000-meter-long bridge extending across two rivers to the lonely Tower of Philip the Fair, the bridge's former tollgate, on the distant side (equally great view from that tower back over Avignon; see below). The island the bridge spanned is now filled with campgrounds. You can pay €3 to walk along a section of the ramparts and do your own jig on pont St. Bénézet (nice view, otherwise nothing special). The castle on the right, St. André Fortress, was once another island in the Rhône. Cross Daladier Bridge for the best view of the old bridge and Avignon's skyline.

Fondation Angladon-Dubrujeaud—This museum mixes a small but enjoyable collection of art from Post-Impressionists (including Cézanne, van Gogh, Daumier, Degas, and Picasso) with recreated art studios and furnishings from many periods. It's a quiet place with a few superb paintings (€4.60, Tue–Sun 13:00–18:00, closed Mon, 5 rue Laboureur, tel. 04 90 82 29 03).

Musée Calvet—This fine-arts museum impressively displays its good collection without any English explanations (€4.60, Wed–Mon 10:00–12:00, 14:00–18:00, closed Tue, on the quieter west half of town at 65 Joseph Vernet; its antiquities collection is a few blocks away at 27 rue de la République, same hours and ticket).

Discovering Avignon's Back Streets—Use the map in this book and the TI's barely adequate, single-sheet-of-paper city map to help navigate this one-hour walk.

Begin at the Agricol Perdiguier **park** by the TI. This lovely park sits on the site of a medieval monastery/college, reminding us of the critical role that monasteries played in the resurgence of medieval cities. Work your way to the eastern edge of the park, passing the children's play area; exit the small doorway on the right and enter place des Corps Saints.

This triangular square, a one-time cemetery, is typical of many smaller squares in Avignon; the plane trees seem to grow right out of the asphalt, providing essential shade for café clients. Walk north to the rue des Lices and turn right. In the 1200s, a defensive wall lined this street, marking Avignon's city limits (*lices* are the areas running along ramparts where knights would practice jousting).

Stroll east along rue de Lices for about 10 minutes (passing recommended Jujubier restaurant), then turn right on **rue des Tenturiers**, ground zero in Avignon for all that's hip. Earthy cafés, galleries, and a small stream with waterwheels line this tie-dyed street that served as the cloth industry's dying and textile center in the 1800s. Go as far as the second waterwheel, then retrace your steps on rue des Tenturiers, crossing back over rue des Lices onto rue de la Bonetterie.

You'll come face to face with Avignon's recently completed and concrete-ugly market hall, **Les Halles** (produce, meats, fish, closes at 12:30). Wander through the air-conditioned market and onto the broad place Pie.

Pass Avignon's medieval lookout tower as you walk up rue Gal Leclerc (lunches in air-conditioned comfort at **Restaurant Francois**, closed Sun, 6 Gal Leclerc). Turn left on rue Carnot, veer right on the narrow street, rue Petite Saunerie, and continue to the charming place des Chataignes (several inexpensive outdoor cafés). Notice the tower of the pope's palace and work your way counter-clockwise around the church of St. Pierre to the intimate place St. Pierre (recommended restaurant, **L'Epicerie**, see "Eating in Avignon," below). Turn left on rue Corderie to the place Carnot to enter Avignon's thriving network of shopping streets. A right on the pedestrian-only rue des Marchands takes you to place de l'Horloge.

Sights near Avignon, in Villeneuve-lès-Avignon
▲**Tower of Philip the Fair (Tour Phillipe-le-Bel)**—Built to protect access to the pont St. Bénézet in 1307, this massive tower offers the best view over Avignon and the Rhône basin. It's best late in the day (€1.50, April–Sept daily 10:00–12:00, 15:00–19:00, Oct–March Tue–Sun 10:00–12:00, 15:00–17:30, closed Mon). To reach the tower from Avignon, it's a five-minute drive (cross pont Daladier bridge, follow signs to Villeneuve-lès-Avignon), boat ride (Bâteau-Bus departs from Mireio Embarcadere near pont Daladier), or a bus ride on #11 (2/hr, catch bus across from train station inside city wall, in front of post office, on cours President Kennedy).

Sleeping in Avignon
(€1.10 = about $1, country code: 33, zip code: 84000)
Hotel values in Avignon pale in comparison to Arles. Still, these are all solid values, listed in the order you would pass them walking north from the train station. The first three are a 10-minute walk from the station; turn right off cours Jean Jaurés on rue Agricol Perdiguier.

At **Hôtel Splendid***, the friendly Pre-Lemoines rent 17 cheery rooms with firm beds and small bathrooms for a fair price (Sb-€26–37, Db-€38–46, breakfast-€4.60, CC, elevator,

17 rue Agricol Perdiguier, tel. 04 90 86 14 46, fax 04 90 85 38 55, www.avignon-splendid-hotel.com).

Hôtel du Parc*, across the street, is a similar value with less personality (D-€27–34, Ds-€35–43, Db-€37–46, CC, ask for room overlooking the park, tel. 04 90 82 71 55, fax 04 90 85 64 86).

Hôtel Colbert** is a fine mid range bet. Parisian refugee Patrice Medy is your host, and his care for this hotel shows in the attention to detail (Sb-€38–44, Db-€44–58, Tb-€58–79, CC, air-con, 7 rue Agricol Perdiguier, tel. 04 90 86 20 20, fax 04 90 85 97 00, e-mail: colberthotel@wanadoo.fr).

Hôtel Blauvac** offers 16 tired rooms (many with an upstairs loft) and stone walls in a grand old manor home near the pedestrian zone (Sb-€52–62, Db-€55–73, Tb/Qb-€73–82, breakfast-€6, CC, 11 rue de La Bancasse, 1 block off rue de la République, tel. 04 90 86 34 11, fax 04 90 86 27 41, www.hotel-blauvac.com).

Hôtel Danieli** is a hello-dolly fluff ball of a place, renting 29 good, modern rooms with faded carpets (Sb-€52–63, Db-€63–72, Tb-€70–78, breakfast-€7, CC, elevator, 17 rue de la République, tel. 04 90 86 46 82, fax 04 90 27 09 24, www.avignon-et-provence.com/danieli).

Hôtel Medieval** is a good value in a stone mansion with unimaginative but comfortable and spacious rooms (Db-€40–56, Tb-€61, extra bed-€7.65, kitchenettes available but require 3-day minimum stay, breakfast-€6, CC, elevator, 15 rue Petite Saunerie, 5 blocks east of place de l'Horloge, behind Eglise St. Pierre, tel. 04 90 86 11 06, fax 04 90 82 08 64, e-mail: hotel.medieval@wanadoo.fr).

For predictable comfort with air-conditioning, elevators, minibars, cable TVs, and unbeatable locations, try one of two **Hôtel Mercures***** (Db-€100–104, extra bed-€12.25, ask about their family rooms, CC, www.mercure.com). **Palais des Papes Mercure** is just inside the walls, near pont St. Bénézet (87 rooms, no CC, rue Ferruce, tel. 04 90 80 93 93, fax 04 90 80 93 94, e-mail: H0549@accor-hotels.com). **Cité des Papes Mercure** is within spitting distance of the Palace of the Popes (73 rooms, many with views over place de l'Horloge, no CC, 1 rue Jean Vilar, tel. 04 90 80 93 00, fax 04 90 80 93 01, e-mail: H1952@accor-hotels.com).

Hôtel Kyriad** is a basic chain hotel, with 38 uninspired but decent rooms in the thick of things on place de l'Horloge (Sb-€56–82, Db-€73–82, Tb-€82–92, Qb-€92–100, includes good buffet breakfast, CC, elevator, 26 place de l'Horloge, tel. 04 90 82 21 45, fax 04 90 82 90 02, www.kyriad-avignon.com).

At **Hôtel d'Europe******, be a gypsy in the palace at Avignon's most prestigious address—if you get one of the surprisingly reasonable standard rooms (standard Db-€120–150, first class-€210, deluxe Db-€285–385, breakfast-€17.50, CC, garage-€13, elevator, every comfort, 12 place Crillon, near pont Daladier, tel. 04 90 14 76 76, fax 04 90 14 76 71, www.hotel-d-europe.fr).

Auberge Bagatelle's hostel/campground offers dirt cheap beds, a lively atmosphere, busy pool, café, grocery store, Laundromat, great views of Avignon, and campers for neighbors (D-€24, dorm bed-€11, no CC, across pont Daladier on the Island (*Ile de la*) Barthelasse, #10 bus from main post office, tel. 04 90 86 30 39, fax 04 90 27 16 23).

Eating in Avignon

Le Jujubier is a delightful place to experience purely Provençal cuisine (€17 *menu*, closed Sun–Tue, 24 rue des Lices, tel. 04 90 86 64 08). **L'Epicerie**, charmingly located on a tiny square a few blocks east of place de l'Horloge, offers a good selection of *à la carte* items (daily, 10 place St. Pierre, tel. 04 90 82 74 22). **D'Ici et d'Ailleurs** ("from here and elsewhere") is Avignon's budget value for discerning diners, with decor as soothing as the prices (*menu* from €13, closed Sun, 4 rue Galande, tel. 04 90 14 63 65). **Auberge le Chevalier** offers an international flavor at a decent price (€13.60 *menu*, 19 rue des Trois Faucons, tel. 04 90 16 03 96).

Transportation Connections—Avignon

Trains

Remember, there are two train stations in Avignon, the new suburban TGV station and the main station in the city center (free shuttle buses connect both stations, 4/hr, 15 min). Some cities are served by slower local trains from the main station and by faster TGV trains from the TGV station; I've listed the most convenient stations for each trip.

By train from Avignon's main station to: **Arles** (12/day, 20 min), **Orange** (16/day, 20 min), **Nîmes** (14/day, 30 min), **Isle sur la Sorgue** (6/day, 30 min), **Lyon** (10/day, 2 hrs, also from TGV station—see below), **Carcassonne** (8/day, 3 hrs, 7 with change in Narbonne), **Barcelona** (2/day, 6 hrs, change in Montpellier).

By train from Avignon's TGV station to: **Nice** (10/day, 4 hrs, a few direct, most require transfer in Marseille), **Lyon** (12/day, 1.5 hrs), **Paris'** Gare du Lyon (14 TGVs/day, 2.5 hrs, 3 with change in Lyon), **Paris'** Charles de Gaulle airport (7/day, 3 hrs).

Buses

The bus station (*halte routière*, tel. 04 90 82 07 35) is in the basement of the building to the right as you exit the train station. You can call STD Gard bus company directly at 04 66 29 27 29. Nearly all buses leave from this station. The main exception is the SNCF bus service that runs from the TGV station to Arles (10/day, 30 min). The Avignon TI should have schedules. Service is reduced or nonexistent on Sunday and holidays.

By bus to **Pont du Gard** (6/day in summer, 4/day off-season,

40 min, see details under "Pont du Gard," below). Consider visiting Pont du Gard, continuing on to Nîmes or Uzès (both merit exploration), and returning to Avignon from there (use the same Pont du Gard bus stop you arrived at to continue on to Nimes and Uzès). Try these plans: Take the 12:00 bus from Avignon, arriving at Pont du Gard at 12:45. Then take either the 14:45 bus from there to Nîmes, where trains run hourly back to Avignon, or a 16:00 bus (Mon–Fri) on to Uzès, arriving at 16:30, with a return bus to Avignon at 18:30. Off-season service can leave you stranded for hours.

By bus to other regional destinations: St. Rémy (6/day, 45 min, handy way to visit its Wed market); **Isle sur la Sorgue** (5/day, 45 min); **Vaison la Romaine, Sablet,** and **Seguret** (all 2/day, 75 min); **Gordes** (via Cavaillon, 1/day, very early, 2 hrs, spend the night or taxi back to Cavaillon); **Nyons** (2/day, 2 hrs).

More Sights in Provence

A car is a dream come true here. Below I've described key sights and two full-day excursions deep into the countryside (see "Villages of the Côtes du Rhône" and "The Hill Towns of Luberon," below), both better done as overnights. Les Baux and St. Rémy work well by car with the Luberon excursion. Orange ties in tidily with a trip to the Côtes du Rhône villages. The Pont du Gard is a short hop west of Avignon and on the way to/from Languedoc for drivers. Travelers relying on public transportation are better off choosing Côtes du Rhône villages over Luberon villages for their rural Provençal experience. However you tour this magnificent area, notice the wind-buffeting rows of bamboo and cypress and how buildings are oriented south, with few or no windows facing north.

LES BAUX

Crowning the rugged Alpilles mountains, this rock-top castle and tourist village is a ▲▲▲ sight, worth visiting for the lunar landscape alone. Arrive by 09:00 or after 17:00 to avoid ugly crowds. Sunsets are sacrosanct and nights in Les Baux are pin-drop peaceful; the castle is beautifully illuminated (though closed after dark).

In the tourist-trampled live city, you'll find the **TI** (daily April–Sept 09:00–19:00, Oct–March 09:00–18:00, in Hôtel de Ville, tel. 04 90 54 34 39), too many shops, great viewpoints, and an exhibit of paintings by Yves Brayer, who spent his final years here (€3, 10:00–12:00, 14:00–18:30, in Hôtel des Porcelets).

A 12th-century regional powerhouse, Les Baux was razed in 1632 by a paranoid Louis XIII, who was afraid of these trouble-making upstarts. What remains is the reconstructed "live city" of tourist shops and snack stands and, the reason you came, the "dead city" (*Ville Morte* or *Citadelle des Baux*) ruins carved into, out of, and on top of a 200-meter-high rock. Climb through the "modern village" to the sun-bleached top where la Citadelle awaits (best early in the morning or early-evening light). Find the perfect view from the highest perch and try to imagine 6,000 people living within these stone walls. Survey the small museum as you enter la Citadelle (good exhibits, pick up the English explanations) and don't miss the slide show on Van Gogh, Gaugin, and Cézanne in the little chapel across from the museum (€6 entry to la Citadelle, includes entry to all the town's sights, Easter–Oct 09:00–19:00, until 20:00 July–Aug, Nov–Easter 09:30–17:00).

The best view of Les Baux day or night is one kilometer north on D-27 near **Caves de Sarragnan**, where you can sample wines in a very cool rock quarry that dates from the Middle Ages (daily April–Sept 10:00–12:00, 14:00–19:00, Oct–March closes at 18:00, tel. 04 90 54 33 58). On the way, you'll pass the **Cathédrale d'Images**, a mesmerizing sound-and-slide show that immerses visitors in regional themes by projecting 3,000 images inside a rock quarry (€7, daily 10:00–18:00, just above Les Baux on D-27).

Four daily buses serve Les Baux from the Arles bus station (30 min, see "Transportation Connections—Arles," above).

Sights between Les Baux and Arles

Abbey de Montmajour—You can't miss this brooding structure, just a few minutes from Arles toward Les Baux. A once-thriving abbey and a convenient papal retreat, it dates from 948. The vast, vacant church of St. Pierre is a massive example of Romanesque architecture, though its subtlety is lost on some (€5.50, April–Sept daily 09:00–19:00, Oct–March 10:00–13:00, 14:00–17:00, tel. 04 90 54 64 17).

▲**Roman Aqueduct**—Coming from Arles, take D-17 toward Fontvieille and look for signs on the right to *L'Aqueduc Romain* just before Fontvieille. Follow that road for a few kilometers to the romantically ruined remains of a Roman aqueduct that served Arles (no sign, look for stone walls on either side of the road). A path allows you to explore this fascinating and largely ignored aqueduct.

Sleeping in and near Les Baux
(€1.10 = about $1, country code: 33)

See also "Sleeping near Arles," above, and "Sleeping in St. Rémy," below.

Hôtel Reine Jeanne** is 50 meters to your right after the main entry to the live city (Db-€46–61, great family suite-€92, CC, most air-con, ask for *chambre avec terasse*, good *menus* from €19, 13520 Les Baux, tel. 04 90 54 32 06, fax 04 90 54 32 33).

Le Mas de L'Esparou *chambre d'hôte*, a few minutes below Les Baux, is welcoming (Jacqueline loves her job, and her lack of English only makes her more animated) and kid-friendly, with spacious rooms, a swimming pool, Ping-Pong, and distant views

of Les Baux. Monsieur Roux painted the paintings in your room
(Db-€60, extra person-€15.25, no CC, a few kilometers north
of Maussane on D-5, look for sign, 13520 Les Baux de Provence,
tel. & fax 04 90 54 41 32, NSE).

Le Mazet des Alpilles, a small home with two tidy rooms
in the unspoiled village of Paradou, may have space when others
don't (Db-€46–52, extra bed-€15.25, no CC, route de Brunelly,
13520 Paradou, tel. 04 90 54 45 89, fax 04 90 54 44 66, e-mail:
ricci@netcourrier.com, Annick NSE).

ST. RÉMY DE PROVENCE
This sophisticated town is famous for its Wednesday market (until
12:30), the ruins of a once-thriving Roman city (Glanum), and the
mental ward where Vincent van Gogh was sent after slicing his ear.

St. Rémy is a scenic 10-minute drive (or a 2-hour walk) over
the hills and through the woods from Les Baux. Almost too close
to Avignon for its own good (though very accessible by bus),
St. Rémy's pleasant old city is ringed by a busy road. The small
streets within the ring road are *très* strollable.

Sights—St. Rémy
▲**Glanum**—These crumbled stones are the foundations of a
Roman market town located at the crossroads of two ancient
trade routes between Italy and Spain. A massive Roman arch and
tower stand proud and lonely near the ruin's parking lot. The arch
marked the entry into Glanum, and the tower is a memorial to the
grandsons of Emperor Caesar Augustus. The setting is stunning,
though shadeless, and the small museum at the entry sets the stage
well. While the ruins are, well, ruined, they remind us of the range
and prosperity of the Roman Empire. Along with other Roman
monuments in Provence, they allow us to paint a more complete
picture of Roman life. The English handout is helpful, but consider buying one of the two English booklets (one has better photos, the other provides much better background). Inside the ruins,
signs give basic English explanations at key locations, and the view
from the *Belvedere* justifies the effort (€5.50, April–Sept daily
09:00–12:00, 14:00–19:00, Oct–March 09:30–12:00, 14:00–17:00).
Cloître St. Paul de Mausole—Just below Glanum is the still-
functioning mental hospital (Clinique St. Paul) that treated Vincent
from 1889 to 1890. The €2.60 entry fee buys a four-minute video
(English and French) and entry into the small chapel, intimate
cloisters, and a re-creation of his room. You'll find limited information in English about Vincent's life. Amazingly, he painted 150
works in his 53 weeks here—none of which remain anywhere close
today. The contrast between the utter simplicity of his room (and
his life) and the multimillion-dollar value of his paintings today is
jarring. The site is managed by VALETUDO, a center specializing

in art therapy (April–Oct daily 09:30–19:00, Nov–March daily 10:30–13:00, 13:30–17:00). Outside the complex, toward Glanum, you can walk on Vincent's favorite footpaths.

Sleeping and Eating in St. Rémy
(€1.10 = about $1, country code: 33)

Auberge de la Reine Jeanne** is central, cozy, and typical of many French hotels in that the rooms take a backseat to the restaurant. The 11 rooms look over a courtyard jammed with tables and umbrellas, and are clean and spacious, with big beds, and decorated in traditional style (Db-€53, Tb-€61, Qb-€62, CC, fine restaurant-€24 *menu*, on the ring road at 12 boulevard Mirabeau, tel. 04 90 92 15 33, fax 04 90 92 49 65).

Mas de Carassins***, a short walk from the center, is impeccably run by friendly Michel and Pierre (2 more Paris refugees). Here luxury is made affordable, and care is given to every aspect of the hotel, from the generously sized pool and gardens to the muted room decor and the optional €23 dinner (Db-€70–115, extra bed-€9, air-con, 1 Chemin Gaulois, look for signs 180 meters toward Les Baux from TI, tel. 04 90 92 15 48, fax 04 90 92 63 47, e-mail: carassin@pacwan.fr).

PONT DU GARD

One of Europe's great ▲▲▲ treats, this perfectly preserved Roman aqueduct was built as the critical link of a 56-kilometer (35-mile) canal that, by dropping one foot for every 300, supplied 44 million gallons of water daily to Nîmes, one of western Europe's largest cities. After years of work, the new **Grande Expo** does this sight justice with a phenomenal museum, a 23-minute movie, and a kid's space (called *Ludo*), all designed to improve your appreciation of this remarkable sight.

Start at the *rive gauche* (left bank of the Pont du Gard). You'll be greeted by the Grande Expo's linear new structure, housing the three exhibits. Begin with the informative but silly movie, if the English times are convenient; otherwise, skip it. Spend most of your time in the museum. The multimedia approach will draw you into daily Roman life: You'll learn about the many uses of water in Roman times; see examples of lead pipes, faucets, and siphons; marvel at the many models; walk through a rock quarry; and learn how they moved those huge rocks into place and how those massive arches were made. English video screens and information displays help make things as clear as spring water. The *Ludo* kid's space does the same for kids (English displays), giving them a scratch-and-sniff experience of various aspects of Roman life and the importance of water (€13, €43 for family of 2 adults and up to 4 kids, Easter–Nov daily 09:30–19:00, mid-June–Aug until 21:30,

Jan–Easter until 18:00, good cafeteria, tel. 04 66 37 50 99). The high-priced entry fees include all three exhibits and your parking (parking costs €4.60 otherwise).

The actual Pont du Gard **aqueduct** is free and open until midnight (the illumination is beautiful after dark). It's a level, 300-meter walk to the aqueduct from the Grande Expo. Inspect it closely and imagine getting those stones to the top. The entire structure relies on perfect stone placement; there's no mortar holding this together. Signs direct you to "panoramas" above the bridge on either side, but you'll get better views by walking along the riverbank below—either up or downstream—or, more refreshing, by floating flat on your back; bring a swimsuit and sandals for the rocks (always open and free).

Consider **renting a canoe** from Collias to Pont du Gard (€27 per 2-person canoe; they pick you up at Pont du Gard—or elsewhere, if prearranged—and shuttle you to Collias, where you float down the river to nearby town of Remoulins; 2-hr trip, though you can take as long as you like, Collias Canoes, tel. 04 66 22 85 54, SE).

Transportation Connections—Pont du Gard

By car: Pont du Gard is an easy 25-minute drive due west of Avignon (follow signs to Nîmes) and 45 minutes northwest of Arles (via Tarascon). The *rive gauche* parking is off the D-981 that leads from Remoulins to Uzès. (Parking is also available on the *rive droite* side but leaves you farther away from the museum.)

By bus: Buses run to Pont du Gard (*rive gauche*) from Nîmes, Uzès, and Avignon. Combine Uzès (see below) and Pont du Gard for a good day excursion from Avignon (5/day in summer, 3/day off-season, 40 min to Pont du Gard; see "Transportation Connections—Avignon," above). The bus stop at Pont du Gard is in the new parking lot near the Grande Expo on the left bank (rive gauche). The return stop to Avignon is to your left before crossing the traffic circle. Make sure you're waiting for the bus on the correct side of the traffic circle.

Sights near Pont du Gard

Uzès—An intriguing, less-trampled town, Uzès is best seen slowly on foot, with a long coffee break in its beautifully arcaded and mellow main square, the *place aux Herbes* (not so mellow during the colorful Wednesday and bigger Saturday-morning market). The city is the sight; there are no important museums, and most of the center city is traffic-free and tastefully restored. (Uzès is officially in Languedoc, not Provence.)

At the **TI**, pick up the English walking tour brochure (June–Sept Mon–Fri 09:00–18:00, Sat–Sun 10:00–13:00, 14:00–17:00, Oct–March Mon–Fri 09:00–12:00, 13:30–18:00,

Sat 10:00–13:00, closed Sun, on the ring road on place Albert 1er
tel. 04 66 22 68 88). Skip the dull and overpriced palace of the
Duché de Uzès (€9, French-only tour). You can enjoy the unusual
Tour Fenestrelle—all that remains of a 12th-century cathedral—
from the outside only.

Uzès is a short hop west (by bus) of Pont du Gard and is
well-served by bus from Nîmes (9/day) and Avignon (3/day).

VILLAGES OF THE CÔTES DU RHÔNE: A LOOP TRIP FOR WINE AND VILLAGE LOVERS

If you have a car (or a bike, best rented in Vaison la Romaine)
and a fondness for wine or beautiful countryside, take the loop
described below through Provence's Côtes du Rhône wine country. Endless vineyards, rugged mountains, and stone villages
fill your windshield (or handlebars). While this trip is doable
as a long daytrip by car from Avignon or Arles, you won't
regret a night or two in one of the villages listed below (Vaison
la Romaine makes the best base and is ideal if you're heading to
or coming from the north). From Avignon, go to Orange, then
connect the wine villages of Vaison la Romaine, Sablet, Seguret,
Gigondas, Vacqueyras, Beaumes de Venise, and Rasteau (figure on a 100-km round-trip from Avignon; 2 buses/day from
Avignon and Orange follow a similar route). The tiny, twisty
D-90 between Baumes de Venise and Malaucene is spectacular,
and those spending a night should drive to the top of Mount
Ventoux and visit the lavender capital village of Sault (this is a
must if you're here anytime from late June to late July, when the
lavender blooms). The Côtes du Rhône is hospitable and offers
relaxed wine-tasting at its best, and most villages have a *Caveau des
Vignerons* (wine-maker cooperative), which are easy places to sample a variety of wines. I've listed places to sleep and eat throughout
this route in the descrip-
tion below.

Provence Wine Country

The less-traveled
Dromme region just north
of Vaison la Romaine
is worthwhile if you're
continuing to the Alps
or if you're here in July
when lavender blooms.
It's laced with vineyards
(producing less-expensive
yet good wines), lavender
fields, and still more postcard-perfect villages.
From Vaison, take the

loop north to Visan, Valreas, Taulignan, and Nyons, and then back to Vaison. Pleasant Nyons is France's olive capital and hosts a dynamite Thursday-morning market. Each village is a detour waiting to happen.

VAISON LA ROMAINE

With bus service from Avignon and Orange, quick access to adorable villages and Mount Ventoux, and vineyards knocking at its door, this thriving little town makes a great base for exploring the Côtes du Rhône region by car or bike. You get two villages for the price of one: Vaison's "modern" lower city is like a mini-Arles, with worthwhile Roman ruins, a lone pedestrian street, and too many cars. The medieval hill town looms above and is car-free, with meandering cobbled lanes, art galleries, cafés, and a ruined castle (good view from its base).

Orientation

The city is split in two by the Ouveze River. The newer city (Ville-Basse) lies on its right bank; the medieval city (Ville-Haute) sits above on the left bank. The impressive Pont Roman (Roman bridge) connects the two.

Tourist Information: The superb TI is in the newer city, between the Roman ruin sites, at place de Chanoine Sautel. Get English tour times for the Roman ruins, ask about festivals and bike rental, and pick up the excellent *Fiches d'Itineraries* (a detailed guide to walks and bike rides from Vaison, ask for English version), and say *bonjour* to charming Valerie, who has worked here for 16 years (May–Sept Mon–Sat 09:00–12:30, 14:00–18:45, Sun 09:00–12:00; Oct–April Mon–Sat 09:00–12:30, 14:00–17:45, closed Sun, tel. 04 90 36 02 11, www.vaison-la-romaine.com).

You can rent **bikes** at Lacombe on avenue Jules Ferry (tel. 04 90 36 03 29) and hire superb **local guide**, Anne-Marie Melard, to bring those ruins to life (reserve ahead through TI, 2 hrs for €114).

Arrival in Vaison la Romaine

By Bus: The stop is in front of Cave la Romaine winery; walk five minutes down avenue de Gaulle to reach the TI.

By Car: Follow signs to *centre-ville*, then *Office de Tourisme*; park free across from the TI.

Sights—Vaison la Romaine

▲**Market Day**—The amazing Tuesday market (until 12:30) is worth organizing your trip and parking plans around.

Roman Ruins—If you've seen Pompeii, this will seem like small potatoes, but the remains of Vaison's two Roman sights—La Villasse and Puymin—are well-presented and give a good picture of life during the Roman Empire. Both ancient sites, separated by a modern road, show the foundations of the same Roman town that once stood here. The museum inside the Puymin ruins has English explanations (€6.25, includes both sets of ruins as well as the cloister at cathedral—Notre Dame de Nazareth; daily June–Sept 09:30–18:00, Oct–March 10:00–12:30, 14:00–18:00, Nov–Feb closes at 16:00; English tours of ruins available April–Sept, several days/week, usually at 11:00, check with TI; or get informative English handout and do tour on your own; even better, call ahead to the TI and reserve local guide Anne-Marie Melard, see above).

In summer, ask about night visits to the ruins. After the fall of the Roman Empire, Vaison's residents headed for the hills and established the Ville-Haute just above. It must have been strange to have peered over the walls to the one-time great civilization that La Villasse and Puymin ruins represented.

Hiking—The TI has good information on relatively easy hikes into the hills above Vaison. It's about 90 minutes to the tiny hill town of Crestet, though the views begin immediately (using the TI's *Fiches d'Itineraries*, follow the *Chemin des Fontaines* route).

Biking—Connect these villages for a great loop ride in just 18 kilometers (11 miles): Vaison la Romaine, St. Romain en Viennois, Puymeras, Faucon, and St. Marcellin les Vaison (the TI has the details).

Wine-Tasting—Cave la Romaine, a five-minute walk up avenue General de Gaulle from the TI, offers a variety of great-value wines from nearby villages in a pleasant, well-organized tasting room (daily 08:30–13:00, 14:00–19:00, avenue St. Quenin, tel. 04 90 36 55 90).

Sleeping in or near Vaison la Romaine
(€1.10 = about $1, country code: 33, zip code: 84110)
Hotels here are a good value, though none have elevators. Those in the medieval town (Ville-Haute) are quieter, cozier, cooler, and a 15-minute walk uphill from the TI (parking available nearby).

Hôtel Burrhus**, easily the best value in the lower city, has artsy decor and is right in the thick of things with a large, shady terrace over the raucous place Montfort (Db-€46–52, extra bed-€7.75, ask for a room off the square if you want to sleep, tel. 04 90 36 00 11, fax 04 90 36 39 05, CC, e-mail: info@burrhus .com). Ask about their adjacent and cushier **Hôtel des Lis***** (Db-€47–72, CC, contact Hôtel Burrhus for reservations and reception). **Le Brin d'Olivier** has a few nice rooms just below the traffic-free street (Db-€61–84, no CC, 4 rue du Ventoux, tel. 04 90 28 74 79, fax 04 90 36 13 36).

The next two listings are in the Ville-Haute. **Hôtel Le Beffroi*****, with wonderful views, is red-tile-and-wood-beamed classy with spacious rooms (some with views), a restaurant, cozy public spaces, and a small pool a few doors away (Db-€73–107, CC, *menus* from €24, rue de l'Eveche, tel. 04 90 36 04 71, fax 04 90 36 24 78, www.le-beffroi.com). **La Fête en Provence's** *chambres* sit above a good restaurant (*menu*-€24) and overlook a stone courtyard (Db-€50–75, huge duplex sleeps up to 5 people-€107, CC, place du Vieux Marche, tel. 04 90 36 36 43, fax 04 90 36 21 49, e-mail: fete-en-provence@wanadoo.fr).

Château Taulignan's *chambres d'hôte*, with six large rooms, offer a kid-friendly and dreamy setting from which to contemplate this beautiful region. Enjoy the big pool, Ping-Pong, and picnic tables (Db-€99, extra bed €15.2, CC, 84110 St. Marcellin, tel. 04 90 28 71 16, fax 04 90 28 75 04, e-mail: chateau@pacwan.fr). It's just five minutes from Vaison's TI; follow *Carpentras* signs and look for brown *chambres d'hôte* signs just as you leave Vaison.

A few kilometers away, below spectacularly situated Crestet (follow Carpentras from Vaison), **l'Ermitage Chambres** is well-run by British ex-pats Nick and Nicole. They have renovated a rustic farmhouse with three big, simple rooms, firm beds, and a pool with magnificent views (Db-€60, Tb-€75, no CC, turn right off D-938 at Loupiotte restaurant, 84110 Crestet, tel. 04 90 28 88 29, fax 04 90 28 72 97, www.lermitage.net).

L'Ecole Buissonniere *chambres* are run by another charming Anglo-France team, Monique and John, who have found complete isolation just 10 minutes from Vaison la Romaine in a tastefully restored farmhouse with three well-appointed rooms, each with very different personalities. I liked the Camargue loft room best (Db-€49, Tb-€59, Qb-€70, no CC, between Villedieu and Buisson on D-75, tel. 04 90 28 95 19, e-mail: ecole.buissonniere@wanadoo.fr).

Eating in and near Vaison la Romaine

La Bartavelle is the place to savor a slow meal in the lower city (€22 *menu*, closed Mon, 12 place Sus-Auze, reserve ahead tel. 04 90 36 02 16). **Le Brin d'Olivier** is also very good (see "Sleeping," above). Of the many cafés on place Montfort, **Pascal Boulangerie/Café** (at the far end) is the best value, though only open for dinner in summer. **Le Tournesol** is the best dinner value in town (34 cours Taulignan, tel. 04 90 36 09 18). The Ville-Haute has a view *crêperie* and a pizzeria with fair prices. The best view in Provence might well be from the simple **Restaurant Le Panorama** in tiny Crestet, a five-minute drive from Vaison la Romaine (cheap *menus* or simple *à la carte*, absolutely call ahead, tel. 04 90 28 86 62), though the relaxed, roadside **Restaurant Loupiote** is where locals go (below Crestet on D-938, tel. 04 90 36 29 50).

Transportation Connections— Vaison la Romaine

The most central bus stop is at Cave Vinicole. **By bus to:** **Avignon** (2/day, 75 min), **Orange** (3/day, 45 min). Bus info: tel. 04 90 36 09 90.

Highlights of the Côtes du Rhône

▲▲**Orange**—This most northern town in Provence is notable for its Roman arch and theater. The 18-meter-tall (60-foot) Roman Arc de Triomphe (from 25 B.C., north of city center on avenue Arc de Triomphe) honors Julius Caesar's defeat of the Gauls in 49 B.C. but is lightweight compared to the best-preserved Roman theater (*Théâtre Antique*) in existence. Information panels in English describe many aspects of the theater. Find a seat up high to appreciate the acoustics and contemplate the idea that, 2,000 years ago, Orange residents enjoyed grand spectacles with high-tech sound and lights effects, such as thunder, lightning, and rain. A huge awning could be unfurled from that awesome 40-meter-high stage wall to provide shade that you might appreciate now. It still seats 10,000 (€4.60, daily April–Sept 09:00–18:30, Oct–March 09:00–12:00, 13:30–17:00). Your ticket includes entrance to the city museum across the street, which has a few interesting renderings of the theater but no English explanations.

Orange has two helpful **TIs**, one that drivers will park near, and another across from the Roman theater (tel. 04 90 34 70 88). Drivers simply follow *centre-ville* signs, then *Théâtre Antique* signs, and park in the big lot near the TI. Trains run hourly between Avignon and Orange (15 min). From Orange's train station, it's a 15-minute walk to the theater (follow signs to *centre-ville*, then *Théâtre Antique*, and if you can't find it, ask a local, *"Oo-ay la tay-aht-ruh on-tique?"*). Buses to Vaison la Romaine and other wine villages depart from the big square, place Pourtoules (turn right out of the Roman theater and right again on rue Pourtoules).

▲**Vaison la Romaine**—This town is a good candidate for a home base for this region; for information, see above.

Gigondas—Nestled enviably at the base of the Dentelles de Montmirail mountains, this prosperous village produces some of the region's best wines and is ideally situated for hiking, mountain biking, and driving into these spectacular mountains. Several good tasting opportunities are on its main square. **Le Caveau des Vignerons** has a vast selection, nifty micro-bottle samples, and a donation-if-you-don't-buy system (daily 10:00–12:00, 14:00–19:00, next to TI). The info-packed **TI** (on the main square, rue du Portail, tel. 04 90 65 85 46) has a list of welcoming wineries, *chambres d'hôtes*, and good hikes or drives into the mountains (the €2.30 map *Chemins et Sentiers du Massif des Dentelles* is helpful, though routes are well-signed). Route 1 takes you on a scenic one-hour walk above Gigondas to great views from the Belvedere du Rocher du Midi (route 2 extends this hike into a 3-hour loop). Drivers can bump their way into incredible scenery by following the dirt road over Col du Cayron (drive past recommended Hostellerie les Florets and go to La Fare village, then hook into D-90 to either Beaumes de Venise or Malaucene; break for a wine tasting en route at Domaine de Cassan, just before La Fare). This drive is better as a two-hour one-way walk.

The comfortable and peaceful **Hostellerie les Florets****, one kilometer above the village, is a complete refuge and a good value. It's huddled at the foot of the Dentelles de Mont-mirail peaks (great hiking from here), with a huge, shady terrace, thoughtfully designed rooms, and an exceptional restaurant (Db-€73, Tb-€88, annex rooms are best, no CC, *menus* from €21, 84190 Gigondas, tel. 04 90 65 85 01, fax 04 90 65 83 80).

Sablet—This perfectly circular wine village, while impressive from a distance, has little of interest except scads of *chambres d'hôte*, well-signed from the road. Sablet wines are reasonable and tasty (the TI and wine cooperative share space in the town center), and its location is central on the wine route.

Seguret—Flawless little Seguret is etched into the side of a hill and has a smattering of shops, two cafés, made-to-stroll lanes, and a natural spring. Come here for compelling vistas and a quiet lunch.

La Bastide Bleue is blue-shutter Provençal, with seven rooms at fair prices and a charming restaurant (Db-€43, €54 July–Aug, includes breakfast, *menus* from €15, CC, just below Seguret, route de Sablet, tel. & fax 04 90 46 83 43).

Rasteau—Another stone village producing great wines. At **Le Domaine des Girasols**, friendly Françoise or John (SE) will take your palate on a tour of some of the area's best wine. It's well-marked and worth a stop. Their wine is a good value.

Cairanne—This least-visited of the wine villages I list is good for a stroll. Sleep surrounded by vineyards and views at the reasonable **Castel Mireio**** (Db-€50–62, CC, route d'Orange, tel. 04 90 30 82 20, fax 04 90 30 78 39).

▲Mount Ventoux and Sault—This sight is worth ▲▲▲ from late June to early August, when lavender blooms. Go only if it's clear and you can see the top of this 1,800-meter (6,000-foot) barren, wind-blown mountain; prepare for much cooler temperatures. Mount Ventoux is Provence's rooftop. You're above the treeline amid wildflowers, butterflies, and views extending from the lower Alps across what seems like all of southern France. The small restaurant **Le Vendran** (with arguably the best views in France) competes for your attention with the old observatory and Air Force control tower. Thirty minutes east, lavender fields forever surround the strollable village of Sault (pronounced "so"), which produces 40 percent of France's lavender essence. From the Vaison area, go to Malaucene, then take the twisty D-974 that loops scenically to and from Mount Ventoux. If continuing to Sault (worthwhile only when the lavender blooms), take D-974, then D-164 to Sault. Return via D-942 and the beautiful Gorges de la Nesque.

▲**Ardeche Gorges**—A 45-minute drive west of Vaison la Romaine, abrupt chalky-white cliffs follow the Ardeche River through immense canyons and thick forests. From Vaison, go to Bollene then follow the villages of Pont St. Esprit to Vallon Pont d'Arc (which offers all-day canoe-kayak floats through the gorge). If continuing north, connect Privas and Aubenas, then head back to the autoroute. Adorable Balazuc, a village north of the gorges, makes a fine stop.

NOT QUITE A YEAR IN PROVENCE: THE HILL TOWNS OF LUBERON

The Luberon region, stretching 50 kilometers along a ridge of rugged hills east of Avignon, hides some of France's most appealing and popular hill towns (including Bonnieux, Lacoste, Oppède le Vieux, Roussillon, Joucas, and Gordes).

Those intrigued by Peter Mayle's *A Year in Provence* will enjoy a day joyriding through the region. Mayle's best-selling book describes the ruddy local culture from an Englishman's perspective, as he buys a stone farmhouse, fixes it up, and adopts the region as his new home. This is a great read while you're here.

The Luberon terrain in general (much of which is a French regional natural park) is as appealing as its hill towns. Gnarled vineyards and wind-sculpted trees separate tidy stone structures from abandoned buildings—little more than rock piles—that seem to challenge city slickers to fix them up.

The wind is an integral part of life here. The infamous *mistral*, finishing its long ride in from Siberia, hits like a hammer—hard enough, it's said, to blow the ears off a donkey. Throughout the region you'll see houses designed with windowless walls facing the *mistral*.

Planning Your Time

To enjoy the windblown ambience of the Luberon, plan a leisurely daytrip visiting three or four of the characteristic towns (impossible *sans* car). Isle sur la Sorgue, located halfway between Avignon and the Luberon, has train service from Avignon (easy daytrip) and Nice (via Marseille) and makes a good biking base.

For the ultimate Luberon experience, hill town connoisseurs with cars should bypass Isle sur la Sorgue and sleep in one of the villages described below. The famous villages are beautiful but attract tourists like flypaper. For a quieter overnight, sleep in Oppède le Vieux, Joucas, or Lacoste. You'll pass *chambres d'hôte* signs everywhere (TIs have long lists), many pricey, and lovingly restored by foreigners..

Getting around the Luberon

Luberon

By Bus: To reach the hill towns such as Roussillon, go to Cavaillon or Apt, then taxi (1 bus/day from Avignon to Gordes, 2 buses/day from Cavaillon to Gordes, bus tel. 04 90 71 03 00).

By Train: Trains get you as far as Isle sur la Sorgue from Avignon (6/day, 30 min) or from Nice (4/day, 4 hrs, transfer in Marseille). Isle sur la Sorgue's train station is called L'Isle Fontaine de Vaucluse.

By Car: Town-hop for a day, side-tripping from your home base, or visit these villages as a detour en route to the French Riviera. Of course, tumbling in for an hour from the parking lot, you'll be just another flash-in-the-pan, camera-toting Provence fan. Spend a night, and you'll feel more a part of the scene. You need Michelin #246 to follow this scenic loop: Take the N-100 east of Avignon toward Apt and find little Lagnes just after Isle sur la Sorgue. Go through Lagnes, then Cabrieres d'Avignon, Gordes, Goult, and Roussillon. From Roussillon, follow Bonnieux and cross the Roman Pont Julien, then find Lacoste, Menerbes and, to complete the loop, Oppède le Vieux. I've listed places to sleep and eat in several of these villages (see below).

ISLE SUR LA SORGUE

This sturdy market town, literally, "Island on the Sorgue River," sits within a split in its happy little river and makes a good base for exploring the Luberon and Avignon. Do not confuse it with the nearby plain town of Sorgue. While Isle sur la Sorgue is renowned for its market days, it is otherwise a pleasantly average town with no important sights and a steady trickle of tourism. It's quiet at night and dead on Mondays.

With crystal-clear water babbling under pedestrian bridges lined with flower boxes, and its old-time carousel always spinning, Isle sur la Sorgue erupts into a market frenzy each Sunday and Thursday, with hardy crafts and local produce (the Sunday market is astounding and renowned for its antiques; the Thursday market is more intimate).

Navigate the town by its mossy waterwheels which, while still turning, power only memories of the town's wool and silk industries. The 12th-century church with its festive Baroque interior seems too big for the town.

Tourist Information: The **TI**, next door to the church, has a line on rooms in private homes, all of which are outside the town (Tue–Sat 9:00–12:30, 14:00–18:00, Sun 9:00–12:30, closed Mon, tel. 04 90 38 04 78). Ask where you can rent a bike. These places make good biking destinations: Velleron (8 km away, flat, a tiny version of Isle sur la Sorgue, with waterwheels, fountains, and an evening farmer's market Mon–Sat 18:00–20:00), Lagnes (5 km away, mostly flat, a pretty, well-restored hill town with views from its ruined château), and Fontaine de Vaucluse (11 km away, uphill, see "Villages of the Luberon," below). A Laundromat is on l'Impasse de la République (open 8:00–20:00).

Sleeping in and near Isle sur la Sorgue
(€1.10 = about $1, country code: 33, zip code: 84800)
Arrive the night before market day to best experience the town.

Hôtel les Nevons**, two blocks from the center (behind the PTT—post office) is motel-modern outside. Inside, however, it seems to do everything right, with comfortable, air-conditioned rooms (a few family suites), small rooftop pool, Internet access, and eager-to-please owners, Mireille and Jean-Philipe (Db-€49–61, Tb/Qb-€73–79, extra bed-€9-15, CC, easy and secure parking-€7.75, 205 Chemin des Nevons, tel. 04 90 20 72 00, fax 04 90 20 56 20, www.hotel-les-nevons .com). The bargain beds in town are sufficiently clean and almost quiet above a local bar at **Hôtel Le Cours de l'Eau** (D-€21, Db-€33, CC, on ring road opposite Café de la Sorgue at place Gambetta, tel. 04 90 38 01 18, no fax, no English). **Loy Soloy Restaurant/Hôtel** is the prow of the ship at the split of the river, with the best view rooms in town right over the water (rooms 1, 2, 3, and 7 have the views—and, sadly, some street noise, Db-€46–61, CC, 2 ave Charles de Gaulle, tel. & fax 04 90 38 03 16).

Eating in and near Isle sur la Sorgue
Begin your meal with a glass of wine at the cozy **Le Caveau de la Tour de l'Isle** (part wine bar, part wine shop, 12 rue de la République). **L'Oustau de l'Isle** is well-suited for a fine dinner (*menus* from €21, closed Wed–Thu off-season, 21 avenue des 4 Otages, near post office, tel. 04 90 38 54 83). The river-front cafés, **Café de la Sorgue** and **Café de Bellevue**, offer fair cuisine with maximum ambience. For a true Provençal experience, head three kilometers toward Velleron to **La Villa** and dine poolside. Mama cooks and Jerome serves a limited but flawless *menu* (€17.50, no CC, reservations necessary, kid-perfect, tel. 04 90 38 25 50).

ROUSSILLON

With all the trendy charm of Santa Fe on a hilltop, this town
will cost you at least a roll of film (and €2 for parking). Climb a
few minutes from either parking lot, past the picture-perfect
square and under the church to the summit of the town (follow
signs to *castum*), where a dramatic view, complete with a howling
mistral and a helpful *table d'orientation* awaits. Then, back under
the church, see how local (or artsy) you can look in what must be
the most scenic village square in the Luberon. On the south
end of town, beyond the upper parking lot, a brilliant ochre
canyon—formerly a quarry—is busy with walkers and explains
the color of this village (€1.50). You could paint the entire
town without ever leaving the red and orange corner of your
palette. Many do. While Roussillon receives its share of daytrippers, evenings are romantically peaceful. Thursday is Roussillon's market day; every day is Christmas for thieves—take
everything out of your car.

Sleeping in Roussillon
(€1.10 = about $1, country code: 33, zip code: 84220)
The **TI**, across from the David restaurant, posts a list of hotels
and *chambres d'hôte* (April–Oct Mon–Sat 09:30–12:00, 13:30–18:30,
Sun 14:00–18:30, Nov–March Mon–Sat 13:30–17:30, closed Sun,
tel. 04 90 05 60 25). For several more hotel and restaurant listings,
see "More Luberon Towns," below.

Hôtel Reves d'Ocres**, the only hotel in the town center,
is run by charming Sandrine and laid-back Web, with reasonably
comfortable, spacious rooms, the best with view terraces (Db-€61,
Tb-€76, balcony room about €8 extra, CC, air-con turned on
at the desk, tel. 04 90 05 60 50, fax 04 90 05 79 74, e-mail:
sables-ocre@web-ingenierie.com).

Madame Cherel rents simple but clean rooms with firm
mattresses and a common view terrace (D-€30–33, no CC, 3
blocks from upper parking lot, between gas station and school,
tel. 04 90 05 68 47). Cherel speaks English, is a wealth of regional
travel tips, and rents mountain bikes to guests only (€15/day).

The next three listings are most easily found by turning north
off the N-100 at the Roussillon/Les Huguets sign: **Les Passiflores**
chambre d'hôte, on D-108 between Roussillon and Bonnieux in
Les Huguets, is everything a *chambre d'hôte* should be: rustic,
charming, comfortable, and owned by the delightful Chantal
(Db-€46–50, includes breakfast, ask her to cook you dinner-€18
for the works, no CC, tel. & fax 04 90 05 69 61, NSE). If you
don't do rustic, try **Chambre d'hôte Les Puches**, offering
smart rooms with terraces and a pool that glissades over the
edge (Db-€61–69, breakfast-€7.75, no CC, 2 km below Roussillon toward Bonnieux on D-104, just past Hôtel Les Sables

d'Ocre, tel. & fax 04 90 05 66 02). **Hôtel Les Sables d'Ocre**** is modern and kid-friendly with good rooms, a big pool, lots of grass, and fair rates (Db-€52, Db with garden balcony-€69, Tb-€87, CC, at intersection of D-108 and D-104, tel. 04 90 05 55 55, fax 04 90 05 55 50).

Eating in Roussillon

Le Piquebaure hangs on a cliff and is the best bet in town for a fine meal (€20 *menus*, €12 garnished *plats du jour*, below Hôtel Reves d'Ocres, route du Gordes, closed Mon off-season, tel. 04 90 05 79 65). Inside the village, **Le Bistrot de Roussillon** is center stage on the square with view tables in the rear (€23 *menu*, closed Thu, tel. 04 90 05 74 45). Just off the main square, **Aux Agapes** does a good wood-fired pizza for €8 (if you like peppers, try their *salade Agapes*).

More Luberon Towns

Fontaine de Vaucluse—You'll read and hear a lot about this sub-limely located village at the source of the river Sorgue, where the medieval Italian poet Petrarch mourned for his love, Laura. This beautiful river seems to magically appear from nowhere (the actual source is a murky green water hole) and flows through Fontaine de Vaucluse, past a lineup of cafés, souvenir shops, and enough tourists to make Disney envious. Arrive by 09:00, after 19:00, or skip it.

Gordes—This is the most touristy and trendy town in the Luberon. Parisian big shots love it. Once a virtual ghost town of derelict buildings, it's now completely fixed up and filled by people who live in a world without calluses. The view as you approach is incredible and merits a detour, though the village has little of interest. The nearby and still-functioning 12th-century **Abbey de Senanque** can be crowded but is splendidly situated and worth a visit. When the lavender blooms (late June–July) this is a ▲▲▲ sight (€4.60, Mon–Sat 10:00–12:00, 14:00–18:00, Sun 14:00–18:00, arrive early to beat crowds).

Joucas—This village is everything Gordes is not: understated, quiet, and overlooked. Tiny cobbled lanes and well-restored homes play host to artists and a smattering of locals. At **La Maison de Mistral**, gregarious Marie-Lucie Mistral (they named the wind after her) has five oh-so-cozy rooms in her *chambre d'hôte* with a breakfast terrace to linger over and access to a nearby pool (Db-€53, extra person-€15.25, includes breakfast, no CC, rue de l'Eglise, tel. 04 90 05 74 01, cellular 06 62 08 15 03, fax 04 90 05 67 04, e-mail: pmistral@free.fr).

Lacoste—Slumbering under its ruined castle, tiny, steep, and quiet-at-night Lacoste has great views of the picturesque town of Bonnieux (listed below). Tuesday is market day here.

    Café de Sade is spotless, with six rooms above a little

restaurant (D-€32, Db-€46, family room-€61, dorm beds-€11.50, no CC, for dorm only, bring your own sheet or pay €3.80 to rent one, tel. 04 90 75 82 29, fax 04 90 75 95 68). **Le Relais du Procureur** is worth the detour for a country-elegant dinner (*menu* €20, closed Tue, tel. 04 90 75 84 78).

Bonnieux—Spectacular from a distance, this town disappoints, as it lacks a pedestrian center, though the Friday morning market briefly creates one.

Oppède le Vieux—This is a windy barnacle of a town, with a few boutiques and a dusty main square at the base of a short, ankle-twisting climb to a ruined church and castle. The Luberon views justify the effort. This way-off-the-beaten-path fixer-upper of a village must be how Gordes looked before it became chic. It's ideal for those looking to perish in Provence.

Goult—Bigger than its sister hill towns, this surprisingly quiet town seems content away from the tourist path. Wander up the hill to the panorama and windmill, and review its restaurants, where you won't compete with tourists for a table.

CASSIS

Cowering in the shadow of impossibly high cliffs, Cassis (cah-see) is what many are looking for when they come to the Riviera: An unpretentious beach town offering a sunny time-out from their busy vacation. Two hours away from the fray of the Côte d'Azur, Cassis is a poor man's St. Tropez. Outdoor cafés line the small port on three sides, where boaters chat up café clients while cleaning their boats. Cassis is popular with the French and close enough to Marseille to be busy on weekends and all summer. Come to Cassis for true *bouillabaisse*, to swim in crystal-clear water, and to scour its fjordlike *calanques*. Cassis is too far from Nice for daytripping.

Orientation

The Massif du Puget encloses Cassis on three of its four sides. The Cap Canaille cliff with the castle (property of the Michelin family) rises from the southeast. All roads spill into the port, and drivers should park at one of the well-signed pay lots above the port to avoid parking purgatory. The train station is three kilometers from Cassis, buses connect with most trains, and taxis cost about €9 with bags.

Tourist Information: The **TI**, just off the port near Hôtel Cassitel, can answer your every question from scuba diving to kayak rental, and help you find a room (May–Sept daily 09:00–18:00, Oct–April Mon–Sat 09:00–12:30, 13:30–17:30, Sun 10:00–12:30, place Baragnon, tel. 04 42 01 71 17, www.cassis.enprovence.com).

A **Laundromat** is up rue Victor Hugo at 9 rue Authemann (daily 09:00–21:00). The **shops** drop in price the farther you get from the port.

les roches blanches

Cassis

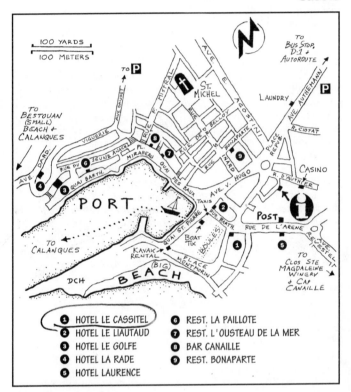

1 HOTEL LE CASSITEL
2 HOTEL LE LIAUTAUD
3 HOTEL LE GOLFE
4 HOTEL LA RADE
5 HOTEL LAURENCE

6 REST. LA PAILLOTE
7 REST. L'OUSTEAU DE LA MER
8 BAR CANAILLE
9 REST. BONAPARTE

Sights—Cassis

Beaches—Cassis' beaches are a sand/pebble mix. You can walk 15 minutes to plage du Bestouan and rent cushy mats, or find a sandy spot at the beach just south of the port.

▲▲**Calanques**—Cassis is all about *Les Calanques* (luh cah-lahnk). That's why most come here—but until you see them, it's hard to understand what all the excitement is about. Splintered, pasty-white rocks create fjordlike inlets with translucent blue water and intimate beaches. Most *calanques* are prickly extensions of cliffs that border the shore, but some rise directly out of the Mediterranean. You can cruise by boat, kayak, or hike to several *calanques*.

Boats will take you to any combination of 10 *calanques*, providing a water-based perspective (3 *calanques*-€9, 2/hr, 45 min; 5 *calanques*-€11.50, 2/day, 65 min; 10 *calanques*-€20, 1/day, 2 hrs). The three-*calanques* tour seems best. Buy tickets at the small booth on the south side of the port where boats depart.

Trails allow hiking/riding to three of the *calanques*. If you plan to spend time at a *calanque*, do so at *Calanque d'En Vau*; a boat provides direct round-trip service (2/hr, €11.50, one-way tickets available). Boats can drop you on a cliff if the sea is calm (short jump), but it's a steep, treacherous hike down to the beach for inexperienced climbers, and an even more difficult hike back up (you'll pay a surcharge to get off unless you buy a one-way ticket, and boats are often reluctant to let you off, so make sure they understand you want to get off at *Calanque d'En Vau* before buying your ticket). Hiking from Cassis to *Calanque d'En Vau* is a safer option, though you must get a map from the TI to follow the correct route. Avoid the shoreline route that requires rappelling skills; take the inland route and you'll do fine (some enjoy taking the boat there and hiking back). The TI has complete information on hiking and boating to the *calanques*. Bring water, sunscreen, and everything you need for the day, as there are no shops.

▲**La Route des Cretes**—Those with cars, or a willingness to hire a taxi (€25 for a good 45 min trip, 4 persons per taxi) can consider this amazing drive straight up to the top of the Cap Canaille to the industrial town of La Ciotat. Acrophobics should skip this narrow, twisty road that provides numbingly high views over Cassis and the Mediterranean at every turn. From Cassis, follow signs to La Citoat/Toulon then *la Route des Cretes*. Drive as far as you like; it's about 40 minutes all the way to La Ciotat.

Sleeping in Cassis
(€1.10 = about $1, country code: 33, zip code: 13260)
Hotels are a bargain compared with those on the Côte d'Azur. Note that many close from November to March.

Le Cassitel**, near the TI, is cute and cozy and located on the harbor over a sprawling café; the rooms with water views have nightlife noise (Db-€46–61, extra bed-€15.25, garage-€11, CC, place Clemenceau, tel. 04 42 01 83 44, fax 04 42 01 96 31, e-mail: cassitel@hotel-cassis.com).

Le Liautaud**, while perfectly located on the port near the TI, has uninspired rooms that are bare-bones modern (Db-€46–64, CC, 2 rue Victor Hugo, tel. 04 42 01 75 37, fax 04 42 01 12 08).

Hôtel le Golfe** is on the northwest corner of the port, over a lunch-only café. Half of its comfortable, long, and narrow rooms come with memorable views and small balconies; the others come with memorable air-conditioning (Db with view-€73, Db without view-€58, extra bed-€15.25, CC, 3 grand Carnot, tel. 04 42 01 00 21, fax 04 42 01 92 08, friendly Michele SE).

La Rade***, a two-minute walk above Hôtel le Golfe, has great views from its teak poolside chairs, and small but adequate rooms with air-conditioning and a busy road below (Db-€92–103, apartments-€150–165, extra bed €12.25, CC, route des Calanques, tel. 04 42 01 02 97, fax 04 42 01 01 32, e-mail: larade@hotel-cassis.com).

Hôtel Laurence**, two blocks off the port beyond Hôtel Cassitel, offers the best budget beds I found, in bland, tight, but clean rooms, some with decks and views (Db-€32–47, Db with terrace-€56, CC, 8 rue de l'Arene, tel. 04 42 01 88 78, fax 04 42 01 81 04).

Eating in Cassis

La Paillote sits on the harbor, with fair prices given its location and tasty cuisine (closed Sun–Mon, quai J-J Barthelemy, tel. 04 42 01 72 14). **L'Oustau de la Mer** has great food and friendly service (closed Thu, 20 quai de Baux, tel. 04 42 01 78 22). **Bar Canaille** is a casual, lunch-only place that has fabulously fresh seafood. It's tucked away in the corner of the port; look for the bright yellow awning (22 quai des Baux, tel. 04 42 01 72 36). **Bonaparte** is off the harbor and cheaper (14 rue du General Bonaparte, closed Sun–Mon, tel. 04 42 01 80 84).

Transportation Connections—Cassis

While the station is three kilometeres from the port, shuttle buses meet most trains and taxis are reasonable.

By train to: Arles (7/day, 2 hrs, change in Marseille), **Avignon** (7/day, 2 hrs, change in Marseille), **Nice** (7/day, 3 hrs, change in Toulon or Marseille), **Paris** (7/day, 4 hrs, change in Marseille).

THE FRENCH RIVIERA

A hundred years ago, celebrities from London to Moscow flocked here to socialize, gamble, and escape the dreary weather at home. The belle époque is today's tourist craze, as this most sought-after fun-in-the-sun destination now caters to budget travelers as well. Some of the Continent's most stunning scenery and intriguing museums lie along this strip of land—as do millions of heat-seeking tourists. Nice has world-class museums, a grand beach-front promenade, and a seductive old city. Daytrips are easy: Monte Carlo welcomes all with open cash registers, Antibes has a romantic port and silky-sandy beaches, and the hill towns present a breezy and photogenic alternative to the beach scene. Evenings on the Riviera, a.k.a. the Côte d'Azur, were made for the promenade and outdoor dining.

Choose a Home Base

I've listed accommodations for three different places: Nice, Antibes, and Villefranche sur Mer. **Nice** is the region's capital and France's fifth-largest city. With excellent public transportation to most regional sights, it's the most practical base for train travelers. Nice also has a full palette of museums and rock-hard beaches, the best selection of hotels in all price ranges, and is ground zero for Riviera nightlife. A car is a headache in Nice. Nearby **Antibes** is smaller, with fewer hotels but fine sandy beaches, good hiking, and the Picasso Museum. It has frequent train service to Nice and Monaco, and is easier for drivers. **Villefranche sur Mer** is the romantic's choice, with a serene setting and small-town warmth. It has finely ground pebble beaches, good public transportation (particularly to Nice and Monaco), and easy parking. Its few hotels leap from simple to sublime, letting Nice handle the middle ground.

Planning Your Time

Most should plan a full day for Nice and at least a half day
each for Monaco and Antibes. Monaco is best at night (sights
are closed but crowds are few, consider dinner here), and Antibes
during the day (good beaches and Picasso Museum). St. Paul
de Vence, Vence, and Eze Village are lower priorities, but offer
a scenic, hilly escape from the beach scene.

Getting around the Riviera

Getting around the Côte d'Azur by train or bus is easy (park
your car and leave the driving to others). For some of the
Riviera's best scenery, follow the coast road between Cannes
and Fréjus (when arriving in or leaving the Côte d'Azur),
take the short drive along *Moyenne Corniche* from Nice to
Eze Village, and take my recommended hill-town drive.
Tune into Riviera-Radio at FM 106.5 for English radio.

Nice is perfectly located for exploring the region.
Monaco, Eze Village, Villefranche, Antibes, St. Paul, and
Cannes are all a 15- to 60-minute bus or train ride apart
from each other. The TI (and probably your hotel) has
information on minivan excursions from Nice (half day-
about €61, full day-€76-107; Tour Azur is one of many,
tel. 04 93 44 88 77, www.tourazur.com).

Bus service can be cheaper and more frequent than
rail service, depending on the destination. At Nice's efficient bus station (*gare routière*), on boulevard J. Jaures
(see map of Nice), you'll find a baggage check (called
messagerie, available Mon–Sat), clean WCs for €0.40, and
several bus companies offering free return trips to some
destinations (keep your ticket). Get schedules and prices
at the helpful information desk in the bus station. Buy
tickets in the station or on the bus.

Here's an overview of public transport options to key
Riviera destinations from Nice (rt = round-trip, ow = one-way):

Destination	Bus	Train
Monaco	4/hr, 40 min, €3, rt	2/hr, 20 min, €3, ow
Villefranche	4/hr, 15 min, €1.40, rt	2/hr, 10 min, €1.40, ow
Antibes	3/hr, 50 min, €4.25, ow	2/hr, 25 min, €3.35, ow
Cannes	way too long	2/hr, 30 min, €4.90, ow
St. Paul	2/hr, 45 min, €3, ow	none
Vence	2/hr, 45 min, €4.60, ow	none
Eze Village	every 2 hrs, 25 min, €2.30, rt	none

Two bus companies, RCA and Cars Broch, provide service on
the same route between Nice, Villefranche, and Monaco; RCA's
buses run more frequently (tel. 04 93 85 61 81 for info on both).

The French Riviera

Cuisine Scene—Côte d'Azur

The Côte d'Azur (technically a part of Provence) gives Provence's cuisine a Mediterranean flair. Local specialties are *bouillabaisse* (the spicy seafood stew-soup that seems worth the cost only for those with a seafood fetish), *bourride* (a creamy fish soup thickened with aioli, a garlic sauce), and *salade niçoise* (nee-swaz; a tasty tomato, potato, olive, anchovy, and tuna salad). You'll also find these tasty bread treats: *pissaladière* (bread dough topped with onions, olives, and anchovies), *fougasse* (a spindly, lacelike bread), *socca* (a thin chickpea crepe), and *pan bagnat* (a bread shell stuffed with tomatoes, anchovies, olives, onions, and tuna). Good Italian cuisine is easy to find and generally a good value. White and rosé Bellet and the rich reds and rosés of Bandol are the local wines.

This is the most difficult region in France in which to find reliable restaurant listings. Because most visitors come more for the sun than the cuisine, and because the clientele is predominantly international, most restaurants aim for the middle and are hard to distinguish from each other. Look for views and ambience and lower your expectations.

Art Scene—Côte d'Azur

The list of artists who have painted the Riviera reads like a Who's Who of 20th-Century Art: Renoir, Matisse, Chagall, Braque, Dufy, Leger, and Picasso all lived and worked here. Their simple, semi-abstract, and, above all, colorful works reflect the Riviera. You'll experience the same landscapes they painted in this bright, sun-drenched region punctuated with views of the "azure sea."

But mostly the artists were drawn to the simple lifestyle of fishermen and farmers that has reigned here since time began. These *très* serious artists, as they grew older, retired in the sun and turned their backs on modern art's "isms" and painted with the wide-eyed wonder of children, using bright, primary colors, simple outlines, and simple subjects.

A remarkable concentration of well-organized contemporary art museums (many described below) litter the Riveria, allowing art-lovers to appreciate these artists' work while immersed in the same sun and culture that inspired them. Many of the museums were designed to blend the art with surrounding views, gardens, and fountains, highlighting that modern art is not only stimulating, but sometimes simply beautiful.

NICE

Nice (neece) is the ultimate tourist melting pot. You'll share its international beaches with the chicest of the chic, the cheapest of the cheap, and everyone else in this scramble to be where the mountains meet the water. Nice's spectacular Alps-to-Mediterranean scenery, thriving old city, eternally entertaining seafront promenade, and fine museums make settling into this city easy. Nice may be nice, but it's hot and jammed in July and August. Get a room with air-conditioning (*avec climatization*). Everything you'll want in Nice is walkable or a short bus ride away.

Orientation

Most sights and hotels recommended in this book are located near the avenue Jean Medécin, between the train station and the beach. It's a 20-minute walk from the train station to the beach (or a €9 taxi ride) and a 20-minute walk along the promenade from the fancy Hôtel Negresco to the heart of Old Nice.

Tourist Information: Nice has four helpful TIs: at terminal 1 at the airport, next to the train station, on RN-7 after the airport on the right, and across from the beach at 5 promenade des Anglais (all open daily 08:00–19:00, until 20:00 July–Aug, can book rooms for a small fee, tel. 04 93 87 07 07 or 04 92 14 48 00).

Pick up the excellent, free Nice map (which lists all the sights and hours), the extensive *Practical Guide to Nice*, information on regional daytrips (such as maps to Antibes), and the museums booklet.

Consider buying the **museum pass**. The regional *Carte Musées* is a great value for those planning to visit more than one museum in a day or several museums over a few days (€5.50/ 1 day, €13/3 consecutive days, €24/7 consecutive days, valid at all museums described in this chapter except Foundation Maeght, sold at any TI or participating museum).

Arrival in Nice

By Train: Nice has one main station (*Nice-Ville*, lockers available) where all trains stop and you get off. Avoid the suburban stations. The TI is next door to the left as you exit the train station, car rental is to the right. To reach my recommended hotels, turn left out of the station, then right on avenue Jean Médecin. To get to the beach and the promenade des Anglais from the station, continue on foot for 20 minutes down avenue Jean Médecin or take bus #12 (stop on Jean Médecin). To get to the old city and the bus station (*gare routière*), catch bus #5 from avenue Jean Médecin.

By Car: Avoid arriving at rush hour (Mon–Fri 17:00–19:30). Stop at the roadside TI just past the airport, then park at the lot at the Nice Etoile shopping center on avenue Jean Médecin (ticket booth on 3rd floor, about €13/day, €7.75 from 20:00–8:00). Most Nice street parking is metered, and garages cost from €9 to €14 per day—your hotel can advise you best.

By Plane: Nice's mellow, user-friendly airport is on the Mediterranean, about 25 minutes west of the city center. The TI and international flights use terminal 1; domestic flights use terminal 2 (airport tel. 04 93 21 30 30). At terminal 1 you'll find the TI, banks (so-so rates), and car rental just outside customs. Taxis wait immediately outside the terminal (allow €25–30 to Nice hotels, €45 to Villefranche). Turn left after passing customs to find the bus information office (taxi vouchers to Villefranche sold here for €43). Three bus lines run to Nice: the Nice-Direct express bus to the SNCF train station (stall #6, €3.50, 2/hr until 21:00, 20 min, drops you within a 10-min walk of many of my hotel listings), local bus #23 (also stall #6, €1.40, 4/hr, 40 min, direction: St. Maurice, serves stops between the airport and SNCF station), and the yellow "NICE" bus to the bus station (*gare routière*, stall #1, €3.50, 3/hr, 25 min). To get to Villefranche from the airport, take the yellow "NICE" bus to the bus station (*gare routière*) and transfer to the Villefranche bus (€1.40, 4/hr). Buses also run to Antibes and Monaco from the airport (both hrly, 50 min).

Helpful Hints

Theft Alert: Nice is notorious for pickpockets. Have nothing important on or around your waist, unless it's in a money belt tucked out of sight (no fanny packs, please); don't leave anything visible in your car; be wary of scooters when standing at intersections; don't leave things unattended on the beach while swimming; and stick to main streets in Old Nice after dark.

U.S. Consulate: If you lose your passport, this is the place to go (31 rue Marechal Joffre, tel. 04 93 88 89 55, fax 04 93 87 07 38).

Medical Help: Dr. Veronique Margery speaks English (26 rue Paul Deroulede, tel. 04 93 87 21 25, cellular 06 12 44 97 85).

Taxis: Taxis allow four passengers in Nice and are handy to some museums. They normally only pick up at taxi stands (*tête de station*) or by a telephoned request. You'll pay €1 per bag and supplements for service on Sunday and after 19:00 any day (tel. 04 93 13 78 78).

Rocky Beaches: To make life tolerable on the rocks, swimmers should buy a pair of the cheap plastic beach shoes (flip-flops fall off in the water) sold at many shops.

American Express: AmEx faces the beach at 11 promenade des Anglais (tel. 04 93 16 53 53).

English Bookstore: Try **The Cat's Whiskers** (closed Sun, 26 rue Lamartine, near Hôtel Star).

Laundromats: Self-serve Laundromats abound in Nice; ask your hotelier for suggestions and guard your load.

Internet Access: It's easy in Nice. Ask your hotelier for the nearest Internet café.

Sights—Nice

▲▲**Promenade des Anglais**—Welcome to the Riviera. There's something for everyone along this seafront circus. Watch the Europeans at play, admire the azure Mediterranean, anchor yourself in a blue chair, and prop your feet up on the made-to-order guardrail. Join the evening parade of tans along the promenade. Start at the pink-domed Hôtel Negresco and, like the belle époque (late 19th-century) English aristocrats for whom the promenade was built, stroll to the old city and Castle Hill (20-min walk).

Hôtel Negresco, Nice's finest hotel and a historic monument, offers the city's most costly beds and a free "museum" interior (reasonable attire is necessary to enter). March through the lobby into the exquisite Salon Royal. The tsar's chandelier hangs from an Eiffel-built dome. Read the explanation, check out the room photos, and stroll the circle. On your way out, pop into the Salon Louis XIV (more explanations).

The next block to your left as you exit has a lush park and the Masséna Museum. The TI is beyond that. Cross over to the promenade.

Nice

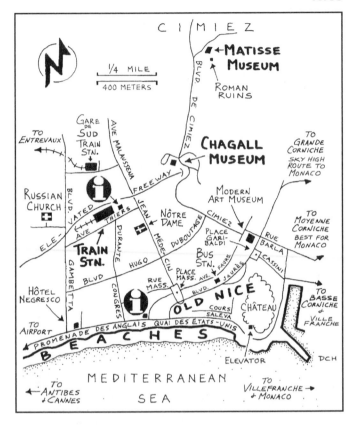

Pull up a chair and admire the scene (beautiful after dark). To your right is the airport, built on a landfill, and, on that tip of land way out there, Cap d'Antibes. Until the late 1800s, Antibes and Nice were in different countries; the Italians gave Nice to the French as thanks for their help during the reunification of Italy in 1860. To the far left lies Villefranche-sur-Mer (beyond that tower at land's end), Monaco, then Italy. Behind you are the pre-Alps (*les Alpes Maritimes*), which gather threatening clouds and leave the Côte d'Azur in sunshine over 300 days per year. Turn around. To the right of Hôtel Negresco sit two other belle epoque establishments: the West End and Westminster hotels. These hotels represent Nice's initiation as a tourist mecca 100 years ago, when the combination of leisure time and a stable economy allowed wealthy tourists to find the sun even in winter. Tourism as we know it today took off after World War II (blame planes, trains, and automobiles), allowing even budget travelers to appreciate this once-exclusive resort. Now get down to that beach.

Beaches—Nice is where the jet set relax *à la plage*. After settling into the smooth pebbles, you can play beach volleyball, Ping-Pong, or *boules*; rent paddleboats, jet skis, or windsurfing equipment; explore ways to use your zoom lens as a telescope; or snooze on comfy beach beds with end tables (mattress-€9, mattress and chaise lounge-€11, umbrella-€4.60). Have lunch in your bathing suit (€9 salads and pizzas). Before heading off in search of sandy beaches, try it on the rocks. As you stroll the promenade, look for the *Plage Publique* signs explaining the 15 beach no-nos (translated in English).

▲▲Old City (Vieux Nice)—The thriving old city is characteristic Nice in the buff. Here Italian and French flavors mix to create a spicy Mediterranean dressing. The modern age drove Old Nice into a triangle of spindly streets filling a corner between Castle Hill and the beach. A broad, park-lined boulevard seals it off. The streets, while straight, are anything but predictable. Stealth pigeons fly under tall, pastel, domestic cliffs, while tattoo shops show their work. The Naples-like rue Droite plays host to simple bars, chic art shops, and shaded strolling; stop by Le Four à Bois bakery (at #38) and watch them make *fougasse*. The fresh pasta shops (almost nonexistent elsewhere in France) and many *gelaterias* remind us how close we are to Italy. Cours Saleya, a long broad square, collects people, produce, and flowers as if in a trough between all this and the sea. Restaurant tables tangle with market stalls and browsers. Dinner here is a treat—not for the cuisine, but for the sea of tables and festive feel. The daily flower and produce market becomes a flea market on Monday. Nearby place Rosetti is more intimate and utterly Italian at night (more average restaurants). Duck into the Cathedral St. Reparate for a dose of Italian Baroque. The fish market on place St. Francois isn't worth the detour.

Castle Hill—Climb or, better yet, take the elevator up this saddle horn in the otherwise flat city center only for exercise or the view (elevator is next to Hôtel Suisse where the bay-front road curves to the right, €0.60 one-way, €1 round-trip). The views over Nice, the port (to the east), the Alps foothills, and the Mediterranean make a decent reward, better if you took the elevator, best at sunset (park closes at 20:00 in summer, earlier off-season). You'll find a waterfall, a playground, two cafés (fair prices), and a cemetery, but no castle on Castle Hill. If you walk down, follow signs from just below the upper café to *Vielle Ville* (not *le Port*), and turn right at the cemetery, then look for the walkway down on your left.

▲Russian Cathedral—Even if you've been to Russia, this Russian Orthodox church, which claims to be the finest outside Russia, is interesting. Its one-room interior is filled with icons and candles.

Tsar Nicholas II gave his aristocratic countryfolk—who wintered on the Riviera—this church in 1912. (A few years later, Russian comrades who didn't winter on the Riviera shot him.) Here in the land of olives and anchovies, these proud onion domes seem odd. But, I imagine, so did those old Russians (€1.85, daily 09:00–12:00, 14:30–18:00, services Sat at 18:00, Sun at 10:00, no shorts, 10-min walk behind station at 17 boulevard du Tsarevitch, tel. 04 93 96 88 02). **Nightlife**—Nice's bars play host to the Riviera's most happening late-night scene, full of jazz and rock 'n' roll. Most activity focuses on Old Nice, near place Rossetti. If you're out very late, avoid walking alone. Plan on a cover charge or expensive drinks.

Museums—Nice

▲▲**Musée National Marc Chagall**—Even if you're suspicious of modern art, this museum—with the largest collection of Chagall's work anywhere—might appeal to you. After World War II, Chagall returned from the United States to settle in nearby Vence. Between 1954 and 1967, he painted a cycle of 17 large murals designed for and donated to this museum. These paintings, inspired by the books of Genesis, Exodus, and the Song of Songs, make up the "nave," or core, of what Chagall called the "House of Brotherhood."

Each painting is a lighter-than-air collage of images drawing from Chagall's Russian-folk-village youth, his Jewish heritage, Biblical themes, and his feeling that he existed somewhere between heaven and earth. He felt the Bible was a synonym for nature, and color and Biblical themes were key ingredients for understanding God's love for his creation. Chagall's brilliant blues and reds celebrate nature, as do his spiritual and folk themes. Notice the focus on couples. To Chagall, humans loving each other mirrored God's love of creation.

Don't miss the stained-glass windows of the auditorium (enter through the garden), early family photos of the artist, and a room full of Chagall lithographs. The small €3 guidebook begins with an introduction by Chagall (€4.60, €5.80 in summer, July–Sept Wed–Mon 10:00–17:40, Oct–June 10:00–16:40, closed Tue, ask about English tours, tel. 04 93 53 87 20). An idyllic café awaits in the garden.

Getting to Chagall and Matisse Museums: The Chagall Museum is a confusing but manageable 15-minute walk from the top of avenue Jean Médecin and the train station; the Matisse Museum (described below) is a 30-minute uphill walk from the Chagall Museum. Buses #15 and #17 serve Chagall and Matisse from the eastern, Italy side of avenue Jean Medécin (both run 6/hr, €1.30). Consider walking to Chagall and taking the bus to Matisse.

To walk to the Chagall Museum, go to the train-station end of avenue Jean Médecin and turn right onto rue Raimbaldi along the overpasses, then turn left under the overpasses onto avenue Comboul. Once under the overpass, angle to the right up rue Olivetto to the alley with the big wall on your right. A pedestrian path soon emerges, leading up and up to signs for Chagall and Matisse. The bus to Matisse is on avenue Cimiez, two blocks up from Chagall.

▲**Matisse Museum (▲▲▲** for his fans)—The art is beautifully displayed in this elegant orange mansion and represents the single largest collection of Matisse paintings. While many don't get Matisse, this museum offers a painless introduction to this influential artist whose style was shaped by the southern light and fellow Côte d'Azur artists, Picasso and Renoir. Watch as his style becomes simpler with time. A room on the top floor has models of his famous Chapelle du Rosaire in nearby Vence and illustrates the beauty of his simple design (€4, April–Sept Wed–Mon 10:00–18:00, Oct–March 10:00–17:00, closed Tue, take bus #15 or #17 to Arènes stop, see directions under Chagall Museum listing above, tel. 04 93 81 08 08).

Modern Art Museum (Musée d'Art Moderne et d'Art Contemporain)—This ultramodern museum features an enjoyable collection of art from the 1960s and 1970s, including works by Andy Warhol and Roy Lichtenstein, and frequent special exhibits (€4, Wed–Mon 10:00–18:00, Fri until 22:00, closed Tue, on promenade des Arts near bus station, tel. 04 93 62 61 62).

Other Nice Museums—These museums offer decent rainy-day options (generally open 10:00-12:00, 14:00-18:00). The **Musée des Beaux Arts** (Fine Arts Museum), with 6,000 works from the 17th to 20th centuries, will satisfy your need for a fine-arts fix (€4, 3 avenue des Baumettes, in western end of Nice, tel. 04 92 15 28 28). The **Musée de la Marine** (Naval Museum) is interesting and relevant, given Nice's huge port (€2.30, in Tour Bellanda, halfway up Château Hill, tel. 04 93 80 47 61). The **Musée Masséna** describes Nice's history (€4, facing beach next to Hôtel Negresco at 65 rue de France, tel. 04 93 88 11 34). The **Musée Archeologique** (Archaeological Museum) displays Roman ruins and various objects from the Romans' occupation of this region (€4, near Matisse Museum at 160 avenue des Arenes, tel. 04 93 81 59 57).

Between Nice and Monaco

▲▲▲**The Three Corniches**—Nice and Monaco are linked with three coast-hugging routes, each one higher than the other, all offering sensational views and a different perspective on this billion-dollar slice of real estate. The *Basse Corniche* (the lower cornice, often called *Corniche Inférieure*) strings ports, beaches, and villages together for a ground-floor view. The *Moyenne Corniche* (middle cornice) is far more impressive and slices its way halfway to the top, connecting hill towns such as Eze Village and providing great views over the Mediterranean below. Napoleon's crowning road-construction achievement, the *Grande Corniche* (Great Cornice), caps the cliffs with staggering views from almost 480 meters (1,600 feet) above the sea. For the best of all worlds, take the Moyenne Corniche from Nice to Eze Village, find the Grande Corniche/La Turbie from there, and drop down to Monaco after La Turbie (see "Sights near Villefranche-sur-Mer," below). Buses travel each route; the higher the cornice, the less frequent the buses (get details at Nice's bus station).

Sleeping in Nice
(€1.10 = about $1, country code: 33, zip code: 06000)
Sleep Code: **S** = Single, **D** = Double/Twin, **T** = Triple, **Q** = Quad, **b** = bathroom, **s** = shower only, **CC** = Credit Cards, **no CC** = Credit Cards not accepted, **SE** = Speaks English, **NSE** = No English, * = French hotel rating (0–4 stars). Hotels have elevators unless otherwise noted.

Don't look for charm in Nice. Go for modern and clean with a central location and, in summer, air-conditioning. Reserve early for summer visits. Prices generally drop €5 to €10 from October to April (the rates listed are for May–Sept) and increase during Carnival (Jan 31–Feb 2) and the Monaco Grand Prix (May 23–27). Most hotels near the station are overrun, overpriced, and loud. I sleep halfway between Old Nice (Vieux Nice) and the train station, near avenues Jean Médecin and Victor Hugo. Drivers can park under the Nice Etoile shopping center (on avenue Jean Médecin and boulevard Dubouchage). Hotels are listed in order of proximity to the train station, the latter being closest to Old Nice and the beach.

Hôtel Excelsior*, one block below the station, is a diamond in the rough with 19th-century decor, a lush garden courtyard with fountain, pleasant rooms with real wood furnishings, and an elegant dining room (*menus* from €19). Rooms on the garden are best in the summer; those streetside have balconies and get winter sun (Db-€72–87, Tb-€87–102, CC, 19 avenue Durante, tel. 04 93 88 18 05, fax 04 93 88 38 69, www.excelsiornice.com).

Hôtel Trianon**, with formal owners, is a small, big-city refuge with very fair rates and bright, spotless rooms, half of which overlook a small park (Sb-€44, Db-€53, CC, 15 avenue Auber, tel. 04 93 88 30 69, fax 04 93 88 11 35).

Hôtel du Petit Louvre*, is basic, but a solid budget bet, with playful owners (the Vilas), art-festooned walls, and adequate rooms (Ds-€35, Db-€39, Tb-€41–46, CC, payment due on arrival, 10 rue Emma Tiranty, tel. 04 93 80 15 54, fax 04 93 62 45 08, e-mail: petilouvr@aol.com).

Hôtel Clemenceau**, is a good value with a homey, family feel and mostly spacious, traditional, and comfortable rooms, some with balconies, all with air-conditioning, but no elevator

Nice Hotels

1. HOTEL DU PETIT LOUVRE
2. HOTEL CLEMENCEAU
3. HOTEL ST. GEORGES
4. HOTEL STAR
5. HOTEL VENDOME
6. HOTEL LORRAIN
7. HOTEL LES CAMELIAS
8. HOTEL MASSENA
9. HOTEL LAFAYETTE
10. HOTEL NOUVEL
11. HOTEL WINDSOR
12. HOTEL EXCELSIOR
13. HOTEL SUISSE
14. HOTEL MERCURE
15. HOTEL TRIANON
16. NISSA SOCCA CAFE
17. ACCHIARDO REST.
18. LOU NISSART REST.
19. L'AUTHENTIC, LE VIN REST. SUR VIN & LE CENAC REST.
20. LE CÔTE GRILL
21. LES VIVIERS REST.
22. CHARCUTERIE JULIEN DELI & LA CAMBOSE REST.
23. REST. LA DIVA
24. HOTEL SPLENDID

(S-€31, Sb-€38, D-€43, Db-€46, Tb-€61, Qb-€77, kitchenette-€7.75 extra and for long stays only, CC, 3 avenue Clemenceau, 1 block west of avenue Jean Médecin, tel. 04 93 88 61 19, fax 04 93 16 88 96, Marianne SE).

Hôtel St. Georges**, a block away, is bigger and brighter with air-conditioning, a peaceful garden courtyard, reasonably roomy and comfortable rooms, and happy Jacques at the reception (Sb-€55, Db-€64, 3-bed Tb-€80, extra bed-€15, CC, 7 avenue

Clemenceau, tel. 04 93 88 79 21, fax 04 93 16 22 85, e-mail: nicefrance.hotelstgeorges@wanadoo.fr).

Hôtel Star**, a few blocks east of avenue Jean Médecin, is immaculate, air-conditioned, comfortable, and a truly great value. It's run by intense Françoise and mellower Georges (SE) who expect you to respect their high standards (Sb-€33–39, Db-€45–55, Tb-€59–69, breakfast-€4.60, CC, fine beds, beach towels, no elevator, 14 rue Biscarra, reserve by fax or e-mail rather than by phone, tel. 04 93 85 19 03, fax 04 93 13 04 23, e-mail: star-hotel@wanadoo.fr, www.hotel-star.com).

Hôtel les Camelias** reminds me of the Old World places I stayed in as a kid traveling with my parents. A well-located, dark, creaky, and floral place burrowed behind a small parking lot and garden, it has linoleum halls, simple rooms (some lumpy beds), and a loyal clientele who give the TV lounge a retirement-home-after-dinner feeling. Some rooms have balconies—request a *chambre avec balcon* (Ss-€40, Ds-€46, Db-€62, includes breakfast, parking-€4.60, CC, 3 rue Spitaleri, tel. 04 93 62 15 54, fax 04 93 80 42 96, formal Madame Vimont and her son Jean Claude SE). The €11 four-course dinner is simple, hearty, and stressless.

Hôtel Vendome***, a mansion, gives you a whiff of *la belle époque*, with pink pastels, high ceilings, and grand staircases. Rooms are small but adequate; the best have balconies—request a *chambre avec balcon*. The most desirable rooms are on the fifth floor (Sb-€82–89, Db-€98–106, Tb-€110–118, Qb-€128, extra bed-€15.25, CC, air-con, limited off-street parking-€8, cable TV, 26 rue Pastorelli, tel. 04 93 62 00 77, fax 04 93 13 40 78, e-mail: contact@vendome-hotel-nice.com).

Hôtel Lafayette*** looks big and average from the outside, but inside it's a cozy, good value offering 18 sharp, spacious, three-star rooms at two-star rates, all one floor up from the street (Sb-€60–76, Db-€75–96, Tb-€90–111, extra bed-€15.50, CC, no elevator, 32 rue de l'Hôtel des Postes, tel. 04 93 85 17 84, fax 04 93 80 47 56, e-mail: lafayette@nouvel-hotel.com).

Hôtel Masséna****, a few blocks from place Massena in a beautiful old building, is a business hotel offering 100 four-star rooms with all the comforts at reasonable rates (Db-€100–137, larger Db-€168, Tb-€198, Qb-€213, CC, reserve a parking space ahead-€15.50, Internet access in lobby, 58 rue Gioffredo, tel. 04 93 85 49 25, fax 04 93 62 43 27, www.hotel-massena-nice.com, SE).

Hôtel Lorrain** offers kitchenettes in all of its simple but spacious rooms and is conveniently located one block from the bus station and Old Nice (Sb-€38, Db-€46, Tb-€53, Qb-€69, CC, 6 rue Gubernatis, push top buzzer to release door, tel. 04 93 85 42 90, fax 04 93 85 55 54, e-mail: hotellorrain@aol.com).

Hôtel Mercure*** is on the water, behind Cours Saleya, and offers predictable, modern rooms at good rates considering the

location (Sb-€84, Db-€94, CC, air-con, some balconies and
views, 91 quai des Etats-Unis, tel. 04 93 85 74 19, fax 04 93 13
90 94, e-mail: H0962@accor-hotels.com).

Hôtel Suisse*** offers Nice's best ocean views for the money
with many balconied rooms. Rooms are comfortable, with air-
conditioning and modern conveniences, and are surprisingly quiet
given the busy street below (Db without view-€67, Db with great
view-€92–107, extra bed-€20, CC, 15 quai Rauba-Capeu, tel. 04 92
17 39 00, fax 04 93 85 30 70, e-mail: nice@hotels-primotel.com).

Hotels near boulevard Victor Hugo: The next three hotels
are on or very near this tree-lined boulevard, several blocks west
of avenue Jean Médecin and about five blocks from the beach.

Hôtel Nouvel** is a well-run, spotless place set on a broad
sidewalk with modern rooms (Sb-€61–76, Db-€67–84, Tb apart-
ment-€112–136, CC, air-con, 19 bis boulevard Victor Hugo, tel.
04 93 87 15 00, fax 04 93 16 00 67, www.nouvel-hotel.com).

Hôtel Windsor***, a snazzy, airy, garden retreat with many
contemporary rooms designed by modern artists, has a swimming
pool, free gym, and €9 sauna (Db-€87–120, extra bed-€15, rooms
over garden are worth the higher price, CC, 11 rue Dalpozzo,
10 blocks west of Jean Medécin and 5 blocks from sea, tel. 04 93
88 59 35, fax 04 93 88 94 57, e-mail: windsor@webstore.fr, SE).

Hôtel Splendid**** is a worthwhile splurge if you miss your
Hilton. The rooftop pool, Jacuzzi, and panoramic breakfast room
alone almost justify the cost—throw in luxurious rooms, a free
gym, Internet access, and air-conditioning, and you're as good
as home (Db-€167–214, suites-€282–300, limited parking-€14,
CC, 50 boulevard Victor Hugo, tel. 04 93 16 41 00, fax 04 93 16
42 70, www.splendid-nice.com).

Eating in Nice

Nice's old city overflows with restaurants in all shapes and sizes.
The dinner scene on Cours Saleya is as entertaining as the food is
average. It's a fun, festive place to compare tans and new outfits.
Comparison shopping is half the fun (I go Italian). **La Cambuse**
is the lone exception, offering a more refined setting and fine cuisine for a bit more (5 Cours Saleya, tel. 04 93 80 02 40). **Charcuterie Julien** is a good deli that sells an impressive array of local
dishes by weight. Buy 200 grams of your choice plopped into a
plastic carton to go (*pour emporter*, poor ahn-por-tay) or eat there
(Thu–Tue 11:00–19:30, closed Wed, rue de la Poissonnerie, at
Castle Hill). **Nissa Socca** café offers good, cheap Italian cuisine
in Old Nice in a lively atmosphere (opens at 19:00, closed Sun,
arrive early, a block off place Rossetti on rue Ste. Reparate, tel.
04 93 80 18 35). Deeper in the old city, **Acchiardo's** is a budget
traveler's best friend, with simple, hearty food at bargain prices
and no fluff (closed Sat–Sun, 38 rue Droite, tel. 04 93 85 51 16).

Just below place Masséna, **Lou Nissart** serves regional specialties to appreciative locals in non-air-conditioned rooms (moderate
prices, across place Masséna at 1 rue de l'Opéra, tel. 04 93 85 34 49).
Across the street, **La Diva** is softer, stylish, and popular (€15–22
menus, closed Sun–Mon, 4 rue de l'Opera, tel. 04 93 85 96 15). For
the best, most authentic Niçoise cuisine in this book (allow €30 for
dinner), reserve a table at the cozy **Les Viviers** (5-min walk west of
avenue Jean Médecin at 22 rue Alphonse Karr, tel. 04 93 16 00 48;
they also run a more elegant restaurant next door).

Several relaxed cafés line the broad sidewalk on rue Biscarra,
just east of avenue Jean Medécin between numbers 16 and 18.
L'Authentic, **Le Vin sur Vin** (with a wine emphasis), and **Le
Cenac** are all reasonable. On the other side of avenue Jean
Medécin, **Le Côte Grill** is bright, cool, and easy, with a salad
bar, air-conditioned rooms, a large selection at reasonable
prices, and a friendly staff (1 avenue Georges Clemenceau,
tel. 04 93 82 45 53).

Transportation Connections—Nice
By train to: Arles (11/day, 3.5 hrs, 10 with change in Marseille),
Paris' Gare de Lyon (14/day, 5.5–7 hrs, 6 with change in
Marseille), **Venice** (3/day, 3/night, 11–15 hrs, 5 require changes),
Chamonix (4/day, 11 hrs, 2–3 changes), **Beaune** (7/day, 7 hrs,
change in Lyon), **Digne/Grenoble** (consider the scenic little
trains that run from Nice to Digne, then on to Grenoble; see
"Travel Notes for La Route de Napoléon" at end of this chapter),
Munich (2/day, 12 hrs with 2 changes, 1 night train with a
change in Verona), **Interlaken** (1/day, 12 hrs), **Florence** (4/day,
7 hrs, changes in Pisa and/or Genoa, night train), **Milan** (4/day,
5–6 hrs, 3 with changes), **Venice** (4/day, 8 hrs, 2 changes required
or a direct night train), **Barcelona** (3/day, 11 hrs, long change in
Montpellier, or a direct night train).

By plane to Paris (hrly, 1 hr, about the same price as a
train ticket).

VILLEFRANCHE SUR MER
Come here for upscale, small-town Mediterranean atmosphere.
Villefranche (between Nice and Monte Carlo, with frequent
15-min buses and trains to both) is quieter and more exotic than
Nice. Narrow cobbled streets tumble into the mellow waterfront,
a scenic walkway below the castle leads to the hidden port, and
luxury yachts glisten in the harbor below. Semisandy beaches, a
handful of interesting sights, and quick access to Cap Ferrat keep
visitors just busy enough.

The **TI** is in the park François Binon, just below the main
bus stop (July–Aug daily 09:00–19:00, Sept–June Mon–Sat 09:00–
12:00, 14:00–18:30, closed Sun, a 20-min walk or €8 taxi from

train station, tel. 04 93 01 73 68). Pick up the brochure detailing a self-guided walking tour of Villefranche and information on boat rides and the Rothschild Villa Ephrussi's gardens (see "Sights near Villefranche," below).

The dramatic interior of **Chapel of St. Pierre**, decorated by Jean Cocteau, is the town's cultural highlight, but at €1.85 it's not worth it for many (daily 10:00–12:00, 16:00–20:30, below Hôtel Welcome). **Boat rides** (*promenades en mer*) are offered several days a week (June–mid-Sept, €12, 2 hrs, across from Hôtel Welcome). Lively *boules* action takes place each evening just below the huge soccer field. Walk beyond the train station for views back to Villefranche and a quieter beach.

Even if you're sleeping elsewhere, consider an ice cream–licking village stroll. The last bus leaves Nice for Villefranche at about 19:45; the last bus from Villefranche to Nice leaves at about 21:00; and one train runs later (24:00). Beware of taxi drivers who overcharge—the normal weekday, daytime rate to central Nice is about €27; to the airport, €38 to €43.

Sleeping in Villefranche-sur-Mer
(€1.10 = about $1, country code: 33, zip code: 06230)
There's precious little middle ground here. Hotels are linoleum-floor cheap or million-dollar-view expensive. The lone *chambre d'hôte* offers the only normal mid-range comfort.

If your idea of sightseeing is to enjoy the view from your bedroom deck, the dining room, or the pool, stay at **Hôtel La Flore***, where most rooms have unbeatable views (Db-€87–120, Tb-€120–151, Qb loft with huge terrace-€151–198, lower rates are Nov–March, CC, air-con, easy parking, fine restaurant, elevator, just off main road high above harbor, 5 boulevard Princess Grace de Monaco, 2 blocks from TI toward Nice, tel. 04 93 76 30 30, fax 04 93 76 99 99, www.hotel-la-flore.fr, e-mail: Hotel -La-Flore@wanadoo.fr, SE).

Hôtel Welcome* is buried in the heart of the old city, right on the water, with most of the 32 rooms overlooking the harbor. You'll pay top price for all the comforts in a very sharp, professional hotel that seems to do everything right and couldn't be better located (standard Db with view but no balcony-€111, "comfort" Db with view and balcony-€132, superior Db with view and balcony-€168, extra person-€30, CC, air-con, 1 quai Courbet, tel. 04 93 76 27 62, fax 04 93 76 27 66, www.welcome-hotel.com, e-mail: steves@welcomehotel.com, SE). The rooms at both Hôtel La Flore and Hôtel Welcome, while different in cost, are about the same in comfort. La Flore has a pool, Welcome is on the harbor.

The hotelesque **Hôtel Provençal** needs a face-lift but offers air-conditioning and fine views from well-worn rooms with awful furniture but nifty balconies (Db-€63–92, Tb-€73–85, extra bed-€9, 10 percent off with this book and a two-night stay, CC, skip the cheaper no-view rooms, a block from TI at 4 avenue Maréchal Joffre, tel. 04 93 76 53 53, fax 04 93 76 96 00, e-mail: provencal@riviera.fr).

At **Le Home**, Madame Repellin-Villard rents the town's best budget beds in 10 simple rooms around a garden bursting with color and a welcoming terrace (Db-€37–40, no CC; from main road near TI, walk between cafés Riche and Regence and then climb the steps and turn left, avenue de Grande Bretagne, tel. 04 93 76 79 88).

Hôtel la Darse**, a simple hotel sitting in the shadow of its highbrow brothers, offers a low-key alternative right on the water in Villefranche's old Port. The rooms are quiet and plain with linoleum floors, and those facing the sea have great view balconies (easily worth the extra cost). Room cleanliness has been a problem, but this hotel will have a new owner in 2002 (Db-€40–58, extra person-€9, CC, from TI walk or drive down avenue General de Gaulle to the old Port de la Darse, tel. 04 93 01 72 54, fax 04 93 01 84 37).

Hôtel Vauban*, two blocks down from the TI, is an odd and basic place with homey, red-velvet decor, and a few cheery, simple rooms (Db-€46–53, Db with view-€53–69, no CC, 11 avenue General De Gaulle, tel. 04 93 76 62 18).

Eating in Villefranche-sur-Mer

Pickings are slim in this land of high rollers. The places lining the port are expensive and vary in quality; less expensive places are off the port. If you want to eat well, spring for dinner at **Hôtel la Flore** (see "Sleeping in Villefranche," above). Or, for a cool view and good-enough food at reasonable prices, try **Restaurant Le Marinières** on the beach below the train station (salads and *à la carte*, open daily, tel. 04 93 01 76 06).

Sights near Villefranche-sur-Mer

Cap Ferrat—This is the peninsula you're staring at across the bay from Villefranche. An exclusive, largely residential community, it's off the Nice-Monaco route and receives less traffic than other towns. Drive, bus, or walk here from Villefranche to visit the sublime gardens of the Rothschild Villa Ephrussi, with stunning views east to Villefranche and west toward Monaco; seven lush and varied gardens and several lavishly decorated rooms (€7.75, €2.25 for English tours generally between 11:00 and 14:00, Feb–Oct daily 10:00–18:00, until 19:00 in July–Aug, Nov–Jan Mon–Fri 14:00–18:00, Sat–Sun 10:00–18:00). From Villefranche, it's a scenic 50-minute walk around the bay past the train station or 10 minutes by bus #111. A few kilometers beyond sits the sophisticated port-village of St. Jean Cap Ferrat, offering more yachts, boardwalks, views, and boutiques in a less-frenzied atmosphere.

▲**Eze Village**—Floating high above the sea, Eze Village (don't confuse it with the seafront town of Eze-Bord de la Mer) mixes perfume outlets, upscale boutiques, outrageously priced hotels, steep, cobbled lanes, and magnificent views. About 15 minutes east of Villefranche on the Moyenne Corniche (6 buses/day from Nice, 25 min), this medieval hill town makes a handy stop between Nice and Monaco. You can drop in on the Fragonard or Galli-mard perfume outlets to learn about the interesting fabrication process and shop the fragrant collections (both daily 08:30–18:00, Gallimard breaks for lunch 12:00–14:00). You can also enjoy the charming church (Eglise Paroissial), but skip the Jardins Exotiques (exotic gardens). For a panoramic view and ideal picnic perch (they say on a clear day you can see Corsica), walk up to the hill town from the parking lot, take a left at the top of the first hill, and walk 20 meters down a dirt path.

▲**La Turbie**—Ten minutes east and uphill of Eze Village lies one of this region's most dramatic panoramas. Follow the winding road up from Eze Village to La Grande Corniche and the village of La Turbie; park in the lot near the view. Inspect all viewpoints. The massive Roman monument in front of you (*La Trophée des Alpes*) was erected to commemorate Caesar Augustus' conquering of the Alps, a less than subtle reminder of who was in charge. The view over Monaco is even greater after dark.

ANTIBES

Antibes is busy and massive compared to Villefranche, but far more manageable than Nice. Come here for yachts, sandy beaches, an enjoyable old town, good hiking, and a great Picasso collection. Twenty-five minutes west of Nice by train (skip the 50-min bus), Antibes' glamorous port glistens below its fortifications—boat lovers are welcome to browse. The Fort Carré that dominates the port was the last fortification before Italy in the 1500s. The festive old city is charming in a sandy-sophisticated way and sits atop the ruins of the fourth-century B.C. Greek city of Antipolis. Hotels aren't a very good value here, so I prefer Antibes as a daytrip.

Orientation

The old city lies between the port and boulevards Albert 1er and Robert Soleau. Place Nationale is the hub of activity in the old city. Lively rue Auberon connects the port and the old city. Stroll along the sea between the Picasso Museum and place Albert 1er (where boulevard Albert 1er meets the sea); the best beaches lie just beyond place Albert 1er, and the path is beautiful. Good children's play areas are on place des Martyrs de la Resistance (near recommended Hôtel Relais du Postillon). Near the port in the old city you'll find **Heidi's English Bookshop** (great selection, daily 10:00–19:00, 24 rue Auberon) and a **Laundromat** (14 rue Thuret).

Tourist Information: The Maison de Tourisme has what you need (July–Aug Mon–Sat 09:00–19:00, Sun 09:00–13:00, Sept–June Mon–Sat 9:00–12:30, 14:00–18:30, closed Sun, located just east of the old city where boulevard Albert 1er and rue de République meet at 11 place de Gaulle, tel. 04 92 90 53 00). Pick up the excellent city map, the interesting walking tour of Old Antibes brochure (in English), ask about tours of the Fort Carré, and get details on the hikes described below. Remember, the Nice TI has Antibes maps; plan ahead.

Arrival in Antibes

By Train: To get to the port (5-min walk), cross the street in front of the station and follow avenue de la Liberation. To reach the TI (15-min walk), exit right from the station on avenue Soleau; follow "Maison du Tourisme" signs to place de Gaulle. A free minibus (*Minibus Gratuit*) circulates around Antibes from the train station and serves place Albert 1er, the old city, and the port (4/hr), or you can call a taxi (tel. 04 93 67 67 67).

By Bus: The bus station is on the edge of the old city on place Guynemer, a block below the TI.

By Car: Follow *centre ville, vieux port* signs and park near the old city walls, as close to the beach as you can (first half hour is free, municipal lots cost about €8/day). Enter the old city through the last arch on the right.

Sights—Antibes

Market Hall (Marché Provençal)—The daily market bustles under a 19th-century canopy and mixes flowers, produce, Provençal products, and beach accessories (in old city behind Picasso Museum on cours Masséna, daily until 13:00, closed Mon off-season). You'll also find antique/flea markets on place Nationale and place Audiberti (next to the port) on Thursdays and Saturdays (7:00–18:00).

▲▲Musée Picasso (Château Grimaldi)—Sitting serenely where the old city meets the sea, this museum offers a remarkable collection of Picasso's work: paintings, sketches, and ceramics. Picasso, who lived and worked here in 1946, said if you want to see work from his Antibes period, you'll have to do it in Antibes. You'll understand why Picasso liked working here. Several photos of the artist make this already intimate museum more so. In his famous *Joie de Vivre* (the museum's highlight), there's a new love in Picasso's life, and he's feelin' groovy (€4.75, June–Sept Tue–Sun 10:00–18:00, closed Mon and Oct–May 12:00–14:00, tel. 04 92 90 54 20).

Musée d'Histoire et d'Archéologie—Featuring Greek, Roman, and Etruscan odds and ends, this is the only place to get a sense

Antibes

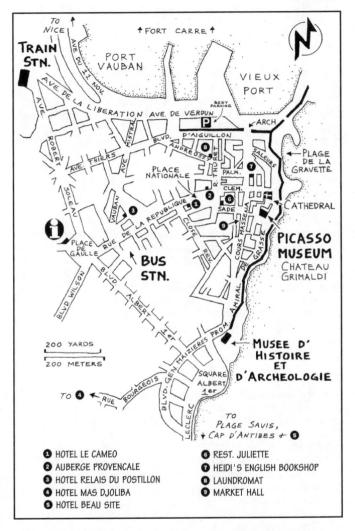

1 HOTEL LE CAMEO
2 AUBERGE PROVENCALE
3 HOTEL RELAIS DU POSTILLON
4 HOTEL MAS DJOLIBA
5 HOTEL BEAU SITE

6 REST. JULIETTE
7 HEIDI'S ENGLISH BOOKSHOP
8 LAUNDROMAT
9 MARKET HALL

of this city's ancient roots. I liked the 2,000-year-old lead anchors (€1.50, no English explanations, Tue–Sun 10:00–12:00, 14:00–18:00, closed Mon, on the water between Picasso Museum and place Albert 1er).

Beaches (Plages)—The best beaches stretch between Antibes' port and Cap d'Antibes, the best (plages Salis and Ponteil) are

just south of Place Albert 1er. All are golden and sandy. Plage
Salis is busy in summer, but it's manageable, with snack stands
every 100 meters and views to the old city. The closest beach
to the old city is at the port (plage de la Gravette) and remains
relatively calm in any season.

Hikes and Day Trips from Antibes

From place Albert 1er (where boulevard Albert 1er meets the
beach), there's a great view of the beach plage Salis and the Cap
d'Antibes. That tower on the hill is your destination for the first
walk described below. The longer hike along the Cap d'Antibes
begins on the next beach, just over that hill (see below).

▲**Chapelle et Phare de la Garoupe**—The chapel and lighthouse, a 20-minute uphill climb from the far end of plage Salis
(follow Chemin du Calvaire up to the lighthouse tower), offer
magnificent views (best at sunset) over Juan les Pins, Antibes,
the pre-Alps, and Nice. Roads allow car access.

**Cap d'Antibes Hike (Sentier Touristique de Tirepoll/Sentier
Littoral)**—At the end of the mattress-ridden plage de la Garoupe
(over the hill from the lighthouse) is a well-maintained trail
around Cap d'Antibes. The beautiful trail follows the rocky coast
for about three kilometers, then heads inland. Take bus #2A from
the bus station (2/hr, get return times) or drive to Hôtel Beau Site
and walk 10 minutes down to plage de la Garoupe (parking available). The trail begins at the far right end of the beach. Allow two
hours for the loop that ends at the recommended Hôtel Beau Site
(see "Sleeping in Antibes," below) and use your Antibes map.

Daytrips from Antibes—Antibes is halfway between Nice and
Cannes (easy train service to both), and close to the artsy pottery and
glass-blowing village of Biot, home of the Fernand Léger Museum
(frequent buses, ask at TI). And while Cannes has much in common
with its sister city, Beverly Hills, and little of interest for your authors,
its beaches and the beachfront promenade are beautiful.

Sleeping in Antibes

(€1.10 = about $1, country code: 33, zip code: 06600)
Central pickings are slim here; most hotel owners seem more
interested in their restaurants.

Hôtel Le Cameo** is a rambling, refreshingly unaggressive old
place above a bustling bar (what reception there is you'll find in the
bar). The public areas are dark, but its nine, very simple linoleum-
lined rooms are almost huggable. All open onto the charming place
Nationale, which means you don't sleep until the restaurants close
(Ss-€35, Sb-€46, Ds-€43, Db-€53, Ts-€53, Tb-€61, CC, 5 place
Nationale, tel. 04 93 34 24 17, fax 04 93 34 35 80, NSE).

Auberge Provençale*, on the same square, has seven reasonably nice rooms (those on the square get all the noise, day and

night) but nonexistent, couldn't-care-less management and a popular restaurant (Db-€53–76, Tb-€61–84, Qb-€92, CC, reception in restaurant, 61 place Nationale, tel. 04 93 34 13 24, fax 04 93 34 89 88). Their loft room, named "Celine," is huge and faces the rear. It comes with a royal canopy bed and a dramatic open-timbered ceiling and costs no more than the other rooms.

Hôtel Relais du Postillon**, on a thriving square, offers 15 small, tastefully designed rooms, accordion bathrooms, and helpful owners who take more pride in their well-respected restaurant (Db-€42–79, extra bed-€9, breakfast-€6.75, CC, *menus* from €30, 8 rue Championnet, tel. 04 93 34 20 77, fax 04 93 34 61 24, www.relais-postillon.com, SE).

Mas Djoliba*** is a good splurge but best for drivers, as it's a 15-minute walk from the beach and old Antibes, and a 25-minute walk to the station. Reserve early for this tranquil, bird-chirping, flower-filled manor house where no two rooms are the same. Dinner (by the pool) is required from May to September (Db with breakfast and dinner-€67–85 per person, off-season Db-€76–107 for two people—room only; several good family rooms, breakfast-€8.50, CC, 29 avenue de Provence, from boulevard Albert 1er, turn right up avenue Gaston Bourgeois, tel. 04 93 34 02 48, fax 04 93 34 05 81, www.hotel-djoliba.com, e-mail: hotel.djoliba @wanadoo.fr).

Hôtel Beau Site***, my only listing on Cap d'Antibes and a 10-minute drive from the old city, is a good value if you want to get away, but not *too* far away. The friendly owners, nice pool, outdoor terrace, easy parking, and 30 pleasant rooms make it worthwhile (Db-€52–107, CC, 141 boulevard Kennedy, tel. 04 93 61 53 43, fax 04 93 67 78 16, www.hotelbeausite.net). From the hotel, it's a 10-minute walk down to the crowded plage de la Garoupe and a nearby hiking trail.

Eating in Antibes

Gourmets should dine at the recommended hotels **Relais du Postillon** or **Auberge Provençale**, while romantics and those on a budget should buy a picnic dinner and head for the beach. Lively place Nationale is filled with tables and tourists (great ambience), while locals seem to prefer the restaurants along the market hall. Just off place Nationale, **Chez Juliette** offers good budget meals (*menus* from €13, 20 rue Sade).

MONACO

Still impressive despite overdevelopment, high prices, and wall-to-wall daytime tourists, Monaco will disappoint anyone looking for something below the surface. This glittering two-square-kilometer country is a tax haven for its miniscule full-time population (30,000, 83 percent foreigners), who pay no income tax, and is the kind of place you visit once and probably don't need to see again. France surrounds Monaco on all sides but the Mediterranean and provides Monaco's telephones (French phone cards work here), electricity, and water. About the only thing you'll use that's made locally are its stamps.

Orientation

Monaco (the principality) is best understood when separated into its three tourist areas: Monaco-Ville, Monte Carlo, and La Condamine (a fourth area, Fontvieille, is of no interest to tourists). Monaco-Ville, dangling on the rock high above, is the oldest section, housing Prince Rainier's palace and all sights except the casino; Monte Carlo is the area around the casino; and La Condamine (the port) divides the two. A brief bus ride on routes #1 or #2 links all areas (10/hr, €1.40, or €3.50 for 4 tickets). It's a 20-minute uphill walk from the port (and train station) to Prince Rainier's palace, 20 minutes to the casino, and a 40-minute down-and-up walk between the palace and the casino.

Tourist Information: There are several TIs, but you shouldn't need one, as sightseeing is straightforward (a map is helpful). The main TI is near the casino (2 boulevard des Moulins), but the handiest one for most is in the train station; pick up a city map (daily 09:00–19:00, tel. 00-377/92 16 61 66). From June to September, you'll find information kiosks in the Monaco-Ville parking garage and on the port.

Telephone Tip: To call Monaco from France, dial 00, then 377 (Monaco's country code), and the eight-digit number. Within Monaco, simply dial the eight-digit number.

Arrival in Monaco

By Bus from Nice and Villefranche: Keep your receipt for the return ride (RCA buses run twice as often as Cars Broch). There are three stops in Monaco, in order from Nice: in front of a tunnel at the base of Monaco-Ville (place d'Armes), on the port, and below the casino (on avenue d'Ostende). The first stop is the best starting point. To walk up to Monaco-Ville and the palace (10 min straight up), or catch a local bus there (lines #1 or #2), cross the street right in front of the tunnel and walk with the rock on your right—the bus stop and steps up to Monaco-Ville are in 70 meters. The bus stop back to Nice is across the major road from your arrival point at the light. The last bus leaves Monaco for Nice at about 19:00 (the last train leaves about 23:30).

By Train from Nice: A dazzling but confusing new train station provides central access to Monaco. The TI, baggage check, and ticket windows are up the escalator at the end of the tracks. To reach Monaco-Ville, walk along the platform toward Nice following *Sortie la Condamine* then *Access Port* signs. The stop for

Monaco

- **①** HOTEL DE FRANCE
- **②** PAN BAGNA SANDWICHES AT RUE BASSE #8
- **③** LOCAL BUS STOPS
- **④** BUS STOPS FROM NICE
- **⑤** BUS STOPS TO NICE

local buses is in front of the station exit. The port is a few blocks downhill, the casino is uphill along the left side of the port, and Monaco-Ville is uphill to the right of the port. The most direct route to the casino from the station is up the escalator from the platform, left past the TI, and up the elevator. Exit the station and turn left on boulevard Princesse Charlotte.

By Car: You'll be directed to parking structures under Monaco-Ville, under the casino, or above at Jardins Exotique (about €1.50/hr).

Sights—Monaco-Ville

Start with a look at Monaco-Ville from the palace square. Buses #1 or 2 leave you a five-minute walk away; turn right off the bus and walk past the fountain down rue Marie de Lorraine to reach the palace (to go directly to the aquarium, walk down the steps at the bus stop). The walkway up from the port ends at the **palace square**. Find a seat overlooking the port for a *magnifique* view (particularly at night).

This funny little country was born on this rock in 1215 and has managed to stay independent for most of its almost 800 years. A medieval castle sat where the palace is today, its strategic setting having a lot to do with Monaco's ability to resist attackers. They still **change guards** the old-fashioned way (11:55 daily, fun to watch but jammed). As you look back over the port, notice the faded green roof above to the right—it's the famous casino. In the mid-1800s, Prince Charles began an aggressive economic development plan for his tiny, isolated country. He built spas and a casino to lure a growing aristocratic class with leisure time. It worked. Today, Monaco has the world's highest per-capita income.

The name Monte Carlo means "Charles' Hill" in Spanish (the Spanish were traditional protectors of Monaco and have 200 guards present today). The famous Monte Carlo Grand Prix started in 1929 and still runs right through the streets of the port and around the casino.

Now walk to the statue of the monk grasping a sword near the palace. Meet François Grimaldi, a renegade Italian who captured Monaco dressed as a monk in 1297, and began the dynasty that still rules the principality. Walk to the opposite side of the square and more Louis XIV cannon balls. Down below is Monaco's newest area, Fontvieille, where much of its post–WWII growth has been. Prince Rainier has continued Monaco's economic growth with land-fills (like Fontvieille), flashy ports, new beaches, and the new rail station. Today, thanks to Prince Rainier's efforts, tiny Monaco is a member of the United Nations.

Hungry? You'll find good *pan bagna* and other sandwiches at 8 rue Basse, on the street leaving the square to the left. You can buy stamps (mail from here!) at the PTT located a few blocks down rue Comte F. Gastaldi.

Palace—Automated and uninspired tours (in English) take you through part of the prince's lavish palace in 30 merciful minutes and yet still manage to describe every painting. The rooms are well-furnished and impressive, but interesting only if you haven't seen a château lately (€4.60, €6 with Napoleon Collection, June–Sept daily 9:30–18:30, Oct 10:00–17:00, closed off-season).

Napoleon Collection—Napoleon occupied Monaco after the French Revolution. This is the prince's private collection of what Napoleon left behind: military medals, swords, guns, letters, and, most interesting, his hat. I found this collection more appealing than the palace (€3, June–Sept daily 09:30–18:30, Oct–May 10:00–12:30, 14:00–17:00, next to palace entry).

Cathédrale de Monaco—This somber cathedral, built in 1878, is where Princess Grace is buried (near the left transept).

Jardins Botanique—Take in sensational views as you meander back to the bus stop through these immaculately maintained gardens (or pick up a *pan bagna* sandwich in the old city and picnic here).

Musée de l'Océanographique (Cousteau Aquarium)—This monumental building overhangs the Mediterranean. It was inaugurated in 1910 and is the largest of its kind, thanks to the oceanographic zeal of Prince Albert I. It can be jammed and disappoints some, though kids love it (€11, ages 6–18–€5.35, April–Sept daily 09:00–19:00, until 20:00 in July–Aug, March and Oct 09:30–19:00, Nov–Feb 10:00–18:00, CC, at opposite end of Monaco-Ville from palace, down the steps from Monaco-Ville bus stop).

Monte Carlo Story—This informative 35-minute film gives a helpful account (English headphones) of Monaco's history and is a comfortable soft-chair break from all that walking (€6, usually on the hour from 11:00–17:00 March–Oct, until 18:00 July–Aug, 14:00–17:00 only Nov–Feb, frequent extra showings for groups that you can join; from the Monte Carlo side of the Aquarium take the escalator into the parking garage, then take the elevator down and follow the signs, it's just past the café).

Leave Monaco-Ville and ride the shuttle bus (the stop is up the steps across from the aquarium) or stroll down through the pedestrian-pleasant port and up to Monte Carlo.

Sights—Monte Carlo

▲**Casino**—Stand in the park, above the traffic circle in front of the casino (opens at noon). The casino is designed to make the wealthy feel comfortable while losing money. Charles Garnier designed this Casino-Opera House in 1878 in part to thank the prince for his financial help in completing the Paris Opéra, which Garnier also designed. The central doors provide access to slot machines, private gaming rooms, and the Opera House. The private gaming rooms take up much of the left wing of the building. Count the counts and Rolls-Royces in front of Hôtel de Paris (built at the same time). Strut inside past the slots and find the sumptuous atrium. This is the lobby for the Opera House; doors open only during performances. There's a model of the Opera at the end of the room and marble WCs on the right. Anyone (even in shorts, if before 20:00) can get as far as the one-armed bandits (open at 12:00, push the button on the slot machines to claim your winnings), though you'll need decent attire to go any farther, and after 20:00 shorts are off-limits anywhere. Only adults 21 and older are allowed to dive deeper and pay €7.75 for the first rooms, Salons Européens (open at 12:00), or €15.50 for the glamorous private game rooms where you can rub elbows with high rollers (these rooms open at 16:00, some at 21:00, a tie and jacket are not necessary until evening, can be rented at the bag check). The scene is great at night and downright James Bond–like in the €15.50 rooms. The park behind the casino offers a peaceful café and a good view of the casino's rear facade and of Monaco-Ville. Entrance is free to all games in the new, plebeian, American-style Loews Casino, adjacent to the old casino. The return bus stop to Nice is at the top of the park above the casino on rue des Moulins. To return to the train station from the casino, walk up the parkway in front of the casino, turn left on boulevard des Moulins, right on impasse de la Fontaine, climb the steps, and turn left on boulevard Princesse Charlotte (the entrance is next to Parking de la gare).

Near Monte Carlo: Menton
Grand, beautiful, and overlooked Menton is a peaceful and relaxing spa/beach town with a fine beachfront promenade and a sandy-cobbled old town (TI tel. 04 93 57 57 00). It's just a few minutes by train (8/day) from Monte Carlo or 40 minutes from Nice.

Sleeping in Monaco
(€1.10 = about $1, country code: 377)
Since Monaco is by far best after dark, consider sleeping here. The perfectly pleasant **Hôtel de France**** is reasonable (Sb-€63, Db-€81, Tb-€100, includes breakfast, CC, 6 rue de la Turbie, near west exit from train station, tel. 00-377/93 30 24 64, fax 00-377/92 16 13 34, e-mail: hotel-france@monte-carlo.mc). You'll find a few affordable restaurants on rue de la Turbie and up in Monaco-Ville.

HILL TOWNS OF THE RIVIERA
Some of France's most dramatic hill towns are ignored in this region more famous for its beaches and casinos. While St. Paul-de-Vence and Vence receive their share of visitors, both are peaceful at night.
▲**Hill Town Drive**—To really get far from the maddening crowds, connect these lost treasures with a scenic drive: Vence, Tourettes sur Loup, Bar sur Loup, and, if you feel like really diving in deep, Gourdon.
    Almost too close to Nice, **St. Paul-de-Vence and Vence,** two different towns, provide a hilly, woodsy escape from the beach (the same bus from Nice's bus station serves both towns, though larger Vence is served by a faster direct bus, saving 20 min). While separated by only five kilometers, Vence faces the mountains while St. Paul-de-Vence faces the Mediterranean.
St. Paul-de-Vence—Small part cozy-medieval-hill-town and large part overrun-artist-shopping-mall, St. Paul is charmingly

artsy but gets swamped with tour buses and daytrippers. Avoid visiting between 11:00 and 17:00 (I avoid it completely). If you must go, meander deep into St. Paul's quieter streets and wander far to enjoy the panoramic views (TI tel. 04 93 32 86 95).

The prestigious, far-out, and pricey **Fondation Maeght** art gallery is a steep (uphill) 15-minute walk from St. Paul (ask the bus driver for best stop). This engaging museum provides a good introduction to modern art; the world-class contemporary-art collection (with works by Leger, Miró, Calder, and Braque, among others) is beautifully arranged between pleasant gardens and well-lit rooms. Don't miss the chapel, designed by Georges Braque, or the frequent special exhibits (€8.50, July–Sept daily 10:00–19:00, Oct–June 10:00–12:30, 14:30–18:00, tel. 04 93 32 81 63).

Vence—Vence disperses St. Paul's crowds over a larger and more engaging city. The mountains are close and the breeze is fresh in this town that bubbles with work-a-day life and tourist activity (no boutique shortage here). Stroll the narrow lanes of the old city (*Cité Historique*), enjoy a drink on a quiet square, and find the small cathedral with its Chagall mosaic. Outdoor markets thrive in the old city on Tuesdays and Fridays until 12:30, and daily on the massive place du Grand Jardin. Vence's TI is at 8 place du Grand Jardin (May–Sept Mon–Sat 09:00–19:00, Sun 09:00–13:00, Oct–April Mon–Sat 9:00–12:30, 14:00–18:00, closed Sun, tel. 04 93 58 06 38). The bus stop for Nice and St. Paul is next to the TI (schedules are posted in the window). Matisse's much-raved-about **Chapelle du Rosaire** may disappoint all but Matisse fans, for whom this is a rich and rewarding pilgrimage (an easy 20-min walk from Vence TI, turn right out of TI and walk down avenue Henri Isnare, then right on avenue de Provence following signs to St. Jeannet). The yellow-, blue-, and green-filtered sunlight does a cheery dance in stark contrast to the brooding tile sketches (€2.30, Tue and Thu 10:00–11:30, 14:00–17:30, Mon and Wed 14:00–17:30; Mass is Sun at 10:00 followed by a visit, closed Nov, tel. 04 93 58 03 26).

If Vence tempts you to stay, the little **Auberge des Seigneurs**** is a short walk from the bus stop and TI and is filled with character (spacious Db-€61, CC, no elevator, place du Frene, tel. 04 93 58 04 24, fax 04 93 24 08 01). **Hôtel la Villa Roseraie*****, an oasis with a pool, lovely garden, and sharply decorated rooms, is on the fringe of the city on the road to Col de Vence (Db-€67–133, CC, parking, easy walk to Matisse's chapel and a 15-min walk to TI, 128 avenue Henri Giraud, tel. 04 93 58 02 20, fax 04 93 58 99 31, e-mail: rvilla5536@aol.fr). **La Pecheur de Soleil Pizzeria** offers inexpensive meals on a quiet square (1 place Godeau, tel. 04 93 58 32 56). The **Auberge des Seigneurs** is a cozy place for a good dinner (*menus* from €26, recommended above).

Travel Notes on Connecting Nice and the Alps—La Route de Napoléon

After getting bored in his toy Elba empire, Napoleon gathered his entourage, landed on the Riviera, bared his breast, and told his fellow Frenchmen, "Strike me down or follow me." France followed. But just in case, he took the high road, returning to Paris along the route known today as La Route de Napoléon. (Waterloo followed shortly afterward.)

By Car: The scenic route between the Riviera and the Alps is beautiful (from south to north follow Digne, Sisteron, and Grenoble). An assortment of pleasant villages with inexpensive hotels lies on this route, making an overnight easy. Little Entrevaux feels forgotten and still stuck in its medieval shell. Cross the bridge, meet someone friendly, and consider the steep hike up to the citadel (€1.50). Sisteron's Romanesque church and view from the citadel above make this town worth a quick leg stretch. If a night in this area appeals, stay farther north, surrounded by mountains. **Hôtel Ferrat****, near the tiny hamlet of Clelles, is a simple, family-run mountain hacienda at the base of Mont Aiguille (after which Gibraltar was modeled) and is a good place to break this long drive. Enjoy your own *boules* court, swimming pool, and good restaurant (Db-€43–58, 38930 Clelles, CC, tel. 04 76 34 42 70, fax 04 76 34 47 47).

By Train: Leave the tourists behind and take the scenic train-bus-train combination that runs between Nice, Digne, and Grenoble through canyons, along whitewater rivers, between snow-capped peaks, and through many tempting villages. Start with a 09:00 departure from Nice on the little *Chemins de Fer de Provence* train to Digne (€17, 25 percent discount with railpass, 4/day, 3 hrs, departs from Gare du Sud station, about 10 blocks behind Nice's main station, 4 rue Alfred Binet, tel. 04 97 03 80 80). In Digne, you can catch a main-line train (covered by railpasses) to other destinations, or, better, the bus (quick transfer, free with railpass) to Veynes (6/day, 90 min) where you can then catch the most scenic two-car train to Grenoble (5/day, 2 hrs). From Grenoble, connections are available to many destinations. To do the entire trip from Nice to Grenoble in one day, you must start with the 09:00 departure from Nice (arrives Grenoble about 18:00), but I'd spend the night in one of the tiny villages en route. Clelles has the best hotel, but Sisteron and Entrevaux are also interesting (see "By Car," above).

THE FRENCH ALPS
(ALPES-SAVOIE)

Savoie, famous for glacier and fondue, is the top floor of the French Alps (the lower Alpes-Dauphiné lie to the south). In the 11th century, this region ruled much of southeastern France, its borders extending from the Riviera to the Rhône Valley. Stubborn Savoie maintained its independence from France until 1860. Home to skier Jean-Claude Killy and the first winter Olympics, today's Savoie is France's mountain-sports capital, with the Alps' highest point, Mont Blanc, as its centerpiece. Savoie feels more Swiss than French.

The scenery is simply spectacular. Serenely self-confident Annecy is a picture-perfect blend of natural and man-made beauty. In Chamonix, it's just you and Madame Nature—there's not a museum or important building in sight. If the weather's right, take Europe's ultimate cable-car ride to the 3,780-meter (12,600-foot) Aiguille du Midi in Chamonix.

Lyon is the southern gateway to the Alps, easily accessible by train or car. This captivating place is France's most interesting major city after Paris. If you need a city fix, linger in Lyon.

Planning Your Time

Surrounded by mountains, lakefront Annecy has boats, bikes, hikes, arcaded walking streets, and good transportation connections (most trains to Chamonix pass through Annecy, making it a convenient stopover). But if you're pressed for time and you're antsy for Alps, go straight to Chamonix. Here you can skip along alpine ridges or stroll tranquil river paths. You can zip down the mountain on a wheeled bobsled or rent a mountain bike. Plan a minimum of two nights and one day in Chamonix and try to work in a night or two in Annecy. Since weather is everything, get the forecast by calling ahead (tel. 08 36 68 02 74) and, if it looks good,

The French Alps

get thee to Chamonix; if it's gloomy, Annecy has more for you to do. Both Chamonix and Annecy are overwhelmed with tourists in summer. (If you're driving or training from here to the Riviera, see "La Route de Napoléon" tips at the end of the previous chapter.) Lyon is France's best-kept urban secret. Strategically situated at the foot of the Alps where the Saone and Rhône Rivers meet, this manageable city merits at least one night and a full day.

Getting around the Alps

Lyon, Annecy, and Chamonix are well-connected by trains. Buses run from Chamonix to nearby villages, and the Aiguille du Midi lift takes travelers from Chamonix to Italy over Europe's most scenic border crossing.

Cuisine Scene—Savoie and Lyon

The **Savoie** offers mountain-country cuisine. Robust and hearty, it shares much with Swiss fare. Specialties include *fondue savoyarde* (melted Beaufort and Comté cheeses and local white wine, sometimes with a dash of cognac), *raclette* (chunks of semimelted cheese served with potatoes, pickles, sausage, and bread), *tartiflettes* (hearty scalloped potatoes with melted cheese), *poulet de Bresse* (the best chicken in France), *morteau* (smoked pork sausage), *gratin savoyarde* (a potato dish using cream, cheese, and garlic), and fresh fish. Local cheeses are Morbier (look for a charcoal streak down the middle), Comté (like Gruyère), Beaufort (aged for 2 years, hard and strong), Reblochon (mild and creamy), and Tomme de Savoie (semihard and mild). Evian water comes from Savoie, as does Chartreuse liqueur. Aprémont and Crépy are two of the area's surprisingly good white wines. The local beer, Baton de Feu, is more robust than other French beers.

Lyon offers French cuisine at its best. Surprisingly affordable, this is an intense palate experience—try the *salad lyonnaise* (croutons, ham, and a poached egg on a bed of lettuce), *andouillettes* (pork sausages), and *quenelles* (large dumplings, sometimes flavored with fish).

ANNECY

There's something for everyone in this lakefront resort city that knows how to be popular: mountain views, flowery cobbled lanes and canals, a château, and swimming in—or boating on—the crystal-clear lake. Sophisticated Annecy (ahn-see) is France's answer to Switzerland's Lucerne, and, while you may not have glaciers knocking at your door as in nearby Chamonix, the distant peaks make a beautiful picture with Annecy's lakefront setting. While Annecy has a few museums, don't kid yourself—you're here for its lovely setting and strollable streets.

Orientation

Modern Annecy sprawls for kilometers, but we're interested only in its compact old city tucked back in the southwest corner of the lake. The old city is bounded by the château to the south, the TI and rue Royale to the north, rue de la Gare to the west, and, above all, the lake to the east.

Tourist Information: The TI is a few blocks from the old city across from the big grass field in the brown-and-glass Bonlieu shopping center (daily in summer 09:00–18:30, off-season 09:00–12:00, 13:45–18:30, 1 rue Jean Jaures, tel. 04 50 45 00 33). Get a city map, the *Vieil Annecy* walking tour brochure, the map of the lake showing the bike trail, and, if you're spending a few days, the helpful *Annecy Guide* with everything a traveler needs to know.

Arrival in Annecy

By Train: To reach the old city and TI, leave the station (baggage check available), veering left at street level, and walk by Hôtel des Alpes along rue de la Poste. Turn left on rue Royale.

By Car: Annecy is a traffic mess. Avoid most of the snarls by taking the Annecy Sud exit from the autoroute and following *Albertville* signs. Upon entering Annecy, either turn left at the roundabout below the hospital for the center city and TI (free parking lot across from hospital) or use Hôtel de Ville parking structure after the roundabout, €1.50/hr), or follow *Château* signs to park free above the old city at Annecy's château (ideal for my first 2 hotels).

Sights—Annecy

Strolling—The canals and arcaded streets of this handsome old city are made for ambling. The TI's *Vieil Annecy* brochure describes a good walking tour with worthwhile historic information (you'll pass the next 2 sights described below). Wander deep past luscious ice-cream shops and waterfront cafés. A thriving outdoor market occupies most of the old-city center on Tuesday, Friday, and Sunday mornings.

Palais de l'Ile—Once a prison, the Museum of Annecy cuts like the prow of a ship through the canal, but is not worth your time or money.

Château Museum (Musée-Château d'Annecy)—This mildly interesting museum mixes local folklore, anthropology, natural history, and modern and fine arts with great views over the lake and city (€4.75, Wed–Sun 10:00–12:00, 14:00–18:00, closed Mon–Tue, no midday closing June–Sept).

▲**Boating**—Rent a paddleboat equipped with a slide (€8/30 min, €12/hr) or a motorboat (€22/30 min, €37/hr) and tool around the lake. It's incredibly clear and warmer than you'd think. Or let a one-hour cruise do the work for you (€10, 7 departures/ day April–Sept, 18/day in summer, Compagnie des Bateaux du Lac Annecy, on lake behind Hôtel de Ville, tel. 04 50 51 08 40, www.annecy-croisieres.com). Get schedules and prices at the TI or at the boat dock right on the lake where the canal meets the old city. Their *Omnibus* boat connects villages along the lake with Annecy, but only three times a day. For a great full-day excursion, take the 10:30 boat to Menthon-St. Bernard, hike the level two hours to lovely Talloires (have lunch and swim here), then catch the 15:00 return boat to Annecy from there (use TI's free map of the lake).

▲**Biking and Rollerblading**—A beautiful bike-and-Rollerbade trail (*piste cyclable*) runs along the entire west side of the lake (TI has free map and list of bike rentals). The small village of Duingt is 17 level kilometers (10 miles) away and makes a good destination. Consider riding to Duingt and taking the *Omnibus* boat back (€7, 3 departures/day, 45 min, bikes allowed). Little Big Shop rents bikes and Rollerblades at 80 rue Carnot (tel. & fax 04 50 67 42 13).

Driving—For the best car-accessible views overlooking Annecy,

Annecy

1. HOTEL DU CHATEAU
2. ANNE-MARIE B & B
3. HOTEL DE SAVOIE
4. HOTEL DU PALAIS DE L'ISLE
5. HOTEL IBIS
6. HOTEL KYRIAD
7. HOTEL SPLENDID
8. HOTEL CENTRAL
9. HOTEL DES ALPES
10. REST. JOHN
11. AUBERGE DU LYONNAIS
12. REST. AU LILAS ROSE
13. REST. L'AVENTURE
14. REST. VIVALDI
15. LAUNDROMAT

drive 20 kilometers to Col de la Forclaz. Take D-508 south along the lake past Duingt and turn left on D-42 a few minutes after leaving the lake (allow 45 min one-way with traffic).

Sleeping in Annecy
(€1.10 = about $1, country code: 33, zip code: 74000)
Sleep Code: **S** = Single, **D** = Double/Twin, **T** = Triple, **Q** = Quad, **b** = bathroom, **s** = shower only, **CC** = Credit Cards accepted, **no CC** = Credit Cards not accepted, **SE** = Speaks English, **NSE** = No English, ***** = French hotel rating system (0–4 stars).

Reserve ahead, particularly in summer and during holiday weekends. Most hotels can help you find free overnight parking. There's a **Laundromat** at the western edge of the old city where the rue de la Gare meets rue Faubourg des Balmettes (4 rue Faubourg des Balmettes).

The first two places lie just below the château (free parking at the château) up the rampe du Château from the old city.

Hôtel du Château** has bright, spotless rooms, some with views, sharp bathrooms, precious few parking spots (free, first come), and a cool view terrace (Sb-€43, Db-€49–55, Tb-€57, Qb-€70, CC, no elevator, 16 rampe du Château, tel. 04 50 45 27 66, fax 04 50 52 75 26, e-mail: hotelduchateau@fnac.net, SE). Just above at the **Bed & Breakfast**, friendly Anne-Marie and Jean-Paul have created the ultimate urban refuge at their chalet *chambre d'hôte*, with a small garden, eight modern yet cozy rooms, and some views and balconies (Db-€57–69, great family rooms-€69–81, no CC, bike rental, open May–Oct, 1 place du Château, tel. & fax 04 50 45 72 28, e-mail: jardinduchateau@wanadoo.fr, SE).

The rest of my listings are in the pedestrian-friendly center and tend to be noisier (ask about free overnight parking deals).

Hôtel de Savoie**, on the canal a block from the lake and run by charming Madame Lavorel, has character and a few view rooms (Db without view-€49–53, Db with canal view-€64–70, extra person-€8, CC, no elevator, place St. François, tel. 04 50 45 15 45, fax 04 50 45 11 99, www.hotel-savoie.com).

Hôtel du Palais de l'Isle*** is romantically located in the thick of the old city with comfortable, ultramodern rooms (Db-€61–86, extra bed-€15, CC, air-con, elevator, 13 rue Perriere, tel. 04 50 45 86 87, fax 04 50 51 87 15, e-mail: palisle@aol.com).

Hôtel Ibis** is a good if sterile option, with tight and tidy rooms and easy parking underneath. It's well-situated on a modern square in the old city, a few blocks from the train station (Db-€56–67, extra person-€7, CC, elevator, 12 rue de la Gare, tel. 04 50 45 43 21, fax 04 50 52 81 08, e-mail: HO538@accor-hotels.com).

Hôtel Kyriad**, a few doors down, is a better hotel-chain option. It's surprisingly cozy with comfortable and well-designed rooms (Db-€58, CC, air-con, no elevator, 1 faubourg des Balmettes, tel. 04 50 45 04 12, fax 04 50 45 90 92, www.annecy-hotel-kyriad.com).

Hôtel Splendid*** is hotelesque, with all the comforts though little personality, on Annecy's busiest street, across from the TI. It makes a striking impression with its almost-lakefront location and grand facade (Sb-€85–95, Db-€95–105, CC, air-con, big beds, 4 quai Eustache Chappuis, tel. 04 50 45 20 00, fax 04 50 45 52 23, e-mail: splenditel@aol.com).

Hôtel Central* is just that, and is simple, homey, and welcoming on a quieter courtyard just off a big pedestrian street (D-€30, Ds-€35, Db-€40, extra person-€6, CC, no elevator, 6 bis rue Royale, tel. 04 50 45 05 37, fax 04 50 51 80 19, e-mail: stefanpicollet@hotmail.com).

Hôtel des Alpes**, with a serious owner and spotless, comfortable, and bright rooms, is to the left across from the train station at a

busy intersection (Sb-€42, Db-€50–56, Tb-€58, Qb-€66, CC, no
elevator, 12 rue de la Poste, tel. 04 50 45 04 56, fax 04 50 45 12 38).

Eating in Annecy

All of these places are in the old city. **Restaurant John** specializes
in tasty regional cuisine at fair prices (€17.50 *menu*, closed Tue
and Thu, at the foot of rampe du Château, 10 rue Perriere, tel.
04 50 51 36 15). **Auberge du Lyonnais** sprawls along the canal and
is a well-respected and classy place for Savoyarde fare (*menus* from
€27.50, daily, 9 rue de la République). **Au Lilas Rose** is a tiny,
funky, and fine place for inexpensive fondue (daily, on canal at passage de l'Evêché, tel. 04 50 45 37 08). If the local food seems too
cheesy, **L'Aventure** specializes in good southwestern French cuisine
(closed Wed, 33 rue Ste. Claire, tel. 04 50 45 45 05). **Restaurant
Vivaldi** offers reasonably priced Italian food (where the old city
meets the lake at 12 faubourg des Annociades, tel. 04 50 51 08 41).

Transportation Connections—Annecy

By train to: Chamonix (8/day, 2.5 hrs, change in St. Gervais),
Beaune (9/day, 5 hrs, change in Lyon), **Nice** (8/day, 7–9 hrs,
change in Lyon or Valence), **Paris'** Gare de Lyon (11/day, 4–5
hrs, many with change in Lyon, night train).

CHAMONIX

Hemmed in by snow-capped peaks, churning with mountain lifts,
and crisscrossed with hiking trails, the resort of Chamonix (shah-
moh-nee) is France's best base for alpine exploration. Officially
called Chamonix-Mt. Blanc, it's the largest of five villages at the
base of Mont Blanc. Chamonix's purpose in life has always been
to accommodate those coming here with some of Europe's top
alpine thrills—it's super busy in the summer and on winter holidays, but peaceful at other times. Chamonix's sister city is Aspen.

Planning Your Time

Ride the lifts early (crowds and clouds roll in later in the morning)
and save your afternoons for lower altitudes. If you have one
sunny day, spend it this way: Start with the Aiguille du Midi lift
(go as early as you can, reservations possible), take it all the way
to Hellbronner (hang around the needle longer if you can't get
to Hellbronner), double back to Plan de l'Aiguille, hike to Montenvers and the Mer de Glace (snow level permitting), and train
down from there. If the weather disappoints or the snow line's
too low, hike the Petit Balcon Sud trail.

Orientation

Eternally white Mont Blanc is Chamonix's southeastern limit;
the Aiguilles Rouges mountains form the northwestern limit.

Chamonix Valley Overview

① GRAND BALCON NORD - BEST HIKE!   ④ LAC BLANC - GREAT HIKE
② GRAND BALCON SUD - GREAT HIKE   ⑤ ARVE RIVERBANK STROLL
③ PETIT BALCON SUD - GOOD HIKE

The frothy Arve River splits Chamonix in two. The small pedestrian zone, just west of the river, and rues du Docteur Paccard and Joseph Vallot make up Chamonix's core. The TI is west of the river, just above the pedestrian zone, while the train station is east of the river.

Tourist Information: Pick up the town and valley map and consider the €4 hiking map called *Carte des Sentiers* (see "Chamonix Area Hikes," below). Ask for hours of lifts (important), biking information, and help with hotel reservations. Weather forecasts are posted near the door (July–Aug daily 08:30–19:30, Sept–June daily 08:30–12:30, 14:00–19:00, on place de l'Eglise, next to Hôtel Mont Blanc, 1 block above pedestrian zone, tel. 04 50 53 00 24, fax 04 50 53 58 90, www.chamonix.com).

Chamonix Quick History

1786—Monsieurs Balmot and Paccard are the first to climb Mont Blanc

1818—First ascent of Aiguille du Midi

1860—After a visit by Louis Napoleon, the trickle of nature-loving visitors to Chamonix turns to a gush

1924—First winter Olympics held in Chamonix
1955—Aiguille du Midi *téléphérique* opens to tourists
2002—Your visit

Arrival in Chamonix

By Train: Walk straight out of the station (lockers available) and up avenue Michel Croz. In three blocks you'll hit the center; turn left at the big clock, then right for the TI.

By Car: For most of my hotels and the TI, take the Chamonix Nord turnoff (second exit coming from Annecy) and park in the lot adjacent to the large traffic circle near Hôtel Alpina or at your hotel. To reach the hotels I list for drivers, take Chamonix Sud exit (first exit). Most parking is metered (€0.60/hr), though your hotel can direct you to free parking.

Getting around the Valley

Note that lifts and cogwheel trains are named for their highest destination (e.g., Aiguille du Midi, Montenvers, and Le Brévent).

By Lifts: Gondolas (*téléphériques*) climb mountains all along the valley, but the best one leaves from Chamonix (see "Sights—Chamonix," below). Sightseeing is optimal from the Aiguille du Midi gondola, but hiking is generally better from the Le Brévent gondola (less snow and plenty of views to Mont Blanc). Kids ages 4 to 11 (*enfants*) ride for 30 percent less, and kids 12 to 15 (*juniors*) ride for 15 percent less. While the lift to Aiguille du Midi stays open year-round, the *télécabines* on the Panoramic du Mont Blanc to Hell-bronner (Italy) are open only from May or June to early October and in good weather (call the TI to confirm). Other area lifts are open from January to mid-April and from July to late October.

By Hiking: See "Chamonix Area Hikes," below.

By Bike: The TI has a brochure proposing the best bike rides and where to rent. The peaceful river-valley trail is ideal for bikes and pedestrians.

By Bus or Train: One road and one rail line lace together the towns and lifts of the valley. Local buses run twice an hour from in front of the TI for local destinations.

Sights—Chamonix

▲▲▲**Aiguille du Midi** (aye-gwee-doo-mee-dee)—This is easily the valley's (and arguably, Europe's) most spectacular and popular lift. If the weather's clear, the price doesn't matter. Pile into the *téléphérique* (gondola) and soar to the tip of a rock needle 3,780 meters (12,600 feet) above sea level. Chamonix shrinks as trees fly by, soon replaced by whizzing rocks, ice, and snow until you reach the top. No matter how sunny it is, it's cold. The air is thin. People are giddy. Fun things can happen at Aiguille du Midi if you're not too winded to join the locals in the halfway-to-heaven tango.

From the top of the lift, cross the bridge and ride the elevator through the rock to the summit of this pinnacle. Missing the elevator is a kind of Alpus-Interruptus I'd rather not experience. The Alps spread out before you. In the distance is the bent little Matterhorn, the tall, shady pyramid behind a broader mountain, listed on the observation table in French as "Cervin—4,505 meters" (14,775 feet). And looming just over there is **Mont Blanc**, at 4,807 meters (15,771 feet), the Alps' highest point. Use the free telescope to spot mountain climbers; over 2,000 climb this mountain each year. Dial English and let the info box take you on a visual tour. Check the temperature next to the elevator. Plan on 32 degrees Fahrenheit even on a sunny day. Sunglasses are essential.

Explore Europe's tallest lift station. More than 150 meters (490 feet) of tunnels lead to a cafeteria, a restaurant, a gift shop, and the icicle-covered gateway to the glacial world. This "ice tunnel" is where summer skiers and mountain climbers depart. Just observing is exhilarating. Peek down the icy cliff and ponder the value of an ice axe.

Next, for your own private glacial dream world, get into the little red *télécabine* (called Panoramic du Mont Blanc) and head south to **Hellbronner Point**, the Italian border station. This line stretches five kilometers (3 miles) with no solid pylon. (It's propped by a "suspended pylon," a line stretched between two peaks 400 meters/ 1,300 feet from the Italian end.) In a gondola for four, you'll dangle silently for 40 minutes as you glide over the glacier to Italy. Hang your head out the window; explore every corner of your view. From Hellbronner Point you can continue down into Italy (see "Transportation Connections," below), but there's really no point unless you're traveling that way.

From Aiguille du Midi, you can ride all the way back to Chamonix or, far better, get off halfway down at **Plan de l'Aiguille** and take a hike plus a train ride down to Chamonix. From Plan de l'Aiguille, hike 20 minutes down to the refuge with great views and reasonable lunches. From the refuge, hike the spectacularly scenic, undulating two- to three-hour trail to Montenvers (overlooking the Mer de Glace glacier; see "Mer de Glace" and "Chamonix Area Hikes, Hike #1," below). From Montenvers, ride the train (€9.75) into Chamonix. Don't hike all the way down to Chamonix from Plan de l'Aiguille or Montenvers (Mer de Glace); it's a long, steep walk through thick forests with few views.

To beat the hordes and morning clouds, ride the **lifts** (up and down) as early as you can. To beat major delays in August, leave by 07:00. If the weather has been bad and turns good, expect crowds in any season (worse on weekends). If it's clear, don't dillydally. Lift hours are weather dependent but generally run daily from 07:00 to 17:00 in summer; 08:00 to 16:45 in May, June, and September; and 08:00 to 15:45 in winter. The last

Over the Alps—France to Italy

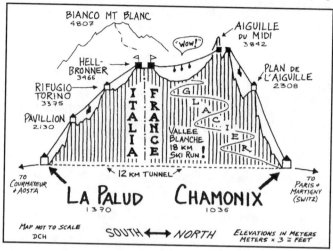

télécabine (called Panoramic du Mont Blanc) departure to
Hellbronner is about 14:00.

Smart travelers reserve the Aiguille du Midi lift in advance
either at the information booth next to the lift (open June–Sept)
or by telephone in any season (toll-free tel. 08 36 68 00 67,
English spoken). You can reserve up to 10 days in advance and
must pick up your reservation at the lift station at least 30 minutes
before your departure. Since you don't pay to reserve, you have
nothing to lose by reserving ahead. Note that you can't reserve
the *télécabines* to Hellbronner.

Costs: These are approximate ticket costs for summer
(slightly less off-season, ask about the special family rates). From
Chamonix to: Plan de l'Aiguille—€13.75 round-trip (€10.50
one-way); Aiguille du Midi—€32 round-trip (€27 one-way, not
including parachute); the Panoramic du Mont Blanc *télécabine*
to Hellbronner—€48 round-trip (€36.50 one-way).

Tickets from Aiguille du Midi to Hellbronner are sold at the
base or on top (€16.75 or €10.75 one-way). It's €22 (about $19,
sold there, other currencies also accepted but no CC) to drop
down into Italy. (Yes, you can bring your luggage.)

Time to allow: Chamonix to Aiguille du Midi—20 minutes
one-way, two hours round-trip, three to four hours in peak season;
Chamonix to Hellbronner: 90 minutes one-way, three to four
hours round-trip, longer in peak season. On busy days, minimize
delays by making a reservation for your return lift time upon
arrival at the top (tel. 04 50 53 30 80).

▲**Mer de Glace (Montenvers)**—From Gare de Montenvers (the little station over the tracks from Chamonix's main train station), the cogwheel Train du Montenvers toots you up to tiny Montenvers (*moan-ton-vare*) and a rapidly moving and dirty glacier called the Mer de Glace (*mayor-duh glahs*, Sea of Ice) and a fantastic view up the white valley (*Vallée Blanche*) to splintered, snow-capped peaks (€12.75 round-trip, €9.75 one-way). The glacier—France's largest, at 10 kilometers long (6 miles)—is impressive from above and below. The **ice caves** are funky—filled with ice sculptures (take the small gondola down, €6.25 round-trip to the caves, includes entry, or hike down 20 min and pay €3 to enter). If you've already seen a glacier up close, you might skip this one. For lunch with great views at Montenvers, consider the Bar Panoramique's sandwiches, or Refuge-Hôtel Montenvers (big salads and pasta dishes; also has cool rooms—see "Sleeping in Chamonix," below).

From Montenvers, you can hike uphill three to four hours to Plan de l'Aiguille (though it's easier the other way) then catch the Aiguille du Midi lift from there. Or just hike toward Plan de l'Aiguille as far as you feel—the views get better and better.

▲**Luge (Luge d'été)**—Here's something for thrill seekers. Ride a chairlift up the mountain and scream down a twisty, banked, concrete slalom course on a wheeled sled. Chamonix has two roughly parallel luge courses. While each course is a kilometer long (half mile) and about the same speed, one is marked for slower bobsledders, the other for the speed demons. Young or old, hare or tortoise, any fit person can manage a luge. Don't take your hands off your stick; the course is fast and slippery. The luges are set in a grassy park with kids' play areas (€5/1 ride, €21.50/5 rides, €38/10 rides, rides can be split with companions, July–Aug daily 10:00–19:30, June and Sept daily 13:30–18:00, call for spring and fall hours, closed in winter, 15-min walk from center, over the tracks from train station, follow signs to *Planards*, tel. 04 50 53 08 97.)

Parapente—For €78, you too can jump off a mountain and sail over Chamonix in a tandem *Parapente* (parasailing) with a trained, experienced pilot (Summits Parapente, reserve ahead, tel. 04 50 53 50 14, fax 04 50 55 94 16, e-mail: summits@summits.fr).

▲▲▲*Téléphériques* **to Le Brévent and La Flégère**—While Aiguille de Midi offers a more spectacular ride, Le Brévent and La Flégère lifts also offer great hiking and viewing options, as you get unobstructed panoramas across to the Mont Blanc range from this opposite side of the valley. The Le Brévent (luh bray-van) lift is in Chamonix; the La Flégère (lah flayj-air) lift is in nearby Les Praz (lay praw). They are connected by a scenic hike or by bus along the valley floor (see "Chamonix Area Hikes, Hike #2," below), and both have sensational view-cafés for nonhikers.

The Le Brévant lift is a 10-minute walk up the road above Chamonix's TI. This *téléphérique* stops halfway up at Planpraz station (€9.50 round-trip, €7.75 one-way, nice restaurant, great views and hiking) and continues to the top (Brévent station) with more views and hikes, though Planpraz offers plenty for me (€13.50 round-trip, €10.50 one-way from Chamonix, daily 09:00–17:00, 08:00–17:30 in summer, closed April–mid-June and Nov). La Flégère lift runs from the neighboring village of Les Praz with just one stop at La Flégère station (€7.75 one-way, €9.50 round-trip, daily 09:00–17:00, 07:40–17:30 in summer, closed April–mid-June and Nov). Hikes to Planpraz and Lac Blanc leave from this station.

Chamonix Area Hikes

Your first stop should be at the full-service *Maison de la Montagne*, across from the TI. You can hire a guide to help you scale Mont Blanc at the *Compagnie des Guides* on the ground floor. Do-it-your-selfers can visit the *Office de la Haute Montagne* on the third floor (Office of the High Mountains, daily 09:30–12:00, 15:30–18:00, closed Sun except summer, no midday closing in summer, tel. 04 50 23 22 08). Here you can pore over trail maps, get up-to-date trail and weather conditions from the English-speaking staff, and study their English guidebooks (and photocopy key pages). Ask for the trail guidebook (€12.50, sold in many stores, includes the good *Carte des Sentiers* trail map) and photocopy the pages of the hikes you're planning. The region's hiking map (*Carte des Sentiers*) is extremely helpful; pick it up at the TI (€4). For your hike, wear warm clothes and good shoes. Pack sunglasses, sunscreen, rain gear, water, and snacks.

I've described three big hikes and two easier walks below (see map on page 280). These hikes give nature-lovers of almost any ability a good opportunity to enjoy the valley in just about any weather. Start early when the weather's generally best. This is critical in summer; if you don't get in the lifts by 08:30, you'll join a conveyor belt of hikers competing for the same views. If starting later or walking longer, confirm lift closing hours, or you'll end up with a long, steep hike down. Trails are rocky and uneven. Take your time, watch your footing, don't take shortcuts, and make sure to say *bonjour* to your fellow hikers.

▲▲▲**Hike #1: Plan de l'Aiguille to Montenvers/Mer de Glace (Grand Balcon Nord)**—This is the easiest way to incorporate a two- to three-hour high-country walk into your ride down from the valley's greatest lift and check out a glacier to boot. The well-used trail undulates (dropping 450 meters/1,500 feet) and is moderately easy, provided the snow is melted (get trail details at the Office de la Haute Montagne, above). From the Aiguille du Midi lift, get off halfway down (Plan de l'Aiguille) and follow signs

Chamonix Valley Hikes and Lifts

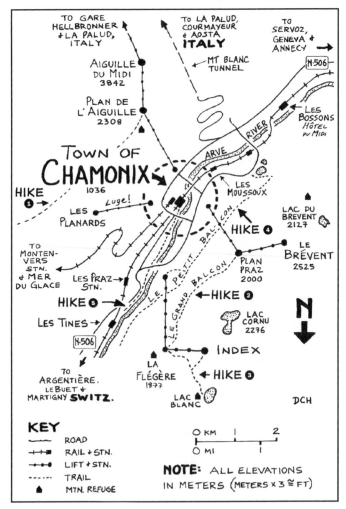

down to the refuge (reasonable food and drinks). From there, follow *Montenvers* signs for about an hour. When the trail splits, follow signs to *Signal Montenvers*, rather than *Montenvers*, as it's more scenic and easier. At this point, you'll climb to the best views of the trail. It's a long, incredibly scenic drop to Montenvers and the Mer de Glace (€9.75 train back to Chamonix at the small gondolas, don't walk it). Snow covers this trail generally until June.

▲▲▲**Hike #2: La Flégère to Planpraz (Grand Balcon Sud)**—
This glorious hike undulates above Chamonix valley, offering
staggering views of Mont Blanc and countless other peaks, glaciers, and wildflowers. With just 113 meters (370 feet) difference in
elevation between La Flégère and Planpraz lift stations, this hike,
while it has its ups and downs, is relatively easy. From Chamonix,
you can drive five minutes, walk 40 minutes along the Arve Rive
(see Hike #5 below), or take the Chamonix bus (10-min ride, every
30 min) to the tiny village of Les Praz and La Flégère lift station.
Ride the lift up to La Flégère (€7.75) and walk down to the
Refuge-Hôtel. Find the signs to Planpraz (you don't want Les
Praz-Chamonix—that's straight down), then hike the undulating
Grand Balcon Sud back to Planpraz station, the midway stop on
the Le Brévent lift line (allow 2.5 hrs). Take the Planpraz lift
down to Chamonix (€7.75); skip the steep hike down (of course,
this route can be done in reverse, but you have to walk backwards).
Ask for the round-trip rate between La Flégère and Planpraz
(Le Brévent) lifts, available at either lift (saves €6).

▲▲▲**Hike #3: La Flégère to Lac Blanc** (lock-blah)—This is
the most demanding trail of those I list, climbing steeply and
steadily over a rough, boulder-strewn trail for 90 minutes to snowy
Lac Blanc (some footing is tricky and good shoes or boots are
essential). I like this trail, as it gets you away from the valley edge
and opens views to peaks you don't see from other hikes. The
destination is a frigid, snow-white lake surrounded by peaks and
capped with a terrific chalet-refuge offering good lunches (and
dinners with accommodations). The views on the return trip are
breathtaking. Check for snow conditions on the trail and go early
(particularly in summer), as there is no shade and this trail is popular. Follow directions from Hike #2 to La Flégère station (above),
then walk out the station's rear doorway past the orientation
table/view area and follow signs to Lac Blanc. The trail is well-
signed and improves in surface quality as you climb. While you
can eliminate much of the uphill hiking by riding the lift up to
Index from La Flégère, the trail from there to Lac Blanc generally
requires serious skill and equipment due to snow—ask.

▲**Hike #4: Petit Balcon Sud**—This two-hour hike parallels the
Grand Balcon Sud at a lower elevation and is ideal when snow or
poor weather make other hikes problematic. No lifts are required—
just firm thighs to climb to the trail. From Chamonix, walk up to Le
Brévent lift station. Follow the asphalt road to the left of the lift leading uphill; it turns into a dirt road that signs mark as the Petit Balcon
Sud trail. After about an hour, look for signs down to Les Praz (not
La Flégère!). When you reach the asphalt road, turn left to explore
the village of Les Praz, or turn right for the bus stop and river trail
back to Chamonix. Return via Chamonix bus or by walking the level
Arve River trail (40 min). This hike works just as well in reverse.

Hike #5: Arve Riverbank Stroll—For an easy forested-valley stroll, follow the Arve River from Chamonix's Hôtel Alpina toward Les Praz. Cross the river from Chamonix's Hôtel Alpina, turn left, and walk until you pass the tennis courts. Cross two bridges to the left and turn right along the rushing Arve River, or keep right after the tennis courts and enter the Le Bouchet woods. Both trails can be linked for a loop, and both will get you to Les Praz—a pleasant destination with several cafés and a charming village green.

Sleeping in Chamonix
(€1.10 = about $1, country code: 33, zip code: 74400)
Reasonable hotels and dormlike chalets abound. With the helpful TI, you can find budget accommodations anytime. Mid-July to mid-August is most difficult, when some hotels have five-day minimum-stay requirements. Prices tumble off-season. If you want a view of Mont Blanc, ask for *côté Mont Blanc* (coat-ay mohn blah). Summertime travelers should seriously consider a night in a refuge-hotel high above. All hoteliers speak English.

Laundromats: One is off rue Joseph Vallot, three blocks north of Hôtel Touring at 40 impasse Primaviere (daily 08:00–20:00), and another is near the Aiguille du Midi lift at 174 avenue du Aiguille du Midi (daily 09:00–20:00).

Hotels in the City Center
Hôtel de l'Arve** has a slick, modern, alpine feel, with sharp view rooms right on the Arve River overlooking Mont Blanc, or cheaper rooms without the view. The fireplace lounge, pleasant garden, sauna, and climbing wall add to this place's appeal (Db-€50–65, extra person-€11, good-value half-pension, good buffet breakfast-€7.50, CC, elevator, behind huge Hôtel Alpina, 60 impasse des Anémones, tel. 04 50 53 02 31, fax 04 50 53 56 92, www.hotelarve-chamonix.com, Isabelle and Beatrice SE).

Richemond Hôtel** is dead center, with a slight retirement-home feel in its alpine-elegant public spaces. The rooms are traditional, comfortable, and generally spacious. There's also an outdoor terrace and a game room with a pool table and Ping-Pong (Sb-€42–48, Db-€62–74, Tb-€74–92, CC, 228 rue du Docteur Paccard, tel. 04 50 53 08 85, fax 04 50 55 91 69, e-mail: richemond@wanadoo.fr).

Hôtel Au Bon Coin**, a few blocks toward the town center from the Aiguille du Midi lift, is a modest, wood-paneled place with great views, private balconies, and thinnish walls in most of its spotless, well-cared-for rooms. The cheaper rooms lack views and private bathrooms (D-€38, Ds-€43, Db with view and balcony-€60, Tb-€62, Qb-€78, CC, usually closed mid-April–June, 80 avenue L'Aiguille du Midi, tel. 04 50 53 15 67, fax 04 50 53 51 51, e-mail: hotel.auboncoin@wanadoo.fr, Dermot and Julie SE).

Boule de Niege* ("Snowball") hotel is a small, simple, and central budget option run by a friendly owner who was born in Chamonix. Two rooms share a huge view terrace (D-€46–51, Db-€52–57, T-€64–73, Tb-€70–79, CC, 362 rue Joseph Vallot, tel. 04 50 53 04 48, fax 04 50 55 91 09, e-mail: laboule@claranet.fr).

Chamonix's most classy *chambre d'hôte*, **Chalet Beauregard**, a short but steep walk above the TI, is relaxed and peaceful, with a private garden. Five of its seven cushy rooms have balconies with grand views (Sb-€46–77, Db-€61–92, Tb-€86–107, no CC, includes breakfast, free parking, may require 5-day minimum in summer, on road to Le Brévent lift, 182 montée La Mollard, tel. & fax 04 50 55 86 30, www.chalet-beauregard.com, Manuel and Laurence SE).

Hôtel la Savoyarde***, a steep but rewarding walk above Chamonix, has views from the outdoor café tables, smart chalet ambience, and a good restaurant. Rooms are chalet-pleasant and all have tubs, not showers (Db-€115, Tb-€145, Qb-€170, CC, includes breakfast, add €14/person for dinner, next to Le Brévent lift, 28 rue des Moussoux, tel. 04 50 53 00 77, fax 04 50 55 86 82, www.lasavoyarde.com).

Hôtel Gourmets et Italy***, with cozy public spaces, a cool riverfront terrace, and balcony views from many of its tastefully decorated rooms, is a good value (Db-€70, Tb-€79, CC, elevator, 2 blocks from casino on Mt. Blanc side of river at 96 rue du Lyret, tel. 04 50 53 01 38, fax 04 50 53 46 74, www.hotelgourmets -chamonix.com, e-mail: hgicham@aol.com).

Hôtel Touring**, with basic but cavernous rooms (many with 4 beds), some saggy beds, and a friendly British staff, is good for families (Ds-€37–49, Db-€47–61, third person-€9, fourth person-€15, CC, 95 rue Joseph Vallot, tel. 04 50 53 59 18, fax 04 50 53 67 25, e-mail: ngulliford@aol.com). They also run the nearby **Hôtel du Midi**** (similar prices and same contact info as Hôtel Touring).

Hotels for Drivers

A few minutes above Chamonix, these places are practical only by car.

Chalet Chantel**, which feels more like a bed-and-breakfast inn, is meticulously kept by friendly Peter (British) and Françoise (French). The place is small, homey, and reasonable, with after-noon tea served during nonsummer months. Balcony rooms facing Mont Blanc are worth reserving (Db-€69–76, includes breakfast, CC, take Chamonix Sud exit and look for red signs, 391 route des Pecles, tel. 04 50 53 02 54, fax 04 50 53 54 52, e-mail: chantel @chamonixleguide.com).

Auberge du Bois Prin****, my only four-star listing, has the best views I found, cozy ambience, and a melt-in-your-chair

Chamonix Town

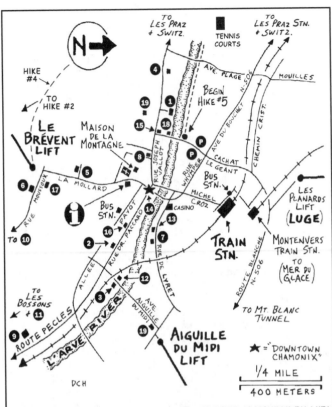

1 HOTEL DE L'ARVE
2 RICHEMOND HOTEL
3 HOTEL AU BON COIN
4 HOTEL BOULE DE NEIGE
5 CHALET BEAUREGARD B & B
6 HOTEL SAVOYARDE
7 HOTEL GOURMETS ET ITALY
8 HOTEL TOURING & SUPER U GROCERY
9 CHALET CHANTEL
10 AUBERGE DU BOIS PRIN & LA GIRANDOLE B & B
11 TO HOTEL L'AIGUILLE DU MIDI
12 LA BOCCALATTE
13 CHEZ NOUS RESTAURANT
14 L'ATMOSPHERE REST.
15 LE GRILLANDIAN
16 LE BIVOUAC
17 LA CABOLEE
18 CASINO GROCERY
19 LAUNDROMATS
P PARKING

restaurant. Ten of the 11 rooms in this flowery chalet come with
a terrace (Db-€175–213, extra person-€44, CC, includes breakfast, sauna, Jacuzzi, elevator, *menus* from €27.50 for guests,
follow Les Moussoux from Chamonix Sud exit, tel. 04 50 53
33 51, fax 04 50 53 48 75, www.boisprin.com).

Chambre d'Hôte la Girandole, just above Auberge du
Bois Prin, may be the highest home in Chamonix, with three
ground-floor rooms, three good bathrooms in the hall, and
immense views from the flowery garden (Sb-€48, Db-€58,
includes breakfast, no CC, 46 Chemin de la Perserverance, tel.
04 50 53 37 58, fax 04 50 55 81 77).

Sleeping near Chamonix

If Chamonix overwhelms you, spend the night in one of the
valley's overlooked, lower-profile villages.

Three kilometers from Chamonix, in the village of Les
Bossons (toward Annecy), lies the best two-star hotel in the valley,
Hôtel l'Aiguille du Midi**. The ultimate hostess, Martine Farini
(SE), runs this mountain retreat in a parklike setting, with a swimming pool, tennis court, Jacuzzi, Ping-Pong, and a laundry room
to boot. The alpine-comfortable rooms aren't big and you won't
care. Chamonix locals come here for their big meal (Db-€58–74,
add 30 percent each for third and fourth person, CC, elevator,
half-pension preferred in summer, €26.75 *menu* or *à la carte*,
easy by train, get off at Les Bossons, tel. 04 50 53 00 65, fax 04
50 55 93 69, www.hotel-aiguilledumidi.com).

Refuges and Refuge-Hotels near Chamonix

Chamonix has the answer for hikers who want to sleep high above
but don't want to pack tents, sleeping bags, stoves, or food: refuges
and refuge-hotels (open mid-June–mid-Sept, depending on snow
levels). Refuges have fewer amenities and require a longer walk
to reach than refuge-hotels. Refuges generally have bunks only
(about €11–14), no hot water, and hearty meals (dinner-€12–23,
breakfast-€6). Refuge-hotels usually have some private rooms (and
dorm rooms), hot showers down the hall, and more full-service
restaurants. You must reserve in advance (a few days are generally
enough), then pack your small bag for a memorable night among
new international friends.

Refuges: Chalet-Refuge Lac Blanc requires a 90-minute
uphill hike but is a fun, cozy, and sharp place with five bed
"cubbies," a friendly caretaker who loves meeting foreigners,
and an English-speaking staff (half-pension-€43/person, kids
under 14-€23, no CC, tel. 04 50 53 49 14, for more information
see "Chamonix Area Hikes, Hike #3," above). **Plan de l'Aiguille
Refuge** is a 20-minute walk down from the Plan de l'Aiguille
du Midi lift and is very basic (beds-€11, no CC, cheap meals,

tel. 06 85 17 31 25). The Office de la Haute Montagne in
Chamonix can explain your options (see "Chamonix Area
Hikes," above).
   Refuge-Hotels: Refuge-Hôtel Montenvers, right at the
Montenvers train stop, is wood-everywhere rustic (S-€23–35,
D-€31–47, T-€60, CC, good showers down the hall, tel. 04 50
53 12 54, fax 04 50 53 98 72; for directions see "Sights—
Chamonix, Mer de Glace," above). **Refuge-Hôtel La Flégère**
hangs on the edge and is simpler but ideally located for hiking to
Lac Blanc or Planpraz (3 private rooms with 5 beds, many dorm
beds, €43/person half-pension, no CC, fireplace, cozy bar/café,
right at La Flégère lift, tel. 04 50 53 06 13, fax 04 50 53 22 65).
For directions, see "Chamonix Area Hikes, Hike #2," above.

Eating in Chamonix

La Boccalatte is a good value with a lively atmosphere and a large
selection of local specialties. It's run by a friendly Alsatian, Thierry
(open daily until 22:00, across from Hôtel au Bon Coin, 59 avenue
de l'Aiguille du Midi, tel. 04 50 53 52 14). For Savoyarde specialties, you can't beat the wood-bench-warm ambience at **Chez
Nous** (€15 *menu*, great fondue comes with a green salad and potatoes, turn right at casino, 78 rue du Lyret, tel. 04 50 53 91 29).
The aptly named **l'Atmosphere** is where locals go when the mood
matters (€18.50 *menu*, better at €24.50, open daily, next to post
office at 123 place Balmat, tel. 04 50 55 97 97). The cute and
unpretentious **Le Bivouac** serves good local and Italian specialties
(€13 *menu*, 266 rue Paccard, tel. 04 50 53 34 08). **La Grillandain**
is a stress-free and sterile cafeteria with a decent salad bar and a
cheap kids' menu (where avenue Mt. Blanc and rue Joseph Vallot
meet). **La Cabolée**, next to the Brévent *téléphérique*, is a hip eatery
with great omelets and a wonderful view from its outdoor tables.
   Grocery stores: The best grocery is Casino, below Hôtel
Alpina. The more central Super U is next to Hôtel Touring at 117
rue Joseph Vallot (Mon–Sat 08:30–19:30, Sun 08:30–12:00).

Transportation Connections—Chamonix

Bus and train service to Chamonix is surprisingly good. You'll
find helpful bus and train information desks at the train station.
   By train to: Annecy (6/day, 2.5 hrs, change in St. Gervais),
Beaune and **Dijon** (7/day, 7 hrs, changes in St. Gervais and Lyon,
sometimes more changes), **Nice** (4/day, 10 hrs, change in St. Gervais and Lyon), **Arles** (8/day, 8.5 hrs, change in St. Gervais and
Lyon), **Paris'** Gare de Lyon (8/day, 7 hrs, change in Martigny and
Geneva or Lausanne, handy night train), **Martigny, Switzerland**
(11/day, 1.5 hrs, scenic trip), **Geneva** (3/day, 3.5 hrs, changes
in St. Gervais, La Roche-sur-Foron, and Annemasse).
   By bus: Buses provide service to destinations not served by

train and also to some cities that are served by train—but at a lower cost and higher speed. Get information at the bus station (*gare routière*) in the SNCF train station (tel. 04 50 53 01 15).

To Italy: See "Itinerary Options," below.

Itinerary Options from Chamonix

A Day in French-Speaking Switzerland—There are plenty of tempting alpine and cultural thrills just an hour or two away in Switzerland. A road-and-train line sneaks you scenically from Chamonix to the Swiss town of Martigny. While train travelers cross without formalities, drivers are charged a one-time 40-SF fee ($24) for a permit to use Swiss autobahns.

A Little Italy—The remote Valle d'Aosta and its historic capital city of Aosta are a spectacular gondola ride over the Mont Blanc range. The side trip is worthwhile if you'd like to taste Italy (spaghetti, gelato, and cappuccino), enjoy the town's great evening ambience, or look at the ancient ruins in Aosta, often called the "Rome of the North."

Take the spectacular lift (Chamonoix-Aiguille du Midi-Hellbronner) to Italy, described in "Sights—Chamonix," above. From Hellbronner, catch the €22 lift down to La Palud and take the bus to Aosta (hrly, change in Courmayeur). Aosta has a train station with connections to anywhere in Italy.

For a more down-to-earth experience, you can take the bus from Chamonix to Aosta. Ask at the TI for the schedules. If buses are allowed in the newly reopened Mont Blanc tunnel, it's a 90-minute trip to Aosta; if buses aren't allowed in the tunnel, it'll take three hours via Martigny. Drivers can simply drive through the Mont Blanc tunnel.

LYON

Straddling the Rhône and Saone Rivers between Burgundy and Provence, Lyon has been among France's important cities since pre-Roman times. Today, overlooked Lyon is one of France's big-city surprises. After Paris, it's the most historic and culturally important city in France. You get two distinctly different-feeling cities: The *molto* Italian cobbled alleys, Renaissance mansions, and colorful facades of Vieux Lyon; and the more staid but classy, Parisian-feeling shopping streets of Presqu'ile. Lyon makes a handy day visit for train travelers, as many trains pass through Lyon and both stations have baggage lockers, but those who invest a night here can experience the most renowned cuisine in France at pleasing prices.

Orientation

Lyon may be France's second-largest city, but inside it feels manageable. Most sightseeing is near the Saone River and can be done on foot. If you stick to the sights listed below, you won't need more than the funicular and a few subway rides to help you get around.

Lyon's sights are concentrated in three adjacent areas: Fourvière Hill is to the west with its white Basilique Notre Dame glimmering over the city; historic Vieux Lyon lies just below on the west bank of the Saone; and the Presqu'ile (home to all my hotels) sits across the Saone river to the east. Huge place Bellecour is in the middle of the Presqu'ile and ground zero for travelers in Lyon.

Start your day on Fourvière Hill (take the funicular near St. Jean Cathedral in Vieux Lyon to Fourvière) and visit the Gallo-Roman Museum, Roman Theater, and Basilique Notre Dame before catching the funicular or walking down to Vieux Lyon. Have lunch in Vieux Lyon and explore the covered passageways called *traboules* (see "Sights—Vieux Lyon," below), then cross over to the Presqu'ile for museums and shopping. Finish your day across the Rhône River at the Resistance museum (take subway or walk 25 min from place Bellecour). Many of Lyon's important sights are closed on Mondays or Tuesdays or both.

Tourist Information: The well-equipped TI and SNCF ticket office share space on the southeast corner of place Bellecour (Mon–Sat 09:00–18:00, until 19:00 mid-June–mid-Sept, Sun 10:00–18:00, closes at 17:00 in winter, tel. 04 72 77 69 69). The good €0.75 English map, which has museum information and a good enlargement of central Lyon, is free at your hotel. Pick up the free magazine on Vieux Lyon (includes a good walking tour) and a schedule of events and concerts (ask about concerts in the Roman theater). The TI sells a useful museum pass for serious sightseers (1 day/€14, 2 days/€25, 3 days/€31; includes all museums, a day pass on Métro/bus system, and a walking tour of Lyon with live guide or audioguide). The well-done €5.50 *World Heritage Excursions* book, sold at the TI, describes interest-ing self-guided walking tours (Vieux Lyon and Presqu'ile North walks are best). Handy audioguides (€6) also offer good, self-guided walking tours, though I prefer the live guided walks (€9.25, English tours depart daily at 14:00 from the TI June–Sept, bilingual tours available off-season).

Arrival in Lyon

By Train: Two train stations serve Lyon: Perrache and Part-Dieu. Many trains stop at both, and through trains connect the two stations every 10 minutes. Both are well-served by Métro, bus, and taxi and have lockers and baggage-checking services, making Lyon an easy stopover visit for train travelers.

The Perrache station is more central and within a 20-minute walk of place Bellecour (leave the station following signs to place

Carnot, then cross place Carnot and walk straight up pedestrian rue Victor Hugo). Or take the Métro (direction Laurent Bonnevay) two stops to Bellecour and follow *sortie rue République* signs. The Resistance museum is one stop away from Perrache station on the T-2 tramway (see "Getting around Lyon," below, for Métro and tramway tips).

To get to the city center from the Part-Dieu station, follow *sortie Vivier Merle* signs to the Métro, take it toward Stade de Gerland, transfer at Saxe-Gambetta to the Gare de Vaise route, get off at Bellecour, and follow signs for *sortie rue République* (see "Getting around Lyon," below, for Métro help).

Figure €9.50 to €12.50 to **taxi** from either train station to the hotels listed near place Bellecour.

By Car: The city center is fairly easy to navigate, though you'll encounter traffic on the surrounding freeways. From the freeways, follow signs to *centre-ville* and *Presqu'ile* and then follow *place Bellecour* signs. Park in the lots under place Bellecour or place des Celestins (yellow P means parking lot) or get advice from your hotel (€0.75/hr, €3 from 19:00–08:00). The TI's map has all public car parks well identified.

By Plane: Lyon's airport, Saint-Exupery (tel. 04 72 22 72 21), has two flights per hour to Paris' Charles de Gaulle airport and 12 TGVs per day from downtown Paris, and is served by flights from most European capitals. Four shuttles per hour run from the airport to both train stations (€8.25).

Getting around Lyon

Lyon has a user-friendly public transit system with two flashy streetcar lines (tramways T-1 and T-2) and four underground Métro lines (A, B, C, and D). While similar to Paris' Métro in many ways (e.g., routes are signed by *direction* for the last stop on the line), Lyon's Métro and tramways are highly automated, cleaner, and less crowded. There are no turnstiles and no obvious ticket windows. Efficient ticket machines (coins only, change given) are located near the platforms (1 ride-€1.30, 10 rides-€10.50, 1 day-€3.75). All tickets are good on buses, tramways, Métros, and funiculars. Buy your ticket (firmly push top button for 1 ticket, then put your coins in), validate it by punching it in a nearby chrome machine, and you're in business (tramway users validate on the trains). Study the wall maps to be sure of your direction; ask a local if you're not certain. Your ticket is good for one hour of travel including transfers between Métro, tramway, and funiculars.

Sights—Fourvière Hill

▲▲**Gallo-Roman Museum (Musée de la Civilisation Galloromaine)**—Constructed in the hillside with views of the Roman Theater, this museum makes Lyon's importance in Roman times

Lyon

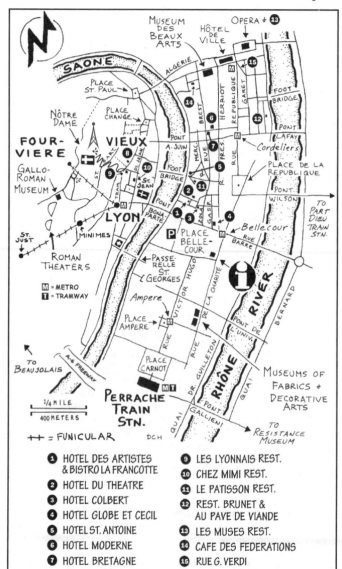

1 HOTEL DES ARTISTES
   & BISTRO LA FRANCOTTE

2 HOTEL DU THEATRE

3 HOTEL COLBERT

4 HOTEL GLOBE ET CECIL

5 HOTEL ST. ANTOINE

6 HOTEL MODERNE

7 HOTEL BRETAGNE

8 REST. LES ADRETS &
   LES RETROUVAILLES

9 LES LYONNAIS REST.

10 CHEZ MIMI REST.

11 LE PATISSON REST.

12 REST. BRUNET &
    AU PAVE DE VIANDE

13 LES MUSES REST.

14 CAFE DES FEDERATIONS

15 RUE G. VERDI

clear. Lyon was the military base that Julius Caesar used to conquer Gaul (much of modern-day France). Admire the bronze chariot from the seventh century B.C. (yes, that's B.C.) and get oriented at the model of Roman Lyon. Your visit continues downhill past Gallo-Roman artifacts allowing you to piece together life in Lyon during the Roman occupation, including 2,000-year-old lead pipes, a speech by Claudius (translated into English), Roman coins, models of Roman theaters complete with moving stage curtains, and haunting funeral masks (€4, free on Thu, open Tue–Sun 10:00–18:00, closed Mon, rooms begin closing 20 min early, helpful English explanations, tel. 04 72 38 81 90).

Basilique Notre Dame de Fourvière—In the late 1800s, the Bishop of Lyon vowed to build a magnificent tribute to God if the Prussians left his city alone (the same reason and vow that built the Sacré-Coeur in Paris). The whipped-cream exterior is neo-everything, and the interior screams "overdone," though the mosaics are impressive and depict key historic scenes. Don't miss the chapel below or the panoramic views from behind the church.

Observatory Tower—You can climb this mini-Eiffel-esque tower for even higher (though not much better) views (€1.50, June–Sept daily 10:00–12:00, 14:00–18:00, Oct–May 13:30–17:30 on weekends only).

Sights—Vieux Lyon (Old Lyon)

▲*Traboules* (**Covered Passageways**)—Lyon is the Florence of France, offering the best concentration of well-preserved Renaissance buildings in the country. From the 16th to the 19th centuries, Lyon was king of Europe's silk industry; at one point, it hummed with more than 18,000 looms. The fine buildings of the old center were designed by Italians and financed by the silk industry. Pastel courtyards, lovely loggias, and delicate arches line the passageways (*traboules*) connecting these buildings. The serpentine *traboules* provided shelter when silk was being moved from one stage to the next and would provide handy cover for the French Resistance in World War II. Several of Lyon's 315 *traboules* are open to the public (press top button next to street-front door to release door when entering; push lit buttons to illuminate dark walkways; pull lever sideways at door handle when leaving; please respect residents' peace when wandering through). The TI's magazine of Vieux Lyon proposes an interesting route connecting some of the most interesting *traboules*, though some are periodically closed. As you wander Vieux Lyon, look for plaques next to doors giving a history of the building and *traboule*. Snoop the courtyards at #26 and #28 rue St. Jean, and, as you walk through Lyon's longest *traboule* at #27 rue de Boeuf (push buttons as you go for mood lights), you'll understand why Lyon made an ideal center for the Resistance.

Cathedral of St. Jean—Stand as far back as you can in the square for the best view. This took 300 years to build and transcends Romanesque and Gothic styles. This cathedral does not soar like northern French cathedrals from the same period; influenced by their Italian neighbors, churches in southern France are typically less vertical than those in the north. Inside you'll find a few beautiful stained-glass windows and an unusual astrological clock with a underwhelming performance at 12:00, 14:00, 15:00, and 16:00 (Mon–Fri 08:00–12:00, 14:00–19:30, Sat–Sun 14:00–17:00). The €0.75 English leaflet is overkill and the treasury is of little interest. Check out the ruins predating the cathedral outside the left transept.

Gadagne Museum—This houses a puppet museum (covering Lyon's famous Guignol puppets) and a Lyon history museum, neither of which are ready for prime time (€4, Wed–Mon 10:45–18:00, closed Tue, place du Petit College).

Sights—On or near Lyon's Presqu'ile

From the Perrache station to place des Terreaux, the Presqu'ile is Lyon's shopping spine, with thriving pedestrian streets and stores in all shapes and price ranges. Join the parade of shoppers on sprawling rue de la République (north of place Bellecour), peruse the *bouchons* (characteristic bistros) of rue Merciere, and relax at a café on place des Terreaux. You'll also find these interesting museums:

▲**Museum of Fine Arts (Musée des Beaux Arts)**—Located around a peaceful courtyard of a former abbey, this fine-arts museum has an impressive collection ranging from Egyptian antiquities to medieval armor to Impressionist paintings. If you need a classical art fix, you'll love it; if you're short on time and going to Paris, it's skippable (€4, Tue–Sun 10:30–18:00, closed Mon, some rooms close between 12:00 and 14:00, pick up a museum layout on entering, great café-terrace, picnic-perfect courtyard, 20 place des Terreaux, Métro: Hôtel de Ville).

Museums of Fabrics and Decorative Arts (Musées des Tissus et des Arts Décoratifs)—These special-interest museums are well-organized and help you to understand Lyon's historic importance, but provide no English explanations. The Musée des Tissus held my interest with a tour of Lyon's important silk industry, including beautiful displays of silk from Napoleon's throne room to dresses, hats, and other clothing. The Musée des Arts Décoratifs is a large manor home decorated with period furniture and art objects (€4.75 covers both museums, Tue–Sun 10:00–17:30, Decorative Arts Museum closes 12:00–14:00, closed Mon, 34 rue de la Charite, Métro: Bellecour).

▲▲**Resistance and Deportation Center (Centre d'Histoire de la Resistance et de la Déportation)**—Located near Vichy, capital of the French puppet state and near neutral Switzerland, Lyon was the center of French Resistance from 1942 to 1945.

This well-done museum, once used as a Nazi torture chamber, uses austere concrete backdrops, headsets, many videos, reconstructed rooms, and, it seems, anything they can get their hands on to help you understand how the Resistance came to be and what life was like for its members. Excellent English explanations throughout provide a good history lesson, and the headsets help, but you need to move slowly with your headset and stand near the remote signal boxes, or you'll feel like you're decoding your own enemy messages. Those with less time should focus on the TV monitors—the film describing the deportation is in a recreated train box car (€4, Wed–Sun 09:00–17:30, closed Mon–Tue, 15-min walk from Perrache station, cross Pont Gallieni and walk 3 blocks to 14 avenue Berthelot; or, easier, take T-2 to Centre Berthelot—1 stop from Perrache—or the Métro to Jean Mace and walk back 3 blocks toward the river).

Sights—Near Lyon

Beaujolais Wine Country—Virtually outside Lyon, the beautiful vineyards and villages of the Beaujolais (relaxed tastings) make a pleasant detour for drivers heading north. The most scenic and interesting section lies between Villefranche sur Saone and Macon, just west of A-6 on D-68. Beaujolais' most important villages lie on this short route: Chiroubles, Fleurie, and Julienas. Look for *Route de Beaujolais* signs. The route continues north into the Maconnais wine region at the famous village of Pouilly-Fuisse. Lyon's TI has information on afternoon bus excursions to the Beaujolais (€31, includes 2 tastings).

Sleeping in Lyon
(€1.10 = about $1, country code: 33, zip code: 69002)

Hotels in Lyon are a steal compared to those in Paris. Weekends are generally discounted in this city that thrives on business travel. Skip the hotels near either train station. All hotels listed below are on the Presqu'ile; the first five are on or near the intimate place des Celestins, two blocks north of place Bellecour (Métro: Bellecour). Hotels have elevators unless otherwise noted, and air-conditioning is a godsend when it's hot.

Hôtel des Artistes*, ideally located right on place des Celestins, is red-velvet plush, comfortable, professional, and the best value in its price range (Sb-€63–87, Db-€69–93, basic buffet breakfast-€8.50, CC, air-con, 8 rue Gaspard-Andre, tel. 04 78 42 04 88, fax 04 78 42 93 76, e-mail: hartiste@clubinternet.fr, SE).

Hôtel du Théâtre*, across the small square from Hôtel des Artistes, is an artsy place with frumpy rooms in all sizes and shapes, some with sliver showers, none particularly luxurious. Those overlooking the place Celestins tend to be larger and are worth the extra cost. Expect laid-back owners and many stairs

(Sb-€50, Db-€47–56, extra bed-€8, CC, no elevator, 10 rue de Savoie, entrance on back side of place des Celestins, tel. 04 78 42 33 32, fax 04 72 40 00 61).

Comfort Hôtel Saint Antoine**, a well-situated and pleasant hotel almost on the Saone River, is a fine value with modern, well-appointed rooms, Internet access, and air-conditioning (Sb-€53–70, Db-€57–75, buffet breakfast-€6, CC, 1 rue du Port du Temple, tel. 04 78 92 91 91, fax 04 78 92 47 37, www.hotel -saintantoine.fr).

Hôtel Colbert**, just off place des Celestins, is spotless, well-located, and warmly run by Sebastian and Veronique. Bright, cheery rooms on the street side are larger but come with street noise (Sb-€53, Db-€58, CC, good buffet breakfast-€6.50, 4 rue des Archers, tel. 04 72 56 08 98, fax 04 72 56 08 65, www.hotel-le-colbert.com).

Hôtel Globe et Cecil*** is the most elegant of my listings, offering refined comfort in tastefully decorated rooms, but with strange hallways (Sb-€91–108, Db-€116–125, CC, includes buffet breakfast, air-con, 21 rue Gasparin, tel. 04 78 42 58 95, fax 04 72 41 99 06, www.globeetcecilhotel.com).

Near Place des Terreaux: These hotels are located closer to place des Terreaux, about 10 to 15 blocks north of place Bellecour; use Métro Cordeliers for both.

Hôtel Moderne** is a reasonable value, with pleasant pastel rooms and a cheery lobby in the heart of the shopping area (Sb-€46–50, Db-€52–55, CC, 15 rue Dubois, tel. 04 78 42 21 83, fax 04 72 41 04 40, www.hotelmodernelyon.com).

Hôtel de Bretagne* is the best one-star value I could find, with tight and tidy rooms and good beds but tired carpeting (Sb-€34, Db-€40, Tb-€47, Qb-€50, CC, no elevator, 10 rue Dubois, tel. 04 78 37 79 33, fax 04 72 77 99 92).

Eating in Vieux Lyon

With an abundance of excellent restaurants in all price ranges, it's hard to go wrong—unless you order *tripes* (cow stomach) or come on Sunday when almost all restaurants close. Look for these classics: *quenelles* (large dumplings), roasted chicken from Bresse, and *salade lyonnaise* (lettuce, ham, and poached eggs).

Bouchons are small bistros that evolved from the days when mama would feed the silk workers. Vieux Lyon is a *bouchon* bazaar, though the rue Merciere on the Presqu'ile also offers many good places. Here are a few to get you started (all are closed Sun):

The epicenter of restaurant activity in Vieux Lyon is place Neuve St. Jean—compare the crowds and sift through their menus. **Les Adrets** is nearby, cozy, and good (€18.50 *menu*, 30 rue de Boeuf, tel. 04 78 38 24 30). At 38 rue de Boeuf, **Les Retrouvailles** offers an excellent €18.50 *menu*, a charming dining room, and a terrific overall experience. A block south,

Les Lyonnais is cheaper, lighthearted, and locally popular, with photo portraits of loyal customers lining the walls (€10 *menu*, 1 rue Tramssac, tel. 04 78 37 64 82). For a salad or quiche and a glass of wine with ambience, consider **Chez Mimi**'s small café one block from the cathedral (inside can be smoky, 66 rue St. Jean).

Eating on the Presqu'ile
The zinc bar bistro **La Francotte** is good for a relaxing drink or a meal and is handy to many hotels (closed Sun, 8 place des Celestins). Vegetarians and nondrinkers will appreciate the fair-priced fine cuisine at **Le Patisson** (€14.50 *menu*, closed Fri–Sun, 2 blocks north of place des Celestins at 17 rue du Port du Temple, tel. 04 72 41 81 71). Near the Opera, these two fine places go unnoticed by tourists (both closed Sun and Mon): The cozy, traditional *bouchon* **Restaurant Brunet** (€15 *menu*, 23 rue Claudia, tel. 04 78 37 44 31) and the more formal **Au Pave de Viande** (€15 *menu*, 15 rue Claudia, tel. 04 78 37 23 89). For lunch or dinner with an exceptional view, ride the elevator to the seventh floor of the Opera House to **Les Muses de l'Opéra** (€16 dinner *menu*, tel. 04 72 00 45 58). For relaxed outdoor dining, window shop the *bouchons* lining rue Giuseppe Verdi. **Café des Federations** is a venerable institution worth a stop for the traditional Lyonnais ambience and good wine selection (€24 *menu*, closed Sun and in Aug, 8 rue Major-Martin).

Transportation Connections—Lyon
After Paris, Lyon is France's most important rail hub. Rail travelers will find this gateway to the Alps, Provence, the Riviera, and Burgundy an easy stopover. Two main stations serve Lyon (Part-Dieu and Perrache). Most trains officially depart from Part-Dieu, though many stop at Perrache, and trains run between the stations every 10 minutes. Double-check which station your train departs from.

By train to: Paris (20/day, 2 hrs), **Dijon** (14/day, 2 hrs), **Beaune** (13/day, 2 hrs, many change in Macon), **Avignon** (24/day, 14 to TGV station in 1.5 hrs, 10 to main station in 2.5 hrs), **Arles** (20/day, 2.5 hrs, most change in Avignon, Marseille, or Nîmes), **Nice** (9 day, 5 hrs, many change in Avignon, Marseille, or Valence, night train), **Annecy** (17/day, 2 hrs, most change in Aix les Bains), **Venice** (7/day, 11–13 hrs, most change in Geneva and Milan, night train), **Rome** (4/day, 12 hrs, at least 1 change in Milan, night train), **Florence** (3/day, 10 hrs), **Geneva** (10/day, 2 hrs), **Barcelona** (1 day train, 7 hrs, change in Perpignan, 2 night trains).

Drivers: En route to Provence, consider a three-hour detour through the spectacular Ardeches Gorges; exit the A-6 autoroute at Privas and follow the villages of Aubenas, Vallon Pont d'Arc (offers kayak trips), and Pont St. Esprit. En route to Burgundy, consider a Beaujolais detour (see "Sights—Near Lyon," above).

BURGUNDY

The rolling hills of Burgundy gave birth to superior wine, fine cuisine, and sublime countryside, crisscrossed with canals and dotted with quiet farming villages. This deceptively peaceful region witnessed Julius Caesar's defeat of the Gauls, and then saw the Abbey of Cluny rise from the ashes of the Roman Empire to vie with Rome for religious influence in the 12th century. Burgundy's last hurrah came in the 15th century, when its powerful dukes controlled an area that stretched north to Holland. Today, bucolic Burgundy is the transportation funnel for eastern France and makes a convenient stopover for travelers (car or train), with quick access north to Paris or the Alsace, east to the Alps, and south to Provence. Only a small part of Burgundy is covered by vineyards, but grapes are what they do best. The white cows you see everywhere are Charolais. France's best beef ends up in *boeuf Bourguignon*.

Planning Your Time

Stay in or near Beaune. It's conveniently located for touring the vineyards and countryside. Plan on a half day in Beaune and a half day for the countryside. Ideally, sleep in Beaune Friday night and awake to the sounds of the Saturday market. If you have more time, visit (or sleep in) unspoiled Semur-en-Auxois and tour its lush countryside and nearby sights.

Getting around Burgundy

Trains link Beaune with ease; less-frequent buses cruise the wine route between Dijon, Beaune, and Chalon-sur-Saone. Bikes and minivan tours get nondrivers from Beaune into the countryside. Buses connect Semur-en-Auxois with Dijon and Montbard rail stations.

Burgundy

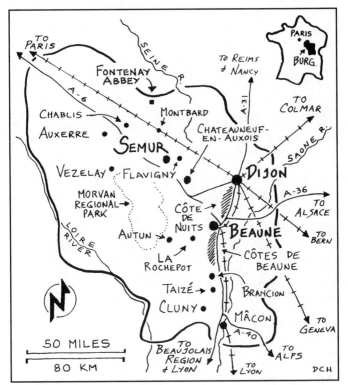

Cuisine Scene—Burgundy

Considered by many to be France's best, Burgundian cuisine is peasant cooking elevated to an art. Several classic dishes were born here: *escargots Bourguignon* (snails served sizzling hot in garlic butter), *boeuf Bourguignon* (beef simmered for hours in red wine with onions and mushrooms), *coq au vin* (chicken stewed in red wine), and *oeufs en meurette* (poached eggs on a large crouton in red wine), as well as the famous Dijon mustards. Look also for *jambon persillé* (cold ham layered in a garlic-parsley gelatin), *pain d'épices* (spice bread), and *gougère* (light, puffy cheese pastries). Native cheeses are Epoisses and Langres (both mushy and great) and, my favorite, Montrachet (a tasty goat cheese). *Crème de cassis* (black currant liqueur) is another Burgundian specialty; look for it in desserts and snazzy drinks (try a *kir*).

With Bordeaux, Burgundy is why France is famous for wine. From Chablis to the Beaujolais, you'll find it all here: great fruity reds, dry whites, and crisp rosés. The three key grapes are Chardonnay (dry, white wines), Pinot Noir (medium-bodied red wines), and Gamay (light, fruity wines such as Beaujolais). Every village produces its own distinctive wine, from Chablis to Meursault to Chassagne-Montrachet. Road maps read like fine wine lists. If the wine village has a hyphenated name, the latter half of its name often comes from the town's most important vineyard (e.g., Gevery-Chamberin, Ladoix-Serrigny). Look for the *Dégustation Gratuite* (free tasting) signs and prepare for serious tasting and steep prices if you're not careful. For a more relaxed tasting, head for the hills: The less prestigious Hautes-Côtes (upper slopes) produce some terrific and overlooked wines. Look for village cooperatives or try my suggestions for Beaune tastings (see "Wine-Tasting in and near Beaune," below). The least expensive (but still tasty) wines are Bourgogne Ordinaire and Passetoutgrain (both red), and whites from the Macon and Chalon areas. If you like rosé, try Marsannay, considered one of France's best.

BEAUNE

You'll feel comfortable right away in this manageable and popular wine capital, where life centers on the production and consumption of the prestigious, expensive Côte d'Or wines. *Côte d'Or* means "golden hillsides," and they are a spectacle to enjoy in late October as the leaves of the vineyards turn colors.

Orientation

Beaune is a compact, prosperous little city (pop. 25,000) with a handful of interesting monuments and vineyards on its doorstep. Limit your Beaune ramblings to the town center, contained within its medieval walls and circled by a one-way ring road, and find a quiet moment to walk into the vineyards just west of the center. All roads and activities converge on the perfectly French place Carnot, as do Wednesday and Saturday markets. Beaune is very quiet on Sundays and on Monday mornings.

    Tourist Information: There are two TIs, one in the city center, the other on the ring road. The city center TI is across the street from Hôtel Dieu on place de la Halle (April–Nov Mon–Sat 09:30–19:00, summers until 20:00, Sun 10:00–17:00, Dec–March daily 10:00–18:00, Sun 10:00–13:00, 14:00–17:00, from place Carnot walk toward thin spire, tel. 03 80 26 21 30). The other TI is handy for drivers in the Porte Marie de Bourgogne on the ring road's southeastern corner (Mon–Sat 09:00–12:00, 14:00–18:00, closed Sun, look for the flags). Both have city maps (with a walking tour described), a room-finding service, a list of *chambres d'hôte*, and bus schedules. Ask about English walking tours (€6.50, usually at noon, June–Sept) and pass on their museum pass.

Arrival in Beaune

By Train: To reach the city center from the train station (lockers available), walk straight out of the station up avenue du Huit (8) Septembre, cross the busy ring road, and continue up rue du Château.

By Bus: Beaune has no bus station—only several stops in the center. Ask the driver for *le centre ville* (luh san-trah veel); the Jules Ferry stop is central and closest to the train station.

By Car: Follow *centre-ville* signs to the ring road. Once on the ring road, turn right at the first signal after the post office (rue d'Alsace) and park for free in the place Madeleine.

Helpful Hints

Best Souvenir Shopping: The **Athenaeum** has a great variety of souvenirs and some books in English, with a great children's section upstairs (daily 10:00–19:00, across from Hôtel Dieu at 7 rue de l'Hôtel Dieu).

Best Wine Stores: Dennis Perret has a good and varied selection in all price ranges and a helpful, English-speaking staff (they can chill a white for your picnic). If you've tasted a wine you like elsewhere, they can usually find a less costly bottle with similar qualities (June–Nov Mon–Sat 09:00–19:00, Dec–May closed 12:00–14:00, closed Sun, 40 place Carnot, tel. 03 80 22 35 47). I also like the wine hardware store, **Comptoir du Vin**, for wine paraphernalia (where the rue d'Alsace runs into place Carnot).

Best Food Store: Peruse the food souvenirs at **Amuse Bouche** (7 place Carnot).

Sights—Beaune

▲▲**Hôtel Dieu**—The Hundred Years' War and the Black Death devastated Beaune, leaving more than 90 percent of its population destitute. Nicholas Rolin, Chancellor of Burgundy and a peasant by birth, had to do something for "his people." So in 1443, he paid to build this Flamboyant Flemish/Gothic charity hospital; it was completed in only eight years. Tour it on your own with the helpful English handout. In the St. Louis wing (where patients replaced the winepresses that once occupied this space), you'll find van der Weyden's dramatic *Last Judgment* polyptych, commissioned by Rolin to give the dying something to ponder. For a closer look, ask the attendant to maneuver the giant roaming monocle. Keep this painting in mind if you see the Isenheim altar piece in Colmar—they were commissioned for similar reasons, but with very different results (€4.75, April–Nov daily 09:00–18:30, Dec–March 09:00–11:30, 14:00–17:30).

▲**Collégiale Notre Dame**—Built in the 12th and 13th centuries, this is a good example of Cluny-style architecture (except for the front porch addition). Enter to see the 15th-century tapestries

Beaune

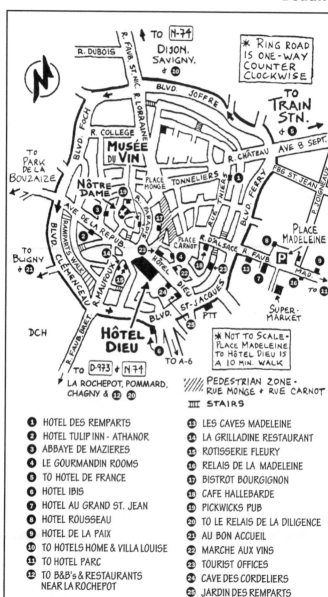

* RING ROAD IS ONE-WAY COUNTER CLOCKWISE

* NOT TO SCALE - PLACE MADELEINE TO HÔTEL DIEU IS A 10 MIN. WALK

PEDESTRIAN ZONE - RUE MONGE + RUE CARNOT

STAIRS

① HOTEL DES REMPARTS
② HOTEL TULIP INN - ATHANOR
③ ABBAYE DE MAZIERES
④ LE GOURMANDIN ROOMS
⑤ TO HOTEL DE FRANCE
⑥ HOTEL IBIS
⑦ HOTEL AU GRAND ST. JEAN
⑧ HOTEL ROUSSEAU
⑨ HOTEL DE LA PAIX
⑩ TO HOTELS HOME & VILLA LOUISE
⑪ TO HOTEL PARC
⑫ TO B&B's & RESTAURANTS NEAR LA ROCHEPOT

⑬ LES CAVES MADELEINE
⑭ LA GRILLADINE RESTAURANT
⑮ ROTISSERIE FLEURY
⑯ RELAIS DE LA MADELEINE
⑰ BISTROT BOURGIGNON
⑱ CAFE HALLEBARDE
⑲ PICKWICKS PUB
⑳ TO LE RELAIS DE LA DILIGENCE
㉑ AU BON ACCUEIL
㉒ MARCHE AUX VINS
㉓ TOURIST OFFICES
㉔ CAVE DES CORDELIERS
㉕ JARDIN DES REMPARTS

(behind the altar, drop in a coin for lights), a variety of stained glass, and what's left of frescoes depicting the life of Lazarus (daily 08:30–19:00). To find the Musée du Vin from here, walk 30 steps straight out of the cathedral, turn left down a cobbled alley (rue d'Enfer), keep left, and enter the courtyard of Hôtel des Ducs—today's Musée du Vin, located in the old residence of the dukes of Burgundy.

Musée du Vin—You don't have to like wine to appreciate this folk-wine museum. The history and culture of Burgundy and wine were fermented in the same bottle. At least wander into the courtyard for a look at the duke's palace, antique winepresses (in the barn), and a model of 15th-century Beaune. Inside the museum you'll find a great model of the region, tools, costumes, and scenes of Burgundian wine history—but no tasting. English explanations are in each room (€4, ticket good for other Beaune museums, daily 09:30–18:00, closed Tue Dec–Jan).

Ramparts Walk, Parc de la Bouzaise, and Vineyards—You can stroll above Beaune on a short segment of its 13th-century wall and get a sense of its once impressive medieval defenses. Find the ramp on the right (Remparts des Dames) where the rue Maufoux meets the ramparts. Wander north to the avenue de la République, drop down and cross the ring road, then follow the stream for three blocks to the park. The vineyards lie just beyond, with small roads and paths.

Wine Tasting

Countless opportunities exist (for a price) for you to learn the fine points of Burgundy's wines. Many shops offer a free tasting (with the expectation that you'll buy), and several large cellars (*caves*) charge an entry fee, allowing you to taste a variety of wines (with less expectation that you'll buy). Most *caves* offer some form of introduction or self-guided tour (also see "Minibus Tours," below). These three places are a block from the TI and stack up conveniently next to each other.

Start or end your tour at the **Athenaeum**, which is a bookstore (with many titles in English), wine bar, and Burgundian wine chamber of commerce all in one (across from Hôtel Dieu, next to TI). You'll pay by the glass (€3–6) to select from a good list (SE).

▲▲▲**Marché aux Vins**—Across the street from the Athenaeum, this is Beaune's wine smørgåsbord and the best way to sample its impressive wines. Hand the mademoiselle €8.50 for a wine-tasting cup (you get to keep it) and scorecard, then plunge into the labyrinth of candlelit *caves* dotted with 18 barrels, each offering a new tasting experience (4 chardonnays, 14 pinot noirs). You're on your own. The best reds are upstairs in the chapel, at the end of the tasting. Buy the €2.50 *gougères* (puff pastries) to cleanse your palate as you taste (mid-June–mid-Sept daily 09:30–17:45, otherwise 09:30–11:45, 14:00–17:45, last entry at 17:15, tel. 03 80 25 08 20).

Caves des Cordeliers—Better for those with less stamina, this *cave* offers self-guided tours of their "museum cellars" (English explanations) and has only six wines to taste (€4.75 April–Sept 09:30–18:30, Oct–March 10:30–12:00, 14:00–17:30, 6 rue de l'Hôtel Dieu, 1 block toward ring road from Marché Aux Vins, tel. 03 80 25 08 85).

Wine Tasting outside Beaune—The TI has a long list of area vintners for those who want to venture into the countryside. Remember, you're expected to buy unless you're with a group tour (see also "The Hautes-Côtes to Châteauneuf-en-Auxois," below, for tastings in the more-relaxed Hautes-Côtes). The famous *Route des Grands Crus* that connects Burgundy's most prestigious wine villages is disappointing north of Aloxe Corton, as you're forced onto the unappealing N-74. Consider instead the villages between Beaune and La Rochepot and south to Santanay (e.g., Monthelie, Nantoux, St. Romain, and St. Aubin are all off the famous path and offer ample tastings; see "Scenic Drive to La Rochepot," below).

Minibus Tours of Vineyards near Beaune—Wine Safari offers minibus wine-tasting tours in three two-hour itineraries (€31, tour #2 is best for beginners, departs from TI, call TI for information, tel. 03 80 26 21 30). These tours are well-run, in English, and get you into the countryside and smaller wineries. Transco buses also run from Beaune through all the great wine villages (see "Getting around the Beaune Region," below).

Sleeping in Beaune
(€1.10 = about $1, country code: 33, zip code: 21200)
Sleep Code: **S** = Single, **D** = Double/Twin, **T** = Triple, **Q** = Quad, **b** = bathroom, **s** = shower only, **CC** = Credit Cards accepted, **no CC** = Credit Cards not accepted, **SE** = Speaks English, **NSE** = No English, * = French hotel rating system (0–4 stars).

A **Laundromat** is between the train station and place Madeleine, at 17-19 rue du Faubourg St. Jean (daily 06:30–21:00).

At **Hôtel des Remparts*****, the formal Epaillys offer classy but affordable rooms in a manor house with beamed ceilings, period furniture, a quiet courtyard, and great family rooms (Db-€51–80, most at €80, Db suites-€100, Tb-€84–95, Qb-€110, CC, cozy attic rooms, parking-€7.50, 48 rue Thiers, between train station and main square, just inside ring road, tel. 03 80 24 94 94, fax 03 80 24 97 08, e-mail: hotel.des.remparts@wanadoo.fr, SE).

Hôtel de France** is ideal for train travelers and handy for drivers with easy parking across from the train station. It's friendly and well-run with spotless rooms, air-conditioning, and Diana the sheepdog (Sb-€37–43, Db-€49, Tb-€59, Qb-€67, CC, 35 avenue du Huit Septembre, tel. 03 80 24 10 34, fax 03 80 24 96 78, e-mail: hotfrance.beaune@wanadoo.fr).

The **Le Gourmandin** restaurant rents three spacious,

comfortable, and air-conditioned rooms right on place Carnot; they are a great value (Db-€53, big Db/Tb or Qb-€70, CC, many stairs, 8 place Carnot, tel. 03 80 24 07 88, fax 03 80 22 27 42, e-mail: gourm01@aol.com).

Hôtel Tulip Inn-Athanor***, with a central location, mixes modern comfort in smaller rooms with a touch of old Beaune (Db-€90–101, most at €90, CC, elevator, 9 avenue de la République, tel. 03 80 24 09 20, fax 03 80 24 09 15, e-mail: hotel.athanor@wanadoo.fr, SE).

Abbaye de Mazieres*** is well-located with 12 quiet, colorful, and big rooms in a 15th-century building over a restaurant near the basilica (Db-€55–114, Tb-€84–117, CC, 19 rue Mazieres, tel. 03 80 24 74 64, fax 03 80 22 49 49, e-mail: abbayedemazieres@wanadoo.fr; if no response contact Hôtel Tulip, above).

Hôtel Ibis**, modern, efficient, and comfortable enough with a pool and airy terrace, is located at the ring road and avenue Charles de Gaulle (Sb-€51, Db-€53–63, CC, tel. 03 80 22 75 67, fax 03 80 22 77 17, e-mail: ibisbeaune@wanadoo.fr). There's another Ibis hotel closer to the autoroute, but it's less central.

Sleeping on Place Madeleine

These hotels are a few blocks from the city center and train station and offer easy parking.

What **Hôtel au Grand St. Jean**** lacks in character, it makes up for in value and location. Like a sprawling motel with ample and safe parking, it's simple, practical, and, with its helpful, English-speaking owner, Monsieur Neaux, plenty French. Color-blind travelers will love the TV lounge (Db-€41, Tb/Qb-€50, CC, on place Madeleine, tel. 03 80 24 12 22, fax 03 80 24 15 43, e-mail: hotel-au-grand-st-jean@wanadoo.fr).

Hôtel Rousseau, across the square, is a no-frills place that turns its back on Beaune's sophistication and will make you smile with cheerful, quirky, and hard-to-find owners, pet birds, and an enclosed garden. The cheapest rooms are simple, generally clean, and fine. The rooms with showers are like grandma's (S-€26, D-€30–37, Db-€47, T-€43, Tb-€54, Q-€46, Qb-€58, showers down the hall-€3, includes breakfast, no CC, free private parking, 11 place Madeleine, tel. 03 80 22 13 59, fax...what's that?).

Hôtel de la Paix***, just off place de la Madeleine, is a good, comfortable value with appealing rooms and an owner who cares (Sb-€49, Db-€69, loft Tb-€90, Qb-€101–116, CC, 45 rue du Faubourg Madeleine, tel. 03 80 24 78 08, fax 03 80 24 10 18, SE).

Sleeping near Beaune

You'll find some exceptional and family-friendly values within a short drive of Beaune. Hotels in famous wine villages are generally pricey and overrated.

Hotels: Hôtel Le Home** is an excellent value, with cushy rooms in an old mansion. It's a kilometer north of town on the N-74. The less-expensive rooms are fine, but the rooms on the parking courtyard (€64) have a nice terrace (Db-€52–64, Tb-€76, Qb-€84, CC, free parking, 138 route de Dijon, tel. 03 80 22 16 43, fax 03 80 24 90 74). Call ahead—it's popular.

Hôtel Parc** is located in the flowery little village of Levernois, down in the valley away from the vines and wine hoopla. This enchanting vine-covered manor house is postcard-perfect, with fine rooms showing great attention to detail surrounding a large grassy garden (Db-€44–82, Tb-€57–95, Qb-€98, CC, 5 min across the autoroute from Beaune, 21200 Levernois, tel. 03 80 24 63 00, fax 03 80 24 21 19, e-mail: hotel.le.parc@wanadoo.fr).

Hôtel Villa Louise*** is burrowed in the prestigious wine village of Aloxe Corton five minutes north of Beaune. It's *très* cozy with thoughtfully decorated rooms and a rear garden made for sipping wine (Db-€92–137, most about €107, CC, 21420 Aloxe Corton, tel. 03 80 26 46 70, fax 03 80 26 47 16, e-mail: hotel-villa-louise@wanadoo.fr).

Chambres d'Hôte: The Côte d'Or has many *chambres d'hôte*; get a list at the TI and reserve ahead in the summer. The cliff-dwelling villages of Baubigny, Orches, and Evelles, just under La Rochepot (zip code for all: 21340) make fine bases and offer many *chambres d'hote*. In Baubigny, **Madame Fussi** has three comfortable rooms (one family-ideal suite) in a modern home over a sweeping lawn (Db-€41, Tb-€47, no CC, tel. & fax 03 80 21 84 66). Just down the road in Evelles, **Madame Lagelee** has a big apartment on a private courtyard (Sb-€28, Db-€40, Tb-€46, Qb-€54, no CC, tel. 03 80 21 79 57). A kilometer above in Orches, charming **Isabelle Raby** has a double room, a good family room, and a third room planned, facing a nice yard with views and a cute pool; ask to see their cellar (Db-€46, Tb-€60, Qb-€72, includes big breakfast, no CC, tel. & fax 03 80 21 78 45, e-mail: praby@wanadoo.fr). Closer to Beaune, **Château de Melin**, home to Paul Dumay wines (tastings available), offers top comfort in a beautifully restored château complete with a small pond, large gardens, and vineyards (Db-€76, Qb-€114, includes breakfast, no CC, 21190 Auxey Duresses, tel. 03 80 21 21 19, fax 03 80 21 21 72, e-mail: derats@chateaudemelin.com).

Eating in Beaune

For a traditional Burgundian setting, step down to the wine-soaked-cellar atmosphere of the 12th-century **Abbaye de Mazieres** (€15 *menu*, closed Tue, see "Sleeping in Beaune," above). For fine traditional Burgundian cuisine (escargot, hot goat-cheese salad, *oeufs en meurette*) at digestible prices, consider **La Grilladine** (I like the €17.50 *menu Bourguignon*, closed Mon, 17 rue Maufoux, tel. 03 80 22 22 36). Or try the nearby and respected **Rotisserie Fleury** (€20–23 *menus*, closed Thu, 15 place Fleury, tel. 03 80 2 35 50). On the place Madeleine, try the relaxed ambience and friendly surroundings of **Les Caves Madeleine** and dine surrounded by shelves of wine (good wines by the glass, reasonable *plats du jour* and *menus*, closed Sun, 8 rue Faubourg Madeleine). Beaune's best budget restaurant is **Relais de la Madeleine**, run by the entertaining "Monsieur Neaux Problem" (€11.50 *menu*, closed Wed, 44 place Madeleine, tel. 03 80 22 07 47). **Le Jardin des Remparts** is ideal for a splurge (*menus* from €29–75, closed Sun–Mon, reserve ahead, on ring road at 10 rue de l'Hôtel Dieu, tel. 03 80 24 79 41, e-mail: lejardin@club-internet.fr).

Beaune's best wine bar is the relaxed **Bistrot Bourguignon** (pricey wines by the glass and a good but limited *menu*, on a pedestrian-only street at 8 rue Monge, closed Sun, occasional jazz concerts, tel. 03 80 22 23 24). Drop by **Café Hallebarde** for a grand selection of draft beer (24 rue d'Alsace); and, if you're tired of speaking French, pop into the late-night-lively **Pickwicks Pub** (behind church at 2 rue Notre Dame).

Eating near Beaune

Five minutes away by car is **Le Relais de la Diligence**, where you can dine surrounded by vineyards and taste the area's best budget Burgundian cuisine with many *menu* options (*menus* from €14, closed Tue–Wed, take N-74 toward Chagny/Chalon and turn left at L'Hôpital Meursault on D-23, tel. 03 80 21 21 32). **Le Pommard,** between Beaune and La Rochepot, is traditional and reasonable (*menus* from €15, on main road from Beaune in Pommard, tel. 03 80 22 08 08). **Au Bon Accueil** is relaxed and country-cozy, on a hill above Beaune, with great outdoor tables, and five-course *menus* for €17.50 (closed Mon–Wed, leave Beaune's ring road and take Bligny-sur-Ouche turnoff, a few minutes outside Beaune you'll see signs, tel. 03 80 22 08 80). For a complete French experience, call ahead for a table at **Auberge du Vieux Pressoir,** below la Rochepot in tiny Evelles (€13–20 *menus*, closed Wed, tel. 03 80 21 82 16).

Transportation Connections—Beaune

By train to: Dijon (17/day, 25 min), **Paris'** Gare de Lyon (12/day, 2.5 hrs, 10 require change in Dijon), **Colmar** (6/day, 4–5 hrs, changes in Dijon and in Besançon, Mulhouse, or Beflort), **Arles** (10/day, 4.5 hrs, 9 with change in Lyon and Nîmes or Avignon), **Chamonix** (7/day, 7 hrs, changes in Lyon and St. Gervais, some require additional changes), **Annecy** (9/day, 5 hrs, change in Lyon), **Amboise** (8/day, 6 hrs, most with changes in Dijon and in Paris, Gare de Lyon, then Métro to Austerlitz or Montparnasse stations).

Getting around the Beaune Region

By Bus: Transco bus #44 runs from Beaune through the vineyards and villages south to Chalon-sur-Saône, west to La Rochepot, and north to Dijon. About 10 buses per day link Beaune and Dijon via the great wine villages; ask at the TI for schedules and stops or call for information (tel. 03 80 42 11 00).

By Bike: Well-organized, English-speaking Florent at **Bourgogne Randonnées** has good bikes, bike racks, maps, and thorough countryside itineraries (get his advice on your plan). He can deliver your bike to your hotel anywhere in France (bikes—€3/hr, €14/day, Mon–Sat 09:00–12:00, 13:30–19:00, Sun 10:00–12:00, 14:00–17:00, near train station at 7 avenue du Huit Septembre, tel. 03 80 22 06 03, fax 03 80 22 15 58).

Sights—Beaune Region

Bike Routes—Immaculate vineyards, lush countryside, and little-traveled roads make this area perfect for biking. Some routes are fairly level; others require realistic self-evaluation of your fitness. Get the local Michelin map and heed the advice from Bourgogne Randonnées (see above). You'll find small paved lanes leading into the vineyards above most villages, offering peaceful alternatives to the busier roads. Bring food and water, as you'll find few shops along these roads. For a relatively easy and rewarding ride, connect Savigny-les-Beaune (consider visiting the château for its motorcycle, racing car, and airplane collection), Pernand Vergeles (have a drink at Café Luxembourg), Aloxe Corton (sample wines at its cooperative), and return toward Savigny-les-Beaune to Beaune. Tiny lanes ideal for biking lead into the vineyards above the main road between Savigny and Pernand Vergeles. The scenic drive to La Rochepot described below is bikeable, though very hilly and rigorous.

▲**Château La Rochepot**—This very Burgundian castle rises above the trees and its village, 12 kilometers (8 miles) from Beaune. It's accessible by car, bike (hilly), or infrequent bus. Cross the drawbridge and knock three times with the ancient knocker to enter. This pint-size castle is splendid inside and out. Tour half on your own and the other half with a French guide (get the English handout, some tours in English, call ahead). The kitchen will bowl you over. Look for the 15th-century highchair in the dining room. Climb the tower and see the Chinese room, sing chants in the resonant chapel, and make ripples in the well. (Can you spit a bull's-eye? It's 72 meters down!) Don't leave without driving, walking, or pedaling up the D-33 a few hundred meters toward St. Aubin (behind Hôtel Relais du Château) for a romantic view (€5.50, June–Aug Wed–Mon 10:00–18:00, Sept–May 10:00–11:30, 14:00–17:30, closed Tue year-round and at 16:30 Nov–March, tel. 03 80 21 71 37).

Scenic Drive to La Rochepot: From Beaune, take D-973 toward La Rochepot. Right after Auxey-Duresses, follow

Beaune Region

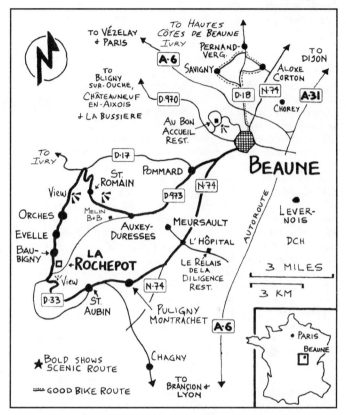

St. Romain and climb to the upper village and find signs to
Château-Pointe de Vue for a great picnic site and nice views.
Leave St. Romain, climbing toward Ivry-en-Montagne (D-17),
then turn left to Orches (spectacular view turnouts soon after
turn), and continue on to La Rochepot. After visiting the château,
leave La Rochepot, continuing over the hill to St. Aubin and
Gamay via the D-33 (it runs behind Hôtel Relais du Château in
La Rochepot). Follow the tiny road to Puligny-Montrachet and
Meursault, and head back to Beaune via the D-973.

▲**Brancion and Chapaize**—An hour south of Beaune by car
(20 km/12.5 miles west of Tournus on D-14) are two churches
that owe their existence and architectural design to the nearby
and once-powerful Cluny Abbey. Brancion's nine-building
hamlet floats on a hill with the purest example of Romanesque

architecture I've seen: a 12th-century church (with faint frescoes inside), a charming château (climb the tower for views), and a 15th-century market hall. **Auberge du Vieux Brancion** offers fine Burgundian cuisine at fair prices (€11 and €17.50 *menus*). For a peaceful break, spend a night in one of the Auberge's simple, frumpy, but cozy rooms (Ds-€36, Db-€54, good family rooms-€54–69, tel. & fax 03 85 51 03 83, www.brancion.fr). A few kilometers closer to Beaune, Chapaize's beautiful church is famous for its 11th-century belfry and its leaning-to-the-leeward interior (English brochure available). Wander around the back for a view of the belfry and pause at the friendly café across the street. To scenically connect these towns from Beaune, follow N-74 south to Chagny (Burgundy's ugliest town), then find Remigny and follow D-109 to Aluze, then follow D-978 east and D-981 south through Givry, Buxy, and on to Chapaize.

Cluny and Taizé—Twenty kilometers (12.5 miles) southwest of Brancion lies the historic town of Cluny. The center of a rich and powerful monastic movement in the Middle Ages is today a pleasant town with very sparse and crumbled remains of its once-powerful abbey. For a new trend in monasticism, consider visiting the booming Christian community of Taizé (teh-zay), just north of Cluny. Brother Roger and his community welcome visitors who'd like to spend a few days getting close to God through meditation, singing, and simple living. Call or write first if you plan to stay overnight. There are dorm beds only. (Taizé Community, 71250 Cluny, tel. 03 85 50 14 14.)

The Hautes-Côtes to Châteauneuf-en-Auxois

This half-day loop trip links vineyards, pastoral landscapes, the Burgundy canal, a Cistercian abbey, and a medieval village. (If you're heading to Paris, Châteauneuf-en-Auxois can be done en route or as an overnight stop). It requires a car, the local Michelin map 243, and navigational patience. Leave Beaune's ring road toward Dijon on N-74. Soon, take the Savigny-les-Beaune turnoff, then connect Pernand Vergelesses with the Hautes-Côtes villages of Echevronne, Magny-les Villiers, Villers la Faye, and Marey-les-Fussey. **Wineries** in these villages offer stress-free tastings. (More serious tasters should consider these wineries: Lucien Jacob in Echevronne, tel. 03 80 21 52 15, SE; Domaine Thevenot Le Brun in Marey-les-Fussey, tel. 03 80 62 91 64, NSE; and Marcel Fribourg in Villers la Faye, tel. 03 80 62 91 74, NSE.) Then head west over the hills to Pont d'Ouche. At Pont d'Ouche, follow the canal toward Pouilly-en-Auxois to Châteauneuf-en-Auxois.

Châteauneuf's medieval **château** towers over the valleys below. This perfectly feudal village huddles securely in the shadow of the castle and merits a stroll. Park at the lot in the upper end of the village and don't miss the panoramic viewpoint near the parking lot. Walk into the courtyard and tour the château if you have time (€4, daily 10:00–12:00, 14:00–19:00, get English handout).

Signs behind Châteauneuf lead to La Bussière's **abbey**, which was founded in the 13th century by Cistercian monks but goes largely unnoticed by tourists today. Stroll the lovely gardens and check out the refectory (look for door in rear of main building marked *Accueil*; enter and walk upstairs). Ask for the key to the *vieux pressoir* (old press). You can dine here under Gothic arches for €15 (includes wine, must call to reserve, tel. 03 80 49 02 29).

The scenic return to Beaune is via Pont d'Ouche (toward Bligny sur Ouche) where you turn left, go uphill through Bouilland, and then downhill through Savigny-les-Beaune.

Sleeping and Eating in or near Châteauneuf-en-Auxois
(€1.10 = about $1, country code: 33, zip code: 21320)

Hostellerie du Château**, in Châteauneuf, offers rooms in two locations. Its main building ("Hôtel") is a better value than its annex up the street called "La Residence" (with larger, less cozy rooms). Many rooms in the Hôtel are half-timbered and have views of the château; the tiny top-floor doubles are adorable, and rooms with showers are small. The Hôtel's garden terrace has tables and swings and faces the château (Db-€45–61, extra bed-€9, CC; restaurant serves fine *menus* from €23, tel. 03 80 49 22 00, fax 03 80 49 21 27, www.hostellerie-chateauneuf.com).

Charming **Annie Bagatelle** has four beautiful rooms, two with lofts (Sb-€40–50, Db-€46–58, extra person-€8, no CC, at upper end of the village, second courtyard down from fountain on the left, tel. 03 80 49 21 00, fax 03 80 49 21 49, e-mail: jean-michel.bagatelle@wanadoo.fr, SE a little).

To sleep floating on a luxury hotel barge at two-star prices with views up to Châteauneuf's brooding castle, find the canal-front village of Vandenesse-en-Auxois. Here the *Lady A* barge offers tight, cozy rooms. Friendly Lisa cooks an elaborate dinner upon request for €20, including wine (Sb-€40, Db-€50, includes breakfast, call way ahead in summer, no CC, tel. 03 80 49 26 96, fax 03 80 49 27 00, SE). The *écluse* (lock house) at the bridge offers small groceries, wine-tastings, and inexpensive *chambres* at **Chez Monique et Pascal** (Sb/Db-€41, Tb-€49, no CC, tel. 03 80 49 27 12, fax 03 80 49 26 05).

Eating: Three Châteauneuf restaurants offer Burgundian cuisine at fair prices: **La Grill du Castel** (meal-sized salads, great escargots, *boeuf Bourguignon*, CC, tel. 03 80 49 26 82), **L'Orée du Bois Créperie** (simple, friendly, and inexpensive), and the country elegant **Hostellerie du Château** (see above), where I splurge for dinner.

SEMUR-EN-AUXOIS

If you have time for one more night in Burgundy, spend it here. This unpretentious little town feels real. There are no important sights to digest—just a seductive jumble of Burgundian alleys and courtyards perched above the meandering Armancon River—all beautifully illuminated after dark. Use Semur as a base to visit the handful of interesting sights nearby, including the *Chocolat* movie-famous hill town of Flavigny, the historic fields of Alesia where Julius Caesar defeated Gaul, and the remarkable abbey of Fontenay—all within 20 minutes of Semur. Semur is also about 45 minutes from the famous church in Vézelay and two hours from Paris, making it a handy first or last-night stop on your trip. Don't miss the smashing panorama of Semur from the viewpoint by the Citroen shop where the D-980 and D-954 intersect.

Tourist Information: The informative TI is across from Hôtel Côte d'Or at Semur's medieval entry (June–Sept Mon–Sat 09:00–19:00, Sun 10:00–12:00, 15:00–18:00, Oct–May Mon–Sat 08:30–12:00, 14:00–18:30, closed Sun, 2 place Gaveau, tel. 03 80 97 05 96). Pick up their city walks brochure, bike routes, and information on the many area sights.

The town has two sights: the Church of Notre Dame (decent English handout), which dominates its small square, and the small Municipal Museum. But Semur is best experienced by following the TI's walking tours. The longer, yellow route takes you down to the river and up to good views over Semur.

Sleeping and Eating in Semur-en-Auxois
(€1.10 = about $1, country code: 33, zip code: 21140)

Hotels and restaurants are a good value here. **Hôtel les Cymaises**** offers three-star comfort for the price of two, with good rooms and big new beds in a manor house with a quiet courtyard (Sb-€46, Db-€50–55, Tb-€66, 2-room Qb-€82–94, CC, 7 rue du Renaudot, private parking, tel. 03 80 97 21 44, fax 03 80 97 18 23, e-mail: hotel.cymaises@libertysurf.fr). The simple and unspoiled **Hôtel des Gourmets*** is good for those on a tight budget who are also seeking a good restaurant (D-€25, Db-€40, T/Q-€32, 5- to 6-person room-€57, traditional *menus* from €12, CC, 4 rue Varenne, tel. 03 80 97 09 41, fax 03 80 97 17 95).

Eating: Franco-American-owned **Le Calibressan** offers tasty *menus* (from €15.50), a cool salad bar, and wood-beam coziness; say hello to friendly Jill (closed Sun–Mon, 16 rue Fevret, tel. 03 80 97 32 40). Tiny, reasonable **Les Minimes** is a local institution (€15 *menu*, closed Sun–Mon, 39 rue des Vaux, tel. 03 80 97 26 86). **L'Entracte** is where everybody goes for pizza, pasta, salads, and more in a relaxed atmosphere (open daily, 4 rue Fevret). The historic *charcuterie* across from the church is ready to supply your dinner picnic.

Transportation Connections— Semur-en-Auxois

By bus to: Montbard (which has a train station and connects with TGV trains; 3 buses/day—early morning, noon, and evening, 20 min), **Dijon** (3/day, 1 hr). Bus info: tel. 03 80 42 11 00.

Sights—Near Semur-en-Auxois

▲▲**Abbey of Fontenay**—This marvelous Cistercian abbey demonstrates the impressive accomplishments of monasteries in the Middle Ages. The abbey was founded in 1181 by St. Bernard as a back-to-basics reaction to the excesses of Benedictine abbeys like Cluny. Fontenay gives you a clearer understanding of abbey life through its many interesting buildings including a massively empty church, the Chapter Hall, the monks' dormitory and warming room, a bakery, and a small iron forge. Get the English translations (€7.25, daily 10:00–12:00, 14:00–17:00, 20-min drive from Semur via Montbard, no bus, €12 taxi from Montbard, tel. 03 80 92 15 00).

Flavigny—Ten minutes from Semur, with its new *Chocolat*-covered Hollywood image, Flavigny is taking the excitement in stride. This unassuming and beautifully situated village feels permanently stuck in the past, with one café and two boutiques. Come here for its setting and walk the grassy ramparts (map at TI), buy the locally produced *Anis* candies, and visit the ancient church of St. Genest. Most important of all, come here for lunch. **La Grange** (the barn) serves farm-fresh fare, including luscious quiche, salad, fresh cheeses, pâtés, and fruit pies (July–mid-Sept daily 12:00–16:00, Sun only rest of year, across from church, no sign, listen for lunch sounds, tel. 03 80 35 81 78). **Le Relais de Flavigny** is a cozy, traditional restaurant with seven bargain rooms above (S/D-€26, Ss/Ds-€30.50, extra bed-€7.65, no CC, on left of main street, see Web site for map, 21150 Flavigny sur Ozerain, tel. 03 80 96 27 77, www.lerelaisdeflavigny.fr). To reach Flavigny from Semur, leave Semur following Venary les Laumes and look for the turnoff to Flavigny via Pouillenay. The approach to Flavigny from Pouillenay on D-9 is photo perfect.

Alise Ste. Reine—A short hop from Flavigny, this vertical little village is allegedly where, in 52 B.C., Julius Caesar defeated the Gallic leader Vercingetorix to win Gaul for the Roman Empire and forever change France's destiny. Drive up and up through the village to the very top and find the park with the huge statue of Vercingetorix overlooking his Waterloo. Stand as he did and imagine yourself trapped on this hilltop. The orientation table under the gazebo shows how the Roman camps surrounded the Gallic stronghold (Camp Gaulois); the red line marks the Roman fortifications. You'll pass signs to the little *Musée et Fouilles* (excavations of the Gallo-Roman town of Alesia) on your way to the top, both of mild interest.

▲▲**Vézelay**—For over seven centuries, pilgrims have overrun this hill town to get to its famous church, the Basilica of St. Madeleine. Built to honor its famous relics (the bones of Mary Magdalene, who had been possessed by the devil and saved) and to welcome pilgrims, this is one of Europe's largest and best-preserved Romanesque churches. Its appeal lies in its simplicity and the play of light on the pleasing patterns of stones. Notice the absence of distracting decoration and bright colors. To appreciate this, compare this to another of the same era, Notre-Dame de Paris. The effect when you enter the Basilica interior is mesmerizing. The tympanum (semicircular area over the door) and capitals provide what decoration there is through astonishing sculptures. These tell Bible stories in much the same way stained-glass windows do in Gothic churches. Notice how unappealing the newer Gothic apse feels in comparison to the older Romanesque nave. One-hour guided tours in English depart from inside the Basilica between 10:00 and 12:00 and from 14:00 to 17:00 (donation requested, tel. 03 86 33 39 50), or you can buy their fine €5 booklet inside the church (free entry to church, open daily 08:00–19:30). The view from the park behind the church is sublime.

Vézelay's **TI** is near the church (rue St. Pierre, tel. 03 86 33 23 69). The **Auberge de la Coquille** is a warm, cozy place to eat with reasonable salads, crepes, and full-course *menus* (halfway up to the church at 81 rue St. Pierre, tel. 03 86 33 35 57). Vézelay is about 45 minutes northwest of Semur (20 min off the autoroute to Paris). Train travelers must either go to nearby Semicelles (via Auxerre) and taxi from there (allow €14 one-way, tel. 03 86 32 31 88) or take the once-a-day bus from Avallon or Montbard (near Semur-en-Auxois) that leaves you in Vézelay for seven hours.

ALSACE AND NORTHERN FRANCE

The French province of Alsace stands like a flower-child referee between Germany and France. Bounded by the Rhine on the east and the softly rolling Vosges Mountains on the west, this is a lush land of Hansel and Gretel villages, sprawling vineyards, and I-could-live-here cities. Food and wine are the primary industry, topic of conversation, and perfect excuse for countless festivals.

Alsace has changed hands several times between Germany and France because of its location, natural wealth, naked vulnerability, and the fact that Germany thinks the mountains are the natural border, while France thinks it's the Rhine River. Having been a political pawn for 1,000 years, Alsace has a hybrid culture: Locals who swear do so bilingually, and the local cuisine features sauerkraut and fine wine. If you're traveling in December, come here for France's most celebrated Christmas markets and festivals.

Strasbourg is a big-city version of Colmar, worth a stop for its grand cathedral. The humbling battlefields of Verdun and the bubbly vigor of Reims in northern France are closer to Paris than Alsace, and follow logically only if your next destination is Paris.

Planning Your Time

Set up in or near Colmar. Allow most of a day for Colmar and a full afternoon for the Wine Road (*Route du Vin*). If you have one day, wander Colmar's sights until after lunch and then set out for the *Route du Vin*. Urban Strasbourg has a soaring cathedral and a lovely center city. If you can spare an extra half day, spend it there, but with limited time, skip it. Reims and Verdun are doable by car as stops between Paris and Colmar—if you're speedy. Train travelers with only one day between Colmar and Paris must choose Reims or Verdun.

Alsace to Champagne

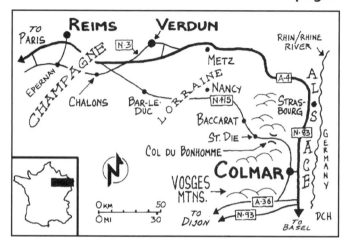

Getting around Alsace

Frequent trains link Colmar and Strasbourg (2/hr, 30 min).
Buses and minivan excursions radiate from Colmar to villages
along the *Route du Vin*, and you can rent bikes in Colmar and
Turckheim if you prefer to pedal (for details on all of these
options, see "Route du Vin," below).

Cuisine Scene—Alsace

Alsatian cuisine is a major tourist attraction in itself. The
German influence is obvious: sausages, potatoes, onions, and
sauerkraut. Look for *choucroute garni* (sauerkraut and sausage—
although it seems a shame to eat it in a fancy restaurant), the
more traditionally Alsatian *baeckeanoffe* (potato, meat, and onion
stew), *rösti* (an oven-baked potato-and-cheese dish), fresh trout,
and foie gras. At lunch, or for a lighter dinner, try a *tarte à l'oignon*
(like an onion quiche but better) or *tarte flambée* (like a thin-crust
pizza with onion and bacon bits). If you're picnicking, buy some
stinky Münster cheese. Dessert specialties are *tarte Alsacienne*
(fruit tart) and *glace Kugelhopf* (a light cake mixed with raisins,
almonds, dried fruit, and cherry liqueur).

Alsatian Wines

Alsatian wines are named for their grapes, unlike in Burgundy
or Provence, where wines are commonly named after villages,
or in Bordeaux, where wines are often named after châteaux.
White wines dominate in the Alsace. The following wines are
made entirely of that grape variety: Sylvaner (fairly light, fruity,

and inexpensive), Riesling (more robust than Sylvaner but drier than the German style you're probably used to), Gerwürtztraminer (spicy, with a powerful bouquet; good with pâtés and local cheeses), Muscat (very dry, with a distinctive bouquet and taste; best as a before-dinner wine), Tokay/Pinot Gris (more full-bodied than Riesling but fine with many local main courses), Pinot Noir (the local red is overpriced; very light and fruity and generally served chilled), and the tasty Crèmant d'Alsace (the region's good and inexpensive champagne). You'll also see *eaux-de-vie*, powerful fruit-flavored brandies; try the *framboise* (raspberry) flavor.

COLMAR

Colmar is a well-pickled old place of 70,000 residents, offering a few heavyweight sights in a warm, midsize-town package. Historic beauty was usually a poor excuse to be spared the ravages of World War II, but it worked for Colmar. The American and British military were careful not to bomb the half-timbered old burghers' houses, characteristic red- and green-tiled roofs, and cobbled lanes of Alsace's most beautiful city.

Today Colmar thrives with colorful, half-timbered buildings, impressive art treasures, and German tourists. Schoolgirls park their rickety horse carriages in front of the city hall, ready to give visitors a clip-clop tour of old town. Antique shops welcome browsers, and hotel managers hurry down the sleepy streets to pick up fresh croissants in time for breakfast.

Orientation

There isn't a straight street in Colmar. Thankfully, most streets are pedestrian-only, and it's a lovely town to be lost in. Navigate by the high church steeples and the helpful signs directing visitors to the various sights. For tourists, the town center is place Unterlinden (a 15-min walk from the train station), where you'll find the TI, Colmar's most important museum, and a huge and handy Monoprix supermarket/department store (Mon–Sat 08:30–20:30, closed Sun). Every city bus starts or finishes on place Unterlinden.

Colmar is most crowded from May through September. Weekends are busiest (reserve ahead). The impressive music festival fills hotels the first two weeks of July, and the local wine festival rages for 10 days in early August. Open-air markets bustle next to the Dominican and St. Martin Churches on Thursdays and Saturdays.

Tourist Information: The TI is next to the Unterlinden Museum on place Unterlinden. Pick up the excellent city map describing a good walking tour of Colmar, a *Route du Vin* map, information on bike rental, and *Colmar Actualités*, a booklet with bus schedules. Get information about concerts and festivals in Colmar and in nearby villages, and ask about Colmar's Folklore Tuesdays (with folk dancing at 20:30 every Tue mid-May–mid-Sept on place de l'Ancienne). The TI reserves hotel rooms and has *chambres d'hôte* listings for Colmar and the region (April–Oct Mon–Sat 09:00–18:00, until 19:00 July–Aug, Sun 10:00–14:00; Nov–March Mon–Sat 09:00–12:00, 14:00–18:00, Sun 10:00–14:00, tel. 03 89 20 68 92). A public WC is 20 meters left of the TI.

Tours: The TI organizes walking tours of the old town and of the Unterlinden Museum (€4, €8.75 includes museum entry, daily July–Aug, weekends only the rest of year, call ahead for times, usually in the mornings). You can also hire a private guide for a walking tour (€75, ask at TI). For minivan tours of the *Route du Vin*, see "Getting around the Wine Road," below.

Arrival in Colmar

By Train: To reach the center from the station (15-min walk, lockers available), walk straight out past Hôtel Bristol, turn left on avenue de la République, and keep walking. Buses #1, #2, and #3 all go from the station to the TI (about €1, pay driver). Allow €10 for a taxi to a hotel in central Colmar. The bus stops here for *Route du Vin* villages.

By Car: Follow signs to *centre-ville* then *place Rapp*. There's a huge pay parking garage under place Rapp, and (for now) free lots at *parking du Musée Unterlinden* (across from Primo 99 hotel), and off the ring road near Hôtel St. Martin (follow signs from the ring road to *parking Hôtel St. Martin*). Several hotels have private parking, and those that don't can advise you where to park.

Self-Guided Tour of Colmar's Old Town

This walk works day or night. Look for handy information plaques with English explanations at various points throughout.

The importance of 15th- to 17th-century Colmar is clear as you wander its pedestrian-friendly old center, decorated with 45 buildings classified as historic monuments. In the Middle Ages, most of Europe was fragmented into chaotic little princedoms and dukedoms. Merchant-dominated cities, natural proponents of the formation of large nation-states, banded together to form "trading leagues" (the World Trade Organizations of their day). The Hanseatic League was the superleague of northern Europe. Prosperous Colmar was a member of a smaller league of 10 Alsatian cities, called the Decapolis (founded 1354).

Start your tour at the old **Customs House** (Koifhus). Here, delegates of the Decapolis would meet to sort out trade issues, much like the European Union does in nearby Strasbourg today. Walk under its archway to place de l'Ancienne Douane and face the Bertholdi statue—arm raised, à la *Statue of Liberty*—and do a 360-degree spin to appreciate a gaggle of gables. This was the center of business activity in Colmar, with trade routes leading from here to several major European cities. Today it's the festive site of outdoor wine-tastings on many summer evenings. The soaring, half-timbered commotion of higgledy-piggledy rooftops just beyond marks the **Tanners' Quarters**. These 17th- and 18th-century rooftops competed for space in the sun to dry their freshly tanned hides; the nearby river channel got rid of the waste products. Walk down to the end of Petite rue des Tanneurs (*not* rue des Tanneurs), turn right, and take the first left along the stream. On your right is the old market hall (fish, produce, and other products were brought here by flat-bottomed boat). Cross the canal and turn right on rue de la Poissonnerie (the fisherman's street), and you'll enter **La Petite Venise** quarter, a bundle of Colmar's most colorful houses lining the small canal. This tourist-popular area is romantic at night with a fraction of the tourists. That beautiful building hanging over the water is the four-star Hôtel Maréchal.

Cross the bridge, take the second right on Grande Rue, and stroll to **Chez Hanzi** restaurant on the rue des Marchands (Merchants' Street), back near the old Customs House. Overhanging roofs such as these were a medieval tax dodge. Since houses were taxed on square footage at street level, owners would expand tax-free up and over the street. Walk up rue des Marchands, and in two blocks you'll come face-to-face with the **Pfister House**, a richly decorated merchant's house from 1537. The external spiral staircase turret and painted walls illustrate the city folk's taste for Renaissance humanism (the wine shop on the ground floor is Colmar's best). The man carved into the side of the building next door (to the left) was a drape maker; he's shown holding a bar, Colmar's measure of about one meter. (In the Middle Ages, it was common for cities to have their own units of length.) One more block on the left is the **Bartholdi Museum** (described below). A passage to the right leads to Colmar's golden **Cathédrale St. Martin** with its lone tower (two were planned), then find your way up rue des Serruriers (Locksmiths' Street) to the **Dominican Church** (worth entering, described below). Compare the soaring St. Martin Cathedral with this low-slung, sober structure that perfectly symbolizes Dominican austerity; both were built at the same time. Continue up rue des Boulangers (Bakers' Street), and then make a hard right down rue des Têtes. The **House of Heads** on the right is Colmar's other famous merchant's house. It was built in 1609 and is decorated with 105 faces and masks. Angle down the rue de l'Eau (Water Street) for a shortcut to the TI and the Unterlinden Museum.

Sights—Colmar

▲▲▲**Unterlinden Museum**—Colmar's touristic claim to fame, this is one of my favorite museums in Europe. Its extensive yet manageable collection ranges from Roman Colmar to medieval

Colmar

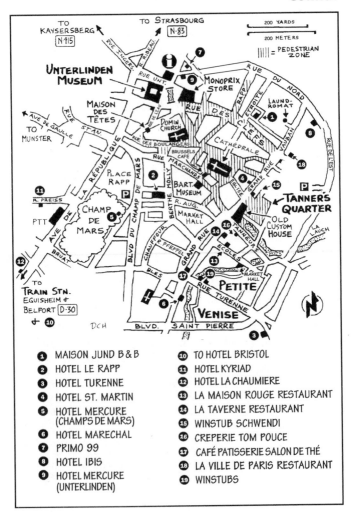

winemaking exhibits, and from traditional wedding dresses to
paintings that give vivid insight into the High Middle Ages.

The highlight of the museum (and, for me, the city) is
Grünewald's gripping *Isenheim Altarpiece*, actually a series of three
different paintings on hinges that pivot like shutters (study the
little model on the wall, explained in English). Designed to help
people in a medieval hospital endure horrible skin diseases (such

as St. Anthony's Fire, later called rye ergotism) long before the age of painkillers, it's one of the most powerful paintings ever produced.

Stand as if you were a medieval peasant in front of the center-piece and let the agony and suffering of the Crucifixion drag its fingers down your face. The point—Jesus' suffering—is drilled home: the weight of his body bending the crossbar, his elbows pulled from their sockets by the weight of his dead body, his mangled feet, the grief on Mary's face. In hopes that the intended viewers—the hospital's patients—would know that Jesus under-stood their suffering, he was even painted to appear as if he, too, had a skin disease. Study the faces and the Christian symbolism.

The three scenes of the painting changed with the seasons of the church year. The happy ending—a psychedelic explosion of Resurrection joy—is the spiritual equivalent of jumping from the dentist's chair directly into a Jacuzzi. The last two panels, showing the meeting of St. Paul the hermit and St. Anthony, are the product of a fertile imagination and the stuff of which nightmares are made.

There's more to the museum. Ringing the peaceful cloister is a fine series of medieval church paintings and sculpture and a room filled with old winepresses. Downstairs you'll find Roman and prehistoric artifacts. The upstairs rooms contain local and folk history, with everything from medieval armor to old-time toys (€5.50, April–Oct daily 09:00–18:00, Nov–March Wed–Mon 09:00–17:00, closed Tue, tel. 03 89 41 89 23).

▲▲**Dominican Church**—Here's another medieval mindblower. In Colmar's Eglise des Dominicains, you'll find Martin Schongauer's angelically beautiful *Virgin in the Rosebush* holding court center stage, dating from 1473 but looking as if it were painted yesterday. Here, Mary is shown as a welcoming mother. Jesus clings to her, remind-ing the viewer of the possibility of an intimate relationship with Mary. The Latin on her halo reads: "Pick me also for your child, O very Holy Virgin." Rather than telling a particular Bible story, this is a general scene . . . designed to meet the personal devotional needs of any worshiper. Here, nature is not a backdrop. Mary and Jesus are encircled by it. Schongauer's robins, sparrows, and gold-finches bring extra life to an already impressively natural rosebush. The contrast provided by the simple Dominican setting heightens the flamboyance of this late-Gothic masterpiece. Dominican churches were intentionally austere, symbolic of their zeal to purify their faith and compete with the growing popularity of 13th-century heretical movements, such as Catharism, whose message was a simpler faith (€1.25, daily 10:00–13:00, 15:00–18:00). This Dom-inican austerity is more apparent after a visit to Colmar's fancier, and Franciscan, St. Martin's Cathedral.

Bartholdi Museum—This little museum recalls the life and work of the local boy who gained fame by sculpting the *Statue of Liberty*. Several of his statues grace Colmar's squares (€3.50, March–Dec

Wed–Mon 10:00–12:00, 14:00–18:00, closed Tue and Jan–Feb, in heart of old town at 30 rue des Marchands).

Sleeping in Colmar
(€1.10 = about $1, country code: 33, zip code: 68000)
Sleep Code: **S** = Single, **D** = Double/Twin, **T** = Triple, **Q** = Quad, **b** = bathroom, **s** = shower only, **CC** = Credit Cards accepted, **no CC** = Credit Cards not accepted, **SE** = Speaks English, **NSE** = No English, * = French hotel rating system (0–4 stars).

Hotels are fairly expensive and are jammed on weekends in May, June, September, and October. Plan ahead. July and August are busy, but there are always rooms—somewhere. Should you have trouble finding a room in Colmar (the TI can help), look in a nearby village where small hotels and bed-and-breakfasts are plentiful; see my recommendations under "Sleeping in Eguisheim," below.

A **Laundromat** is near Maison Jund at 1 rue Ruest, just off the pedestrian street rue Vauban (usually open daily 08:00–21:00).

Maison Jund offers my favorite budget beds in Colmar. This easygoing B&B is the home of a winemaker. The ramshackle yet magnificent half-timbered home feels like a medieval tree house soaked in wine and filled with flowers. The rooms are simple but adequately comfortable, spacious, and equipped with kitchenettes. Most rooms are generally available only April to mid-September, though two rooms are rented year-round (D-€26, Db/Tb-€32–38, CC, 12 rue de l'Ange, tel. 03 89 41 58 72, fax 03 89 23 15 83, e-mail: martinjund@hotmail.com). Leave your car at the lot across from the Primo 99 hotel, walk from Unterlinden Museum past Monoprix, and veer left on rue des Clefs, left on rue Etroite, and right on rue de l'Ange. This is not a hotel, so there is no real reception, though friendly Myriam (SE) seems to be around, somewhere, most of the time.

Hôtel Le Rapp**, just off place Rapp, is the best-located two-star hotel in town, with 40 just-large-enough rooms, a small basement pool, sauna, Turkish bath, and an indoor/outdoor bar-café. It's well-run (friendly Sylvie SE) and family-friendly with a big park one block away (Sb-€46–51, Db-€64–70, good buffet breakfast-€7.50, CC, elevator, 1 rue Berthe-Molley, tel. 03 89 41 62 10, fax 03 89 24 13 58, www.rapp-hotel.com, SE). Its restaurant serves a classy Alsatian *menu* with impeccable service (closed Fri).

Hôtel Turenne** is very sharp and a good value with 83 rooms in a historic building. It's a 10-minute walk from the city center, a 15-minute walk from the train station, and is located on a busy street with easy parking. Rooms are well appointed, although some have tight bathrooms. Thirty percent of the rooms are non-smoking; air-conditioning is planned for 2002 (Sb-€42, Db-€55–62, Tb-€65, family-friendly studios-€95, CC, parking-€4.75, elevator for one wing, cozy bar, from train station walk straight out to avenue

Raymond Poincaré, turn left on rue des Americains, 10 route du Bale, tel. 03 89 21 58 58, fax 03 89 41 27 64, www.turenne.com, SE).

Hôtel St. Martin***, near the old Customs House, is a classy, family-run place that began as a coaching inn (since 1361). It's small, with traditional yet well-equipped rooms woven into its antique frame. Half of its 24 rooms are in the annex, opposite a peaceful courtyard. While just as comfortable, these cheaper rooms have showers instead of tubs and no elevator or air-con. Eighteen new rooms are planned for 2002 (Sb-€57–95, Db-€65–116, most about €92, Tb-€99–132, CC, free public parking nearby, 38 Grand Rue, tel. 03 89 24 11 51, fax 03 89 23 47 78, www.hotel-saint-martin.com, Winterstein family SE).

Mercure Hôtels (Unterlinden and Champs de Mars)***: You can sleep comfortably in either of these chain hotels for about the same price as Hôtel St. Martin but without a hint of the Old World (Sb-€88, Db-€98, extra person-€15.25, CC, air-con, elevators, easy parking). The Champs de Mars Mercure is better located, near place Rapp (2 avenue de la Marne, tel. 03 89 21 59 59, fax 03 89 21 59 00, e-mail: h1225@accor-hotels.com). The other Mercure is near the Unterlinden Museum (5 rue Golbery, tel. 03 89 41 71 71, fax 03 89 23 82 71, e-mail: h0978@accor-hotels.com).

Hôtel Maréchal**** provides Colmar's most famous and most characteristic digs in this most-photographed building in the heart of La Petite Venise (standard Db-€95–135, Db with whirlpool tub-€130–190, suite Db-€255, CC, 4 place des Six Montagnes Noirs, tel. 03 89 41 60 32, fax 03 89 24 59 40, www.hotel-le-marechal.com). Their well-respected restaurant will melt a romantic's heart; you will be encouraged to dine here (*menus* from €32, reserve ahead).

Primo 99**, near Unterlinden Museum, is an efficient, bright, nothing-but-the-plastic-and-concrete-basics place to sleep for those who consider ambience a four-letter word (S/D/T-€27, Sb-€44, Db-€47–58, third person-€7.75, CC, 5 rue des Ancêtres, free parking in big square in front, rooms held until 18:30 if you call, friendly staff, tel. 03 89 24 22 24, fax 03 89 24 55 96, www.hotel-primo.com, SE). Half the beds have footboards—a problem if you're taller than six foot two.

Hôtel Ibis**, on the ring road, sells white, efficient comfort with pleasant rooms but small bathrooms (Sb-€52, Db-€58, extra person-€9.25, CC, parking-€6.25, 11 rue St. Eloi, tel. 03 89 41 30 14, fax 03 89 24 51 49).

Sleeping near the Train Station

Hôtel Bristol*** couldn't be closer to the station and, in spite of its Best Western plaque, has some character with pleasant public spaces and good rooms (Db-€74–119, most Db about €85, CC, 7 place de la Gare, tel. 03 89 23 59 59, fax 03 89 23 92 26, www.grand-hotel-bristol.fr).

La Chaumière*, on a big street two blocks from the station, is above and behind a truly French café and has been run by gentle Madame Servor for 40 years. Most of its modest, good-value rooms surround a courtyard off the street (S/D-€28, Sb/Db-€38–40, CC, parking-€4, 74 avenue de la République, walk straight out of the station and turn left on avenue de la République, tel. 03 89 41 08 99, SE a smidgen).

Kyriad Hôtel** is another modern chain hotel and a reasonable value (Db-€49, Tb-€60, CC, elevator, 1 rue de la Gare, turn left immediately when leaving station and walk 10 min, tel. 089 41 34 80, fax 03 89 41 27 84, e-mail: kyriadcolmar@aol.com).

Eating in Colmar
(Also see "Eating in Eguisheim," below.)

For reasonably priced, good, traditional Alsatian cuisine, I like **La Maison Rouge** (€15.25 and 20 *menus*, try the endive salad and *tarte flambée forestiere*, closed Sun, 9 rue des Écoles, tel. 03 89 23 53 22). Nearby, **La Taverne** serves *tartes flambées* and other regional specialties to appreciative locals (closed Sun, 2 impasse de la Maison Rouge, tel. 03 89 41 70 33). Join the fun in wood-cozy ambience at **Winstub Schwendi;** try one of their robust Swiss *rösti* plates (€8–9.50, facing old Custom House at 3 Grand Rue). For crepes and salads with atmosphere, eat at **Crêperie Tom Pouce** (daily, 10 rue des Tanneurs). Closer to the Unterlinden Museum, **La Ville de Paris** is reasonable, friendly, and serves Alsatian dishes (€17.50 *menu*, place Jeanne d'Arc, tel. 03 89 24 53 15).

For canal-front dining, head into La Petite Venise to the photo-perfect bridge on rue Turenne, where you'll find two lively **Winstubs** (both cheap and fun for *tartes flambées*). On the other side of the bridge lies the **Café-Pâtisserie Salon de Thé** with melt-in-your-mouth quiches, *tarte flambées*, and salads (to go or eat there, closed Mon, open until 22:00, until 19:00 off-season, on place des Six Montagnes Noires).

Hôtel Restaurant Le Rapp is a traditional place to savor a slow, elegant meal served with grace and fine Alsatian wine (*menus* start at €15.25, the *baeckeanoffe* is great, good salads, closed Fri, air-con, 1 rue Berthe-Molley, tel. 03 89 41 62 10, SE). The recommended **Hôtel Maréchal** is the place to go for a truly special occasion with gourmet cuisine and Colmar's most romantic tables (*menus* from €31, reserve ahead).

Brussels Café is Colmar's liveliest café (facing right transept of Cathedral St. Martin on place de la Cathédrale).

Transportation Connections—Colmar
By train to: Strasbourg (hrly, 50 min), **Reims** (6/day, 6 hrs, changes in Strasbourg or Mulhouse and Metz or Chalon), **Beaune** (6/day, 4–5 hrs, changes in Besançon, Mulhouse, or Beflort and

Dijon), **Paris**, Gare de l'Est (12/day, 5.5 hrs, change in Strasbourg, Dijon, or Mulhouse), **Amboise** (8/day, 9 hrs, via Paris),
Basel, Switzerland (13/day, 1 hr), **Karlsruhe**, Germany (10/day,
2.5 hrs, best with change in Strasbourg; from Karlsruhe it's 90 min
to Frankfurt, 3 hrs to Munich).

ROUTE DU VIN (THE WINE ROAD)

Alsace's *Route du Vin* is an asphalt ribbon tying 145 kilometers
(90 miles) of vineyards, villages, and feudal fortresses into an
understandably popular tourist package. The generally dry, sunny
climate has made for good wine and happy tourists since Roman
days. Colmar and Eguisheim are ideally located for exploring the
30,000 acres of vineyards blanketing the hills from Marlenheim
to Thann. If you have only a day, focus on towns within easy
striking range of Colmar. Top ones are Eguisheim, Kaysersberg,
Hunawihr, Ribbeauvillé, and the too-popular Riquewihr. As you
tour this region, you'll see storks' nests on many church spires
and city halls, thanks to a campaign to reintroduce the birds to
this area (the big nests weigh over 1,000 pounds). Get a map of
the *Route du Vin* from any TI.

Most towns have wineries that give tours (some charge a fee).
The modern cooperatives at Eguisheim, Bennwihr, Hunawihr, and
Ribbeauvillé, created after the destruction of World War II,
provide a good look at a more modern and efficient method of
production. Try the tasty Muscat and Gerwürztraminer wines.
Crèmant, the Alsatian "champagne," is very good—and much
cheaper. The French term for headache, if you really get
"Alsaced," is *mal à la tête*.

Getting around the Wine Road

Pick up a Michelin regional map before heading out.

By Bus: Public buses connect Colmar's train station with
most of the villages along the *Route du Vin*. The schedules are
fairly convenient but close to nonexistent on Sunday (Mon–Sat
schedules from Colmar to Eguisheim: 6/day, 5 min; to Kaysersberg: hrly, 30 min; to Riquewihr, Bennwihr, Hunawihr, and
Ribbeauvillé: 6/day, 30–45 min; to Turckheim: 6/day, 20 min).
Get schedules from the TI and buy tickets from the driver
(about 12F from Colmar to most Route du Vin villages).

By Minivan Tour: Friendly Jean-Claude Werner organizes
daytrips around the Alsace at Les Circuits d'Alsace (half-day
tours-€43, 09:00–13:00, office open Mon–Fri 09:00–12:30, 14:00–
18:30, Sat 09:00–13:00, across from train station at 6 place de la
Gare, tel. 03 89 41 90 88).

By Bike: The Wine Road's level terrain makes biking a
good option. In Colmar, try Cycles Geiswiller (6 boulevard du
Champs de Mars, tel. 03 89 41 30 59) or Cyclothèque (31 route

Alsace's Wine Road

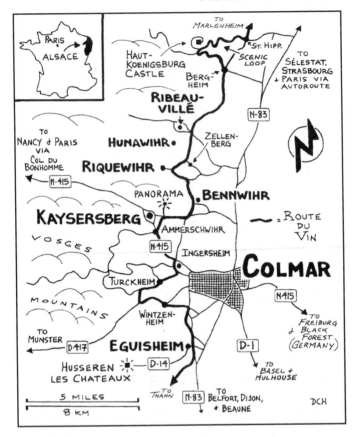

d'Igersheim, tel. 03 89 79 14 18). Or, to save yourself the ride
out of Colmar, you can rent a bike in Turckheim (84 Grand Rue,
tel. 03 89 27 06 36) on the *Route du Vin*. Turckheim, Kaysersberg,
Riquewihr, and Hunawihr make good biking destinations (get
advice and a good map from a bike shop and avoid major roads;
leave Colmar following directions under "By Car," below).

By Car: To reach the Wine Road north of Colmar, leave
Colmar from the station following signs to Epinal. In Wintzen-
heim, follow signs to Turckheim, then find D-10 (*Route du Vin*) to
Ingersheim (Kaysersberg is a short detour from here), Riquewihr,
Hunawihr, Ribbeauvillé, and Château de Haut-Koenigsbourg.
Look for *Route du Vin* signs. For Eguisheim, leave Colmar on N-
83 toward Belfort.

By Foot: A few signed walking trails connect *Route du Vin* villages through the vineyards (get info at local TIs), and hikers can climb to the higher ruined castles of the Vosges Mountains (Eguisheim and Ribbeauvillé are good bases). Kayserberg to Riquewihr is a pleasant one- to two-hour walk (return by bus).

Sights Along the Wine Road, North of Colmar

These sights are listed from south to north.

Turckheim—This pleasant town, with a small castle, is just enough off the beaten path to be overlooked.

Kaysersberg—Albert Schweitzer's hometown is cute, but its main drag is usually swamped. Browse the boutiques, check out the church and its notable 400-year-old altarpiece, look for the stork's nest near the fortified town bridge, and enjoy the colorful jumble of 15th-century houses. Drop by **Dr. Schweitzer's house** (€1.50, May–Oct daily 10:00–12:00, 14:00–18:00, closed rest of year, 126 rue Général de Gaulle), then climb the castle tower for a great view and wander into nearby vineyards on the north side of town. Kaysersberg's **TI** is inside Hôtel de Ville near the town's main entry (closed 12:00–14:00, tel. 03 89 78 22 78). Walking trails through the vineyards to Riquewihr (1.5–2.5 hrs) and other *Route du Vin* towns are well-marked; walk under the arch (10 meters to the right of the TI as you face it), and you'll see signs.

Alsatian Panorama at WWII Monument—This remarkable viewpoint, easiest to reach by car, is at the WWII monument and military cemetery (also called Negrophile Nationale or Cimitière Militaire). The spectacular setting, best at sunset, houses a monument to the American divisions that helped liberate Alsace in World War II (find the American flag), a beautiful cemetery for French and North African soldiers who died for the cause, and a brilliant panorama over the southern section of the *Route du Vin* and into Germany.

To find this poorly marked place, go to Sigolsheim (between Kaysersberg and Bennwihr). The road to the monument leaves from the town center (look for French flags at Pierre Sparr winery and follow small signs to Cimitière Militaire or Negrophile Nationale). After you check out the monument to the Americans, take the small road to the top to find the viewpoint and cemetery.

Riquewihr—Overly picturesque, this walled village is crammed with tourist shops, cafés, galleries, cobblestones, and flowers. Try the excellent tasting and tour at Caves Dopff et Irion (Cour du Château, tel. 03 89 47 92 51, TI tel. 03 89 47 80 80).

Zellenberg—This town has an impressive setting and is worth a quick stop for the views from either side of its narrow perch.

Hunawihr—This bit of wine-soaked Alsatian cuteness is far less visited than its more famous neighbors and comes complete with a 16th-century fortified church that today is shared by Catholics and Protestants (the Catholics are buried next to the church; the Protestants are buried outside the church wall). Park below the church in the village at the sheltered picnic tables and follow the trail up to the church, then loop back through the village. Kids will enjoy Hunawihr's small stork park (Parc des Cygognes, April–Nov daily 10:00–12:00, 14:00–18:00, other animals take part in the afternoon shows). You'll find a few *chambres d'hôte* and a good wine cooperative in Hunawihr. Eat well at **Winstub Suzel** near the church (closed Tue, 2 rue de l'Eglise, tel. 03 89 73 30 85).

Ribbeauvillé—Come here to hike. Two brooding castles hang above this pleasant town, seldom visited by Americans. The steep castle trail leaves from the top of the town (at Hôtel Trois Châteaux, park in city lot here). Allow 45 minutes one-way, or just climb 10 minutes for a view over the town.

Château de Haut-Koenigsbourg—If you haven't yet visited an Alsatian castle, here's your chance. Strategically situated high above the flat Rhine plain, it protected passage between Alsace and Lorrain for centuries for its famous German dynasties. Rebuilt in the early 20th century, this furnished castle illustrates Germanic influence in Alsatian history (€6.50, audioguide-€4, May–Sept daily 09:00–18:00, Oct–April 09:00–12:00, 13:00–17:30, about 15 min north of Ribbeauvillé above St. Hippolyte, consider the longer scenic route via Thannenkirch).

EGUISHEIM

Just a few kilometers south of Colmar's suburbs (a flat and easy bike ride on busy roads), this circular, flower-festooned little wine town is nearly too cute. It's ideal for a relaxing lunch and makes a good small-town base for exploring Alsace. It's a cinch by car (easy parking) and accessible by bus (6/day, 10 min, departs Colmar's train station). The helpful **TI** (on the street that bisects Eguisheim) has information on accommodations, festivals, walks in the vineyards, and hikes into the Vosges (June–Sept Mon–Fri 09:00–12:30, 14:00–18:30, Sat until 17:00, Sun 10:00–12:00 only, Oct–May Mon–Fri 09:00–12:00, 14:00–18:00, Sat until 16:00, closed Sun, 22 Grand Rue, tel. 03 89 23 40 33, www.ot-eguisheim.fr). Eguisheim is best explored by walking around its narrow circular road (rue des Remparts) and then cutting through the middle. Visit the colorful church and one of Eguisheim's countless cozy **wineries** or the big and modern **Wine Cooperative** (Wolfberger, Cave Vinicole d'Eguisheim, daily 08:00–12:00, 14:00–18:00, tours and tastings available, 6 Grand Rue, tel. 03 89 22 20 20). If you have a car, follow signs up to Les Husseren and Les 5 Châteaux for a pleasant walk to the **ruined castle towers** and a good view of the Vosges above and vineyards below. Without wheels, stroll above the town into the vineyards above Eguisheim for good views (TI has a map).

Sleeping and Eating in Eguisheim
(€1.10 = about $1, country code: 33, zip code: 68420)
Chambres d'Hôte: While none of the owners speak English, they're creative at communicating. Please remember to cancel if you reserve a room and can't use it.

Your Alsatian grandmother, **Madame Hertz-Meyers**, welcomes you with big rooms in a mansion surrounded by vineyards only 75 meters from the village center. Rooms in the main house are perfect for families and are better than her two modern apartments (Sb-€38, Db-€54, Tb-€69, includes breakfast, no CC, 3 rue Riesling, no sign, tel. 03 89 23 67 74, fax 03 89 23 99 23). Formal **Madame Dirringer**'s five comfortable rooms have big beds and face a traditional courtyard (Db-€31–33, breakfast-€4.75, no CC, 11 rue Riesling, tel. 03 89 41 71 87). It's hard to imagine a better location, more comfortable rooms, or a more charming owner than **Monique Freudenreich**, who is learning English (Db-€38, includes breakfast, no CC, 1 block from TI, 4 cour Unterlinden, tel. & fax 03 89 23 16 44). **Madame Alleman** has simple, traditional rooms above her gift shop and bakery (Db-€28.50, breakfast-€4.75, no CC, 28 Grande Rue, tel. 03 89 41 40 25). Gentle **Madame Bombenger**'s modern home has nice views into the vineyards and over Eguisheim (Db-€40, includes breakfast, no CC, 3 rue de Trois Pierres, tel. & fax 03 89 23 71 19).

Hotels: Hotels are a good value here, although most care more about their restaurants than their rooms. The picturesque **Auberge Alsacienne***** is a good value with small, tastefully designed rooms and rental bikes for guests (Db-€50–60, Tb-€70, CC, 12 Grand Rue, tel. 03 89 41 50 20, fax 03 89 23 89 32). The five cozy rooms above the **Auberge du Rempart** are a great value (Db-€47, CC, 3 rue des Rempart Sud, near TI, tel. 03 89 41 16 87, fax 03 89 41 06 50). The snazzy **Hostellerie du Château*****, part art gallery, part hotel, is ideally located in front of the church and provides stylish, contemporary luxury (Sb-€64, Db-€77–90, extra bed-€15.25, CC, no elevator, 2 rue du Château St. Leon IX, tel. 03 89 23 72 00, fax 03 89 41 63 93). Overlooking the village, the modern yet tasteful **Hôtel St. Hubert***** offers polished comfort, an indoor pool and sauna, vineyards out your window, and free pickup at Colmar's train station if reserved in advance (Db-€76–96, extra bed-€15.25, CC, 6 rue des Trois Pierres, tel. 03 89 41 40 50, fax 03 89 41 46 88, e-mail: hotel.st.hubert@wanadoo.fr).

Eating in Eguisheim: Auberge de Trois Châteaux is cozy and good (26 Grand Rue, tel. 03 89 23 11 22). The recommended **Auberge Alsacienne** offers fine meals (2 courses-€16.50, 3 courses-€23), and the recommended **Auberge du Rempart** has good *tarte flambée* and outdoor tables surrounding a fountain (for address and tel. of both, see above). **Le Pavillon**

Gourmand is at the top of the town and is the place to go for a special meal (*menus* from €18, closed Tue–Wed, 101 rue Rempart Sud, tel. 03 89 24 36 88.)

STRASBOURG

Strasbourg is urban Alsace at its best and feels like a giant Colmar with water. It's one of France's most livable big cities, with generous space devoted to pedestrians, bike lanes, meandering waterways, and a young, lively population of university students and Eurocrats. Situated on the west bank of the Rhine River, Strasbourg provides the ultimate blend of Franco-Germanic culture, architecture, and ambience. Since 1949, Strasbourg has been home to the European Parliament, sharing administrative responsibilities for the European Union with Brussels, Belgium. Strasbourg is a fine daytrip from Colmar or a handy stop en route to Paris. Plan on two hours, starting at Strasbourg's dazzling cathedral (try to be here by 12:15 for the clock's best performance, see below) and ending with La Petite France (for lunch).

Tourist Information: There are two TIs. One is at the train station (outside and one floor down, June–Sept daily 09:00–18:00, Oct–April Mon–Sat 09:00–12:30, 13:30–17:30, closed Sun, Nov–March until 16:30). The main office is at 17 place de la Cathédrale (daily 09:00–19:00, tel. 03 88 52 28 28, www.strasbourg.com). Call ahead for a schedule of walking tours in English. Buy the €0.50 city map (the free map is useless); it describes a decent walking tour in English, or spring for the €6 audioguide tour that covers the cathedral and old city.

Arrival in Strasbourg

By Train: After stopping by the station TI (lockers available), walk 15 pleasant minutes to the cathedral. Walk past Hôtel Vendome up rue Marie Kuss, cross the river, and continue straight on rue 22 November to place Kleber. Cross place Kleber and turn right on rue des Grandes Arcades and follow that spire. (You'll return to the station via La Petite France.) A sleek tram runs from the station one floor below the TI (€1.10, Tram A, direction: Illkirch) to the Grande Rue stop, two blocks from the cathedral (return to the station, *Gare central*, from same stop, direction: Hautpierre).

By Car: Follow *centre-ville/cathédrale* signs and park as close to the center as you can. Parking lots are well-marked—place Gutenberg and place du Château are most convenient, though the larger Austerlitz lot works fine.

Helpful Hints

U.S. Consulate: It's at 15 rue d'Alsace (tel. 03 88 32 67 27, fax 03 88 23 07 17).

Airport: The user-friendly Strasbourg-Entzheim airport (tel. 03 88 64 67 67) has frequent and often inexpensive flights to Paris and is easily accessible via tram and shuttle bus.

Sights—Strasbourg

▲▲**Strasbourg Cathedral (Cathédrale de Notre Dame)**— Stand in front of Hôtel de la Cathédrale and crane your neck up. If this church makes an impression today with its single soaring spire and pink sandstone color, imagine the impact it had on medieval peasants. The delicate Gothic style of the cathedral (begun in 1176, not finished until 1429) is another Franco-German mixture that somehow survived the French Revolution, the Franco-Prussian war, World War I, and World War II. As you enter, notice the sculpture over the left portal (complacent, spear-toting Virtues getting revenge on those nasty Vices). Enter and walk about halfway down the center. The stained glass on the lower left shows various rulers of Strasbourg, while the stained glass on your right is the Bible for the poor (read: illiterate). A beautiful organ hangs above. Walk to the choir and stare at the stained-glass image of Mary and find the European Union flag at the top. In the right transept is a high-tech 15th-century astronomical clock (restored in 1883), operating every 15 minutes (better on the half hour, best at 12:30, arrive by 12:15 to hear an explanation of its workings just outside the door, €0.75). For €3 you can climb 330 steps up the tower for an amazing view (access on right side of cathedral, cathedral open daily 07:00–11:40, 12:45–19:00; tower open daily April–Sept 09:00–18:30, Oct–March 09:00–16:30). Before leaving this area, stroll the impressive network of pedestrian streets that connect the cathedral with the huge place Kleber (home to various outdoor markets depending on the day of the week).

Museums Near the Cathedral—These museums, all close to the cathedral, are interesting only for aficionados with a full day in Strasbourg. The Palais Rohan houses three museums: the Museum of Decorative Arts (big, boring rooms with red velvet chairs), the Museum of Fine Arts (modest but well-presented collection of paintings from Middle Ages to Baroque), and the Archaeological Museum, the best of the three with an excellent presentation of Alsatian civilization over the millennia and English explanations (€3/museum, €6 for all 3, Mon and Wed–Sat 10:00–12:00, 13:30–18:00, Sun 10:00–17:00, closed Tue, 2 place du Château). The Museum of the Cathedral (Musée de l'Oeuvre Notre Dame) has many artifacts from the cathedral but no English explanations (€4.75, Tue–Sun 10:00–18:00, closed Mon, 3 place du Château). The Museum of Alsace's (Musée Alsacien) costumes and cultural exhibits are a good presentation of local traditions, with many stairs and walkways connecting furnished rooms in traditional homes (€3, Mon and Wed–Sat 10:00–12:00, 13:30–18:00, Sun 10:00–17:00, closed Tue, across river from tourist boat dock at 23 quai St. Nicholas).

Boat Ride on the Ill River—Do a loop trip on the Ill River and get a different perspective on the city (€6.25, 70 min, English commentary via live guide or audioguide, boats depart 2/hr from 09:30–21:00, dock is 2 blocks outside cathedral's right transept, where rue Rohan meets the river).

La Petite France—Historic home to Strasbourg's tanners, this delightful area is laced with canals, grand half-timbered homes, cobblestones, and tourists. From the cathedral, walk to place Gutenberg, then follow rue Gutenberg, which turns into the pedestrian-only Grande Rue. Turn left off Grand Rue onto rue des Bouchers, and drop down to the river at the bridge. Wander deep—the best cafés line the canal on quai de la Bruche at the far end, and the small parks that lie between the canals are picnic and siesta perfect (cross bridge at rue des Moulins to reach the parks). Climb the grassy wall (Barrage Vauban) for a great view back over Strasbourg's medieval towers, city center, and waterways. The glass structure behind you is the new modern-art museum (interesting more for its architecture than its collection). From here, it's a 10-minute walk back to the station (with river on your left, cross the third bridge and find rue Marie Kuss).

Sleeping in Strasbourg
(€1.10 = about $1, country code: 33, zip code: 67000)
Hôtel Cathédrale*** lets you stare point-blank from your room at the cathedral, and is a comfortable, stylish place (Db without view-€75, larger Db with view-€100, extra person-€15.50, breakfast buffet-€9.20, CC, parking-€15.50, air-con, elevator, 12 place de la Cathédrale, tel. 03 88 22 12 12, fax 03 88 23 28 00, www.hotel-cathedrale.fr). **Hôtel des Suisses****, across from the cathedral's right transept and off place du Château, is a quiet, dark and centrally solid two-star value (Sb-€46–55, Db-€61–70, Tb-€76–86, CC, elevator, 2 place de la Rape, tel. 03 88 35 22 11, fax 03 88 25 74 23, e-mail: hotel.suisse.strasbourg@gofornet.com).

Transportation Connections—Strasbourg
Strasbourg makes a good side trip from Colmar or stop on the way to or from Paris.

By train to: Colmar (hrly, 50 min), **Paris'** Gare de l'Est (14/day, 4.5 hrs, 6 require changes), **Karlsruhe**, Germany (16/day, 1.5 hrs, 11 with change in Appenweier), **Basel**, Switzerland (hrly, 2 hrs).

VERDUN

Little remains in Europe today to remind us of World War I,
but Verdun provides a fine tribute to the million-plus lives lost
in the battles fought here. While the lunar landscape of World
War I is now forested over, countless craters and trenches are
visible. Millions of live bombs lie in vast cordoned-off areas.
Drive through the eerie moguls surrounding Verdun, stopping
at melted-sugar-cube forts and plaques marking where towns
once existed. With two hours and a car, or a full day and a bike
(and a strong heart), you can see the most stirring sights and
appreciate the tremendous scale of the battles. The town of
Verdun is not your destination but a starting point for your
visit into the nearby battlefields.

Tourist Information: The TI is on place Nation (May–
Sept daily 8:30–18:30, Oct–April closed 12:00–14:00 and at
18:00, tel. 03 29 86 14 18).

Arrival in Verdun

By Train: Walk straight out of the station and down avenue
Garibaldi to the town center.

By Car: Follow signs to *centre-ville*, place Nation, and Porte
Chatel; you'll pass the TI just before crossing the river.

Getting around the Verdun Battlefield

The TI has good maps of the battlefields. French-language **minivan tours** of the battle sites are available June through September
and leave the TI around 14:00 (€23 guides usually speak some
English, and English handouts are available). You can rent a bike
opposite Verdun's train station at **Cycles Flavenot** (tel. 03 29 86
12 43). To reach the battlefields by car or bike (about 30 km/18.5
mi round-trip), take D-112 from Verdun (look for signs to
Douaumont) and then take D-913 to Douaumont.

The battlefield remains are situated on two sides of the
Meuse River; the Rive Droite has more sights. By following signs
to Fort Douaumont and the Ossuaire, you'll pass Musée Fleury.

Sights—Verdun

▲▲**Battlegrounds**—The most compelling sights are Mémorial-
Musée de Fleury, l'Ossuaire, and Fort Douaumont. Start with
Mémorial-Musée de Fleury, built around an impressive re-
creation of a battlefield, hard-hitting photos, weapon displays,
and a worthwhile 15-minute movie narrated in English with headphones (€3, March–Dec 9:00–18:00, until 17:00 in winter).
The museum is built on the site of a village (Fleury) that was
obliterated during the fighting.

L'Ossuaire is the tomb of 130,000 French and Germans,
whose last homes were the muddy trenches of Verdun (March–early

Verdun

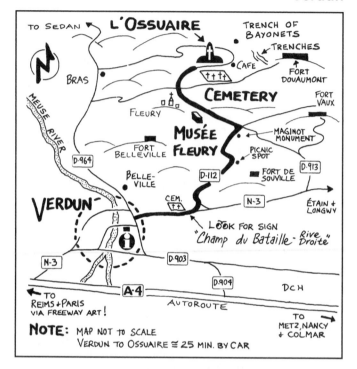

Sept daily 9:00–18:00, late-Sept–Feb closes 12:00–14:00 and at 17:30). Look through the low windows for a bony memorial to those whose political and military leaders asked them to make the "ultimate sacrifice" for their countries. Enter the monument and experience a humbling and moving tribute. Ponder a war that left half of all Frenchmen aged 15 to 30 dead or wounded. Climb the tower for a territorial view (€1) and don't miss the thought-provoking 20-minute film (€2.50, €3 includes tower, closed Nov–March; theater in basement, ask for English version). The little €0.30 coin-op picture boxes in the gift shop are worth a look if you don't visit Mémorial-Musée de Fleury (turn through all of the old photos before time expires).

Before leaving, walk to the cemetery and listen for the eerie buzz of silence and peace. You can visit the nearby **Tranchée des Baionnettes**, where an entire company of soldiers was buried alive in their trench (the soldiers' bayonets remained above ground until recently).

The nearby **Fort Douaumont** was a strategic command

center for both sides at various times. It's more interesting from the outside than the inside (walk on top and notice the round, iron-gun emplacements that could rise and revolve). A walk inside (€2.50) completes the picture, with long, damp corridors and a German memorial where 1,600 Germans were killed by a single blast. Halfway between l'Ossuaire and Fort Douaumont (on either side of the road) are clearly visible trenches. *Village Détruit* signs indicate where villages were entirely destroyed; only monuments remain to mark their existence.

Citadelle Souterraine—This is a disappointing train ride through the tunnels of the French Command in downtown Verdun. While it tries to re-create the Verdun scene, it's not worth your time.

Transportation Connections—Verdun

By train to: Colmar (5/day, 4–6 hrs, best with changes in Metz and Strasbourg), **Reims** (4/day, 3 hrs, most with change in Chalons), **Paris'** Gare de l'Est (5/day, 3hrs, change in Metz or Chalon).

REIMS

Deservedly famous for its cathedral and champagne, contemporary Reims is a prosperous, modern city. Rebuilt after being leveled in World War I, Reims is 90 minutes from Paris by car or train and makes a good daytrip or handy stop for travelers en route elsewhere. Most sights of interest (champagne caves included) are within a 20-minute walk from the cathedral.

To best experience contemporary Reims, wander the thriving shopping streets between the cathedral and the train station; rue de Vesle, rue Condorcet, and place d'Erlon are best.

Tourist Information: The TI is outside the cathedral's left transept (Easter–mid-Oct Mon–Sat 09:00–19:00, Sun 10:00–18:00; mid-Oct–Easter Mon–Sat 09:00–18:00, Sun 09:00–17:00, free map shows champagne *caves*, tel. 03 26 77 45 25). Ask about tours of the cathedral in English (generally summer afternoons only) and skip the €7.75 audioguide tour.

Arrival in Reims

By Train: Walk out of the station (lockers available), cross the huge boulevards Joffre and Foch, and stroll up the pedestrian place Drouet d'Erlon. Turn left on rue Condorcet, then right on rue Talleyrand to reach the cathedral.

By Car: Follow *centre-ville* and *cathédrale* signs and park on the street approaching the cathedral (rue Libergier) or in the well-signed *Parking Cathédrale* structure.

Sights—Reims

▲▲▲**Cathedral**—The cathedral of Reims is a glorious example of Gothic architecture, with the best west portal (inside and outside) anywhere. (Since medieval churches always face east, you enter the west portal.) Clovis, the first king of the Franks, was baptized here in A.D. 496 (thus determining France's religion). Ever since, Reims' cathedral has served as the coronation place of French kings and queens. Self-assured Joan of Arc led a timid Charles VII here to be coronated in 1429. This event rallied the French around their king to push the English out of France and end the Hundred Years' War. The cathedral houses many treasures, great medieval stained glass, and a luminous set of Marc Chagall stained-glass windows from 1974 that somehow fit in well with this ancient stone structure. Informative English explanations are provided along the right aisle (including the Chagall windows) and offer sufficient historical detail for most travelers (daily 07:30–19:30).

Palais de Tau—This Archbishop's Palace houses artifacts from the cathedral (mostly tapestries and stone statues) in impressive rooms—these guys lived well. There is sadly little English information. I enjoyed seeing eye to eye with the original statues from the cathedral's facade, particularly the huge Goliath that hangs above the entry's rose window, but, for most, this museum isn't worth the time (€5.50, daily 09:30–12:30, 14:00–18:00, July–Aug 09:30–18:30).

▲**Champagne Tours**—Reims is the capital of the Champagne region. While the bubbly stuff's birthplace was closer to Epernay, you can tour a champagne *cave* right in Reims. All charge for tastings and are open daily; the last tours usually depart about an hour before midday and afternoon closings. All but the four listed below must be reserved in advance to visit.

Mumm is a major producer, offering the cheapest tours in English that include a tasting (€4.75, tours daily 09:00–11:00, 14:00–17:00, 4 blocks left out of the train station at 34 rue du Champs de Mars, tel. 03 26 49 59 70). The next three places cluster near each other about 15 minutes by foot southeast of the cathedral (from behind cathedral's right transept, walk down rue de l'Université, then rue de Barbatre). **Taittinger** does a great job trying to convince you they're the best. After seeing their movie (in comfortable theater seats), follow your guide down into some of the five kilometers (3 miles) of chilly chalk caves, many dug by ancient Romans. Popping corks signal when the tour's done and the tasting's begun (€5.50, includes tasting, Mon–Fri 09:30–12:00, 14:30–16:30, Sat–Sun 09:00–11:00, 14:00–16:30, 9 place St. Nicaise, tel. 03 26 85 45 35). **Piper Heidsieck** offers a Disneyesque train-ride tour and tasting (€6.25, 9:00–11:45, 14:00–17:15, 1 block beyond Taittinger up boulevard Victor Hugo to 51 boulevard Henri-Vasnier, tel. 03 26 84 43 44). **Comte de Noiron** is nearby and less famous, with a we-try-harder attitude. Their €4.75, 50-minute tour includes a film, a tour of their cellars, and a tasting of three different champagnes. It's open through lunch (daily 10:00–19:00, last tour departs at 18:00, 17 rue des Créneaux, tel. 03 26 82 70 67).

Sights—Near Reims

Epernay—Champagne purists may want to visit Epernay (26 km away, well-connected to Paris and Reims), where the granddaddy of champagne houses, **Moët et Chandon**, offers tours (€6.25 with tasting, daily 09:30–11:30, 14:00–16:30, tel. 03 26 51 21 00). According to the story, it was near here in about 1700 that the monk Dom Perignon, after much fiddling with double fermentation, stumbled onto this bubbly treat. On that happy day he ran through the abbey shouting, "Brothers, come quickly… I'm drinking stars!"

Route de la Champagne—Drivers can joyride through the scenic and prestigious vineyards just south of Reims. Follow D-9 south to Cormontreuil, then Louvois, then Bouzy, to see the chalky soil and vines that produce Champagne's costly wines. Many of the villages have small hotels if you'd like to sleep surrounded by vineyards.

Sleeping and Eating in Reims
(€1.10 = about $1, country code: 33, zip code: 51100)

It's hard to differentiate among the scads of hotels lining the vast pedestrian place Drouet d'Erlon. The modern and friendly **Hôtel des Arcades**** is a simple, solid value (Sb-€39, Db-€42, CC—Visa only, 16 passage Sube, off rue Condorcet in mall opposite merry-go-round, tel. 03 26 88 63 74, fax 03 26 40 66 56).

Grand Hôtel Continental*** is a business hotel offering reasonable three-star comfort, pleasant public spaces, and frequent specials (Db-€53–100, Tb/Qb-€100–165, CC, parking-€4.75, 93 place Drouet d'Erlon, tel. 03 26 40 39 35, fax 03 26 47 51 12, www.grandhotelcontinental.com).

Eating: La Coupole is *the* belle époque place to be seen dining (€18.50 *menus*, 70 place Drouet d'Erlon, tel. 03 26 47 86 28), but **l'Apostrophe** wins the cozy contest, with a librarylike interior and lively bar scene in the rear (look for their specials, 59 place Drouet d'Erlon, tel. 03 26 79 19 89).

Transportation Connections—Reims

By train to: Epernay (12/day, 30 min), **Verdun** (4/day, 3 hrs, most with change in Chalons), **Paris'** Gare de l'Est (12/day, 1.5 hrs), **Colmar** (6/day, 6 hrs, several changes).

BELGIUM

- 19,200 square kilometers (12,000 square miles), a little larger than Maryland
- 10 million people (520 people per square kilometer)
- €1.10 = $1

Belgium falls through the cracks. It's nestled between Germany, France, and Britain and it's famous for waffles, sprouts, and endive—no wonder many travelers don't even consider a stop here. But many who visit remark that Belgium is one of Europe's best-kept secrets. There are tourists—but not as many as the country's charms merit.

The country is split between the French-speaking Walloons in the south and the Dutch-speaking Flemish people (60 percent of the population) in the north. Talk to locals to learn how deep the cultural rift is. Belgium's capital, Brussels, while mostly French-speaking, is officially bilingual. The country also has a small minority of German-speaking people. Because of Belgium's international importance as the capital of the European Union, more than 25 percent of its residents are foreigners.

It is in Belgium that Europe comes together: Where Romance languages meet Germanic languages, Catholics meet Protestants, and the BeNeLux union was established, planting the seed 40 years ago that today is sprouting into the unification of Europe. Belgium flies the flag of Europe more vigorously than any place on the Continent.

Bruges and Brussels are the best two first bites of Belgium. Brussels is simply one of Europe's great cities. Bruges is a wonderfully preserved medieval gem that expertly nurtures the tourist industry, bringing the town a prosperity it hasn't enjoyed since 500 years ago, when—as one of the largest cities in the world— it helped lead northern Europe out of the Middle Ages.

Belgians brag that they eat as much as the Germans and as well as the French. They are among the world's leading beer consumers and carnivores. In Belgium, never bring chrysanthemums to a wedding. And tweaking little kids on the ear is considered rude.

Ten million Belgians are packed into a country only a little bigger than Maryland. At 520 people per square kilometer (833 people per square mile), it's the second most densely populated country in Europe (after the Netherlands). This population concentration, coupled with a dense and well-lit rail and road system, causes Belgium to shine at night when viewed from space, a phenomenon NASA astronauts call the "Belgian Window."

Rail Deals: Belgium's train system is tops, and its various rail sales are worth considering. The second-class Multipass gives groups of three to five people any two trips in Belgium: three people pay €34, four pay €39, and five pay €43 (at least one of the Multipass users must be age 26 or older). People under age 26 can get a Go Pass: €39 for 10 rides anywhere in Belgium. (The one-way Brussels–Bruges fare is €10 per person.) Seniors age 60-plus can get any six rides for €45 (available in first class only). Expect a modest increase in pass prices in February. Those traveling on the weekend should ask for the weekend discount for round-trips (40 percent off for 1 person, 60 percent off for any traveling companions).

BRUGES
(BRUGGE)

With Renoir canals, pointy gilded architecture, time-tunnel art, and stay-awhile cafés, Bruges is a heavyweight sightseeing destination as well as a joy. Where else can you ride a bike along a canal, munch mussels, wash them down with the world's best beer, savor heavenly chocolate, and see Flemish Primitives and a Michelangelo, all within 300 meters of a bell tower that rings out "Don't worry, be happy" jingles every 15 minutes? And there's no language barrier.

The town is Brugge (broo-gha) in Flemish, Bruges (broozh) in French and English. Before it was Flemish or French, the name was a Viking word for "wharf" or "embarkment." Right from the start, Bruges was a trading center. In the 11th century, the city grew wealthy on the cloth trade. By the 14th century, Bruges' population was 40,000, as large as London, which was one of the biggest cities in the world. At the time, Bruges was the most important cloth market in northern Europe. In the 15th century, Bruges was the favored residence of the powerful Dukes of Burgundy. Commerce and the arts boomed. The artists Jan van Eyck and Hans Memling had studios here. But by the 16th century, the harbor had silted up and the economy collapsed. The Burgundian court left, Spain conquered Belgium in 1548, and Bruges' golden age abruptly ended. For generations, Bruges was known as a mysterious and dead city. In the 19th century, a new port, Zeebrugge, brought renewed vitality to the area. And 20th-century tourists discovered the town. Today Bruges prospers because of tourism: It's a uniquely well-preserved Gothic city and a handy gateway to Europe. It's no secret, but even with the crowds it's the kind of city where you don't mind being a tourist.

Bruges has been selected, along with Salamanca, Spain, to be a "Cultural Capital of Europe" in 2002 (www.brugge2002.be).

This means that the city will boast even more special events—and tourist crowds—than usual. There has been a flurry of renovation and new construction to prepare for the event, but the scaffolding and cranes disappear in 2002, when visitors enjoy sparkling new facades and landmarks: A pavilion in front of the Burg by Japanese architect Toyo Ito and a concert hall near t'Zand. The Groeninge Museum's collection will be traveling in Belgium (like you are) for most of the year to make way for a special exhibition of the works of Jan van Eyck (Jan–June).

Planning Your Time

Bruges needs at least two nights and a full, well-organized day. Even nonshoppers enjoy browsing here, and the Belgian love of life makes a hectic itinerary seem a little senseless. With one day, the speedy visitor could do this: 09:30-Climb the belfry, 10:00-Tour the Burg sights (visit the TI if necessary), 11:30-Take a boat tour, 12:15-Walk to the brewery, have lunch, and catch the 13:00 tour, 14:30-Walk through the Begijnhof, 15:00-Tour the Memling Museum (6 paintings), 15:45-See the Michelangelo in the church, 16:00-Tour the Groeninge Museum if you like Eyck (closes at 18:00, ideally buy tickets in advance, see "Groeninge Museum," listed under "Sights"). Rent a bike for an evening ride through the quiet backstreets (or take a €27.50 half-hour horse-and-buggy tour). Lose the tourists and find a dinner. (If this schedule seems insane, skip the belfry and the brewery—or stay another day.) Note that churches generally close from 12:00 to 14:00.

Orientation

The tourists' Bruges (you'll be sharing it) is contained within a one-kilometer-square canal, or moat. Nearly everything of interest and importance is within a cobbled and convenient swath between the train station and Market Square (a 15-min walk).

Tourist Information: The main office is on Burg Square (April–Sept Mon–Fri 09:30–18:30, Sat–Sun 10:00–12:00, 14:00–18:30, Oct–March Mon–Fri 09:30–17:00, Sat–Sun 09:30–13:00, 14:00–17:30, lockers and money-exchange desk, tel. 050-448-686, www.brugge.com, public WC in courtyard). The other TI is at the train station (April–Sept Mon–Sat 10:30–13:15, 14:00–18:30, Oct–March Mon–Sat 09:30–13:15, 14:00–17:30, closed Sun year-round). Both TIs sell a great €0.75 all-inclusive Bruges visitors guide with a map and listings of all of the sights and services. You can also pick up a bimonthly English program *events@brugge*, as well as a schedule of special events related to the "Brugge 2002" cultural capital celebration. Consider the TI's "combo" museum ticket, which may tie into the 2002 festivities. If you're fond of Flemish art and visiting before July, ask about the Jan van Eyck exhibition. The TIs also have train-schedule information and specifics on the various kinds of tours available. Bikers will want the *5X on the Bike around Bruges* map/guide, which sells for €1.25 and shows five routes through the countryside.

Internet Access: The relaxing Coffee Link, with mellow music and pleasant art, is located between the train station and the center of town (Mon–Sat 10:00–21:30, Sun 10:00–19:30, across from Church of Our Lady at Mariastraat 38, tel. 050-349-973).

Arrival in Bruges

By Train: From the train (and from the TI near the station), you'll see the square belfry tower marking the main square. Upon arrival, stop by the station TI (has lockers) to pick up the Bruges visitors guide (map in centerfold). There are no ATMs at the station, but you can change money at ticket windows.

Buses marked *Centrum* speed to the Market Square, near most recommended hotels (€1 ticket, buy from driver, good for 1 hr). Buses #4 and #8 go farther, to the northeast part of town (to the windmills and a recommended B&B on Carmersstraat). The **taxi** fare to most hotels is around €6.

It's a 15-minute **walk** from the station to the center: Cross the busy street and canal in front of the station, head up Oost-meers, and turn right on Steenstraat to reach Market Square. You could rent a **bike** at the station for the duration of your stay (ticket window #3, daily 07:00–20:00, €9/day, €6.50/half day after 14:00, €12.50 deposit, tel. 050-302-421), but other bike-rental shops are closer to the center (see "Bruges Experiences," below).

By Car: Park at the train station for just €2.50 per day; show your parking receipt on the bus to get a free ride into town. The pricier underground parking garage at t'Zand costs €8.70 per day.

Helpful Hints

Shops are open from 09:00 to 18:00; a little later on Friday. Grocery stores are usually closed on Sunday. **Market days** are Wednesday morning (Market Square) and Saturday morning (t'Zand). On Saturday and Sunday afternoons, a flea market hops along Dijver in front of the Groeninge Museum.

The information number for all **museums** is 050-448-711. October through March is off-season (when some museums close on Tue).

The **post office** is on Market Square near the belfry (Mon–Fri 09:00–19:00, Sat 09:30–12:30, closed Sun, tel. 050-331-411).

Sights—Bruges

Bruges' sights are listed here in walking order, from Market Square to the Burg to the cluster of museums around the Church of Our Lady to the Begijnhof (10-min walk from beginning to end). Like Venice, the ultimate sight is the town itself, and the

Bruges

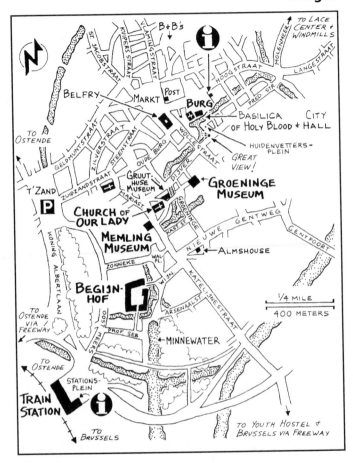

best way to enjoy that is to get lost on the backstreets, away from the lace shops and ice-cream stands.

Market Square (Markt)—Ringed by banks, the post office, lots of restaurant terraces, great old gabled buildings, and the belfry, this is the modern heart of the city. Most city buses go from here to the station. Under the belfry are two great Belgian French-fry stands, a quadrilingual Braille description of the old town, and a metal model of the tower. In Bruges' heyday as a trading center, a canal came right up to this square. **Geldmuntstraat**, just off the square, is a delightful street with many fun and practical shops and eateries.

▲▲**Belfry (Belfort)**—Most of this bell tower has stood over Market Square since 1300. The octagonal lantern was added in 1486, making it 88 meters high—that's 366 steps (daily 09:30–17:00, ticket window closes 45 min early, WC in courtyard). The view is worth the climb and the €5. Survey the town. On the horizon you can see the towns along the coast. Just before you reach the top, peek into the carillon room. The 47 bells can be played mechanically with the giant barrel and movable tabs (as they do on each quarter hour) or with a manual keyboard (as it does for regular concerts) with fists and feet rather than fingers. Be there on the quarter hour, when things ring. It's *bellissimo* at the top of the hour. Carillon concert times are listed at the base of the belfry (year-round Sun at 14:15, also Oct–mid-June Wed and Sat at 14:15). Back on the square, with your back to the belfry, turn right onto pedestrian-only Breidelstraat and thread yourself through the lace and *wafels* to Burg Square.

▲▲**Burg Square**—The opulent square called Burg is Bruges' civic center, historically the birthplace of Bruges and the site of the ninth-century castle of the first Count of Flanders. Today it's the scene of outdoor concerts and home of the TI (with a €0.25 WC). It's surrounded by six centuries of architecture. Sweeping counterclockwise 360 degrees, you'll go from **Romanesque** (the round arches and thick walls of the brick basilica in the corner, best seen inside the lower chapel) to the pointed **Gothic** arches of the City Hall (with its "Gothic Room") to the well-proportioned **Renaissance** windows of the Old Recorder's House (next door, under the gilded statues), and past the TI and the park to the elaborate 17th-century **Baroque** of the Provost's House. Complete your spin and walk to that corner.

▲**Basilica of the Holy Blood**—Originally the Chapel of Saint Basil, it's famous for its relic of the blood of Christ which, according to tradition, was brought to Bruges in 1150 after the Second Crusade (and is displayed only during Friday worship services). The lower chapel, accessed through the door labeled *Basiliek*, is dark and solid—a fine example of Romanesque style (with some beautiful statues). The upper chapel (separate entrance, climb the stairs) is decorated Gothic and usually accompanied by appropriately contemplative music. A €0.25 English flier tells about the relic, art, and history. The small but sumptuous Basilica Museum (well described in English) contains the gem-studded hexagonal reliquary (c. 1600) that carries the relic on its yearly Ascension Day trip through the streets of Bruges (museum is next to upper chapel, €1.25, April–Sept daily 09:30–12:00, 14:00–18:00, Oct–March Thu–Tue 10:00–12:00, 14:00–16:00, Wed 10:00–12:00 only).

▲**City Hall's Gothic Room**—Your ticket gives you a room full of old town maps and paintings and a grand, beautifully restored "Gothic Hall" from 1400. Its painted and carved wooden ceiling features hanging arches (explained by an English flier). Notice the New Testament themes carved into the circular "vault keys." The wall murals are late-19th-century Romantic paintings of episodes from the city's history (described in the flier). The free ground-level lobby (closed on weekends) is a picture gallery of Belgium's colonial history, from the Spanish Bourbon king to Napoléon (€2.50, includes audioguide and admission to Renaissance Hall, daily 09:30–17:00, Burg 12).

Renaissance Hall (Brugse Vrije)—This is just one ornate room with an impressive Renaissance chimney. If you're into heraldry, the symbolism (explained in the free English flier) makes this worth a five-minute stop. If you're not, you'll wonder where the rest of the museum is (€3.75, includes admission to City Hall, daily 09:30–17:00, entry in the corner of the square at Burg 11a).

From Burg to Fish Market to View—From Burg, walk under the Goldfinger family down Blinde Ezelstraat. Just after you cross the bridge, the persistent little fish market (*Vismarkt*, fresh North Sea catch sold Tue–Sat 06:00–13:00) is on your left. Take an immediate right to Huidevettersplein, a tiny, picturesque, restaurant-filled square. Continue a few steps to Rozenhoedkaai Street, where you can get a great photo of the belfry reflected in the canal. Can you see its tilt? It leans about four feet. Down the canal (past a flea market on weekends) looms the huge spire of the Church of Our Lady (tallest brick spire in the Low Countries). Between you and the church are the next three museums.

▲▲▲Groeninge Museum—This museum usually houses a classy collection of mostly Flemish art, from Memling to Magritte. But for the first half of 2002, the building will be taken over by a special exhibition of the works of Flemish artist **Jan van Eyck** and his influence on the Mediterranean world (€10, daily 10:00–18:00, Wed until 21:00, reservations are recommended, same-day advance tickets available at TI, can book further in advance for an additional fee at tel. 070-223-302, in the U.S. call 1-800-669-8687).

After the Eyck exhibition ends on June 30, the Groeninge Museum will close to reshuffle art, then reopen probably in fall, starring its regular collection.

If you're visiting in fall: Rooms 1 through 18 take you from 1400 to 1945. While the museum has plenty of worthwhile modern art, the highlights are its vivid and pristine Flemish Primitives. ("Primitive" here means before the Renaissance.) Flemish art is shaped by its love of detail, its merchant patrons' egos, and the power of the Church. Lose yourself in the halls of Groeninge: Gaze across 15th-century canals, into the eyes of reassuring Marys, and through town squares littered with leotards, lace, and lopped-off heads (€6.20, daily 09:30–17:00, Oct–March closed Tue, Dijver 12, tel. 050-448-751).

The **Brangwyn Museum** (Arentshuis) next door is only interesting if you are into lace or the early-20th-century art of Brangwyn (€2, daily 09:30–17:00, Oct–March closed Tue, Dijver 16, tel. 050-448-763).

▲**Gruuthuse Museum**—A wealthy brewer's home, this is a sprawling smattering of everything from medieval bedpans to a guillotine (€5, daily 09:30–17:00, audioguides planned for 2002, Oct–March closed Tue, Dijver 17). Leaving the museum, contemplate the mountain of bricks towering 120 meters (394 feet) above as they have for 600 years.

▲▲**Church of Our Lady**—The church stands as a memorial to the power and wealth of Bruges in its heyday. A delicate *Madonna and Child* by Michelangelo is near the apse (to the right if you're facing the altar). It's said to be the only Michelangelo statue to leave Italy in his lifetime (thanks to the wealth generated by Bruges' cloth trade). If you like tombs and church art, pay to wander through the apse (€1.75, Michelangelo free, art-filled apse April–Sept Mon–Fri 10:00–12:00, 14:00–17:00, closes at 16:00 on Sat, Sun 14:00–16:00, Oct–March closes at 16:30, on Mariastraat).

▲▲**St. Jans Hospital/Memling Museum**—This medieval hospital (newly opened after 2 years of renovation) contains six much-loved paintings by the greatest of the Flemish Primitives, Hans Memling. His *Mystical Wedding of St. Catherine* triptych deserves a close look. Catherine and her "mystical groom," the baby Jesus, are flanked by a headless John the Baptist and a pensive John the Evangelist. The chairs are there so you can study it. If you understand the Book of Revelation, you'll understand St. John's wild and intricate vision. The St. Ursula Shrine, an ornate little mini-church in the same room, is filled with impressive detail (€7, daily 09:30–17:00, off-season closed Wed, across the street from the Church of Our Lady, Mariastraat 38).

▲▲**Straffe Hendrik Brewery Tour**—Belgians are Europe's beer connoisseurs. This fun and handy tour is a great way to pay your respects. The happy gang at this working family brewery gives entertaining and informative 45-minute, four-language tours (usually by friendly Inge, €3.75 including a beer, lots of very steep steps, great rooftop panorama, daily on the hour 11:00–16:00, 11:00 and 15:00 are your best times to avoid groups, Oct–March 11:00 and 15:00 only, 1 block past church and canal, take a right down skinny Stoofstraat to #26 on Walplein square, tel. 050-332-697). At Straffe Hendrik ("Strong Henry") they remind their drinkers: "The components of the beer are vitally necessary and contribute to a well-balanced life pattern. Nerves, muscles, visual sentience, and a healthy skin are stimulated by these in a positive manner. For longevity and lifelong equilibrium, drink Straffe Hendrik in moderation!"

Their bistro, where you'll be given your included-with-the-tour beer, serves a quick and hearty lunch plate (the €8.70 "meat selection and vegetables" is a beer-drinker's picnic for two; try some Belgian cheese or quiche, a house specialty). On sunny summer days, they offer a barbecue and salad bar for €10. You can eat indoors with the smell of hops or outdoors with the smell of hops. This is a great place to wait for your tour or to linger afterward. From here the lacy cuteness of Bruges crescendoes as you approach the Begijnhof.

▲▲**Begijnhof**—For military (and various other) reasons, there were more women than men in the medieval Low Countries. Towns provided Begijnhofs (buh-HINE-hofs), dignified places in which these *begijns* could live a life of piety and service (without having to take the same vows a nun would). You'll find Begijnhofs all over Belgium and Holland. Bruges' Begijnhof—now inhabited not by begijns but by Benedictine nuns—almost makes you want to don a habit and fold your hands as you walk under its wispy trees and whisper past its frugal little homes. For a good slice of Begijnhof life, walk through the simple museum (Begijn's House, left of entry gate, €1.50 with English explanations, daily 10:00–12:00, 13:45–17:30, off-season closes at 17:00).

Minnewater—Just south of the Begijnhof is Minnewater, an idyllic, clip-clop world of flower boxes, canals, swans, and tour boats packed like happy egg cartons.

Almshouses—Walking from the Begijnhof back to the center, you might detour along Nieuwe Gentweg to visit one of about 20 almshouses in the city. At #8, go through the door marked "Godshuis de Meulenaere 1613" (free) into the peaceful courtyard. This was a medieval form of housing for the poor. The rich would pay for someone's tiny room here in return for lots of prayers. The Diamond Museum (at the start of Nieuwe Gentweg) is less interesting than an encyclopedia (€5, daily 10:30–17:30).

Bruges Experiences

Chocolate—Bruggians are connoisseurs of fine chocolate. You'll be tempted by chocolate-filled display windows all over town. Godiva is the best big-factory/high-price/high-quality local brand, but there are plenty of smaller, family-run places in Bruges that offer good handmade chocolates.

You can find Bruges' smoothest, creamiest chocolate at **Dumon** (€1.60/100 grams). Stefaan makes the chocolate, his twin brother Christophe sells it near the Straffe Hendrik brewery (closed Mon, Walstraat 6, tel. 050-340-043), and their sister Nathalie runs a shop in a precious little gingerbread house just off Market Square (closed Wed, Eiermarkt 6, check out the basement display of old chocolate molds, tel. 050-346-282, www.chocolatierdumon.com).

Locals and tourists alike flock to **The Chocolate Line** (€3/100 grams), which feels more elegant and offers over 80 varieties. While you're sampling their ginger chocolate (shaped like a Buddha) or their saffron curry chocolate (a white elephant), you can watch them pouring chocolate into plastic molds in the back room (daily 09:30–18:30, Sun open at 10:30, Simon Stevinplein 19, between Church of Our Lady and Market Square, tel. 050-341-090).

The smaller **Sweertvaegher**, near Burg Square, features top-quality chocolate (€2.45/100 grams) made with fresh ingredients and no preservatives (Tue–Sun 09:30–18:15, closed Mon, Philip-stockstraat 29, tel. 050-338-367).

Lace and Windmills by the Moat—A 10-minute walk from the center to the northeast end of town brings you to four windmills strung out along a pleasant grassy setting on the "big moat" canal (between Kruispoort and Dampoort, on Bruges side of the moat). One of the windmills (St. Janshuismolen) is open to visitors (€2, daily 09:30–12:30, 13:30–17:00, closed Oct–April, at the end of Carmersstraat).

To actually see lace being made, drop by the nearby **Lace Centre**, where ladies toss bobbins madly while their eyes go bad (€1.50 includes afternoon demonstrations and a small lace museum called Kantcentrum, as well as the adjacent Jerusalem Church; Mon–Fri 10:00–12:00, 14:00–18:00, until 17:00 on Sat, closed Sun, Peperstraat 3, tel. 050-448-764). The **Folklore Museum**, in the same neighborhood, is cute but forgettable (€2, daily 09:30–17:00, Oct–March closed Tue, Rolweg 40, tel. 050-330-044). To find either place, ask for the Jerusalem Church.

▲▲**Biking**—While the sights are close enough for easy walking, the town is a treat to bike through, and you can to get away from the tourist center. Consider a peaceful evening ride through the backstreets and around the outer canal. Rental shops have maps and ideas. The TI sells a handy *5X on the Bike around Bruges* map/guide for €1.25; it narrates five different bike routes (18–30 km) through the idyllic countryside nearby. The best trip is 30 minutes along the canal out to Damme and back. The Netherlands/Belgium border is a 40-minute pedal beyond Damme. Two shops rent bikes in the center of town (€2.50–2.75 for 1 hr, €5–5.60 for 4 hrs, or €8/day). Both offer free city maps and child seats. **Fietsen Popelier** doesn't require a deposit and sells a good map of the countryside for €1.85 (July–Sept daily 10:00–20:00, Oct–June Tue–Sun 10:00–18:00, closed Mon winter through Easter, 50 meters from Church of Our Lady at Mariastraat 26, tel. 050-343-262). **'T Koffieboontje** asks for a €25 deposit, your passport, or a credit-card imprint (Hallestraat 4, closer to belfry, tel. 050-338-027). The less central **De Ketting** rents bikes for less (€5/day, daily 09:00–20:00, Gentpoortstraat 23, tel. 050-344-196).

Tours of Bruges

Bruges by Boat—The most relaxing and scenic (though not informative) way to see this city of canals is by boat, with the captain narrating. Boats leave from all over town (€5.50, 4/hr, 10:00–17:00, copycat 30-min rides). Boten Stael offers a €0.50 discount with this book (just over the canal from the Memling Museum at Katelijnestraat 4, tel. 050-332-771).

City Minibus Tours—"City Tour Bruges" gives 50-minute/ €9.50 rolling overviews of the town in an 18-seat, two-skylight minibus with dial-a-language headsets and video support. The tour leaves hourly (on the hr, 10:00–19:00 in summer, until 18:00 in spring and fall, less in winter) from Market Square. The narration, while clear, is slow-moving and boring. But the tour is a lazy way to cruise by virtually every sight in Bruges.

Walking Tours—Local guides walk small groups through the core of town daily in July and August and Saturday and Sunday in June and September (€3.75, depart from TI at 15:00). The tours, while earnest, are heavy on history and in two languages, so they may be less than peppy. Still, to propel you beyond the pretty gables and canal swans of Bruges, they are good medicine. A private guided tour costs €40 (reserve at least 3 days in advance through TI). Beginning in April 2002, special theme tours— including medieval Bruges, culinary Bruges, literary Bruges, and "twilight zone" Bruges—will celebrate the city's tenure as a cultural capital of Europe; ask for specifics at the TI or call ahead to reserve (tel. 050-448-685).

Bus Tours of Countryside—Quasimodo Tours offers those with extra time two excellent all-day tours through the rarely visited Flemish countryside. The "Flanders Fields" tour concentrates on World War I battlefields, trenches, memorials, and poppy-splattered fields (Sun, Tue, and Thu 09:00–16:30). The other is "Triple Treat": the port of Damme, a castle, a monastery, a brewery, and a chocolate factory, as well as a sampling of the treats—a waffle, chocolate, and beer (Mon, Wed, and Fri 09:00–16:00). Hardworking Lote leads all the tours himself, in English only (€45, €38 if under 26, CC, 29-seat nonsmoking bus, includes lunch, lots of walking, pickup at your hotel or the train station, tel. 050-370-470 to book, fax 050-374-960, www.quasimodo.be).

Bruges by Bike—The Backroad Bike Company, also run by Quasimodo Tours, leads daily bike tours in and around Bruges (€13.50, 10:00 and 19:00, 8 km, 2 hrs) and through the nearby countryside to Damme (€16, 13:00, 25 km, 3–4 hrs, tel. 050-370-470).

Bus and Boat Tour—The Sightseeing Line offers a bus trip to Damme and a boat ride back (€16.50, April–Sept daily at 14:00, 2 hrs, leaves from Market Square).

Sights—Near Bruges

Dolfinarium—At Boudewijnpark, just outside of town, dolphins make a splash several times a day (call for show times— tel. 050-383-838, €7.50 for 40-min show, Debaeckestraat 12, www.boudewijnpark.be). The theme park's roller-skating rink is open in the afternoon (and turns into an ice-skating rink off-season). From Bruges, catch the "Sint Michiels" bus #7 or #17 from Kuipersstraat.

Flanders Fields—This World War I museum, 60 kilometers southwest of Bruges, provides a moving look at the battles fought near Ieper (Ypres in French). Use interactive computers to trace the wartime lives of individual soldiers and citizens. Powerful videos and ear-shattering audio complete the story (€10, March–Nov special exhibition with expanded coverage and more computers, otherwise €7.50, April–Sept daily 10:00–18:00, Oct–March Tue–Sun 10:00–17:00, ticket sales stop one hour before closing, Grote Markt 34, Ieper, tel. 057-228-584, fax 057-228-589, www .inflandersfields.be). From Bruges, catch a train to Ieper via Kortrijk (2 hrs). Drivers follow A17 to Kortrijk, then take A19 to Ieper.

Sleeping in Bruges
(€1.10 = about $1, country code: 32, area code: 050, zip code: 8000)

Sleep Code: **S** = Single, **D** = Double/Twin, **T** = Triple, **Q** = Quad, **b** = bathroom, **s** = shower only, **CC** = Credit Cards accepted, **no CC** = Credit Cards not accepted. Everyone speaks English.

Most places are located between the train station and the old center, with the most distant (and best) being a few blocks beyond Market Square to the north and east. B&Bs offer the best value. All include breakfast, are on quiet streets, and (with a few exceptions) keep the same prices throughout the year. Bruges is most crowded Friday and Saturday evenings Easter through October—with July and August weekends being worst. Since Bruges has been designated a Cultural Capital of Europe in 2002, accommodations will fill up more quickly than usual. Book in advance.

Bruges' most convenient place to do laundry is **Mr. Wash** (self-service open daily until 22:00, just off Market Square at Sint Jakobsstraat 33 in an arcade, tel. 050-335-902). A less central Laundromat is at Gentportstraat 28 (daily 07:00–22:00).

Hotels

Hansa Hotel offers 24 rooms in a completely modernized old building. It's tastefully decorated in elegant pastels and has all the amenities. It's a great splurge (Sb-€115–195, Db-€125–205, depending on room size, extra bed-€40, suites available, CC, air-con, nonsmoking, elevator, free Internet access, sauna, tanning bed, fitness room, bike rental for €6.20/half day, €11/day, Niklaas Desparsstraat 11, a block north of Market Square, tel. 050-338-444, fax 050-334-205, www.hansa.be, e-mail: information@hansa.be, cheery and hardworking Johan and Isabelle).

Hotel Adornes is small, new, and classy—a great value.

It has 20 comfy rooms with full, modern bathrooms in a 17th-century canalside house, and offers free parking, free loaner bikes, and a cellar game and video lounge (Sb-€75–95, Db-€80–100 depending upon size, Tb-€115, Qb-€125, CC, elevator, near Van Nevel B&B, mentioned below, and Carmersstraat at St. Annarei 26, tel. 050-341-336, fax 050-342-085, e-mail: hotel .adornes@proximedia.be, Nathalie runs the family business).

Hotel Aarendshuis, an old merchant's mansion, is well-worn but comfortable. It's family-run and has 25 spacious rooms, dingy carpets, chandeliered public places, and a small garden (prices vary with size and luxury: Sb-€76, Db-€80–104, Tb-€112, Qb-€124, kids under 10 free, car park-€10, CC, elevator, 2 blocks off Burg Square at Hoogstraat 18, tel. 050-337-889, fax 050-330-816, e-mail: hotelaarendshuis@village.uunet.be). The owner, Danny, will take you on a one-hour sightseeing tour of Bruges in his turn-of-the-century "old-timer" car for the same price as a buggy ride (€25 for 2 people).

Hotel Cavalier, which has more stairs than character, serves a hearty buffet breakfast in a royal setting (Sb-€50–52, Db-€55–62, Tb-€70–75, Qb-€77–82, lofty "backpackers' doubles" on fourth floor-€40 or €45 with WC, CC, Kuipersstraat 25, tel. 050-330-207, fax 050-347-199, e-mail: hotel.cavalier@skynet.be, run by friendly Viviane De Clerck).

Hotel Egmond is quietly located in the middle of the placid Minnewater. Its 18th-century rooms have all the comforts (Sb-€82–102, Db-€112–120, Tb-€132–142, no CC, for longer stays ask about their apartments a few blocks away, Minnewater 15, tel. 050-341-445, fax 050-342-940, www.egmond.be).

Hotel Cordoeanier, a family-run place, rents 22 bright, simple, modern rooms on a quiet street two blocks off Market Square (Sb-€48–62, Db-€57–67, Tb-€72–80, Qb-€85, Quint/b-€97, higher prices are for weekends or luxury rooms, larger groups should ask about holiday house across the street, CC, nearly free Internet access, Cordoeanierstraat 16, tel. 050-339-051, fax 050-346-111, www.cordoeanier.be, Kris and Veerle).

Hotel Botaniek has three stars, nine small rooms, and a quiet location a block from Astrid Park (Sb-€65, Db-€75–85, Tb-€90, Qb-€100, CC, elevator, Waalsestraat 23, tel. 050-341-424, fax 050-345-939, e-mail: hotel.botaniek@pi.be).

Hotel De Pauw is tall, skinny, and family-run, with straightforward rooms on a quiet street across from a church (S-€40, Sb-€50, 2 top-floor D-€50, Db-€60–65, CC, free and easy street parking or pay garage, Sint Gilliskerkhof 8, tel. 050-337-118, fax 050-345-140, www.hoteldepauw.be, Philippe and Hilde).

Hotel Rembrandt-Rubens has 15 rooms in a creaky 500-year-old building with tipsy floors, a mysterious layout, tacky rooms, ancient dippy beds, elephant tusks, a gallery of creepy

Hotels in Bruges' Center

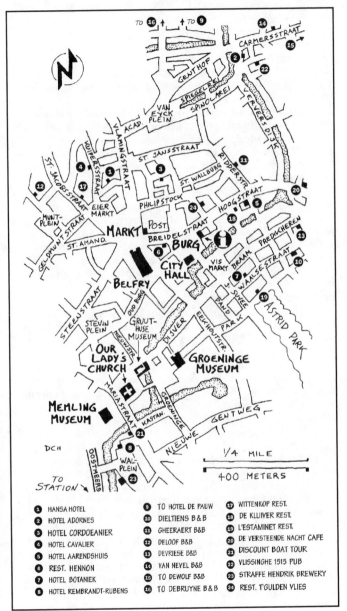

1. HANSA HOTEL
2. HOTEL ADORNES
3. HOTEL CORDOEANIER
4. HOTEL CAVALIER
5. HOTEL AARENDSHUIS
6. REST. HENNON
7. HOTEL BOTANIEK
8. HOTEL REMBRANDT-RUBENS
9. TO HOTEL DE PAUW
10. DIELTIENS B&B
11. GHEERAERT B&B
12. DELOOF B&B
13. DEVRIESE B&B
14. VAN NEVEL B&B
15. TO DEWOLF B&B
16. TO DEBRUYNE B&B
17. WITTENKOP REST.
18. DE KLUIVER REST.
19. L'ESTAMINET REST.
20. DE VERSTEENDE NACHT CAFE
21. DISCOUNT BOAT TOUR
22. VLISSINGHE 1515 PUB
23. STRAFFE HENDRIK BREWERY
24. REST. T'GULDEN VLIES

old paintings, and probably the Holy Grail in a drawer somewhere (S-€30, Ss-€40, one D-€40, Ds-€55, Db-€60, Tb-€75, Qb-€100, no CC, locked up from 24:00–7:30, on a quiet square between the Memlings and the brewery at Walplein 38, tel. 050-336-439, fax 050-677-780). The breakfast room (which must have been the knights' hall) overlooks a canal (while Rembrandt and Rubens overlook you from an ornately carved and tiled 1648 chimney). There's a little warmth behind Mrs. De Buyser's crankiness. The hotel has been in her family for 50 years.

Crowne Plaza Hotel Brugge is the most modern, comfortable, and central hotel option. Each of its 96 air-conditioned rooms comes with a magnifying mirror and trouser press (Db-€210–240, prices drop as low as €170 on weekdays and off-season, CC, elevator, pool, Burg 10, tel. 050-446-844, fax 050-446-868, www.crowneplaza.com).

Near Train Station: The **Hotel t'Keizershof** is a dollhouse of a hotel that lives by its motto, "Spend a night, not a fortune." It's simple and tidy, with seven small, cheery, old-time rooms split between two floors, a shower and toilet on each (S-€25, D-€36, T-€54, Q-€65, no CC, free and easy parking, laundry service-€7.50, Oostmeers 126, a block in front of train station, tel. 050-338-728, e-mail: hotel.keizershof@12move.be, Stefaan and Hilde).

Bed-and-Breakfasts

These places, run by people who enjoy their work, offer the best value. Each is central and offers lots of stairs and three or four doubles you'd pay €100 for in a hotel. Parking is generally easy on the street.

Koen and Annemie Dieltiens are a friendly couple who enjoy getting to know their guests and sharing a wealth of information on Bruges. You'll eat a hearty breakfast around a big table in their bright, comfortable, newly renovated house (Sb-€45, Db-€50, Tb-€70, Qb-€90, 1-night stays pay €5 extra per room, no CC, nonsmoking, Waalse Straat 40, 3 blocks southeast of Burg Square, tel. 050-334-294, fax 050-335-230, http://users.skynet.be/dieltiens, e-mail: koen.dieltiens@skynet.be). The Dieltiens also rent a cozy studio and apartment for two to six people in a nearby 17th-century house (2 people pay €350 per week for studio, €403 per week for apartment, prices higher for shorter stays and more people, cheaper off-season).

Debruyne B&B, run by Marie-Rose Debruyne and her architect husband Ronny D'Hespeel, offers artsy, original decor (check out the elephant-sized doors—Ronny's design) and genuine warmth (Sb-€45, Db-€50, Tb-€70, Qb-€90, 1-night stay-€5 extra per room, no CC, 5-min walk north of Market Square, look for Ronny's architect sign at Lange Raamstraat 18, tel. 050-347-606, fax 050-340-285, www.bedandbreakfastbruges.com).

Paul and Roos Gheeraert live on the first floor, while their guests take the second. This neoclassical mansion with big, bright, comfy rooms is another fine value (Sb-€45, Db-€50, Tb-€70, no CC, rooms have coffeemakers, TVs, and fridges, Ridderstraat 9, 4 blocks east of Market, tel. 050-335-627, fax 050-345-201, http://users.skynet.be/brugge-gheeraerte-mail: gheeraert.brugge @skynet.be,). They also rent three modern, fully equipped apartments and a large loft nearby (3-night minimum).

Chris Deloof's big, homey rooms are a good bet in the old center. Check out the fun, lofty A-frame room upstairs (Sb-€45, Ds/Db-€47–52, pleasant breakfast room, no CC, nonsmoking, Geerwijnstraat 14, tel. & fax 050-340-544, www.sin.be /chrisdeloof, e-mail: chris.deloof@ping.be). Chris also rents a nearby apartment (Qb-€87) and a holiday house (Qb-€100), great for a family or group.

The **Van Nevel family** rents two attractive top-floor rooms with built-in beds in a 16th-century house (S-€33–40, D-€40–55, T-€63, includes breakfast, CC but cash preferred, nonsmoking, no sign but ring the bell at Carmersstraat 13, 10-min walk from Market Square, or bus #4 or #8 from train station or Market Square to Carmersbridge, tel. 050-346-860, fax 050-347-616, http://home.worldonline.be/~rvanneve, e-mail: Robert.VanNevel @advalvas.be). Robert enthusiastically shares the culture and history of Bruges with his guests.

Yvonne De Vriese rents three tidy B&B rooms on a corner overlooking two canals (S-€25, D-€37, Db-€44.65, third or fourth person-€12.40 extra, breakfast served in your room, CC, Predikherenstraat 40, 4 blocks east of Burg Square, take bus #6 or #16 from station and get off at the first stop on Predikheren Rei, tel. 050-334-224, fax 050-336-491, e-mail: ivonne.de.vriese @pandora.be).

Arnold Dewolf's B&B is in a stately, quiet neighborhood (S-€25, D-€35–37, T-€45, Q-€55, 5-bed-€60, no CC, family-friendly, near windmills, Oostproosse 9, tel. 050-338-366, www .ardewolf.be). From the train station, take bus #4 to Sasplein. Walk to the path behind the first windmill and turn left on Oostproosse.

Absoluut Verhulst is a modern-feeling B&B in a 400-year-old building (Sb-€50, Db-€75–93 depending on size of room, Tb-€115, Qb-€125, no CC, 5 min east of Market Square at Verbrand Nieuwland 1, tel. & fax 050-334-515, www.b-bverhulst .com, Frieda and Benno).

Hostels

Bruges has several good hostels offering beds for around €10 to €12 in two- to eight-bed rooms (singles go for around €15). Pick up the hostel info sheet at the station TI. The American-style **Charlie Rockets** bar and hostel is the liveliest and most central

(56 beds, €12.50 per bed, 2–6 per room, no CC, Hoogstraat 19, tel. 050-330-660, fax 050-343-630, www.charlierockets.com). These hostels are small, loose, and central: the dull **Snuffel Travelers Inn** (Ezelstraat 47, tel. 050-333-133), **Bauhaus International Party Hotel** (Langestraat 135, tel. 050-341-093, www.bauhaus.be), and the funky **Passage** (Dweerstraat 26, tel. 050-340-232; its hotel next door rents €35 doubles).

Eating in Bruges

Specialties include mussels cooked a variety of ways (one order can feed two), fish dishes, grilled meats, and French fries. Touristy places on the square come with great views and are affordable; candle-cool bistros flicker on backstreets. Don't eat before 19:30 unless you like eating alone. Tax and service are always included.

Bistro in den Wittenkop is very Flemish—a cluttered, laid-back, old-time place specializing in the beer-soaked equivalent of beef Bourguignon (€10–17 main courses, Tue–Sat 18:00–24:00, closed Sun–Mon, terrace in back, Sint Jakobsstraat 14, tel. 050-332-059).

De Kluiver is a pub serving hot snacks, light €10 meals, and great "sea snails in spiced bouillon" simmered in a whispering jazz ambience (Wed–Mon 18:00–24:00, closed Tue, Hoogstraat 12, tel. 050-338-927).

Pannekoekenhuisje—the little pancake house—is a cute restaurant serving delicious, inexpensive pancake meals and home-made *wafels* (daily 10:00–22:00, just off Geldmuntstraat at Helmstraat 3, tel. 050-340-086). Enthusiastic chefs Mario and Rik have just opened **The Flemish Pot** next door at #5, offering vintage Flemish cuisine (same hours and tel. as above).

Lotus Vegetarisch Restaurant serves good veggie lunches only (€8 plates, Mon–Sat 11:45–13:45, closed Sun, just off Burg at Wapenmakersstraat 5, tel. 050-331-078).

Check out these two youthful, trendy, jazz-filled eateries: For hearty budget spaghetti (€6), head for **L'Estaminet**, on the northern border of peaceful Astrid Park (11:30–24:00, closed Mon afternoon and all day Thu, Park 5, tel. 050-330-916). Or try **De Versteende Nacht Jazzcafe** on Langestraat 11 (€12.50 meals, Tue–Thu 19:00–24:00, Fri–Sat 18:00–24:00, closed Sun–Mon, tel. 050-343-293).

Herberge Vlissinghe, the oldest pub in town (1515), serves hot snacks in a great atmosphere (open from 11:00 on, closed Mon–Tue, Blekersstraat 2). **Restaurant 't Gulden Vlies**, just off Burg, is good for a late dinner (€16 plates, Wed–Sun 19:00–03:00, closed Mon–Tue, Mallebergplaats 17, tel. 050-334-709).

Bistro de Eetkamer (the living room) offers stay-a-while elegance, fine service, and fine food (Thu–Mon 12:00–14:00, 18:30–23:00, Sat until 24:00, closed Tue–Wed, just south of

Markt, Eeekhout 6, tel. 050-337-886). Drop by **Bistro De Schaar** for good food and fun atmosphere (Fri–Wed 12:00–14:30, 18:00–23:00, Hooistraat 2, tel. 050-335-979).

The popular grill house **The Hobbit,** near two recommended bars (below), features an entertaining menu, including all-you-can-eat spareribs (daily 18:00–24:00, Kemelstraat 8-10, tel. 050-201-827).

Picnics and fast meals: Geldmuntstraat is a handy street when you're hungry. A block off Market Square, **Pickles Frituur** serves the best sit-down fries in town (ask about their deep-fried vegetarian food, Mon–Sat 11:00–24:00, sometimes later in summer, closed school days 14:00–16:30 and all day Sun, at the corner of Geldmuntstraat and Sint Jakobsstraat, tel. 050-337-957). A block farther from Market Square on Geldmuntstraat, **Nopri Supermarket** is great for picnics (push-button produce pricer lets you buy as little as one mushroom, Mon–Sat 09:00–18:30, Fri until 19:00, closed Sun). The small **Delhaize grocery** is on Market Square opposite the belfry (Mon–Sat 08:00–12:00, 13:30–18:00, closed Sun). For midnight munchies, you'll find Indian-run corner grocery stores.

Frietjes: These local French fries are a treat. Proud and traditional *frituurs* serve tubs of fries and various local-style shish kebabs. Belgians dip their *frietjes* in mayonnaise, but ketchup is there for the Yankees (along with spicier sauces). For a quick, cheap, and scenic meal, hit a *frituur* and sit on the steps or benches overlooking Market Square, about 50 meters past the post office.

Beer: Belgium boasts more than 350 types of beer. Straffe Hendrik ("Strong Henry"), a potent and refreshing local brew, is, even to a Bud Lite kind of guy, obviously great beer. Among the more unusual to try: Dentergems (with coriander and orange peel) and Trappist (a dark, malty, monk-made beer). Non-beer drinkers enjoy Kriek (a cherry-flavored beer) and Frambozen Bier (raspberry-flavored beer). Each beer is served in its own unique glass. Any pub carries the basic beers, but for a selection of more than 300 types, including brews to suit any season, drink at **t'Brugs Beertje** (16:00–24:00, closed Wed, Kemelstraat 5, tel. 050-339-616). When you've finished those, step next door, where **Dreupel Huisje** serves more than 100 Belgian gins and liqueurs (Sun–Fri 18:00–24:00, Sat 18:00–02:00; if you're hungry, drop by The Hobbit, across the street). Another good place to gain an appreciation of the Belgian beer culture is **de Garre**. Rather than a noisy pub scene, it has a sit-down-and-focus-on-your-friend-and-the-fine-beer ambience (huge selection, off Breidelstraat, between Burg and Markt, on tiny Garre alley, daily 12:00–24:00, tel. 050-341-029).

Belgian Waffles: While Americans think of "Belgian" waffles for breakfast, the Belgians (who don't eat waffles or pancakes for breakfast) think of *wafels* as Liege style (dense, sweet, eaten plain and heated up, served take-away) and Brussels style (lighter, often with powdered sugar or whipped cream and fruit, served in tea-houses only in the afternoons from 14:00–18:00). For the best Liege-style *wafels* in town, stop by **Restaurant Hennon** for a *Luikse Wafel* (€1.50, May–Oct Tue–Sun 08:30–21:00, rest of year closes at 19:00, between Market Square and Burg at Breidelstraat 16, tel. 050-332-800). Rudy Hennon's extremely tasty *wafels*—and other dishes—are made with fresh ingredients.

Transportation Connections—Bruges

From Brussels, an hour away by train, all of Europe is at your fingertips (see "Brussels Connections," next chapter). Train info: tel. 050-302-424.

By train to: Brussels (2/hr, usually at :33 and :59, 1 hr), **Ghent** (4/hr, 40 min), **Ostende** (3/hr, 15 min), **Köln** (6/day, 4 hrs), **Paris** (hrly via Brussels, 2.5 hrs, must pay supplement of €10.50/second class, €21/first class, even with a railpass), **Amsterdam** (hrly, 3.5 hrs, transfer in Antwerp or Brussels).

Trains from England: Bruges is an ideal "welcome to Europe" stop after London. Take the Eurostar train from London to Brussels under the English Channel (10/day, 3 hrs), then transfer to Bruges (hrly, 1 hour). Or, if you'd prefer to cross the Channel by boat, catch the London-to-Dover train (2 hrs, from London's Victoria station), then the catamaran to Ostende (2 hrs; train station at Ostende catamaran terminal), then the Ostende-to-Bruges train (15 min). Five boats run daily (€37 one-way, same price for cheap five-day return ticket, reserve by phone with CC and pick up your ticket at the dock, tel. 059-559-955).

BRUSSELS

Brussels, the capital of Belgium, is also the capital of Europe. Since World War II it's been the convenient home of both NATO and the "government of Europe," working busily to move things toward unity. It's Europe's linguistic hinge, too (60 percent of all Belgians speak the Germanic Flemish; 40 percent speak the Romantic French). It's easy to miss Brussels as you zip from Amsterdam to Paris on the train, but its rich, chocolaty mix of food and culture pleasantly surprises those who stop.

Brussels, like Belgium, is officially bilingual. Most maps and signs here list place-names in French and Flemish (Dutch). Since 80 percent of Brussels speaks French, I list mostly French names in this chapter.

Planning Your Time

Brussels is low on great sights and high on ambience. On a quick trip, a day and a night are enough for a good first taste. It could even be done as a day trip from Bruges (1 hr away by train) or a stopover on the Amsterdam-Paris ride (hrly trains). The main reason to stop—La Grand Place (*Grote Markt* in Flemish)—takes only a few minutes to see. With very limited time, skip the indoor sights and enjoy a coffee or a beer on the square. Even travelers not "into art" can spend an enjoyable three hours at Brussels' ancient- and modern-art museums, and even the tone-deaf will appreciate the Musical Instruments Museum. To see the auto and military museums (side by side), plan on a three-hour trip from the town center. If you're in Brussels on a Monday, when most sights are closed, consider Autoworld, Atomium, shopping, a walking tour, or a minibus tour. Most important, this is a city to browse and wander.

Orientation

Central Brussels is defined by a ring of roads (which replaced the old city wall) called the Pentagon. All hotels and nearly all the sights I mention are within this circle. The epicenter is the main square (La Grand Place), TI, and Central Station (3 blocks away). To get to La Grand Place from Central Station, walk downhill from the station (through the arch in Le Meridien Hôtel, across the street) and turn right in front of the church; after a block, you'll reach a small square with a fountain. For La Grand Place, turn left at the far end of the square; for the TI, continue straight past the square for one block. For the restaurant streets, take the first right (an alley) past the TI (see "Eating," below).

Tourist Information: Although the office at rue du Marché-aux-Herbes 63 is for all of Belgium, it does Brussels just fine (July–Aug daily 09:00–19:00; Sept–June Mon–Fri 09:00–18:00, Sat–Sun 09:00–13:00, 14:00–18:00, Jan–March closed Sun afternoon, downhill 3 blocks from Central Station, tel. 02-504-0390; two fun Europe stores are across the street). Another TI is in the City Hall in La Grand Place (daily 9:00–18:00, closed Sun off-season, tel. 02-513-8940). Among their countless fliers, pick up *Brussels, Yours to Discover*, the weekly *What's On*, a city map, and a public transit map. The €2 *Brussels Guide & Map* booklet is worthwhile if you want a series of neighborhood walks and a more complete explanation of the city's many museums. If your next destination is Bruges, get your Bruges information here.

Theft Alert: As the capital of a united Europe, Brussels is on the rise. Unfortunately, so is its violent crime rate. Muggings do occur. Some locals warn that it's not safe to be out late, especially after the Métro shuts down at midnight; troublemakers prey on people who missed that last ride. As in any other big city, use common sense and consider taking a taxi back to your hotel at night (try Taxi Bleu: tel. 02-268-0000).

Arrival in Brussels

By Train: Brussels can't decide which of its three stations (Central, Nord, and Midi) is the main one. Most international trains leave and land at the Nord and Midi Stations. The Eurostar leaves from Midi Station (also called Zuid or South), getting you to London in three hours. The area around the Midi Station is a rough-and-tumble immigrant neighborhood (with a towering Ferris wheel); the area around the Nord Station is a seedy red-light district. Central Station has handy services (grocery store, fast food, a luggage storage, waiting rooms, and so on) and is nearest to the sights. Normally only Belgian and Amsterdam trains stop at Central. Don't assume your train stops at more than one station. Confirm your plan with the conductor.

Trains zip under the city, connecting all three stations every

Brussels

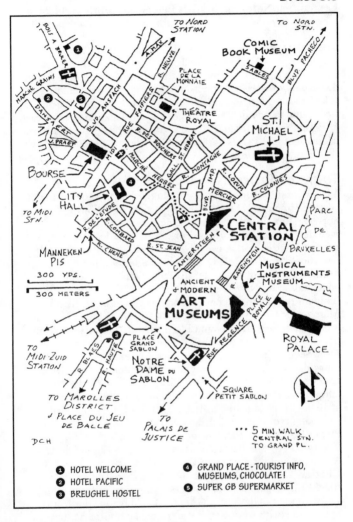

HOTEL WELCOME ①
HOTEL PACIFIC ②
BREUGHEL HOSTEL ③

④ GRAND PLACE - TOURIST INFO, MUSEUMS, CHOCOLATE!
⑤ SUPER GB SUPERMARKET

two minutes or so. It's an easy three-minute chore to connect from Nord or Midi to Central. You technically must buy a €1.35 ticket (or use your railpass) to go between Brussels' stations, but the conductors rarely check. As you wait on the platform for your train, look at the track notice board that tells which train is approaching. They zip in and out constantly. Anxious travelers often board the wrong train on the right track.

By Plane: Shuttle trains run between the three stations (Midi, Central, and Nord) and Brussels International Airport, 14 kilometers away (€2.35, 3/hr, 25 min). Airport info: tel. 0900-70-000.

Getting around Brussels

Most of Brussels' sights are walkable. For a few of the sights, such as the auto and military museums, take the Métro. The TI's free *Métro Tram Bus Plan* is excellent. The integrated system uses one €1.35 ticket that's good for one hour (notice the time when you first stamp it; buy tickets on bus or at Métro stations). The deals (5 tickets/€6, 10 tickets/€9) are available at TIs, newsstands, and Métro stations. TIs also sell a one-day ticket for €3.60 (cheaper than 3 rides, transit info: tel. 02-515-2000).

Tours of Brussels

Visit Brussels Hop-on Hop-off Bus—This makes a 90-minute, 14-stop circuit (including the corny Atomium), allowing you to hop off, see a sight, and catch the next bus (€12.50/24 hours, includes discounts to various sights, runs daily 10:00–18:00, departs Central Station every half hour at :00 and :30, headphone narration, tel. 02-513-7744, www.brussels-city-tours.com).

Human Profile of Brussels Minibus Tour—This company, which takes six visitors on three-hour tours, has a sincere commitment to teaching an understanding of Brussels (€30, mid-March–Oct Mon, Wed, Fri, Sat at 10:00 and 15:00, reservation required, departs from Grand Place 10, near Brewery Museum, tel. 02-715-9120).

De Boeck's City Tours—This typical three-hour, guided bus tour provides the handiest way to get the grand perspective on Brussels (€18.60, starts with a walk around La Grand Place before jumping on a tour bus at rue de la Colline 8, April–Oct daily at 10:00, 11:00, and 14:00, also at 15:00 on Fri–Sat and daily July–Aug; Nov–March daily at 10:00 and 14:00; buy tickets a block off La Grand Place at rue de la Colline 8 or at TI, tel. 02-513-7744). You'll see (and learn about) the Royal Palace, Atomium, and the European Union Headquarters.

Chatter Tour—This 2.5-hour tour tries to make hard-to-understand Brussels more than a collection of sights. But some guides are disappointingly short on chatter. You'll be on your feet much of the time (with some limited use of public transportation). The groups are small, and the better guides explain the delicate balance between French and Flemish through the architecture and art of the city. Starting with medieval and moving through modern styles, this is a study in how a region in an almost-perpetual state of flux until the 19th century somehow managed to find some cohesion and create a modern state (€7.50, mid-June–mid-Sept daily at 10:00, also Sat at 14:00 through Dec, meet at Galeries

Royales Saint-Hubert, rue Marché-aux-Herbes 90, near La
Grand Place, tel. 02-673-1835). They also offer other tours.

Sights—Brussels

▲▲▲**La Grand Place**—Brussels' main square, aptly called La
Grand Place, is the heart of the old town and Brussels' greatest
sight. Any time of day, it's worth swinging by to see what's going
on. Concerts, flower markets, sound-and-light shows, endless
people watching—it entertains (as do the streets around it).
In mid-August during the Flower Festival, the square will be
carpeted with 600,000 flowers.

The museums on the square are well advertised but dull.
The **Hôtel de Ville**, or City Hall, with the tallest spire, is the
square's centerpiece but no big deal to see (€2.50, visits only by
30-min tours, April–Sept Tue–Wed 15:15, Sun 12:15; Oct–March
Tue–Wed 15:15, no Sun tour). The **City Museum**, opposite City
Hall, is in a neo-Gothic building (1875) called "the King's House"
(in which no king ever lived). The top floor has an entertaining
room full of costumes the *Manneken* statue has pissed through,
the middle floor features maps and models of old Brussels, and
the bottom floor has a few old paintings and tapestries (€2.50,
Tue–Fri 10:00–17:00, Sat–Sun 10:00–13:00, closed Mon). Opposite
the King's House is the **Brewery Museum**, with one room of
old brewing paraphernalia and one room of new (all explained in
Flemish and French). It's pretty lame... but a good excuse for a
beer (€3 including an unnamed local beer, daily 10:00–17:00, sometimes open later July–Sept, Grand Place 10). The **Museum of
Cocoa and Chocolate**, next door, is a delightful concept. But offering a meager set of displays, a second-rate video, a look at a "chocolate master" at work, and a choco-sample for €5, it's way overpriced
(Tue–Sun 10:00–17:00, last entry 16:30, Grand Place 13).

For many, the best thing about La Grand Place is **chocolate**
at Godiva's (to the right as you face the City Museum), Leonidas,
or Galler's (both to the left). Each has an inviting display case
of 20 or so chocolates and sells a minimum of 100 grams—
your choice of six to eight pieces. Most consider Godiva the
very best (handmade, €3.45/100 grams). But most locals sacrifice
10 percent in quality to double their take by getting their fix at
Leonidas (machine-made, €1.25/100 grams, white is their specialty). Galler's chocolate, the royal favorite, rivals Godiva. Only
their display includes English descriptions, so you'll know what
you're enjoying (handmade, €3.25/100 grams).
Manneken-Pis—Brussels is a great city, but its mascot (apparently
symbolizing the city's irreverence) is a statue of a little boy urinating.
For his story, read any postcard stand. It's three short blocks off La
Grand Place, but, for exact directions, I'll let you ask a local, "*Où est
le* Manneken-Pis?" The little squirt may be wearing some clever out-

La Grand Place

1 HOTEL LE MADELEINE	**9**	CAFE A LA BECASSE
2 HOTEL OPERA	**10**	TO CAFE A LA MORT SUBITE
3 HOTEL FLORIS	**11**	GALLER'S CHOCOLATE
4 HOTEL IBIS	**12**	LEONIDAS CHOCOLATE
5 T'KELDERKE REST.	**13**	GODIVA CHOCOLATE
6 REST. LEON	**14**	AD DELHAIZE SUPERMARKET
7 PANOS SANDWICHES	**15**	TO OTHER LISTED HOTELS
8 CAFE LE CIRIO		(SEE BRUSSELS MAP)

fit as costumes are sent to Brussels from around the world. Cases full of these are on display in the City Museum (described above).
Costume and Lace Museum—This is worthwhile only to those who have devoted their lives to the making of lace (€2.50, Mon–Tue and Thu–Fri 10:00–12:30, 13:30–17:00, Sat–Sun 14:00–16:30, closed Wed, Violette 6, a block off La Grand Place, tel. 02-512-7709).
▲▲▲**Museum of Ancient Art and Modern Art**—These are two separate museums, connected by a tunnel and covered by the same ticket (enter either through the main foyer). The Ancient Art museum, featuring Flemish and Belgian art of the 14th to 18th centuries, is packed with a dazzling collection of masterpieces

by Van der Weyden, Breughel, Bosch, and Rubens. Consider the €2.50 *Twenty Masterpieces of the Art of Painting—A Brief Guided Tour* booklet, available in the shop. Tour the rooms of this museum in numerical order (starting with 10). Highlights are room 31—busy with Breughel—and rooms of Rubens (with delightful mini-cartoons used as designs to produce the big canvases).

The Museum of Modern Art gives an easy-to-enjoy walk through the art of the 19th and 20th centuries. Highlights include David's famous neoclassical portrait of Marat (1793; on floor +1, on the Yellow Tour), the stirring Social Realism of the early industrial age, and the surreal fantasies of Rene and Georgette Magritte.

The same ticket covers both museums (€5, Tue–Sun 10:00–17:00, closed Mon, half the rooms close for lunch 12:00–13:00, the other half close 13:00–14:00, last entry 30 min before closing time, decent cafeteria with salad bar, rue de la Regence 3, tel. 02-508-3211).

▲**Belgian Comic Strip Centre**—This strip joint is housed in an industrial warehouse designed by Horta, the local Art Nouveau great. It's free to get inside to visit the brasserie and bookstore. Upstairs in the comics museum, only Belgians get the jokes (€6.20, Tue–Sun 10:00–18:00, closed Mon, rue des Sables 20, tel. 02-219-1980).

Sights—Away from the Center

▲**Park of the Cinquantenaire**—This park sprawls out from under a massive triumphal arch, which was built in 1880 to celebrate the 50th anniversary of Belgian independence. While precious few of the governmental buildings of the European Union (EU) are visually exciting, you can emerge from the Métro's Schuman stop to be surrounded by the political headquarters of a more or less united Europe. The huge, star-shaped Berlaymont Building (built in 1963 to house the Commission of the European Union) was contaminated by asbestos insulation but has just been renovated. From there, walk 10 minutes through the park to the Autoworld and military museums (under giant arch). The next Métro stop (Merode) is closer to the museums.

▲**Autoworld**—Starting with Mr. Benz's motorized tricycle of 1886, you'll walk through a giant hall filled with 400 historic cars. It's well described in English (€5, April–Sept daily 10:00–18:00, Oct–March 10:00–17:00, in Palais Mondial, Parc du Cinquantenaire, Métro: Merode, tel. 02-736-4165).

▲**Royal Museum of the Army and Military History**—Wander through a vast collection of 19th-century weaponry and uniforms and a giant hall dedicated to airplanes of war (free, Tue–Sun 09:00–12:00, 13:00–16:30, closed Mon, tel. 02-737-7811). There's a good display from the Belgian struggle for independence (early 1800s).

Museum of Natural Sciences—Dinosaur enthusiasts come here for the world's largest collection of iguanodon skeletons (€3.75, Tue–Fri 09:30–16:45, Sat–Sun 10:00–18:00, closed Mon, last entry 30 min before closing time, rue Vautier 29, bus #34 from Bourse Stock Exchange, tel. 02-627-4238).

Royal Museum of Central Africa—Remember the Belgian Congo? Brussels has an excellent museum of the Congo and much more of Africa (ethnography, sculptures, jewelry, colonial history, flora, and fauna) an hour from the center. Take Métro 1B to Montgomery and then catch tram #44 to its final stop, Tervuren. From there, walk 200 meters through the park to a palace (€4, Tue–Fri 10:00–17:00, Sat–Sun until 18:00, closed Mon, tel. 02-769-5211).

Antoine Wiertz Museum—This 19th-century artist painted some of the world's largest canvases, with themes from biblical to political (free, 10:00–12:00, 13:00–17:00, closed Mon and every other weekend, rue Vautier 62, bus #34 from Bourse Stock Exchange, tel. 02-648-1718).

Atomium—This giant molecule, with escalators connecting the various "atoms" and a restaurant with a view in the top sphere, was the symbol of the 1958 Universal Exhibition held in Belgium (€5.50, combo-ticket with Mini-Europe-€15, April–Aug daily 09:00–19:30, Sept–March daily 10:00–17:30, Métro: Heysel, tel. 02-474-8977). Today it's the cheesy nucleus of a park on the edge of town that has the kid-pleasing **Mini-Europe**, with 1:25-scale models of 350 famous European landmarks such as Big Ben, the Eiffel Tower, and Venice (€11, combo-ticket with Atomium-€15, March–June and Sept daily 09:30–17:00, July–Aug daily 09:30–19:00, Oct–Feb 10:00–17:00, some weekends in Aug open until 23:00 with fireworks, tel. 02-474-1313).

▲▲**Musical Instruments Museum**—One of Europe's best musical museums is housed in one of Brussels' most impressive Art Nouveau buildings, the newly renovated Old English department store. Inside you'll be given a pair of headphones and set free to wander several levels: folk instruments from around the world on the ground floor, a history of Western musical instruments on the first, and an entire floor devoted to strings and pianos on the second. As you approach an instrument, you hear it playing on your headphones (which actually work, most of the time). The museum is skimpy on English information—except for a €16 visitors' guide—but the music you'll hear is an international language. The sixth floor has a restaurant, terrace, and great view of Brussels (€5, Tue–Fri 09:30–17:00, Thu until 20:00, Sat–Sun 10:00–17:00, closed Mon, last entry 30 min before closing time, concerts every Thu at 20:00, rue Montagne de la Cour 2, just downhill and toward La Grand Place from the art museum, tel. 02-545-0130).

Sleeping in Brussels
(€1.10 = about $1, country code: 32, area code: 02, zip code: 1000)

Sleep Code: **S** = Single, **D** = Double/Twin, **T** = Triple, **Q** = Quad, **b** = bathroom, **s** = shower only, **CC** = Credit Cards accepted, **no CC** = Credit Cards not accepted. Everyone speaks English. Prices include breakfast unless noted otherwise.

Like everything else, hotel prices are high in central Brussels. You have three budget options: modern hostels with double rooms, safe but dingy old places, and business hotels offering summer or weekend specials. April, May, September, and October are very crowded, and finding a room without a reservation can be impossible.

Business Hotels with Summer Rates

The fancy (Db-€125–150) hotels of Brussels survive off the business and diplomatic trade. They are desperately empty in July and August (sometimes June, too) and on weekends (most Fri, Sat, and Sun nights). If you ask for a summer/weekend rate you'll save about a third. If you go through the TI, you'll save up to two-thirds. Four-star hotels in the center abound with summer rates between €62 and €75. If you are willing to sink as low as three stars, you'll probably get a double with enough comforts to keep a diplomat happy, including a fancy breakfast, for as low as €50.

While the TI assured me that every day in July and August there are tons of business-class hotel rooms on the push list, you can book in advance by calling the BTR **room-booking service** (tel. 02-513-7484). You will, however, get an even bigger discount by just showing up at the TI (for same-day booking only). In July and August, I would arrive without a reservation, walk from the Central Station down to the TI, and let them book me a room within a few blocks. These seasonal rates apply only to business-class hotels. Because of this, budget accommodations, which charge the same throughout the year, go from being a good value one day to a bad value the next. I like the first three listings best.

Hotels near La Grand Place

Hôtel Welcome is farthest away from the Grand Place (a 10-min walk) but is the best value. Owned by a bundle of hospitality energy named Meester Smeesters, it offers small but business-class rooms. Each room has a different geographic theme, from India to Japan to Provence (where Brigitte Bardot once slept). With just 10 rooms, it brags it's the smallest hotel in the Brussels city center (prices the same for 1 or 2 people, all rooms with b; 1 smaller "budget" room-€60, larger room-€70, "business-class" room-€80, "executive-class" room-€95, "junior suite" with view-€120, large suite-€130, extra bed-€12, breakfast-€7.50, parking-

€7.50, CC, elevator, airport pickup for a fee, 23 Quai au Bois a Bruler, Métro: Ste. Catherine, tel. 02-219-9546, fax 02-217-1887, www.hotelwelcome.com, run by Sophie and Michael Smeesters). Guests get a 5 percent discount at the pricey attached restaurant, La Truite d'Argent.

Hôtel La Madeleine, on the small square between the station and La Grand Place, is comfortable and hotelesque, with 52 fine rooms (S-€47, no shower at all for this room; Ss-€65, Sb-€85, Db-€93; "executive" rooms: Sb-€100, Db-€105, Tb-€120, CC, elevator, rue de la Montagne 22, tel. 02-513-2973, fax 02-502-1350, www.hotel-la-madeleine.be).

Hôtel Pacific is gently run by Paul Powells, whose motto is "safe, clean, and cheap." While the charming breakfast room is from the 19th century, the ramshackle upstairs feels like a Jackson Pollock thrift shop. Even with the wrinkly linoleum and funky furnishings, Paul gives the place an enjoyable calmness (S-€32, D-€45–50, Ds-€60, T-€75, showers-€2, prices include a cheese-omelet breakfast, no CC, nonsmoking rooms, elevator, 24:00 curfew, easy phone reservations, rue Antoine Dansaert 57, tel. 02-511-8459).

Hôtel Ibis has six locations in or near Brussels; the best is well situated halfway between the Central Station and La Grand Place—a huge modern place offering 184 quiet, simple, industrial-strength-yet-comfy rooms (Db-€125–135, extra person-€12.50, CC, air-con, elevator, smoke-free rooms, Grasmarkt 100, tel. 02-514-4040, fax 02-514-5067, www.ibishotel.com).

Hôtel Opera, on a great people-filled street near the Grand Place, is professional, dark, and classy, with street noise and 49 boxy rooms (Sb-€68, Db-€80–85, Tb-€93, Qb-€107, courtyard rooms are quieter, CC, elevator, Internet access, rue Gretry 53, tel. 02-219-4343, fax 02-219-1720, www.hotel-opera.be, e-mail: hotel.opera@skynet.be).

Hôtel Floris, with wood floors and some beamed ceilings, has 12 spacious rooms just off La Grand Place and right across from the TI (Sb-€75–100, Db-€100–125, Tb-€160–175, 2-person suite-€150–200, third person-€30–62, CC, elevator, rue des Harengs 6-8, tel. 02-514-0760, fax 02-548-9039).

Hostels

Three classy and modern hostels, in buildings that could double as small, state-of-the-art, minimum-security prisons, are within a 10-minute walk of Central Station. Each accepts people of all ages, serves cheap hot meals, takes credit cards, and charges about the same price. All rates include breakfast and showers down the hall. **Breughel Hostel**, a fortress of cleanliness, is handiest and most comfortable. Twenty-two of its rooms are bunk-bed doubles (open 7:00–10:00, 14:00–24:00, S-€20, D-€30, beds in quads-€12.65, beds in bigger dorms-€10.65, sheets-€3.25; nonmembers pay up to €2.50 extra per night, rue de St. Esprit 2, midway between Midi and Central Stations, behind Chapelle church, tel. 02-511-0436, fax 02-512-0711, www.vjh.be, e-mail: brussel@vjh.be). **Sleepwell**, surrounded by high-rise parking lots, is also comfortable (S-€20, D-€14.75 per person, T-€14.25 per person, €9–13 for beds in larger rooms, sheets-€3.25, nonsmoking, 03:00 curfew, laundry nearby, offers Internet access and walking tours-€2.50/person, rue de Damier 23, tel. 02-218-5050, fax 02-218-1313, www. sleepwell.be, e-mail: info@sleepwell.be). **Jacques Brel** is a little farther out but still a reasonable walk from everything (S-€22.50, D-€17.50 per person, T/Q-€14.50 per person, bed in dorm-€12.50, includes breakfast and sheets, no curfew, nonsmoking rooms, laundry available, rue de la Sablonniere 30, tel. 02-218-0187, fax 02-217-2005, www.laj.be, e-mail: brusselsbrel@laj.be).

Eating in Brussels

Eat mussels in Brussels. They're served everywhere. You get a big-enough-for-two bucket and a pile of fries. Use one empty shell to tweeze out the rest of the *moules* (mussels). When the mollusks are in season, from about mid-July through April, you'll get the big Dutch mussels. Locals take a break in May and June, when only the puny Danish kind are available. For an atmospheric cellar just off the Grand Place, step into the **t'Kelderke** (daily 12:00–24:00, La Grand Place 15, tel. 02-513-7344). It serves local specialties, including mussels, a splittable 2-kilo bucket for €15.50). Locals claim the best mussels are served at the touristy **Restaurant Chez Leon**, which offers a small "Formula Leon" €12.25-*menu* of a small bucket, fries, and a beer (daily 12:00–23:00, rue des Bouchers 18, tel. 02-511-1415).

Brussels' **restaurant streets** are touristy but fun (exit left from TI on rue Marché-aux-Herbes and take the first right). Many of these restaurants take advantage of tourists by tacking on extra charges.

Looking for a good place to enjoy that famous Belgian beer? Brussels is full of atmospheric cafés to savor. Across from the Borse, **Le Cirio**'s dark wooden tables boast the skid marks of over a century's worth of beer steins (rue de la Bourse 18-20, tel. 02-512-1395). Just around the corner towards the Grand Place, hidden away at the end of a courtyard, the lower-profile **A la Becasse** is a favorite of local students (enter at rue de Tabora 11, tel. 02-511-0006). Beyond the restaurant streets, visit **A la Mort Subite** and ponder whether the mustard-yellow walls got that way because of paint—or time (rue Montagne-aux-Herbes Potageres 7, tel. 02-513-1318).

If Brussels puts you in an Art Nouveau mood, have a meal or coffee at the city's most atmospheric hangout, **De Ultieme**

Hallucinatie (exotic €10–19 meals, Mon–Fri 11:00–24:00, Sat from 16:00, closed Sun, beautiful patio, rue Royale 316, tel. 02-217-0614).

You'll find *frites* (French fries) and sandwich shops throughout Brussels. **Panos** has good, cheap sandwiches (on Grasmarkt, across from entrance of Galleries Royales St. Hubert).

Two **supermarkets** are about a block from the Bourse Stock Exchange and a few blocks from La Grand Place. The **AD Delhaize** is at the intersection of Anspachlan and Marché-aux-Poulets (Mon–Sat 09:00–20:00, Fri until 21:00, Sun 09:00–18:00), and the **Super GB** is a half block away at Halles and Marché-aux-Poulets (Mon–Sat 09:00–20:00, Fri until 21:00, closed Sun).

Transportation Connections—Brussels

By train to: Bruges (2/hr, 1 hr, from Central, Midi, and Nord stations), **Amsterdam** (hrly, 3 hrs, from Central, Midi, or Nord, sometimes from just one but sometimes all three), **Berlin** (7/day, 7.5–8 hrs, from Central or Midi, transfer in Köln, 9-hr direct night train from Midi), **Bern** (5/day, 8–9.5 hrs, from Central, Midi, or Nord with complicated transfers; consider the direct 8.5-hr night train from Nord), **Frankfurt** (9/day, 5.5 hrs, from Midi; or Central, Midi, and Nord, transfer in Köln), **Munich** (9/day, 8.5–9.5 hrs, from Central, Midi, and Nord, most transfer in Köln and sometimes also Mannheim), **Rome** (3/day, 17 hrs, from Nord, transfer in Milan, Zurich, or Paris), **Paris** (fast trains zip to Paris—hrly, 90 min, from Midi—it's best to book by 20:00 the day before or risk limited availability on same day; even railpass holders need to pay the supplement of €11/second class, €21/first class. Every day there are two slow, no-supplement trains leaving Brussels Midi for Paris: the 17:11 departure takes 4.5 hours and requires transfer in Charleroi Sud, the night departure at 1:30 is direct and takes 5.5 hrs; confirm schedule at station). Train info: tel. 02-528-2828 (long wait).

To London: Brussels and London are just three hours apart by Eurostar train (10/day, under the English Channel in 20 min). For the latest prices, call U.S. tel. 800/EUROSTAR or Belgian tel. 0900-10366, or visit www.raileurope.com or www.eurostar .co.uk (you can order online at either site). In 2001, "full-fare" tickets cost $279 for first class and $199 for second class. Full-fare tickets are exchangeable and fully refundable even after your departure date. The cheaper "Leisure" tickets cost $219 for first class and $139 for second class; these are nonrefundable but exchangeable up to three days before departure. Railpass holders get discounts. Cheaper 7- and 14-day advance-purchase tickets are usually available if you order your ticket in Europe (can call from home). To order your ticket in Belgium by phone, call 0900-10177 (expensive toll line costs €0.50/min from pay phone and €1.50/min from hotel); you can either pay with a credit card or simply reserve a seat (and pay at the station at least an hour before the train leaves).

You can also buy your Eurostar tickets in the United States (tel. 800/EUROSTAR) or at any major train station in Europe. If you buy tickets in person in Belgium, go to a major train station rather than a travel agency; you'll get your tickets immediately (travel agencies can't deliver until the next day).

Another option is the slooooow train and ferry combination (8/day, 4.5–7.5 hrs). Or save a little money by riding a Eurolines bus ($46 one-way, $71 round-trip, tel. 02-203-0707 in Brussels).

By plane: Virgin Express flies cheap between Brussels and London (hrly, starting at $72), Milan, Rome, Nice, Barcelona, Madrid, Ireland, and Copenhagen (Belgian tel. 02-752-0505, www.virgin-express.com). Airport info: tel. 0900-70000.

THE NETHERLANDS

- 22,400 square kilometers (14,000 square miles), a little larger than Maryland
- 15 million people (670 per square kilometer; 15 times the population density of the United States)
- €1.10 = $1

The Netherlands, Europe's most densely populated country, is also one of its wealthiest and best organized. A generation ago, Belgium, the Netherlands, and Luxembourg formed the nucleus of a united Europe when they joined economically to form BeNeLux.

Efficiency is a local custom. The average income is higher than that in the United States. Though only 8 percent of the labor force is made up of farmers, they cultivate 70 percent of the land, and you'll travel through vast fields of barley, wheat, sugar beets, potatoes, and flowers.

"Holland" is just a nickname for the Netherlands. North Holland and South Holland are the largest of the 12 states that make up the Netherlands. The word Netherlands means

"lowlands." Half the country is below sea level, reclaimed from the sea (or rivers). That's why the locals say, "God made the Earth, but the Dutch made Holland." Modern technology and plenty of Dutch elbow grease have turned much of the sea into fertile farmland. While a new, 12th state—Flevoland, near Amsterdam—has recently been drained, dried, and populated, Dutch reclamation projects are essentially finished.

The Dutch generally can speak English, pride themselves on their frankness, and like to split the bill. Traditionally, Dutch cities have been open-minded, loose, and liberal (to attract sailors in the days of Henry Hudson). And today, Amsterdam is a capital of alternative lifestyles—a city where "victimless crime" is a contradiction in itself. While freewheeling Amsterdam does have a quiet side, many travelers enjoy more sedate Dutch evenings by sleeping in a small town nearby and side-tripping into the big city.

The country is so small, level, and well covered by trains and buses that transportation is a snap. Major cities are connected by speedy trains that come and go every 10 or 15 minutes. Connections are excellent, and you'll rarely wait more than a few minutes. Round-trip tickets are discounted. Buses take you where trains don't, and bicycles take you where buses don't. Bus stations and bike-rental shops cluster around train stations. The national bus system, both within and between cities, runs on a uniform "strip card" system (though single-ride tickets are also available). You can buy various strip cards on the bus or more cheaply (15 strip card, €5.75) at train stations, post offices, and some tobacco shops. If you're caught riding without a card, you have to take off your clothes.

Holland is a biker's dream. The Dutch, who average four bikes per family, have put small bike roads (with their own traffic lights) beside every big auto route. You can rent bikes at most train stations and drop them off at most others. (And you can take bikes on trains, outside of rush hour, for €4.75.)

Smaller shops are open from 9:00 to 18:00 and until 21:00 on Thursdays (closed Sun). Larger stores and supermarkets are open weekdays from 8:00 to 20:00 and until 17:00 on Saturdays (closed Sun). The businesslike Dutch know no siesta, but many shopkeepers take Monday mornings off.

The best "Dutch" food is Indonesian (from the former colony). Find any Indisch restaurant and experience a *rijsttafel* ("rice table"). With as many as 30 spicy dishes, a rijsttafel can be split and still fill two hungry tourists. *Nasi rames* is a cheaper, smaller version of a rijsttafel. Local taste treats are cheese, pancakes (*pannenkoeken*), Dutch gin (*jenever*, pronounced "ya nayver"), light pilsner beer, and "syrup waffles" (*stroopwafel*). Yogurt in the Netherlands (and throughout northern Europe) is delicious and drinkable right out of its plastic container. *Broodjes* are sandwiches of fresh bread and delicious cheese—cheap at snack bars, delis, and *broodje* restaurants. For cheap fast food, try a Middle Eastern *shwarma*, roasted lamb in pita bread. Breakfasts are big by continental standards. Lunch and dinner are served at American times.

Experiences you owe your tongue in Holland: a raw herring (outdoor herring stands are all over), lingering over coffee in a "brown café," an old *jenever* with a new friend, and a giant *rijsttafel*. Tipping is not expected, but locals round the bill up (not more than 5 percent) as thanks for good service.

AMSTERDAM

Amsterdam is a progressive way of life housed in Europe's most 17th-century city. Physically, it's a city built upon millions of pilings. But, more than that, it's a city built on good living, cozy cafés, great art, street-corner jazz, stately history, and a spirit of live and let live. It has 800,000 people and as many bikes. It also has more canals than Venice and as many tourists. While Amsterdam may box your Puritan ears, this great, historic city is an experiment in freedom.

Planning Your Time

While I'd sleep in nearby Haarlem, Amsterdam is worth a full day of sightseeing on even the busiest itinerary. While the city has a couple of must-see museums, its best sight is its own breezy ambience. The city's a joy on foot. It's a breezier and faster joy by bike. And the sights are conveniently laced together by circular tram #20. Here are the essential stops for a day in Amsterdam:

Start the day with a circular orientation tour on tram #20 (described below). Break this morning overview with a stop at the city's two great art museums: the Van Gogh and the Rijksmuseum (cafeteria lunch). Because of a huge special exhibit at the Van Gogh Museum, those visiting before June 2, 2002, will need a reservation with an entry time in order to get into this museum (explained below).

After the museums, if you have limited time, you can pick up tram #20 where you got off and complete the circle back to the station.

With more time, walk from the museums to Spui via Leidsestraat. Spend midafternoon taking a relaxing hour-long canal cruise from the dock at Spui. Near Spui, consider seeing the peaceful

Begijnhof, Amsterdam Historical Museum, and flower market.

Visiting the Anne Frank House after 18:00 (it's open until 21:00) will save you an hour in line.

On a balmy evening, Amsterdam has a Greek-island ambience. Wander the Jordaan for the idyllic side of town and wander down Leidsestraat to Leidseplein for the roaring café and people scene. Wander the Red-Light District while you're at it.

With extra time: With two days in Holland, I'd side-trip by bike, bus, or train to an open-air folk museum and visit Edam or Haarlem. With a third day, I'd do the other great Amsterdam museums. With four days, I'd do the "historic triangle" of Enkhuizen, Hoorn, and Medemblik, or visit The Hague (for details, see "Sights— Near Haarlem and Amsterdam," in the next chapter).

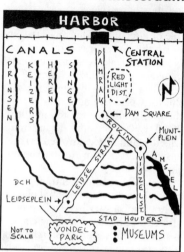

Orientation (area code: 020)

Amsterdam's central train station is your starting point (TI, bike rental, and trams—including #20—fanning out to all points). Damrak is the main street axis, connecting the station with Dam Square (people watching and hangout center) and its Royal Palace. From this spine, the city spreads out like a fan, with 90 islands, hundreds of bridges, and a series of concentric canals (named "Prince's," "Gentleman's," and "King's") laid out in the 17th century, Holland's Golden Age. Amsterdam's major sights are within walking distance of Dam Square.

Tourist Information

Avoid Amsterdam's inefficient VVV offices if you can ("VVV" is Dutch for tourist information office; TI inside train station open Mon–Sat 08:00–20:00, Sun 09:00–17:00). Most people wait 30 min-utes just to pick up information brochures and get a room. At the VVV in front of the station (daily 09:00–17:00), avoid this line by studying the display of publications for sale and going straight to the sales desk (where everyone ends up anyway, since any information of substance will cost you). Consider buying a city map (€2), *Day by*

Day entertainment calendar (€1.25), and any of the €1 walking-tour brochures (*Discovery Tour through the Center, The Former Jewish Quarter, Walks through Jordaan*). The Amsterdam Pass, offering free or discounted admissions to some sights and boat rides, isn't worth the clutter or cost (€29, doesn't include Anne Frank House). Nor does it make sense to stand in line at the VVV to buy prepaid same-cost admissions to various Amsterdam sights.

The TI on Leidsestraat is less crowded (daily 09:00–17:00). But for €0.50 a minute, you can save yourself a trip by calling the tourist information toll line at 0900-400-4040 (Mon–Fri 09:00–17:00). If you're staying in nearby Haarlem, use the helpful, friendly, and rarely crowded Haarlem TI (see next chapter) to answer most of your Amsterdam questions and provide you with the brochures.

At Amsterdam's Central Station, **GWK Change** has two hotel reservations windows that sell phone cards and cheaper city maps (€1.60) and answer basic tourist questions with shorter lines. They also change money, including coins, for a hefty €2.25 fee (one office is at track 4/5, the other is in the west tunnel at the right end of the station as you leave the platform, tel. 020/627-2731).

Don't use the TI (or GWK) to book a room; you'll pay €2.25 and your host loses the 13 percent deposit. The phone system is easy, everyone speaks English, and the listings in this book are a better value than the potluck booking you'd be charged for at the TI.

Helpful Hints

Theft Alert: Tourists are considered green and rich, and the city has more than its share of hungry thieves—especially on trams. Wear your money belt.

Street Smarts: A *plein* is a square, *gracht* means canal, and most canals are lined by streets with the same name.

Shop Hours: Many shops close all day Sunday and Monday morning.

Telephones: Calling the United States from a phone booth is now very cheap—you'll get about five minutes for a dollar. Handy telephone cards (€4.50, €11.50, or €23) are sold at TIs, the GVB public-transit office (in front of station), tobacco shops, post offices, and train stations.

Happy Birthday: On the Queen's Birthday on April 30, Amsterdam turns into a gigantic garage sale/street market.

Internet Access: It's easy at cafés all over town. The Internet Café is a couple blocks from the station and is open until the wee hours (20 min free with each drink you buy, Sun–Thu 09:00–24:00, Fri–Sat 09:00–03:00, must buy at least 1 beverage, Martelaarsgracht 11, tel. 020/627-1052). A monstrous Internet café, easyEverything, has several hundred computers and cheap access (daily 24 hrs, at Damrak 33, across the bridge and then a block in front of the station, and another branch at Reguliersbreestraat 22, next to Rembrandtplein). "Coffee shops" (which sell marijuana) also offer Internet access, letting you surf the Net with a special bravado.

Arrival in Amsterdam

By Train: Amsterdam swings, and the hinge that connects it to the world is its perfectly central Central Station. Walk out the door, and you're in the heart of the city. You'll nearly trip over trams ready to take you anywhere your feet won't. Straight ahead is Damrak Street, leading to Dam Square. With your back to the entrance of the station, the TI and GVB public-transit offices and circular tram #20A are just ahead and to your left. And on your right is a vast, multistoried "bike garage."

By Plane: From Schiphol Airport, take the train to Amsterdam (6/hr, 20 min, €3). If you're staying in Haarlem, take a direct express bus to Haarlem (#236 or #362, 2/hr, 30 min, €3.25).

Getting around Amsterdam

The helpful GVB transit-information office is next to the TI. Its free multilingual *Public Transport Amsterdam Tourist Guide* includes a transit map and explains ticket options and tram connections to all the sights.

By Bus, Tram, and Métro: Individual tickets cost €1.50 and give you an hour on the buses, trams, and Métro system (on trams and buses pay as you board; buy Métro tickets from machines). **Strip cards** are cheaper than individual tickets. Any downtown bus or tram ride costs two strips (good for 1 hr of transfers). A card with 15 strips costs €5.75 at the GVB public-transit office, train stations, post offices, airport, or tobacco shops throughout the country; shorter strip tickets (2, 3, and 8 strips) are also sold on some buses and trams. Strip cards are good on buses all over the Netherlands (e.g., 6 strips for Haarlem to the airport), and you can share them with your partner. A €5 **Day Card** gives you unlimited transportation on the buses and Métro for a day in Amsterdam; you'll almost break even if you take three trips (valid until 06:00 the following morning; buy as you board or at the GVB public-transit office, which also sells a better-value 2-day version for €8; sometimes costs €0.50 more if you buy it on board). If you get lost in Amsterdam, 10 of the city's 17 trams take you back to the central train station.

By Foot: The longest walk a tourist would take is 45 minutes from the station to the Rijksmuseum. Watch out for silent but potentially painful bikes, trams, and crotch-high curb posts.

By Bike: One-speed bikes, with "brrringing" bells and two locks (use them both; bike thieves are bold and brazen here), rent for €5.75 per day at the central train station (daily 08:00–22:00, €91 deposit or your credit-card imprint and passport required;

as you exit the station go left, then down the ramp; at east end of station; tel. 020/624-8391). In the summer, arrive early or make a telephone reservation (they hold bikes until 11:00). If the station has rented all its bikes, walk 10 minutes to Rent-a-Bike Damstraat near Dam Square (€7/day, daily 09:00–18:00, deposit of €22.75 plus I.D., or a credit-card imprint, just down alley that begins at Damstraat 20, tel. 020/625-5029).

By Boat: While the city is great on foot or bike, there is a "Museum Boat" with an all-day ticket that shuttles tourists from sight to sight. Tickets cost €12.50 (with discounts to sights worth about €2.25). The sales booths in front of the central train station (and the boats) offer handy free brochures with museum times and admission prices. The narrated ride takes 90 minutes if you don't get off (every 30 min in summer, every 45 min off-season, 6 stops, live quadrilingual guide, departures 10:00–17:00, discounted after 13:00 to €10.25, tel. 020/530-1090). A similar "Canal Bus" is nearby. If you're looking for a floating nonstop tour, the real canal tour boats (without the stops) give more information, cover more ground, and cost less (see "Tours of Amsterdam," below).

By Taxi: Amsterdam's taxis are expensive (€2.75 drop and €1.40 for each kilometer). Given the fine tram system, taxis are only a good value for airport connections (Schiphol Airport to Amsterdam costs €27.25).

By Car: Forget it—frustrating one-ways, terrible parking.

Circle Tram #20 Orientation Tour

If this is still running in 2002 (light use is threatening its existence), Amsterdam's Circle Tram #20 offers a great one-hour, self-guided tour for €1.50. Catch this designed-for-tourists circle route at the train station. Board #20A (not #20B) from tram lane (or *spoor*) #2 on the left as you leave the station. The free tourist guidebooklet—there's a stack on the desk in the transit office 50 meters away—comes with a route map and lists each stop. Tram #20 runs daily every 10 minutes from 09:00 to 18:00 only.

0. Train Station: Leaving the station, you pass both the canal bus and museum boat docks (left). The *Rondvaart* sign (right) means round-trip. Boats like these all over town offer similar one-hour city tours. Gliding up the tacky commercial cancan called the Damrak (which was once the Amstel River), you're following the same route taken by boats loaded with spices and goodies from the East Indies in the city's early trading days. The buildings across the water are Amsterdam's oldest. Behind them are the Red-Light District and the old sailor's quarter. The huge redbrick Beurs building (left) is the Dutch stock exchange.

1. Dam Square: This is the city center, where the original dam was built across the Amstel River, giving the town its name. To your right is the Royal Palace (1655); next to it is the New

Amsterdam

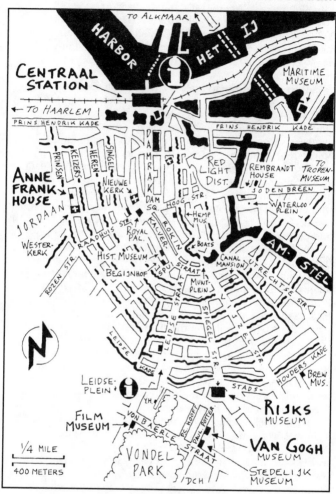

Church, the coronation church of Dutch royalty. To your left is the World War I Memorial, now becoming a generic peace memorial; behind that is a strip of head shops. Straight ahead is one of many diamond-polishing centers. Beyond Dam Square, you continue down Rokin. Parallel and a block to the right is the bustling Kalverstraat pedestrian shopping mall.

2. Spui Square: This marked the end of the city in the 14th century. Spui (rhymes with cow) is near the Begijnhof and the University of Amsterdam's archaeology museum, which has a fine Egyptian collection.

3. Muntplein: This lively area is marked by the Mint Tower from 1620 (on the right). Behind that, a charming flower market lines the Singel Canal (see the row of greenhouses, thriving Mon–Sat 09:00–17:00). Turning left you enter a noisy neon nightlife center.

4. Rembrandtplein: Look for Rembrandt's statue in the leafy park (right). This is the center of gay Amsterdam; you'll pass lots of discos and a Planet Hollywood. A bridge will take you over the Amstel River. The modern brown-and-white building (left) is City Hall. Adjacent is the round Opera House. Notice the charming counterbalance bridges (right).

5. Waterlooplein: This is famous for its flea market (daily except Sun, on left). The Jewish Quarter (right) features the impressive Jewish History Museum (renovated brick synagogues with blue-and-white banner). Crossing the bridge (funny paintings revealed when opened), you enter green Amsterdam (gardens and hothouses of University of Amsterdam all around, zoo nearby).

6. Plantage Kerklaan: Immediately to the right of this tram stop, the white facade of the old Dutch Theater (Hollandsche Schouwburg) survives. Used by Nazis as a holding zone for Jews being deported, today it's a memorial. The Dutch Resistance Museum and the zoo are half a block to the left. Passing through many University of Amsterdam buildings, notice the "XXX" symbol of the city (the three Xs stand for the adversities that Amsterdammers have overcome throughout their history: fire, plague, and floods). Crossing the Amstel River again, see the City Hall and the Opera House again in the distance (right), the palatial Amstel Hotel (behind on the left), and, farther off, Holland's tallest skyscraper—the Philips Electronics corporate headquarters.

7. Frederiksplein: Notice the houseboats; they're a common sight in Amsterdam. Also in Frederiksplein, you'll see the huge Albert Cuyp Market. Perhaps the town's most interesting market, it shows off Amsterdam's ethnic mix daily except Sunday. Now, passing through a nondescript area, notice how the city works: Shops at street level—with homes above—keep neighborhoods vital, people friendly, and safe. Bike lanes even have their own little traffic lights. New buildings still lean out and come with planks and pulleys for hoisting furniture past too-narrow stairways. Many of these are brick and built in the Art Deco "Amsterdam School" from the 1920s—a time when architects considered entire blocks as integrated works of art. Notice street signs with the district listed. You're in the *oud-zuid* (old south) quarter. Mail slots have green and orange decals saying yes or no to junk mail. And now public phone booths stand next to curbside computers for Internet access (locals use prepaid "chip cards"—the first step toward the cash-free society of the future—to access things such as these).

8. Museumplein: A huge park (right) leads to the grand, redbrick Rijksmuseum (built in 1885 by the same guy who designed Central Station). The new addition to the Van Gogh Museum juts into the park in the foreground. The Concertgebouw (on the left) is Amsterdam's main concert hall. A huge underground parking lot keeps things uncluttered.

9. Van Baerlestraat: Rounding the corner, you stop at the Stedelijk Modern Art Museum (right) and the Van Gogh Museum (see crowd on right). An ice rink (right) faces the Coster Diamond House (left).

10. Hobbemastraat: This is the stop for the Rijksmuseum (right). A fancy gate marks the entrance to the sprawling, in-love-with-life Vondelpark (left). Pass a casino (right) as you cross a canal and enter the noisy, people-filled Leidseplein area.

11. Leidseplein: Your tram just skirts Amsterdam's liveliest café, people watching, and entertainment district. Be sure to loiter in Leidseplein later on. The huge modern parking lot (Texaco station, left) marks the line between the protected old town (right) and the anything-goes new one (left). Turning right you cut through the proud, fashionable, and trendy Jordaan district. Ahead stands the much-loved tallest church spire in town, marking the Westerkerk (West Church). Anne Frank hid out just down the street. As you continue ahead, the canal system is evident as you cross the Prinsen (prince's), Keizers (king's), Herren (gentlemen's, actually medieval business fat cats), and Singel Canals and head toward the back side of the Royal Palace we saw at Dam Square. Hop out here or glide back to your starting point at the Central Station.

Sights—Amsterdam's Museum Neighborhood

▲▲▲**Rijksmuseum**—Built to house the nation's greatest art, the Rijksmuseum packs several thousand paintings into 200 rooms. To survive, focus on the Dutch masters: Rembrandt, Hals, Vermeer, and Steen. For a list of the top 20 paintings, pick up the cheap €.50 leaflet *A Tour of the Golden Age* and plan your attack (or follow the self-guided tour, one of 25, in my *Mona Winks* guidebook, written with Gene Openshaw). Audioguide tours are available, allowing you to dial up descriptions of over 200 paintings (€4).

Follow the museum's chronological layout to see painting evolve from narrative religious art, to religious art, to the Golden Age, when secular art dominated. With no local church or royalty to commission big canvases in the post-1648 Protestant Dutch republic, artists had to find different patrons. They specialized in portraits of the wealthy city class (Hals), pretty still lifes (Claesz), and nonpreachy slice-of-life art (Steen). The museum has four quietly wonderful Vermeers. And, of course, a thoughtful brown soup of Rembrandt, including *The Night Watch*. Works by Rembrandt show his excellence as a portraitist for hire (*De Staalmeesters*) and offer some powerful psychological studies, such as *St. Peter's Denial*—with a betrayed Jesus in the murky background (€8, daily 10:00–17:00, great bookshop, decent cafeteria, tram #2, #5, or #20 from station, Stadhouderskade 42, tel. 020/674-7000).

▲▲▲**Van Gogh Museum**—Near the Rijksmuseum, this outstanding and user-friendly museum houses the 200 paintings owned by Vincent's younger brother Theo. It's a stroll through a beautifully displayed garden of van Gogh's work and life. While the main floor dominates, don't miss the top two floors (€7.25, daily 10:00–18:00, Paulus Potterstraat 7, www.vangoghmuseum.nl, tel. 020/570-5200). The museum also focuses on the late-19th-century art that influenced van Gogh (much of which happened to be in his brother Theo's collection). The new exhibition hall (usually included with admission) features temporary art exhibits from 1840 to 1920. The €4 audioguide includes insightful commentaries about van Gogh's paintings, along with related quotations from Vincent himself. *Note that until June 2, 2002, this museum is only open by appointment as the special van Gogh and Gauguin Exhibition takes it over (see details below).*

▲▲▲**Van Gogh and Gauguin Exhibition (Feb 9–June 2, 2002)**—The Van Gogh Museum hosts a major exhibition examining the personal and artistic development of van Gogh and Gauguin. With 120 works from 65 lenders from around the world assembled in the museum's exhibition wing, art lovers are able to explore the intense and almost legendary relationship of these two artists like never before. The climax of the exhibition is the work they produced during their short but turbulent collaboration at the Yellow House in Arles, France, in late 1888. Together they evolved ambitious plans to reinvigorate modern art through what van Gogh called a "Studio of the South." Ultimately, the alliance couldn't survive their philosophical differences. Van Gogh wanted to paint what he saw and show the actual process of painting. Gauguin wanted the painter's technique to remain unnoticed while portraying things beyond what the eye could see. This philosophical debate got physical, culminating in the famous argument in which van Gogh threatened his friend with a razor and then cut off a piece of his own ear. Anticipating huge crowds, the museum is selling tickets with admission time blocks. Visitors can only enter with a reservation and within the time block assigned. Once inside, they can stay as long as they like. Since only a few tickets are available at the museum, assure your entry by getting tickets in advance at www.vangoghgauguin.com or in Amsterdam at Uit Buro (Leidseplein 26), VVV Ticketpoints, or Tracks Multitronics (at Schiphol Airport). For more information, see the above Web site. During this special exhibition, the museum costs more (€13, includes audio-guide) and is open longer (Tue–Wed and Fri–Sun 09:00–21:00, Mon and Thu 09:00–18:00). If crowds are huge, a reservation several days in advance will be necessary. If crowds are moderate, you can drop by the ticket window and get a time that same day. Do this early in the day and plan to visit the Rijksmuseum if you need to kill a couple of hours.

Stedelijk Modern Art Museum—Next to the Van Gogh Museum, this place is fun, far-out, and refreshing. It has mostly post-1945 art but also a sometimes-outstanding collection of Monet, van Gogh, Cézanne, Picasso, and Chagall, and a lot of special exhibitions (€4.50, daily 11:00–17:00, tel. 020/573-2737).

Sights—Near Dam Square

▲▲**Anne Frank House**—A pilgrimage for many, this house offers a fascinating look at the hideaway of young Anne during the Nazi occupation of the Netherlands during World War II. Pick up the English pamphlet at the door. Recently expanded, the exhibit now offers more thorough coverage of the Frank family, the diary, the stories of others who hid, and the Holocaust. Why do thousands endure hour-long daytime lines when they can walk right in by arriving after 18:00? Last entrance is 20:30. Visit after dinner (€6.50, April–Aug daily 09:00–21:00, Sept–March daily 09:00–19:00, Prinsengracht 263, near Westerkerk church, tel. 020/556-7100, www.annefrank.nl). For an interesting glimpse of Holland under the Nazis, rent the powerful movie *Soldier of Orange* before you leave home.

Westerkerk—Near the Anne Frank House, this landmark church has a barren interior, Rembrandt somewhere under the pews, and Amsterdam's tallest steeple. It's worth climbing for the view (€1.40, ascend only with a guide, departures on the hour, April–Sept Mon–Sat 10:00–17:00, last trip at 16:00, closed Sun and in winter, tel. 020/612-6856).

Royal Palace (Koninklijk Paleis)—The palace, right on Dam Square, was built as a lavish city hall for Amsterdam, when the country was a proud new Dutch Republic and Amsterdam was awash in profit from trade. When constructed (around 1660), this building was one of Europe's finest. Today it's the official (but not actual) residence of the Queen and has a sumptuous interior (€4.50, €2.25 audioguide, June–Aug daily 11:00–17:00, Sept daily 12:30–17:00, closed off-season, tel. 020/624-8698).

▲**Begijnhof**—Stepping into this tiny, idyllic courtyard in the city center, you escape into the charm of old Amsterdam. Notice house #34, a 500-year-old wooden structure (rare since repeated fires taught city fathers a trick called brick). Peek into the "hidden" Catholic church, dating from the time when post-Reformation Dutch Catholics couldn't worship in public. It's opposite the

English Reformed church, where the Pilgrims worshiped while waiting for their voyage to the New World (marked by a plaque near the door). Be considerate of the people who live around the courtyard (free, daily 10:00–17:00, on Begijnensteeg Lane, just off Kalverstraat between #130 and #132, pick up flier at office near entrance, open weekdays 10:00–16:00).

Amsterdam Historical Museum—Offering the town's best look into the age of the Dutch masters, this creative and hardworking museum features Rembrandt's paintings, fine English descriptions, and a carillon loft. The loft comes with push-button recordings of the town bell tower's greatest hits and a self-serve carillon "keyboard" to ring a few bells yourself (€6.50, Mon–Fri 10:00–17:00, Sat–Sun 11:00–17:00, good-value restaurant, next to Begijnhof, Kalverstraat 92, tel. 020/523-1822). Its free pedestrian corridor—lined with old-time group portraits—is a powerful teaser.

Sights—East Amsterdam

To reach these sights from the train station, take tram #9, #14, or #20. The first six sights listed make an interesting walk.

▲**Rembrandt's House**—Rembrandt's reconstructed house is filled with exactly what his bankruptcy inventory of 1656 said he owned. You'll find no paintings but 65 of his etchings and a workshop with demonstrations (€7, Mon–Sat 10:00–17:00, Sun 13:00–17:00, 10-min English video explains reconstruction of home, Jodenbreestraat 4, tel. 020/520-0400).

Holland Experience—Bragging "Experience Holland in 30 minutes," this show takes you traveling with three clowns through an idealized montage of Dutch clichés. There are no words but lots of images and special effects as you rock with the boat and get spritzed with perfume while viewing the tulips (€8, 2 enter for price of 1 with this book, or show this book and get €1.25 off the €11.50 combo Rembrandt's House/Experience ticket, daily 10:00–18:00, Jodenbreestraat 8, near Rembrandt's House and Waterlooplein street market, Métro: Waterlooplein, tel. 020/422-2233. www.holland-experience.nl). The men's urinal is a trip to the beach. Plan for it.

Waterlooplein Flea Market—For over a hundred years, the Jewish Quarter flea market has raged daily except Sunday behind the Rembrandt House.

▲**Jewish History Museum**—Four historic synagogues have been joined by steel and glass to make one modern complex telling the story of the Jews in Amsterdam through the centuries (€4.50, daily 11:00–17:00, good kosher café, Jonas Daniel Meijerplein 2, tel. 020/626-9945).

▲**Dutch Theatre (Hollandsche Schouwburg)**—This is a moving memorial. Once a great theater in the Jewish neighborhood, this was used as an assembly hall for local Jews destined for Nazi

Central Amsterdam

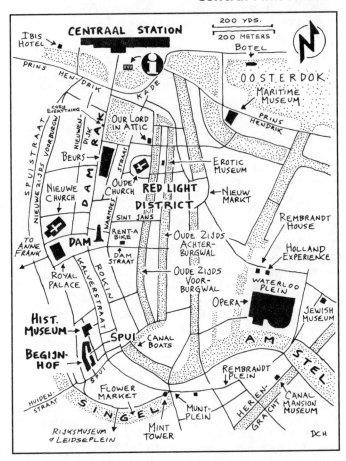

concentration camps. On the wall, 6,700 family names pay tribute to the 104,000 Jews deported and killed by the Nazis. Upstairs is a small history exhibit on Jews here during World War II. Otherwise, there's little to actually see but plenty to think about (free, daily 11:00–16:00, Plantage Middenlaan 24, tel. 020/626-9945).

▲▲**Dutch Resistance Museum (Verzetsmuseum)**—This is an impressive look at how the Dutch resisted their Nazi occupiers from 1940 to 1945. You'll see propaganda movie clips, study forged ID cards under a magnifying glass, and read of ingenious, clever, and courageous efforts to hide local Jews from the Germans. And at the end of the war, Nazi helmets were turned into bedpans (€4.50, Tue–Fri 10:00–17:00, Sat–Mon 12:00–17:00, closed April 30, well described in English, café, tram #9 or #20A from station, Plantage Kerklaan 61, tel. 020/620-2535). Amsterdam's famous zoo is just across the street.

▲**Tropenmuseum (Tropical Museum)**—As close to the Third World as you'll get without lots of vaccinations, this imaginative museum offers wonderful re-creations of tropical-life scenes and explanations of Third World problems (€7, daily 10:00–17:00, tram #9 to Linnaeusstraat 2, tel. 020/568-8215).

Netherlands Maritime (Scheepvaart) Museum—This huge collection of model ships, maps, and sea-battle paintings fills the 300-year-old Dutch Navy Arsenal. Given the Dutch seafaring heritage, I expected a more interesting museum. Sailors may disagree, but—even with its recreation of an 18th-century Dutch East India Company ship manned with characters in old costumes—I found the place pretty lifeless (€6.75, daily 10:00–17:00, closed Mon off-season, English explanations, don't waste your time with 30-min movie, bus #22 or #32 to Kattenburgerplein 1, tel. 020/523-2222).

Sights—Red-Light District

▲**Our Lord in the Attic (Amstelkring)**—Near the station, in the Red-Light District, you'll find a fascinating hidden Catholic church (1661) filling the attic of a hollowed-out row of 17th-century merchants' houses (€4.50, Mon–Sat 10:00–17:00, Sun 13:00–17:00, Oudezijds Voorburgwal 40, tel. 020/624-6604).

▲**Red-Light District**—Europe's most touristed ladies of the night shiver and shimmy as they have since 1700 in 450 display-case windows between the Oudezijds Achterburgwal and Oudezijds Voorburgwal, surrounding the Oude Kerk (Old Church). Druggies make the streets uncomfortable late at night, but it's a fascinating walk at any other time after noon.

The neighborhood, one of Amsterdam's oldest, has had prostitutes since 1200. Back then they were run by the sheriff and his men. Prostitution is entirely legal here and woman are generally entrepreneurs, renting a space and running their own business. Women typically rent their space for eight-hour shifts for about €60 a day. Popular prostitutes make €300 a day (S&F, €34–45), fill out tax returns, and many belong to a loose union called the Red Thread. Rather than pimps, prostitutes are protected by the law. Each one has a buzzer. If she needs help, she rings this to call the police.

The Prostitution Information Center welcomes visitors. They have a map showing exactly where prostitution is legal and print a small and frank booklet answering most common questions tourists have about Amsterdam's Red-Light District (free, Tue, Wed, Fri, and Sat 11:30–19:30, facing Old Church at Enge Kerksteeg 3, www.pic-amsterdam.com).

Amsterdam has two **sex museums**, one in the Red-Light District and one a block in front of the train station on Damrak. While visiting one can be called sightseeing, visiting both is hard to explain. Here's a comparison:

The Red-Light District sex museum is less offensive, with five sparsely decorated rooms relying heavily on badly dressed dummies acting out the roles that women of the neighborhood play. It also has videos, phone-sex phones, and a lot of uninspired paintings, old photos, and sculpture (€2.25, daily 11:00–24:00, along the canal at Oudezijds Achterburgwal 54).

The Damrak sex museum goes deeper and has more rooms. It tells the story of pornography from Roman times through 1960. Every sexual deviation is uncovered in its various displays, and the nude and pornographic art is a cut above that of the other sex museum. Also interesting are the early French pornographic photos and memorabilia from Europe, India, and Asia. You'll find a Marilyn Monroe tribute and some S&M displays, too (€2.25, daily 10:00–23:30, Damrak 18, a block in front of station).

More Sights—Amsterdam

▲**Herengracht Canal Mansion (Willet Holthuysen Museum)**—This 1687 patrician house offers a fine look at the old rich of Amsterdam, with a good 15-minute English introductory film and a 17th-century garden in back (€4.50, Mon–Fri 10:00–17:00, Sat–Sun 11:00–17:00, tram #1, #2, #4, #5, or #9 to Herengracht 605, tel. 020/523-1870).

Vondelpark—This huge and lively city park is popular with the Dutch—families with little kids, romantic couples, hippies sharing blankets and beers, oldsters strolling, and free summer concerts. On a sunny afternoon, it's a hedonistic scene that seems to say "parents...relax" (tel. 020/523-7790).

Amsterdam Film Museum—This museum, next to Vondelpark, has a massive archive and a theater that shows a variety of films, from small foreign productions to 70-mm classics (€5.75, at least 3 showings/night, often English subtitles, Vondelstraat 69, tel. 020/523-7790, www.filmmuseum.nl).

Heineken Brewery—The popular brewery welcomes visitors (€5 for self-guided tour, price includes 3 drinks, must be over age 18, in full slosh Tue–Sun 10:00–18:00, closed Mon, tram #16, #24, or #25, Stadhouderskade 78, near Rijksmuseum, tel. 020/523-9666).

Leidseplein—Brimming with cafés, this people- and pigeon-watching square is an impromptu stage for street artists, accordionists, jugglers, and unicyclists. Sunny afternoons are liveliest. Stroll nearby Lange Leidsedwarsstraat (1 block north) for a taste-bud tour of ethnic eateries from Greece to Indonesia. The Boom Chicago theater fronts this square.

Boom Chicago—This R-rated comedy theater act was started

10 years ago by a group of Americans on a graduation tour. They have been entertaining tourists and locals alike ever since. The show is a series of rude, clever, and high-powered skits offering a raucous look at Dutch culture and local tourism (€16, nightly at 20:15, dinner seating early, Leidseplein Theater, Leidseplein 12, tel. 020/423-0101, www.boomchicago.nl). Meals are optional and a good value. Their irreverent free *Boom Chicago Amsterdam Guide* magazine is packed with practical tips and counter-cultural insights (and gives a €2.25 discount on their show).

Shopping—Amsterdam brings out the browser even in those who were not born to shop. Ten general markets, open six days a week, keep folks who brake for garage sales pulling U-ies. Shopping highlights include Waterlooplein (the flea market); the huge Albert Cuyp street market; various flower markets (such as the Singel Canal market near mint tower/*Munttoren*, daily except Sun); diamond dealers (free cutting and polishing demos at shops behind the Rijksmuseum and on Dam Square); and Kalverstraat, Amsterdam's teeming pedestrian/shopping street (parallel to Damrak).

Tours of Amsterdam

▲▲**Canal-Boat Tour**—These long, low, tourist-laden boats leave continually from several docks around the town for a relaxing, if uninspiring, one-hour quadrilingual introduction to the city (€6.50, 2/hr, more frequent in summer). One very central company is at the corner of Spui and Rokin, about five minutes from Dam Square (daily 10:00–22:00, tel. 020/623-3810). No fishing allowed—but bring your camera. Some prefer to cruise at night, when the bridges are illuminated.

Biking Tours—The Yellow Bike Tour company offers a city tour (€16, at 09:30 and 13:00, 3 hrs) and a tour of the countryside (€21, April–Nov daily at 11:00, 6 hrs, 35 km/22 mi, Nieuwezijds Kolk 29, 3 blocks from train station, tel. 020/620-6940).

Do-It-Yourself Bike Tour of Amsterdam—A day enjoying the bridges, bike lanes, and sleepy off-the-beaten-path canals on your own one-speed is the essential Amsterdam experience. The real joys of Europe's best-preserved 17th-century city are the countless intimate glimpses it offers: the laid-back locals sunning on their porches under elegant gables, rusted bikes that look as if they've been lashed to the same lamppost since the 1960s, wasted hedonists planted on canalside benches, and happy sailors permanently moored but still manning the deck.

For a good day, rent a bike at the station. Head west down Haarlemmerstraat, working your wide-eyed way down the Prinsengracht (along the canal, pop into the Café 't Papeneiland at Prinsengracht 2) and detouring through the gentrified small streets of the Jordaan area before popping out at Westerkerk under the tallest spire in the city.

Pedal past the palace, through Dam Square, and down Kalver-straat (the city's bustling pedestrian mall), and poke into the sleepy Begijnhof. Catch the hour-long cruise at Spui (lock your bike at the dock). Continue down Rokin to the Mint Tower, biking along the Singel Canal flower market to Leidsestraat. Dodge trams and people down Leidsestraat and enjoy the lush and peaceful Vondelpark. Then pedal back to Dam Square. To detour through seedy, sexy, pot-smoking Amsterdam, roll down Damstraat and then turn left down Oudezijds Voorburgwal through the land of Rastafarian "coffee shops," red lights over black tights, and sailors lost without the sea. You'll come out near the station.

To finish your day, escape into the countryside by hopping on the free ferry behind the Amsterdam station. In five minutes, Amsterdam will be gone, and you'll be rolling through your very own Dutch painting. (See "Getting around Amsterdam," above, for info on bike rental).

Wetlands Safari, Nature Canoe Tours near Amsterdam— If you'd like to "turn your back on Amsterdam" and get a dose of the *polder* country and village life along with some exercise, consider this tour. Majel Tromp, a young village woman who speaks great English, takes groups of no more than 15. The pro-gram: Meet at the VVV tourist office outside the central train station at 09:30, catch a bus, stop for coffee, take a canoe trip with several stops, munch a village picnic lunch (included), canoe and bus back into the big city by 14:30 (€30, 10 percent off with this book, May–mid-Sept Mon–Fri, reservations required, tel. 020/ 686-3445 or 06/53-552-669, www.wetlandssafari.nl).

Sleeping in Amsterdam
(€1.10 = about $1, country code: 31, area code: 020)
Sleep Code: **S** = Single, **D** = Double/Twin, **T** = Triple, **Q** = Quad, **b** = bathroom, **s** = shower only, **CC** = Credit Cards accepted, **no CC** = Credit Cards not accepted. Nearly everyone speaks English in the Netherlands, and prices include breakfast unless noted.

While I prefer sleeping in cozy Haarlem (see next chapter), those into more urban charms will find that Amsterdam has plenty of beds. The Queen's Birthday (April 30) and summer weekends get booked well in advance.

Sleeping near the Station
Amstel Botel, the city's only remaining "boat hotel," is a shipshape, bright, and clean floating hotel with 175 rooms (Sb/Db-€75, Tb-€84, worth the extra €5 for canalside view, breakfast-€7, €19.50/ day parking pass, CC, elevator, 400 meters from train station, on your left as you leave station, you'll see the sign, Oosterdokskade 2-4, 1011 AE Amsterdam, tel. 020/626-4247, fax 020/639-1952, www.amstelbotel.com).

Amsterdam's Hotels

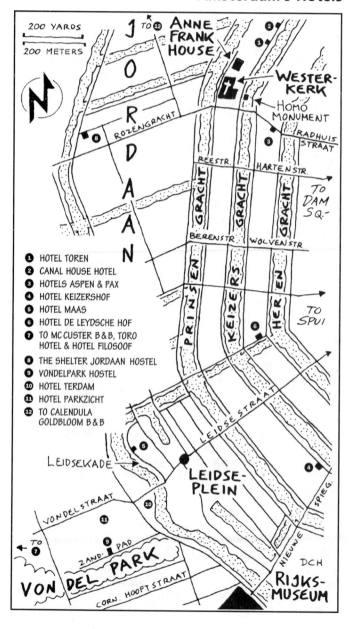

200 YARDS
200 METERS

N

J
O
R
D
A
A
N

TO ⑫ ANNE FRANK HOUSE

②
①

WESTER-KERK

HOMO MONUMENT

RADHUIS STRAAT

ROZENGRACHT

⑧

③

REESTR.

HARTENSTR.

TO DAM SQ.

BERENSTR. WOLVENSTR.

PRINSEN GRACHT

KEIZERS GRACHT

HEREN GRACHT

TO SPUI

⑥

① HOTEL TOREN
② CANAL HOUSE HOTEL
③ HOTELS ASPEN & PAX
④ HOTEL KEIZERSHOF
⑤ HOTEL MAAS
⑥ HOTEL DE LEYDSCHE HOF
⑦ TO MC CUSTER B&B, TORO HOTEL & HOTEL FILOSOOF
⑧ THE SHELTER JORDAAN HOSTEL
⑨ VONDELPARK HOSTEL
⑩ HOTEL TERDAM
⑪ HOTEL PARKZICHT
⑫ TO CALENDULA GOLDBLOOM B&B

LEIDSE STRAAT

⑤

LEIDSEKADE

LEIDSE-PLEIN

④

NIEUWE SPIEG.

VONDELSTRAAT

⑩

⑪

TO ⑦

⑨

ZAND. PAD

VON DEL PARK

CORN. HOOFT STRAAT

DCH

RIJKS-MUSEUM

Ibis Amsterdam Hotel is a modern and efficient 180-room place towering over the station. It offers a central location, comfort, and good value without a hint of charm (Db-€136, family-€176, skip breakfast and save €11 per person, CC, book long in advance, air-con, smoke-free rooms on request, Stationsplein 49, tel. 020/638-3080, fax 020/620-0156, www.ibishotel.com.

Sleeping between Dam Square and the Anne Frank House

Hotel Toren is a chandeliered historic mansion in a pleasant, quiet canalside setting in downtown Amsterdam. This splurge, run by Eric and Annemika Toren, is classy yet friendly, two blocks northeast of the Anne Frank House (Sb-€95–128, Db-€110–190, Tb-€140–170, bridal suites for €205–217 make you want to get married, prices vary with view and Jacuzzi, 10 percent discount for 3 nights and cash with this book, breakfast buffet-€10, CC, air-con, Keizersgracht 164, 1015 CZ Amsterdam, tel. 020/622-6352, fax 020/626-9705, www.toren.nl).

Well-heeled readers enjoy the similar 17th-century **Canal House Hotel**, a few doors down, for its beautiful antique interiors, candlelit evenings, and soft music (Sb-€134, Db-€129–166, CC, elevator, Keizersgracht 148, 1015 CX Amsterdam, tel. 020/622-5182, fax 020/624-1317, www.canalhouse.nl).

Cheap hotels line the convenient but noisy main drag between the town hall and the Anne Frank House. Expect a long, steep, and depressing stairway, noisy front rooms, and quieter rooms in the back. **Hotel Aspen**, a good value for a budget hotel, is tidy, stark, and well maintained (S-€32, D-€41, Db-€64, Tb-€75, Qb-€87, no breakfast, CC, Raadhuisstraat 31, 1016 DC Amsterdam, tel. 020/626-6714, fax 020/620-0866, e-mail: hotelaspen@planet.nl, run by Esam). A few doors away, **Hotel Pax** has large, plain, but airy backpacker-type rooms (S-€25–34, D-€37–57, T-€50–68, Q-€55–77, no breakfast, prices vary with size and season, CC, 2 showers and 2 toilets for 8 rooms, Raadhuisstraat 37, tel. 020/624-9735, run by brothers Philip and Peter).

Calendula Goldbloom's B&B, run by an American couple, offers two comfortable rooms in a classy old home in a quiet Jordaan neighborhood a five-minute walk northwest of the Anne Frank House (D-€100, extra bed €34, CC, 3-night minimum, books out long in advance, good breakfasts, Goudsbloemstraat 132, tel. 020/428-3055, fax 020/ 776-0075, www.calendulas.com, e-mail: info@calendulas.com, Lynn and Dennis).

Sleeping in the Leidseplein Area

The area around Amsterdam's museum square (Museumplein) and the rip-roaring nightlife center (Leidseplein) is colorful, comfortable, convenient, and affordable. These three canalside places are a 5- to 10-minute walk from Leidseplein.

Hotel Keizershof is wonderfully Dutch, with six bright, airy rooms in a 17th-century canal house. A steep spiral staircase leads to rooms named after old-time Hollywood stars. The enthusiastic hospitality of the De Vries family has made this place a treat for 40 years (S-€45, D-€64, Ds-€68, Db-€82, T-€91, Tb-€115, 3-night minimum, CC, nonsmoking, classy breakfast, tram #16, #24, or #25 from station; Keizersgracht 618, where Keizers canal crosses Spiegelstraat, ring bell at street-level door instead of up the stairs, 1017 ER Amsterdam, tel. 020/622-2855, fax 020/624-8412, www.vdwp.nl/keizershof).

Hotel Maas is a big, well-run, elegant, quiet, and stiffly hotelesque place (S-€68, Sb-€102, one D-€91, Db-€142–157, suite-€200, prices vary with view and room size, extra person-€20, CC, hearty breakfast, air-con, elevator, Leidsekade 91, tram #1, #2, #5, or #20 from station, 1017 PN Amsterdam, tel. 020/623-3868, fax 020/ 622-2613, www.hotelmaas.nl).

Hotel De Leydsche Hof is canalside with simple, quiet rooms. Its peaceful demeanor almost helps you overlook the flimsy cots and old carpets (Ds-€60, Ts-€90, Qs-€110, no breakfast, no CC, Leidsegracht 14, near where Keizersgracht hits Leidsegracht, 10-min walk from Leidseplein, 1016 CK Amsterdam, tel. 020/ 623-2148, run by friendly Mr. Piller).

Best Western Hotel Terdam is an 89-room American-style hotel well situated on a quiet street just across the bridge from bustling Leidseplein (Db-€130–170 depending on season and air-con, CC, elevator, Tesselschadestraat 23, tel. 020/612-6876, fax 020/683-8313, www.ams.nl).

Sleeping near Vondelpark

These options connect you with the sights via an easy tram ride, a pleasant 15-minute walk, or a short bike ride through Vondelpark.

Karen McCuster, a friendly Englishwoman, rents cozy rooms in her shoes-off home. Rooms are clean, white, and bright, with red carpeting and green plants. One room has a private rooftop patio (D-€64–82 depending on room size, suite-€114, includes buffet breakfast, no CC, Zeilstraat 22, tram #2 from station to Amstelveenseweg, 3rd floor, 1075 SH Amsterdam, tel. 020/679-2753, fax 020/ 670-4578, www.bedandbreakfastamsterdam.net, e-mail: pgaldermans@chello.net).

Toro Hotel, in a peaceful residential area at the edge of Vondelpark, is your personal 19th-century hotel/mansion, with a plush lounge, elegant dining hall, and 22 rooms with TVs, safes, and phones. Rooms in the back overlook the park, canal, and garden, which is yours for relaxing (Sb-€120, Db-€147, Tb-€164, Qb-€200, CC, elevator, metered parking at door,

Koningslaan 64, tram #2 from station to Koningslaan, then walk to intersection of Emmalaan and Koningslaan, 1075 AG Amsterdam, tel. 020/673-7223, fax 020/675-0031).

Hotel Filosoof greets you with Aristotle and Plato in the foyer and classical music in its lobby. Its 30 rooms are decorated with themes; the Egyptian room has a frieze of hieroglyphics. Philosophers' sayings hang on the walls, as thoughtful travelers wander down the halls or sit in the garden, rooted deep in discussion. The rooms are small (and split between two buildings), but the hotel is endearing (Sb-€39–102, Db-€93–111, Tb-€116–134, CC, elevator, Anna Vondelstraat 6, 5-min walk from tram #1 line, get off at Jan Peter Heierstraat, tel. 020/683-3013, fax 020/685-3750, www.hotelfilosoof.nl).

Hotel Parkzicht is an old-fashioned place with lots of extremely steep stairs and 13 big, plain rooms on a quiet street bordering Vondelpark (S-€34, Sb-€43, Db-€77–84, as low as €50 in winter, Tb-€109, Qb-€118, CC, Roemer Visscherstraat 33, tram #1, #2, or #5 from station, exit Leidseplein, tel. 020/618-1954, fax 020/618-0897, e-mail: hotel@parkzicht.nl). This street is in a charming neighborhood and lined with other small hotels.

Hostels

The Shelter Jordan is scruffy, friendly, well run, and in a great neighborhood. These are Amsterdam's best budget beds, in 14- to 20-bed dorms (€13–15, includes sheets and breakfast, no CC, free Internet access, maximum age 35, nonsmoking, 02:00 curfew, Bloemstraat 179, near Anne Frank House, tel. 020/624-4717, www.shelter.nl, e-mail: reservations@jordan.shelter.nl). It serves hot meals, runs a snack bar, offers lockers, leads nightly Bible studies, and closes the dorms from 10:30 to 13:00. Its sister Christian hostel, **The Shelter City**, in the Red-Light District, is similar but definitely not preaching to the choir (€13–15, includes breakfast, no CC, maximum age 35, curfew, Barndesteeg 21, tel. 020/625-3230, fax 020/623-2282, www.shelter.nl, e-mail: city@shelter.nl).

The city's two HI hostels are **Vondelpark**, Amsterdam's top hostel (€18–24 with breakfast, D-€66, nonmembers pay €2.25 extra, no CC, lots of school groups, 4–20 beds per dorm, right on the park at Zandpad 5, tel. 020/589-8996, fax 020/589-8955, www.njhc.org/vondelpark) and **Stadsdoelen** (€17 with breakfast, nonmembers pay €2.25 extra, no CC, Kloveniersburgwal 97, just past Dam Square, tel. 020/624-6832, fax 020/639-1035, www.njhc.org, e-mail: stadsdoelen@njhc.org). While generally booked long in advance, a few beds open up each day at 11:00.

Eating in Amsterdam

Dutch food is basic and hearty. *Eetcafés* are local cafés serving budget sandwiches, soup, eggs, and so on. Cafeterias, *broodje* (sandwich shops), and automatic food shops are also good bets for budget eaters. Picnics are cheap and easy. A central supermarket is **Albert Heijn**, at the corner of Koningsplein and Singel Canal near the flower market (Mon–Sat 10:00–20:00, Sun 12:00–18:00).

Of Amsterdam's thousand-plus restaurants, no one knows which are best. I'd pick an area and wander. The major action is around Leidseplein. Wander along restaurant row: Leidsedwarsstraat. For fewer crowds and more charm, find something in the Jordaan district. The best advice: your hotel's. Most keep a reliable eating list for their neighborhood and know which places keep their travelers happy. Here are a few handy places to consider:

Eating near Spui in the Center

The city university's **Atrium** is a great budget cafeteria (€4.50 meals, Mon–Fri 11:00–15:00, 17:00–19:30; from Spui, walk west down Landebrug Steeg past the canalside Café 't Gasthuys 3 blocks to Oudezijds Achterburgwal 237, go through arched doorway on the right, tel. 020/525-3999). **Café 't Gasthuys**, one of Amsterdam's many "brown" cafés (named for their smoke-stained walls), makes good sandwiches and offers indoor or canalside seating (daily 12:00–24:00, walk west down Landebrug Steeg to Grimburgwal 7, tel. 020/624-8230).

La Place, a cafeteria on the ground floor of a department store, has islands of entrées, veggies, fruits, desserts, and beverages (Mon–Sat 10:00–20:00, Thu until 21:00, Sun 12:00–20:00, near Mint Tower, corner of Rokin and Muntplein, tel. 020/620-2364).

De Jaren Café ("The Years") features eclectic energy, an upstairs restaurant, and drinks at its canalside patio (daily 10:00–24:00, Nieuwe Doelenstraat 20-22, just up from Muntplein, tel. 020/625-5771).

Eating in the Train Station

The train station has a surprisingly classy, budget, self-service **Stationsrestauratie** on platform 1 (Mon–Sat 07:00–22:00, Sun from 08:00).

Eating near the Anne Frank House

For pancakes in a family atmosphere, try the **Pancake Bakery** (€8.25 pancakes, splitting OK, offers an Indonesian pancake for those who want 2 experiences in 1, daily 12:00–21:30, Prinsengracht 191, 1 block north of Anne Frank House, tel. 020/625-1333). Across the canal, **De Bolhoed** serves serious vegetarian food (daily 12:00–22:00, Prinsengracht 60, tel. 020/626-1803). **Dimitri's** is the place for a hearty salad (€9 main-course salads, daily 08:00–22:00, Prinsenstraat 3, tel. 020/627-9393).

Café 't Papeneiland is a classic "brown café." With Delft tiles, an evocative old stove, and a stay-awhile perch overlooking a canal, it's been the neighborhood hangout since the 17th century (overlooking the northwest end of Prinsengracht at #2).

Eating near Vondelpark
Café Vertigo offers a fun selection of French, Italian, and Spanish dishes. Grab an outdoor table and watch the world spin by (daily 11:00–24:00, beneath Film Museum, Vondelpark 3, tel. 020/612-3021).

Bars
Try a *jenever* (Dutch gin), the closest thing to an atomic bomb in a shot glass. While cheese gets harder and sharper with age, *jenever* grows smooth and soft. Old *jenever* is best.

Drugs
Amsterdam, Europe's counterculture mecca, thinks the concept of a "victimless crime" is a contradiction. While hard drugs are definitely out, marijuana causes about as much excitement as a bottle of beer. Throughout the Netherlands "coffee shops" are pubs selling marijuana. Menus dangling from strings look like the inventory of a drug bust. Display cases show various joints or baggies for sale. The Dutch roll a little tobacco into their joints. To avoid the tobacco, you need to get a baggie and papers. Baggies usually cost €11.50—smaller contents…better quality. Walk east from Dam Square on Damstraat for a few blocks and then down to Nieuwmarkt. While several Bulldog Cafés are popular with tourists, less-glitzy neighborhood places (farther from the crowds) offer a better value and a more comfortable atmosphere.

Pot should never be bought on the street in Amsterdam. Well-established "coffee shops" are considered much safer. Up to five grams of marijuana per person per day can be sold in "coffee shops". Minimum age for purchase: 18 years.

The tiny **Grey Area** coffee shop is a cool, welcoming, and smoky hole-in-the-wall appreciated among local aficionados as a seven-time winner of Amsterdam's Cannabis Cup award. Judging by the proud autographed photos on the wall, many of America's most famous heads have dropped in. You're welcome to just nurse a bottomless cup of coffee (open high noon to 21:00, closed Mon, between Dam Square and Anne Frank House at Oude Leliestraat 2, tel. 020/420-4301, www.greyarea.nl, Steven and John).

Near the corner of Leidsestraat and Prinsengracht, **Tops** coffee shop has Internet access. **Homegrown Fantasy**'s coffee shop and gallery, about two blocks northwest of Dam Square, has a gentle Dutch atmosphere, cosmic rest room, and a grow shop next door (daily 12:00–24:00, Nieuwe Zijds Voorburgwal 87a, tel. 020/627-5683).

▲**Marijuana and Hemp Museum**—This is a collection of dope

facts, history, science, and memorabilia (€5.75, daily 11:00–22:00, Oudezijds Achterburgwal 148, tel. 020/623-5961). While small, it has a shocker finale: the high-tech grow room in which dozens of varieties of marijuana are cultivated in optimal hydroponic (among other) environments. Some plants stand five feet tall and shine under the intense grow lamps. The view is actually through glass walls into the neighboring "Sensi Seed Bank" Grow Shop, which sells carefully cultivated seeds and all the gear needed to grow them. It's an interesting neighborhood. The Cannabis College Foundation, "dedicated to ending the global war against the cannabis plant through public education," is next door at #124 (daily 11:00–22:00, tel. 020/423-4420, www.cannabiscollege .com or www.marijuananews.com). As you wander through the Foundation, ponder the 400,000 Americans serving time in jail because of U.S. marijuana laws.

Transportation Connections—Amsterdam

Amsterdam's train-information center requires a long wait. Save lots of time by getting train tickets and information in a small-town station or travel agency. For phone information, dial 0900-9292 for local trains or 0900-9296 for international trains (€0.75/min, daily 7:00–24:00, wait through recording and hold...hold...hold...).

By train to: Schiphol Airport (6/hr, 20 min, €3.25), **Haarlem** (6/hr, 15 min, €5.50 round-trip), **The Hague** (2/hr, 50 min), **Rotterdam** (4/hr, 1 hr), **Brussels** (2/hr, 3 hrs), **Ostende** (hrly, 4 hrs, change in Antwerp), **London** (2/day, 8 hrs, train to Hoek van Holland, then ferry across Channel, then train from Harwich to London; or 8/day, 6.5 hrs, with transfer to Eurostar Chunnel train in Brussels, Eurostar discounted with railpass, www.eurostar.com), **Copenhagen** (5/day, 10 hrs, transfer in Osnabrück and Hamburg; or 3-hr train to Duisberg and transfer to 11-hr night train), **Frankfurt** (8/day, 5–6 hrs, transfer in Köln or Duisburg), **Munich** (7/day, 9 hrs, transfer in Mannheim, Hanover, or Köln, one 11-hr direct night train), **Bonn** (10/day, 3 hrs, some direct but most transfer in Köln), **Bern** (5/day, 9 hrs, one direct but most transfer in Basel, Köln, or Brussels), **Paris** (5/day, 5 hrs, required fast train from Brussels with €11 supplement). If you don't have a railpass, the cheapest way to get to Paris is by bus (about $33 compared to $100 second-class by train; bus station in Amsterdam at Julianaplein 5, Amstel Station, 5 stops by Métro from Central Station, tel. 020/560-8788, www.eurolines.com).

Amsterdam's Schiphol Airport: The airport, like most of Holland, is English speaking, user-friendly, and below sea level. Its banks offer fair rates (24 hrs daily, in arrival area). Schiphol Airport has easy bus and train connections (11 km/7 miles) into

Amsterdam or Haarlem. The airport also has a train station of its own. (You can validate your Eurailpass and hit the rails immediately or, to stretch your train pass, buy an inexpensive ticket into Amsterdam today and start the pass later.) Schiphol flight information (tel. 0900-0141) can give you flight times and your airline's Amsterdam number for reconfirmation before going home (€0.45/min to climb through its phone tree). To reach airlines, dial KLM at 020/649-9123 and Martainair at 020/601-1222.

HAARLEM

Cute, cozy, yet real and handy to the airport, Haarlem is a fine home base, giving you small-town, overnight warmth with easy access (15 min by train) to wild and crazy Amsterdam.

Haarlem is a busy Dutch market town buzzing with shoppers biking home with fresh bouquets. Enjoy the market on Saturday (general) and Monday (clothing), when the square bustles like a Brueghel painting with cheese, fish, flowers, and families. Make yourself at home; buy some flowers to brighten your hotel room.

The town will be more popular than ever in 2002. The **Floriade** world horticultural exhibition puts down roots in Haarlemmermeer, just five kilometers outside the city (April 6– Oct 20, 2002). Organizers expect up to 3 million visitors for the event, which is held only once every 10 years. Hotels will fill quickly and some will increase their rates dramatically. If you plan to visit Haarlem during the exhibition, book long in advance. For more information, ask at the TI or visit www.floriade.nl.

Orientation (area code: 023)

Tourist Information: Haarlem's TI (VVV), at the train station, is friendlier, more helpful, and less crowded than Amsterdam's. Ask your Amsterdam questions here (Mon–Fri 09:30–17:30, Sat 10:00–14:00, closed Sun, tel. 0900-616-1600, €0.45/min, helpful parking brochure, their €0.90 *Holidaymagazine* is not necessary).

Arrival in Haarlem: As you walk out of the train station (has lockers), the TI is on your right and the bus station is across the street. Two parallel streets flank the train station (Kruisweg and Jansweg). Head up either one, and you'll reach the town square and church within 10 minutes. If you need help, ask a local person to point you toward the *Grote Markt?* ("Main Square?")

Helpful Hints

The handy GWK **change office** at the station offers fair exchange rates (Mon–Fri 08:00–20:00, Sat 09:00–18:00, Sun 10:00–18:00). The train station rents **bikes** (€5.50/day, €45 deposit and passport number, Mon–Sat 06:00–24:00, Sun 07:30–24:00). For **Internet access**, try Hotel Amadeus (nonguests welcome, facing Market Square), High Times (if you don't mind marijuana smoke, Lange Veerstraat 47), or the Global Hemp Museum (Spaarne 94). On April 20, 2002, an all-day **Flower Parade** of floats wafts through eight towns, including Haarlem.

Sights—Haarlem

▲▲**Market Square (Grote Markt)**—Haarlem's market square is the town's delightful centerpiece. To enjoy a coffee or beer here, simmering in Dutch good living, is a quintessential European experience. In a recent study, the Dutch were found to be the most content people in Europe. And later, the people of Haarlem were found to be the most content in the Netherlands. Observe. Just a few years ago trolleys ran through the square and cars were parked everywhere. But today it's a people zone, with market stalls filling the square on Mondays and Saturdays and café tables on others. The local drunk used to hang out on the bench in front of the town hall, where he'd expose himself to newlyweds. The Dutch, rather than arrest the man, moved the bench. The big statue in the square is of Coster, the man only Haarlemers think invented printing. The little shops around the cathedral have long been church owned and rented to bring in a little cash. The fine building nearest the cathedral is the old meat hall—decorated with carved bits of early advertising.

▲**Church (Grote Kerk)**—This 15th-century Gothic church (now Protestant) is worth a look, if only for its Oz-like organ (from 1738, 30 meters/100 feet high, its 5,000 pipes impressed both Handel and Mozart). Note how the organ, which fills the west end, seems to steal the show from the altar. Pick up the English flier, which lists spots of interest, including Frans Hals' tomb (under black lantern in choir). To enter, find the small *Entrée* sign behind the church at Oude Groenmarkt 23 (€1.50, Mon–Sat 10:00–16:00). Consider attending (even part of) a concert to hear Holland's greatest pipe organ (regular free concerts Tue at 20:15 mid-May–mid-Oct, additional concerts Thu at 15:00 July–Aug, confirm schedule at TI).

▲▲**Frans Hals Museum**—Haarlem is the hometown of Frans Hals, and this refreshingly easy museum—an almshouse for old men back in 1610—displays many of his greatest paintings (€5, Mon–Sat 11:00–17:00, Sun 12:00–17:00, may be closed Mon in 2002, tel. 023/511-5775). Enjoy lots of Frans Hals group portraits (rooms 21, 25, 28) and the take-me-back paintings of old-time

Haarlem

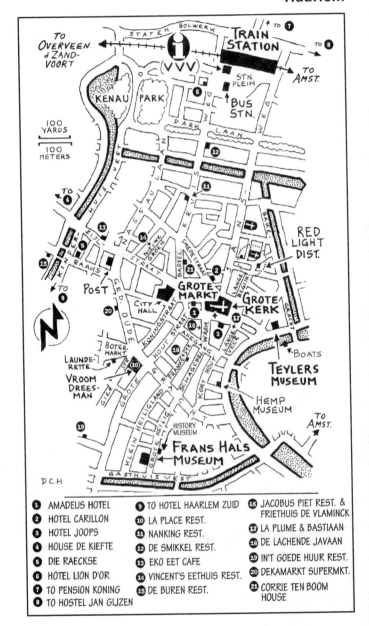

1 AMADEUS HOTEL	**9** TO HOTEL HAARLEM ZUID	**16** JACOBUS PIET REST. & FRIETHUIS DE VLAMINCK
2 HOTEL CARILLON	**10** LA PLACE REST.	**17** LA PLUME & BASTIAAN
3 HOTEL JOOPS	**11** NANKING REST.	**18** DE LACHENDE JAVAAN
4 HOUSE DE KIEFTE	**12** DE SMIKKEL REST.	**19** IN'T GOEDE HUUR REST.
5 DIE RAECKSE	**13** EKO EET CAFE	**20** DEKAMARKT SUPERMKT.
6 HOTEL LION D'OR	**14** VINCENT'S EETHUIS REST.	**21** CORRIE TEN BOOM HOUSE
7 TO PENSION KONING	**15** DE BUREN REST.	
8 TO HOSTEL JAN GIJZEN		

Haarlem. Peter Brueghel the Younger's painting *Proverbs* illustrates 72 old Dutch proverbs. To peek into old Dutch ways, identify some with the help of the English-language key.

History Museum—Across the street from the Frans Hals Museum, this small museum gives a peek into old Haarlem. Request the English version of the 10-minute video. Study the large-scale model of Haarlem in 1822 before the town's fortifications were demolished, and enjoy the new "time machine" computer and video display that shows you various aspects of life in Haarlem at different points in history (€1, Tue–Sat 12:00–17:00, Sun 13:00–17:00, closed Mon, Groot Heiligland 47, tel. 020/542-2427). The adjacent architecture museum (free) may be of conceivable interest to architects.

Corrie Ten Boom House—Haarlem is home to Corrie Ten Boom, popularized by *The Hiding Place*, an inspirational book and movie about the Ten Boom family's experience hiding Jews from Nazis. The Ten Boom House is open for 60-minute English tours (donation accepted, April–Oct Tue–Sat 10:00–16:00, Nov–March Tue–Sat 11:00–15:00, closed Mon, 50 meters north of Market Square at Barteljorisstraat 19, the clock-shop people get all wound up if you go inside—wait at the door, where tour times are posted, tel. 023/531-0823). The Ten Boom family had for generations hosted a prayer meeting for peace here, for both Jews and Christians. On the 100th anniversary of the prayer meetings, the Gestapo came, tipped off that the family was harboring Jews. It's a great and inspirational story (although some may be put off by the preaching mixed in).

▲Teylers Museum—Famous as the oldest museum in Holland, it's interesting mainly as a look at a 200-year-old museum—fossils, minerals, and primitive electronic gadgetry. New exhibition halls (with rotating exhibits) have freshened up the place. Stop by if you enjoy mixing, say, Renaissance sketches with pickled extinct fish (€4.50, Tue–Sat 10:00–17:00, Sun 12:00–17:00, Spaarne 16, tel. 023/531-9010).

Canal Cruise—Making a scenic loop through and around Haarlem, these little trips by Woltheus Cruises are more relaxing than informative (€6, daily 10:00–17:00, 70 min, 5/day, across the canal from Teylers Museum at Spaarne 11a, tel. 023/535-7723).

Red Lights—Wander through a little red-light district as precious as a Barbie doll (2 blocks northeast of Market Square, off Lange Begijnestraat, no senior or student discounts). Don't miss the mall marked by the red neon sign reading *t'Steegje*. The nearby *t'Poortje* (office park) costs €3.40.

Global Hemp Museum—More a hemp-products store and hub of Haarlem's coffee-shop action, this friendly place runs a humble hemp museum out back (shop free, museum €2.25, Internet access-€1.35/30 min, Mon–Sat 11:00–20:00, summer Sun

12:00–20:00, down the canal from Teylers Museum at Spaarne 94, tel. 023/534-9939).

Hofjes—*Hofjes* are peaceful courtyards surrounded by small row homes. The courtyards, open to a quiet public, are often accessed through an archway off the street (see map for location of *hofjes*).

Amsterdam to Haarlem Train Tour

Since you'll be commuting from Amsterdam to Haarlem, here's a tour to keep you entertained. Departing from Amsterdam, grab a seat on the right (with your back to Amsterdam, top deck if possible). Everything is on the right unless I say on the left.

You're riding the oldest train line in Holland. Across the harbor behind the Amsterdam station, the tall brown skyscraper is the corporate office of **Shell Oil**. The Dutch had the first multi-national corporation (the United East India Company back in the 17th century). And today this international big-business spirit survives with companies like Shell and Phillips.

Leaving Amsterdam, you'll see the cranes and ships of its harbor—sizable but nothing like the world's biggest in nearby Rotterdam.

On your left, find the old **windmill**. In front of it, the little garden plots and cottages are escapes for big-city people who probably don't even have a balcony.

Coming into the Sloterdijk Station (where trains connect for Amsterdam airport), you'll see huge office buildings, such as Dutch Telecom KPN. These grew up after the station made commuting easy.

A kilometer past Sloterdijk Station, about 50 meters to the right of the tracks, a yellow sign says, "Tippel Zone—open 21:00." (*Tippel* is the sound a mouse makes when it runs through the house at night.) This is a **drive-in brothel**. See the oval driveway with pink "bus stops" for browsing, the lounge building, and the blue privacy stalls behind (including 2 for bikers). The lounge has a clinic with a nurse and counselors to keep the women healthy. If a prostitute is diagnosed with AIDS, she gets a subsidized apartment to encourage her to quit the business. Shocking as this may seem to some, it's a good example of a pragmatic solution to a problem—getting the most dangerous prostitutes off the streets and combating AIDS.

Passing through a forest and by some houseboats, you enter a *polder*—reclaimed land. This is an ecologically sound farm zone, run without chemicals. Cows, pigs, and chickens run free—they're not raised in cages. The train tracks are on a dike, which provides a solid foundation not susceptible to floods. This way the transportation system functions right through any calamity. Looking out at the distant dike, remember you're in the most densely populated country in Europe. On the horizon, sleek modern windmills whirl.

Passing the tall smokestack and the Sony Music Building, find a big, unnamed, beige-and-white building. This is the **mint**, where currency is printed (top security, no advertising). This has long been a family business.

As the train slows down, you're passing through the Netherlands' biggest train-car maintenance facility and entering Haarlem. Look left. The domed building is a **prison**, built in 1901 and still in use. As you cross the Spaarne River, you'll see the great **church spire** towering over Haarlem as it has since medieval times—back when a fortified wall circled the town. Hop out into one of Holland's oldest stations. Art Nouveau—decor from 1908—survives all around.

Nightlife in Haarlem

Haarlem's evening scene is great. The bars around the Grote Kerk and Lange Veerstraat are colorful and lively. You'll find plenty of music.

The best show in town: the café scene on Market Square. In good weather, café tables tumble happily out of the bars.

For trendy local crowds, consider a drink at **Studio Café** (daily 12:00–24:00, on the main square, next to Hotel Carillon). Tourists gawk at the old-fashioned belt-driven ceiling fans in **Café 1900** across from the Corrie Ten Boom House (daily 9:00–00:30, live music Sun night except in July, Barteljoris-straat 10, tel. 023/531-8283).

Coffee Shops: Haarlem has 16 "coffee shops" where marijuana is casually sold and smoked by easygoing, noncriminal types. The **Frans Hals Coffee Shop** is one of the best established (daily 09:00–24:00, in front of station at Kruisweg 46). The display case-type "menu" explains what's on sale (€2.50 joints, €11.50 baggies, space cakes—but no alcohol, only soft drinks). At **High Times**, smokers can choose from 16 varieties of joints in racks behind the bar (neatly prepacked in trademarked "Joint Packs," €2–3.50, daily 12:00–23:00, Internet access, Lange Veerstraat 47). If you don't like the smell of pot, avoid places sporting Rastafarian yellow, red, and green colors; wildly painted walls; or plants in the windows.

Crack is the wild and leathery place to go for loud music, pool, darts, and smoking (Lange Veerstraat 32). **Taverna Imperial** has live music Sunday through Thursday (daily 20:00–02:00, best to arrive around 00:30 on weekends, a few doors down from Crack at Korte Veerstraat 3, tel. 023/531-8283).

Sleeping in Haarlem
(€1.10 = about $1, country code: 31, area code: 023)
Sleep Code: **S** = Single, **D** = Double/Twin, **T** = Triple, **Q** = Quad, **b** = bathroom, **s** = shower only, **CC** = Credit Cards accepted, **no CC** = Credit Cards not accepted.

The helpful Haarlem TI, just outside the train station, can nearly always find you a €17 bed in a private home (for a €4.50-per-person fee plus a cut of your host's money). Avoid this if you can; it's cheaper to reserve direct.

Haarlem is most crowded in April, on Easter weekend, in May, and in July and August. Because of the once-in-a-decade Floriade festival (April 6–Oct 20, 2002), hotels are likely to fill even more quickly than usual, so it will be smart to book far in advance.

Nearly every Dutch person you'll encounter speaks English. The listed prices include breakfast (unless otherwise noted) and usually include the €1.70-per-person-per-day tourist tax. To avoid this town's louder-than-normal street noises, forgo views for a room in the back. Hotels and the TI have a useful parking brochure.

For a **Laundromat**, try My Beautiful Launderette—handy, self-service, and cheap (€5 wash and dry, daily 08:30–20:30, bring lots of change, near Vroom Dreesman department store at Boter Markt 20).

Sleeping in the Center

Hotel Amadeus, on Market Square, has 15 small, bright, and basic rooms. Some have views of the square. This characteristic hotel, ideally located above an early 20th-century dinner café, is relatively quiet. Its lush old lounge/breakfast room, on the second floor, overlooks the square (Sb-€50, Db-€70, Tb-€87, Qb-€100, includes tax, 2-night stay and cash get you a 5 percent discount, 12-min walk from train station, CC, steep climb to lounge, then an elevator, Grote Markt 10, 2011 RD Haarlem, tel. 023/532-4530, fax 023/532-2328, www.amadeus-hotel.com, Mike and Inez take good care of their guests).

Hotel Carillon also overlooks the town square but comes with a little more traffic and bell-tower noise. Many of the 22 well-worn rooms are small, and the stairs are ste-e-e-p. The front rooms come with great town-square views and street noise (tiny loft singles-€30, Db-€70, Tb-€95, Qb-€102, includes tax, 12-min walk from train station, CC, no elevator, Grote Markt 27, 2011 RC Haarlem, tel. 023/531-0591, fax 023/531-4909, www.hotelcarillon.com, e-mail: info@hotelcarillon.com).

Hotel Joops is an innovative concept. Mr. Joops rents rooms in his own hotel, just behind the cathedral (Db-€70–90), and also administers a corral of 80 other rooms, all within a block of the church. These are a mixed bunch, ranging from cheap, well-worn, depressing rooms (S-€30, D-€55, T-€75) to modern new suites with kitchenettes (Db-€58–75 depending upon size, Tb-€20 extra, breakfast-€8.50, save about 5 percent with cash, CC, Oude Groenmarkt 20, 2011 HL Haarlem, tel. 023/532-2008 or 023/512-5300, fax 023/532-9549, www.joops.hotelinformation.com).

Bed and Breakfast House de Kiefte, your get-into-a-local-home budget option, epitomizes the goodness of B&Bs. Marjet (mar-yet) and Hans, a fun-to-know Dutch couple who speak English fluently, rent four bright, cheery, nonsmoking rooms (with a good breakfast and travel advice) in their quiet, 100-year-old home (Ds-€50, T-€70, Qs-€90, Quint/s-€105, cash only, minimum 2 nights, all rooms with very steep stairs, family loft sleeps up to 5, kids over 4 welcome, Coornhertstraat 3, 2013 EV Haarlem, tel. 023/532-2980, cellular 06-5474-5272). It's a 15-minute walk or €7 taxi ride from the train station and a five-minute walk from the center. From Grote Markt (Market Square), walk to the right of City Hall straight out Zijlstraat and over the bridge and take a left on the fourth street.

Die Raeckse Hotel is not as central as the others, with less character and more traffic noise, but its rooms are decent and comfortable (Sb-€55–70, Db-€80, Tb-€92, Qb-€100, extra bed-€25, CC, Raaks 1, 2011 VA Haarlem, tel. 023/532-6629, fax 023/531-7937).

Hotel Lion D'Or is a classy 34-room business hotel with all the professional comforts and a handy location. Don't expect a warm welcome (Sb-€104–118, Db-€136–154, extra beds-€23, prices much higher during Floriade from April–Oct, CC, elevator, some nonsmoking rooms, across the street from the station at Kruisweg 34, 2011 LC Haarlem, tel. 023/532-1750, fax 023/532-9543, www.goldentulip.nl/hotels/gtliondor).

Sleeping near Haarlem

The 300-room, very American **Hotel Haarlem Zuid** is sterile but a good value for those interested only in sleeping and eating. It sits in an industrial zone, a 20-minute walk from the center on the road to the airport (Db during Floriade-€126, otherwise €80, breakfast included or skip and save €8 each, CC, elevator, easy parking, laundry service, fitness center, inexpensive hotel restaurant, Toekanweg 2, 2035 LC Haarlem, tel. 023/536-7500, fax 023/536-7980, www.hotelhaarlemzuid.nl, e-mail: haarlemzuid@valk.com). Buses #5, #70, #71, #72, and #80 connect the hotel to the station and Market Square every 10 minutes. Bus #80 makes runs to the beach or Amsterdam. Fast buses (#236 and #362) zip to the airport.

Pension Koning, a 15-minute walk north of the station or a quick hop on bus #71, has five simple rooms in a row house in a residential area (S-€23, D-€46, T-€69, 2-night minimum, includes breakfast, no CC, Kleverlaan 179, 2023 JC Haarlem, tel. 023/526-1456).

Hostel Jan Gijzen, completely renovated and with all the youth-hostel comforts, charges €18 to €21 for beds in eight-bed dorms (€2.25 extra for nonmembers, a few D-€42–45, includes breakfast and sheets, no CC, daily 07:30–24:00, Jan Gijzenpad 3, 3 km from Haarlem station—take bus #2 from platform A1, or a 5-min walk from Santpoort Zuid train station, tel. 023/537-3793, fax 023/537-1176, www.njhc.org/haarlem, e-mail: haarlem@njhc.org).

Eating in Haarlem

Eating between Market Square (Grote Markt) and Train Station

Enjoy an Indonesian rijsttafel feast at the **Nanking Chinese-Indonesian Restaurant** (daily 16:00–22:00, Kruisstraat 16, a few blocks off Grote Markt, tel. 023/532-0706). Couples eat plenty, heartily, and cheaply by splitting a €12.50 Indonesian "rice table" for one; each eater should order a drink. Say hi to gracious Ai Ping and her daughter, Fan. Don't let them railroad you into a Chinese (their heritage) dinner. They also do cheap and tasty takeout.

Pancakes for dinner? **Pannekoekhuis "De Smikkel"** serves a selection of over 50 dinner (meat, cheese, etc.) and dessert pancakes. The pancakes (€8 each) are filling. With the €1.25-per-person cover charge, splitting is OK (daily 12:00–22:00, Sun from 16:00, closed Mon in winter, 2 blocks in front of station, Kruisweg 57, tel. 023/532-0631).

Eat well and surrounded by trains and 1908 architecture in the classy **Brasserie Haarlem Station Restaurant** (€13.75 for 3 courses, daily 9:00–21:00, between tracks #3 and #6).

Eating on or near Zijlstraat

Eko Eet Café is great for a cheery, tasty vegetarian meal (€9 *menu*, daily 17:30–21:30, Zijlstraat 39, tel. 023/532-6568). Because they serve only fresh food, the *menu* gets sparse by 21:00.

Vincent's Eethuis serves the best cheap, basic Dutch food in town. This former St. Vincent's soup kitchen now feeds more gainfully employed locals than poor (€5, free seconds on veggies, friendly staff, Mon–Fri 12:00–14:00, 17:00–19:30, Nieuwe Groenmarkt 22).

The cheery **De Buren** offers handlebar-mustache fun and traditional Dutch food (such as *draadjesvlees*, beef stew with apple-sauce, and *oma's kippetje*, grandmother's chicken) to happy locals (€11–16 dinners, Wed–Sun 17:00–22:00, closed Mon–Tue, out-side the tourist area at Brouwersvaart 146, follow Raaks Straat west across the canal from Die Raeckse Hotel, tel. 023/534-3364). Gerard and Marjo love their work. Enjoy their creative menu, made especially for you.

Eating between the Market Square and Frans Hals Museum

Jacobus Pieck Eetlokaal is popular with locals for its fine-value "global cuisine" (€9 plate of the day, Tue–Sat 10:00–22:00, Sun–Mon 10:00–17:00, Warmoesstraat 18, tel. 023/532-6144).

For a (€1.35) cone of old-fashioned French fries, drop by **Friethuis de Vlaminck** on Warmoesstraat 3 (Tue–Sat until

18:00). Notice the old-time shop sign cobbled into Warmoes-straat's brick sidewalk.

La Plume steak house is noisy with a happy, local, and carnivorous crowd (€13.75 meals, daily from 17:30, CC, Lange Veerstraat 1, tel. 023/531-3202).

Bastiaan serves good Mediterranean cuisine in a classy atmosphere (€13.75 dinners, Tue–Sun from 18:00, closed Mon, CC, Lange Veerstraat 8, tel. 023/532-6006).

De Lachende Javaan ("The Laughing Javanese") serves the best real Indonesian food in town. Their €17 rijsttafel is great (light eaters can split this extravaganza—€3.85 for extra plate, Tue–Sun from 17:00, closed Mon, CC, Frankestraat 25, tel. 023/532-8792).

For a candlelit dinner of cheese and wine, consider **In't Goede Uur** (Tue–Sun 17:00–24:00, Fri–Sat until 01:00, closed Mon, Korte Houtstraat 1, tel. 023/531-1174).

For a healthy budget lunch with Haarlem's best view, eat at **La Place**, on the top floor or roof garden of the Vroom Dreesman department store (Mon 11:00–17:30, Tue–Sat 09:30–17:30, Thu until 20:30, closed Sun, on the corner of Grote Houtstraat and Gedempte Oude Gracht, tel. 023/515-8700).

Picnic shoppers head to the **DekaMarkt** supermarket (Mon 11:00–20:00, Tue–Sat 08:30–20:00, Thu until 21:00, closed Sun, Gedemple Oude Gracht 54, between Vroom Dreesman department-ment store and post office).

Transportation Connections—Haarlem
By train to: Amsterdam (6/hr, 15 min, €3.20 one-way, €5.45 same-day return, ticket not valid on "Lovers Train," a misnamed private train that runs hrly), **Delft** (2/hr, 38 min), **Hoorn** (4/hr, 1 hr), **The Hague** (4/hr, 35 min), **Alkmaar** (2/hr, 30 min), **Schip-hol Airport** (2/hr, 40 min, €4.55, transfer at Amsterdam-Sloterdijk); the direct buses #236 (use a strip card) and #362 (local cash) to the airport are faster (2/hr, 30 min, €3.20); by taxi it's €32.

Sights—Near Haarlem and Amsterdam
The Netherlands are tiny. The sights listed below are an easy day trip by bus or train from Haarlem or Amsterdam. Match your interest with the village's specialty: flower auctions, folk museums, cheese, delft porcelain, beaches, or modern art.

Floriade—This horticultural exhibition, which sounds like the world's biggest garden show, takes place every 10 years in the Netherlands. In 2002, it's coming to Haarlemmermeer, just five kilometers outside of Haarlem (April 6–Oct 20, 2002). Horticul-turalists from all over the world converge to show off their plants. The main entrance features a huge, flat "floating roof" (100 by 300 meters). The lake has been dolled up with Oriental pavilions

Daytrips from Haarlem and Amsterdam

and an open-air theater. Towering above everything is the center-piece of the park—"Big Spotters Hill." The man-made hill rises 40 meters (130 feet) above the countryside (which doesn't sound like much, but hey—it's Holland), giving you a bird's-eye view of the surrounding gardens and displays (€17, kids 4–12 €8.50, daily 09:30–19:00, ticket office open 09:00–18:00, Floriadepark 1, main entrance near town of Vijfhuizen, tel. 023/562-2002, www.floriade.nl). After this Floriade officially closes, the park will remain for people to enjoy.

▲▲**Enkhuizen's Zuiderzee Museum**—This lively, open-air folk museum in the salty old town of Enkhuizen has a "Living on Urk" village (patterned after an old Dutch fishing town), populated by people who do a convincing job of role-playing no-nonsense 1905 Dutch villagers. No one said "Have a nice day" back then. You can eat herring hot out of the old smoker and see barrels and rope made. Children enjoy playing at the dress-up chest, trying out old-time games, and making sailing ships out of old wooden shoes (€10, early April–late Oct daily 10:00–17:00, July–Aug free tours at 14:00, private guide for €40, tel. 0228/

351-111, www.zuiderzeemuseum.nl). Take the train from Amsterdam direct to Enkhuizen, where a boat shuttles you to the museum, avoiding a pleasant 15-minute walk.

▲**Zaanse Schans**—This 17th-century Dutch village turned open-air folk museum puts Dutch culture—from cheese making to wooden-shoe carving—on a lazy Susan. Take an inspiring climb to the top of a whirring windmill (gather a group and ask for a tour). Located in the town of Zaandijk, this is your easiest one-stop look at traditional Dutch culture and the Netherlands' best collection of windmills (entrance to grounds free, but you must pay around €1–2 to go in windmills and other sights in the park, daily 08:30–17:30, until 17:00 in winter, parking €3.40/hr, 15/day, tel. 075/616-8218). It's 15 minutes by train north of Amsterdam; take the Alkmaar-bound train to Station Koog-Zaandijk and then walk, following the signs—past a fragrant chocolate factory—for 10 minutes.

▲▲**Aalsmeer Flower Auction**—Get a bird's-eye view of the huge Dutch flower industry. Wander on elevated walkways (through what's claimed to be the biggest commercial building on earth) over literally trainloads of freshly cut flowers. About half of all the flowers exported from Holland are auctioned off here in four huge auditoriums. Stop at one of the "listening posts" for on-the-spot information (€4, Mon–Fri 7:30–11:00, the auction wilts after 09:30 and on Thu but the warehouse swarms, gift shop, cafeteria; bus #172 from Amsterdam's station, 2/hr, 1 hr; from Haarlem take bus #140 and transfer to bus #172 or #77 in Aalsmeer, 2/hr, 1 hr; tel. 0297/392-185). Aalsmeer is close to the airport and a handy last fling before catching a morning weekday flight.

▲▲▲**Keukenhof**—This is the greatest bulb-flower garden on earth. Each spring 6 million flowers, enjoying sandy soil behind the Dutch dunes, conspire to make even a total garden hater enjoy them. This 100-acre park is packed with tour groups daily from about March 21 to May 20 for the 2002 spring show (€11, daily 08:00–19:30, last tickets sold at 18:00) and early August to mid-September for the summer exhibition (€7, daily 09:00–18:00, last ticket sold at 17:00; from Haarlem take the train to Leiden, then catch bus #54, tel. 0252/465-555, www.keukenhof.nl). Go late in the day for the best light and the fewest groups.

The 2002 Flower Parade will be held April 20. This all-day parade, featuring floats decorated with blossoms instead of crepe paper, runs through eight towns, including Lisse and Haarlem.

Zandvoort—For a quick and easy look at the windy coastline in a shell-lover's Shangri-La, visit the beach resort of Zandvoort, a breezy 45-minute bike ride or an eight-minute car or train ride west of Haarlem (from Haarlem, follow signs to Bloemendaal). South of the main beach, bathers work on all-over tans.

▲**Hoorn**—This is an elegant, quiet, and typical 17th-century Dutch town north of Amsterdam. Its TI can rent you a bike or give you a walking-tour brochure. Any TI offers the flier describing the "Historic Triangle," an all-day excursion from Amsterdam that connects Hoorn, Medemblik, and Enkhuizen by steam train and boat (€18 plus €3 for train back to Haarlem; train: 2/day in July–Aug and Sat–Sun, otherwise 1/day: boat: 1/day, Sept–June doesn't run on Mon, tel. 0229/214-862).

De Rijp—This sleepy town is worth visiting if you're driving north of Amsterdam.

Volendam, Marken, and Monnikendam—These famous towns are quaint as can be (although Volendam is very touristy).

▲**Delft**—Peaceful as a Vermeer painting (he was born here) and lovely as its porcelain, Delft is a typically Dutch town with a special soul. Enjoy it best by simply wandering around, watching people, munching local syrup waffles, or daydreaming from the canal bridges. The town bustles during its Saturday antiques market (09:00–17:00). Its colorful Thursday food-and-flower market attracts many traditional villagers (09:00–17:00). The TI on the main square has a €1.85 brochure outlining Delft's sights, including a "Historical Walk through Delft" (Mon–Sat 09:00–17:30, April–Sept also Sun 11:00–15:00, tel. 015/213-0100). The town is a museum in itself, but, if you need a turnstile, it has an impressive Army Museum (€4.30, Mon–Fri 10:00–17:00, Sat–Sun 12:00–17:00, tel. 015/215-0500). Or tour the Royal Porcelain Works to watch the famous 17th-century blue delftware turn from clay into art (€2.25, Mon–Sat 09:00–17:00, summer Sun 09:30–17:00, tel. 015/256-9214).

▲**Alkmaar**—Holland's cheese capital is especially fun (and touristy) during its weekly cheese market (Fridays April–Aug 10:00–12:30). TI tel. 072/511-4284.

▲▲**Edam**—For the ultimate in cuteness and peace, make tiny Edam your home. It's sweet but palatable and 30 minutes by bus from Amsterdam (2/hr). The Edam Museum is a small, quirky house offering a fun peek into a 400-year-old home and a floating cellar (€2, Tue–Sat 10:00–16:30, Sun 13:30–16:30, closed in winter, on main square, tel. 0299/372-644). Wednesday is the town's market day (09:00–13:00). In July and August, market day includes a traditional cheese market (10:30–12:30).

Sleeping and Eating: The **TI** (tel. 0299/315-125) has a list of inexpensive rooms in private homes. **Hotel De Fortuna**, an eccentric canalside mix of flowers, a cat of leisure, a pet turtle, and duck noises, offers steep stairs and low-ceilinged rooms in several ancient buildings in the old center of Edam (Db–€85–97.50, includes breakfast, CC, garden patio, attached restaurant, Spui-straat 3, 1135 AV Edam, tel. 0299/371-671, fax 0299/371-469, www.fortuna-edam.nl). The centrally located **Damhotel** (on a

canal around corner from TI) has attractive, comfortable rooms
with a plush feel (Sb-€52, Db-€86, Tb-€122.50, Qb-€163,
includes breakfast, CC, attached restaurant, Keizersgracht 1,
1135 AZ Edam, tel. 0299/371-766, fax 0299/374-031, www
.damhotel.nl). **Tai Wah** has take-out Chinese/Indonesian (eat
in De Fortuna garden) and indoor seating (Mon and Wed–Sat
16:00–21:00, Sun 13:00–21:00, closed Tue, Lingerzijde 62, tel.
0299/371-088).

▲**Rotterdam**—This city, the world's largest port, bounced back
after being bombed flat in World War II. See its towering Euro-
mast, take a harbor tour, and stroll its great pedestrian zone (TI
tel. 0900/403-4065, toll call-€0.45/min).

▲▲**The Hague (Den Haag)**—Locals say the money is made
in Rotterdam, divided in The Hague, and spent in Amsterdam.
The Hague is the Netherlands' seat of government and the home
of several engaging museums. The Hague's TI is at the train station (Mon–Sat 09:00–17:30, later in summer, Sun 10:00–17:00,
tel. 06/3403-505, €0.45/min).

   The **Mauritshuis'** delightful, easy-to-tour art collection stars
Vermeer and Rembrandt (€7, Tue–Sat 10:00–17:00, Sun 11:00–
17:00, Korte Vijverberg 8, tel. 070/302-3456). Across the pond,
the **Torture Museum** (Gevangenpoort) shows the medieval mind
at its worst (€3.75, Tue–Fri 11:00–17:00, Sat–Sun 12:00–17:00,
closed Mon, required tours on the hour, last one at 16:00, ask
ticket taker if film and talk will be in English before you commit,
tel. 070/346-0861). For a look at the 19th century's attempt at
virtual reality, tour **Panorama Mesdag**, a 360-degree painting
of nearby Scheveningen in the 1880s with a 3-D sandy-beach
foreground (€4, Mon–Sat 10:00–17:00, Sun 12:00–17:00, Zee-
straat 65, tel. 070/310-6665). The nearby **Peace Palace**, a gift
from Andrew Carnegie, houses the International Court of Justice
(€3.40, Mon–Fri, required guided tours only at 10:00, 11:00,
14:00, or 15:00, closes without warning—call ahead or check at
TI, tram #7 or #8 from station, tel. 070/302-4137).

   Scheveningen, the Dutch Coney Island, has a newly renovated pier and is liveliest on sunny summer afternoons (take tram
#1, #8, or #9 to Gevers Deynootplein/Kurhaus and walk via Palace
Promenade to the Boulevard). **Madurodam**, a mini-Holland
amusement park, is a kid pleaser (€10, kids 4–11-€7, Sept–
mid-March daily 09:00–18:00, mid-March–June until 20:00,
July–Aug until 22:00, George Maduroplein 1, tram #1 or #9,
tel. 070/355-3900, www.madurodam.nl).

Utrecht—The Museum von Speelklok tot Pierement has free
and necessary guided 55-minute tours on the hour demonstrating
its musical clocks, calliopes, and street organs (€6, Tue–Sat
10:00–17:00, Sun 12:00–17:00, closed Mon, last tour at 16:00,
10-min walk from station, Buurkerkhof 10, tel. 030/231-2789).

▲▲**Arnhem's Open-Air Dutch Folk Museum**—An hour
east of Amsterdam, Arnhem has the Netherlands' first and
biggest folk museum. You'll enjoy a huge park of windmills,
old farms, traditional crafts in action, and a pleasant education-
by-immersion in Dutch culture. The English guidebook (€3.85)
explains each historic building (€11, Easter–Oct daily 10:00–
17:00, cool new multimedia exhibit, tel. 026/357-6111, www
.openluchtmuseum.nl). The park has several good budget restaurants and covered picnic areas. Its rustic Pancake House serves
hearty (splittable) Dutch flapjacks.

Trains make the 70-minute trip from Amsterdam to Arnhem
twice an hour (likely transfer in Utrecht). At Arnhem station, take
bus #3 (direction: Alteveer) or, even better, #13 (faster, 4/hr, 15
min, runs July–Aug only) to the *Openluchtmuseum*. By car from
Haarlem, skirt Amsterdam to the south on E9, follow signs to
Utrecht, and take A12 east to Arnhem. Just before Arnhem, take
the Arnhem Nord exit *Openluchtmuseum* (exit #26) and follow
signs to the nearby museum. For the Kröller-Müller Museum,
follow white signs to Hoge Veluwe.

▲▲**Kröller-Müller Museum and Hoge Veluwe National
Park**—Near Arnhem, Hoge Veluwe National Park is the Netherlands' largest (13,000 acres) and is famous for its Kröller-Müller
Museum. This huge, striking modern-art collection, including
55 paintings by van Gogh, is set deep in the forest. The park
has hundreds of white bikes you're free to use to make your
explorations more fun (€4.50 to enter park, €4.50 more for the
museum, museum open Tue–Sun 10:00–17:00, closed Mon, easy
parking, tel. 031/859-1041). Pick up information at the Amsterdam or Arnhem TI (tel. 026/442-6767). Bus #12 connects the
Arnhem train station with the Kröller-Müller Museum (April–Oct,
check ahead for times as #12 runs infrequently). A visit to the park
and the open-air museum makes a great day trip from Amsterdam.

APPENDIX

"La Marseillaise"
There's a movement in France to soften the lyrics of their national anthem. Sing it now ... before it's too late.

Allons enfants de la Patrie, (Let's go, children of the fatherland,)
Le jour de gloire est arrivé. (The day of glory has arrived.)
Contre nous de la tyrannie (The blood-covered flagpole of tyranny)
L'étendard sanglant est levé, (Is raised against us,)
L'étendard sanglant est levé. (Is raised against us.)
Entendez-vous dans nos campagnes
    (Do you hear what's happening in our countryside?)
Mugir les féroces soldats? (The ferocious soldiers are howling.)
Qui viennent jusque dans nos bras (They're nearly in our grasp)
Egorger nos fils et nos compagnes.
    (They're slitting the throats of our sons and our women.)
Aux armes citoyens, (Grab your weapons, citizens,)
Formez vos bataillons, (Form your battalions,)
Marchons, marchons, (March on, march on,)
Qu'un sang impur (So that their impure blood)
Abreuve nos sillons. (Will fill our trenches.)

French History in an Escargot Shell
Around the time of Christ, Romans "Latinized" the land of the Gauls. With the fifth-century fall of Rome, the barbarian Franks and Burgundians invaded. From this unique mix of Latin and Celtic cultures evolved today's France.

While France wallowed with the rest of Europe in medieval darkness, it got a head start in its development as a nation-state. In 507, Clovis established Paris as the capital of his Christian Merovingian dynasty. Clovis and the Franks would eventually become Louis and the French. Charles Martel stopped the spread of Islam by beating the Spanish Moors at the Battle of Poitiers. And Charlemagne, the most important of the "Dark Age" Frankish kings, was crowned Holy Roman Emperor in 800 by the pope. Charles the Great presided over the "Carolingian Renaissance" and effectively ruled a vast-for-the-time empire.

The Treaty of Verdun, which in 843 divided Charlemagne's empire among his grandsons, marks what could be considered the birth of Europe. For the first time, a treaty was signed in vernacular languages (French and German) rather than in Latin. While this split established a Franco/Germanic divide, it also heralded an age of fragmentation. While petty princes took the reigns, the Frankish king ruled only Ile-de-France, a small region around Paris.

Vikings, or Norsemen, settled in what became Normandy. Later, in 1066, these "Normans" invaded England. The Norman king, William the Conqueror, consolidated his English domain, accelerating the formation of modern England. But his rule also muddied the political waters between England and France, kicking off a centuries-long struggle between the two nations.

In the 12th century, Eleanor of Aquitaine (a separate country in southwest France) married Louis VII, king of France, bringing Aquitaine under French rule. They divorced, and she married Henry of Normandy, soon-to-be Henry II of England. This marital union gave England control of a huge swath of land from the English Channel to the Pyrenees. For 300 years, France and England would struggle over control of Aquitaine. Any enemy of the French king would find a natural ally in the English king.

In 1328, a French king (Charles IV) died without a son. The English king (Edward III) was his nephew and naturally was interested in the throne. The French resisted. This pitted France, the biggest and richest country in Europe, against England, which had the biggest army. They fought from 1337 to 1453 in what was modestly called the Hundred Years' War.

Regional powers from within France sided with England. Burgundy actually took Paris, captured the royal family, and recognized the English king as heir to the French throne. England controlled France from the Loire north, and things looked bleak for the French king.

Enter Joan of Arc, a 16-year-old peasant girl driven by religious voices. France's national heroine left home to support the dauphin Charles VII (boy prince, heir to the throne but too young to rule). Joan rallied the French, inspiring them to ultimately throw out the English. In 1430, Joan was captured by the Burgundians, who sold her to the English, who convicted her of heresy and burned her at the stake in Rouen. But the inspiration of Joan of Arc lived on, and, by 1453, English holdings on the Continent had dwindled to the port of Calais.

By 1500, a strong centralized France had emerged with borders similar to today's borders. Her kings (from the Renaissance François I through the Henrys and all those Louises) were model divine monarchs, setting the standards for absolute rule in Europe.

Outrage over the power plays and spending sprees of the kings, coupled with the modern thinking of the Enlightenment—whose leaders were the French *philosophes*—led to the French Revolution (1789) and the end of the Old Regime and its notion that some are born to rule while others are born to be ruled.

But the excesses of the Revolution led to the rise of Napoléon, who ruled the French empire as a dictator until his excesses ushered him into a South Atlantic exile. The French settled on a compromise role for their ruler. The modern French king was himself ruled by a constitution. Rather than dress in leotards and powdered wigs, he went to work in a suit with a briefcase.

The 20th century spelled the end of France's reign as a military and political superpower. Devastating wars with Germany in 1870, 1914, and 1940 and the loss of her colonial holdings left France with not quite enough land, people, or production to be a top player on a global scale.

France in the 21st century is the cultural capital of Europe and a leader in the push to integrate Europe into one unified economic power. When that happens, Paris will once again emerge as a superpower capital.

Contemporary Politics in France

The key political issues in France today are high unemployment (about 12 percent), a steadily increasing percentage of ethnic minorities, and a recognized need to compete in a global marketplace. The challenge is to address these issues while maintaining the social benefits the French expect from their government. As a result, national policies seem to conflict with each other (e.g., France supports the lean economic policies of the European Union but has recently reduced the French work week to 35 hours).

The unification of Europe has been powered by France and Germany. The 15-member European Union, which is well on its way to becoming a "United States of Europe," is dissolving borders, freeing up trade, and sharing a common currency, the euro.

French national politics are fascinating. While only two parties dominate American politics, France has five major parties. From left to right, these include the reformed Communists (PCF-Parti Communiste Française), the moderate Socialists (PS-Parti Socialiste), the aristocratically conservative UDF (Union pour la Democratie Française), the center-right RPR (Rassemblement pour la République), and the racist Front National. In general, the UDF and RPR split the conservative middle ground and the Socialists dominate the liberal middle ground. But, in France (unlike the United States), coalitions are generally necessary for any party to "rule." At the fringes, you'll read about the racist Front National Party, led by Jean-Marie Le Pen. Le Pen's "France for the French" platform calls for the expulsion of ethnic minorities and broader police powers. As unemployment has gone up, so has the popularity of this far-right party. Garnering 15 percent of a recent national vote, Le Pen has been able to force center-right parties farther in his direction. On the far left, the reformed Communists, still recovering from the fall of the Soviet Union, have had to work more flexibly with the less-radical Socialists and the environmental parties.

While the French president is elected by popular vote every seven years (which may be shortened to five), he is more of a figurehead than his American counterpart. The more powerful prime minister is elected by the parliament (every three years). With five major parties, a single majority is rare—it takes a coalition to elect a prime minister. Currently the left is working together better than the right, and France has a liberal prime minister (Socialist Lionel Jospin) with a conservative president (Jacques Chirac). This "cohabitation" is similar to an American president having to deal with a Congress controlled by an opposing party.

Let's Talk Telephones

Here's a primer on making direct phone calls. For information specific to France and the Low Countries, see "Telephones," in the introduction.

Making Calls within a European Country: About half of all European countries use area codes (like we do); the other half uses a direct-dial system without area codes.

To make calls within a country that uses a direct-dial system (Belgium, Denmark, France, Italy, Portugal, Norway, Spain, and Switzerland), you dial the same number whether you're calling across the country or across the street.

In countries that use area codes (such as Austria, Britain, Czech Republic, Finland, Germany, Ireland, Netherlands, and Sweden), you dial the local number when calling within a city, and you add the area code if calling long-distance within the particular country.

Making International Calls: You always start with the international access code (011 if you're calling from America or Canada, or 00 from Europe), then dial the country code of the country you're calling (see chart below).

What you dial next depends on the phone system of the country you're calling. If the country uses area codes, drop the initial zero of the area code, then dial the rest of the number.

Countries that use direct-dial systems (no area codes) vary in how they're accessed internationally by phone. For instance, if you're making an international call to Denmark, Italy, Norway, Portugal, or Spain, simply dial the international access code, country code, and phone number. But if you're calling Belgium, France, or Switzerland, drop the initial zero of the phone number.

International Access Codes

When dialing direct, first dial the international access code of the country you're calling from. For the United States and Canada, it's 011. Virtually all European countries use "00" as their international access code; the only exceptions are Finland (990) and Lithuania (810).

Country Codes

After you've dialed the international access code, dial the code of the country you're calling.

Austria—43
Belgium—32
Britain—44
Canada—1
Czech Rep.—420
Denmark—45
Estonia—372
Finland—358
France—33
Germany—49
Gibraltar-350

Greece—30
Ireland—353
Italy—39
Morocco-212
Netherlands—31
Norway—47
Portugal—351
Spain—34
Sweden—46
Switzerland—41
United States—1

Calling-Card Operators

	AT&T	MCI	Sprint
France	0800-990-011	0800-990-019	0800-990-087
Belgium	0800-100-10	0800-100-12	0800-100-14
Netherlands	0800-022-9111	0800-022-9122	0800-022-9119

Telephone Directory
Useful Parisian Phone Numbers and Addresses
Emergency: Dial 17 for police
Emergency Medical Assistance: 15
Train Schedules and Reservations: 08 36 35 35 35.
Paris & France Directory Assistance (some English spoken): 12
American Church: 01 40 62 05 00
American Express: 11 rue Scribe, Mo: Opéra, 01 47 77 77 07
American Hospital: 01 46 41 25 25
American Pharmacy: 01 47 42 49 40
Office of American Services (lost passports, etc.): 01 43 12 48 45
Sunday Banks: 115 and 154 avenue des Champs-Elysées

U.S. Embassies
Paris: 2 rue St. Florentin, tel. 01 43 12 22 22,
    www.amb-usa.fr/consul/consulat.htm
Brussels: Regentlaan, 25 Boulevard du Regent, tel. 02-508-2111,
    www.usembassy.be
Amsterdam: Museumplein 19, tel. 020/575-5309, www.usemb.nl

Festivals in France, Belgium, and the Netherlands
This is just a partial list. For specifics, contact the national TIs
(listed in Introduction) and visit www.whatsgoingon.com,
www.festivals.com, and www.franceguide.com.

January	Monte Carlo Motor Rally, Monaco
Jan–Feb	Carnival Celebrations, Belgium, Holland, France
April	Flower Parade (April 20), Haarlem, Netherlands;

	Queen's Day (April 30—street fairs, parades), Amsterdam
May	Festival de Versailles (arts); Cannes Film Festival; Grand Prix (May 23–27), Monaco; Ascension Day (religious procession), Bruges, Belgium; Festival Jeanne d'Arc (pageants), Rouen, France
June	Festival du Marais (arts), Paris; Holland Festival of Performing Arts, Amsterdam; North Sea Jazz Festival, The Hague, Holland
July	Ommegang (historical pageant), Brussels; Bastille Day (July 14—fireworks, celebrations), France; Grand Parade du Jazz, Nice, France; Festival d'Avignon (arts), Avignon, France; Tour de France (ends in Paris); Les Tombées de la Nuit (arts festival), Rennes, France; Beaune International Music Festival; Fête de la Musique—17th (free concerts), France; Belgian National Day (July 21—parades, feasts), Brussels
August	Canal Festival (historic fair, performances), Bruges
September	Opening of Parliament (pageantry), The Hague, Holland; Fête d'Automne (arts festival), Paris
December	Christmas Market, Strasbourg, France

Numbers and Stumblers

- Europeans write a few of their numbers differently than we do: 1 = 1 , 4 = 4 , 7= 7. Learn the difference or miss your train.
- Europeans write dates as day/month/year (Christmas is 25/12/02).
- Commas are decimal points, and decimals are commas. A dollar and a half is 1,50. There are 5.280 feet in a mile.
- When pointing, use your whole hand, palm downward.
- When counting with fingers, start with your thumb. If you hold up your first finger to request one item, you'll probably get two.
- What we Americans call the second floor of a building is the first floor in Europe.
- Europeans keep the left "lane" open for passing on escalators and moving sidewalks. Keep to the right.

Metric Conversion (approximate)

1 inch = 25 millimeters	32 degrees F = 0 degrees C
1 foot = 0.3 meter	82 degrees F = about 28 degrees C
1 yard = 0.9 meter	1 ounce = 28 grams
1 mile = 1.6 kilometers	1 kilogram = 2.2 pounds
1 centimeter = 0.4 inch	1 quart = 0.95 liter
1 meter = 39.4 inches	1 square yard = 0.8 square meter
1 kilometer = 0.62 mile	1 acre = 0.4 hectare

Climate

First line, average daily low temperature; second line, average daily high; third line, days of no rain.

	J	F	M	A	M	J	J	A	S	O	N	D
FRANCE • Paris												
	34°	34°	39°	43°	49°	55°	58°	58°	53°	46°	40°	36°
	43°	45°	54°	60°	68°	73°	76°	75°	70°	60°	50°	44°
	14	14	19	17	19	18	19	18	17	18	15	15
Nice												
	35°	36°	41°	46°	52°	58°	63°	63°	58°	51°	43°	37°
	50°	53°	59°	64°	71°	79°	84°	83°	77°	68°	58°	52°
	23	22	24	23	23	26	29	26	24	23	21	21
BELGIUM • Brussels												
	30°	32°	36°	41°	46°	52°	54°	54°	51°	45°	38°	32°
	40°	44°	51°	58°	65°	72°	73°	72°	69°	60°	48°	42°
	10	11	14	12	15	15	14	13	17	14	10	12
NETHERLANDS • Amsterdam												
	31°	31°	34°	40°	46°	51°	55°	55°	50°	44°	38°	33°
	40°	42°	49°	56°	64°	70°	72°	71°	67°	57°	48°	42°
	9	9	15	14	17	16	14	13	11	11	9	10

Basic French Survival Phrases

Hello (good day).	**Bonjour.**	bohn-zhoor
Do you speak English?	**Parlez-vous anglais?**	par-lay-voo ahn-glay
Yes. / No.	**Oui. / Non.**	wee / nohn
I'm sorry.	**Désolé.**	day-zoh-lay
Please.	**S'il vous plaît.**	see voo play
Thank you.	**Merci.**	mehr-see
Goodbye.	**Au revoir.**	oh vwahr
Where is...?	**Où est...?**	oo ay
...a hotel	**...un hôtel**	uhn oh-tehl
...a youth hostel	**...une auberge**	ewn oh-behrzh
	de jeunesse	duh zhuh-nehs
...a restaurant	**...un restaurant**	uhn rehs-toh-rahn
...a grocery store	**...une épicerie**	ewn ay-pee-suh-ree
...the train station	**...la gare**	lah gar
...the tourist info office	**...l'office du tourisme**	loh-fees dew too-reez-muh
Where are the toilets?	**Où sont les toilettes?**	oo sohn lay twah-leht
men / women	**hommes / dames**	ohm / dahm
How much is it?	**Combien?**	kohn-bee-an
Cheaper.	**Moins cher.**	mwan shehr
Included?	**Inclus?**	an-klew
Do you have...?	**Avez-vous...?**	ah-vay-voo
I would like...	**Je voudrais...**	zhuh voo-dray
...a ticket.	**...un billet.**	uhn bee-yay
...a room.	**...une chambre.**	ewn shahn-bruh
...the bill.	**...l'addition.**	lah-dee-see-ohn
one	**un**	uhn
two	**deux**	duh
three	**trois**	twah
four	**quatre**	kah-truh
five	**cinq**	sank
six	**six**	sees
seven	**sept**	seht
eight	**huit**	weet
nine	**neuf**	nuhf
ten	**dix**	dees
At what time?	**À quelle heure?**	ah kehl ur
Just a moment.	**Un moment.**	uhn moh-mahn
Now.	**Maintenant.**	man-tuh-nahn
today / tomorrow	**aujourd'hui / demain**	oh-zhoor-dwee / duh-man

Road Scholar Feedback for
FRANCE, BELGIUM, AND THE NETHERLANDS 2002

*We're all in the same travelers' school of hard knocks. Your feedback helps us improve this guidebook for future travelers. Please fill this out (or use the online version at www.ricksteves.com/feedback), attach more info or any tips/favorite discoveries if you like, and send it to us. As thanks for your help, we'll send you our quarterly travel newsletter free for one year. Thanks! **Rick***

Of the recommended accommodations/restaurants used, which was:

Best _____

     Why? _____

Worst _____

     Why? _____

Of the sights/experiences/destinations recommended by this book, which was:

Most overrated _____

     Why? _____

Most underrated _____

     Why? _____

Best ways to improve this book:

_____

_____

I'd like a free newsletter subscription:

_____ Yes   _____ No   _____ Already on list

_____
Name

_____
Address

_____
City, State, Zip

_____
E-mail Address

    Please send to: ETBD, Box 2009, Edmonds, WA 98020

Faxing Your Hotel Reservation

Use this handy form for your fax (or find it online at
www.ricksteves.com/reservation). Photocopy and fax away.

One-Page Fax

To: _____ @ _____
                    hotel   *fax*

From: _____ @ _____
                    name   *fax*

Today's date: ____ / ____ / ____
              day   month   year

Dear Hotel _____,

Please make this reservation for me:

Name: _____

Total # of people: _____   # of rooms: _____   # of nights: _____

Arriving: ____ / ____ / ____ My time of arrival (24-hr clock): _____
          day   month   year   (I will telephone if I will be late)

Departing: ____ / ____ / ____
           day   month   year

Room(s): Single___ Double___ Twin___ Triple___ Quad___

With: Toilet___ Shower___ Bath___ Sink only___

Special needs: View___ Quiet___ Cheap___ Ground Floor___

Credit card: Visa___ MasterCard___ American Express___

Card #: _____

Expiration date:_____

Name on card: _____

You may charge me for the first night as a deposit. Please fax, e-mail, or
mail me confirmation of my reservation, along with the type of room
reserved, the price, and whether the price includes breakfast. Please also
inform me of your cancellation policy. Thank you.

_____
Signature

_____
Name

_____
Address

_____
City   *State*   *Zip Code*   *Country*

_____
E-mail Address

INDEX

FREE-SPIRITED TOURS FROM
Rick Steves

Great Guides

Big Buses

Small Groups

No Grumps

Best of Europe ■ **Village Europe** ■ **Eastern Europe** ■ **Turkey** ■ **Italy** ■ **Britain**
Spain/Portugal ■ **Ireland** ■ **Heart of France** ■ **South of France** ■ **Village France**
Scandinavia ■ **Germany/Austria/Switzerland** ■ **London** ■ **Paris** ■ **Rome**

Looking for a one, two, or three-week tour that's run in the Rick Steves style? Check out Rick Steves' educational, experiential tours of Europe.

Rick's tours include much more in the "sticker price" than mainstream tours. Here's what you'll get with a Europe or regional Rick Steves tour...

■ **Group size:** Your tour group will be no larger than 26.

■ **Guides:** You'll have two guides traveling and dining with you on your fully guided Rick Steves tour.

■ **Bus:** You'll travel in a full-size 48-to-52-seat bus, with plenty of empty seats for you to spread out and read, snooze, enjoy the passing scenery, get away from your spouse, or whatever.

■ **Sightseeing:** Your tour price includes all group sightseeing. There are no hidden extra charges.

■ **Hotels:** You'll stay in Rick's favorite small, characteristic, locally-run hotels in the center of each city, within walking distance of the sights you came to see.

■ **Price and insurance:** Your tour price is guaranteed for 2002. Single travelers do *not* pay an extra supplement (we have them room with other singles). ETBD includes prorated tour cancellation/interruption protection coverage at no extra cost.

■ **Tips and kickbacks:** All guide and driver tips are included in your tour price. Because your driver and guides are paid salaries by ETBD, they can focus on giving you the best European travel experience possible.

Interested? Call (425) 771-8303 or visit www.ricksteves.com for a free copy of Rick Steves' 2002 Tours booklet!

Rick Steves' Europe Through the Back Door
130 Fourth Avenue North, PO Box 2009, Edmonds, WA 98020 USA
Phone: (425) 771-8303 ■ Fax: (425) 771-0833 ■ www.ricksteves.com

FREE TRAVEL GOODIES FROM

Rick Steves

EUROPEAN TRAVEL NEWSLETTER

My *Europe Through the Back Door* travel company will help you travel better *because* you're on a budget—not in spite of it. To see how, ask for my 64-page *travel newsletter* packed full of savvy travel tips, readers' discoveries, and your best bets for railpasses, guidebooks, videos, travel accessories and free-spirited tours.

2002 GUIDE TO EUROPEAN RAILPASSES

With hundreds of railpasses to choose from in 2002, finding the right pass for your trip has never been more confusing. To cut through the complexity, ask for my 64-page *2002 Guide to European Railpasses.* Once you've narrowed down your choices, we give you unbeatable prices, including important extras with every Eurailpass, **free:** my 90-minute *Travel Skills Special* video or DVD; your choice of one of my 16 country guidebooks and phrasebooks; and answers to your "top five" travel questions.

RICK STEVES' 2002 TOURS

We offer 18 different one, two, and three-week tours (180 departures in 2002) for those who want to experience Europe in Rick Steves' Back Door style, but without the transportation and hotel hassles. If a tour with a small group, modest family-run hotels, lots of exercise, great guides, and no tips or hidden charges sounds like your idea of fun, ask for my 48-page 2002 Tours booklet.

YEAR-ROUND GUIDEBOOK UPDATES

Even though the information in my guidebooks is the freshest around, things do change in Europe between book printings. I've set aside a special section at my website (www.ricksteves.com/update) listing *up-to-the-minute changes* for every Rick Steves guidebook.

*Call, fax, or visit **www.ricksteves.com** to get your...*

- ☑ **FREE EUROPEAN TRAVEL NEWSLETTER**
- ☑ **FREE 2002 GUIDE TO EUROPEAN RAILPASSES**
- ☑ **FREE RICK STEVES' 2002 TOURS BOOKLET**

Rick Steves' Europe Through the Back Door

130 Fourth Avenue North, PO Box 2009, Edmonds, WA 98020 USA
Phone: (425) 771-8303 ■ Fax: (425) 771-0833 ■ www.ricksteves.com

Rick Steves' Phrase Books

Unlike other phrase books and dictionaries on the market, my well-tested phrases and key words cover every situation a traveler is likely to encounter. With these books you'll laugh with your cabby, disarm street thieves with insults, and charm new European friends.

Each book in the series is 4" x 6", with maps.

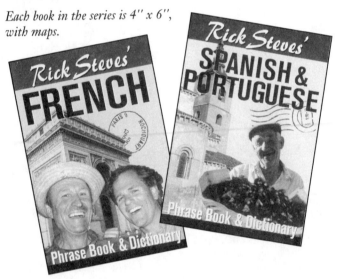

RICK STEVES' FRENCH PHRASE BOOK & DICTIONARY
U.S. $6.95/Canada $10.95

RICK STEVES' GERMAN PHRASE BOOK & DICTIONARY
U.S. $6.95/Canada $10.95

RICK STEVES' ITALIAN PHRASE BOOK & DICTIONARY
U.S. $6.95/Canada $10.95

RICK STEVES' SPANISH & PORTUGUESE PHRASE BOOK & DICTIONARY
U.S. $8.95/Canada $13.95

RICK STEVES' FRENCH, ITALIAN & GERMAN PHRASE BOOK & DICTIONARY
U.S. $8.95/Canada $13.95

Free, fresh travel tips, all year long.

Call (425) 771-8303 to get Rick's free
64-page newsletter, or visit
www.ricksteves.com for even more.

AVALON
TRAVEL
publishing

How far will our travel guides take you? As far as you want.

Discover a rhumba-fueled nightspot in Old Havana, explore prehistoric tombs in Ireland, hike beneath California's centuries-old redwoods, or embark on a classic road trip along Route 66. Our guidebooks deliver solidly researched, trip-tested information—minus any generic froth—to help globetrotters or weekend warriors create an adventure uniquely their own.

And we're not just about the printed page. Public television viewers are tuning in to Rick Steves' new travel series, *Rick Steves' Europe*. On the Web, readers can cruise the virtual black top with *Road Trip USA* author Jamie Jensen and learn travel industry secrets from Edward Hasbrouck of The *Practical Nomad*.

In print. On TV. On the Internet.

We supply the information. The rest is up to you.

Avalon Travel Publishing

Something for everyone

www.travelmatters.com

Avalon Travel Publishing guides are available at your favorite book or travel store.

 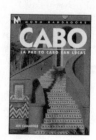 

MOON HANDBOOKS

provide comprehensive coverage of a region's arts,
history, land, people, and social issues in addition
to detailed practical listings for accommodations,
food, outdoor recreation, and entertainment. Moon
Handbooks allow complete immersion in a region's
culture—ideal for travelers who want to combine sightseeing with insight for an extraordinary travel experience
in destinations throughout North America, Hawaii,
Latin America, the Caribbean, Asia, and the Pacific.

WWW.MOON.COM

Rick Steves shows you where to travel
and how to travel—all while getting the most value
for your dollar. His Back Door travel philosophy
is about making friends, having fun, and avoiding
tourist rip-offs.

Rick has been traveling to Europe for more
than 25 years and is the author of 22 guidebooks,
which have sold more than a million copies. He
also hosts the award-winning public television
series *Rick Steves' Europe*.

WWW.RICKSTEVES.COM

ROAD TRIP USA

Getting there is half the fun, and Road Trip USA
guides are your ticket to driving adventure. Taking
you off the interstates and onto less-traveled, two-
lane highways, each guide is filled with fascinating
trivia, historical information, photographs, facts
about regional writers, and details on where to
sleep and eat—all contributing to your exploration
of the American road.

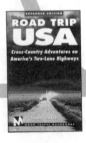

*"[Books] so full of the pleasures of the
American road, you can smell the upholstery."*
                                        ~BBC radio

WWW.ROADTRIPUSA.COM

FOGHORN OUTDOORS guides are for campers, hikers, boaters, anglers, bikers, and golfers of all levels of daring and skill. Each guide focuses on a specific U.S. region and contains site descriptions and ratings, driving directions, facilities and fees information, and easy-to-read maps that leave only the task of deciding where to go.

"Foghorn Outdoors has established an ecological conservation standard unmatched by any other publisher." ~Sierra Club

WWW.FOGHORN.COM

TRAVEL SMART guidebooks are accessible, route-based driving guides focusing on regions throughout the United States and Canada. Special interest tours provide the most practical routes for family fun, outdoor activities, or regional history for a trip of anywhere from two to 22 days. Travel Smarts take the guesswork out of planning a trip by recommending only the most interesting places to eat, stay, and visit.

"One of the few travel series that rates sightseeing attractions. That's a handy feature. It helps to have some guidance so that every minute counts." ~San Diego Union-Tribune

CiTY·SMaRT™ guides are written by local authors with hometown perspectives who have personally selected the best places to eat, shop, sightsee, and simply hang out. The honest, lively, and opinionated advice is perfect for business travelers looking to relax with the locals or for longtime residents looking for something new to do Saturday night.

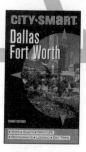